AA

WHERE TO GO IN BRITAIN

WHERE TO GO IN BRITAIN

AA

Produced by the
Publications Division of the Automobile Association
Fanum House,
Basingstoke, Hampshire RG21 2EA

Produced by the Publishing Division of the Automobile
Association
Editor **Rebecca King**
Assistant Editor **Richard Powell**
Art Editor **Keith Russell**

Research by the Publications Research Unit of the Automobile
Association

All maps by the Cartographic Department, Publishing Division of
the Automobile Association
Based on the Ordnance Survey Maps, with the permission of the
Controller of HM Stationery Office
Crown Copyright Reserved
Town Plans produced by the Cartographic Department,
Publishing Division of the Automobile Association, copyright
reserved by the Automobile Association

Filmset by Vantage Photosetting Co Ltd, Eastleigh and London
Printed and bound by New Interlitho SPA, Milan, Italy

Reprinted with amendments 1986
Reprinted with amendments 1982
First edition 1980

Published by the Automobile Association, Fanum House, Basing
View, Basingstoke, Hampshire RG21 2EA

ISBN 0 86145 455 3

Reference AA. 54438

**Boats have to be pulled high
up the shingle beach at
Hastings because this
seafaring Sussex town has
no harbour**

Contents

The rolling countryside of
Northamptonshire and
Oxfordshire spreads out below the
ancient hill village of Aynho

Introduction

Britain is packed with exciting places to go and interesting things to discover – magnificent castles where history can be traced as far back as Norman times; ruined forts built by the Romans; elegant stately homes filled with priceless treasures giving a glimpse of a grander past; fascinating cities with ancient houses and churches at every turn; seaside resorts with all the fun of the promenade; sleepy villages to wander around and beautiful countryside to explore.

It would be impossible to include all of Britain's many attractions in one book, so we have picked over 400 of the best from England, Scotland and Wales. The places have been selected because of their accessibility, variety and wide general appeal, catering for as many different tastes as possible. There is something here to suit every occasion – a family day out with the children, a trip whilst on holiday, a weekend away, a school outing, or just a Sunday drive to somewhere new.

With details of opening times accompanying each description where appropriate, street plans of cities and larger towns, twelve pages of road maps clearly locating every place in the gazetteer and hundreds of colour photographs, *Where To Go In Britain* is an invaluable guide to exploring Britain.

How to Use this Book

All the places in the gazetteer are listed in alphabetical order. Each entry has a page number beside it which refers to the road atlas at the back of the book, and a map reference locating the place on the map. For example, Bath *p 212 E4* will be found on page 212 of the atlas in square E4.

When planning a trip to a particular area, use the key map on page 210 to find out which map you need to refer to. All the gazetteer entries are printed in red type on the maps, so it is easy to see exactly where the places of interest are.

With every map there is an alphabetical list of all the places of interest in that area, and beside each name its gazetteer page number and its grid reference. These enable you to turn quickly back to the gazetteer to find out about a place and to pinpoint it easily on the map.

Abbreviations and Ancient Monument Opening Times

NT   Indicates properties in England and Wales administered by the National Trust for Places of Historic Interest or Natural Beauty, 42 Queen Anne's Gate, London SW1H 9AS.

NTS   National Trust for Scotland, 5 Charlotte Square, Edinburgh EH2 4DU.

AM   Ancient Monuments in England are in the care of the Historic Buildings and Monuments Commission for England, popularly known as English Heritage, PO Box 43, Ruislip, Middlesex HA4 0XW, with the exception of seven properties in and around London which are administered by the Department of the Environment.

Ancient Monuments in Scotland (with the exception of Holyrood House) are the responsibility of the Scottish Development Department, 3–11 Melville St Edinburgh EH3 7QD.

Ancient Monuments in Wales are the responsibility of Cadw, Brunel House, Fitzalan, Cardiff CF2 1UY.

Except where otherwise stated, the standard times of opening for all Ancient Monuments, except Scotland, are as follows:

16 Oct to 14 Mar weekdays 9.30–4   Sunday 2–4
15 Mar to 15 Oct weekdays 9.30–6.30   Sunday 2–6.30

Standard times of opening for all Ancient Monuments in Scotland are as follows:
Apr to Sep: weekdays 9.30–7   Sunday 2–7
Oct to Mar: weekdays 9.30–4   Sunday 2–4

All monuments in England and Wales are closed on 1 January and 24 to 26 December.
Those in Scotland on 25 and 26 December, also 1 and 2 January

Some of the smaller monuments may close for the lunch hour and may be closed for one or two days a week.

Churches, cathedrals and abbeys are usually open at all reasonable times.

As far as possible, the opening times given in the book are believed correct at the time of printing. However, as these details may be altered at the discretion of individual establishments, it is advisable to check that they are correct before making a special visit to a place.

Town Plan

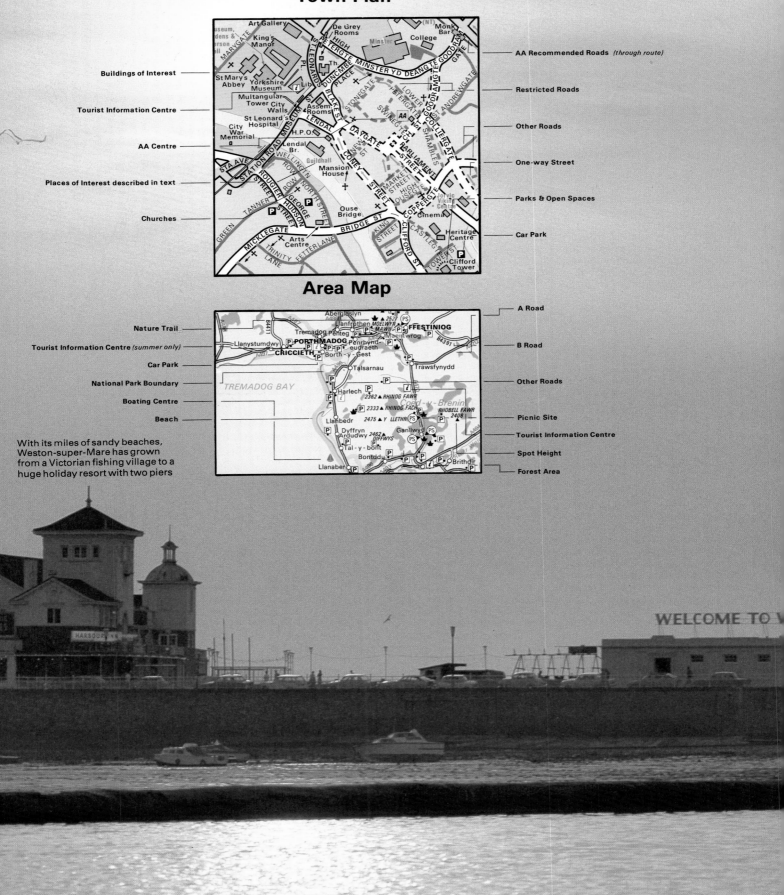

Buildings of Interest

Tourist Information Centre

AA Centre

Places of Interest described in text

Churches

AA Recommended Roads *(through route)*

Restricted Roads

Other Roads

One-way Street

Parks & Open Spaces

Car Park

Area Map

Nature Trail

Tourist Information Centre *(summer only)*

Car Park

National Park Boundary

Boating Centre

Beach

A Road

B Road

Other Roads

Picnic Site

Tourist Information Centre

Spot Height

Forest Area

With its miles of sandy beaches, Weston-super-Mare has grown from a Victorian fishing village to a huge holiday resort with two piers

Abbotsbury

Dorset *p212 E2*

This picturesque yellow-stone and thatch village is located on the western end of the sweep of Chesil Beach.

In the village itself is a huge medieval tithe barn which is all that is left of a Benedictine abbey. Up on the hill just behind the village is St Catherine's Chapel, also built by the monks in the fifteenth century. It is a small, austere building from which there are panoramic views of the surrounding gentle countryside.

It was the monks who established the famous swannery just south of the village. It has existed here for over six centuries and today is the largest in England. The swannery provides a safe breeding ground for hundreds of mute swans and is home for many species of wild fowl.

Another attraction nearby are the sub-tropical gardens about one mile west of Abbotsbury. Twenty acres of walled grounds enclose numerous unusual trees and an extensive collection of rare shrubs and plants. There are also magnolias and camelias, all of which are proudly surveyed by the resident peacocks, pheasants and turkeys.

Swannery open mid May to mid Sep daily.
Gardens open mid Mar to mid Oct daily. Refreshments available.

Over 500 swans nest and feed on the waters of the Fleet

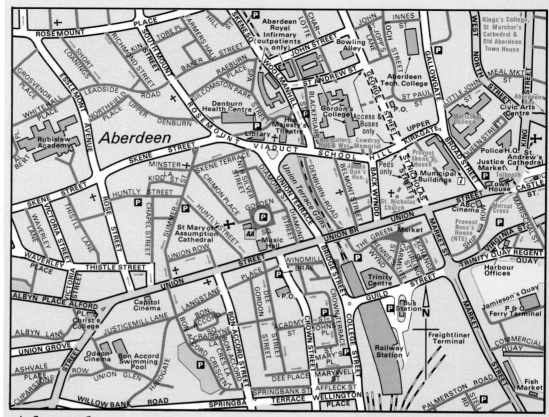

Aberdeen Grampian *p222 F2*

The Royal Town, or Burgh, of Aberdeen was first patronized by the Crown in the twelfth century when William the Lion granted it two royal charters. Since then it has prospered as a port and become one of Scotland's most important commercial, religious and scholastic centres.

Aberdeen was the main seaport in the north of Scotland as far back as the thirteenth century. Its shipping trade gradually grew and by the mid-nineteenth century the Aberdeen clippers which raced over to China for their cargo of tea had reached their zenith – the *Thermopylae* was reputed to be the fastest clipper in the world and the *Cutty Sark* was built in Clyde to compete with it.

The trawling industry also developed here in the nineteenth century and Aberdeen became an important fishing port. Although vast catches of fish are still handled in the harbour, the oil industry tends to dominate the docks.

Aberdeen is an austere city of grey buildings built from the granite which is quarried locally. However, this severity contrasts with the many parks in the city, all beautifully laid out with flower gardens. Thousands of roses create a blaze of colour every year which have won the city the Britain in Bloom trophy many times.

For ten days during June the Aberdeen Festival transforms the city into a riot of entertainment. Competitions, dancing displays, concerts, vintage car and steam rallies and special markets seem to fill the streets.

Aberdeen Bay

The city stands at the entrance to the valley of the river Dee and the sands here provide wide golden beaches which stretch from the harbour to the Don Estuary. The resort of Aberdeen is located along these two miles of coastline known as Aberdeen Bay. The beaches are backed by Promenades, golf links and extensive recreation and picnic areas. Amusement arcades, a sportsground, an adventure playground and a

fairground are all to be found at the end of Beach Boulevard.

King's College
The focal point of Old Aberdeen has always been the complex of university buildings known as King's College which date back to 1494. Its most splendid feature is the dominating tower which supports a huge stone crown built in honour of James IV who aided in the founding of the university. The other gem is the eighteenth-century chapel which is the best preserved example of a medieval college church in the British Isles. Of particular interest here is the wealth of intricate wooden carving inside.

St Machar's Cathedral
The fortification of this fifteenth-century cathedral reflects the political climate of those times. Aberdeen then was a dangerous place to live as it was so open to attack. On the seaward side it was likely to be attacked by the English landing, and on the other side by Celtic Highlanders approaching from the mountains.

The site for Aberdeen's cathedral was allegedly chosen because St Machar, a follower of St Columba from Iona, was guided there in the sixth century after being told to travel until he found a bend in the river resembling a shepherd's crook.

Old Aberdeen Town House
This is the most charming of Aberdeen's Georgian buildings and is situated on an island facing down a street lined with attractively restored houses – the High Street. Displayed above the door are the Lilies of Aulton, the coat of arms depicting heaven, virginity and the Holy Trinity.

Mercat Cross
The oldest part of new Aberdeen is Castlegate, which has been recognised as the city centre for the past 600 years although the castle has long since disappeared.

Situated in Castlegate is the Mercat Cross – undoubtedly the finest burgh cross in Scotland today. It is a circular structure made of red sandstone and has a pillar rising up from the centre of the roof supporting a unicorn made of white marble.

Shiprow
A few steps from Castlegate is Shiprow which may have even

Mercat Cross, built in 1686

earlier origins. Today its main feature of interest is Provost Ross's House, the city's oldest surviving building, which overlooks part of the harbour to which Shiprow descends. It now houses the Maritime Museum.

Marischal College
This was founded by the 5th Earl of Marischal as a Protestant rival to King's College, but the two merged in 1860 to become the University of Aberdeen. It is an elaborate building and around the archway through to the quadrangle there is a frieze of shields bearing the coats of arms belonging to past worthies of Aberdeen.

Attached to the college is an anthropological museum with a collection of treasures from all over the world, ranging from whale-tooth necklaces to tom-toms.

Provost Skene's House
Nearby in Guestrow, (off Broad Street), is Provost Skene's House dating from the seventeenth century. The chapel is particularly interesting here as, during restoration work in 1951, a painted ceiling was uncovered illustrating religious scenes thought to be seventeenth century. The top storey of the house has been turned into a folk museum housing exhibits ranging from swords and muskets to domestic items, including a spinning wheel.

St Nicholas' Church
Among the many churches of Aberdeen, St Nicholas' is the main city church and has always functioned as the ecclesiastical centre of the city. It has the distinction of possessing the largest carillon in Britain – a set of forty-eight bells which can either be played mechanically or by hand. They may be visited during the summer after recitals. Other features include the Jameson tapestries and St Mary's Chapel.

Art Gallery
The gallery houses a wide range of visual art spanning painting, sculpture, photography and silverwork. Artists contributing to the collections include Hogarth, Degas, Renoir, Augustus John, and Henry Moore.

James Dun's House
This restored eighteenth-century house is home for a museum concentrating on the social and domestic aspects of Scottish history.

Union Terrace Gardens
There are a number of parks and gardens in and around Aberdeen and this is one of the most central and attractive. Bands play here during summer evenings and there are entertainments for all including four outdoor draughts boards.

Anthropological Museum Marischal College, open Mon to Fri, also Sun pm only.
Maritime Museum Provost Ross's House, open all year Mon to Sat (except Christmas and 1, 2 Jan)
Provost Skene's House open as Maritime Museum. Refreshments available.
James Dun's House open as above.
Aberdeen Art Gallery open as above, also Sun, pm only. Refreshments available.

The granite clock-towers of Aberdeen rise above the old harbour

Aberystwyth

Dyfed *p216 C1*

Two rivers flow into Cardigan Bay at Aberystwyth – the Ystwyth which gave the town its name, and the Rheidol.

Aberystwyth is a pleasant seaside resort with some attractive nineteenth-century architecture, particularly in South Marine Terrace, Queen's Square and Laura Place.

On the headland between the two beaches are the ruins of its castle. Built in 1277 by Edward I, it soon fell into disrepair and was eventually blown up by the Roundheads in 1649. The headland is attractively laid out with gardens and seats at one or two view-points.

Perched high on a hill overlooking the town is the huge National Library of Wales. It offers unparalleled research facilities on all sorts of Welsh subjects and has over four million books and documents. Here too is the oldest Welsh manuscript in existence – the twelfth-century Black Book of Carmarthen.

Wales is famous for its Great Little Trains and Aberystwyth is the terminus of one of the most popular narrow-gauge steam lines – the Vale of Rheidol Railway, which follows the course of the river Rheidol for twelve miles through some magnificent scenery. It climbs from sea-level up to 680 feet where the line ends at Devil's Bridge. At this famous beauty spot the river Mynach cascades down a 300 foot gorge, spanned by three bridges each at different levels.

Castle open at all times.
National Library of Wales open all year Mon to Sat (except Bank Holidays).
Parking available.
Vale of Rheidol Railway operates Easter to Oct, journey time one hour each way. Parking available.

Abingdon

Oxfordshire *p213 A3*

Abingdon is a pleasant Thamesside town of great historic interest, now relieved from the burden of heavy traffic by a by-pass.

Its origins can be traced back to the seventh century when a Benedictine abbey was founded here. Some of the abbey buildings still remain, notably the long gallery, the thirteenth-century building known as the Checker with its vaulted undercroft, and the adjacent Checker Hall. The Hall has been converted into the delightful little Elizabethan-styled Unicorn Theatre.

Abingdon's County Hall has been described as the 'grandest market house in England', as it is alleged to be the work of a student of Sir Christopher Wren. The first floor of the Hall is now the home of the Town Museum which has collections of local history and archaeological finds.

Other historic buildings in the town include the Guildhall with its fine collection of paintings, the churches of St Helen and St Nicholas' and the sixteenth-century Christ's Hospital almshouses.

Abbey open all year daily (except Mon), pm only.
Museum open all year daily (except Bank Holidays), pm only.

Alfriston

Sussex *p214 C2*

This typically picturesque Sussex village has a fourteenth-century church, known as the 'Cathedral of the Downs' because of its unusually large size. Alfriston also has a number of old inns and an enchantingly peaceful village green. Close to the green is the Clergy House. It was first built in 1350 in timber and thatch and used as a residence for priests. Later it became labourers' cottages, but has since been carefully restored retaining many of the original building materials. The large medieval hall is particularly interesting.

One-and-a-half miles north of Alfriston is Drusillas Zoo which specialises in rare breeds of farm animals. There are collections of small mammals with which children are allowed to play, penguins, a flamingo lagoon, a butterfly house, an adventure playground and a miniature railway.

There is also an authentic Japanese garden, an English vineyard (offering the visitor tours and tastings), a cottage bakery and a pottery and leather-craft shop.

Clergy House open Easter to Oct daily. Shop only open, Nov to Xmas. NT.
Drusillas Zoo Park open daily (except Christmas).
Attractions end Mar to Oct only. Parking and refreshments available.

Allington Castle

Kent *p213 C3*

This charming thirteenth-century moated castle is set amongst woodlands and green fields beside the river Medway.

Originally built by Stephen of Penchester in 1282, it was intended as a home as well as a military stronghold, and consequently has more the air of a large, well-fortified manor house than a castle. Although it was extensively restored during the early part of this century, structural alterations were kept to a minimum and it still retains its massive gatehouse, inner courtyard, castellated curtain walls and Great Hall.

Today the castle is occupied by the Carmelite Order of Friars who run it as a Christian centre.

Open all year daily (except Christmas) pm only. Parking available.

Alnwick

Northumberland *p220 F3*

Standing on the banks of the river Aln, this beautiful and ancient market town, provides an excellent base for touring the rugged Northumbrian countryside.

Standing high on a rocky escarpment overlooking the river and dominating the town is the huge castle, an eleventh-century border fortress built for protection from the Scots. This stronghold was the principal seat of the Percy family who virtually ruled the north-east of England for over 600 years.

The interior of the castle differs entirely from the formidable exterior, as it has been redecorated in the Italian Renaissance style. The treasures of the magnificently elaborate staterooms include many objects by renowned

Fine views of Aberystwyth as the cliff railway descends the north cliff

Alton Towers

Staffordshire *p216 F2*

Charles, 15th Earl of Shrewsbury, created Alton in the nineteenth century out of 600 acres of lovely wild woodland in the Churnet Valley. The house which once stood in the grounds was called Alveton Lodge. Charles lived here while his gardens were being landscaped and renamed it Alton Abbey. Later, in 1831, his nephew enlarged the house and called it Alton Towers. Having been used as a training centre during World War II, the Towers then fell into decay and as they were never restored only the shell remains.

However, the gardens which took twelve years to build are magnificent. Lakes, pools, terraces and valleys complement each other perfectly and are covered with thousands of ornamental flowering plants, shrubs and trees.

Various buildings were also installed to enhance the gardens and these include a Chinese pagoda fountain, a Chinese temple and a Swiss cottage. The latter was built for a blind Welsh harpist. From here he played for walkers in the gardens.

Today Alton Towers is Europe's premier leisure park and can boast some of the world's most famous rides and shows.

Open Easter to Oct daily. Parking and refreshments available.

---

craftsmen: a pair of cabinets looted from Louis XIV during the French Revolution; and impressive porcelain collection; armoury; and paintings by famous artists including Van Dyck and Titian.

Surrounding the castle are grounds landscaped by Capability Brown which stretch down to the river and the footpath along its banks.

Castle open May to Sep daily (except Sat, other than Bank Holidays), pm only. Parking available.

Alresford

Hampshire *p213 A2*

New Alresford and Old Alresford make up this charming village which stands on either side of the river Alre, a tributary of the river Itchen. New Alresford's aptly named Broad Street, lined with lime trees and Georgian buildings, is one of the finest village streets in Hampshire. North of

The grim walls of Alnwick Castle from the banks of the river Aln

---

A fully restored N Class 2–6–0 steam loco leaving Ropley Station

the town there is a pleasant walk through watercress beds, and another route follows the south side of the river passing a picturesque fulling mill on the way.

Perhaps the most nostalgic feature of the village is Alresford Station, a terminus of the Mid-Hants 'Watercress' Line, so called because of the large amounts of cress once carried by British Rail from Alresford.

Today a steam railway line runs between Alresford and Alton along ten miles of the old Winchester to Alton line. The stations are typical examples of Victorian country-station architecture.

Since the line was re-opened in April 1977, visitors have been able to take a pleasant journey through beautiful Hampshire countryside and to see steam locomotives dating back over the last sixty years, the oldest of which was built in 1920. Most of the coaching stock on the line was built between 1954 and 1956.

The shed and workshop at Ropley house a variety of steam locomotives are at different stages of restoration.

Open early Mar to late Oct weekends and Bank Holidays only, but also Wed and Thu late May to late Jul, and daily late Jul to Aug. Parking and refreshments available.

The monument in Alton Towers commemorates their creator, Charles Talbot

Arundel's huge castle shows little evidence today of the damage it suffered during the Civil War

Argyll Forest Park

Strathclyde *p219 B4*

This was the first Forestry Commission Forest Park to be created in Britain. It lies on the Cowal Peninsula between Loch Fyne and Loch Long, covering some 66,000 acres of rugged West Highland Countryside, and consists of three forests: Ardgartan, Glenbranter and Benmore.

The scenery here is magnificent, with lofty peaks soaring to heights above 3,000 feet from the shores of sea lochs, their foothills clad in woods of pine and spruce. A network of forest roads covers the park and with their signposted forest walks and numerous picnic sites are ideal for walkers.

Besides the rugged highland scenery the park encompasses the beautiful Younger Botanic Garden and the nearby Kilmun Arboretum. The Younger Botanic Garden situated at Benmore on the southern end of the Park. Their delightful woodlands and fine gardens feature conifers, rhododendrons and azaleas. The Kilmun Arboretum and Forest Plots extend to a hundred acres on a hillside overlooking th Holy Loch.

Younger Botanic Garden open Apr to Oct daily. Refreshments and parking available.
Kilmun Arboretum and Forest Plots open all year during daylight hours. Entrance and car park at Forestry Commission District Office, Kilmun.

Arley Hall

Cheshire *p216 E3*

Arley Hall lies at the centre of an estate which has been in the possession of one family for over 500 years. It is an example of an early Victorian house in the 'Jacobean' style, containing fine plasterwork, oak-panelling, furniture and pictures.

The gardens rank among the best in the country and are of great variety and charm. They feature an unusual avenue of Ilex trees, walled gardens, a scented garden and a woodland garden.

Open Easter to early Oct, Tue to Sun and Bank Holidays, pm only. Parking and refreshments.

Arlington Court

Devon *p212 C3*

Arlington Court was the home of the Chichester family until it was bequeathed to the National Trust in 1949.

It was the last owner, Miss Rosalie Chichester, who left her mark here and gave the house its present character. Her mementoes and trinkets adorn every room. She collected many things, including shells, pewter, porcelain, period costumes and, not least, over a hundred model ships, some of which were made by French prisoners during the Napoleonic wars.

The 2,775 – acre park also owes much to Miss Chichester as she established the flock of Jacobs sheep, the Shetland ponies and the heronry which can be seen today from the nature trail. There is also a large collection of horse-drawn vehicles housed in the stable block.

Open Easter to Oct daily (House closed Sat, except Sat before Bank Holidays). Park and gardens open all year daily. Refreshments available.

Arundel

Sussex *p213 B2*

Narrow, hilly streets, antique shops and austere Victorian architecture lend Arundel charm and atmosphere.

Overlooking the Arun valley and the town is Arundel's superb castle – home of the dukes of Norfolk for over 500 years. The interior of the eleventh-century castle is packed with interesting treasures including paintings by Reynolds, Van Dyck and Gainsborough. Although it was virtually rebuilt in the eighteenth and nineteenth-centuries, much of the furniture and furnishings are classic period-pieces from William and Mary to Victorian.

Another building of note in the town is the Roman Catholic church of St Philip Neri. It was built to the design of Joseph Hansom, the man who invented the Hansom Cab, in French Gothic style. The church is, in fact, a cathedral since in 1965 Arundel was chosen as the seat of the bishopric of Brighton and Arundel. Light streams through the modern stained glass windows into the spacious interior. The high vaulted ceiling is patterned with alternating stripes of chalk and stone.

Just north of the town lies the Arundel Wildfowl Trust covering some fifty-five acres of woodland. Many birds not easily visible in the wild can be seen here.

Castle open Easter to late Oct Sun to Fri, pm only.
Wildfowl Trust open all year daily (except 25 Dec). Parking available.

Audley End House

Essex *p213 C4*

Built on the site of a Benedictine abbey, Audley End was at one time the home of the first Earl of Suffolk. The original house, with the two large courtyards, was reputed to be comparable to Hampton Court in its splendour and magnitude. Although much of the building was demolished due to the lack of resources of subsequent earls, it remains one of the most impressive Jacobean mansions in England.

The palatial interiors of the state rooms which remain are particularly magnificent. These include the alcove room, saloon and drawing room, and the exquisite state bed to be found in the Neville Room is still hung with

Capability Brown's lake enhances the distinguished stone facade of 17th-century Audley End House

the original embroidered drapes. The house also has a large collection of stuffed birds.

In the rolling parkland grounds are several elegant outbuildings, some of which were designed by Robert Adam. Amongst these are an icehouse, a circular temple and the Springwood Column. A miniature railway runs in the grounds and over the river Cam.

Open Apr to Sep; Tue to Sun and Bank hols pm only. Parking and refreshments available. AM.

Avebury

Wiltshire *p212 F4*

A ring of ancient banks and ditches almost a mile in circumference, and the remains of the largest stone circle in Europe surround the tiny village of Avebury. Many of the stones have now gone, but the line of the outer circle can still be easily followed. Some huge stones, although apparently placed at random, are the remains of two inner circles.

The Alexander Keiller Museum in the village traces the history of the stones and also that of the many prehistoric sites in the area. On the edge of the circle is the romantic Elizabethan Manor House, home of the Marquess and Marchioness of Ailesbury. Carefully restored, the house contains some fine panelling and plasterwork.

The surrounding garden and parkland are equally intriguing, featuring topiary, walled gardens, a wishing well and a magnificent old dovecote.

Museum see AM info. Also open Sun am, Apr to Sep. Parking available. **Avebury Manor** open Apr to Sep, daily; Oct to Mar, weekends pm, only. Parking and refreshments available.

Aviemore

Highland *p221 D2*

Aviemore, lying between the Monadhliath and Cairngorm mountains, is now the nucleus of Britain's principal winter sports region. The Aviemore Centre, which was developed in 1965, is a huge concrete holiday complex open all the year round.

Within the centre are hotels, restaurants, bars and shops. Recreational facilities include a dry ski-slope, chair lifts, skating and curling rinks, a swimming pool and a go-kart track. The Strathspey Steam Railway can be boarded at Aviemore for the short but very scenic haul to the village of Boat of Garten.

Railway open Easter; early to late Apr and early to mid Oct, Sun only; Sat to Mon (except Jul to late Aug, daily, except Fri).

The huge stones at Avebury are thought to have been placed by the nomadic Beaker peoples, as part of a religious circle, in about 1800 BC

Ayr Strathclyde *p220 C3*

Ayr is a busy market town overlooking the Firth of Clyde. Its excellent sandy beaches, attractive fishing harbour and associations with Robert Burns make it one of Scotland's most popular resorts.

Scotland's national poet, Robert Burns, was born south of the town at Alloway and in Ayr his spirit is never far away. The poet was christened at the Auld Kirk and his statue stands near the station, gazing back to Alloway. Relics of his life and work can be seen in the Tam O'Shanter Museum.

The Twa Brigs

These are two bridges close to one another spanning the river Ayr on its path through the town to the Clyde. The oldest of these, the Auld Brig, dates from the thirteenth century and for five hundred years was the only bridge in the town over the river. Burns wrote of it in his poem *The Brigs of Ayr* as 'a poor narrow footpath of a street where two wheel-barrows tremble when they meet'. The Auld Brig was renovated in 1910 and today carries only pedestrians. The second of the Twa Brigs, New Bridge, is a modern replacement of a structure first erected in 1788.

Auld Kirk of Ayr

Now hidden by modern buildings in the High Street, the Auld Kirk dates from 1654 and was built with money given by Oliver Cromwell as compensation for his take-over of the Church of St John. The church was renovated in 1952 and has three galleries known as the 'Merchants', 'Sailors', and 'Traders' lofts. It still retains its original pulpit, and in the churchyard is a tombstone commemorating the Covenanting Martyrs. In the lych-gate are some heavy iron grave-covers which were commonly used to deter body-snatchers.

St John's Tower

A notable landmark providing panoramic views, St John's Tower is the only substantial remainder of the twelfth-century Church of St John. In 1315 the church played host to Robert Bruce's parliament which was to decide his successor to the Scottish throne. Cromwell incorporated the church into a citadel built in 1652; its remains can be seen nearby.

Tam O'Shanter Inn

An old thatched inn, a brewhouse in Burns' day, stands in the High Street and was bought for the town in 1943. It now houses a Burns museum. This is by tradition the start of Tam's ride as depicted in Burns' famous poem, *Tam O'Shanter*. Every June, the town celebrates the journey with the commemorative Burns Ride. This procession follows Tam's route which ends at the Auld Brig O'Doon, Alloway.

Wallace Tower

This neo-Gothic tower is a conspicuous feature of the High Street. Built in 1832, the 113-foot-high tower incorporates a statue of Sir William Wallace – a fervent champion of Scottish independence.

Burns' Cottage (Alloway)

Burns' Cottage a two-roomed clay and thatch house, contains many furnishings and domestic implements used in Burns' day. Adjoining the cottage, set in pretty gardens, is the Burns Museum. This has an interesting exhibition of original manuscripts, a copy of the Kilmarnock edition of poems, and other of Burns' possessions, including his family Bible. Nearby stands the Burns' Monument and sculptures of characters from Burns' poems stand in the grounds.

Tam O'Shanter Museum open all year Mon to Sat (Oct to Mar, pm only). Also Sun Jun to Aug, pm only. **Burns' Cottage & Monument** open Apr to mid Oct, Mon to Sat. Also Sun Mar to May, Sep and Oct, pm only. Refreshments available.

Above: A stained-glass portrait of Burns in his cottage at Alloway
Below: Ayr's harbour forms part of the river which flows into Ayr Bay

Balmoral Castle

Grampian *p222 E2*

Balmoral Castle lies in a curve of the river in the beautiful wooded valley of Royal Deeside. It is one of the private residences owned by Her Majesty the Queen and is used by the Royal Family as a summer holiday estate. The estate itself dates back to the late fifteenth century when it was known as 'Bouchmorale', Gaelic for 'majestic dwelling'. It first came into the hands of the Royal Family in 1848 when Sir Robert Gordon, who developed the deer forest and enlarged the original buildings, died suddenly. After leasing the estate for four years it was bought by Prince Albert for the sum of £31,000.

The most striking feature of the house is a square tower rising to eighty feet, which is then surmounted by a turret, extending the total height to 100 feet.

Although the castle itself is not open to the public the grounds and gardens can be visited when members of the Royal Family are not in residence. There is an exhibition of paintings and works of art in the Castle Ballroom.

Grounds and Castle Ballroom Exhibition open May to July Mon to Sat. Refreshments available.

Bamburgh

Northumberland *p220 F1*

The small seaside resort of Bamburgh is dominated by its castle standing some 150 feet high on a rocky crag overlooking the North Sea. The town was of considerable importance as a border stronghold against invading Scots, and the castle has suffered much damage throughout its history as a result.

From the 1400s the castle was left to deteriorate and was not restored until the eighteenth century. It has since been completely renovated, and although partly residential, is still open to the public.

The most notable part of the castle is the great square keep

The countryside around Balmoral includes Ballochuie Forest, which was added to the estate by Queen Victoria

Bath see page 18

Battle

East Sussex *p213 C2*

Located near the site of the Battle of Hastings is the town of Battle. William the Conqueror built a church here to commemorate his victory in 1066 and the high altar was positioned on the spot where Harold fell. Later, Benedictine monks built St Martin's Abbey close by, although only the gatehouse and the refectory have survived. The abbey house is now a school for girls and the grounds and outer buildings are open to the public. Nothing remains of the Conqueror's church now, but excavations revealed its plan and a monument called Harold's Stone was erected in 1903 on the site of the original high altar.

There are many items connected with the battle, including a half-scale reproduction of the Bayeux tapestry, housed in the Battle Historical Society Museum located in Langton House. The museum also exhibits pieces from the local ironwork industry which prospered in Sussex for over 1,000 years.

Museum open Easter to Sep daily, Sun pm only.

which has a turret at each corner. Within its walls are many treasures including paintings, tapestries, and a cradle which belonged to Queen Anne. Also on view is an impressive weapon collection housed in the armoury. Opposite the church is the Grace Darling Museum. This contains various relics associated with the heroine, including the rowing boat in which she and her father rescued nine survivors from the wrecked SS *Forfarshire* one stormy night in 1838. When Grace Darling died of tuberculosis at twenty-six, she was buried in the churchyard of St Aidan – a thirteenth-century church with a vaulted crypt.

Castle open Apr to Sep daily, pm only. Parking available.
Grace Darling Museum open early Apr to mid Oct daily. Parking.

Banham

Norfolk *p213 D5*

Over twenty acres of Norfolk countryside are occupied by Banham Zoo, which specialises in monkeys and apes. Apart from rarer primates, there is a worldwide collection of other animals and birds including otters, llamas, penguins and sealions.

Next to the zoo is a motor museum containing Lord Cranworth's collection of over forty cars, motor cycles and children's pedal cars, all dating from the 1920s to the 1960s. Here can be found Bentleys, famous for their racing success at Le Mans, a rare Gullwing Mercedes and a supercharged Cord.

Zoo open all year. Parking available.
Motor Museum open daily, Apr to Oct. Parking available.

Bamburgh Castle became a 14th-century stronghold of the Percy family

Barnard Castle

Co Durham *p220 F1*

This historic town on the banks of the Tees is still dominated by the castle from which it takes its name. Originally called Bernard's Castle, it was built by Bernard Baliol around the late eleventh century and quickly gained importance, as did the family when, in 1292, John Baliol was crowned King of Scotland.

In 1569 the castle was besieged during the rising of the Northern Earls and fell into disrepair until 1630 when a large part of the fabric was carried off to build Raby Castle. The ruin that remains covers about six and a half acres on its cliff-top site eighty feet above the river Tees.

The Bowes family were also significant in the history of the town and it was John Bowes and his French wife, Josephine, who built the Bowes Museum in the late nineteenth century. Standing in its own park, the museum looks like an impressive French chateau and contains superb collections of paintings, furniture and porcelain, together with childrens' galleries and exhibits of local historic interest.

There are many pleasant walks in the area, one of which follows the river south-east to the lovely ruins of Egglestone Abbey, founded in 1190 for the Premonstratensian Order.

Castle see AM info. Also open Sun am, Apr to Sep.
Bowes Museum open all year daily ('except Christmas period and New Year's Day). Sun pm only. Parking and refreshments available.
Abbey open any reasonable time. AM.

The Bowes collected the museum's contents themselves, although they died before its completion in 1892

Bath Avon *p212 E4*

Secured in the bend of the river Avon between the Cotswold and Mendip Hills, Bath can surely claim to be one of England's most beautiful cities. The Romans built their city around the hot springs and eleven centuries later Georgian architects did the same. Today Bath is a carefully preserved tribute to both those eras.

The origins of Bath are related to the hot springs which probably first reached the earth's surface at this point over one million years ago. However, it took the Romans to discover that the water had some possible therapeutic value and they first utilised it by building the sophisticated baths that, second to Hadrian's Wall, remain Britain's greatest monument to the Roman Empire.

Towards the end of the sixteenth century the hot springs were important to the city because the visitors eventually created more revenue than the established wool industry. Despite this, Bath was not an attractive place to live – the sanitation was appalling and thieving and debauchery were rife.

It was not until the eighteenth century that a gradual change was wrought which transformed Bath to the place we know. The baths became a social centre as well as a source of healing.

When a young dandy named Beau Nash arrived in Bath and became Master of Ceremonies, he impregnated the city with his personality. He was a man of tremendous elegance and style and became the sole arbiter of taste, etiquette and fashion.

Whereas Nash controlled the social structure of Bath, it was one-time postmaster Ralph Allen who instigated the building of the Georgian city. He made his fortune by radically improving the postal system and with the money bought two of the local limestone quarries. With the building material available, Allen, in conjunction with architect John Wood, was thus able to build the city of his dreams.

The Roman Baths

Serious excavations began in the nineteenth century but it was not until 1925 that the full extent of the Roman complex was uncovered. It consisted of the Great Bath, lined with lead, swimming pools, mineral-water baths and a series of rooms heated by hot air under the floors.

Attached to the baths was a temple built as a dedication to the god Sulis Minerva, and fragments have survived to this day. Part of the outside decoration shows, intact, a gorgon's head.

The many treasures which have been retrieved from the ground are housed in the adjoining Roman Baths Museum. Exhibits range from domestic utensils to a bronzed head of Minerva that survived destruction.

The Pump Room

Forming part of the Great Bath complex is the Pump Room. The present building dates from 1796 when the townsfolk decided that a larger room was needed than the one used in Nash's reign. The interior is much the same as it has

The Great Bath, below the present street level, still has its original Roman masonry and bases of the huge pillars

Bath's famous bridge spans the Avon

always been, including the two sedan chairs – one of which was privately owned and the other used as a taxi. The room is filled with tables where either tea or spa water may be drunk to the sound of discreet chamber music.

Pulteney Bridge

This is the only piece of Robert Adam's work in Bath, but it is certainly one of the most beautiful features of the city. The bridge was copied from the Florentine Ponte Vecchio and has the same three arches. It is lined on both sides with shops, and at the back of the arcade is a central window.

Bath Abbey

The abbey is in the centre of the town and it is easy to see why it is called The Lantern of the West. Inside, enormous plain-glass windows above the nave and the choir soar up to the stone fan-vaulted ceiling seventy feet above.

The tower is rectangular rather than square because its foundations were built on the nave pillars of the previous Norman cathedral. The architects of the abbey also designed the chapel at Westminster and the chapel of St George in Windsor Castle

The contents of the abbey include a rare eighteenth-century portable oak font which is still used for abbey baptisms, and more tablets and memorials than any other English church excluding Westminster Abbey; one of these tablets commemorates Beau Nash.

The Assembly Rooms

The upper floors are a fine suite of rooms, which used to be the scene of high society events in the eighteenth century. Eminent figures such as Dickens, Johann Strauss and Liszt were known to grace the rooms. Unfortunately in 1942 the building was gutted by fire and was not reopened until 1963. Since then, however, the Rooms have again provided a sumptuous setting for balls, banquets and conferences.

On reopening, a section was allocated to the Museum of Costume which exhibits one of the largest collections of costumes in the world. The clothing ranges from the Tudor period to the present day.

Royal Crescent

This magnificent sweep of thirty elegant houses, fronted by a total of 114 Ionic columns, was the first

The grandeur of Royal Crescent

terrace ever to be built as a crescent. It remains one of the finest examples of its kind in Europe.

Number One has been taken over by the Bath Preservation Trust to display Georgian furnishings in an authentic setting.

The Circus

The elegant houses which form the Circus are built in three blocks of eleven, all ornamented by Tuscan, Ionic and Corinthian columns. One complete frieze depicting the arts and sciences stretches across the front of the three arcs.

In the Mews behind the Circus is the Bath Carriage Museum, housed in the original coach houses and stables of the Circus houses. Here over 40 carriages are carefully looked after and displayed with all their various accessories such as whips, harness and liveries. Carriage rides are available daily.

Burrows Toy Museum

This relatively new museum, opened in 1976, is housed in a building next to the Roman Baths. Curious and amazing toys of all sorts including books and games are on display and provide a fascinating insight into children's lives over the past two centuries.

Victoria Art Gallery and Library

This is housed above the library at the western end of Pulteney Bridge. It is a particularly interesting museum with some unusual collections, including Bohemian glass, mint coins and trade notes of Bath, and the Horstmann collection of antique watches.

Baths and Pump Room open all year. Refreshments available.

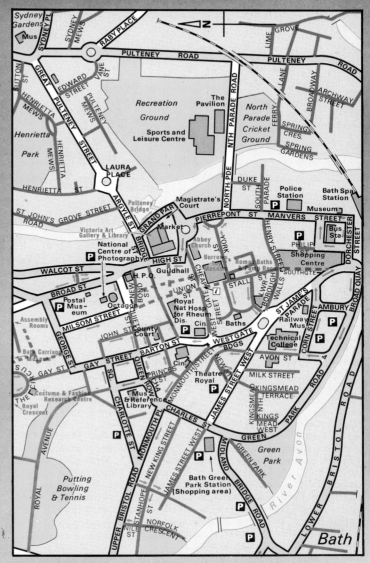

Abbey open all year.
Assembly Rooms open all year, daily. Refreshments available, NT.
Royal Crescent No 1 open Mar to Oct, daily (except Mon and Good Fri) but open Bank Holiday Mon. Sun pm only.

Carriage Museum open all year. Parking available.
Burrows Toy Museum open daily (except Christmas Day and Boxing Day).
Victoria Art Gallery and Library open all year (except Sun and Bank Holidays).

Palace House at Beaulieu with a *Planet* loco replica

Beaulieu

Hampshire *p213 A1*

There are a variety of attractions at Beaulieu comprising the Palace House, the abbey ruins and the National Motor Museum, all set amidst beautiful New Forest scenery. Once through the entrance hall to this complex, the path leads first to the Motor Museum building with its 70,000 square feet of exhibition floor space. Over 300 motor vehicles are displayed here from the magnificent 1909 Silver Ghost to the humble Mini; from the first petrol-driven car of 1895 to one of the recent Formula 1 racing models. There are comprehensive collections here of motor cycles and commercial vehicles, a few bicycles, prototypes and the huge land-speed record breakers such as Donald Campbell's *Bluebird*. There are also displays of the components and accessories of motor transport and the whole museum is often alive with the sound of engines running and the clatter of spanners from the workshops next door. Work being carried out here may be viewed from a special window in the motorcycle gallery.

Moving on from the world of transport, visitors can either stroll through the pleasant grounds or take a monorail trip to the Palace House. Built in the fourteenth century as the abbey gateway, it was transformed in the nineteenth century and today is a charming blend of historic

building and family home of Lord Montagu.

Behind the house are the ruins of a Cistercian Abbey founded by King John in 1204 and destroyed by Henry VIII. Much of the building is gone now, but the refectory serves as the parish church of Beaulieu village and the Domus building contains an exhibition of Monastic Life at Beaulieu. Other attractions in Beaulieu include veteran bus rides, rallies, steam fairs, a model railway and a monorail.

Open all year except Christmas Day. Parking and refreshments available.

Beaumaris

Gwynedd *p216 C3*

The Norman invaders called this area *Beau Marais*, a Norman-French name meaning fair marsh. Situated on the eastern shore of the Isle of Anglesey was Beaumaris castle, and the town grew up around it. For centuries the town was the administrative capital of the island.

In contrast to many other Welsh castles which are built on limestone rocks or cliffs, Beaumaris castle stands on a vast area of flat ground. This accounts for its grand, spacious layout. The outer walls are surrounded by an octagonal moat which is fed from the sea.

In Steeple Lane, in the town centre, is the county gaol which was built in 1829 by architect and inventor Joseph Hansom. Inside

is a perfect example of a wooden treadmill and this was the last one to be used in Britain. Prisoners serving hard labour in the nineteenth century had to serve between six and eight hours a day on the treadmill, fifteen minutes on the wheel then fifteen minutes rest. Confinement to a sound-proofed cell in total darkness was the harsh punishment prisoners received for offences such as swearing, insolence or refusal to work. High on the outer wall of the prison is the door through which condemned men stepped for execution. The last public execution was in 1862. A documented exhibition of nineteenth-century prison life gives a complete illustration of the conditions of that time.

The fifteenth-century Tudor Rose in Castle Street is a fine example of Tudor half-timber work. It was bought and restored by artist Hendrik Lek, and today houses an art gallery exhibiting his work and that of his son, who is the present owner.

Castle see AM info. Also open Sun am, Apr to Sep. Parking available.
Beaumaris Gaol open May to Sep daily.
Tudor Rose open July to mid Sep daily and also Easter and Whitsun weekends.

Bekonscot Model Village

Buckinghamshire *p213 B3*

This model village, situated within the town of Beaconsfield, has been honoured with several

Royal visits over the years. It contains many working models including an airport, docks, a funfair and a model railway complete with five stations. In a colourful rock-garden setting visitors can walk among miniature houses, shops and churches built to a scale of one inch to one foot. There are also castles, a racecourse and a polo ground – all constructed in minute detail.

Open Easter to Oct, daily, with limited display before Easter. Parking available.

Belton House, Park and Gardens

Lincolnshire *p217 C1*

Belton House has been the home of the Brownlow family since it was built in 1685 to a design by Christopher Wren. The house is decorated with wood carvings by Grinling Gibbons and the furnishings include pieces of porcelain, some Aubusson carpets and many great paintings, including one by Leonardo da Vinci which closely resembles his famous *Mona Lisa*. Of more recent interest is the collection of memorabilia connected with the late King Edward VIII, including, probably, the only portrait painted of him during his brief reign.

The old kitchens stood across the courtyard from the house, and were connected to it by an under-

The windmill and lilyponds in the tiny model village of Bekonscot

ground railway which still exists.

The grounds vary from formal gardens to deer parkland. They contain a small church housing the tombs of the Brownlows and an orangery. An extensive children's adventure playground is a more recent addition.

Open Easter to Oct, Wed to Sun and Bank Holiday Mons (closed Good Friday) pm only. Refreshments available. NT.

Belvoir Castle

Leicestershire *p217 C1*

Home of the Rutland family since Tudor times, the present Belvoir Castle is the third to be built on this superb site above the lovely Vale of Belvoir.

The first castle was Norman, built by Robert de Todeni who came ashore with William the Conqueror, but this was destroyed during the Wars of the Roses. The second castle met a similar fate during the Civil War and the third, although almost destroyed by fire, was extensively rebuilt and restored during the early nineteenth century.

The exterior of the castle is medieval in appearance with towers, turrets and battlements, but the interior is furnished in a more classical style with painted ceilings, panelling and rich Regency furnishings. Works of art include paintings by Poussin, Reynolds, Gainsborough, Van Dyck, Hogarth and Holbein, and Gobelin tapestries adorn the walls of the Regent's Gallery. There is also a military museum devoted to the 17th/21st Lancers.

Special events take place in the grounds on most Sundays in season such as jousting tournaments, band concerts, car rallies, folk dancing and steam rallies.

Open end Mar to early Oct, Tue to Thu, weekends and Bank Holidays. Also open Sun in Oct, pm only. Parking and refreshments available.

Berkeley

Gloucestershire *p212 E4*

This quiet little Georgian town is dominated by its splendid castle. Built between 1117 and 1153, it remained the ancestral home of the Berkeley family for over 800 years.

The castle has been splendidly preserved and beautifully furnished over the years by the various earls of Berkeley. It was here that the barons of the west gathered in 1215 before setting out for Runnymede to witness the sealing of the Magna Carta by King John, and the deposed King Edward II was gruesomely murdered in 1327 at the behest of his wife and the Earl of Mortimer.

This feudal stronghold is entered by a bridge over a moat and has a solid circular keep. Today visitors can see the dungeon, the fourteenth-century hall, the state apartments with their tapestries and furniture, the medieval kitchens, and the actual cell in which Edward was murdered. There are also Elizabethan terraced gardens, which include a bowling alley, and close by is a large well-stocked deer park.

In the town, the fine early English church, which contains many memorials to the Berkeleys, has a Norman doorway and a detached tower built in 1783. The churchyard contains the grave of Edward Jenner (1749–1823), pioneer of smallpox vaccination, who was born here. The Jenner Museum is housed in The Chantry, the house in which he lived for most of his life.

Castle open Apr to Sep daily (except Mon) but Apr, Sep and all Suns pm only. Also open Oct (Sun pm only) and Bank Holidays. Parking available.
Jenner Museum open Apr to Sep daily (except Mon, but including Bank Holidays).

Betws y coed

Gwynedd *p216 C3*

This oft-painted, much-photographed village has been a busy

15th-century Pont-y-Pair bridge across the Llugwy at Betws y coed

touring centre since Victorian times and shows no sign of losing its popularity. It is set in a fairytale area of wooded slopes and white water where the rivers Conwy and Gwydyr tumble over the rocks and through the valleys.

One of Betws y coed's most famous attractions is the Swallow Falls, an enchanting series of cascades and rapids. Along their course runs a railed footpath.

There are historic bridges here too; the fifteenth-century Pont-y-Pair, Telford's iron Waterloo Bridge, built in the same year as the battle, and the curious Miners' Bridge which climbs from one bank to the other like a ship's gangplank.

In the former goods yard of Betws y coed station is the Conwy Valley Railway Museum which displays railway items of both narrow and standard gauge with North Wales connections.

Also to be seen are operating model railway layouts and a steam-hauled miniature railway. Among the many walks through the nearby Gwydyr Forest is the Cyffty Lead Mine Trail, taking in the old mine buildings which are currently being restored.

Railway Museum open Easter to Oct. Parking available.

19th-century Belvoir Castle, pronounced 'Beever' Castle

The choir of Beverley Minster with its curious illusion of 3-D flooring

A tiered fountain in the formal Italian gardens at Bicton

Beverley

Humberside *p217 C3*

This flourishing market town boasts one of the finest examples of ecclesiastical architecture in Europe, the twin-towered Beverley Minster. The most notable feature of the Minster is the beautifully ornamented Percy tomb, a shrine to the family who once owned much of the land in the area.

The other great church in the town, the church of St Mary, is a worthy tribute to fine English Gothic workmanship. The chancel is particularly impressive with its ceiling of forty panels representing the kings of England up to Henry VI.

Also in Beverley is a fine art gallery, museum and heritage centre, as well as a museum of army transport.

Another notable feature of the town is the eighteenth-century Lairgate Hall, famed for its Adam ceiling and delicately hand-painted Chinese wallpaper.

Wednesday Market is a small square surrounded by attractive Georgian houses, whilst Saturday Market contains the Market Cross, bearing four shields: those of Queen Anne; Beverley Borough and the Hotham and Warton families who together contributed to the building costs of the cross.

Art Gallery, Museum and Heritage Centre open all year daily (except Sun) Thu am only. Parking available.
Lairgate Hall open all year, Mon to Fri. Parking available.
Museum of Army Transport open all year daily (except Christmas Day). Parking and refreshments available.

Bickleigh

Devon *p212 D2*

The thatched cottages of this charming village lie peacefully on the east bank of the river Exe.

Bickleigh Castle, also known as the Court, lies on the opposite side of the river from the village and was built on the site of a Norman castle. All that remains now from that period is the lovely little chapel with its thatched roof. The present building dates mainly from the Tudor period, although it was considerably devastated by Parliamentarians in the Civil War. However, the great hall, armoury guard room and Stuart farmhouse have survived, and the tower can be climbed for extensive views. For generations it was the home of the Carew family; and Bamfylde Moat Carew, the 'king of the gipsies', was born in the castle and is buried in the village churchyard.

To the north of the village lies Bickleigh Mill Craft Centre and Farm. This picturesque old working watermill is now given over to craft-work including pottery, wood-turning and the making of jewellery and corndollies. Adjacent to the mill is a living example of a nineteenth-century Devon farm, which has working shirehorses, many rare breeds of farm animals and a museum.

Bickleigh Castle open Easter to early Oct, Wed, Sun and Bank Holiday Mon. Between end May and early Oct daily (except Sat), pm only. Parking and refreshments available.
Bickleigh Mill Craft Centre and Farm open all year. Jan to Mar, weekends only. Apr to Dec daily. Parking and refreshments available.

Bicton Park

Devon *p212 D2*

The gardens which form part of Lord Clinton's estate were landscaped in 1735 by Henry Rolle, to the designs of Andre Le Notre, French designer of the gardens at Versailles.

The mile-long narrow-gauge Bicton Woodland Railway provides a good chance to view the lake and one of the finest collections of coniferous trees in Britain, the Pinetum. On the shores of the lake is a nineteenth-century summer house called the Hermitage.

Set amidst magnificent trees is the James Countryside Collection, a pageant of agricultural history. For a complete contrast the 'World of Tomorrow' features a space station and space travel simulator.

Open end Mar to Oct daily and other times during winter. Parking and refreshments available.

Bignor Roman Villa

West Sussex *p213 B2*

Evidence was found in 1811 of a Roman Villa at Bignor and the excavations which followed revealed one of the largest villas ever to be discovered in Britain. The buildings, which were inhabited from the second to the fourth century, enclosed a large courtyard and had farm buildings to the rear of them.

There are extensive remains of the Roman mosaic floors and pavements, now protected by wooden buildings. The cold plunge-bath and the floor of its undressing room lie beyond what is now the car park. A museum on the site contains various Roman relics and a plan of the original complex.

Open end Mar to Oct daily (closed Mon except Bank Hols and Jun to Sep). Parking available.

Roman mosaics often depict legends, gods or geometric patterns

Blackpool Lancashire *p216 D4*

Blackpool is England's mecca of entertainment and has attained this position through sheer size, extravagance and wholehearted devotion to the big business of holiday-making. The world famous tower, illuminations and beach are the resort's star attractions, but they merely spearhead the endless amusements Blackpool has to offer.

Over the last two centuries Blackpool has exploded from a small fishing village with a population of less than 1,000, to become one of the largest, most spectacular holiday centres in Europe with well over 150,000 resident inhabitants.

It was the advent of the railway that opened up to Lancastrians and Yorkshiremen the possibility of going away for holidays. With this new-found mobility people flocked to the coast; Blackpool was quick to see the opportunities which existed and the town plunged into the industry of entertainment. Now, during the summer months, approximately eight million people flock to Blackpool and for at least half of them it is their annual holiday resort.

It is difficult to imagine the vastness of a resort which has to cater for such numbers. From the town itself seven miles of sandy beaches stretch southwards, backed by entertainments of every kind. During September and October five miles of the promenade are ablaze at night with dazzling coloured lights. These are Blackpool's famous illuminations.

As well as the promenade display, gigantic animated tableaux are mounted on the cliffs and many of the electric tramcars are transformed into creations such as a Moon Rocket; Mississippi Showboat and the Santa Fe Express. New additions are being made all the time to incorporate current popular fictional characters.

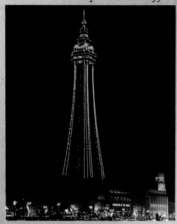
Glittering Blackpool Tower

The Tower
Standing 518 feet high is the town's landmark, Blackpool Tower. It is a fairytale showpiece which was built in imitation of the Parisian Eiffel Tower. Weather permitting, a lift takes people up to the top for the tremendous views along the coast.

At the base of the Tower is a family entertainment complex housing the Ballroom, Undersea World, Dome of Discovery and the world famous Tower Circus.

The Space Tower
Another tower has been added to Blackpool's coastline recently, the Space Tower. This construction of tubular steel is one of the main attractions on the Pleasure Beach and has a glass-fronted observation cabin. Which travels up and down the cylindrical tower.

The Promenade
The three piers, each with a sundeck and a theatre, the Winter Gardens and Opera House, the Golden Mile and the only electric trams still operating in Britain, are all characteristic features of Blackpool's seafront.

The piers, trams and Winter Gardens are almost all that is left of the Victorian days that established Blackpool's popularity. The rest of the promenade is crammed with every kind of amusement gimmick and entertainment novelty imaginable. Amongst the more recent entertainment complexes are Coral Island, Wonderful World and the Star Entertainment centre. Tram rides can be taken along the length of the promenade.

Stanley Park
Behind the town can be found a more restful aspect to Blackpool's character – Stanley Park. Around the large boating lake gardens are laid out in Italian style and many rose gardens adorn the park.

Next to Stanley Park is Zoo Park, one of Britain's newest zoos. Over 500 large and small mammals and birds are kept in thirty-two acres of landscaped gardens.

Grundy Art Gallery and Central Library
Situated in the town itself, the gallery houses a permanent collection of paintings by nineteenth and twentiety-century artists.

Tower Buildings open Easter to Oct daily and winter weekends only. Refreshments available.
Pleasure Beach (Space Tower) open Easter to Oct daily.
Zoo Park open all year (except Christmas Day). Parking and refreshments.
Grundy Art Gallery open all year (except Sun and Bank Holidays).

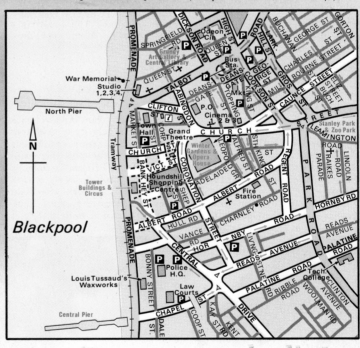
Blackpool

Blair Castle

Tayside *p221 D1*

Beside the highland village of Blair Atholl on the banks of the river Garry, Blair Castle stands amidst its sweeping parkland. It is still the seat of the Duke of Atholl, who is the only British subject permitted to keep a private army, the Atholl Highlanders. The oldest part of the building remaining is the thirteenth-century Comyn's Tower which was renovated during the nineteenth century.

Although the present Duke still lives in the castle, thirty-two of the rooms are open to the public. They contain one of the best collections of weaponry in Scotland, many beautiful tapestries and a marvellous china collection. Several family portraits adorn the walls, and there are many extremely fine examples of period furniture here, including work by Chippendale and Sheraton.

Open Easter week; each Sun and Mon in Apr; end Apr to mid Oct daily. Sun pm only. Parking and refreshments available.

Blickling Hall

Norfolk *p218 F1*

This superb example of Jacobean architecture was designed by Robert Lyminge in the early seventeenth century for Sir Henry Hobart.

The splendid interior contains many rooms of the Georgian era. The hall and Jacobean staircase were remodelled by Thomas Ivory and his family who were architects from Norwich, and have life-size carvings of Elizabeth I and Anne Boleyn set into the walls. The long gallery contains a carved Jacobean ceiling. The library is reputed to have one of the finest collections of pre-sixteenth-century books in England.

The exquisite gardens are mainly the work of Humphrey Repton. They contain many formal flower beds and great arcades, an orangery and a temple. Here too is the pyramid-shaped mausoleum designed by the Italian architect, Joseph Bonomi in 1793 for the Earl and Countess of Buckinghamshire.

A crescent-shaped lake in the grounds has been enlarged to stretch almost a mile in length and provides an attractive contrast to the formal gardens.

Open late Mar to late Oct daily, except Mon and Thu (other than Bank Holiday Mon), pm only. Refreshments available. NT.

Bluebell Railway

East Sussex *p213 C2*

The Bluebell steam railway line is operated largely by a volunteer work force of steam enthusiasts and is one of the most successful of its kind in Britain. It runs for five miles through lovely Sussex countryside between Sheffield Park and Horsted Keynes. Sheffield Park Station, built in 1882, is being restored to its original state

The Lily Pool below Bodnant House decorates the third garden terrace

and on Platform 2 is a museum of railway relics. Visitors can also see the signal box and the locomotives which are not in service.

Horsted Keynes station is being restored as well, and it is here that the collection of old carriages and wagons are kept. (See *Sheffield Park.*)

Steam trains run at weekends throughout the year (Sun only in Dec, Jan and Feb), weekends and Wed in May and Oct, daily from June to Sep and daily during Easter week. The museum is open on days when trains are running, and on other days is open for limited viewing. Parking and refreshments available.

Bodiam Castle

East Sussex *p213 C2*

In the fourteenth century when the river Rother was navigable as far as Bodiam and the French were becoming hostile, Richard II granted Sir Edward Dallyngrigge permission to build Bodiam Castle as a military stronghold. From the outside the castle looks very much the same as it did then because its defences were never seriously put to the test. However, since it was besieged in the Civil War the castle has not been inhabited and it is little more than an empty shell, although restoration work is in progress to enable visitors to view more of the interior. The exterior was restored during the first half of this century by Lord Curzon.

Much of the castle's romantic appearance results from its reflection in the waters of the moat. This is shaped like a lake and is dotted with lovely water lillies. Various objects dicovered during excavations may be viewed in the small museum which is attached to the castle.

Open all year daily (except Sun Nov to Easter, and Christmas period). Parking and refreshments NT.

Bodnant Gardens

Gwynedd *p216 C3*

These are undeniably the finest gardens in Wales and they occupy a superb position above the Conwy Valley with views across to Snowdon. They were first developed in 1875 and were in the care of the Aberconway family until donated to the National Trust.

Five large terraces lead down from the house. The canal terrace is perhaps the most beautiful of these, with its open-air theatre at one end and eighteenth-century Pin Mill at the other. The Pin Mill is a small building which was last used as a pin factory in Gloucestershire. It was rescued when practically in ruins and brought to Bodnant. The theatre has a raised grass stage and the

The gables, turrets and open-topped lantern of Blickling Hall

The gaunt shell of Bodiam Castle reflected in the still waters of its wide moat

wings and back-drops are constructed of clipped yew hedges. The gardens are at their best in the spring when the mass of rhododendrons and camellias are in glorious bloom.

Open mid Mar to Oct daily. Refreshments available. NT.

Bolsover Castle

Derbyshire *p217 B2*

Bolsover Castle stands some 600 feet above sea level and commands lovely views of the locality. Built on the site of a former Norman keep, the present castle dates back to the seventeenth century when Sir Charles Cavendish had the buildings erected to imitate the earlier romantic medieval style. The battlements, turrets and decorative domes achieved this effect. King Charles I and Queen Henrietta were entertained here after the completion of the lavish staterooms in 1634.

The 170-foot long riding school and gallery, added at a later date by Sir Charles's son, is now used by a Spanish riding school.

See AM info. Also open Sun am, Apr to Sep. Parking available.

Bolton Abbey

North Yorkshire *p217 A3*

The skeleton of this twelfth-century Augustinian priory lies on the banks of the river Wharfe. A foot-bridge spans the river here and there is a way across via stepping stones. After the Dissolution only the nave of the priory was saved which subsequently became the parish church of the village, known as Bolton Abbey. The priory gatehouse was incorporated in the nearby Bolton Hall, home of the Dukes of Devonshire.

So attractive is the spot, that the painter Landseer immortalised it in his poem *Bolton Abbey in Olden Time*.

The abbey View at any time.

Border Forest Park

Northumberland, Cumbria and Borders *p220 E3*

Only a few main roads give access to these 145,000 acres of forest and fell which extend along the Cheviots and neighbouring hills in Northumberland, Cumbria and the Scottish Borders Region.

At the heart of the park is Kielder Water, Western Europe's largest man-made lake, which occupies seven-and-a-half miles of the North Tyne Valley. Peel Fell is the highest peak in the park at 1,975 feet and stands right on the border, affording excellent views over northern England and southern Scotland. Spruce trees account for most of the park's woodlands and provide shelter for the growing wildlife community. Every few years each plantation is harvested and the timber, which visitors can see being felled and trimmed, is transported for use in timber industries.

The area is rich in history, hill circles and hill forts of prehistoric man are scattered over the moors. There are also Roman camps, fortified farmsteads and castles in the park which is crossed by the 250-mile Pennine Way footpath.

Boscastle

Cornwall *p211 B2*

The small fishing village of Boscastle lies in the Valency Valley on the north coast of Cornwall. The main village lies behind the harbour and is surrounded by steep woods. The harbour, built into the cliffs, forms a natural haven for boats. However, its narrow entrance can be difficult to negotiate, especially if the river in spate meets a strong tide which causes a dramatic surge of current.

The harbour's inner jetty dates from 1584, when it was rebuilt by the Elizabethan seafaring hero Sir Richard Grenville. The outer breakwater was built in the early nineteenth century when Boscastle was used by the slate industry.

Boscobel House

Shropshire *p216 E2*

This modest house in the Brewood Forest was built at the beginning of the seventeenth century by John Giffard of Chillington Hall. It was intended for use both as a hunting lodge and as a refuge against religious persecution (the Giffards were staunch Catholics). Not until some fifty years later was its effectiveness as a place of concealment put to the test. On 3 September, 1651, Charles II's army was soundly beaten at the Battle of Worcester and the Royal escape party reached Brewood Forest. Luckily the owner of Boscobel was with them. Charles spent one tense night in a hiding-hole within the house which can still be seen. The more famous refuge is the Royal Oak in which the King spent his days hiding from the Roundhead search party. A descendant of the original oak in the grounds marks the spot today.

See AM info. Also open Sun am, Apr to Sep. Parking available.

Boughton House

Northamptonshire *p213 B5*

Boughton House was erected around a fifteenth-century abbey in a picturesque village built mostly of ironstone and thatch. Sir Edward Montagu was the first to buy the property but there is little left of the original architecture. Four generations later, the house was in the possession of the third Lord Montagu, who was appointed Ambassador to France in 1669, and maintained his fortune by wisely marrying a series of wealthy widows. His love of French architecture inspired him to restore the building in the style of the famous Versailles. The left wing was never completed and was left without floors or ceilings.

Inside the house varying styles of decoration are employed. Mythological scenes cover the ceilings and walls, whilst many of the rooms are oak-panelled in a more sombre manner. Amongst the furnishings are examples of velvet upholstery and marquetry pieces. Italian paintings adorn the walls and there is a splendid collection of luxurious Persian carpets.

The house is surrounded by water gardens and broad avenues of lime and elm trees which include a spacious picnic area, nature trail, and woodland adventure playground.

Open Aug, daily. Grounds also open May to Jul and Sep, daily (except Fri). Open pm only. Refreshments available.

Originally an abbots' residence, Boughton House was bought in 1683 by Sir Edward Montague (one of Henry VII's executors)

Boscastle was once a busy port with a flourishing slate industry

Bournemouth Dorset *p212 F2*

This distinguished resort was, until the Victorian love-affair with the seaside, a place of wild heathland where the tiny Bourne stream meandered its way to the sea. Today Bournemouth provides all the attractions of a high-class resort with its mild climate, sandy beaches, acres of gardens and fine coastal views.

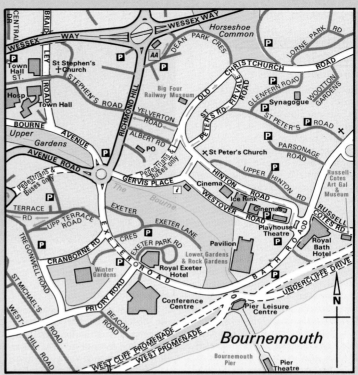

Bournemouth

The sandy shoreline of Bournemouth lies in the shelter of 100-foot cliffs which spread along Poole Bay. These steeply rising cliffs, with their lifts, steps and footpaths leading to the seafront, provide a magnificent background to the town and almost traffic-free promenades. Just to the west of the town these sandstone cliffs are penetrated by a series of deep, wooded valleys called chines that open out to the sea.

The character of this dignified resort is enhanced by the acres of beautiful parks and public gardens which have been landscaped around the natural beauty of the valley and the Bourne stream. Behind the promenades and gardens spreads a modern town of shops, hotels, cinemas and theatres. The two piers, the museums, and the Victorian villas which stand in shaded streets of pine are reminders of Bournemouth's Victorian heyday.

Bournemouth offers the visitor a fine selection of entertainment ranging from variety shows to theatre, cinemas and opera. The renowned Bournemouth Symphony Orchestra has its permanent home at the Winter Gardens, whilst the pier and surrounding areas provide the more traditional seaside amusement arcades, children's pools and playgrounds.

The resort has become a major, and popular, centre for exhibitions and conferences. Pride of place goes to Bournemouth International Centre, a multi-purpose centre, built on the West Cliff. As well as the exhibition halls, which offer seating for up to 4,000 delegates, there is an indoor lagoon-

One of Bournemouth's gardens

type swimming pool with a wave machine, plus a range of other facilities.

Bournemouth is also known for its language schools and colleges which attract a large number of students from all over the world.

Russell-Cotes Art Gallery and Museum

East Cliff Hall (housing the museum) is an interesting example of Victorian architecture. It contains period rooms, a section on Oriental art, the Henry Irving theatrical collection and a freshwater aquarium.

Big Four Railway Museum

This museum contains over 1,000 railway items, including one of the largest collections of locomotive nameplates, number plates and work plates in the country. There is also a large display of model locomotives and a shop selling books and models.

The Lower, Central and Upper Gardens

These attractive gardens follow the Bourne stream through the heart of the town. The Lower Gardens form the hub of Bournemouth's seafront. They lie in the valley amongst footpaths and pines and in spring are ablaze with flowering cherry trees. As the gardens follow the Bourne they become the Central Gar-

Some of the fascinating contents of the Russell-Cotes Museum

dens, with their azaleas, rhododendrons and magnolias. The Upper Gardens come next with their pretty willow trees.

Russell-Cotes Art Gallery and Museum open all year, daily (except Sun). Refreshments available.

Big Four Railway Museum open all year, daily (except Sun and Bank Holidays).

Bourton-on-the-Water

Gloucestershire *p212 F5*

Bourton is a delightful Cotswold-stone village, with the river Windrush flowing through it beside sloping lawns and beneath picturesque low-arched bridges.

Interesting features of this popular spot include the restored parish church which has a fourteenth-century chancel. In the eighteenth-century watermill is a collection of cars and motorcycles ranging from vintage to the 1950s.

In the garden behind the Old New Inn the Model Village portrays Bourton to a scale one-ninth actual size and includes a replica of the river Windrush, working waterwheel, churches, shops and the Inn all in real Cotswold stone.

The nearby Birdland Zoo Gardens covers four acres of ponds, groves and aviaries and is home to some 1200 species of foreign and exotic birds.

Cotswolds Motor Museum open Feb to Nov, daily.
Model Village open all year daily (closed 25 Dec).
Birdland Zoo Gardens open all year daily (except 25 Dec).

Footbridges over the river Windrush in Bourton-on-the-Water

Bradgate Park

Leicestershire *p213 A5*

This area of woods and heathland was donated to the county of Leicester in 1928 to be used as an open space for public use. There are many pleasant walks through its 850 acres, and the native Fallow and Red deer are protected now where once they were mercilessly hunted.

The area known as Swithland Woods used to contain a prosperous slate-quarrying industry which only declined when cheaper Welsh slate came on to the market in the nineteenth century. The disused quarries are now fenced off for safety.

Standing on the highest point of the park is a tower known as Old John, used by hunting parties and reputedly built to commemorate Old John, a local miller who died in an accident on this hill.

Between the hill and the Cropston Reservoir are the ruins of Bradgate House, built around 1500 by Thomas Grey, 1st Marquess of Dorset. He was the grandfather of Lady Jane Grey, the ill-fated nine-day-Queen who was born and brought up here before the plotting of her family cost her her head. On the edge of the Park at Newtown Linford is Marion's Cottage which serves as the park's information centre and bookshop.

Park open all year, no vehicles allowed except those carrying invalids at certain times. Parking.
Ruins open Apr to Oct, Wed, Thu and Sat pm only. Sun am only.
Marion's Cottage open all year Sat and Sun pm only, also Wed and Thu pm Apr to Oct.

Braemar

Grampian *p222 E2*

This summer and winter resort is divided by Clunie Water and surrounded by the heather-clad slopes of the eastern Cairngorms. It is probably most famous for its annual Highland Gathering, an extravaganza of pipe-bands, athletics and, of course, tossing the caber. This event is often attended by members of the Royal Family.

Reminders of Braemar's past exist in the scant remains of Kindrochit Castle near the Cluny Bridge, already a ruin in 1600; in

the cottage in Castleton Terrace where Robert Louis Stevenson wrote *Treasure Island*; and in the picturesque Braemar Castle just outside the village.

Built overlooking the Dee in 1628 by the 2nd Earl of Mar, the castle was a gesture of strength against the Farquharsons who later burned it down. Ironically, it was this same family who purchased and rebuilt the castle during the eighteenth century. Still their family home today, the castle has many notable features including the solidly built round tower, star-shaped curtain wall, barrel-vaulted ceiling and the massive iron gateway.

Royal Highland Gathering first Sat in Sep.
Braemar Castle open May to early Sep daily. Parking available.

Bramall Hall

Gt Manchester *p216 F3*

One of the finest examples of half-timbered houses in the country, Bramall Hall, is now a museum. Most of the Hall in its present form dates from 1590 and the Davenport family have held the property for 500 years, restoring it in 1819.

The south wing, said to be the oldest, contains the Banqueting Room and Chapel and dates back to approximately 1400. In the master bedroom there is a tapestry worked by Dame Dorothy Davenport which apparently took thirty-six years to complete. She was one of the Hall's owners in the 1590s.

Open all year (except Dec) Tue to Sun and Bank Holidays, pm only. Parking and refreshments available.

Breamore House

Hampshire *p212 F3*

This red-brick Elizabethan manor was not completed until three years after William Dodington first bought the wooded estate in 1580. In 1856 a fire swept through the interior of the house, and some of the original structure was destroyed.

The Hulses, who owned the property for almost 200 years, collected many treasures which can be seen today. The walls are hung with family portraits dating back as far as the early eighteenth

A Victorian cottage kitchen recreated in the Countryside Museum at Breamore House

century. All the furnishings are magnificent, including rare examples of early English mahogany carpentry, unusual Dutch marquetry-work, and an extremely rare feather fan from India.

The grounds contain the Breamore Countryside Museum, which is an interesting exhibition of rural crafts and agricultural machinery, and the Carriage Museum. This has many horse drawn vehicles, and is housed appropriately in the old stables.

Open Easter to Sep, Tue to Thu, Sat, Sun and all Bank Holidays, pm only. Parking and refreshments available.

Bressingham Gardens and Live Steam Museum

Norfolk *p213 D5*

Bressingham Hall's gardens are said to be the largest of their kind in Europe. Alpine plants and perennials are lavishly displayed in five acres of informal gardens with some 5,000 species of hardy plants. A glittering roundabout accompanied by a brassy steam organ can also be seen in the grounds.

The most comprehensive collection of steam-powered engines in Britain is housed in the Live Steam Museum which exhibits standard-gauge locomotives.

Apart from the locomotives, traction and road engines are on show; in particular a ten-ton machine called *Bertha* which was mainly used in farm work and was the first exhibit to start the steam engine museum.

Another feature of the museum is a separate narrow-gauge railway with miniature trains which give the visitor the chance to take a steam-hauled ride through the Bressingham estate.

Open May to Sep, Sun pm also Thu pm from late May to mid Sep and Wed pm during Aug. Bank Holidays (except winter) pm only. Parking and refreshments available.

Alan Bloom, owner of Bressingham Museum, with the *Oliver Cromwell*

Magnificent views over Braemar, with Clunie Water snaking away into the distance between the Cairngorm Hills

Brighton Sussex p213 C2

From a small village called Brighthelmstone tucked away beneath the South Downs, grew the town of Brighton – destined to become one of the most fashionable seaside resorts in the south of England. It reached its heyday in Victorian times but since then its character has shifted away from that of the resort to that of a modern town. Now, rich in cultural and commercial amenities, it remains a popular holiday centre offering a diverse range of entertainment and interests.

The Pavilion – first built in 1787 at a cost of £50,000

Brighton's fame began when a certain Dr Russell published a book in 1750, extolling the curative powers of the sea air, and moved his practice to Brighthelmstone. When the Prince of Wales heard of this and consequently visited the village, it soon became a very fashionable place basking in the glory of royal patronage. A considerable amount of building subsequently took place and the Regency architecture of the eighteenth century gave Brighton the style which distinguishes it from many other resorts. Regency Square, Clifton Terrace and Royal Crescent are particularly fine with their well-proportioned houses, white façades, bow windows and wrought-iron balconies.

Brighton is a curious mixture of styles, however, and offsetting its Regency elegance are the seventeenth-century Lanes, the nineteenth-century pier and the vast ultra-modern marina which is the largest in Europe.

The Royal Pavilion

This curiosity was first built as a classical domed structure to serve as a seaside retreat for the Prince of Wales – such was the fancy he had taken to Brighton. Later, architect John Nash rebuilt the Pavilion after the style of an Indian palace to indulge the exotic taste of the Prince. Inside the flavour becomes oriental and is richly furnished and decorated in the classical Chinese style which was in vogue at the time. The decor is lavish in the extreme; especially splendid is the Banqueting Hall with its forty-five-foot-high domed ceiling, from

Good advertising in the Lanes

Pier, beach and sea – still the great holiday attractions

which hangs a glittering silver dragon dangling from a huge chandelier by its claws. The Great Kitchen is also particularly interesting as it contains hundreds of pieces of cooking equipment for every purpose.

The Lanes

This famous part of the town consists of a maze of narrow streets and alleys lined with bow-fronted one-time fishermen's cottages. Now they sell hundreds of antiques and curios of every description and the browser may stop at any one of the number of attractive pubs and cafés which also abound here.

The Piers and Promenade

The piers and promenade of Brighton are still an integral part of the town's popularity. Although the beach is shingle, it is nearly always crowded with holiday makers in the summer as Brighton is known for its mild sunny climate.

The promenade follows the whole of the front and deck chairs may be hired here in time-honoured tradition. In the 1930s it was extended eastwards from Black Rock as an undercliff path to prevent erosion of the cliffs by the sea. In stormy weather the

waves crash over the sea wall in a spectacular fashion.

The pleasures of two piers were once enjoyed in Brighton but at present only the newer Palace Pier is open. West Pier, closed when it caught fire, is under restoration. There are still amusement arcades and refreshment stalls on Palace Pier but they are a far cry from the numerous entertainments which flourished in the Victorian era.

Apart from walking along the promenade, the front may be viewed from the Volks railway. This was Britain's first public electric railway which opened in 1883. In the summer it provides rides along to Black Rock from the Aquarium.

Aquarium and Dolphinarium

There has been an Aquarium in Brighton for over one hundred years and thousands of aquatic wonders can be seen amidst its Victorian subterranean arches.

Museum and Art Gallery

Next to the Pavilion in Church Street is the Museum and Art Gallery. The buildings were originally stables to the Pavilion – the interior being a far cry from the one which offsets the treasures housed there now. There are paintings by English and continental masters, as well as a gallery devoted to Fine Art of the twentieth century. Also to be seen here are collections of Sussex archaeology and folk life, natural history, the Willett Collection of English pottery and several wax busts of Georgian personalities.

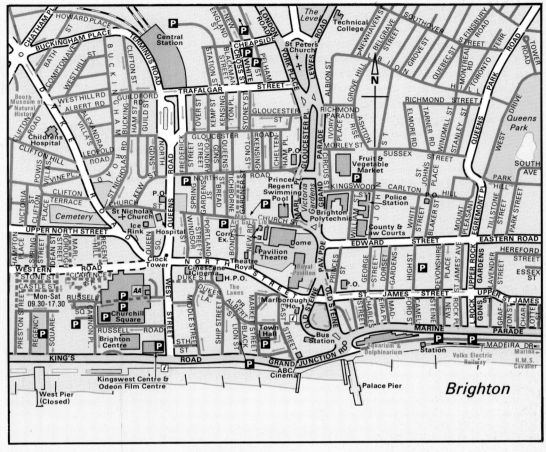

Brighton

Booth Museum of Natural History

Stuffed British birds are attractively and realistically displayed here in models of their natural habitat. There are also skeletons here of both rare and extinct animals and over one million pinned butterflies.

HMS Cavalier

The only surviving destroyer to have seen active service in World War II is preserved in the Brighton Marina and offers a unique opportunity to see how sailors lived and fought in these famous small ships.

Royal Pavilion open all year daily (except Christmas). Refreshments.

Aquarium open all year daily (except Christmas Day). Parking and refreshments available.

Museum and Art Gallery open all year (except Mon, Good Fri, Christmas). Sun pm only. Refreshments.

Booth Museum of Natural History open all year (except Thu), Sun pm only. Closed Good Friday, Christmas and New Years Day.

HMS Cavalier open all year daily. Parking and refreshments available.

Bristol Avon *p212 E4*

The Flower of Bristowe, commonly known as non-such, and the phrase 'all ship-shape and Bristol Fashion' give a clue to the city's past. The former was brought here by merchants from the Middle East and the latter reflects the sea-faring history of this bustling centre. Although new shopping centres, car parks and entertainment complexes intermingle with the old buildings, Bristol still has the salty air of a sea-trading port.

Amateur yachtsmen sailing in the shelter of Bristol's harbour

As an Anglo-Saxon settlement, *Brigstoc,* as it was known, grew up around the harbour on the river Avon. Silver coins have been found that were minted in Bristol during the reign of Ethelred the Unready (978–1013) and these indicate the commercial importance of the city even then.

The Normans built a castle on the strip of land separating the rivers Avon and Frome and from the time of the Conquest, Bristowe (the medieval name) grew steadily in importance during the twelfth and thirteenth centuries, doubling in size and increasing its wharfage area to cope with the growth of trade.

Late in the fifteenth century sailors brought from Iceland stories of a distant land to the west. The tales stirred the merchants of Bristol to dispatch their ships in search of these lands, spurred by economic need to find new markets. They were successful and Cabot's Tower, erected in 1897, stands a hundred feet high on Brandon Hill to commemorate the discovery of North America by John Cabot in 1497.

Trade grew and flourished but during the seventeenth century Bristol's wealth was bought dearly, for a large part of its income was derived from slave trading. When slavery was abolished in the nineteenth century Bristol suffered a serious setback and found herself in fierce competition with Liverpool.

Bristol is still a busy port and from Prince Street Bridge, Prince's Wharf and Wapping Wharf can be seen where Baltic timber and Dutch merchandise is unloaded. From Hotwells Road a good view may be had of the Albion Dockyards and Cumberland Basin which accommodate ocean-going ships coming in from the Avon.

The Cathedral

The cathedral has stood on College Green since the twelfth century. Originally founded in the 1140s as the church of an Augustinian abbey, Henry VIII granted it the status of cathedral in 1542. The Norman chapter house, the gatehouse, the entrance to the abbot's lodging, the

The cathedral's ornate interior

south-east transept walls and the east walk of the cloister remain from the original building. The superbly carved choir stalls were added in the sixteenth century, and later Grinling Gibbons built the fine organ case.

One particular feature are the bosses in the roof of the north transept and there is also some fine fourteenth-century glass.

In the nineteenth century a nave was built to match the choir. There are fascinating tombs and monuments here and some interesting candlesticks. These were donated in 1712 by the rescuers of Alexander Selkirk, the man on whom Daniel Defoe based his character of Robinson Crusoe.

Museum and Art Gallery

The museum has fine collections of archaeological, natural history, scientific and transport exhibits and the art gallery has displays of ceramics, glass and sculpture. Among the fine art collections are paintings by Sir Thomas Lawrence, a Bristol man. There is also an aquarium in the museum.

Bristol's history, until the Reformation can be found in the St Nicholas Church Museum. There is a special collection of church art and displays of eighteenth and nineteenth-century watercolours of Bristol. A notable attraction is the Hogarth altar piece originally intended for the St Mary Redcliffe church.

Early engraving of the
Clifton Suspension Bridge

St Mary Redcliffe

Elizabeth I described this thirteenth-century church as 'the fairest, goodliest, and most famous parish church in the Kingdom'. The nineteenth-century 250-foot spire rests on the thirteenth-century tower and within the church the long nave, open parapets, flying buttresses and huge glass windows resemble the interior of a cathedral. The hexagonal north porch contains carvings of beasts and men which have survived restoration, extension and rebuilding.

The Exchange

Situated in Corn Street this splendid building was designed by John Wood the Elder, famous for his work in Bath. The exchange stands back from the street so its carefully proportioned façade may be more easily viewed.

Outside on the pavement stand four 'nails'. These are bronze pillars on which merchants conducted their business, giving rise to the saying 'to pay on the nail'.

The entrance hall is divided by four Corinthian columns. There are niches along the walls with a frieze of flowers and fruit and a head in the middle of each section. The doorways leading off to the east, west and south have exuberant decorations above them arranged around allegorical heads depicting Asia, Africa and America.

Theatre Royal

Down cobbled King Street, one of the oldest in Bristol, is the longest working theatre in England. Built in 1764–6 the interior is 120 feet by fifty feet and was originally all wood. It has a semi-circular auditorium, which was unusual for that time, and this has been kept.

Also in its original condition is Red Lodge in Park Row. This sixteenth-century house was altered in the eighteenth century

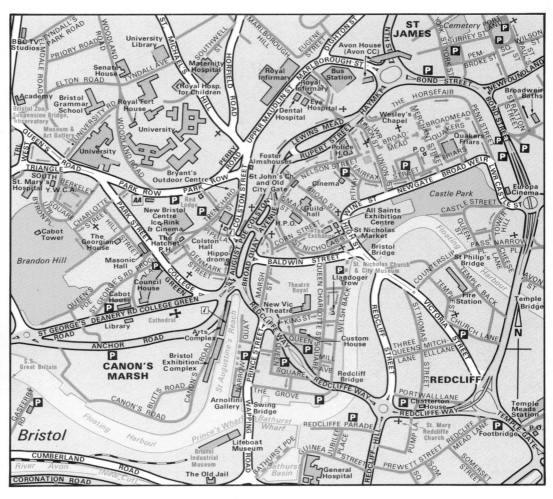

and contains fine oak carvings and furnishings from both periods.

SS *Great Britain*

Prince Albert launched Isambard Kingdom Brunel's *Great Britain* in Bristol in July, 1843. It was the beginning of a new era in ocean travel. The 322-foot-long ship was the largest in the world and also the first one of this size to use an iron hull and be driven by a screw propeller.

Brunel's SS *Great Britain*

Great Britain sailed until 1886 when she was abandoned in the Falkland Islands after being wrecked by a storm. In 1970 she was rescued and brought back to Bristol on a specially constructed raft, and is being restored in the dock in which she was built.

A converted dockside transit shed 400 yards from SS *Great Britain* serves as the Bristol Industrial Museum. Vehicles, both horse-drawn and motorised, aircraft and aero engines and various kinds of manufacturing machinery used locally compete for attention with railway exhibits, which include a full-size locomotive.

Clifton

This elegant, attractive suburb of Bristol is interesting in its own right. Here Brunel's best known work, Clifton Suspension Bridge, hangs like a cobweb between the sides of the Avon Gorge 245 feet above the river. It sways slightly as one walks across it and at night is lit up with fairy lights.

Nearby on the Bristol side of the bridge is the Observatory. Formerly a snuff-mill, it now contains a camera obscura. Beneath is a passage to Giant's Cave which opens out into a ledge high above the river below.

Also in Clifton is Bristol Zoo. This has a good collection of unusual animals including the only white tigers in Europe.

Cabot Tower open all year daily.
Museum and Art Gallery open Mon to Sat (except Bank Holiday, and following Tue, Christmas and New Years Day but open Easter Mon and late Summer Bank Holiday). Refreshments available.
St Nicholas Church Museum open daily.
The Exchange open daily.
Red Lodge open as Museum and Art Gallery.
SS *Gt Britain* open all year (except Christmas). Parking and refreshments available.
Bristol Industrial Museum open all year (except New Year's Day, and Christmas). Sat to Wed.
Bristol Zoo open daily all year (except Christmas). Parking and refreshments available.
Observatory and Giants Cave open all year, daily.

Guests, dressed in Dickensian costume, attending a garden party at Bleak House during the Dickens Festival, which takes place in June

Broadstairs

Kent *p214 E3*

During the Regency period Broadstairs was a fashionable 'watering place'; the Victorians continued the fashion by holidaying here and today it is both a popular residential and holiday resort.

The several miles of sand in small bays beneath chalk cliffs make this stretch of coastline particularly attractive.

The town has many links with Charles Dickens. Bleak House, now a Dickens' and maritime museum, was his home whilst writing *David Copperfield*. It contains many pieces of Dickens' own furniture, as well as some original editions of his novels, drawings and photographs. Close to Bleak House is the Dickens House Museum immortalised as the home of Betsey Trotwood in *David Copperfield*.

A Dickens Festival is held each year in mid June and the old town with its buildings round the jetty recall Dickensian days as the townsfolk dress up as Dickens' most famous characters.

Bleak House open Easter to Sep daily pm only.

Dickens House Museum open Apr to Oct daily, pm only. (Tue and Wed, evenings June to Sep.)

In fine weather several counties can be seen from Broadway Tower

Broadway

Hereford and Worcester *p212 F5*

Broadway, the epitome of a Cotswold village, is built entirely of the honey-coloured local stone. Most of its houses are of Tudor, Jacobean or Georgian origin, and many have been turned into antique shops.

To the east of the village Fish Hill rises to 1,024 feet, surmounted by a fifty-five-foot tower—a folly built in 1800 by the Earl of Coventry. The tower contains an observation room, an exhibition on Broadway and the history of the tower; and the nearby Tower Barn contains a countryside exhibition. This forms the focal point of the Broadway Tower Country Park with its nature trails and picnic areas.

Country Park grounds open all year. Tower and Tower barn Apr to early Oct daily. Parking and refreshments available.

Brougham Castle

Cumbria *p220 E1*

This imposing building stands on the banks of the river Eamont near its junction with the river Lowther. The oldest surviving part of the castle is the keep. It was built during the latter part of the twelfth century although it

is not just confined to the Reserve. The colony of rare red squirrels may be a little shy, but there are 200 peacocks and large numbers of ducks, geese, waders, heron, gulls and tern to be seen.

It was here that in 1907 General Baden-Powell held a camp for twenty boys which was the small beginning of the Boy Scout Movement.

Open Apr to Sep daily. Reached by boat from Poole Quay or Sandbanks. No dogs. Refreshments available. NT.

Buckfast

Devon *p212 D2*

The village of Buckfast lies within Dartmoor National Park. Perhaps of most interest in the village is the beautiful Buckfast Abbey. It was built between 1908 and 1933 by a succession of small teams of French Benedictine monks. The Abbey stands on the site of the original medieval monastery. This was replaced by a Gothic mansion in 1806 which was subsequently incorporated into the present abbey. Inside there is a particularly fine mosaic pavement.

Today, the monks take part in the daily services, and form the choir of the abbey. They run farms, are prominent honey producers from their own beehives, and also produce the famous Buckfast tonic wines.

was heightened in the following century. The groove for the portcullis can still be seen in the outer gatehouse. On the south wall is an inscription detailing the renovations carried out by the owner, Lady Anne Clifford, and the north wall leads to a guard room. Below the floor is a store chamber which was probably once used as a dungeon.

The Roman fort of *Brocavun*, where two Roman roads crossed, can be seen outside the castle walls. Lady Anne Clifford also rebuilt the nearby church of St Ninian in 1660, as well as St Wilfred's Chapel, the interior of which is decorated with richly carved oak and carved wall scenes.

Castle see AM info. Also open Sun am Apr to Sep. Parking available.

Brownsea Island

Dorset *p212 F2*

This lovely unspoilt island covering 500 acres lies within the sheltered waters of Poole Harbour. It makes a perfect contrast to the bustling seaside resorts just across the water.

About half of the island is a Nature Reserve run by the Dorset Naturalists' Trust and guided tours lasting one-and-a-half hours are available around it. However, the wealth of wildlife

Buckfast Abbey always accessible.

Buckfastleigh

Devon *p212 D2*

This pleasant little market town lies south of Buckfast in the lowlying Dart Valley, and it has long been associated with the woollen industry.

An interesting attraction here is the Buckfast Butterfly Farm. Visitors can walk under cover around a specifically designed tropical landscaped garden where living butterflies and moths from many parts of the world can be seen.

Buckfastleigh Station is the terminus of the Dart Valley Railway, a steam-operated service which follows the river Dart for seven miles to Totnes. The station at Buckfastleigh is an attraction in itself. It has locomotives undergoing restoration, a museum, workshops public viewing gallery, scented garden, adventure playground and an extensive picnic area beside the river. From here there are also good riverside walks.

Trains operate during the Easter period, Bank Holidays and Jun to mid Sep, daily. Parking and refreshments available.
Buckfast Butterfly Farm open late Mar to Oct daily. Parking and refreshments available.

Bucklers Hard

Hampshire *p213 A1*

Walking into Bucklers Hard village is like stepping back in time. Two rows of cottages, unchanged since the eighteenth century, face each other across a wide green which slopes down to the banks of the Beaulieu River. One of the cottages was lived in by Henry Adams – Nelson's shipbuilder. No roads pass through the village and visitors must leave their cars in the nearby car park.

Bucklers Hard was not always so tranquil, however. It was once a busy shipbuilding yard where many of the ships which fought at Trafalgar were built, including Nelson's *Agamemnon*. Remnants of the docks such as slipways and lengths of rusty chain can be seen along the river bank.

The importance of the shipbuilding industry here is illustrated in the Maritime Museum which contains models, drawings, documents and various seafaring relics.

Visitors may also take trips along the river by launch from the village during the summer.

Museum open all year daily (except Christmas Day). Parking and refreshments available.

There are no cars to interrupt the grazing of these New Forest ponies by the roadside in Bucklers Hard

Bungay

Suffolk *p213 D5*

Bungay is a historic market town and a popular yachting centre situated on the river Waveney in the heart of rural Suffolk. Its many interesting buildings include the domed Butter Cross which used to contain a cage where wrongdoers were held.

Saxons once lived within the banks and ditches of the ancient earthworks now known as the Castle Hills, and it was upon this vantage point that Hugh Bigod, Earl of Norfolk, chose to build his castle in 1165. This castle and its successor both fell to ruin and much of the masonry went into road repairs in the eighteenth century. However, visitors today can see the foundations which reach up to the ground floor windows and parts of the curtain wall.

A unique feature of the castle is the unfinished mine gallery. It was begun with the intention of destroying the castle, following Hugh Bigod's rebellion against Henry II. Over the last few decades the castle has been restored and the site excavated.

One mile west of Bungay at Earsham is Philip Wayre's Otter Trust, one of the best collections of otters in the country. The Trust aims to promote the conservation of otters in the wild and to breed them for zoos and wildlife parks.

Castle open all year; guide book and keys available from Sayer's shop or Council Offices, both in Earsham Street.
Otter Trust open Apr to Oct daily. Refreshments and parking available.

Otters are becoming increasingly rare in Britain today

Burford

Oxfordshire *p213 A3*

The wide high street of this picturesque town is lined with old houses and inns of every variety of Cotswold stone. At the bottom of the main street a narrow triple-arched bridge of old Cotswold stone spans the river Windrush.

The Old Tolsey, formerly a toll house, is now an interesting little museum exhibiting local craft work, as well as a dolls house with eighteenth-century décor and furnishings.

South of the town is the Cotswold Wildlife Park where animals and birds live in natural surroundings. Exotic birds and small mammals can be seen in the walled garden. and a tropical house contains a variety of colourful birds and many tropical plants. Larger animals including rhinos, zebras and camels can be seen in the African enclosure. An easy and pleasant way of getting around the park is by the narrow-gauge railway.

The park is in the centre of Bradwell Grove Estate and several events take place here during the summer including vehicle rallies and dog shows. Other features here are woodland walks and informal gardens.

Tolsey Museum open Easter to early Nov, pm only.
Cotswold Wildlife Park open all year daily (except 25 Dec). Parking and refreshments available.

Burton Constable Hall

Humberside *p217 D3*

This fine Elizabethan house, home of the Constable family for hundreds of years, is set amidst two hundred acres of parkland landscaped by Capability Brown.

There are twenty-two acres of lakes, an arched bridge, an island, a bird sanctuary and four acres of lawns and gardens. The grounds incorporate an official country park which has a nature trail and facilities for seasonal fishing, boating and birdwatching. Other attractions include a model railway, a children's playground, a picnic area by the lake, a pets corner and a collection of vintage agricultural machinery, vintage motor-cycles and Lilian Lunn miniature figures.

The great house dates from 1570, although the interior was remodelled in the eighteenth century by craftsmen such as Robert Adam, Wyatt and Lightoler. The superb staterooms, the drawing room with its rare Chippendale furniture and the Chinese room are particularly notable. In the Alice in Wonderland room—once used as a small theatre—is a fascinating collection of dolls.

A caravan site is available in the summer and special events are held in the grounds.

Hall open Easter Sun to Sep, Sun and Mon pm only. Also Tue to Thu in Aug.
Grounds Easter Sun to Sep daily pm only. Parking and refreshments available.

The central block of Burton Constable is built around a courtyard

Bury St Edmunds Suffolk p213 D4

Bury, as it is locally known, is a town of colourful history. Here the last King of East Anglia was buried, and King John's Barons swore to force him to accept the Magna Carta. Today it is a pleasantly laid out market and county town with many interesting buildings.

Bury was named after Edmund, the martyred King of East Anglia, whose body was interred in the Saxon monastery thirty-odd years after his death at the hands of the Danes in AD870.

The town has many fine civic and domestic buildings. Angel Hill, for centuries the scene of Bury Fair, is a spacious square which leads into the central complex of the city. On the south side of Angel Hill is the Athenaeum, an eighteenth-century assembly room and formerly the social hub of Regency Bury where Dickens is known to have given two readings. He used the Angel Hotel as a setting in *Pickwick Papers*.

The Abbey

Little remains of this once great and prosperous abbey although there is enough to indicate its former splendour. Behind the abbey gateway and gatehouse, where the portcullis grooves are still visible, lie the abbey gardens flanked by the river Lark which flows under the thirteenth-century Abbot's Bridge. The gardens are filled with flowers, trees, ruins and large areas of grass. Serving now as a bell tower for the cathedral is the solid Norman tower. The ragged remains of the west front of the abbey church have houses built into them.

St Mary's Church

This magnificent fifteenth-century Perpendicular church has a superb hammerbeam angel roof in the nave and a wagon roof in the chancel. The chancel contains the grave of Mary Tudor and a fine porch over the north door.

Pentecostal Church

Built in the style of Wren in 1711, and one of the finest non-conformist churches in existence, it retains the original double-decker pulpit and box pews.

Moyses Hall

This twelfth-century flint and stone building is possibly the oldest domestic building in East Anglia. The ground floor is vaulted with stone arches springing

Moyses Hall – the Jew's house in Kipling's The Law and the Treasure

from massive pillars. It now houses a museum of local history, archaeology and natural history. Exhibits include Bronze Age weapons.

The Market Cross

The Market Cross, also the Town Hall, dates from 1771 and was constructed to Robert Adam's design. It was originally built as a theatre but the upper rooms now serve as an art gallery.

The Cathedral

Formerly the parish church, it did not become a cathedral until 1914. Although it has been considerably extended and restored its origins are fifteenth century. It has a fine interior with particularly beautiful stained glass windows.

Angel Corner

This Queen Anne mansion contains the Gershom-Parkington memorial collection of clocks and watches which is one of the largest such collections in Britain.

Moyses Hall open all year daily (except Sun and some Bank Hols.)
Market Cross Art Gallery open all year Tue to Sat.
Angel Corner open all year daily (except Sun, and some Bank Hols).

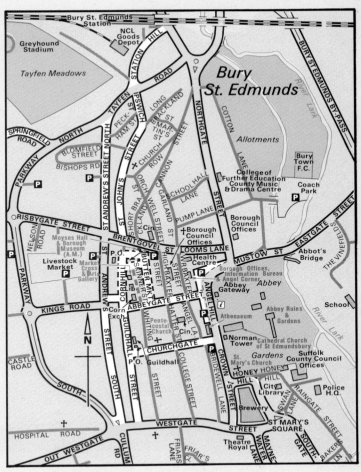

The 14th-century Great Gate of the abbey in Bury St Edmunds

Caerleon

Gwent *p212 E4*

One of the many places associated with Arthurian legends, City of The Legion and seat of Welsh princes, sits on the banks of the river Usk. Beneath present day roads and houses lies the greater part of the Roman fortress of *Isca*, which was established in AD75 and inhabited until the fourth century. It covered over fifty acres and housed 5,600 men of the 2nd Augustan Legion. The parish church stands on the site of the old Roman basilica which would have been the centre of the fort.

Excavation of part of the north-west corner of the fort has exposed the remains of the legionary barrack block, the only one yet found in Britain, and turrets of the fortress wall. The other

area to have been preserved and excavated is the amphitheatre, which actually lay outside the walls of the fort. It was an oval arena hollowed out of the hillside with tiered timber seats, eight entrances and competitors' waiting rooms. Before the amphitheatre was discovered, the site was known locally as King Arthur's Round Table.

The Legionary Museum, which, at the time of going to press, is being redeveloped, contains many of the finds from the site. Among these is the remains of a pipe burial – a pipe was left sticking out of the ground to enable relatives to pour wine down it as a religious offering.

Amphitheatre see AM info. Also open Sun am Apr to Sep. Parking available.
Legionary Museum closed until 1987 for redevelopment.

Caernarfon

Gwynedd *p216 C3*

Caernarfon was an important settlement long before its famous castle was built. The Romans came here in AD78 and built their fort, *Segontium*, on Llanbebig Hill.

Above: Caernarfon Castle, where the first Prince of Wales was born, seen from the banks of the river Seiont

Left: The Roman amphitheatre at Caerleon was able to seat about 6,000 spectators at the gladitorial contests

It was one of the four corner stations of the town which were established to control the Welsh territories. Excavations in the 1920s revealed the foundations which can be seen today, and the Roman museum here contains many of the articles found on the site including many of the personal possessions of the Legionaries.

The castle was part of Edward I's plan to show his supremacy in North Wales. Begun in 1283, it was never completed but is nevertheless one of the most impressive castles in Britain, covering a three-acre site between the Menai Straits and the river Seiont.

Much of the castle's interior was dismantled following the Civil War, but the shell remains intact with its unusual stratified brickwork, battlements and picturesque towers forming an irregular hourglass shape. The walls, up to nine-feet thick in places, were originally extended to encircle the whole of the town, but over the centuries the town has spread far beyond its original limits. Nevertheless the walls are still almost intact, and follow the promenade and quay to the north of the castle

Today the town is a busy market centre with good shopping facilities and the sportsman is well catered for with yacht clubs, golf courses, tennis courts and river and sea fishing.

Castle see AM info. Also open Sun am Apr to Sep. Parking available.
Segontium Roman Fort and Museum open all year daily (except some Bank Hols), Sun pm only.

Caerphilly

Mid Glamorgan   *p212 D4*

The industrial market town of Caerphilly is renowned for its cheese and its castle. Although cheese-making has really died out in the town because Devon and Somerset took over as the main producers, the huge castle remains. The first concentric castle to be built in Britain, it is second only to Windsor Castle in size and covers some thirty acres. It was built by Gilbert de Clare, Lord of Glamorgan, in 1266 as protection against invasion from the north. The extensive moats, dams and lakes he created formed a marvellous defence system and now, decorated with swans, provide a beautiful setting for the castle. Parts of the building lie in ruins as a result of repeated attacks and one attempt by Oliver Cromwell in the seventeenth century to blow up the castle caused the slant of one of the huge towers.

Castle see AM info. Also open Sun am Apr to Sep. Parking available.

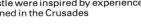

The double defences of Caerphilly Castle were inspired by experience gained in the Crusades

Cambridge

Cambridge revolves around its famous university and there are reminders of this at every turn. The beautiful college buildings and their gardens, students on bicycles, punts on the river Cam and huge bookshops, all blend to create the peaceful scholarly atmosphere of this enchanting Fenland city.

King's College Chapel seen from across the meadows. This masterpiece was begun in 1446 and was not finished until nearly 70 years later

The scholastic origins of Cambridge date back as far as the thirteenth century. At that time several religious orders had established themselves in and around the town and, as schools were then attached to monasteries and cathedrals, this may have had some influence over the gathering of scholars there, particularly since many had to leave Oxford after disagreements with the inhabitants of the town.

The academic community in Cambridge was quickly established and although it called itself a university, it had not acquired any buildings of its own. The colleges as such began in 1284 with the building of Peterhouse College, which was named after the neighbouring St Peter's church. This was the first of the collection of buildings that give Cambridge its unique beauty. Over the next two centuries eleven more colleges were built, together with hostels to accommodate the students who had hitherto lodged wherever they could find room. As the university became a more powerful and influential factor in the town, disputes arose between the scholars and the townsfolk and as a result the expression 'town and gown' was coined. The situation reached such a pitch that in 1381 several riots occurred.

It is impossible to visit Cambridge and not explore the colleges, and although not all are mentioned here, they are all worthy of exploration and admiration.

King's College

Henry VI was the founder of King's College. He established Eton School at the same time and they share the same coat of arms. In fact, however, the chapel was the only part of his plans that came to fruition and no more was added until the eighteenth century, when the Fellow's Building was built. However, the chapel has remained as the splendid centre-piece to the buildings which have gradually surrounded it. Its ceiling is a superb example of delicate fan vaulting and the Renaissance windows portray the story of the New Testament. Above each one the equivalent story from the Old Testament is depicted. Reuben's magnificent painting, *Adoration of the Magi*, takes pride of place behind the altar.

Queens' College

Both the Queen of Henry VI and of Edward IV founded this college. It is built of red brick, and arching from it over to the opposite bank of the river is the well-known Mathematical Bridge, so named because it was allegedly constructed without using nails – based solely on geometrical principles. However, when a curious Victorian took it apart, he was unable to put it back together again without using iron bolts to secure it.

St John's College

Originally, the site of this college held the Hospital of St John, established in 1135, but after the hospital fell into decay it was converted into a college in 1509. The main gate is decorated with St John, the coat of arms of Lady Margaret Beaufort (Henry VII's mother and foundress of the college), and marguerites to commemorate her name.

Two bridges cross the river from St John's – the Kitchen Bridge and the more famous 'Bridge of Sighs', modelled on the bridge in Venice. The bars in the arched windows were put in to prevent undergraduates getting out at night when codes of conduct were rather more rigid than today.

Trinity College

Two exceptional features of this college are the beautiful ornate fountain of 1602, and the library built by Sir Christopher Wren. Inside the library can be seen examples of Grinling Gibbons' carving and plate dating from the seventeenth century.

St Mary's Church

There are many churches in Cambridge but the official university church is that of St Mary the Great. A climb to the top of the tower affords a good view of the market and most of the main colleges. The clock tower chimes, composed for the Cambridge church in 1793, are the same as the chimes of Big Ben.

The Round Church

One of only four round churches in Britain, it was built to commemorate the Holy Sepulchre and dates from about 1130. Although the conical roof was added in the nineteenth century to replace a crumbling fifteenth-century bell tower, the interior has been carefully preserved and restored.

The Mathematical Bridge crossing the Cam from Queens' College

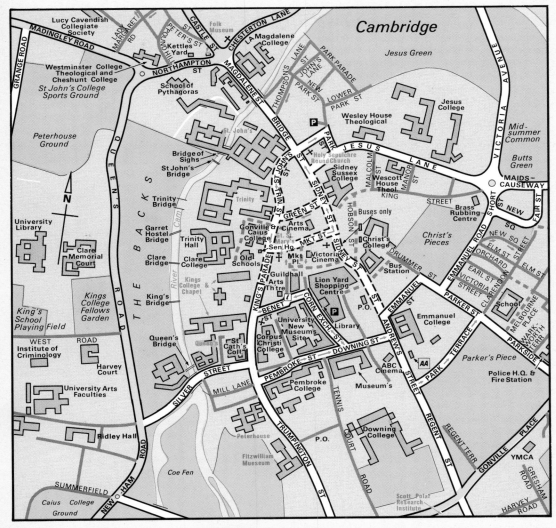

vided up into groups such as kitchen equipment and children's toys, and a room is devoted to each. In the courtyard is an eighteenth-century shop front which was rescued from the town.

The Scott Polar Research Institute

The Institute was founded to commemorate the great explorer Captain Scott and his comrades. The ground floor of the premises in Lensfield Road have been converted to an interesting display area. Souvenirs, records, photographs and relics of the South Pole Expedition can be seen, as well as the latest findings of Antarctic geographical and geological research.

The River

The river Cam has played an important part in the history and development of Cambridge, and the present charm of the city is intrinsically bound up with it.

The most popular stretch of the river in the city, known as The Backs, passes behind the colleges between well-kept open gardens and lawns. Along here punting, rowing and canoeing may be enjoyed. Further downstream, beyond Jesus Lock, motor boats are permitted.

A familiar sight on the river is that of colleges and schools practising sculling and rowing to the encouraging shouts of their instructors.

For those who prefer to remain on dry land, there are lovely walks and many unspoiled picnic spots along the towpaths, as the river continues on through restful pastoral scenery.

Colleges open to the public on most days, though some restrictions during term times.
Fitzwilliam Museum open all year Tue to Sat, Sun pm only. Closed some Bank Holidays.
Cambridge and County Folk Museum open all year (except Mon). Sun pm only.
Scott Polar Research Institute open all year Mon to Sat pm only. Closed some Bank Holidays.

The Fitzwilliam Museum

This belongs to the university and is the largest museum in Cambridge. Amongst its many collections are those of Roman, Greek and Egyptian antiquities; medieval and Renaissance objects of art; paintings ranging from early Italian to pre-Raphaelite and the French Impressionists; and Meissen china.

Cambridge and County Folk Museum

An extensive and varied selection of items familiar to every family in Cambridge over the past half dozen centuries or so are on exhibition here. The items are di-

The Great Gateway and Nevile Fountain of Trinity College

Camperdown Park

Tayside *p220 E5*

Situated to the north east of Dundee, off the A923, the park and its many recreational facilities comprise some four hundred acres, formed round the neo-classical Camperdown House. The parklands were extensively planted with a wide variety of trees, the most famous of these being the Camperdown Elm, a weeping form of Wych Elm.

Today, the recreational and leisure attractions within the park are varied. They include a Wildlife Centre with a large collection of indigenous and domestic animals, an extensive network of footpaths, forest trails and bridleways, as well as a large adventure play area which incorporates kiddies cars and trampolines.

An interesting golf museum is situated beside the restaurant, located in the manor house, and an eighteen hole golf course is a feature of the parkland.

Open Apr to Sep daily. Other times by arrangement. Refreshments and parking available.

Canterbury Kent *p213 D3*

The birthplace of English Christianity and the seat of the Primate of all England, Canterbury's past reaches back to prehistoric times when Iron Age peoples settled by the banks of the river Stour.

When the Romans invaded Canterbury in AD43, it became a trading centre on the most direct route between London and Europe. The Romans were succeeded by the Anglo-Saxons and in 597 St Augustine arrived to spread the teachings of Christ and build his cathedral. The city, standing on flat land and within reasonable reach of the Channel, was easy prey to invaders and in 851 fell to the Vikings and in 1011 was captured by the Danes. When the Normans arrived they characteristically fortified the city with a wall and castle. A mile or so of the wall remains, but of the castle only the ruined keep has survived.

Although Canterbury was heavily bombed during World War II, it still retains much of its medieval flavour. The massive cathedral bears down on the city from its central position, shadowing narrow streets, old hospitals, hostelrys and churches, which are scattered amongst the newer buildings.

The Cathedral

Nothing remains of St Augustine's cathedral, nor of the Norman one that replaced it, but the present nave and transepts do stand on the latter's foundations.

It was in this cathedral that Thomas à Becket was murdered and Chaucer's *Canterbury Tales* give a vivid account of pilgrims journeying to his shrine here in late medieval times.

St Michael's Chapel stands off the south-west transept and is now the Memorial Chapel of the Buffs, the Kent Royal East Regiment. Every morning at eleven o'clock a bell is rung by a soldier who turns a page of the Book of Memory which lists the names of men who died in battle. Just short of 250 feet high, the central Bell Harry Tower dates from 1498.

The Old Weaver's House – a picturesque timber-framed building of 1507

The crypt is the oldest part of the cathedral and has a fine vaulted roof which is the largest of its kind in the country.

The cathedral contains many splendid tombs; Henry IV lies beside his queen in Trinity Chapel, and one of the finest tombs is that of the Black Prince, son of Edward III. Above it are replicas of his armour and weaponry. The originals (over 600 years old) are contained in a glass show-case nearby. St Augustine's Purbeck marble chair is also in the chapel and has been used for centuries to enthrone successive archbishops.

Dane John

One of Canterbury's most attractive amenities is centred upon a prehistoric mound which was re-shaped in 1790, and turned into a pleasure garden in the nineteenth century. The mound was probably a sister to three further mounds which were once beyond the city wall, and possibly part of an early defence system.

A column on top of Dane John commemorates the gardens and overlooks a memorial to Christopher Marlow, Elizabethan playwright and contemporary of Shakespeare. Part of the medieval wall skirts the bottom of the mound, and with its round towers, is still an impressive sight.

Westgate

Built between 1375 and 1381 the only surviving city gate now stands across the busy London Road. There was no need for a wall here as the river Stour formed a natural barrier, and the Westgate had its own drawbridge across it.

For many years, the Westgate was used as a prison, but since 1906 has been a museum. The rooms hold a variety of old weapons, handcuffs, manacles, the timbers of old gallows and other reminders of a violent past. Less dour is a penny farthing bicycle and a 1868 'boneshaker'. There is a splendid view across the roof tops of the city to the cathedral from the museum.

Old Weaver's House

Elizabeth I welcomed Flemish refugees of the sixteenth and seventeenth centuries, and gave them permission to ply their trade of weaving in Canterbury. Furthermore they were given a special place of worship in the cathedral, and today, there is still a service held every week in French.

The weavers worked in what is now one of the most attractive

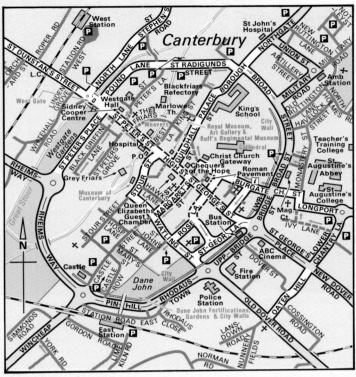

buildings in the city. A white half-timbered building with walls rising up sheer from the river, it has three gables overlooking the road and five more over the river Stour.

Old bobbins, threads and coins were discovered in the house when it was restored earlier this century, and today a resident weaver using an early Victorian loom carries on the weaving tradition of the past.

Royal Museum, Art Gallery and Buffs Regimental Museum

The museum of the Buffs, tells the story of one of England's oldest regiments. There are collections of medals, uniforms, weapons and trophies pertaining to the Regiment.

The museum also holds a rich store of archaeological finds, and Anglo-Saxon glass and jewellery. An art gallery includes work by local artist Sidney Cooper, and collections of engravings and photographs.

Museum of Canterbury

Housed in the fully restored Poor Priest's Hospital, the museum traces Canterbury's history from the Roman era to the present day. Exhibits include Roman cavalry swords, pagan Anglo-Saxon gold and Viking finds. Among the displays are a reconstruction of Becket's tomb, a medieval street and the city in the Civil War.

Westgate Museum open all year Mon to Sat. Oct to Mar pm only.
Old Weaver's House open shop hours.
Royal Museum open all year Mon to Sat.
Museum of Canterbury open Apr to Sep Mon to Sat. Oct to Mar reduced opening hours.

Canterbury Cathedral dominates its city and rises as a landmark which can be seen for miles around

Cardiff

South Glamorgan *p211 D4*

The name of Cardiff conjures up images of docks and industry and rugby football, but it is much more than this. It is an ancient city that was first established by the Romans and parts of their stone walls have been restored.

The Normans chose the same site for their castle which now dominates the modern development of the city centre. It was always an occupied castle, and when military and defensive requirements ceased, it began to be transformed by the addition of new buildings. It is in these newer parts of the castle that the guided tour reveals a wholly nineteenth-century character with its richly ornate décor. One of the most notable features is the banqueting hall fireplace which is surmounted by a medieval castle, complete with a knight on horseback and trumpeters on the battlements.

Within the walls is a vast grassy area where the original Norman keep is perched high on its mound, once surrounded by a moat.

Cardiff is home to one of the largest museums in Britain, the National Museum of Wales, which is primarily concerned with the story of Wales, but also has a fine collection of European art and sculpture, including work by artist Augustus John.

The Welsh Industrial and Maritime Museum in the heart of Cardiff's dockland, houses eight huge engines, including a beam engine and a triple-expansion steam engine.

Outside the museum there are collections of boats, locomotives and cranes.

Castle open for conducted tours all year daily. Closed Christmas and New Year.
National Museum open all year daily (except Christmas, New Year, Good Fri, May Day), Sun pm only. Refreshments available.
Welsh Industrial and Maritime Museum open as above.

Carlisle

Cumbria *p220 E2*

Situated just to the south of Hadrian's Wall, the city of Carlisle has frequently been the scene of battles between the English and the Scots and in 1092, William Rufus (the Conqueror's son) built the castle here. Although the castle has suffered many conflicts throughout history, the outer walls, an impressive keep, the main gate and Queen Mary's Tower remain today. The latter houses the Border Regiment and Kings Own Border Regiment Museum, exhibiting trophies, weapons and documents which depict 300 years of the Regiment's history.

Carlisle's red-sandstone cathedral, begun in 1123 as a Norman church, is the second smallest cathedral in England. It boasts one of the finest stained glass windows – the east – in the country, and other notable features include the carved choir stalls, and a painted barrel-vault ceiling. In the cathedral grounds is a thirteenth-century pele tower, called the Prior's Tower. The ceiling is made up of forty-five painted panels bearing coats of arms of well-known Cumbrian families.

Just outside the cathedral stands the fifteenth-century tithe barn built of stone with huge roof beams by Prior Gondibour. It is now the parish hall.

Between the castle and the cathedral stands Tullie House, a Jacobean town house with Victorian extensions which serves as the museum and art gallery. It contains many items relating to Hadrian's Wall, and a collection of Roman and prehistoric relics, together with English porcelain and pre-Raphaelite paintings.

The Carlisle Cross which stands in front of the old Town Hall of 1717 is surmounted by a fearsome lion. Important proclamations are read from its steps, and it was here, in 1745, that Bonnie Prince Charlie declared his father king of Scotland.

The Guildhall in Greenmarket is a splendidly renovated early fifteenth-century timbered building containing displays concerning guild, civic and local history.

Castle see AM info. Also open Sun am Apr to Sep. Parking available. Museums open as castle.
Museum and Art Gallery open all year Mon to Sat. Also Sun pm June to Aug.
Prior's Tower open all year Mon to Sat (pm only Oct to Apr).
Guildhall open mid May to mid Sep, pm only.

Carlton Towers

North Yorkshire *p217 C3*

The estate here has been owned by the Stapleton's since Norman times, and it is still their family home.

Extensive alterations were made to the exterior of the house during the nineteenth century, and these created a forbidding array of battlements, towers and turrets.

John Francis Bentley, designer of Westminster Cathedral, created the elaborate state rooms. Richly furnished with heraldic detail in their stained glass windows, they are hung with Italian paintings.

In contrast are some delightful smaller rooms with family portraits and photographs, an exhibition of family uniforms and coro-

Colourful Cathays Park, once part of the castle grounds, is now the site of Cardiff's finest public buildings

Tullie House in Carlisle – now used as a museum and art gallery

nation robes and an intriguing priests' hiding hole which has recently been opened. The extensive grounds contain several attractive picnic areas.

Open Easter (Sat to Tue), May Day (Sun and Mon), Spring Bank Holiday and Aug (Sat to Tue). May to Sep, Sun pm only. Parking and refreshments available.

Carnglaze Slate Caverns

Cornwall *p211 C2*

Near St Neot, the second largest parish in Cornwall, in the beautiful wooded valley of the river Loveny, are the Carnglaze Slate Caverns. Ever since the fourteenth century, the slate from the quarry has been used as a roofing material, but today its uses include building stone, crazy paving and hard core.

The route into the caverns allows the visitor to view the upper chamber, some 300 feet high, which was once used as a rum store. Many drilling holes made by blasting to raise the roof can be seen, as well as the tramway which was built to haul the stone from the depths of the quarry to the surface.

Patches of lichen which collect droplets of water, grow on the roof and reflect the daylight in a most remarkable manner. The underground lake a little further on is a magnificent pool of blue-green water of extraordinary clarity.

Outside the caves stands the proprietor's house, an unusual structure primarily erected to house the machinery once used in the quarry.

Open Easter to Sep daily. Parking available.

Castle Bolton

West Yorkshire *p220 F1*

This romantic-looking castle commands beautiful views of open Wensleydale countryside. It was built in 1379 by Richard Scrope, the Lord Chancellor of England, but not actually completed until nearly eighteen years later.

The gateway and living quarters surround a central courtyard, the entrance being extremely well defended with five doorways and a portcullis at either end. The lord's quarters are spacious and comfortable, and built away from

those of the servants as protection against internal strife. Mary Queen of Scots was held captive here for over five months from 1568–69.

The castle now houses a folk museum in which there is a replica of a Dales kitchen as it would have looked a hundred years ago.

Open all year daily (except Mon). Parking and refreshments available.

Castle Combe

Wiltshire *p212 F4*

Castle Combe, lying deep in a wooded valley, is one of the most

photographed places in the country. The twisting Bye Brook passes under a triple-arched bridge which provides the foreground for the Perpendicular church beyond. Much of the history of the village can be traced in the church, which was built with the help of wealthy clothiers as Castle Combe was an important weaving centre in the fifteenth century.

The church contains a thirteenth-century font, and beautiful fan vaulting. Also inside the church is an effigy to Walter Dunstanville, dated 1270, to commemorate the man who built the original castle from which the vil-

Castle Bolton was dismantled after the Civil War, and one of the four corner towers was lost in a storm

lage subsequently took its name.

The seventeenth-century Dower House, the ancient, roofed market cross, and quaint stone cottages with their uneven mossy roofs, help make this one of England's most beautiful villages.

On the outskirts of the village is a popular circuit for motor racing enthusiasts.

Bye Brook winds through Castle Combe – one of England's prettiest villages

Hawksmoor's magnificent Mausoleum stands in the grounds of Castle Howard

Castle Howard

North Yorkshire *p217 C3*

Castle Howard is one of the largest houses in the country, and everything about it is on the grandest scale. The splendid five-mile-long approach is lined with lime and beech trees, and at a bend a huge obelisk stands to commemorate the rebuilding and replanting of the avenue.

The house was built in 1670 of pale yellow local stone by Sir John Vanbrugh and Nicholas Hawksmoor.

Inside is particularly magnificent although most of the rooms are surprisingly small which give the house a pleasant atmosphere. The marbled entrance hall is lit by a multi-windowed dome – the first to be put on an English house, although the original was gutted by fire in 1940. Near the main staircase hang tapestries by John Vanderbank depicting the four seasons, and paintings by Rubens, Canaletto, Van Dyke and Holbein adorn the walls. The beautiful staterooms are vast and luxurious (only two survived the fire) and are filled with magnificent examples of Sheraton and Chippendale furniture and many fine pieces of porcelain.

In the stables is Britain's largest collection of eighteenth to twentieth-century costume which contains beautiful period-dress lavishly embroidered and trimmed, and costumes belonging to famous artistes.

The grounds surrounding the house extend for some 1,000 acres and sparkle with lakes and fountains, while peacocks strut amongst the parkland. Scattered around the gardens are elegant ornamental structures such as Hawksmoor's circular Mausoleum, and Vanbrugh's charming domed Temple of the Four Winds.

Open Late Mar to Oct daily. Parking and refreshments available.

Castle Rising

Norfolk *p218 E1*

Situated in this one-time seaport is the castle built by William de Albini, Earl of Sussex, in the twelfth century. The great keep is one of the largest surviving in England, and the exterior walls are decorated with ornate arches. A staircase leads up to the entrance of the castle, which is only two storeys high and once contained a great hall, kitchens, a small, domestic chapel and a gallery.

Also of interest in the village is the Trinity Hospital, now used as alms-houses. The building has a towered gatehouse and chapel and visitors are able to see the rooms furnished with Jacobean furniture and the common-room which has its original fireplace.

Castle See AM info. Also open Sun am Apr to Sep. Parking available.
Trinity Hospital open all year Tue, Thu and Sat.

Castleton

Derbyshire *p217 B2*

This pretty stone village is set in the heart of the magnificent Peak District, amid such famous natural beauty spots as Winnats Pass and Mam Tor.

With its older buildings grouped around the grassy square, the village is overlooked by the ruins of Peveril Castle, now only a shadow of its former strength. It was built in the eleventh century by William Peveril, then later became the property of Henry II, and was featured in Sir Walter Scott's novel *Peveril of the Peak*.

Castleton is most famous for its four caverns which attract countless visitors each year. The Peak Cavern is the largest, extending some 2,000 feet into the mountain, while the Speedwell Cavern is the only one in Britain which has to be toured by boat. The half-mile trip takes visitors to the famous 'bottomless pit'.

The Blue John Cavern is named after the Blue John spar which is found there. It is the rarest rock formation in the country and this area is reputed to be the only source of it in the world. Blue John was mined here as long ago as Roman times and vases made of Blue John were found among the ruins of Pompeii. The Treak Cliff Cavern is also rich in Blue John and includes a solid pillar of it, six feet high.

Castle See AM info. Also open Sun am Apr to Sep. Parking available.
Peak Cavern open Easter to mid Sep daily. Parking available.
Speedwell Cavern open all year daily (except Christmas). Parking available.
Blue John Caverns and Mine open as above.
Treak Cliff Cavern open as above.

The Blue John Cavern at Castleton. Jewellery is made from the famous spar of blue rock and is on sale in the nearby shop

Cawdor Castle

Highland *p221 D3*

Cawdor Castle is considered to be one of Scotland's finest and most picturesque medieval buildings. It is famous as the scene of Duncan's murder in Shakespeare's play *Macbeth*.

The fourteenth-century tower is the oldest part of the castle, surrounded by sixteenth-century buildings which have been gradually converted, changing what was once a small defensive fort into a large family mansion.

The interior has several attractive rooms giving a good impression of both the family's history and present life at Cawdor. There are tapestries in the family bedroom, specially made in Arras in 1682, depicting biblical scenes; the drawing room has an elegant minstrel gallery and some fine paintings. However, perhaps the most charming room is the blue room, a panelled sitting room with a curious ornate fireplace.

The flower and wild gardens are delightful and there is also a pitch and putt course, several nature trails and a picnic area in the grounds.

Open May to early Oct daily. Parking and refreshments available.

Charlecote Park

Warwickshire *p216 F1*

An avenue of lime trees leads down from Charlecote village to Charlecote Park, where a large Elizabethan mansion stands. Built in 1558 and the home of the Lucy family since the twelfth century, the house contains many fine furnishings and paintings collected by the family. The great park, set beside the river Avon, was landscaped by Capability Brown, and Spanish sheep and fallow deer peacefully graze here together. It was in this park that a youthful Shakespeare is traditionally supposed to have poached deer.

Opposite the entrance farm buildings have been converted to house a display of historic carriages, including a carriage once owned by Alphonso XII, the last King of Spain.

Open Apr and Oct, Sat and Sun pm only; May to Sep daily (except Mon and Thu but including Bank Holidays). Refreshments available. NT.

Chartwell

Kent *p213 C2*

Sir Winston Churchill bought this unpretentious red-brick Victorian house in 1922 as the home where he could pursue his various interests, and he lived here until his death over forty years later. He extensively altered the house and grounds, building a swimming pool and a wall enclosing some 300 acres of grounds.

The character of the house is that of a real home and still has the air of being occupied. It was from Chartwell House that Churchill wrote most of his historical works, and the study remains virtually as he left it. On the writing table are photographs of his wife Clemmie, his children and his grandson Winston, and the walls are decorated with a painting of Blenheim Palace, where he was born, and a portrait of his mother and father. An unfinished canvas stands on an easel in the studio, and his paintings that afforded him such pleasure adorn the walls.

At the front of the house a long terraced lawn stretches down to the combe and the lakes that Churchill had built. The flower garden was created by Lady Churchill and is ablaze with fuchsias, lavender and flowering shrubs. White geraniums and tulips give it an informal, pleasant country garden charm.

House open Mar and Nov, Wed and Sat. Apr to Oct Tue to Thu pm only; Sat, Sun Bank Holiday all day.
Garden and Studio Apr to mid Oct, times as above.

Chartwell, home of Sir Winston Churchill from 1922 to 1965

The Emperor Fountain at Chatsworth was built for a visit by Tsar Nicholas I and throws up water 290 feet high

Chatsworth

Derbyshire *p216 F3*

The ancestral home of the Dukes of Devonshire, Chatsworth House is set in lovely gardens and parkland. It was built in 1687 by the 4th Earl of Devonshire on the site of an earlier house and estate which had been established by the Earl's grandmother, the famous Bess of Hardwick. Coming from a family of modest means, Bess outlived four husbands, becoming progressively richer as she did so. Her fourth husband, the Earl of Shrewsbury, was for some time the keeper of the captive Mary Queen of Scots. Although the house is now a quite different one, some of its rooms are named after the ill-fated Queen.

The house is palatial and the furnishings, décor and state apartments are said to be 'unsurpassed in any house in Europe'. The tour of the house passes through grand rooms with painted ceilings by Verrio and Laguerre (both specialists in that field), exquisite oak panels and carvings and fine sculpture. Both the sculpture gallery and the orangery contain more works of art, and exhibitions of family treasures are held in the theatre gallery.

The gardens were re-landscaped by Capability Brown and subsequent additions and alterations have given them their individual charm. One of the outstanding features is the huge Emperor Fountain which was installed in 1844. An artificial lake had to be created on a hill behind the house in order to supply enough pressure to raise the water to 260 feet. More recent additions include a yew maze which was planted in the early 1960s and a modern greenhouse containing a water-lily pool.

The farmyard at Chatsworth is open during the summer months and the life-cycles of the various breeds of animals are explained. A woodland walk gives a good insight into the management of forestry on the estate.

House and Garden open late Mar to late Oct daily.
Farmyard open late Mar to late Sep daily. Parking and refreshments available.

Cheddar

Somerset *p212 E3*

Famous for its gorge, its caves and its cheese, Cheddar is one of Britain's most popular spots. Gift shops and incongruous modern buildings have sprung up at the foot of the gorge around the entrances to the caves, but no amount of commercialisation can detract from the grandeur of the scenery.

It is best to approach from the north and travel down the gorge where each bend in the winding road takes you deeper into this spectacular ravine, its cliffs rising to some 450 feet on either side. The caves too are a natural phenomenon, a fact which is somewhat disguised by the constructed entrances, the paved floors and the discreet lighting. These man-made additions, however, make it easier to see the magnificent rock formations of stalactites and stalagmites.

Gough's Cave is the most extensive and the most spectacular, stretching into the cliffside for a quarter of a mile. Here evidence was found of inhabitation by prehistoric man over 10,000 years ago. The almost complete skeleton, christened Cheddar Man, which was found here in 1903, now takes pride of place in the museum near the cave entrance. The museum also exhibits flint and bone implements dating from the last phase of the Ice Age and evidence of Iron Age and Romano-British occupation.

Further down the road towards the village is Cox's Cave, which also has some beautiful formations, and the man-made Waterfall Grotto with waterfalls and fish tanks set into the rocks. Here too is the entrance to Jacob's Ladder, a steep flight of 322 steps up the face of the gorge. The view from the top is breath-taking.

Gough's Cave open all year daily (except 25 Dec). Parking and refreshments available.
Museum open Easter to Sep daily. Refreshments available.
Cox's Cave, Waterfall Grotto and **Jacob's Ladder** open Easter to Sep daily. Parking and refreshments available.

Chedworth Roman Villa

Gloucestershire *p212 F4*

This is situated in the wooded valley of the river Coln close to the Fosse Way: the Roman road linking Lincoln and Exeter. The villa is the finest and most fully excavated of its kind in Britain, first discovered accidentally in 1864 by a gamekeeper. After excavations in the 1960s, it was apparent that the building ranged from the mid-second century to the early fourth century.

The living rooms and bedrooms, part of which can still be seen, were all served by under-floor hot-air heating. The most remarkable aspect of the house are the baths, which give a clear picture of the elaborate procedures carried out in Roman days. They had steam baths and dry hot baths which worked on the same principles as sauna baths.

Beautiful mosaic floorings have also been unearthed. The dining room pattern consisted of a central octagon with eight main panels surrounding it which were ornately decorated with nymphs and satyrs, and pieces of them remain today. Many other elaborate mosaic pavements have also survived and are on display. The spring which supplied the occupants of the villa with fresh water has a shrine featuring water nymphs built above it.

Open Mar to Oct, Tue to Sun and Bank Holiday Mons. Feb and Nov to mid Dec, Wed to Sun. NT.

Lime deposits from dripping water cause these formations in Cox's Cave

Cheltenham Gloucestershire *p212 F5*

Cheltenham is a town of spacious elegance. The whole town is a well-proportioned pattern of stately squares, sweeping terraces, broad avenues and well-placed trees and gardens.

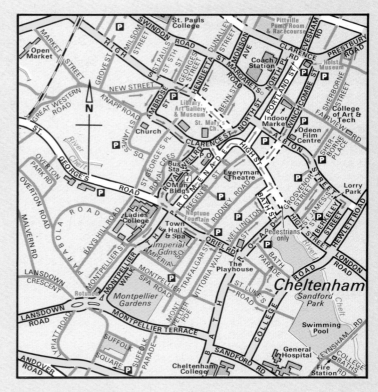

Once just a little place on the banks of the river Chelt, its development as a major spa town began with the discovery of a mineral spring in 1715. By 1738 the first pump room was built and fifty years later its future was assured when George III, accompanied by his family, came here to take the waters. The medicinal reputation of the spa grew so rapidly that a select few of the most eminent architects of the day were employed to plan an entirely new town.

On the whole Cheltenham has retained its unique character and the houses and villas still have their splendid Regency ironwork balconies and verandas. Of particular note is Montpellier Walk which is modelled on the Erechtheion Temple in Athens and, lined with female figures, is one of the most unusual shopping precincts in the world. Other fine examples of Regency architecture can be found in Landsdown Place, Suffolk Place, and the Rotunda, which is modelled on the huge Pantheon in Rome. The culmination of this period of planning and design was the Promenade, with its fountain of Neptune, completed in 1825.

Cheltenham is a major centre for music and literary festivals and several of international repute are held here throughout the summer. A contrasting attraction is the race-course at Prestbury Park, home of the Cheltenham Gold Cup, one of the premier National Hunt races which is held in March.

Pittville Pump Room

Built between 1825 and 1830 for Joseph Pitt MP, as a place to entertain his friends, it stands in regal splendour amidst spacious parkland and lakes. The building consists of a great hall surmounted by a gallery and dome, fronted by a colonnade of Ionic columns.

Art Gallery and Museum

The permanent collection here includes Dutch and British paintings, English and Chinese ceramics, pewter, glass, modern art and art and craft exhibitions. In addition there is a large local section which includes regional archaeology, Cotswold crafts, Cheltenham prints, Edward Wilson (companion of Scott to the Antarctic) personalia and general social history items.

Gustav Holst Museum

This modest terraced house was the birthplace of the composer Gustav Holst and he spent the first eight years of his childhood here. The house has been carefully renovated and is now not only a museum portraying the composer's life and music, but also contains fine examples of typical Regency and Victorian rooms.

Cheltenham's Pittville Pump Room dispenses the only drinkable alkaline waters in Britain

St Mary's Parish Church

This, the only medieval building left standing in the town, dates back to the early twelfth century. It is best known for its fourteenth century window tracery and its fine Victorian stained glass.

Pittville Pump Room open Apr to Oct Tue to Sun; Nov to Mar Tue to Sat. Closed Good Fri and some Bank Hol Mons.

Art Gallery and Museum open all year (except Sun and Bank Hols.

Gustav Holst Museum open all year Tue to Sat (except Bank Holidays).

Chepstow Castle on the river Wye

Chepstow

Gwent *p212 E4*

On the outskirts of old market town of Chepstow, with its steep narrow streets lies an ancient fortress – Chepstow Castle. It stands on limestone cliffs at the Welsh/English border, above the river Wye which forms a natural moat. The castle has spread over the centuries along the natural ridge of land as new defences and buildings were built. Martens Tower was added during the thirteenth century and Henry Marten, a signatory of Charles I's death warrant, was imprisoned in the tower until his death in 1680.

The castle has four courtyards, a forty-foot-high keep and is surrounded by walls which are strengthened by towers. A walk through the dell to its western end reveals a delightful view of the castle and river.

See AM info. Also open Sun am Apr to Sep. Parking available.

Chester Cheshire *p216 E3*

This, the one-time Roman fortress of Deva, is now a dignified mixture of medieval and Victorian architecture. The two-mile circuit of ancient walls, black and white buildings, galleried streets, flights of uneven steps and double-tiered shops, give Chester its unique atmosphere of medieval England.

The Romans chose their site well when they built their stronghold on the river Dee. As it was situated at the head of the tidal estuary on a sandstone plateau, sea-going vessels were able to moor virtually under the walls of the settlement, and the bend of the river protected its southern and western sides. However, when the Romans left Britain, Chester, like so many of their settlements, fell into decay and obscurity and remained so for several centuries.

Under Norman rule Chester was turned into a virtually independent state governed successively by eight earls over a period of 106 years. This ended because the last of these powerful rulers had no male heir and the King, rather than let the city fall into female hands, took over the city and conferred the earldom on his son. Ever since then Chester has been a property of the eldest son of the reigning monarch.

Chester flourished most profitably between the twelfth and fourteenth centuries as a port. Its position on the west coast meant easy trading with Ireland, and a flourishing import and export trade developed. However, this only lasted until the fifteenth century because the estuary began to silt up and was no longer navigable to ships. Trade subsequently declined rapidly and was diverted to the nearby village of Liverpool.

The Walls

These provide a pleasant two-mile walk around the city. The northern and eastern walls are mostly the original Roman structure, but those to the west and south have been replaced over the centuries and their perimeter extends down to the river and the castle.

Towers have been added to the walls at various times; Eastgate is particularly attractive with its ornate clock. Arched over the roads are the four main gates through the walls.

The walls have always been important to the inhabitants of the city and at one time people known as 'murages' were appointed as officials to collect taxes for maintenance.

From the walls are good views both of the city and its environs. To the south-east of the walls is the racecourse known as the Roodee. Originally a harbour in Roman times, the name is derived from two Anglo-Saxon words meaning island of the cross. It has been the scene of horse-racing for 400 years and the Chester Cup is held here annually.

The Rows

These unique shops are probably the most famous features in Chester and have characterised the city since the Middle Ages. Situated in Bridge Street, Watergate and Eastgate Street, they consist of shops on two levels so arranged that the top row is overhung by its upper storeys. The result is an attractive fully-covered shopping precinct which is a delight to explore.

Chester Visitor Centre

Part of the Rows, reconstructed exactly as they were in the nineteenth century, can be seen here, as well as an exhibition illustrating 2,000 years of Chester's history.

Roman Amphitheatre

This is the site of the largest amphitheatre excavated in Britain to date. The Roman Garden next to it has re-erected Roman columns, as well as other remains which have been found in the city, including part of an underground heating system.

The Grosvenor Museum

The museum is best known for its galleries of Roman antiquities but it also devotes a considerable amount of space to natural history, local history, costume, furniture and Victoriana.

The Cathedral

Built of sandstone, the cathedral was originally a Norman Benedictine abbey, but when many monasteries were abolished in the Dissolution it was turned into a cathedral. Although it was restored quite considerably in the nineteenth century, architecture spanning eight centuries can be seen in different parts of the

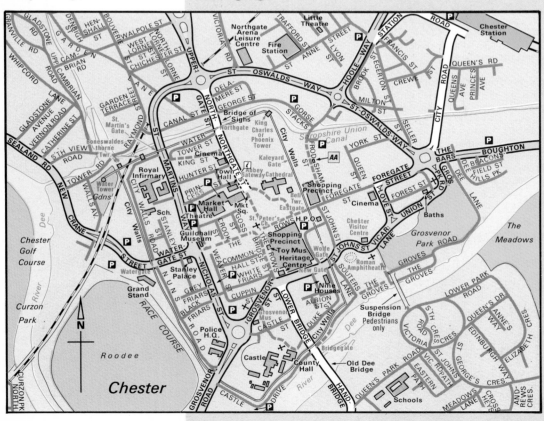

Chester

cathedral. The stalls which were carved in the 1300s are particularly interesting as they depict in wood a variety of creatures and figures.

The Groves

Alongside the river are the tree-lined Groves providing a pleasant respite from the city centre. In the summer, band concerts are held here and the river is always alive

with pleasure boats.

Behind the Groves are the neat, colourful gardens of Grosvenor Park – donated by the 2nd Marquis of Westminster in 1867 for the enjoyment of Chester's inhabitants.

Chester Visitors Centre open all year daily. Refreshments available.
Grosvenor Museum open all year daily (except Good Fri and Christmas) Sun, pm only.

Above: The Cross, seen here from Watergate Street Rows
Below: The ironwork clock tower of 1897 on Eastgate

An engraving of Chester Castle

Chichester West Sussex *p213 B2*

Chichester, standing between the South Downs and the sea, combines the flavour of both. Its busy yachting harbour and weekly cattle market reflect the seafaring and agricultural past of the town.

The Romans called the place *Noviomagus* and in AD200 they built a wall around it of which large stretches remain. Although the remains are mainly medieval, the Roman foundations and core still exist.

Most of the best architecture in the town is Georgian. The area known as The Pallants is particularly elegant and here, and in West Street, are many fine buildings that were once wool merchants' houses. During the fourteenth century wool was Chichester's main source of revenue and a flourishing export trade existed from the town's port. The harbour is now one of the south coast's most popular yachting centres and a path leads down to it from the old canal basin.

The Cathedral

The bishopric, originally at Selsey, moved to Chichester after the Norman Conquest. In 1245 St Richard of Chichester became Bishop and was subsequently adopted as the town's saint.

The graceful 277-foot spire of the cathedral dominates the skyline and is clearly visible from the sea and nearly every point in the city. In 1861 the old spire collapsed in a gale; Sir Gilbert Scott's successful reconstruction preserved the original design however. Some notable features inside the cathedral are the double aisles of the nave with its fine Norman arches and fourteenth-century choir stalls. Two more modern works of art are the

vividly-coloured altar tapestry designed by John Piper in 1966 and Graham Sutherland's oil painting, depicting the appearance of Christ to Mary Magdalene on the first Easter morning. The composer Gustav Holst is buried in the north transept.

Roman remains including mosaic pavements have recently been discovered under the foundations of the cathedral and are now kept in the Guildhall Museum. On the south side access can be gained to the formal gardens of Bishop's Palace through a gateway adjoining the cloisters.

District Museum

Exhibits in Chichester museum date from prehistoric to modern times and relate particularly to the town and surrounding area. The Royal Sussex Regiment also have a collection here dating from 1701 – the year it was established. An annexe to the museum is the Guildhall Museum located in Priory Park, which mainly houses Roman relics.

The Market Cross

The city is crossed by four main streets and in the middle stands the fifty-foot high Market Cross, a complex eight-sided arcaded structure crowned with an octagonal stone cupola. It was built in 1500 and provided shelter for countryfolk while they sold their produce. Farmers and growers still gather from a wide area to attend a weekly cattle market here.

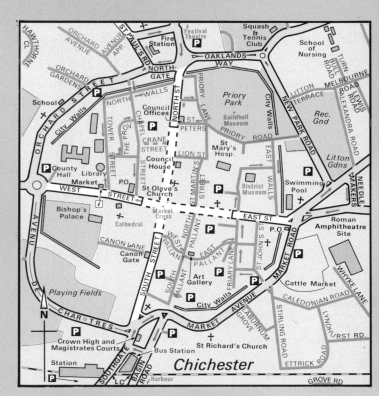

Festival Theatre

Just outside the city walls is the distinctive hexagonal-shaped theatre which opened in 1962. It has gained an international reputation for staging the best in classical and contemporary works.

District Museum open all year Tue to Sat.
Guildhall Museum open June to Sep, Tue to Sat pm only.

The cathedral spire rises above the compact city of Chichester

Chichester's Festival Theatre

Chilham

Kent *p213 D2*

Chilham's magnificent central square, surrounded by timbered black and white houses, makes it one of the most attractive villages in Kent. Amongst these Tudor buildings is a fifteenth-century flint church which contains several fine monuments, including a group sculpted by Sir Francis Chantrey. He left the large fortune he had accrued to found the art collection now housed in the Tate Gallery (London).

The gates of Chilham Castle stand in the village and through them the hexagonal Jacobean mansion, built in 1616, can be seen. Close to the house is a massive flintstone Norman keep – the only remains of an earlier castle which in turn stood on the site of ancient Saxon fortifications.

The present house is set in a great park overlooking the river Stour, and interesting features and events which take place in the grounds include jousting tournaments, eagle and falconry displays, woodland and lake-side walks and extensive gardens.

Chilham Petland has been created to show a wide-ranging collection of hand-reared, and domestic animals in readily accessible enclosures. Some of the pets may be stroked and fed.

Castle not open to the public.
Grounds open Easter to Oct (except Mon and Fri). Jousting Suns. Parking and refreshments available.

The gardens of Chilham Castle were landscaped by Capability Brown

Chipping Campden

Gloucestershire *p212 F5*

This ancient town of gabled stone buildings of varying levels has remained unspoilt for centuries. Between the thirteenth and sixteenth centuries Chipping Campden was a major wool centre, and the merchants' prosperity is reflected in the town's beautiful architecture. Perhaps the finest example of this is the Jacobean Market Hall with its pointed gables, open arcade and timber roof.

The impressive 120-foot pinnacled tower on the fifteenth-century church of St James, enhances one of the finest wool churches in the Cotswolds. Inside, kept safely in a glass case, is a rare collection of English embroidery, some dating back to Richard II's reign.

The mid fourteenth-century Woolstaplers Hall in the High Street contains an unusual collection of relics from bygone days, including cine equipment, kitchen utensils, farm tools, coins and exhibits from the wool industry.

The word 'chipping' keeps on recurring in the Cotswolds. It is an Old English word for 'market' or 'trading centre', which perfectly sums up the character and history of this delightful little town.

Woolstaplers Hall open May to Sep daily, weekends only Oct.

Chirk Castle

Clwyd *p216 D2*

Chirk Castle stands high on a hilltop on the Welsh border, commanding breath-taking views of the surrounding countryside. It was built as a frontier fortress in a style similar to many other Welsh castles built by Edward I. It is rectangular, with round towers at each of its corners, and surrounds a large quadrangle which is entered through a splendid archway.

Today the castle is an elegant stately home which has been in the possession of the Myddleton family since 1595.

The entrance hall is richly panelled in oak – the work of the English architect Pugin, and is bedecked with weapons and armoury from the Civil War. Beyond is an elegant sweeping staircase after the style of Robert Adam. At the foot of the stairs hangs a portrait of Sir Thomas Myddleton, who bought the castle in 1595. The regal state dining room bears a magnificent brass and crystal chandelier and has been restored to its original eighteenth-century splendour. Rich furnishings abound throughout the chambers, including the Mortlake tapestries, and many interesting paintings adorn the walls, including those of royalty and striking local landscapes.

In the Tudor block are rooms which have been unchanged since Elizabethan days, and the original Tudor room houses a bed where Charles I once slept.

The grounds of the castle are heralded by superb eighteenth-century ornamental gates, wrought with intricate tracery bearing elaborate crests and flower designs, which are the work of the Davies Brothers of Bersham.

Open Easter to late Sep, Tue to Thu, Sun and Bank Holiday Mon, pm only. Oct Sat and Sun only. Parking and refreshments available.

Chirk Castle stands in the valley of the river Ceiriog which divides England and Wales

Chysauster

Cornwall *p211 A1*

For nearly 1,600 years the site of this ancient village lay overgrown and neglected. When excavations first began to take place in the 1860s one of the best preserved Iron Age villages in England was discovered. Although only the bottom half of the walls can be seen, it is enough to give a good indication of the layout of the houses. Built with walls fifteen feet thick against the elements they may either have been roofed with thatch or stone. The village was lived in between about 100 BC to the third century AD and the inhabitants probably smelted tin and existed on small-scale mixed farming. A short distance from the houses is an underground chamber, or fogou, which was probably used by the village as a central storage area.

See AM info. Also open Sun am Apr to Sep. Parking available.

Cilgerran Castle

Dyfed *p211 C5*

Romanticism has popularised this striking slate-grey castle. It was from here that the beautiful

Chysauster – where the oval plans of Iron Age houses can be seen

wife of Gerald of Windsor, Nesta, was abducted by an admirer in 1109 and subsequently became something of a legend, often referred to since as the Helen of Wales.

However, the castle has had a turbulent political history; it was fought over and changed hands many times before falling to ruin in 1326. The remaining parts of the curtain walls and the huge twin-towers have been an inspiration to poets and painters such as Turner, and an attraction to

countless visitors. Today the ruins dominate the valley of the river Teifi and the quiet old-fashioned village below.

See AM info.

Cirencester

Gloucestershire *p212 F4*

Once one of the chief centres of the wool industry in the Middle Ages, Cirencester became a

centre for agriculture when the cloth industry declined during the Industrial Revolution.

Known as *Corinium* by the Romans, the town became the second largest in Britain. The Romans were quick to realise the strategic position of Cirencester, which accounts for the Roman roads radiating from it, including the great Fosse Way and Ermin Street.

In the middle of this mellow Cotswold town is the colourful Market Place where weekly open-air markets are still held. The rest of Cirencester is a maze of fascinating streets lined with quaint old houses including workmen's cottages, almshouses and seventeenth-century bow-fronted shops.

However, the most striking feature of the town is the 120-foot tower of the church of St John the Baptist, built by the prosperous wool merchants, which overlooks Market Place.

A large collection of Roman antiques recovered by archaeologists is kept in the Corinium Museum, and the atmosphere of *Corinium* life is recaptured here for the visitor in a reconstructed dining room, and part of a kitchen in a Roman town house. A cut-away

section shows part of an underground Roman central heating system.

The museum entrance looks across to the gateway of Cirencester Park, a 3,000-acre estate belonging to Earl Bathurst. Although the house is not open to the public, the park is available for riding and walking and on most Sundays polo matches take place there.

A Norman arch is all that is left of the abbey, but the grounds make an attractive centrepiece to the town with the river Churn winding through the well kept lawns into a large lake populated by swans and wildfowl.

Corinium Museum open all year daily (except Christmas), Sun pm only. Oct to Apr closed Mon.

Clandon Park

Surrey *p213 B2*

In 1735, the 2nd Lord Onslow commissioned the Venetian architect Leoni to rebuild his Elizabethan family home. The result was a grand, square, red-brick house decorated in a mixture of Baroque and Palladian styles, with Italian, French and English trimmings.

A nineteenth-century porch

In the late 18th century Clandon Park was one of the grandest Palladian houses in England

leads into the beautiful marble hall which is splendidly embellished with Italian plasterwork and fascinating mythological scenes. The staterooms contain plasterwork by Artari and Bagutti and are lavishly decorated; the exact colours and materials of the eighteenth century have been restored where possible. Flock wallpaper from France covers the Palladio room, and the saloon has a magnificent ceiling in pastel shades. In the hunting room there is a collection of Chinese porcelain birds, and the morning room has satinwood furnishings and pieces of Chelsea porcelain.

Other treasures in the house include a highly ornamented state bed dating from the eighteenth century, with a matching set of chairs, a Chippendale marquetry dressing table, and some early Staffordshire pottery.

Open Apr to mid Oct daily (except Mon and Fri) pm only. Also open Bank Holiday Mon but closed following Tue. Parking and refreshments available. NT.

Claydon House

Buckinghamshire *p213 A4*

Claydon House, in the small village of Middle Claydon, has been the home of the Vernay family since 1620. The stone-faced westwing is the only surviving part of the house, and its sober exterior belies the beautiful rococo state rooms within.

The pink parlour and north hall are particularly fine adjoining rooms. Each is richly embellished with exuberant tracery, magnificent wood carvings depicting fruits and flowers, and birds and beasts on the ceilings and walls. In the fantastic Chinese room is a rare example of eighteenth-century Chinoiserie, decorated with ornate carvings and furniture, and tiny bells hanging from

Cirencester Park stretches away beyond the house, home of Earl Bathurst, which lies on the western edge of the town

the walls. The staircase is a masterpiece of wrought ironwork. It winds into garlands and scrolls, and has ears of corn so delicate they faintly rustle as one climbs the stairs.

Florence Nightingale and her sister Frances Parthenope Vernay lived at Claydon for some years, and both have left their impression on the house. Florence's bedroom can be seen in its original Victorian state, and adjoining this is a room containing items from her Crimean mission, and other treasures relating to the military history of the Vernay family.

The eighteenth-century library was created by Frances, although its earlier plasterwork and Ionic doorframes were retained.

Open Apr to Oct daily, pm only (except Mon, Fri and Tue following Bank Holiday). NT.

Cleeve Abbey

Somerset *p212 D3*

The only Cistercian abbey in Somerset, Cleeve Abbey, was founded by the Earl of Lincoln in 1198 and became the most prosperous religious foundation in the county. After its decline, the abbey was sometimes used as a shelter for farm animals and for storage of farm implements but, now in the care of the Department of the Environment, it has been well renovated. The buildings that remain include the refectory, chapter house, common-room and the cloisters, which stand on the banks of the Washford River.

See AM info. Also open Sun am Apr to Sep. Parking available.

The formal design of the box hedges probably dates from the 1850s, when the present Cliveden House was built

Cliveden

Buckinghamshire   *p213 B3*

Cliveden Reach, with its sweeping views, is a beautiful wooded stretch of the river Thames. The grounds of the 327-acre estate of Cliveden contain rambling wooded walks, avenues, terraced gardens and delightful water gardens. Hidden around the grounds are sculptures and statues set in niches and ornamental temples of Italian design.

Cliveden House, former home of the Astor family, is now a luxury hotel but three rooms are still on view to the public.

Gardens open Mar to Dec daily.
House Apr to Oct, Thu and Sun pm only. Refreshments available. NT..

Clovelly

Devon   *p212 C3*

The beautiful village of Clovelly is world-famous for its picturesque, unspoilt charm; unspoilt largely because no traffic can enter the village. All vehicles must be left in the large cliff-top car park, and visitors have to make their way on foot down the cobbled streets, so steep that they have been stepped in places.

Pretty, white-painted cottages line the streets, bright with window-boxes and flowering shrubs

which somehow defy their north-facing situation, and flower as early and as long as in more southerly resorts.

At the bottom of the cliff-side village is the tiny harbour where fishing boats take shelter, and ancient cannon barrels have been upturned to serve more peacefully now as mooring bollards. Visitors who cannot face the steep climb back to the car park can make use of a Land-Rover service available from the harbour.

All around the village the densely wooded cliffs rise to some 400 feet, providing lovely walks and superb sea views, particularly from Gallantry Bower.

The most attractive way into Clovelly is via Hobby Drive, a three-and-a-half-mile toll road which runs from the main road near Buck's Cross to Clovelly car park, passing through pleasant woodland with panoramic views.

Clumber Park

Nottinghamshire   *p217 C2*

This lovely park of nearly 4,000 acres was landscaped by the Dukes of Newcastle. Much of the credit, however, must go to Capability Brown who laid out lawns and shrubberies, planted trees and created the lake all in his own distinctive style.

In the mid nineteenth century

an unusual double avenue of limes was planted, three miles long and containing some 3,000 trees, which remains one of the outstanding features of the park.

The palatial mansion, once the centrepiece of the estate, was demolished in the 1930s, but the lodges and gate-piers remain at the entrances and two garden temples and a fine classical bridge still exist

By far the most impressive remaining structure in the park is the Clumber Chapel, the word 'chapel' doing little justice to the size of the building. Described as 'a cathedral in miniature', it was designed by G F Bodley and is a superb example of Gothic Revival architecture based on the four-teenth-century Decorated style. It is built of contrasting sandstone and white Streetly stone and is surmounted by a graceful

180-foot spire. The interior had the benefit of the finest nineteenth-century craftsmen to create the intricate rood-screen, stone and wood carvings, and stained glass.

Today the whole park is a pleasure ground with shops, cycle hire and fishing available.

Park open all year. Chapel temporarily closed for repairs. Parking and refreshments available. NT.

Cockermouth

Cumbria   *p220 D1*

The Cumbrian town of Cockermouth, lying to the west of Bassenthwaite Lake and the distant, lofty height of Skiddaw, is a good starting point for exploring the Lake District. It sprung up around the Norman castle, strategically placed at the junction of the rivers Cocker and Derwent. Much of the castle was destroyed by Parliamentary forces during a Civil War siege, but a surviving older part contains an oubliette, or subterranean dungeon, that was for life prisoners.

The town is particularly famous as the birthplace of the Lakeland poet William Wordsworth. Wordsworth House, the family home, is at the west end of the broad, tree-lined main street where the garden backs on to the river Derwent, which he recalls in *The Prelude*. A simple Georgian house, it contains many of its original features including the staircase and some of the fireplaces and panelling.

All Saints, a nineteenth-century church occupying part of the site of an old grammar school attended by Wordsworth, contains a stained glass window commemorating the poet.

Wordsworth House open Apr to Oct daily (except Thu). Refreshments available. NT.
Castle not open to the public.

Donkeys may be hired to carry luggage up the hill at Clovelly

Colchester Essex *p213 D4*

The garrison and market town of Colchester stands in the midst of rolling East Anglian countryside, presided over by its lofty Town Hall and an enormous Victorian water tower called Jumbo. The famous Colchester oysters are cultivated on beds in the lower reaches of the river Colne which skirts the northern edge of the town.

The timbers of Old Siege House are riddled with Civil War bullets

Colchester is England's oldest recorded town, and goes back to the seventh century BC when a settlement was first established on the site. Evidence of the huge system of earth works which protected pre-Roman Colchester can be seen to the west and the oldest part of the town is still surrounded by its Roman walls including the Balkerne Gate – the west gate of the Roman town. Later occupations are marked by the Norman Castle, the house of the Flemish weavers in 'The Dutch Quarters' to the west of the castle and the Civil War scars visible on the walls of Siege House in East Street.

Castle and Museum
This Norman castle was built mainly of Roman bricks and constructed on the site of the temple of the Emperor Claudius. The keep, the largest ever built in Europe, is all that remains and now houses the Castle Museum. The museum contains an interesting collection of Roman, Iron Age and medieval relics.

Holly Trees Museum
A fine Georgian house, situated close to the castle, Holly Trees houses a collection of costumes and antiquities. It was purchased for the town by Viscount Cowdray in 1920 and opened as a museum.

Natural History Museum
The museum is situated in the former All Saints church with its fine flint tower, and its existence saved the church from demolition in 1958. Exhibits illustrate the natural history of Essex, with special reference to the Colchester area, and the museum includes a diorama and an aquarium.

Museum of Social History
This interesting museum contains historical displays of rural craft and country life. It is housed in the historic church of Holy Trinity in Trinity Street, and is the only Saxon building left in the town.

The Minories Art Gallery
The Minories is a late Georgian house rebuilt in 1776 from an original Tudor building and is a centre for the visual arts. It has a

The keep of Colchester Castle

continuous programme of concerts, exhibitions and lectures as well as Georgian furnishings and paintings by William Constable.

Bourne Mill
This striking stepped and curved gabled building was constructed in 1591 with stone from St John's Abbey and was originally a fishing lodge. It was converted into a mill in the nineteenth century and can be seen in working order.

St Botolph's Priory
These ruins consist of a great Norman church of which the west front – with a particularly fine doorway – and part of the nave, have survived.

Colchester Zoo
In the forty-acre park of Stanway Hall, with its sixteenth-century mansion and church dating from the fourteenth century, is Colchester Zoo. Founded in 1963, it has a variety of attractions including an aquarium, birdland, all the breeds of large cats, and a model railway.

Castle and Museum open all year Mon to Sat, except Christmas and Good Fri, also Sun pm Apr to Sep.
Holly Trees Museum open all year (except Christmas and Good Fri) Mon to Sat.
Natural History Museum open all year Mon to Sat (except Christmas and Good Fri).
Museum of Social History open as above.
The Minories open all year Tue to Sat; Sun, pm only. Refreshments available.
Bourne Mill open Easter to mid Oct weekends and Bank Hols only. Also Tue, Jul to Sep. Afternoons only. NT.
Colchester Zoo open all year daily. Parking and refreshments available.

Compton Acres Gardens

Dorset *p212 F2*

Thomas William Simpson bought the house at Compton Acres just after World War I and his idea was to surround the house with gardens, designed in such a way that only one of them could be seen at a time. It is not hard to believe that this ambitious plan, begun in 1919, took several years to accomplish.

There are seven gardens in all; English, Heather, Japanese, Italian, Roman, Rock and Water, each with its own individual beauty. Most of them contain a priceless collection of bronze and marble statues which have come from all over the world. There are particularly fine views of Poole Harbour and the Purbeck Hills from the English garden. The careful lay-out of the gardens includes paths and bridges over streams and ponds to avoid steps and stepping stones for the less agile. Many of the plants grown at Compton Acres can be purchased.

Open Apr to Oct daily. Parking and refreshments available.

Above: The Italian garden at Compton Acres – one of seven designed by owner T W Simpson

Compton Castle

Devon *p212 D2*

Battlements and towers lend Compton Castle a charmingly romantic air. Actually a fortified manor house, it belonged to the Gilbert family for six hundred years and the hall, reconstructed in the 1950s, contains an assortment of Gilbert mementoes. Other rooms on view include the old kitchen and the chapel which date from the fifteenth century.

Surrounded by grounds extending to 346 acres, the house is beautifully set in a combe and there is a thatched barn standing next to it.

Open Apr to Oct, Mon, Wed and Thur. Parking available. NT.

Compton House

Dorset *p212 E3*

In 1839 an architect from Bath by the name of John Pinch created the present mansion known as Compton House. Although Victorian, the house – featuring gables, tall chimneys, dormer windows and window gables –

has a distinctly Tudor appearance.

The Gooden family bought the original house in 1746 and they have owned the estate ever since. During the 1970s one enterprising member of the family, Robert Gooden, transformed the house and grounds into a home for his spectacular collection of butterflies. Locally known as Worldwide Butterflies Ltd, the house contains species from all over the world. There is also a natural jungle, where living butterflies fly free, and a tropical palm-house.

Another great attraction of Compton House is the Lullingstone Silk Farm where live silk worms and demonstrations of silk-making can be seen. Silk has been produced by this company for the last two coronations and Queen Elizabeth's wedding dress was made from Lullingstone silk.

Open Apr to Oct daily. Parking and refreshments available.

Compton Castle's magnificent façade was built in about 1500 to protect the earlier house of 1420 from the threat of French invasion

Conwy Gwynedd *p216 C3*

This ancient walled town and its castle stand out against tree-clad hills which rise steeply from the broad estuary of the river Conwy, over which span a trio of very differently styled bridges — a suspension, a tubular railway and a modern road bridge.

The massive town walls, some thirty-five feet high and six feet thick, extend right down to the shoreline and, with their twenty-one crenellated towers, make Conwy one of the most formidable towns in Britain. The Quay is one of the pleasantest parts of the town, now mainly used by pleasure craft and small fishing boats. Fresh fish is sold here and trips to Trefriw, where old wharves remain as reminders of the days when slates were shipped down the river, are available.

The Castle
Edward I drew workmen from all over England in 1283 to build this giant fortress as a means of controlling the newly defeated Welsh armies. It remained as a powerful military stronghold until after the Civil War when, having survived a three-month siege, was surrendered to Parliamentary forces who rendered it useless for military purposes.

Plas Mawr
On the corner of Crown Lane and the High Street stands a perfectly restored Elizabethan house, which is now an art gallery and the headquarters of the Royal Cambrian Academy of Art. Of particular note is the ornate plasterwork which was covered until the nineteenth century and is consequently remarkably well preserved. The banqueting hall is particularly fine.

The smallest house in Britain beside the river-quay in Conwy

Aberconwy
This claims to be the oldest house in Wales, dating mainly from the fifteenth century. Over the years the road level has risen so much that the upper storey has to be approached by outside stairs. Inside an exhibition depicts the life of the borough since Roman times.

St Mary's Parish Church
The church is all that remains of the former abbey which stood here before being moved to Maenan to make way for the castle. It is reached by narrow lanes which lead up to the open grassy churchyard. Inside is a stone figure of the daughter of John Williams, Archbishop of York and a bust of the sculptor John Ginson.

The Smallest House
With its frontage of only six feet and only ten feet in height, its claim to being the smallest house in Britain may well be justified. The only two rooms are linked by an almost vertical staircase and resemble a mid Victorian cottage.

Castle see AM info. Also open Sun am Apr to Sep. Parking available.
Plas Mawr open Feb to Mar and Nov Wed to Sun; Apr to Oct daily.
Aberconwy open Etr to Sep daily (except Tue). Oct weekends only. NT.
Smallest House open Apr to mid Oct daily.

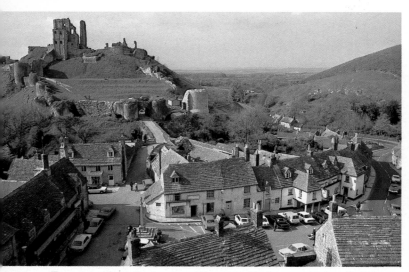

The ruins of Corfe Castle where Edward the Martyr was murdered in 978

Corfe Castle

Dorset *p212 F2*

Overlooking the village of the same name, are the dramatic ruins of Corfe Castle, a stronghold in the Purbeck Hills which was fortified by Saxon kings. Besieged during the Civil War, the owner's wife, Lady Banks, defended the castle after her husband died, against Parliamentary troops, but it was eventually seized and reduced to its present condition and much of the stone was removed to construct buildings in the village. The ruins cover more than three acres, with the keep at the hill's summit.

The central point of this quaint village is the little square with its church, old inns and houses. In the Middle Ages a marble carving industry existed in the village and the Ancient Order of Marblers still meet in the Council Chamber every Shrove Tuesday. Located in the same tiny buildings as the Chambers is the small museum which shows old village relics and dinosaur footprints one hundred and thirty million years old.

Castle open all year daily, pm only Nov to Feb.
Museum open all year daily.

Cotehele House

Cornwall *p212 C2*

Granite-built Cotehele House, standing in lovely gardens above the river Tamar, is a perfect example of an early Tudor manor house.

Most of the furniture in the house dates from between the six-teenth and seventeenth century and was all collected by the Edg-cumbe family. The hall is deco-rated with armour, weaponry and hunting trophies, and seven-teenth-century tapestries hang from floor to ceiling in most of the rooms.

The grounds cover over a thousand acres and fall down in terraces of gardens and pools to the valley of the river Tamar where there is a restored water-mill. A small shipping museum and the restored sailing barge 'Shamrock' can be seen at the quay.

Open Apr to Oct daily, (House closed Fri, except Good Fri); Nov to Mar garden only open daily. Refreshments available. NT.

Coughton Court

Warwickshire *p216 F1*

This Elizabethan house is situated in pleasantly wooded countryside close to the Forest of Arden. The building, which once had a moat, has a central stone Tudor gatehouse flanked by two half-timbered wings which form an open courtyard to the east.

The house is most famous for its association with the Gunpowder Plot; the wives of the conspirators awaited the result of their hus-band's conspiracy in the gate-house dining room. The house is interesting for its Jacobite relics, fine panelling and the early six-teenth-century staircase brought from Harvington Hall in 1910.

Open Apr and Oct Sat, Sun and Bank Hol Mons. May to Sep daily (except Mon and Fri). Also open Easter Sat to Thu. Afternoons only. NT.

Courage Shire Horse Centre

Berkshire *p213 B3*

Set amidst pleasant Berkshire countryside, the Courage Shire Horse Centre has a fine collection of up to twelve Shire horses. The centre was created to arouse in-terest in this breed and to help ensure its survival.

The timber-built stables con-tain a coach house for the show drays and the loose boxes where the horses can be seen. In the display room are many rosettes and shining horse brasses as well as a static exhibition of the an-cient craft of barrel-making.

Around the centre is a collection of farm carts and agricultural equipment. Other features of the centre include a farrier's shop, a small animals' enclosure, and a children's playground.

Opposite stands a famous coaching inn, once called The Coach and Horses, but now re-named the Shire Horse Inn, whose deeds go back some 300 years.

Open Mar to Oct daily (except Mon unless Bank Holiday). Parking and refreshments available.

The stone ruins of Criccieth Castle – built in the 13th century

Crathes Castle

Grampian *p222 F2*

Crathes Castle has been the an-cestral home of the Burnett family since 1323. Its romantic little tur-rets and gables were added at the end of the sixteenth century and it was around this time that the magnificent painted ceilings were completed in the Chamber of the Nine Worthies, the Chamber of the Nine Muses and the Green Lady's Room. This is supposed to be haunted, and the ghost is apparently undisturbed by the biblical inscriptions on the beams.

The ghost of the Green Lady is said to walk Crathes Castle

The great hall was restored to its original state during the 1930s and contains a curved granite fireplace dating back to Elizabethan times. Paintings by Jameson adorn the walls of the hall, but by far its proudest possession is the Horn of Leys, a jewelled horn of fluted ivory believed to have been given to the Burnetts by Robert the Bruce. At the very top of the house, stretching across its entire width, is the long gallery with a superbly carved oak ceiling and panelling.

As one of the most visited properties in Scotland, Crathes Castle is equally famous for its gardens, dating from the eighteenth century. A magnificent array of plants glorifies the formal gardens which are separated by dense yew hedges – planted in 1702.Each section has been carefully planned so the colours of the plants complement each other. The rest of the grounds extend almost 600 acres to the north of the river Dee and contain several nature trails.

Castle open Easter and May to Sep daily. Refreshments available.
Gardens and grounds open daily all year. NTS.

A team of four, from the Courage Shire Horse Centre, pulling a brewer's dray in the Cart Horse Parade on Whit Monday, in Regent's Park, London

Criccieth Castle
Gwynedd *p216 C2*

Perched high on its headland between two sandy bays, Criccieth Castle looks down over the quiet but popular holiday resort below. Criccieth is the only North Wales resort to face due south and from this unique position the castle enjoys panoramic views across Tremadog Bay to the south and inland to the foothills of Snowdonia in the north.

During the fifteenth century the castle was captured by Owain Glyndwr who then set fire to it; the damage is still evident today from the scorch-marked walls and stones cracked by the heat. Since that time the castle was left to decay, but there are substantial parts of the curtain walls and towers remaining. Particularly notable are the Leyburn Tower and the Engine Tower; the latter is so named because it once contained a stone-throwing machine called an 'engine', to defend its northern face.

See AM info. Also open Sun am Apr to Sep.

Cricket St Thomas Wild Life Park
Somerset *p212 E3*

This beautiful and historic 1,036-acre estate belonged to the famous naval family, the Hoods, between 1757 and 1897. The Park is approached over Windwhistle Ridge and along a tree-lined drive which sweeps down to Cricket House, a fine Ham-stone early nineteenth-century building.

The Wild Life Park is surrounded by the rolling acres of the Cricket St Thomas dairy farms and contains a collection of wild animals and birds. Many of them, which include llamas, wallabies and flamingoes, are allowed to roam free in spacious paddocks. There are sixteen acres of landscaped gardens and a stream was dammed to form the waterfalls and series of lakes.

The park is also the home of the National Heavy Horse Centre and has four shire horses in Victorian stalls, a dray, and showcases displaying harness. A country life museum in the walled area of the park houses farming implements of bygone days.

Other facilities for visitors include a picnic area, a garden shop, a gift shop and a restaurant.

Open all year daily. Parking and refreshments available.

Culloden Battlefield
Highland *p222 D2*

It was here on 16 April, 1746, on the windswept plateau of Culloden Moor that the last battle fought on the soil of the United Kingdom took place. It was between the Jacobites of Prince Charles Edward Stuart and the Hanoverian army, led by the Duke of Cumberland. The defeat of the Prince's men, who were outnumbered by two to one, marked the end of the struggle for supremacy by the Stuarts. The battle is remembered for the particular savagery of the Duke of Cumberland's troops towards the defeated Highlanders, who were slaughtered indiscriminately both in the battle and in the subsequent pursuit. No mercy was shown and over 1,200 men died. This event caused the Duke to become known by Scotsmen as 'Butcher' Cumberland.

A tall cairn erected in 1881 stands at the side of the road, which was constructed across the moor in 1835. On both sides of the road are scattered stones, which mark the graves of the Highlanders and are engraved with the names of the clans that took part. Old Leanach Farmhouse, around which the battle raged, still stands and now houses a museum.

Nearby is the Field of the English where seventy-six of the Hanoverian dead are buried, as well as the inscribed 'Cumberland Stone' which is said to mark the position taken by Cumberland during the battle. The Well of the Dead is reputed to be where wounded Highlanders were butchered when trying to drink.

A National Trust Centre has been erected and houses an audio-visual exhibition, and an information desk.

National Trust Centre open Good Fri to mid Oct, daily. Parking available. NTS.

Culzean Castle and Country Park

Strathclyde *p219 B3*

The powerful Kennedy family's ancestral home has been at Culzean Castle since the sixteenth century, but the present castle was not built until about 1780. It is, in fact, not so much a castle as a palatial mansion, designed by Robert Adam in typical eighteenth-century style with classical lines and an elegant interior.

A collection of Kennedy family portraits hangs on the walls of the castle, which has an unusual circular drawing room and a superb central staircase. The castle tour also includes three rooms set out as a memorial to the late General Eisenhower who was presented with a flat here to use as his official Scottish residence.

The gardens and grounds form the Culzean Country Park, occupying over 500 acres overlooking the Firth of Clyde. It includes a walled garden, an orangery, a camellia house, an aviary and a swan pond. Robert Adam also designed the Home Farm buildings which have now been converted to form a reception and interpretation centre for the Country Park.

Castle open Apr to Oct daily, (pm only Oct).
Country Park open all year. Centre open Apr to Oct daily. NTS.

Cwmcarn Scenic Forest Drive

Gwent *p212 D4*

This seven-mile drive through mountain forest, passes through an area which totals 10,000 acres. It includes twenty miles of valleys between the river Ebbw in the north to Newport in the south. Partly a twentieth-century recreation of the thirteenth-century Forest of Machen, the forest is comprised largely of larch, spruce and pine which provide timber for coal mining, local sawmills and the paper and packaging industries.

The drive offers spectacular views of the surrounding countryside as far as the Brecon Beacons and the Bristol Channel. There are forest and mountain paths especially set aside for the walker, along which viewpoints are marked.

Open daily Easter to Sep. Parking available.

D

Dalemain

Cumbria *p220 E1*

The Hasel family has occupied this historic house, with its distinctive façade of locally quarried dusty-pink sandstone, since 1679. Set in parkland amidst wooded

Left: a monument to local industry along the Cwmcarn Forest Drive

vice on 27 September, 1825. This famous locomotive is now preserved in the North Road Station Railway Museum, housed in what is possibly the oldest railway station in the world, certainly the oldest in Britain. The station, built in 1842, has a long plasterwork façade and a cast-iron colonnade and staircase. In the museum are six other nineteenth-century locomotives, a railway coach (c 1845), a chaldron wagon and an extensive model railway layout. There are also paintings, drawings, photographs and railway documents.

Darlington's town museum includes many items of natural and local history, geology and archaeology. One of its more interesting features is an observation beehive exhibited during the summer months. The art gallery contains a permanent collection which includes John Dobbin's painting of the opening of the first public railway.

Among the modern development in Darlington are some interesting historical features, particularly a fine clock tower and the ancient parish church of St Cuthbert. Built by Bishop Pudsey of Durham in about 1180, it contains intricately carved misericords.

Railway Museum open all year daily, Sun pm only. Parking available.

Museum open all year daily (except Good Fri, Christmas Day and New Year's Day, Sun and Thu pm).

Art Gallery open all year daily (except Sun and Bank Holidays).

Left: The grand gardens of Culzean Castle

Locomotion No 1 in the North Road Railway Museum at Darlington

hills, Dalemain lies to the north of Ullswater, on a site which once supported a Saxon settlement. A Norman pele-tower (a tower built to protect crops and livestock) is still the main part of the house, and formed part of the chain of strongholds established along the Scottish marches as a defensive measure against Border raids. Over the centuries the tower has been added to, resulting in the Elizabethan and Georgian mixture seen today.

A museum located in the base of the pele-tower contains military relics of the Westmorland and Cumberland Yeomanry, as well as the militia and volunteer forces which preceded it. In the six-teenth-century cobbled courtyard beside the pele-tower is a countryside museum with many interesting agricultural tools. Other attractions on the estate are the gardens and deer park.

Open Easter to mid Oct Sun to Thu. Parking and refreshments available.

Darlington

Co Durham *p217 B4*

The industrial town of Darlington is undoubtedly best known for its railway associations, for it was here that George Stephenson's *Locomotion No. 1* made its first journey as a public passenger ser-

Dartmoor Devon

Dartmoor National Park is one of the few wide open spaces left in the south of England, and its wild beauty is free to all. The moor actually covers some 365 square miles between Okehampton and Ivybridge, Tavistock and Christow, and manages to combine mountains, moors, valleys, woods, market towns and villages.

Many of Dartmoor's ponies are sold each autumn as pets for children

It is the great variety of landscape and colour of Dartmoor which never fails to strike the visitor. Rolling upland, occasionally broken by rugged outcrops of grey granite, rises to summits crowned by massive tors sculptured by centuries of weathering into fantastic shapes, some of which have become strangely recognizable, such as Vixen Tor near Merrivale.

The heather, moss and lichens which predominate in the upland combine to produce soft browns, olives and purples which contrast strongly with the close-cropped green grass along the peat banks of the river valleys, dotted with browsing sheep. Many streams and rivers criss-cross the moor and these rise in the moors to the north and south. The fens and mires provide the headwaters for such rivers as the West Dart and Cowsic in the north and the Avon, Erme and Plym in the south. The going here is too soft for larger animals such as sheep and wild ponies, but, curiously, there are few smaller animals either. It seems an area devoid of inhabitants and even few birds breed here. However, the patient observer can spot the occasional curlew, lapwing or merlin.

The heather and grass moors surround the bogs and it is on these that the wild Dartmoor ponies roam. It is believed these sturdy little animals were first turned out on the moor by our ancestors in the Dark Ages. Although allowed to wander freely over the moor, all the ponies have owners, and are rounded up once a year so the foals can be branded. The open country is ideally suited to riding, and pony trekking is a popular way of seeing the less accessible parts of the moor. Rabbits too, are plentiful here, thanks to the Normans who brought them over from France. The addition of the word warren (as in Trowlesworthy Warren) to many place-names is testimony to the rabbits' long occupation of the

Bowerman's Nose Tor – the name is derived from its curious shape

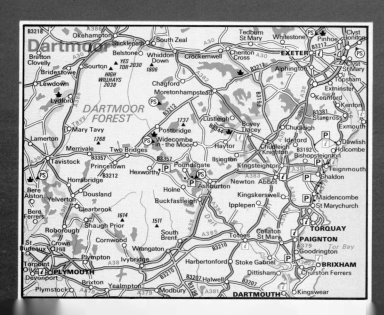

This noble tower belongs to the parish church of Widecombe-in-the-Moor, scene of the famous Widecombe Fair

Spinster's Rock, near Drewsteighton, is a Megalithic tomb which dates from Neolithic times. Remains of villages of the same period are also scattered over the moor and one of these hut circles can be seen at Grimspound on Hameldon. There are also Bronze Age kistvaens (small burial chambers) and standing stones (mysterious monuments where sacred rites were performed). These either take the form of a great monolith such as Beardown Man and Menhir on Petertavy Common, or as long rows of smaller stones – the row which runs between Stall Moor and Green Hill is two and a quarter miles long. On the edges of the moor are Celtic hill-forts of the Iron Age, such as the ones at Cranbrook near Moretonhampstead and at Prestonbury near Drewsteighton.

Medieval legacies to Dartmoor are the wayside crosses marking the old track used by the monks of Buckfast and Buckland Abbeys, and the 'clapper' bridges which were built by the tin miners out of huge granite slabs.

moor. The fox is another common inhabitant, and badgers and otters live here undisturbed.

Wistman's Wood, Black Tor Beare and Piles Copse are ancient uplands oak copses, where stunted, gnarled oaks festooned with mosses, lichens and ferns, create a fairyland atmosphere. Other plantations, mostly of conifers, date back to the beginning of this century and the forests at Archerton and Fenworthy and Bellever are even younger. The lower river valleys have their own indigenous oak woods.

Interesting characteristics of this wild tract of land are the relics of prehistoric communities who lived on the moor long before Celtic, Roman and Saxon times.

Kingswear, set on the river Dart, is linked by car ferry to Dartmouth on the opposite bank

Dartmouth

Devon p212 D2

On the west bank of the beautiful river Dart lies Dartmouth, an interesting ancient town and fishing port with narrow, hilly streets.

The wide tidal river is alive with private, pleasure, and naval craft which must avoid the two car ferries plying back and forth across the Dart at the north and south end of the embankment. A regatta is held here in August and there are regular boat trips to Totnes during the summer. Around the town are a number of fifteenth, seventeenth and eighteenth-century buildings, including those on the waterfront in Bayards Cove with its cobbled quay. On a wooded hill to the north of the town is the magnificent Britannia Royal Naval College (not open to the public). Built in 1905, it replaced HMS *Britannia*, a former training ship for Royal Naval Cadets and here, for the past one hundred years, most of the regular officers of the Royal Navy have started their service careers.

Dartmouth has two castles, one in Bayards Cove, built by Henry VIII as part of his coastal defence system, which has been restored, and Dartmouth Castle opposite, near St Petros Church. The two castles were attached by a chain during times of war to make a barrier across the estuary.

One of the oldest (c 1725) Newcomen Engines (so it is claimed), is housed in a glass-fronted com-memorative building in Royal Avenue Gardens. Almost opposite is The Butterwalk, an attractive colonnaded arcade built in the 1630s. On the first floor of number six is a nautical museum which displays over one hundred and fifty ship models, as well as other objects of local interest.

Bayards Cove Castle accessible at all reasonable times. Parking available. AM.
Dartmouth Castle See AM info. Also open Sun am Apr to Sep. Parking available.
Newcomen Memorial Engine open Easter to end Oct Mon to Fri.
Butterwalk Museum open all year daily (except Sun); pm only Nov to Mar.

Deal

Kent p214 E2

This peaceful, old-fashioned seaside resort is tucked beneath the chalk cliffs which border it to the north and south. Here the shingle beach is lined by fleets of fishing boats and its open seascape provides splendid views of shipping passing the notorious Goodwin Sands. These vast, shifting beds lie just five miles offshore and have caused hundreds of wrecks.

Much of the character of old Deal can be found around Middle Street, where narrow lanes run back from the seafront. This eighteenth-century quarter is said to have been the haunt of smugglers.

Deal's first claim to fame is that Julius Caesar made his initial invasion on the beach here between Deal and Walmer in 55 BC. The main historical monument however is Deal Castle, one of a line of defensive forts built by Henry VIII when there was a threat of invasion from France. The castle stands near the foreshore to the south of the town and was built in the symmetrical shape of a six-petalled flower, or clover leaf design, in 1540. Two rings of semi-circular bastions surround the central keep. The castle has been returned to its original architectural form and now houses a small museum exhibiting Iron Age weapons, early pottery and relics of Deal's history. Also of interest here is the Maritime and Local History Museum in St George's Road, which has an interesting collection of items on Deal. Exhibits include local boats, model sailing-ships, maps, photographs and naval relics.

The old Time Ball Tower on the seafront was built in 1854 and indicated Greenwich Mean Time to passing shipping by dropping a large black ball, induced by electric current direct from the Greenwich Observatory itself, down a shaft on the top of the tower at 1.00 pm each day. The time ball ceased to function in 1927 when regular radio broadcasts to shipping became commonplace.

Near the foreshore at Walmer stands Walmer Castle, also built by Henry VIII as part of his coastal defence systems. The castle is now the official residence of the Lord Warden of the Cinque Ports. Over the years many alterations and modifications have changed much of its original at-

Middle Street typifies the character of old Deal

mosphere, so that today it is more like a stately home than a fort. It houses a fine collection of items associated with the Duke of Wellington and other Lord Wardens, and is set in magnificent gardens.

Deal Castle See AM info. Also open Sun am Apr to Sep. Parking available.
Maritime and Local History Museum open Spring Bank Holiday to Sep daily, pm only.
Walmer Castle See AM info. Also open Sun am Apr to Sep closed Mon (except Bank Holidays) Gardens closed in winter. Parking available.

Deene Park

Northamptonshire *p213 B5*

Deene is a house built over six centuries having grown from a typical quadrangular-plan medieval manor into a Tudor and Georgian mansion. Its main front faces south across a large park and lake.

Before the Norman conquest and for 150 years afterwards, the Manor of Deene belonged to the Abbey of Westminster. Various families, including the Colets and Lyttons, rented the property until in 1514 it was acquired by Sir Robert Brudenell. Today it is still owned by his descendants.

The exterior is dominated by a massive tower, which has heraldic shields around its top and by a number of rectangular turrets. The building has had many additions over the years and therefore offers differing styles of architecture. It is still fully occupied as a family home and among its interesting rooms are the Great Hall with its elaborate sweetchestnut roof, an oak-panelled parlour and a drawing room. All contain fine examples of period furniture, family portraits and beautiful paintings. There are also interesting records and historical relics of the 7th Earl of Cardigan and his role in the Crimean War.

The gardens have been developed from lawns and trees into an area containing large borders of shrubs, with roses and flowers of every variety. Two wooden bridges in the Chinese style and statues of the four seasons adorn the garden.

Open Easter, Spring and Summer Bank Holidays Sun and Mon, also Sun in Jun, Jul and Aug, pm only. Parking and refreshments available.

Dorchester Dorset *p212 E2*

This pleasant market town, lying in the heart of Thomas Hardy country on the banks of the river Frome, contains many relics of its interesting, and occasionally violent, past. It was here that Judge Jeffreys held his Bloody Assize in 1685, and 1834 saw the trial of the famous Tolpuddle Martyrs.

Despite its ancient origins which stretch back to pre-Roman times, Dorchester has retained very few of its medieval buildings. The exceptions are the Napier Almshouses (founded in 1610 and now converted into shops) and the predominantly sixteenth-century church of St Peter. Most of their contemporaries were destroyed in fires which occurred during the seventeenth and eighteenth centuries, and the greater part of the town has been rebuilt in pleasing grey Portland stone.

However, Dorchester is probably best known for its associations with the author and poet Thomas Hardy who spent most of his life in the area, and immortalised the town as Casterbridge in his novel *The Mayor of Casterbridge*. A life-sized statue of him stands at the top of The Grove.

Dorset County Museum

This contains an interesting collection of archaeological finds and items relating to natural and local history. Exhibits also include the original manuscript of Hardy's novel, *The Mayor of Casterbridge* and a reconstruction of Hardy's study. Relics of Dorchester's other literary figure, William Barnes, noted for his Dorset dialect poetry during the nineteenth century, are also here.

Dorset County Museum

Dorset Military Museum

The museum, housed in the keep which was once the entrance to the Dorset Regiment barracks, covers almost 300 years of local military history. It includes a fascinating collection of uniforms, badges, weapons and souvenirs ranging from a pair of boots and a sword worn during the Charge of the Heavy Brigade at Balaclava, to a desk captured from Hitler's Chancellery in 1945.

Old Crown Court

The six famous Tolpuddle Martyrs stood trial here in 1834. They had formed the Friendly Society of Agriculture Labourers, the forerunner of the Trade Union Movement, and were charged under the Unlawful Oaths Act of 1797. The Martyrs were harshly sentenced to seven years transportation, but were officially pardoned two years later following a public outcry. The Trades Union Congress purchased the Court as a public memorial in 1956.

Judge Jeffreys' Lodging and The Antelope Hotel

When Judge Jeffreys came to Dorchester to preside over the trial of those accused of taking part in Monmouth's unsuccessful rebellion of 1685, he took up lodging in a house in the High Street which has now been converted into a restaurant named after him. His Bloody Assize was probably held in a room at the rear of the Antelope Hotel, which is preserved with its original Tudor panelling. Some 300 men came before Jeffreys and he sentenced seventy-four of them to public hanging and mutilation, and 175 to transportation.

Maumbury Rings

This Roman amphitheatre was built on the site of a prehistoric stone circle. It could accommodate 13,000 spectators for the gladiatorial contests and it was the scene of beast-baiting and public executions during the Middle Ages.

Maiden Castle

This huge prehistoric earthwork, consisting of a complicated system of ditches and ramparts, is perhaps, the most famous in the country. Despite its impressive defences, the Romans stormed and seized the castle in AD43.

Dorset County Museum open all year (except Sun, Good Fri, Christmas and New Years Day).
Dorset Military Museum open all year (except Sun, and Christmas); Sat am only from Oct to June. Parking available.
Old Crown Court open all year Mon to Fri (except Bank Holidays).
Maiden Castle open at any reasonable time. Parking available. AM.

16th-century St Peter's church in the historic centre of Dorchester

The keep of Doune Castle – the residential apartments were never built

Doune

Central *p220 C4*

The superb fourteenth-century castle of Doune with panoramic views of the surrounding countryside, stands near the confluence of the river Teith and Ardoch Burn on the outskirts of the village. The castle was last used by royalty when Bonnie Prince Charlie housed prisoners here in 1746, but has since been privately owned by the Earls of Moray.

The Doune Park Gardens were laid out in the nineteenth century and the walled garden has the traditional fruit, house, spring and autumn gardens.

Situated about one-and-a-half miles west of the village is Lord Doune's collection of motor vehicles, which includes such cars as Bentleys, MGs and Rolls-Royces. There is also an immaculate 1924 Hispano Suiza, and saloon, sports and racing cars of the 1920s and 1930s. They are all displayed in appropriately converted farm buildings in the grounds of the Doune estate. All of the vehicles are in pristine condition and some compete in the Doune Hill Climb events which take place in April, June and September.

Castle open Apr to Oct daily (except Thu in Apr and Oct). Parking available.
Motor Museum open Apr to Oct daily. Parking and refreshments.

Dover

Kent *p213 D2*

Dover, looking out over the English Channel, has been the Gateway of England for some 2,000 years. During the second century, it was the headquarters of the Roman fleet in Britain and is now our busiest passenger port. Ships were guided to the harbour by a lighthouse, and the one which still stands on the famous white cliffs as part of the castle is known as the Pharos.

The castle was built during the second half of the twelfth century on the site of an earlier castle and has been remarkably well preserved. Two walls with numerous towers protect a formidable massive keep which stands ninety-five-feet high, forming an almost perfect cube with walls up to twenty-one-feet thick.

Some interesting features within the castle are a 242-foot well with remains of the medieval plumbing, and a collection of weapons and armour. Cut into the chalk cliffs beneath the castle are a series of underground passages, first constructed during the siege of 1216 by Prince Louis of France. They were extended during the early nineteenth century and were put to use as an air-raid shelter during World War II. When Napoleon's army were gathering on the French coast and Dover once more became a garrison town, Crabble Mill was built to provide flour for the troops. The six-storey mill driven by the waters of the river Dour ceased working in 1890. It is at present undergoing further restoration.

Dover has many other historic buildings including tiny St Edmund's Chapel and the Town Hall which incorporates the thirteenth-century Hall of Maison Dieu and a museum. It was not until 1970 that the exciting discovery was made of Roman remains beneath the streets of Dover. A part of the site has since been permanently excavated to show extensive remains of a fine town house, its richly painted walls still standing up to ten feet high in places. Also on show is a section of the hypocaust, or underfloor heating system, displays relating to Roman Dover, and items found during excavation.

Castle and underground passages see AM info. Also Sun am Apr to Sep.
Crabble Watermill closed for the foreseeable future due to extensive restoration work.
Town Hall (including Maison Dieu and museum) open daily (except Wed and Sun).
Roman Painted House open Apr to Oct daily (except Mon). Parking available.

Drayton Manor Park and Zoo

Staffordshire *p216 F2*

Drayton was the home of Sir Robert Peel in the nineteenth century, but the manor house has since been demolished. In the extensive grounds are two lakes teeming with small pleasure craft, and a replica of a stern wheel paddle boat. On the lower and smaller lake is a cruise through the Jungle and Lost World, which has life-size model animals and natives. Amongst the magnificent lions, leopards and bears in the zoo are lovable monkeys, exotic birds, paddocks, a farm section and children's corner. There is also an amusement park and a miniature railway along the lakeside, with passenger compartments hauled by a scale model of a nineteenth-century North American locomotive.

A chair lift operates from the main gate across the park and affords an aerial view of the estate and lakes which in all cover over 160 acres.

For the nature lover there is a marked trail and walks through forty acres of woodland.

Open Easter to Oct daily. Parking on parkland and refreshments available.

Dover Castle on the lofty site where an Iron Age fort once stood

Drumlanrig Castle

Dumfries and Galloway *p220 D3*

The cost of building Drumlanrig Castle in about 1680 was so great that the horrified owner, the 1st Duke of Queensberry, spent only one night there. The castle is now the property of the Dukes of Buccleuch.

It is a superb Renaissance building of pink sandstone with lead cupola turrets and ballustrading overlooking the Nith Valley. Its works of art include Rembrandt's *Old Woman Reading*, and there is also some fine Louis XIV furniture, a silver chandelier which weighs nine stones, and souvenirs of Bonnie Prince Charlie and his highland followers. Lovely walks can be taken through the grounds and there is an exciting adventure playground for children.

Open May to late Aug daily (except Fri). May, June and Suns, pm only. Parking and refreshments available.

Dryburgh Abbey

Borders *p220 E3*

Standing on a beautiful wooded horseshoe-bend of the river Tweed is the ruin of Dryburgh Abbey – the site of which was once a holy place for Druids.

It is one of a famous group of

Border monasteries which were attacked by English invaders in 1322, 1385 and 1544. Although there was extensive damage, the west front of the church remains, with its thirteenth-century portal; the transepts, parts of the nave and chapter house have also survived.

The cloister buildings, however, are more complete than those of any other monastery in Scotland, with the exception of Iona and Incholm. Sir Walter Scott, his biographer J. G. Lockhart, and the former Commander-in-Chief of the British Army, Field Marshal Earl Haig, are all buried in the abbey grounds.

See AM info. Parking available.

Dudley Castle and Zoo

West Midlands *p216 F1*

Standing above an escarpment, in the midst of a heavily built-up area, are the impressive ruins of a castle constructed by Roger de Somery in the thirteenth century. This excellent viewpoint is reached by a chairlift which starts from the main entrance 200 feet below the castle.

Housed in the forty-acre wooded castle grounds is Dudley Zoo, famous for the breeding of rare species of animals such as the ring-tailed lemur and the silvery marmoset. The pits which were left after mineral excavations have been cleverly adapted to accommodate some of the larger animals, which include bears, tigers, lions, monkeys and reptiles.

The Land of the Dinosaurs exhibition has lifesize prehistoric monsters, and the children's farm includes a collection of small animals. There is also a fair, and, for the more adventurous, a ski slope.

Open all year daily. Parking and refreshments available.

Dufftown

Grampian *p222 E2*

Dufftown is chiefly famous for its malt whisky distilleries. It was founded by James Duff, the 4th Earl of Fife, and is laid out with two streets running at right angles to a central clock tower, with smaller streets leading off them.

On the northern outskirts of the town stands Balvenie Castle, a

substantial ruin overlooking the river Fiddich. The thirteenth-century castle was originally a stronghold of the Comyns, but was converted to a mansion in the fifteenth century by the 4th Earl. The front entrance still has its original wrought iron gate, known as a yett; and it is the only one of its kind left in Scotland.

A small local history museum in the town contains items of civil regalia and interesting relics from the Mortlach Kirk, which is one of the oldest churches in Scotland.

Perhaps the most famous distillery is the Glenfiddich, situated by the Robbie Dubh – the Black Robert stream. It was founded in 1887 by Major William Grant, and is one of the few distilleries where one can see each stage of the production right through to the bottling process. The visitors reception centre has a bar and Scotch Whisky Museum.

Balvenie Castle See AM info. Parking available.
Dufftown Museum open May to Sep Mon to Sat, also Sun in Aug.
Glenfiddich Distillery open all year Mon to Fri (except Christmas and New Year). Mid May to mid Oct also Sat and Sun pm. Parking.

Dumfries

Dumfries and Galloway *p220 D2*

Affectionately known as Scotland's Queen of the South, Dumfries is delightfully situated on the broad waters of the river Nith.

In 1791 the poet Robert Burns made his home in Dumfries. He wrote some of his most famous songs here and the house where he died in 1796, now called Burns' House, has been made into a museum in his honour. Many of the poet's personal belongings can be seen here, and the road in which the house stands has been renamed Burns Street.

Not far from the house is St Michael's churchyard, where Burns, his wife Jean Armour and their five sons lie buried in the now famous mausoleum. St Michael's Church itself dates from 1744 and a brass plate in the church marks the pew where Burns sat. A fine statue of him, erected in 1882, stands in front of the present Greyfriars Church.

The central point of the town is an eighteenth-century complex of buildings known as Midsteeple, comprising the old municipal buildings, courthouse and prison. A tablet on the wall inscribed

The six-arched Old Bridge over the river Nith at Dumfries. Down river is the Caul – a weir built to drive grain mills in the 18th century

with distances includes Huntingdon, and this serves as a reminder of the times when Scottish cattle drovers herded their animals south to trade in the lucrative English markets. Another detail on the steeple is a relief map of the town, showing it as it was in Burns' days.

Unusually housed in a restored mid eighteenth-century windmill in Church Street, is the Dumfries Museum with a camera obscura on top of it. The museum itself has a large collection covering local history, archaeology, geology, birds and animals. Close by is yet another museum in the seventeenth-century Old Bridge House, on the end of the medieval bridge. Here period rooms portray the local way of life of the past. The Old Bridge or Devorgilla Bridge itself, now closed to traffic, is a six-arched stone structure and the most famous of five bridges which cross the river Nith on its course through the town. Another attraction here is the Caul, an early eighteenth-century weir, which lies just downstream from the bridge and was built to provide power for riverside grain mills.

Burns' House open all year Tue to Sat. Also Mon and Sun pm. Apr to Sep.
Burns' Mausoleum open as Burns' House by arrangement with curator.
Dumfries Museum and Camera Obscura open as Burns' House (Camera Obscura Apr to Sep only).
Old Bridge House Museum open as Burns' House but Apr to Sep only.

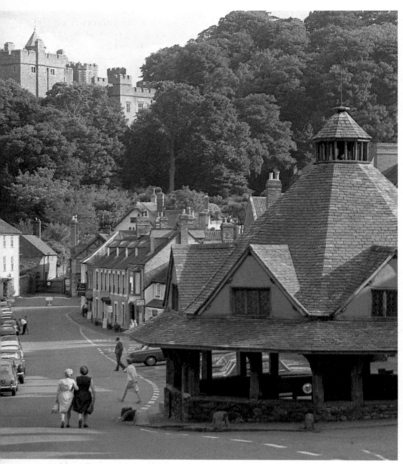

Dunster's yarn-market. The town was a busy trading point in the 17th century

Dunrobin Castle

Highland *p221 D3*

Built in 1275, Dunrobin is the oldest castle in Scotland which is still inhabited and has been the home of the Dukes of Sutherland for 500 years. Most of the existing building was designed in 1856 by Sir Charles Barry, architect of the Houses of Parliament, although much of it was restored after a fire in 1915.

Inside are some fine tapestries, paintings by Reynolds and Canaletto and Louis XV furniture, and various trophies and regimental colours belonging to the 93rd Sutherland Highlanders.

In the grounds a magnificent formal garden borders a hundred-yard terrace.

Open Jun to mid Sep, daily, Sun pm only. Parking and refreshments available.

Dunster

Somerset *p212 D3*

The unspoilt village of Dunster lies off the main road, two miles from Minehead. The wide main street is overlooked by the well-preserved castle which stands in a prominent position, surrounded by trees, commanding excellent views of the Bristol Channel, Exmoor and the Quantock Hills.

Originally built by the Earl of Somerset, the castle was the home of the Luttrells for some 600 years. The seventeenth-century plasterwork ceilings and the beautifully carved balustrade of the staircase, depicting a stag hunt, have been well preserved. In the banqueting hall there are some unusual Dutch painted leather panels and portraits.

At the centre of the village is a yarn-market built by George Luttrell when the trade cloth was flourishing. The fifteenth-century church has monuments to the Luttrells and a fine rood screen. A twelfth-century dovecote with a revolving ladder to reach the nesting boxes stands in a walled garden attached to the church.

Castle open Apr to Sep Sat to Wed, Oct pm only. Parking available. NT.
Old Dovecote open Easter to mid Oct daily.

Durham Co Durham *p217 B5*

County town, cathedral city and seat of a university, Durham is one of Britain's most pleasing cities to explore, with the cathedral and castle standing together high on a rocky outcrop surrounded by steep wooded banks leading down to the river Wear.
Gathered about these two Norman giants are old buildings spanning several centuries, pleasant lawns and gardens.

The origins of Durham are related to St Cuthbert who was one of the founders of Christianity in northern England. His shrine was brought to Durham in 995 after being removed from Holy Island in 875 to escape Viking raids, and by 998 a church had been built to house it.

Legend has it that the coffin became immovable on a neighbouring hill until the saint revealed his chosen resting place to his followers in a vision. The spot quickly became a place of pilgrimage, and the pilgrims brought the wealth which enabled the town to grow.

The history of Durham is a peaceful one, although it was a military base from Norman times when the castle was built, until the seventeenth century. The only battle fought in the vicinity was in 1346 when Philip VI of France, having lost a war against Edward III, exhorted his Scottish allies to invade England. Edward III's wife, Philippa, raised an army in her lord's absence and defeated the invaders at Neville's Cross, named after one of her commanders, now a suburb of the city.

The oldest regatta in England is held in Durham, and the renowned miners' gala on every third Saturday of July fills the city with marching feet and music.

The Castle

This was the Bishop's fortress until 1832, when the university was founded, and it now houses University College. The oldest part of the castle is the beautiful little Norman chapel. Original paving, laid in a herringbone pattern, lies under a vaulted roof and the heads of the pillars are carved with geometrical designs, serpents, flowers, human figures and leopards.

The senate room, placed directly above the Norman chapel, is one of the best of the splendid apartments in the castle, and has a sixteenth-century Flemish tapestry depicting the life of Moses.

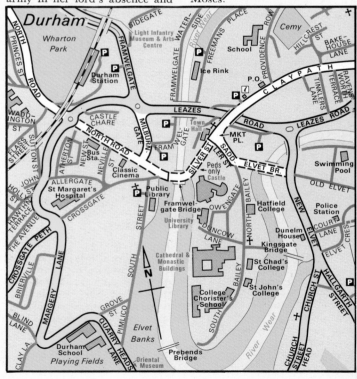

Monks of Lindisfarne chose the site of the cathedral in Saxon times

In 1840 the battlemented keep was rebuilt to house students and it still serves this function. Opposite is the great hall, a magnificent dining room in which royalty has been entertained since 1322, decorated with carvings and banners.

The Black Staircase, built by Bishop Cosin in 1663, is mainly made of oak with pierced panels of richly carved willow. It rises fifty-seven feet through four storeys. There is much fine carving in St Tunstall's Gallery and Pudsey's Gallery which are connected by the staircase.

The Cathedral
The Cathedral Church of Christ and Blessed Mary the Virgin was built between 1093 and 1133. The vast interior of this, the finest Norman building in Europe, is breathtaking. What first strikes the visitor are the great round pillars, seven feet in diameter. They are adorned with bold zig-zag carvings which lead the eye up to the earliest rib-vaulted ceiling in the country. A splendidly elaborate stone screen stands behind the high altar and here too is the shrine of St Cuthbert, whose body was laid there in 1104. He is in good company with the Venerable Bede who lies at the opposite end of the cathedral. The fourteenth-century throne of Bishop Hatfield is the tallest known.

Otherwise practically unspoiled Norman architecture, the only two major additions, the Galilee chapel built between 1170 and 1175, and the Chapel of the Nine Altars built between 1242 and 1280, successfully enhance the beauty of the cathedral rather than detract from it.

The Galilee chapel has a roof supported by clusters of Purbeck marble and stone of remarkably light construction, giving the chapel an airiness distinct from the rest of the cathedral. The Chapel of the Nine Altars, built for women worshippers who were denied access to the rest of the cathedral, has pointed arches and richly carved pillar heads.

In the monks dormitory, a timbered hall 194 feet by thirty-nine feet, is a display of the cathedral's prized possessions, including illuminated manuscripts, a collection of crosses and the reconstructed oak coffin of St Cuthbert.

Town Hall
This Victorian hall was built by public subscription and opened in 1851. Relics of Count Boruwalski, a Polish dwarf who died in 1837 at the age of ninety-eight, are kept here, including his violin which he played adeptly. He was buried in the cathedral and an inscribed brass, rejected by the Dean for its wording, states he 'mesured no more than three feet three inches in height, but his form was well proportioned and he possessed a more than common store of understanding and knowledge'.

Durham University
All around the Palace Green the collection of buildings ranging from the fifteenth to the twentieth century, once courts, hospitals, almshouses and residences, now houses the university. It was the third university to be founded in England and has inherited an aura of antiquity and distinction rivalling Oxford and Cambridge.

Durham Castle stands guard high on a wooded terraced hill above the city

Oriental Museum
Housed withing the university on Elvet Hill, this collection of oriental art and archaeology is the finest in England. The displays in the multi-level hall of Egyptian and Mesopotamian antiquities, Chinese and Japanese pottery and porcelain, exquisite jades, ivories, textiles and paintings are stunning. Particularly interesting are the colourful Tibetan paintings or tankas; a Tibetan magician's apron of human bones, and fifty-feet-long series of carved teak panels from a Burmese palace.

Durham Light Infantry Museum and Arts Centre
The history of the Light Infantry Regiment is traced back to 1757 in the museum, with exhibits that include uniforms, medals, armoury and Victoria Crosses won by the regiment. The Arts Centre has family exhibitions and films.

Castle open first 3 weeks in Apr, then July to Sep, Mon to Sat. Rest of the year Mon, Wed and Sat pm only. Occasionally closed for University functions.
Town Hall open all year daily (except Sun).
University Grounds open all year daily.
Oriental Museum open all year Mon to Fri. Also Sat and Sun pm Mar to Oct. Closed Christmas.
Light Infantry Museum and Arts Centre open all year Tue to Sat and Bank Holiday Mon, Sun pm only.

Dyrham Park

Avon *p212 E4*

This long, low, many-windowed mansion overlooks a beautiful 263-acre deer park. The house was built between 1691 and 1702 for William Blathwayt, Secretary at War to William III, and the furnishings have hardly changed since Blathwayt first completed them, according to his house-keeper's inventory of 1710.

During his career, Blathwayt frequently visited Holland. Consequently many of the furnishings are Dutch, and include several pieces of blue and white Delftware, beautiful bird paintings by Hondecoeter and leather wall hangings from the Hague. Blathwayt also had connections with the American colonies which enabled him to obtain some fine cedarwood for one of the staircases. There is Virginian walnut panelling in the Diogenes room.

The orangery which is attached to the house resembles the style of Versailles with its massive Tuscan columns. Formal pleasure gardens, laid out by George London, feature terraces with fountains, cascades and a canal. The deer park, as it is now, dates from the late eighteenth century, but Fallow deer have roamed the estate since Saxon times. It is thought that Dyrham comes from the Saxon word 'doer-hamm' meaning deer enclosure.

Open Apr, May and Oct daily (except Thu and Fri) pm only. June to Sep daily (except Fri) pm only. Park all year daily, pm only. NT.

East Bergholt

Suffolk *p213 D4*

On 11th June, 1776, John Constable – one of Britain's best-loved landscape artists, was born in East Bergholt. When talking of his home village, Constable once said 'these scenes made me a painter' and some of those scenes have scarcely changed from the day he committed them to canvas. His famous painting *The Hay Wain*, was modelled on Flatford Mill – the family home. Willy Lott's cottage, lived in by a friend of Constable, stands near the mill.

Flatford Lock resembles the locks in some of Constable's paintings and a restored Stour lighter – a flat bottomed barge – can be seen on request.

In the village itself are many cottages dating back to Elizabethan times, and the church has a number of interesting features, including memorials inside to Constable and his wife, and a bell-house stands in the church yard. This is a timber building dating from the sixteenth century, and the bells are hung upside down and rung by hand.

Flatford Mill and **Willy Lott's Cottage** not open but exteriors viewable at all times. NT.
Flatford Lock open at all times.

Eastbourne

East Sussex *p213 C2*

Eastbourne is a popular south coast resort which has retained much of its nineteenth-century elegance. Rather than bingo halls and amusement arcades, its promenade is backed by splendid hotels and beautiful gardens, notably the Carpet Gardens. Along with all the usual seaside attractions, Eastbourne plays host to international tennis tournaments and, during the summer season, top military bands perform daily on the seafront bandstand encircled by a large covered arena.

There are some pleasant walks from Eastbourne, particularly westwards to Beachy Head which rises to 575 feet and helps to shelter the resort from sea winds.

During the early nineteenth century, when Napoleon was threatening to invade Britain's shores, Eastbourne was in the front line of defence and some of its fortifications can still be seen. The Circular Redoubt was the most extensive, and now contains the Sussex Combined Services Museum which illustrates the military history of Sussex. There is access to the gun platform and the area also includes an aquarium and the popular Treasure Island Play Centre. Tower 73, or The Wish Tower, incorporates a Martello tower and is the home of the Coastal Defence Museum where Napoleonic defence methods and equipment are displayed. Nearby is the Lifeboat

Easton Farm Park
Suffolk *p213 D4*

A working farm is the focal point of this country park near the picturesque village of Easton.

Early farm machinery and country bygones are on show in the Victorian farm buildings, built by the Duke of Hamilton in 1870 as a model dairy farm. The dairy itself is sparkling clean, decorated with floral tiles and a fountain. Visitors may observe the collection of farm livestock, including some rare breeds such as St Kilda sheep and Longhorn cattle, and watch demonstrations of steam machines and horse-drawn equipment.

There are nature trails in the park through woodland and riverside meadows, and other features here include an apiary, a children's pets paddock, an adventure play pit and a craft shop. Coarse fishing is also available.

Open Easter to Sep daily. Parking and refreshments available.

Left: Willy Lott's cottage, an enchanting 17th-century house on the banks of the river Stour owned by Constable's father

Below: The many colourful cliff gardens at Eastbourne provide one of the resort's most attractive features

Museum which, when opened in 1937, was the first one in Britain.

Eastbourne is justifiably proud of its parks and gardens and it is within one of these that the Towner Art Gallery is situated. This lovely Georgian manor house contains a fine collection of nineteenth- and twentieth-century British paintings and Georgian caricatures.

Circular Redoubt open Easter to Oct. Parking and refreshments.
Coastal Defence Museum open Easter to Oct daily.
Royal National Lifeboat Museum open Apr to Dec daily, Jan to Mar weekends only.
Towner Art Gallery and Local History Museum open all year daily (except Mons in winter), Sun pm only. Parking available.

Edinburgh Lothian *p220 D4*

Watched over by the great castle, the Old Town of pre-eighteenth century Edinburgh huddles about the foot of Castle Rock, while to the north stands the gracious New Town of Georgian buildings, broad streets, squares and circuses.

The Castle

Edinburgh's history centres around its castle and records show that Castle Rock was a tribal stronghold as early as 600BC. Very little now remains of the original eleventh-century castle, and the present building is a mixture of additions made until the seventeenth century.

On the eastern side of the Palace Yard are the royal apartments, among them the tiny bedroom where Mary Queen of Scots gave birth to a son who became James VI of Scotland and James I of England.

The great hall, built by James IV, now houses a fascinating collection of weapons and armour. In the Crown Room displays of Scottish regalia include the crown, the sceptre and the sword of state.

The famous Military Tattoo takes place under the castle walls and is the highlight of Edinburgh's annual international festival held in late summer. All the arts are included in the official programme which attracts thousands of visitors from all over the world every year.

Holyroodhouse and Abbey

The abbey, now a picturesque ruin, was founded in 1128 by David I and the Palace was built for Charles II in 1671. Mary Queen of Scots spent six years of her reign here during which time her jealous husband murdered her secretary, David Riccio. The place where he fell is marked by a brass tablet.

One hundred and eleven portraits of Scottish kings hang in the picture gallery in the Palace, and the state apartments here are decorated with Flemish tapestries.

Gladstone's Land

This six-storey tenement, completed in 1620, is remarkable for its painted ceilings. The main rooms have been refurbished as a home typical of the period and the ground floor includes a shop front and goods typical of the seventeenth century.

Lady Stair's House

Here important manuscripts and relics of three of Scotland's most famous literary figures – Robert Burns, Sir Walter Scott and Robert Louis Stevenson – are housed. They include Scott's writing desk and printing press and Stevenson's riding accessories.

Museum of Childhood

In this unique museum are historical toys, books, costumes, and dolls' fashions providing a picture of childhood over the past centuries.

Royal Museum of Scotland
(Queen Street)

Extensive collections here include treasures from all over Scotland depicting the Scottish way of life from the Stone Age to modern times. Outside, the building is decorated with statues of eminent Scotsmen.

Royal Museum of Scotland
(Chambers Street)

Here collections from all over the world cover archaeology, natural history, geology, technology and science as well as the decorative arts. There are also a large number of fossil fish here.

Canongate Tolbooth

When Canongate was a separate burgh from Edinburgh the Tolbooth, built in 1591, was the municipal building and civic centre. It is an interesting building with outside steps, a turreted tower and a projecting clock. On the ground floor it houses a brass rubbing centre.

National Gallery of Scotland

This is one of the most distinguished of the smaller galleries in Europe with its collection of Old Masters, Impressionists and Scottish paintings. Exhibits include work by Constable, Van Gogh and Turner.

John Knox's House

The great Scottish reformer and theologian John Knox is said to have lived here from 1561 to 1572. The house was built in 1490 and may well be the oldest in Edinburgh. His day study and his bedroom can be seen on the second floor.

The Cathedral

A church has stood on this site since the ninth century, but most of the existing building of St Gile's Cathedral is fourteenth or fifteenth century. The most recent addition to this lofty structure is the Thistle chapel, built in 1911, which has a superbly carved interior. John Knox is buried in the churchyard and a statue of him stands here too.

The North-East View of EDINBURGH CASTLE

The unfinished Parthenon on Calton Hill was started as a monument to Scotsmen killed in the Napoleonic Wars

Scottish National Gallery of Modern Art

Home of the national collection of twentieth-century painting, sculpture and graphic art. Modern artists represented include Picasso, Henry Moore and Barbara Hepworth.

Mons Meg cannon stands by the chapel door of the castle

Princes Gardens

The huge Scott Monument in the East Princes Street Gardens is 200-feet-high and has a statue of Sir Walter Scott himself beneath its arches. Placed in niches around the monument are sixty-four statuettes of characters created by him in his novels and poems. The 287 steps up to the top lead to fine views over the city.

The Floral Clock at the east end is a famous trysting place. It was built in 1903, and over 24,000 plants cover its huge face.

Castle open all year daily, Sun pm only Nov to Apr. Subject to Tattoo requirements. Parking available. AM.
Holyroodhouse and Abbey open all year daily (except Sun Nov to Apr and when occupied by the Royal Family).
Gladstone's Land open Good Fri to Oct daily, Sun pm only; Nov Sat and Sun pm only. NTS.
Lady Stair's House open all year Mon to Sat, aslo Sun pm during Festival.
Museum of Childhood open as above.
Royal Museum of Scotland (Queen St) open all year daily, Sun pm only.
Royal Museum of Scotland (Chambers St) open all year daily, Sun pm only. Refreshments available Mon to Sat.
Canongate Tolbooth open all year daily, Sun pm only during Festival.
National Gallery of Scotland open all year daily, Sun pm only.
John Knox's House open all year Mon to Sat.
Scottish National Gallery of Modern Art (Belford Rd) open all year daily, Sun pm only. Parking and refreshments available.

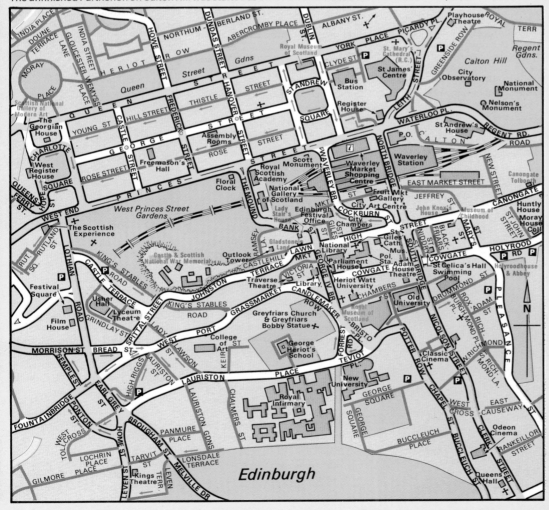

Edinburgh

Elan Valley Reservoirs

Powys *p216 D1*

This wild and remote valley, where the river Elan flowed down to the Wye, enchanted the poet Shelley when he occupied a house here with his young wife Harriet, early in the nineteenth century. From the west bank near the mouth of the Nant Gwyllt stream, long stretches of the garden wall can be seen when the water level is low. However, in 1871 the Corporation of Birmingham decided to look to mid-Wales as a suitable source for its water supply and chose the Elan Valley.

Work on forming the great reservoirs began in 1892 by damming the river, and they were completed in 1904. The complex of lakes, which enhanced the beautiful scenery is sometimes referred to as the Welsh Lake District and lies to the west of the little market town of Rhayader. Elan Village in its wooded setting below Caban Coch dam was built by Birmingham Corporation to house the workforce.

Craig Goch, enclosing over 200 acres of the highest part of the Elan Valley, is the topmost reservoir and its stern and rugged shoreline is a popular picnic spot. From Craig Goch the waters cascade over the top dam dropping sheer into the next lake Pen-y-garreg. Its 124 acres are set in wooded surroundings with a fir-covered island in its centre. The long, sinuous shape of Garreg-Ddu follows, with its submerged causeway and woods sweeping across the lake. Caban Coch is the final lake in the complex, which covers some 500 acres and is surrounded by crags and steep, wooded slopes.

Elgin

Grampian *p222 E3*

Elgin is a busy market town and royal burgh lying south of the river Lossie. Well situated for exploring the coast of the Moray Firth to the north, and the hills and Spey Valley to the south, it is also ideal for the trout and salmon angler.

The town has many buildings of architectural interest, the most famous being the beautiful ruins of the thirteenth-century cathedral. Both the town and the cathedral were burnt down in 1390 by Robert II's outlawed son who terrorized the area. However there are well preserved sections of its vaulted roof, and carved stonework can still be seen. Close by is the remaining wing of the fifteenth-century Bishop's Palace and the East Gate of the precincts, which is the only one surviving.

Also of interest in the town are Gray's Hospital, Braco's Banking House and, occupying an island-site in the High Street, St Giles Church with its huge portico supported by six giant columns. The town museum stands at the entrance to Cooper Park and contains a world-wide collection of fossils, as well as a display on the heritage of Elgin and Moray.

Elgin Cathedral see AM info.
Museum open Apr to Sep Mon to Fri. Sat am all year.

Elvaston Castle and Country Park

Derbyshire *p217 B1*

When this neo-Gothic mansion was built in 1817, it incorporated an earlier seventeenth-century house to surround a large courtyard. In the middle of this there stands a large water tower.

The entrance hall with its high vaulted ceiling is particularly strikingly decorated in black and gold.

The gardens were landscaped by William Barron, and include a kitchen garden and an old english garden. A remarkable number of trees and bushes, including some rare specimens, were planted in the gardens, and an elaborate topiary garden with yews cut into intricate designs can still be seen today. The church in the castle grounds contains memorials to the Stanhopes who lived here for many years, and an interesting sculpture by Canova, the famous Venetian artist.

The Country Park covers some 200 acres of woodland, gardens and parkland, and is the home of many species of animal and bird life. A marked nature trail and reserve has been developed here, as well as an estate museum, riding centre, bridle paths and picnic areas.

Castle and **Park** open all year. Parking available. Refreshments available Easter to Oct.

Ely

Cambridgeshire *p213 C5*

Ely is one of Britain's oldest religious foundations, and there has been a cathedral here for some 1,300 years.

Before the Fens were drained for agriculture during the eighteenth and nineteenth centuries, Ely was an island. Today the cathedral rises like a beacon from the flat fenland country, a landmark for miles around. It has always had a measure of good luck, having survived the Dissolution, the Puritans and the Death Watch Beetle. However, the cathedral has had its disasters too. In February, 1322, the Norman tower came crashing down, demolishing part of the choir in the process. Nevertheless, from the rubble arose what is now the cathedral's most characteristic feature – the magnificent octagon. The very best medieval craftsmen were employed to create this unique structure which supports an octagonal lantern. The cathedral building is principally Norman, evident in the style of its lofty nave, with some superb intricate stone carving. The most notable example of this is the Bishop Alcock's lovely chantry, built in 1488.

Erddig

Clwyd *p216 E2*

Erddig is set in a magnificent 1,900-acre estate on the south bank of the river Clywedog. This late seventeenth-century red

Lovely scenery is very much a feature of the Elan Valley Reservoirs

brick mansion has been the home of the Yorke family since 1733. Erddig owes much of its character to John Meller, an uncle of the Yorkes, who acquired the property in 1715. He enlarged the house and furnished it exquisitely with tapestries, oriental porcelain and silver. Its collection of gilt and silver furniture is considered to be one of the finest and best documented in any country house. Especially fine is the state bed, made in London in 1720, and upholstered in beautifully embroidered Chinese silk. The garden has been skilfully remodelled by the National Trust, following the layout of an old engraving of Erddig. It is a fine example of typical eighteenth-century formal design with walks,

a canal, a pond and an avenue of lime trees.

Perhaps the most fascinating facet of Erddig is the amount of information about the life of the domestic staff who worked here. The Yorkes were particularly good to their servants and kept their portraits with poetic descriptions of them which are now in the servants' hall. The Trust has also carefully restored the old service equipment and buildings. These include the smithy, sawmill, stable, laundry, kitchens and the bakehouse. There is also an agricultural museum here.

Open Good Fri to mid Oct daily (except Fri) pm only. Tapestry and Chinese rooms open on Wed and Sat only. Refreshments available. NT.

Evesham

Hereford and Worcester *p212 F5*

Lying at the heart of the market gardening area called the Vale of Evesham, is a small market town nestled in a bend of the river Avon. The river, with its tree-lined walks, lends Evesham much of its peaceful charm.

Two churches have the honour of sharing Evesham's churchyard, entered through an attractive timbered gateway, and between them stands Clement Lichfield's beautiful 110-foot-high bell tower. Abbot Lichfield is buried in All Saints' Church (the oldest of the two) in a marble tomb, although there is no inscription because it was lost during the Puritan régime.

Ely Cathedral's crowning glories – seen from the south side – are the octagon and lantern which were built over 600 years ago

A stroll around the compact town takes in a number of fine old buildings. Probably the best of these is the close-timbered Booth Hall or Round House – now a bank, and Dresden House with its huge iron brackets over the doorway.

The Abbey Almonry in Vine Street is used as a museum of local history which includes many curious old agricultural implements.

Almonry open Good Fri to Sep daily (except Mon and Wed), Sun pm only. Also open Bank Hol Mons.

Exeter Devon *p212 D2*

The charming, historic city of Exeter, capital of rural Devon, has often experienced strife and hardship in the past, but today reigns peacefully as the gateway to the beauty of the West Country.

During the course of its lively history the Danes took the city twice and William the Conqueror laid siege to it for eighteen days in 1068 before capturing it. During the Wars of the Roses, although the citizens were really supporters of Warwick the Kingmaker, they persuaded the victorious Edward IV that they had been loyal to him so successfully that he presented the city with a sword in gratitude. Exeter collected a second sword to hang in the Guildhall from Henry VII for resisting the rebellion in 1497 of Perkin Warbeck, an impostor who claimed succession to the throne.

The town was an important cloth manufacturing and trading centre from Norman times up until the eighteenth century, and Tucker's Hall in Fore Street, which was built for the Guild of Weavers, Fullers and Shearmen in 1471, is evidence of this.

Unfortunately the city was badly damaged by German bombers in May, 1942, and many medieval buildings were lost. In their place new complexes such as the huge Guildhall shopping centre have been built, incorporating much of the Civic Hall of 1838 and the thirteenth-century St Pancras Church.

There are many different aspects to Exeter now, as its huge twice-weekly livestock market, its attractive canal, and its modern university buildings prove.

The Cathedral

Near Southernhay Gardens in the attractive cathedral close, stands the Cathedral of St Peter, notable for the two great Norman towers and fourteenth-century west front which is decorated with a superb array of sculptures. The cathedral was established in 1050, rebuilt by the Normans between 1107 and 1137, and in 1260 demolished except for the two towers, between which the new cathedral was subsequently built. Among the finest features inside the cathedral are the rib-vaulted ceiling, the choir with its finely carved screen, the minstrel's gallery decorated by carvings of a heavenly choir playing musical instruments, the chantry chapels and the fifty-nine-feet-high Bishop's throne, which was carved in Devon oak between 1313 and 1317. A most unusual astrological clock of 1376 adorns the north wall of the transepts.

In the Close, next to the little church of St Martin, stands Mol's Coffee House, where Sir Francis Drake and Sir Walter Raleigh, amongst others, used to meet. The room is now an art shop.

Rougemont and Northernhay Gardens

Running through Northernhay Gardens is a fine piece of the Roman city wall, and the remains of the Norman castle are here too. At the northernmost corner of the wall stands Athelstan's Tower, named after a grandson of King Alfred, first King of All England, who had a palace here. An arch in the wall by the tower leads to the Rougemont Gardens. In a corner of these pleasant gardens is

The spire of St Michael and All Angels Church above Exeter

Rougemont House, a fine Georgian town house, soon to play host to a costume and lace museum.

St Nicholas' Priory

Nearby is the Norman priory of St Nicholas. It has a room with massive Norman pillars and a vaulted roof, a prior's cell, a medieval guest hall with a fine oak ceiling, a Tudor room with an oriel window and a fifteenth-century kitchen. There are also displays of pewter, furniture and wood carving here.

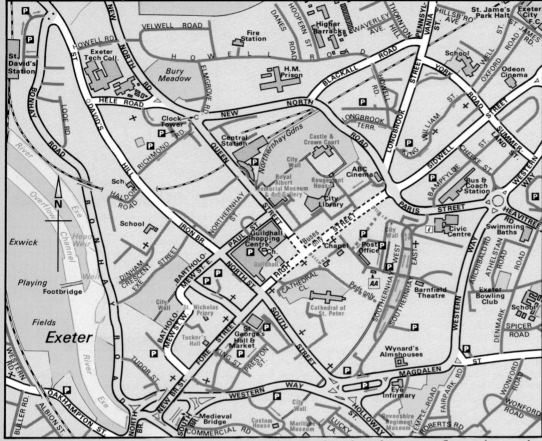

Royal Albert Memorial Museum, Maritime Museum and Custom House

There is a large and fascinating museum dedicated to Prince Albert in Queen Street, which was founded in 1865. Here can be found permanent displays of fine and applied art in the gallery, and exhibits of local industry. Particularly interesting are the collections of Devon paintings and Exeter glass, silver, and local natural history.

The exciting Maritime Museum at Town Quay and Canal Basin has the biggest boat collection in the world. Over a hundred and thirty old rowing, sail and steam vessels are on display, some afloat, others under cover. Amongst them is the world's oldest working steamboat and the renowned Ellerman collection of Portuguese craft.

Nearby is the Custom House of 1681, which was the first building in the city to be constructed with bricks. The interior features fine plaster ceilings.

Guildhall

Perhaps the oldest municipal building in the country, the Guildhall, was built in 1330 although the roof dates from 1466 when much rebuilding was carried out. The heavy portico which overhangs the High Street was added in Elizabethan days and the beautiful roof of gilded beams rests on carved figures of bears holding staffs – the badge of Warwick the Kingmaker. Inside is an unusual collection of early civic seals.

Devonshire Regiment Museum

The Devonshire Regiment was gathered in 1685 to help fight an illegitimate son of Charles II when he landed at Lyme Regis to claim his right as heir. Collections of uniforms, medals and weapons reflect its history since that time, until 1958 when it amalgamated with the Dorset Regiment.

Tucker's Hall open all year Tue, Thu, Fri am only (Oct to May, Fri only).
Rougemont House Mueseum Closed for redevelopment. Due to re-open in 1987.
St Nicholas' Priory open all year daily (except Sun and Mon).
Royal Albert Memorial Museum open as above.
Maritime Museum open all year daily (except Christmas). Parking and refreshments available.
Custom House shown by arrangement with HM Customs and Excise – casual visitors usually accepted.
Guildhall open all year, Mon to Sat except when in use for meetings.
Devonshire Regiment Museum open all year (except Sat, Sun and Bank Holidays).

A state barge – just one of the Maritime Museum's fascinating boats

Farnborough Hall

Warwickshire *p213 A4*

Farnborough is a place of great period charm. The home and landscaped gardens have undergone little alteration in the last 200 years and survive largely as William Hotbeach, owner in the mid eighteenth century, left them. William, influenced by Italian art and architecture, transformed the old house into the style of a Palladian villa to display his sculptures and paintings by Canaletto and Panini.

The landscaped gardens have a beautiful Terrace Walk, a temple, a pavilion and an obelisk; they are notable for their magnificent views.

Open Apr to Sep Wed, Sat and May Day Holiday (Sun and Mon), pm only. Terrace Walk only Thu, Fri and Sun, pm only. NT.

Farway Countryside Park

Devon *p212 D2*

The park, covering some 189 acres, in unspoilt Devon countryside, opened in 1971. Here visitors can enjoy seeing animals in their natural surroundings, in particular Roe, Red, Fallow and Sika deer. As well as present day farm animals there are some rarer breeds such as St Kilda sheep and red, hairy Tamworth pigs. Other features include a children's pets corner, nature trails and pony and donkey rides.

For the more energetic visitor Ball Hills close to the park is a good place to wander and take in magnificent views of the whole of the Coly valley; a walk along a marked track reveals Bronze Age burial mounds.

Open Good Fri to Sep daily (except Sat). Parking available.

Festiniog Railway

Gwynedd *p216 C2*

This narrow-gauge railway was originally built to take slate from the quarries around Blaenau Ffestiniog down to the sea at Porthmadog. At first trucks ran down from the quarries by gravity, but then steam trains eventually came into operation and were used for commercial purposes for over a century.

The line re-opened as a passenger service, with the help of railway enthusiasts, in 1955. The trains, hauled by historic little engines, now operate between Porthmadog and intermediate stations to Blaenau Ffestiniog. On leaving Porthmadog the trains pass over the Cob, built across the Glaslyn estuary, and wend their way up to a height of approximately 600 feet. The scenery through which they pass is spectacular and includes panoramic views of Snowdonia, Harlech Castle and the sea. They travel up the side of the river Dwyryd valley and the Vale of Ffestiniog, passing through a nature reserve to Dduallt Station. The line continues and goes through a new tunnel prior to running along the side of the Tanygrisiau Reservoir and passing the Hydro-electric power station before reaching Tanygrisiau.

At the Harbour Station at Porthmadog is the railway museum housing ancient rolling stock, maps, and diagrams.

Railway Daily service late Mar to early Nov, also 26 Dec to 1 Jan and weekends in Feb and Mar.
Festiniog Railway Museum open Feb to Dec all weekends and Mar to Nov when train service is operating. Parking and refreshments available.

Part of the fascinating mosaics at Fishbourne Roman Palace

Fishbourne Roman Palace

West Sussex *p213 B2*

Fishbourne Roman Palace is the largest residence of this period so far discovered in England. It was built in AD70 with many mosaic-floored rooms and is thought to have been constructed round a great central court, half of which is now laid out in its original pattern.

A fire at the end of the third century unfortunately destroyed the whole building and the palace was buried until 1960, when several walls and mosaic floors were accidentally uncovered by workmen laying a water pipe. Finds of the 1960s excavation including the superb mosaic floors, sections of walls and bath and heating systems, are preserved under a modern cover; an adjoining museum explains the history of the palace and surrounding area. Species of herbs and plants grown in Roman times can be purchased from the old palace garden.

Open Mar to Nov daily, Dec to Feb Sun.

Flamingo Land

North Yorkshire *p217 C4*

Over 1,000 birds, animals and reptiles live here at Kirby Misperton Hall. One of the most spectacular sights here is the flock of pink flamingos standing in a handsome lake edged by willow trees. Many species of animals roam in large paddocks including several elephants, llama, zebra, wallabies and deer, and some of the tamer animals are housed in the Contact Corner, allowing close inspection.

Linda is one of two engines owned by the Festiniog Railway that were built in 1893 by the Hunslet Engine Co

For model railway enthusiasts, there is a landscaped layout incorporating train sets ranging from vintage steam models to modern diesel electric engines.

Other attractions include a circus, dolphin shows, fantasy caves, an adventure playground and a jungle cruise, through jungle scenes and Zulu villages. Also for the children there is a real working farm with a milking parlour and a chicken hatchery. Both supply some of the produce made here.

A pottery workshop allows each stage of the craft to be watched, and the finished products may be purchased in the pottery shop.

Open Easter to Sep daily. Parking and refreshments available.

Fleet Air Arm Museum

Somerset *p212 E3*

This interesting museum, situated within the Royal Naval Air Station at Yeovilton, traces the progress of naval aviation since 1903. The collection includes more than fifty restored historic aircraft including a Swordfish, a Sea Fury and a Sea Vampire. There are also many engines, ships, aircraft models, armaments, uniforms and photographs. It is interesting to listen to recorded pilot communications on the special telephones provided.

The museum area has been extended to include an exhibition hall which graphically portrays the progress of passenger supersonic flight. Pride of place has already been given to Concorde 002 which can be inspected inside and out by visitors. On most weekdays flying can be watched from a special viewing area.

Open daily (except 24, 25 Dec). Parking and refreshments available.

Folkestone

Kent *p213 D2*

The old and the new mix well in Folkestone; modern development failing to detract from the picturesque charm of the old harbour area. It is both a holiday resort and a busy passenger port with all the facilities and attractions expected of both.

On top of the 200-foot cliffs there is a lovely long stretch of gardens known as The Leas. From here access to the beach is obtained either via pleasant wooded paths or the cliff-lift. Built in 1890, it is one of the few remaining lifts in the country to be operated by water pressure.

More formal gardens have been planted at East Cliff and in complete contrast is a rugged area known as the Warren, where wild flowers abound and many fossils can be found among the cliffs.

Among Folkestone's historic buildings is the interesting parish church of Saints Mary and Eanswythe, founded by the latter in 1138 and still containing her remains. A window commemorates Folkestone-born William Harvey who discovered how the blood circulates round the human body and became physician to James I.

Folkestone's museum and art gallery in Grace Hill specialises in local and Kentish history.

Museum and Art Gallery open all year (except Wed pm, Sun and Bank Holidays).

Forde Abbey

Dorset *p212 E3*

Forde Abbey, home of the Roper family since 1864, lies to the south-east of Chard on the south bank of the river Axe. The magnificent ham-stone structure dating from the twelfth century when it was built by Cistercian monks, embraces a mixture of Tudor and mid-seventeenth-century styles. Much of the earlier medieval stone work is in evidence, in the dormitories for example, and the splendid Tudor entrance tower is particularly picturesque.

Set in beautiful grounds with delightful water and rock gardens, Forde Abbey has a fine south front when viewed from across the lake.

Its most famous contents are the large Mortlake Tapestries, the work of Flemish weavers brought to England by Charles I. They are tapestry copies of Raphael's cartoons, depicting scenes from the Act of the Apostles.

Open May to Sep, Wed, Sun and Bank Holidays, pm only. Parking and refreshments available.

Fort Newhaven

East Sussex *p213 C2*

This Victorian fortification, built in 1860 to protect the valuable port of Newhaven and the surrounding area against an attack from the French, has recently been restored. The fortress and its collection of authentic armaments is a mecca for enthusiasts of military history. Covering some ten acres, it comprises a parade ground with perimeter casemates, which provided quarters for the officers and men. They are now used by several craftworkers and also house a pub named after the designer of the Fort, Major General Ardagh.

There are underground passages and rooms devoted to various military themes, including the Allied commands raid of Dieppe in 1942. The surrounding concrete ramparts have gun emplacements on the seaward side and a deep moat on the landward side. A children's assault course contains an original Churchill tank.

The garrison adjoins seventy acres of coastal parkland which offers beautiful views of the sea and Downs.

Open all year daily (except Christmas Day). Parking and refreshments available.

Fort William

Highland *p221 C1*

Fort William is a popular touring centre lying at the junction of Lochs Linnhe and Eil, at the foot of Ben Nevis, Britain's highest mountain. The town originates from 1655 when General Monk built an earth and wattle fort here as an English military base. This was rebuilt of stone in 1690 by William III, and the town was named after him.

In the High Street is the West Highland Museum, housing many personal belongings of Prince Charles Edward Stuart (Bonnie Prince Charlie), including the famous secret portrait, a picture which only becomes apparent when reflected in a small polished metal cylinder. Also in the museum is a bed in which the Prince once slept, and a sandalwood fan presented to Flora Macdonald on behalf of the Prince, after she had served a brief sentence for helping him to flee to France.

Ben Nevis is probably the most popular mountain in Scotland for both hill walkers and mountaineers. There is a well defined path climbing the Ben, which starts at Achintree Farm about two miles south-east of Fort William. Ben Nevis is not visible from the town itself, but it can be clearly seen from the peak of the 942-foot Cow Hill, which rises behind the town. From here the splendid views incorporate the lower reaches of the spectacular Glen Nevis – a deep and rugged valley on the south face of the mountain, and the beautiful white quarzite peak of Squrr a'Mhaim reaching to some 3,601 feet.

Museum open all year (except Sun).

Ben Nevis provides a magnificent backdrop to Fort William

Cistercian monks used to teach or study in the cloisters of Fountains Abbey

Fountains Abbey

North Yorkshire *p217 B3*

The largest, possibly the best preserved, and certainly the most famous ruined abbey in Britain is Fountains Abbey, standing majestically beside the river Skell. It was founded in the twelfth century by a handful of monks who had split from their brothers at York. Devoted to a life of poverty, the Cistercians farmed the land and built the large, but austere abbey. Ironically, their farming was so efficient that it eventually became the wealthiest abbey in Britain.

After the Dissolution the abbey and its grounds were sold by Henry VIII to Sir Richard Gresham. It then gradually fell to ruin, some of the stones being used in the building of nearby Fountains Hall. It was saved from total neglect, however, by the new owner's interest in landscaping the area and today its lofty walls share the site with ornamental gardens, ponds, monuments and temples of the hundred-acre deer park. On summer evenings the ruins are spectacularly floodlit.

Open all year (except 25 Dec). Refreshments available. NT.

Framlingham Castle

Suffolk *p213 D4*

The little market town of Framlingham lies in a green valley on the banks of the river Ore. Framlingham Castle stands above the river on the outskirts of the town, for centuries the home of a

number of powerful families and successive Dukes of Norfolk.

This site was originally occupied by a fortified house, which was later developed into a castle by members of the Bigod family, the first Earls of Norfolk, at the end of the twelfth century. Its history has been an eventful one, as it was a stronghold of King John in his struggle with the barons, and later the sanctuary of Mary Tudor during the attempt by the Duke of Northumberland to make Lady Jane Grey Queen.

The massive curtain walls incorporate thirteen flanking towers, some of which rise to a

height of sixty feet, and are then topped by attractive brick chimneys. The chimneys, added in the sixteenth century by members of the Howard family are all dummies except those on the eighth and ninth towers. In the seventeenth century the castle was given to Pembroke College, Cambridge, by Sir Robert Hitcham. Much of the inside was then demolished and the great hall converted into a poorhouse. Since 1913 it has been open to the public as an Ancient Monument.

See AM info. Also open Sun am Apr to Sep. Parking available.

The high walls of Framlingham Castle rise up above the village

Furness Abbey

Cumbria *p216 D5*

Standing in a deep wooded valley known as the Vale of the Deadly Nightshade is the ruin of the abbey of St Mary of Furness, better known as Furness Abbey.

Founded in 1127 the order was originally Benedictine, then changed to Cistercian in 1147 and became one of the most powerful religious houses in England.

Much of the soft red sandstone ruins which remain are of the twelfth and thirteenth centuries, although the east end transepts and belfry tower were rebuilt in the fifteenth century. Outstanding features are the late Norman arches of the cloisters, three fine transitional arches and the Early English chapter house. In the presbytery the basin used for washing the Communion vessels, and the priests' seats, are among the finest examples to have survived from the twelfth and thirteenth centuries.

See AM info. Parking available.

Furzey Gardens

Hampshire *p213 A2*

In the picturesque village of Minstead are the eight acres of Furzey Gardens with their winter and summer heathers, flowering trees and shrubs. The gardens are of botanical interest throughout the year, but are probably at their best in springtime when they burst into a blaze of colour.

Also of interest here is the 400-year-old thatched cottage with its Will Selwood Art and Craft Gallery displaying work by many local artists and craftsmen.

Open all year daily (except Christmas). Parking available.

Galloway Forest Park

Dumfries and Galloway *p220 C2*

Actually comprised of seven forests, the Galloway Forest Park covers almost 250 square miles of south-west Scotland. It is mountainous country, its highest point being the 2,764 foot Merrick, and hill walkers here are rewarded with some superb views.

The park is well watered with many rivers, streams, tarns and lochs which are particularly popular with anglers for their salmon and trout. These waters also provide much of the beauty of the area, with pretty little streams cascading through wooded glens and glass-like stretches of water surrounded by hills. Large herds of Red and Roe deer live within the forest and birds of prey such as buzzards, kestrels, owls and sparrowhawks can often be seen. Occasionally the native Golden eagle may be seen by the alert observer.

The Galloway area has strong associations with Robert the Bruce who won two battles against the English here in 1307. The Battles of Glen Trool and Rapploch Moss are commemorated with inscribed stones, one by the viewpoint looking down Glen Trool, the other by the Clatteringshaws Reservoir. More modern monuments are the impressive dams and power stations of the Galloway Hydro-Electric scheme. The area is particularly beautiful, taking in mountains, forests and moors. Forest trails and forest walks have been laid out for walkers, and the less energetic can enjoy driving along some lovely quiet roads.

Gawsworth Hall

Cheshire *p216 F3*

This charming black and white Tudor manor with its varying roof levels, is now the home of the Roper-Richards family. The most decorative side of the house with its compass window, faces a courtyard of lawn and flower beds and a lawn beyond. Overlooking the lawns and lake is the north façade, with a sixteenth-century coat of arms of the Fitton family, who were owners of the property for over four centuries.

Of particular interest in the beautiful beamed interior is the bedroom with its fourposter; the carved mantlepieces in the drawing room and library; the tables and seventeenth-century oak coffer in the long hall; the refectory table supported by eight carved bulbous legs in the dining room and above the main staircase the seventeenth-century Waterford crystal chandelier.

The charming little chapel has some beautiful stained glass windows, and over 200 oil paintings and water colours collected over

the centuries are hung throughout the house.

In the grounds is a museum housing a collection of coaches and carriages from the early eighteenth century onwards, and a medieval jousting ground.

Open late Mar to Oct daily, pm only. Parking and refreshments.

Glamis

Tayside *p222 E1*

Glamis is best known for its romantic-looking castle – associated with Shakespeare's *Macbeth*, the thane of Glamis, who became King of Scotland by killing King Duncan. The lands of Glamis were granted to the Lyon family (Earls of Strathmore) in 1372 and the castle's origins are thought to be fourteenth century. Standing in fine grounds bordered by Dean Water, it was rebuilt in the style of a French chateau during the late seventeenth century by Patrick Lyon, 1st Earl of Strathmore and Kinghorne.

The castle contains fine collections of china, tapestry, furniture, paintings and armour. In the beautiful grounds is a massive sundial with eighty-four dials.

An attractive terrace of restored nineteenth-century cottages in the village houses the Angus Folk Museum. Here a display of local domestic and agricultural life illustrates how people in the area have lived over the past 200 years or so.

Castle open Easter then May to Sep Mon to Fri, and Sun, pm only. Parking and refreshments.
Angus Folk Museum open Easter then May to Sep daily pm only and on request. NTS.

Turreted Glamis Castle – once used by kings as a hunting lodge

Glastonbury

Somerset *p212 E3*

This ancient Isle of Avalon, surrounded by mist-covered marshland and colourful legends, has long been associated with Joseph of Aramathea and King Arthur.

It was likely that Glastonbury was founded in Celtic times, but its most popular legend says it was created by Joseph of Aramathea who came from the Holy Land in AD60 to preach the gospel. While leaning on his staff on Wearyall Hill it magically took root and flowered. Joseph took this as a sign that he should settle here, and a wattle and daub church was subsequently built on the site now occupied by the present abbey ruins.

The Arthurian legend has it that both Arthur and Queen Guinevere were buried in the

abbey, and yet another story says that St Patrick was one of the first abbots here.

Without doubt Glastonbury's chief glory is the ruined abbey, and although little of its early history is known, it certainly became one of the richest and most famous in England. The majestic ruins of today consist largely of St Mary's Chapel, the abbey church and various monastic buildings. By far the best of these is the superb Abbot's Kitchen. It was built in the fourteenth century and stands intact with its vaulted domed roof and a fireplace in each corner. The gatehouse now houses a small museum, showing a model of the abbey as it was in 1539.

What was once the principal tithe barn of the abbey is now the Somerset Rural Life Museum. This contains relics of pre-mechanised farming in Somerset and has displays concerning cider making, peat and withy (young willow) cutting.

A walk to the nearby steep, conical hill called Glastonbury Tor, which rises up out of the flat Somerset Plain, provides panoramic views from its top. The tower there is all that remains of the fifteenth-century St Michael's Church. At the foot of the Tor is the Chalice Well beneath which Joseph is supposed to have buried the Holy Grail – the cup used by Christ at the Last Supper.

Abbey (including Abbot's Kitchen and Abbey Gatehouse Museum) open all year.
Somerset Rural Life Museum open all year daily, Sat and Sun pm only.
Chalice Well open all year daily (Oct to Mar pm only).

The ruins of Glastonbury Abbey, which was built in the 12th century

Glencoe

Highland *p221 C1*

The fame of the battles at Glencoe has spread far from this remote corner of Scotland, but it is the very remoteness which contributes so much to its rugged beauty. The Glen itself stretches for some seven-and-a-half miles from Rannoch Moor down to Loch Leven through magnificent mountain scenery. Its lofty peaks attract mountaineers, skiers and hill-walkers, but the more leisurely visitor can enjoy the views from special viewpoints, particularly the 1,000-foot summit of the main road at The Study, or Studdie.

Besides being a famous beauty spot, Glencoe is historically important for it was here that on 13th February, 1692 the shameful massacre of the Macdonalds took place. By order of King William III, a party of troops, mostly of the Campbell clan, turned on the families who had been their hosts for twelve days, mercilessly slaughtering men, women and children. Many escaped into the snowy hills of Glen Coe only to perish in the bitter cold. The only crime of the Macdonald clan was that their chief was unavoidably delayed on his journey to swear allegiance to the new King, arriving on the 6th January rather than 1st. A memorial to the Macdonalds stands near the old Invercoe road and another reminder is the Signal Rock near the Clachaig Inn, reputedly the place from which a signal was sent to the Campbells to proceed with the dreadful deed.

Macdonald relics are among the exhibits in the Glencoe and North Lorn Folk Museum, housed in

Mountains tower behind the village of Glencoe as a spectacular backdrop

two heather-thatched cottages. There are also local domestic and agricultural exhibits, Jacobite relics, costumes and embroidery. At the north end of Glencoe is the National Trust's Visitor Centre which provides information and a ranger-naturalist service.

Museum open mid May to Sep daily (except Sun).
Visitor Centre open Good Fri to Oct daily. Parking available. NT.

Glen More Forest Park

Highland *p221 D2*

The Glen More Forest Park which lies to the north of the Cairngorms National Nature Reserve is sometimes referred to as the Queen's Forest of Glen More. The reserve, one of the largest in Britain, covers nearly sixty-four square miles incorporating Rothiemurchus Forest and the Ben Macdui, Britain's second highest peak. Aviemore, the winter-sports and holiday centre, lies to the west of Glen More.

The forest was originally held by the Grants before passing to the Dukes of Gordon, who used it as a deer preserve. In 1923 it was acquired by the Forestry Commissioners who subsequently established it as a forest park.

The forest of Glen More contains some 9,100 acres of mountainside and 3,400 acres of spruce and pine woods. For centuries it was a completely isolated area and has featured little in history.

When approached from Aviemore via Coylumbridge, the road enters the forest by skirting the shores of Loch Morlich; a central feature of Glen More. Loch Morlich and its surrounding area offers various facilities including bathing, camping and sailing. Beyond the loch to the east lies Glen More Lodge, the National Outdoor Training Centre. Within the park the Forestry Commission has marked a variety of walks and Red deer, Golden eagles, ospreys and reindeer can be seen from them.

Rugged moorland scenery along the Lairig Ghm nature trail in Glen More Forest Park

Gloucester Gloucestershire *p212 F5*

In Roman times Gloucester was a fortified port which guarded the lowest Severn crossing and the legions' route into Wales. Since then the city has had a chequered history as a port, but nevertheless survived to become a thriving export point for local industries.

Since Saxon times the Cross has been the junction of the main thoroughfares of the city which still follow the pattern of the original Roman roads. In the streets leading off from the Cross are a number of interesting buildings including the handsome Guildhall of 1890, the galleried New Inn dating from the fifteenth century and Robert Raike's House, a fine timber-framed house said to have been the home of Raike, the founder of Sunday schools.

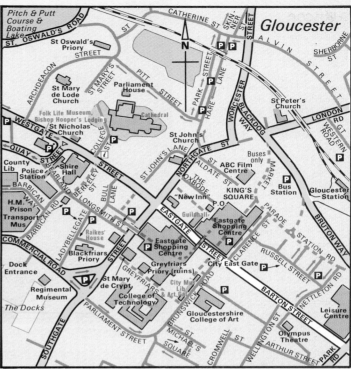

The Cathedral

Although mainly Norman in origin, extensive rebuilding has produced an example of architectural development hard to better throughout Europe. The massive Norman pillars dominate the 174-foot long nave with its thirteenth-century vaulting above. The east window is the largest left from medieval England and celebrates the victory at Crécy in 1346 by a glorious profusion of coloured glass saints, popes and kings. The cloisters, with their exquisite fan vaulting, surround a delightful garden which has a well in the middle.

Bishop Hooper's Lodging

This early sixteenth-century timber-framed house is so called because the Protestant martyr sup-

Carved saints adorn the façade of Gloucester's cathedral

posedly stayed here the night before he was burnt at the stake in 1555. It now houses one of the best folk museums in the country and illustrates crafts and industries of the county down to the minutest detail. There is also a section of relics from the Civil War siege of Gloucester in 1643.

City Museum and Art Gallery

Virtually all the finds left from the Roman occupation are kept here, amongst which are fragments of a bronze statue of an emperor on horseback. Many examples of Celtic craftsmanship in bronze are kept here too, including the Birdlip Mirror made in AD25.

Bishop Hooper's Lodging open all year Mon to Sat (except Bank Holidays).

Museum and Art Gallery open as above.

The tomb of the murdered Edward II lies in Gloucester Cathedral

Grasmere

Cumbria *p220 E1*

This unspoilt village sits on the fringe of lake Grasmere, surrounded by high fells, offering protection from cold north and east winds.

Dove Cottage, a simple six-room slated and limewashed stone cottage is delightfully situated on the east side of the lake at Town End. Dating from the early seventeenth century, it was originally a small inn named The Dove and Olive-Bough, serving weary travellers on the old Ambleside to Keswick road. It became the home of William Wordsworth and his family in 1799 and was the scene of some of the poet's most creative years. He wrote most of *The Prelude*, his autobiographical poem, here.

Thomas De Quincy, the essayist, lived in the cottage after Wordsworth left and remained there until about 1830. During this time he wrote *The Confession of an English Opium Eater* and *Recollections of the Lakes and the Lake Poets*.

The cottage is open to the public and has been arranged so the rooms look as they did during Wordsworth's tenancy. Much of the furniture actually belonged to the poet and his family, and the garden, climbing up the hillside at the back of the house, has been carefully kept as it was in Wordsworth's day. Opposite the cottage is the Wordsworth Museum housing a collection of his possessions. An exhibition there displays newly-discovered manuscripts of letters and poems,

Dove Cottage was the unassuming home of the poet William Wordsworth and his family in Grasmere

as well as portraits on loan from the Wordsworth Circle and the National Portrait Gallery. Wordsworth, his wife Mary and sister Dorothy are buried in the churchyard of the thirteenth-century St Oswald church in Grasmere village. The poet is commemorated in the church with a bust by Woolner.

An annual attraction of the village is the Grasmere Sports, held on the Thursday falling closest to 20th August. Wrestling contests, fell-racing and fox-hound training feature among the events.

Dove Cottage and Wordsworth Museum open Mar to Oct and early Dec to early Jan daily.

The waterfront at Great Yarmouth with its old merchants' houses

Great Dixter

East Sussex *p213 D2*

Great Dixter is a superb example of a late medieval manor house, half-timbered with oak from the Forest of Weald. Built around 1450, it was acquired in 1911 by Nathaniel Lloyd, an architectural historian who employed Sir Edwin Lutyens to restore the building. During this time Lloyd and Lutyens found a decaying sixteenth-century house in Benenden, encased in corrugated iron and in use as a barn. By re-erecting this building at Great Dixter, Lutyens skilfully merged the two to form a sizeable house of great character. Particularly notable is the hall with its timbered roof. The house contains some fine antiques and a late sixteenth-century Flemish tapestry. The delightful gardens complement the house perfectly with yew hedges and a sunken garden.

Open Apr to mid Oct, Tue to Sun and Bank Holiday Mon, pm only. Parking available.

Great Yarmouth

Norfolk *p214 E5*

The town lies on a spit of land between the river Yare and the North Sea with five miles of golden sands on its doorstep. All the attractions of a popular holiday resort are in Great Yarmouth, which mingle well with the quaint houses lining the waterfront. To the north-east of the large open

air market place are some interesting almshouses called the Fishermen's Hospital. Nearby is St Nicholas Church, considered to be the largest parish church in England. Originally twelfth-century, the interior was restored after parts of the church were damaged during World War II; the Norman tower and Early English west end have been preserved. Next to the church is Anna Sewell House, a seventeenth-century Tudor fronted building, birthplace of the authoress of *Black Beauty*.

Leading from the town walls (one evening a week during July and August there are conducted tours of these) near the South Quay are The Rows, a number of narrow lanes based on a grid system. Although damaged during World War II air raids, several rows remain, one of which has been renovated, providing a typical example of small town houses in the seventeenth century. Close by is the restored Old Merchant's House, a 300-year-old building exhibiting local building craftsmanship of the seventeenth to nineteenth centuries.

The Tolhouse, which houses the local museum, illustrates the long history of the town. Formerly the civic building and dungeons, the original cells of which can still be seen, the building dates back to the fourteenth century and has been completely restored. Also near here are the fourteenth-century Greyfriar Cloisters and

Elizabethan House, now a museum, which has a late Georgian façade. The interior contains modern furniture, domestic utensils from the nineteenth century, a sixteenth-century panelled room and collections of Victorian toys and Lowestoft porcelain.

There are two piers in the town, each with a theatre, and between the two is the Maritime Museum for East Anglia, showing development of marine equipment past and present and the oil and gas industry. It also includes exhibits depicting the herring fishery and inland waterways. Near Wellington Pier is Merrivale Model Village, set in an acre of landscaped gardens and including a model railway and radio-controlled model boats. The models are to a scale of 1 : 12 and illuminated after dusk from June to September.

Old Merchant's House open Apr to Sep Mon to Fri by guided tour only starting from Row 111 Houses. Ticket includes Row 111 Houses and Greyfriars Cloister. AM.
Tolhouse Museum open all year Sun Jun to Sep only (except Good Fri, Christmas, New Year, and Sat).
Elizabethan House Museum open as above.
Maritime Museum for East Anglia open as above.
Merrivale Model Village open late May to Sep daily. Refreshments available.

Greys Court

Oxfordshire *p213 A3*

Three miles west of Henley-on-Thames stands this attractive brick and stone gabled house in some 280 acres of gardens.

In the fourteenth century it belonged to Lord de Grey, who fought at the Battle of Crécy and from whom the house obtained its name. The medieval great tower and the smaller towers still stand, but the present house, with a battlemented bay window on one end, is mainly sixteenth century, although over the years various alterations have been made.

The well-house has a nineteen-foot-wide wooden donkey wheel which was used until 1914 to raise water from the 200-foot-deep well to supply the house with water.

Another feature of interest is the 'Archbishop's' Maze.

Open Apr to Sep.
Grounds Mon to Sat, House, Mon Wed and Fri, pm only. Refreshments available (Wed to Sat only). NT.

Grime's Graves

Norfolk *p213 C5*

The 350 or so holes in the ground here are not, in fact, graves but the workings of the largest prehistoric flint mines in Europe. First worked around 4,000 years ago, both Stone Age and Bronze Age man extracted flints from the ground for their own use and for trading throughout southern England. The shafts sink vertically for between twenty to forty feet, and passages lead off following the seams of flint. Some of them link up underground to form a labyrinth of tunnels where primitive man hacked at the rock using antlers as pickaxes. They were excavated for the first time in 1870, and have fascinated modern man for many years and it is now possible to go down a shaft and inspect these ancient workings, although it is wise to take a torch.

See AM info. Parking available.

Guildford

Surrey *p213 B2*

The ancient capital of Surrey, Guildford is a pleasant town and busy shopping centre with an attractive cobbled High Street up the hill. This is lined with historic buildings, including the very decorative seventeenth-century Guildhall with its balcony, bell-tower and ornate gilded clock. Its neighbour, Guildford House,

built in 1660, is a timber-framed building, with a carved staircase and finely decorated plaster ceilings. It is now an art gallery. Further up the High Street is the Hospital of the Blessed Trinity, better known as the Abbot's Hospital after its founder, George Abbot, who was Archbishop of Canterbury in 1619. A magnificent arched gateway with four turrets leads to an enclosed courtyard in front of this Tudor brick building, which has been in continuous use as an almshouse for old people since it was built.

Guildford's oldest building is the castle, behind Quarry Street, built by Henry II during the twelfth century. Only the square keep remains and it is surrounded by colourful gardens. At the entrance, in Castle Arch, is the town museum containing items of local history and archaeology and needlework. The town's connection with Charles Lutwidge Dodgson – better known as Lewis Carrol, who lived in Quarry Street, is also illustrated here. He died in Guildford in 1898 and is buried in the Mount Cemetary.

One of Guildford's newest buildings is also its most impressive – the Cathedral of the Holy Spirit which looks down over the town from the top of Stag Hill. Completed in 1961, it was built in the shape of a cross with pink bricks made from Stag Hill clay.

The river Wey with its weeping willows provides a lovely setting for the Yvonne Arnaud Theatre,

The clock on Guildford's Guildhall is its most striking feature

and in summer boats can be hired along the river.
Guildford House Gallery open all year daily (except Sun).
Hospital of the Blessed Trinity closed for repairs at time of going to press. Due to reopen in 1987.
Castle open daily (except Christmas Day). Grounds all year.
Keep open Apr to Sep.
Museum open all year daily (except Sun and some Bank Holidays).

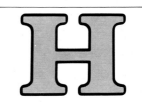

Haddon Hall

Derbyshire *p217 B2*

This estate was first owned by William Peveril, illegitimate son of William the Conqueror. The fine stone-built manor situated on the river Wye at the foot of a densely wooded incline was probably originally no more than a modest residence, but through the ages has been developed into a delightful rambling manor house.

Although the Hall was extensively restored in the early part of this century, the same basic materials were used, and it looks much as it did over 300 years ago. Its special features include the long gallery which is beautifully panelled in oak and walnut and has a decorated ceiling. Heraldic panelling and carving decorate the dining room, and the staircase landing is hung with three Mortlake tapestries. Ancient troughs used for water storage are kept in the kitchen, and the butcher's shop contains the original equipment used for salting and chopping.

A small museum has been set up within the Hall which has interesting items found during the restoration. To the south of the house are beautiful stone-walled terraced gardens, a series of lawns, flower beds and yews. Masses of roses adorn the grounds: they can be seen almost everywhere, in formal flower beds and climbing along the stone walls, providing the perfect setting for an English country house.

Open Apr to Sep, Tue to Sun (Jul and Aug, Tue to Sat and Bank Holidays). Parking and refreshments available.

Hadrian's Wall

Cumbria, Northumberland, Tyne and Wear

The barrier across Britain between Solway and Tyne was built because the Emperor Hadrian wanted to separate the Romans from the barbarians. Roman soldiers, who were also skilled engineers and craftsmen, began work on the wall in AD 122. The wall took just over seven years to complete, and twenty-seven million cubic feet of stone were used in the process.

All that remains of the temple to Mithras at Carrawburgh fort

Huge though the actual wall was, it only formed part of Hadrian's complete defence system. On the north side a steep ditch ran parallel to the wall, whereas south of it ran a flat-bottomed ditch with earth ramparts built up on either side, known as the vallum. The system extended beyond the wall in the form of small forts at one-mile intervals and watchtowers down the Cumbrian coast, outpost forts north of the wall, and a Roman port on the Tyne at South Shields.

On the wall at intervals of 1,620 yards (one Roman mile) there were milecastles, which held between eight and sixty-four men and had gateways opening north and south. Turrets, used as watchtowers, were built between the milecastles every third of a (Roman) mile. In addition to these were seventeen forts, or garrisons, placed strategically on or near the wall which were each manned by troops or cavalry. Altogether the wall garrison consisted of about 15,000 men.

Although the wall has been virtually derelict since the end of the fourth century, the surviving remains are nevertheless quite extensive and very impressive, not least because of their beautiful setting. Working from east to west, the first visible remains are at South Shields which was the port of the Roman wall. In Roman Remains Park, Baring Street, parts of the fort have been preserved, and there is also a museum here of finds from the excavations there.

Just before Heddon-on-the-Wall, about 110 yards of the wall has been preserved, but beyond this point until Shield-on-the-Wall, evidence of the wall has disappeared because the Hanoverians used it in 1781 to construct their military road, and only a few short stretches have survived. However, at Brunton there is a fine piece of wall and a well preserved turret.

The fort at Chesters (*Cilurnum*), south of the wall on the west bank of the North Tyne, housed a regiment of cavalry. Opposite the north gateway is the headquarters building, with a strong-room beneath the paymaster's office. The Commanding Officer's house, east of the headquarters, had heated rooms and a bath suite. Between the fort and river, set into the riverbank, is a large building which housed the fort baths.

West of Chesters the wall rises

to 1,230 feet, following the geological ridge known as Whin Sill. The central sector of the wall begins here and it runs through magnificent wild countryside. Lonely moors stretch away to the north with the hills of south Scotland and north Northumberland in the distance, while to the south lies the fertile valley of the Tyne.

The next Roman fort to the west is Carrawburgh (*Brocolitia*) where only grass covered ramparts are visible, but to the south a temple of Mithras has been excavated and preserved. He was a God that seemed to appeal to soldiers as a number of temples were dedicated to him.

Beyond Shield-on-the-Wall, where the military road finally leaves the wall, is Housesteads (*Vercovicium*), the best and most exciting of the Roman forts. Its ramparts and gateways have been very well preserved, and the granaries, headquarters, commandant's house, hospital, latrines, some barracks and civilian settlements have been uncovered. The remains of a fourth-century man and woman were found beneath the floor of one of these settlements and their end was

clearly not a happy one as the point of a sword was embedded in the man's ribs. The south gateway tower of Housesteads was a stronghold of the Armstrong's – a notorious gang of cattle raiders and bandits in the sixteenth and seventeenth centuries.

Farther along the wall is the fort at Chesterholm (*Vindolanda*) which was built before the wall in the AD 80s, and subsequently incorporated into the wall system in the AD 160s. There is a military bath-house west of the fort and considerable remains of another civilian settlement. An interest-

ing feature here is a full-scale replica of a section of wall which includes a stone turret. In a valley below the fort is a museum of the site, containing some remarkable finds from the pre-Hadrianic forts, including writing tablets, footwear and leather items.

From the line of the wall at South Shields are magnificent views. The hills of south-west Scotland are visible on a fine day, and to the south Skiddaw, Saddleback and Cross Fell of the Pennines.

Still following the Whin Sill, the wall continues on to Cawfields

An 18th-century engraving of the great Roman wall

where there is a well preserved milecastle, and beyond to the fort at Greatchesters (*Aesica*) with its ramparts, two gateways, barracks and an underground strong-room.

Continuing westwards the wall is rather tumbledown, but at Walltown a lone turret still survives. Beyond the point where the river Irthing intersects it, a fine stretch of wall leads up to Birdoswald fort (*Camboglanna*), where some believe King Arthur fought his last battle. From here to the Solway the land becomes gentler, although no less beautiful, and red sandstone takes over from limestone. Since the wall has provided building materials in the past, few remains of it are visible beyond Walton village, except the ditch and earthworks.

Chesters Roman Fort and Museum see AM info. Also open Sun am Apr to Sep. Parking available.
Carrawburgh Roman Fort open at any reasonable time. Parking available.
Housesteads Roman Fort and Museum see AM info. Also open Sun am Apr to Sep. Parking available.
Chesterholm open all year daily (except 25 Dec). Parking and refreshments available.

Hailes Abbey and Museum

Gloucestershire *p212 F5*

In beautiful countryside, secluded in trees, stand the ruined walls of this Cistercian abbey and its cloisters, founded in 1246 by the Earl of Cornwall. Although relatively little remains above ground, excavations have revealed the massive plan of this once impressive abbey.

The adjoining museum contains roof bosses, armorial tiles and other relics which came to light during the excavations.

See AM info. NT. Parking available.

Hardwick Hall

Derbyshire *p217 B1*

This striking Elizabethan building, surrounded by a country park, was built by Robert Smythson for the famous Dowager Countess of Shrewsbury, best known as Bess of Hardwick.

It is a plain, symmetrical, stone building with four huge towers at each corner, topped with decorative open stonework incorporating the initials of the Countess, ES, and surmounted with a crown. The exterior has such enormous windows that it seems to be more glass than wall. The lavish interior has an abundance of tapestries and fine needlework, furniture and portraits. It also has magnificent plasterwork and stone and marble fireplaces. Of special interest are the coloured plasterwork frieze and beautiful walls and fireplace in the great high chamber, the fourposter bed in the state bedroom and the seventeenth-century tapestry on the landing of the main staircase.

Open Apr to Oct, Wed, Thu, Sat, Sun and Bank Holiday Mon, pm only. Park open all year daily. Parking and refreshments, Apr to Oct, available. NT.

Harewood House and Bird Garden

West Yorkshire *p217 B3*

Harewood House, the West Yorkshire home of the Earl and Countess of Harewood was designed by John Carr of York and decorated by Robert Adam in the eighteenth century.

It is beautifully sited for views over the surrounding countryside and the yellow-stone house itself is set in timbered parkland created by Capability Brown.

The interior is outstanding, offering a glittering display of eighteenth-century craftsmanship, which includes furniture by Thomas Chippendale, said to be the finest ever made in England. Many of the rooms reflect Robert Adam's passion for designing complete rooms, including the ceilings, mirrors and carpets which complement each other perfectly. A fine collection of Sèvres and Chinese porcelain is also to be seen, as well as many fine paintings including work by Reynolds, Tintoretto, Titian and Turner.

The eighteenth-century stable block has been converted into exhibition rooms showing the history of the house, and next to it children can explore the adventure playground. Between the stables and the lake, covering an area of some four acres, is the Harewood Bird Garden containing numerous species of exotic birds. In these natural, delightful surroundings many of the birds wander freely on the lawns and amongst the trees. Other attractions within the Bird Garden include a tropical house, a penguin pool and a walk-around aviary.

Open daily Apr to Oct, but Sun only Feb, Mar and Nov. Parking and refreshments available.

Harlech Castle

Gwynedd *p216 C2*

Harlech Castle standing, high on a rock, is one of the most imposing fortresses in the country. On one side lies the little holiday town of Harlech, on the other a wide expanse of sand dunes and the sea.

Harlech is one of the four biggest castles in Wales

The castle built by Edward I, was first put to the test just a few years after its completion in 1290 and subsequently suffered repeated attacks. Today it remains as impressive as ever, remarkably well-preserved and still dominating the entire area. From its walls and towers there are panoramic views across Tremadoc Bay, across the Morfa Harlech Nature Reserve to the north and inland towards the mountains of Snowdonia.

Castle see AM info. Also open Sun am Apr to Sep. Parking available.

Harrogate

North Yorkshire *p217 B3*

Harrogate grew up around its eighty-nine mineral springs, and developed to accommodate the fashionable society of the nineteenth century who came to 'take the waters'. Much of its Victorian architecture remains, and the mellow stonework, wide tree-lined streets and colourful gardens lend an air of elegant spaciousness to the busy town centre.

The Royal Pump Room was built in 1842 over a sulphur well which had previously enjoyed the name The Stinking Spaw. This well can still be seen in the basement, and the rest of the building

Springtime at Hardwick Hall, where there is 'more glass than wall'

mile south of the town, best viewed from the A61. Built by the York and Midland Railway Company in 1847, it carried the main Leeds to Thirsk line across the Crimple Beck.

Looking to the future, Harrogate's most modern landmark is the magnificent multi-million pound International Centre on Kings Road, providing conference and entertainment facilities comparable with the best in the world. The 12,000 square metres of space houses trade fairs and exhibitions in a futuristic setting. The central feature of the Centre, however, is the turn-of-the-century Royal Hall, an atmospheric building rich in baroque architecture.

Royal Pump Room Museum open all year daily, Sun pm only.
Art Gallery open all year daily.
Harlow Car Gardens open all year daily. Parking and refreshments available.

Harvington Hall

Hereford and Worcester
p216 F1
This moated, rambling gabled brick house, with stone and mullioned windows masking part of an earlier timber framed building, was one of Worcestershire's great Roman Catholic homes, whose history is linked with the days of Catholic persecution during the seventeenth-century.

In 1630 it was the home of the Catholic Throckmorton family who had been implicated in the Gunpowder Plot. The amazing honeycomb of secret passages, sliding panels, trapdoors, and hidden rooms or attics called priests' holes, where persecuted Catholic priests found refuge or held secret services, can all be seen.

The Hall also contains some re-

has been turned into a museum of local history. Exhibits include costume, pottery and a lovely antique dolls house containing some 300 household items.

Harrogate's art gallery is in the library and has a permanent collection of oils and water-colours.

On the edge of the town are the outstanding Harlow Car Gardens which contain one of the most comprehensive collections of garden plants in the north of England, all laid out in a pleasant landscape of flower beds, rockeries, woodland and shrubberies. Of industrial and archaeological interest is the half-mile-long Crimple Viaduct one

The park of Harewood House lost 20,000 trees in the gales of 1962

All Saints Street in Hastings shows some of its Tudor architecture

markable wall paintings from the Elizabethan or earlier periods, together with fine oak furniture.

John Wall, a Roman Catholic priest and one of the last men in England to be martyred for his faith, frequently used the house as a hiding place. His portrait is in the Roman Catholic church here and a stone lies in the churchyard commemorating him.

Open Feb to Nov, Tue to Sat pm only. Easter to Sep all day, also Sun pm. Open Bank Hol Mons. Parking and refreshments available.

Hastings

Sussex *p213 D2*
The old town of Hastings, between Castle Hill and the East Cliff, is an interesting huddle of houses dating from medieval times. Its roots are in the fishing industry which still thrives despite the silting up of the harbour. The motor vessels now used are winched up onto the shingle beach when not at sea, but the tall, narrow, fishermen's huts, are a reminder of past traditions. In these huts the nets are hung to dry and fishing paraphernalia is stored. Nearby is the Fishermen's Museum, built as a chapel in 1854. Now it contains a fascinating collection of photographs, documents and mementos as well as the lugger *Enterprise,* the last vessel to be built in Hastings before the shipyard was closed in 1909. In spite of its change of use, a Harvest Festival service is held annually, and the font is used for christenings.

The two-tier promenade separates a busy road, fronted by shops and hotels, from the beach which is coarse shingle, except at low tide when sand is exposed and rock pools can be explored. Most of the beaches provide safe bathing and are patrolled by lifeguards, and a number of indoor and outdoor swimming pools are provided. Sea trips are available and for those who prefer to row their own boat and there

are vessels for hire both on the beach and at the two boating lakes. Other sports are well catered for, fishing being a favourite pastime, and there is plenty of entertainment, from concert orchestra or brass band to Punch and Judy, with, at Playland, amusements and visual delights to keep the children happy. For those who like to get away from the town, Hastings Country Park provides 520 acres of cliff-top walks with beautiful views of sea and downs.

Hastings is known internationally for its annual chess congress and the Town Criers' Championship, when officials come from all over the country to show off their colourful uniforms and the power of their lungs.

Most people connect the town with the Battle of Hastings where Harold Godwinson got an arrow in his eye and the bastard William became the first Norman King of England. That encounter actually took place six miles inland at the place now called Battle. However, William's arrival is remembered in Hastings itself by the Conqueror's Stone on the seafront near the pier, and is reputed to have been used as a table when he enjoyed his first meal in England, and the ruined Norman castle on the cliff top above the old town, built in 1068 to replace a temporary wooden fort. To commemorate the 900th anniversary of the Norman landing, the Royal School of Needlework designed and made a 243 foot-long tapestry depicting eighty-one major events in British history since 1066; this is now on display in the town hall. Near the castle on West Hill is a series of caves – St Clement's – once used by smugglers, where dances are held on summer evenings.

Fishermen's Museum open Spring Bank Hol to Sep daily (except Fri).
Hastings Castle open Apr to Sep daily.
St Clement's Caves open Apr to Sep daily; Sat and Sun only in winter.

The rich furnishings in the long gallery are typical of Hatfield House

Hatfield House

Hertfordshire *p213 B3*

Erected early in the seventeenth-century for Robert Cecil, 1st Earl of Salisbury, the house has been occupied by his descendants ever since. Today it is the home of the Marquess of Salisbury.

A brick and stone Jacobean building of mammoth proportions, it has two enormous wings with square turrets at each corner, joined by a colonnaded central section which is crowned by an imposing domed clock tower.

Particularly interesting inside are the elaborately carved screen, the tapestries depicting the four seasons hanging in the marble hall, the decorated plasterwork ceiling, the fine fireplace in the long gallery, and the stained glass of the chapel. Another point of interest is the beautiful carved staircase which has supporting posts adorned with figures, and wooden gates (to prevent children falling down the stairs) on the the first floor landing.

In the gardens is the remaining wing of the original Palace, a royal residence in the early sixteenth century, now used as a tea room.

Open late Mar to mid Oct (except Good Fri and Mon but open Bank Holiday Mon) Sun, pm only. Gardens open all year daily. Parking and refreshments available.

Haworth

West Yorkshire *p217 A3*

To the south of the Aire Valley lies an area immortalized in English literature by the novels of the Brontë sisters. At its centre in a valley on the edge of rugged moorland is Haworth, a small, bleak, grey West Yorkshire village. Its narrow streets still contain buildings dating from the sixteenth century, such as the Elizabethan Emmott Hall at the foot of Old Kirkgate. At the top of the steep main street, looking down on the valley below, is a hilltop church and old parsonage.

It was to the bleak Georgian parsonage that the Brontë family came in 1820 and the sisters lived and wrote here until 1849. Now the house is a museum containing the family's belongings including Branwell's portraits of his sisters, Charlotte's sewing box and Mr Brontë's spectacles.

The tower is all that remains of Haworth Old Church, in which the Brontës worshipped, as the rest of the existing church was rebuilt in 1881. A Memorial Chapel was built for them in 1964 and beneath the base of one of the stone entrance pillars is the family vault.

In the village itself at the top of the hill the Black Bull Inn, where Branwell Brontë drank himself to death, may still be seen.

Some two miles west of the churchyard on Haworth Moor, along a favourite footpath of the sisters, lies the Brontë Bridge and waterfall.

Brontë Parsonage open all year daily (except first 3 weeks in Feb and Christmas).

Heaton Hall

Gt Manchester *p216 E3*

This superb country house looks down over the conurbation of Greater Manchester and enjoys a very different view from that in 1772 when it was built. The Earl of Wilton commissioned James Wyatt to design this, the architect's first country house, and the result was one of the finest of its sort in the country. The interior decorations are magnificent and there are eighteenth and nineteenth-century furniture, paintings, ceramics, silver and glass. The music room is particularly notable for its collection of early keyboard instruments, including an organ built by Samuel Green in 1790. The house stands in lovely parkland with lawns, woods, a lake and a playground.

Open Easter Mon to Sep Mon and Wed to Sat, also Sun pm only.

Hereford Hereford and Worcester *p212 E5*

Hereford lies in the rich farmland area of rural England famed for its cider and white-faced red-brown cattle, and the busy market town itself with its famous cathedral, centre around these thriving industries.

Hereford began as a stronghold on the Welsh border around AD 700 and obtained its name from Army Ford. The town's position has caused it to suffer over the centuries from opposing English and Welsh armies, the English finally capturing it in 1645 during the Civil War.

The street plan of Hereford has remained virtually unaltered since its Saxon layout and attractive seventeenth and eighteenth-century buildings now line the streets. One of the pleasantest parts of the town is to the south where it borders the river Wye. Here the cathedral grounds, Castle Green and well-kept Redcliffe Gardens with its bowling green, provide views of the surrounding farmland.

The Cathedral

The pink-stone cathedral church of St Mary the Virgin and St Ethelbert the King dates back to 1080, although the first Bishop was installed in 676. Ethelbert, the Christian King of East Anglia was buried here after being beheaded by Offa, King of Mercia.

The interior is very interesting, boasting one of the finest collections of brasses in any cathedral. It also contains a vast chained library where all the books are chained to the shelves. This dates from the time when books were rare and valuable objects and liable to be stolen. The Mappa Mundi map is kept here too — it is a map of the world as known in 1290, drawn on vellum.

The Old House

Built in 1621, the Old House is a fine restored Jacobean black and white timbered house. It was once part of the picturesque Butchers' Row, which was pulled down in Victorian times by public subscription. Wood carving decorates both the exterior and interior and the outside porch features an amusing butchers' coat

The Old House – once part of Butchers' Row

of arms. The fascinating Jacobean contents include solid oak furniture and paintings of the acting families, the Siddons and Garricks.

Museum and Art Gallery

Although the museum houses mainly modern water colours by

Hereford Cathedral's Lady Chapel dates from the 12th century

local artists, a number of Roman remains are kept here too. Amongst these are sections of tesselated pavements which were excavated from Kenchester, the nearby Roman garrison stronghold called *Magna*.

A natural history and geological section includes domestic items of

byegone days and military uniforms and relics.

St John and Coningsby Museum

Almshouses were added in 1614 to the older dining hall of the Knights of St John (c1170) to form the present museum. Its

contents consist of armour and relics belonging to the Knights.

Churchill Gardens Museum and Brian Hatton Art Gallery

The interesting exhibits here include costumes, water colours, glass, porcelain, jewelry and dolls. There is also a Victorian nursery and butler's pantry equipped, as they would have been in those days.

Bulmers Railway Centre

Hereford claims to have the world's biggest cider factory – Bulmers, which was founded in 1887. They now have on the premises of their factory a Railway Centre which is open at weekends during the summer. On Easter Monday and Spring Bank Holiday locomotives can be seen in full steam.

The Old House open Mon to Sat. Limited opening hours on Mon, also Sat in winter.
Museum and Art Gallery open all year Tue to Sat.
St John and Coningsby Museum open Easter to Sep Tue to Thu, Sat and Sun, pm only.
Churchill Gardens Museum and Brian Hatton Art Gallery open pm only Tue to Sat; Sun summer only.

Herstmonceux

East Sussex *p213 C2*

Although the village of Herst-monceux is noted for its wood-crafts (traditional in this part of Sussex), it is much more famous for its beautiful mellow-brick castle. Formerly a Norman manor house, it was transformed into a castle in 1440 and was one of the first to be designed for residential comfort as well as defensive strength. In 1777 it was largely demolished, but careful restoration in 1913 has recreated its impressive array of battlements and turrets, so that it stands now in perfect condition within its wide moat.

In 1948 the Royal Greenwich Observatory moved here from its outdated premises in Greenwich Park, and it contains one of the largest telescopes in the world.

Grounds and Observatory open Easter to end Sep daily. Occasional castle openings.
Parking and refreshments available.

Heveningham Hall

Suffolk *p214 E5*

One of the finest and loveliest Georgian mansions in the country, Heveningham Hall is set on a hill above its lake and the winding river Blyth. Sir Gerald Vanneck, MP, inherited the estate with its small Queen Anne house from his father in 1777, and had it enlarged by Sir Robert Taylor, court architect to George III. Taylor screened the front with Corinthian columns and added pedimented wings to either side, creating today's imposing building in the Palladian tradition. The Victorian architect James

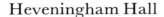

The beautiful red-brick exterior of Herstmonceux Castle is perfectly mirrored in the still moat which surrounds it

Wyatt designed the Hall's attractive interior, along with some of its furnishings, now considered to be his best surviving work. The magnificent painted decorations are the work of the Italian artist Biagio Rebecca.

Amongst the highlights of the interior are the famous entrance hall, with its semi-circular vaulted ceiling and screens of columns, the dining room, the Etruscan room and the library — all of which contain much of their original furniture and contents.

The grounds including the majestic lake, were laid out by Capa-bility Brown and contain an attractive red-brick crinkle-crackle wall that snakes in and out and so protects delicate plants, and a beautiful orangery by Wyatt.

Open Due to fire damage extensive renovation work in progress. Hoped to re-open to public during 1987. Specific opening dates unavailable.

Hever Castle

Kent *p213 C2*

Hever Castle owes much of its present splendour to Lord Astor who spent vast sums of money on restoring it during the early part of this century. The castle dates back to the thirteenth century and in Tudor times was the home of the Boleyn family.

Henry VIII reputedly courted his ill-fated second wife, Anne, here and following her execution he confiscated the castle, later installing the discarded Anne of Cleves.

Lord and Lady Astor modernised the interior of the castle without detracting in any way from its character. The exterior, surrounded by a wide moat, is superbly complemented by the formal gardens which the Astors laid out and filled with Italian sculptures.

There is also an interesting maze using over 1,000 yew trees, and the outstanding topiary work includes a complete set of chessmen.

Castle and Gardens open Easter to Oct daily, Castle pm only. Parking and refreshments available.

Hever Castle, one-time home of Anne Boleyn, looks more like a manor house than a castle

High Force Waterfall

Co Durham *p217 A4*

The river Tees cascades down over a drop of seventy feet from a cliff of the Great Whin Sill, creating one of the most spectacular waterfalls in England. It plunges into a deep pool enclosed by rocks and shrubs set in a charmingly wooded glen. The best time to see the fall is when the river is in full spate following heavy rain. Access to the falls is by way of a short wooded path which leads down the bank from an entrance opposite the High Force Hotel on the B6277.

A causeway, revealed at low tide, links Holy Island to the mainland

Highland Wildlife Park

Highland *p221 D2*

Amidst mountainous Speyside scenery, the Highland Wildlife Park contains animals that once roamed the Highlands, as well as those species that still do. The drive-through park gives one a close view of free-ranging herds of Red deer, European bison, wild goats, wild horses, Highland cattle and Soay sheep from the isles of St Kilda. Over the hill are enclosures housing bears, wild-cat, eagles, grouse and other mammals and birds. Above the road is the wolf enclosure, where the first cubs to have been raised in the Highlands since 1742 live.

A children's park includes a selection of tame animals, and an Alpine-style chalet incorporates a cafe and souvenir shop overlooking the wildfowl lochan.

Open Apr to Oct daily. Parking and refreshments available.

Hodnet Hall Gardens

Shropshire *p216 E2*

These beautiful landscaped gardens surround the large Elizabethan red-brick house (not open) which stands on the bank of a small valley.

Beginning in 1922, Brigadier Heber-Percy spent over thirty years creating the sixty acres of gardens which are laid out with lakes, pools and sweeping lawns. These provide a perfect setting for the rare shrubs and trees which blend with the blaze of colour roses, rhododendrons and azaleas produce. Primulas, irises and other moisture-loving plants grow beside the water.

Next to the house is a pretty half-timbered seventeenth-century building which is used as a tea-room. The inside is unusually adorned with big game trophies.

Open Good Fri to Sep daily, pm only. Parking available. Refreshments Sun and Bank Holidays and daily May to Aug.

Holker Hall

Cumbria *p216 D5*

This handsome red-sandstone house, ancestral home of the Cavendish family, is a magnificent spectacle. The west wing is particularly fine with its square tower, copper dome and numerous windows of varying sizes and shapes.

The spacious interior has a wealth of carved panelling and woodwork, tapestries and elaborate plasterwork ceilings. Of particular note are the carved twisted columns, made from oakwood taken from the park, of the dining room fireplace. The huge library, an airy room with large windows, houses some 3,500 books. Many are scientific works collected by Henry Cavendish, the eighteenth century scientist who discovered the properties of hydrogen. Several fine paintings hang in the ground floor rooms, including portraits by Richmond and landscapes by Jacob Raysdael. The magnificent staircase has beautiful panelling and elaborately carved balustrades, each one having its own individual design created by local craftsmen. The bedrooms are still furnished in the Victorian style, some with four-poster beds, and toilet sets and wash basins by Copeland and Minton.

The formal and woodland gardens have many different flowering shrubs and trees including a large monkey puzzle tree, said to be the oldest in England. Herds of deer, Shetland ponies, Highland cattle and Jacob sheep roam happily around the parkland. Other attractions here are the Lakeland Motor Museum and an adventure playground.

Open Easter Sun to late Oct, Sun to Fri. Parking and refreshments.

Holkham Hall

Norfolk *p218 E1*

This vast mansion has remained largely unaltered since its construction in 1734. It was built by William Kent for Thomas Coke, 1st Earl of Leicester, who wanted a fitting home for his remarkable collection of works of art. This he certainly achieved, for the hall and state rooms are truly magnificent with marble columns, a classical frieze and rich furnishings. Old Masters which hang on the walls include works by Poussin, Rubens, Van Dyck and Claude, and the sculpture gallery contains fine marble statues.

The estate was inherited by the Earl's nephew, another Thomas Coke, who was a prominent figure in the Agricultural Revolution. Much of his work concerning soil improvement, crop rotation and sheep breeding was carried out on the Holkham estate. A large monument to Coke of Norfolk, as he was fondly known, stands at the entrance. The gardens include a fine terrace by Nesfield, with a fountain featuring Perseus and Andromeda.

Open Jun to Sep, Sun, Mon and Thu; also Wed Jul and Aug; pm only. Open Spring and late Summer Bank Holiday Mon.

Holy Island

Northumberland *p220 F3–4*

Off the bold, uncluttered Northumberland coastline to the south of Berwick-upon-Tweed, lies Holy Island. This fascinating island, complete with castle and ruined priory, is rich in atmosphere and memory. Often referred to as Lindisfarne, it is commonly regarded as the seventh-century birthplace of English Christianity. For centuries pilgrims crossed the wet sand at low tide to set foot on a place associated with St Aidan and St Cuthbert. Today a three-mile-long causeway enables visitors to drive or walk across at low tide. However, the island is completely cut off from the mainland for some two-and-a-half hours before high tide and remains so for some three hours afterwards. Tide tables are posted at each end of the causeway.

Lindisfarne Castle is a small sixteenth-century Tudor building romantically perched on a pinnacle of high rock, overlooking the tiny harbour. Built as a border fort some of its thick walls were constructed with stones from the ruined abbey nearby. Only ever garrisoned by twenty men, its defences, perhaps fortunately, were never put to the test. The castle fell into ruins in the period after the Civil War, but was acquired by Edward Hudson in 1903 who commissioned Sir Edwin Lutyens to convert it into a comfortable home.

The first Lindisfarne monastery, established by St Aidan in AD 635, was destroyed by raiding Danes in the ninth century. The island then lay deserted until Benedictines from Durham founded the priory two centuries later. All that now remains of the Norman priory are the picturesque red sandstone ruins which look out over the North Sea.

Lindisfarne mead, once the drink of monks, is made on the island and the mead factory close to the priory ruins is open.

Lindisfarne Castle open when tidal conditions permit; Apr, Wed, Sat and Sun; May to Sep daily (except Fri); Oct, Sat and Sun only. NT
Lindisfarne Priory see AM info. Also open Sun am Apr to Sep. Parking available.

Hopetoun House

Lothian *p220 D4*

As one approaches this Palladian mansion down the long drive, its elegance can be fully appreciated. A wide flight of stone steps lead up to the entrance of the central block, which is flanked by two single-storey wings topped with domed central towers.

Inside is no less elegant with beautiful panelling and plaster ceilings. The two drawing rooms are particularly attractive, one being furnished in yellow and the other in red. Amongst a number of fine paintings here are works by Rubens, Van Dyke, Titian and Canaletto.

The rolling parkland has a specially laid out nature trail, from which Fallow and Red deer and St Kilda sheep can be seen.

Open Easter then end April to mid Sep daily. Parking and refreshments available.

Hornsea Pottery

Humberside *p217 D3*

This famous pottery attracts many thousands of visitors every year to the guided factory tour, and an inspection of the award-winning designs in their various stages of production. However the factory tour is by no means the only thing to do here. Surrounding the factory are twenty-eight acres of gardens including a landscaped picnic area, a lake, a tea garden and a country craft centre. To keep children amused there is a playground, pony rides, an aviary, a model village and a mini zoo.

The factory shop sells a wide range of Hornsea pottery and bargains can be found on the low priced 'seconds' section.

Open all year daily. Model village open early May to Sep. Parking and refreshments available.

Houghton Hall

Norfolk *p218 E1*

One of the finest examples of Palladian architecture in England is Houghton, built in the eighteenth century for Sir Robert Walpole, first Prime Minister of England and Earl of Orford.

Walpole spent some thirteen years, between 1722 and 1735, rebuilding the original Hall into today's sumptuous masterpiece. His architects were Colen Campbell and Thomas Ripley, and James Gibbs created the striking domes on the four corners of the

Hopetoun House – perhaps the greatest of architect William Adam's houses – was completed in 1748

building. Walpole commissioned William Kent to create the magnificent interior decorations and furniture, including the beautiful painted ceilings. All that Walpole achieved has survived today with the exception of his superb art collection which, unfortunately, was sold to the Empress of Russia after his death.

The present owner of the Hall is the Marquess of Cholmondley whose parents restored the house during this century and also added paintings, French furniture and porcelain.

The exterior of the house is faced in beautiful Yorkshire stone and its façade has a Classical portico with a richly carved pediment. The Hall is set in a vast park which was laid out by Bridgeman. In the grounds are stables of heavy horses and Shetland ponies, a coach house, pleasure grounds and picnic areas.

Walpole himself is buried in the parish church, a small building of flint and stone which stands in the park. The original village of Houghton also once stood within the park, but was moved by Walpole because it spoilt his view.

Open Easter Sun to last Sun in Sep and Bank Holidays, Thu and Sun. Parking available.

Mrs Disraeli had Hughenden Manor totally remodelled and faced in brick

House of the Binns

Lothian *p220 D4*

Although this estate is mentioned in documents dating as far back as 1335, the house itself is chiefly seventeenth century. It was then the home of the Dalyell family and in 1681 General Tam Dalyell raised the Royal Scots Greys here. Many of his personal possessions, including his sword and bible, have remained. The magnificently moulded plaster ceilings in four of the main rooms are a particularly attractive feature of the house.

Within the grounds is a beautiful woodland walk which leads to a panoramic viewpoint overlooking the Forth.

Open Easter then May to Sep daily (except Fri) pm only. Parkland open all day. NTS.

Hughenden Manor

Buckinghamshire *p213 B3*

This large and dignified house was considerably remodelled in Victorian times by its equally impressive and dignified owner – Benjamin Disraeli, twice Prime Minister and later Earl of Beaconsfield. Disraeli and his wife, Mary Anne, were extremely fond of Hughenden Manor which they bought in 1847, and spent as much time there as possible. Although some alterations have been made to much of the Manor, its furnishings and its contents remain as Disraeli knew them.

a 104-foot-high rotunda, decorated with a terracotta frieze. On top is a dome-shaped roof with a balustraded parapet surrounding a central skylight. Semi-circular wings join the rectangular outer pavilions to the rotunda.

The huge rooms are hung with paintings by Reynolds and Gainsborough. A marble statue, *Fury of Athamas,* sculptured by Flaxman, forms the centre piece, and is illuminated naturally from the skylight a hundred-feet above. The house contains many fine pieces of English and French furniture from the eighteenth and nineteenth centuries and pictures by Hogarth hang in the library. Part of the silver collection dates back to the seventeenth century, and includes elaborate designs by French Huguenot craftsmen.

The beautiful park was landscaped by Capability Brown, and magnificent oak and cedar trees provide the house with an effective natural screen.

Open Apr and Oct weekends only. May to Sep Tue, Wed, Fri, Sat, Sun and Bank Hol Mon, pm only. Park open all year daily. NT.

Frederick Hervey built Ickworth to house his great art collection

His study is quite unchanged and contains many of his personal items, such as letters from Queen Victoria, Mary Anne's diaries, manuscripts of the novels which he wrote here and portraits of his parents. The house is surrounded by lovely parkland with woods, lawns and a stream, and become more formal near the house where a terraced garden was created in the Italian style.

Open Apr to Oct, Wed to Sat, Sun and Bank Holiday Mon, pm only, Mar, Sat and Sun pm only. Closed Good Fri. NT.

Ightham Mote

Kent *p97 C2*

Ightham Mote, one of the few moated manor houses remaining in England, lies just south of the delightful Tudor village of Ightham, considered one of the prettiest in Kent.

The house was originally built more than 600 years ago and derives its name from the 'moot' or council which met here in medieval times. Despite alterations and additions, much of the early fabric remains, along with a strong sense of the past. This is especially noticeable in the Great

Hall, Old Chapel and Crypt, and the Drawing Room with its Jacobean fireplace and frieze. Also of interest is an eighteenth-century Palladian window and hand-painted Chinese wallpaper.

Open Apr to Oct Mon, Wed, Fri and Sun, also Good Fri and Bank Holiday Mon. Parking available. NT.

I

Ickworth House

Suffolk *p213 C4*

Probably one of the most unusual houses in England, is this impressive eighteenth-century mansion lying in the small village of Horringer. Frederick Hervey, 4th Earl of Bristol and Bishop of Derry, conceived the idea from designs by the Italian architect Asprucci. Unfortunately Hervey died in 1803 before the building had been completed, but further work was carried out by his successors.

The centre block of Ickworth is

Ightham Mote, one of the finest moated houses in the country

Inveraray Castle

Strathclyde *p219 B5*

Standing in beautiful country on the edge of Loch Fyne, Inveraray Castle looks more like a French château than a Scottish castle, with its light-coloured brick walls, round towers and tall conical turrets. It was built during the eighteenth century on the site of an earlier castle for the Dukes of Argyll, chiefs of the powerful Campbell clan.

Inside there are portraits by Landseer and Gainsborough, Beauvais tapestries and Louis XIV furniture. The armoury hall contains a huge collection of early Scottish weaponry including the dirk handle and sporran which belonged to Rob Roy.

In the grounds is a Spanish cannon salvaged from the sunken Armada vessel, the *Florida*, and pleasant walks may be taken in the well-wooded parkland.

There are excellent views of the whole area from the top of the Inveraray Bell Tower, standing 126 feet high. It contains vestments and campanology (bell ringing) exhibits and the ten bells which hang in the bell chamber are rung daily during Inveraray Week at the end of July.

Castle open Apr to mid Oct daily Sun pm only. Closed Fri (except Jul and Aug). Parking and refreshments available.
Bell Tower open May to Sep daily, Sun pm only.

Impressive Inveraray Castle – an early example of neo-Gothic architecture

Inverewe Gardens

Highlands *p221 B3*

The little West Highland village of Poolewe stands where the salmon-filled river Ewe flows into the head of Loch Ewe after its short journey from Loch Maree. One mile north of the village, on a rock promontory jutting out into Loch Ewe, lie the gardens of Inverewe House. Originally barren land supporting no more than a lone dwarf willow, the gardens were founded by Osgood Mackenzie in 1862. In order to establish the right conditions, soil had to be brought to the site and rows of trees were planted to act as wind breaks against the salt-laden Atlantic gales.

The gardens, with their magnificent mountain background, offer something of interest all year round. However, benefiting from the warm, moist climate of the Gulf Stream they are at their best from May to early June. Among the many rare and sub-tropical plants are flowering eucalyptus trees, Australian tree-ferns and Monterey pines. The gardens include a Visitors Centre.

Open all year daily. Visitors Centre open Apr to late Oct daily, Sun pm only. Parking and refreshments (Apr to Sep) available. NTS.

Inverness

Highland *p221 D2*

Inverness, Capital of the Highlands, lies partly ringed by mountains on either side of the grassy tree-lined banks of the river Ness, just inland from the Moray Firth. The town has long been the historical and administrative centre of the Highland region and its origins can be traced back to the fourth century by the vitrified fort standing on the summit of Craig Phadrig to the west of the town.

One of the oldest buildings in Inverness today is Abbertarff House in Church Street. It dates from 1593 and contains the last remaining example of turnpike stairs, an ancient type of spiral staircase. The house is now the Highland Regional Office of The National Trust for Scotland and contains a Trust Information Centre and shop.

The present castle (now housing a Sheriff Court House and administrative offices) dates from 1834, although there has been a castle on this site since the twelfth century. A statue of Flora Macdonald stands on the castle esplanade. It was erected in 1899 and shows her looking southwards towards the hiding place of Bonnie Prince Charlie whom she helped escape after his defeat in 1746.

In front of the Town House, a Gothic-style building where Lloyd George and his cabinet met, is the Clach-na-Cudaiann (stone of tubs), where the women of Inverness used to rest on their way back from the well loaded with full tubs of water. Tradition has it that a seer predicted that so long as the stone was preserved Inverness would flourish.

Just off Shore Street is Cromwell's Clock Tower, the only part of the large citadel built by Cromwell's army to escape demolition on the restoration of Charles II. The Tolbooth steeple in Church Street, built in 1791, is the former jail steeple where dangerous prisoners were kept.

St Andrews Cathedral, built in 1866, is richly decorated with illuminated windows and carved pillars. Other religious houses include the High Parish Church which was rebuilt between 1770 and 1772, although the four-

teenth-century vaulted tower remains from an earlier building. In the churchyard a bullet-marked stone marks the place where the Duke of Cumberland's victorious army summarily executed prisoners after the Battle of Culloden, fought just six miles away.

The Northern Meeting Park is the venue for entertainment during the summer months and among the attractions here are pipe band concerts, Highland and Scottish dancing. At Holm Mills tartan and tweed spinning and weaving can be watched. The town also boasts a particularly fine theatre in the Eden Court. The Museum and Art Gallery in Castle Wynd depicts the history of the Highlands and includes a reconstruction of the last taxidermist's workshop in the region. Also on display is an important collection of Highland silver. The art collection includes many views of old Inverness.

Holm Mills Mill and showroom open Mon to Fri, showroom only Sat am.
Museum and Art Gallery open all year Mon to Sat.

Ironbridge Gorge Museum

Shropshire *p216 E2*

The Ironbridge Gorge Museum represents a unique monument to the Industrial Revolution. It was here, in 1709, at Coalbrookdale, that Abraham Darby first smelted iron using coke as a fuel instead of charcoal, and the Museum illustrates the growth of the iron and allied industries which blossomed in this area, following the experiment.

In the midst of this complex the impressive Ironbridge spans the gorge. Designed in 1779 by Abraham Darby III, this was the first bridge to be constructed entirely of cast-iron and each segment of its 380-ton structure was produced by local workmen.

Blists Hill Open Air Museum occupies a forty-two-acre woodland site with buildings and machines which trace the industrial and social history of the area. Particularly interesting is the 1,000-yard-long tunnel known as the Tar Tunnel under Blists Hill. This gives access to the artificial wells of natural bitumen.

Coalbrookdale Furnace and

The old kilns and buildings of Coalport pottery at Ironbridge

Museum of Iron is a collection of indoor and outdoor exhibitions, including the original furnace used by Abraham Darby. It illustrates the history of the Coalbrookdale Company which progressed from producing iron cooking pots, to the construction of the first iron boiler for a locomotive, the Ironbridge itself, and the iron gates which stand between Hyde Park and Kensington Gardens in London, made for the Great Exhibition of 1851.

Coalport China was manufactured, in what is now the China Works Museum, from the late eighteenth century until 1926 when the company moved to Staffordshire – where they still operate. The works once covered both banks of the Shropshire Canal, used for the transportation of goods, and many of the original buildings have been restored to form this museum which includes workshops, ovens, kilns and displays of porcelain.

The Severn Warehouse and Visitor Centre – a nineteenth-century building and its adjoining wharf, has been restored and the Warehouse now contains displays and slide shows which introduce the history of the Ironbridge Gorge.

A useful Tourist Information Centre has been installed in the old Ironbridge toll-house.

Open all year daily (except 25 Dec).

The river Ness flows towards the Moray Firth past Inverness Castle

Isle of Wight

p213A1

This compact little island is perfectly suited to the traditional family holiday by the sea with its miles of sandy beaches, rugged cliffs, unspoilt countryside, high chalk downs, little old villages and seaside resorts.

The mainly 14th-century church in the delightful village of Godshill

The island was Queen Victoria's favourite holiday resort and she died at Osborne House, her much loved family home near Cowes. It is now open to the public and among the Victorian opulence and Indian finery can be seen domestic reminders of the Royal Family's daily life.

Cowes itself contains many fine Georgian and Victorian buildings, but is most famous for its yachting tradition. Situated on the mouth of the river Medina, the town is renowned throughout the world for Cowes Week, when the famous yacht races draw competitors from all over the globe.

The Maritime Museum in Beckford Road illustrates the maritime history of the island with models, photographs, paintings and books.

Cowes is the home of the Royal Yacht Club and the club house stands on the site of a castle built originally by Henry VIII. Twenty-two brass cannons stand on the semi-circular platform of Victoria's Parade, and are used to start races and fire royal salutes.

Beyond East Cowes behind Old Castle Point lies turreted Norris Castle, set in attractive grounds. Its rooms are crammed with pictures, furniture and armour.

Carisbrooke was capital of the island long before Newport (the present capital), because Carisbrooke Castle, built by a kinsman of William the Conqueror shortly after the Conquest, was the home of the 'Governor' of the island. Visitors can walk round the high parapets, see the chapel and museum, or visit the fascinating wheel-house, where a donkey turns a wheel to draw water from a 160-foot-deep well.

Brighstone and Godshill are picture postcard villages complete with thatched cottages, cafés and gift shops. Godshill has a Model Village in the Vicarage gardens and a small but interesting Natural History Centre, with a display of butterflies and birds, tropical shells and corals, and semi-precious stones.

One mile to the south of Godshill are the ruins of Appuldurcombe House, damaged by a German landmine in 1943. This shell of a grand mansion is surrounded by beautiful grounds landscaped by Capability Brown.

Another inland village of the island is the pretty, unspoilt Calbourne. Winkle Row – a group of ancient cottages – is a popular subject for photographers here. The Caul Bourne stream flowing through the village used to power Calbourne Mill, which stopped grinding flour in 1955, and is now a Rural Museum. The quiet well-ordered grounds are paraded by peacocks, and the mill-pond is well stocked with water-fowl.

The chief coastal resorts are on the south coast, except Ryde and Seaview. Ryde, on the north coast and east of Cowes, was turned from a small village into a fashionable holiday resort in the early nineteenth century, and is still as popular today. There is five miles of sandy beach, a pier nearly half a mile long with an electric railway, and an esplanade which leads to pleasant gardens, a boating lake, aviaries, aquariums and parks.

Seaview, farther east, is a quieter resort and more residential. The Flamingo Park bird sanctuary has an attractive collection of native and foreign water-fowl.

On the eastern tip of the island is the quiet village of Bembridge, best known as a yachting centre. Here there is a lifeboat station, a windmill owned by the National Trust, and a small Maritime

Museum – all open to the public.

Inland from Bembridge is Brading, once a seaport on the tidal river Yar in the nineteenth century. The Town Hall has a stone lock-up, a whipping post and stocks, and the sixteenth-century building close-by houses a clever and amusing wax museum, which includes a spine chilling torture-chamber. The Lilliput Dolls Museum here has an interesting collection of dolls and toys displayed in a small, charming cottage.

Sandown is the largest resort on the island, and with its neighbour Shanklin forms a continuous holiday complex three miles long. The old village of Shanklin has been restored although most of it has retained its Victorian atmosphere. Shanklin Chine is a commercially exploited river gorge filled with various amusements.

Ventnor, another major resort, is built on terraces leading down a cliff to a small seafront and pier. Its sheltered position gives it a warm, almost sub-tropical climate and exotic plants flourish in the Botanic Gardens. Close by is the fascinating Museum of Smuggling History, and also Blackgang Chine, a pleasure park set on the cliff complete with a cowboy town, giant dinosaurs, a maze and an adventure play ground.

The island countryside affords

The Needles and Needles Lighthouse lie off the western tip of the island

many opportunities for pleasant walks, whether on open high ground with magnificent views as on Brighstone Down, or Tennyson Down where the great chalk stacks of the Needles can be seen standing in the sea, or in the cool, shady woodland of Brighstone Forest or Parkhurst Forest.

Robin Hill Country Park, on Arreton Down, covers eighty acres of grass and woodland where a collection of wild and domestic animals roam free. There is also a selection of caged animals here.

Above: The brass cannons of the Royal Yacht Squadron in Cowes

Osborne House open early Easter Mon to Sep Mon to Sat. Parking available. AM.

Norris Castle At present closed. Due to re-open during 1987. Dates unavailable.

Maritime Museum (Cowes) open all year daily (except Sun).

Carisbrooke Castle see AM info. Museum closed Oct to Easter. Also open Sun am Apr to Sep. Parking and refreshments available.

Godshill Model Village open Apr to Sep daily, Sun pm only.

Natural History Centre open Mar to Oct daily.

Appuldurcombe House see AM info.

Calbourne Watermill and Rural Museum open Easter to Oct daily.

Bembridge Windmill open Apr to Sep daily. NT.

Maritime Museum open Apr to Oct daily. Parking available.

Flamingo Park open Easter to Sep daily, Oct Wed to Sun. Afternoons only Easter to mid May and Oct. Parking and refreshments available.

Wax Museum and Animal World open all year daily.

Lilliput Museum open mid Mar to mid Jan daily.

Museum of the History of Smuggling open Easter to Sep daily. Parking and refreshments available.

Blackgang Chine open Apr to late Sep daily. Parking and refreshments available.

Robin Hill Country Park and Zoo open Mar to Oct daily. Parking and refreshments available.

J

Jedburgh

Borders *p220 E3*

One of the four famous border monasteries founded by David I, now a roofless red sandstone ruin, stands by this most attractive lowland town.

The abbey is still impressive, with its eighty-six-foot high Norman tower, richly carved Norman doorway, splendid nave and fine rose window. A small museum houses monuments from the abbey and many carved fragments of medieval work.

The original Jedburgh Castle, built in the twelfth century, was a residence of Scottish kings. However, because of its vulnerable position (to English attack) the Scottish parliament decided to demolish it in 1409. The present

Georgian building, erected in 1823 on the site of the old castle, became the county prison and is now a museum of penal methods in the nineteenth century.

Mary Queen of Scots came to Jedburgh in 1566, and almost died of illness here. The house in which she lodged, known as Mary Queen of Scots' House, is a picturesque L-shaped, building, built for defence rather than comfort. It stands in pleasant gardens and today is a museum of relics associated with the ill-fated queen.

Abbey see AM info. Oct to Mar closed 1½ days per week.
Castle Jail open Apr to mid Sep daily, Sun pm only.
Mary Queen of Scots House open Apr to Oct daily, (Sun pm only, Nov to May).

Jervaulx Abbey

North Yorkshire *p217 B4*

The ruins of this eleventh-century Cistercian monastery lie in a magnificent garden setting on the edge of the Yorkshire Dales.

The monastery was founded in 1156 by an order not allowed to eat meat, although many bones were found here. Fifteen masons' marks are discernable on remain-

ing stones and the best feature is the wall of the monks' dormitory with its high lancet windows.

Until it was dissolved by Henry VIII in 1538, the abbey thrived and was particularly noted for its cheese making. Although little remains of its former grandeur, the mellowed remains scattered amidst the trees and shrubs which abound here, are enough to indicate the original plan of the abbey buildings.

Abbey always accessible. Parking available.

Jodrell Bank

Cheshire *p216 E3*

In 1957 the first and largest of the two radio telescopes at Jodrell Bank came into operation to track Russian and American satellites and space probes. Two-hundred-and-fifty-feet in diameter and weighing 850 tons, it is one of the largest fully steerable radio telescopes in the world. In 1964 the 125-feet diameter telescope was completed and both are now engaged in a variety of research programmes.

The Concourse Building houses a fascinating exhibition on space

Above: The house at which Mary Queen of Scots stayed when she visited Jedburgh in the 16th century

and astronomy, and working models include a twenty-five-foot radio telescope which visitors can operate to pick up radio emissions from the sun. There is also a Planetarium which presents images and explanations of the night sky.

Open mid Mar to Oct daily Nov to mid Mar weekends pm only (closed Christmas and New Year). Parking and refreshments available.

Below: One of the huge radio telescopes used for research purposes at Jodrell Bank

K

Kelling Park Aviaries

Norfolk *p218 E1*

The Kelling Park Aviaries house a fine collection of European and tropical birds in some four acres of exquisite gardens.

Ornamental pheasants, cockatoos, macaws and flamingos are amongst some of the colourful and exotic inhabitants.

Entertainment within the park includes a children's playground, and a picnic area.

Open all year daily. Parking and refreshments available.

Kendal

Cumbria *p220 E1*

Famous for Kendal Green cloth, mint cake and snuff, Kendal is South Lakeland's largest town and its administrative centre. The river Kent flows through the town and it is surrounded by the gentle countryside of the fells on the edge of the Lake District National Park.

Kendal is very conscious of its past and has a particularly good museum, notable for its huge collection of world-wide animals and birds. There is also an exhibition here of Lake District natural history and items of archaeology and geology.

The Abbot Hall Art Gallery and Culture Centre is housed in the skilfully converted eighteenth-century mansion which stands in the Abbot Hall Park. Paintings by such artists as Turner, Reynolds, Raeburn and Romney are displayed here in carefully re-

Kendal – the Auld Grey Town – has many grey limestone buildings

stored rooms, with valuable pieces of china, glass and silver. The stable block of the mansion has also been converted to house the fascinating Museum of Lakeland Life and Industry. Here realistic model displays illustrate how a family would have lived and how rural craftsmen carried on their trades.

The Castle Dairy in Wildman Street is a very well preserved Tudor building with oak beams and fine carvings. It is now a licensed restaurant but is open to visitors during the afternoon. Almost opposite is the Kendal Studio Pottery, an historic building housing a permanent exhibition of lakeland-stone pottery and paintings by local artists.

Just to the east of the town is Kendal's most historic feature – the castle. It dates back to the twelfth century and was the birthplace of Catherine Parr, Henry VIII's sixth wife. Although scant remains exist today it is well worth the pleasant walk to its summit.

Museum open all year Mon to Fri, Sat pm only. Parking available.
Abbot Hall Art Gallery and Museum open all year daily (except Good Fri and two weeks over Christmas/New Year) Sat and Sun pm only. Parking available.

Kenilworth

Warwickshire *p216 F1*

The town of Kenilworth lies between Coventry and Warwick in an area commonly regarded as the heart of England. It is a pleas-

ant residential area with a number of charming half-timbered houses dating from the fifteenth century. The interesting remains of an Augustinian Abbey may be seen in Abbey Fields and, close by, the mainly Perpendicular parish church of St Nicholas with its fine Norman doorway.

The town's chief glory, however, is Kenilworth Castle, immortalised by Sir Walter Scott in *Kenilworth*, his historical novel of Elizabethan England. The novelist once stayed at the Kings Arms and Castle Hotel in the Square and used the castle as the setting for many of the events in the book.

It is situated on the north-west edge of the town and is remarkable for its size, having been referred to as the grandest fortress ruin in England. Built by the Norman de Clinton family in the twelfth century on an original Saxon site, the castle was remodelled by John of Gaunt in the fourteenth century and Robert Dudley, Earl of Leicester, entertained Queen Elizabeth I there in the sixteenth century. From the seventeenth century onwards the castle fell into ruin, but nevertheless conveys an impression of past great strength. The massive keep, its walls over seventeen feet thick in places, still stands although damaged by Parliamentary forces during the Civil War. A sixteenth-century gatehouse, known as Lord Leicester's Buildings, and parts of the banqueting hall, also survive.

See AM info. Also open Sun am Apr to Sep. Parking available.

Keswick

Cumbria *p220 D1*

Keswick stands between Skiddaw and Derwentwater on the river Greta. A market town of intriguing narrow streets and buildings of old grey stone, possibly its finest building, dominating the Market Place, is Moot Hall, built in 1813.

Keswick Park Museum and Art Gallery in Station Road contains manuscripts and relics of the author Hugh Walpole, and of Robert Southey (a notable poet of the nineteenth century) who both lived in Cumbria. There are two manuscripts by Wordsworth here as well. Apart from its literary collection, the museum also has geological exhibits and a scale-model of the Lake District. The art gallery includes works by Turner and Wilson Steer.

On the west side of the town, there are excellent views of Derwentwater from the churchyard of St John's. The church was built in 1838 and is the burial place of Hugh Walpole. North-west of the town centre is the parish church; memorials here include one to Canon Rawnsley who was vicar at the church for twenty-five years and co-founder of the National Trust, and another to Robert Southey.

To the south-west of the town on the west shore of Derwentwater is Lingholm, with its formal gardens and one-and-a-half-mile woodland walk full of azaleas and rhododendrons.

East of Keswick is a prehistoric circle of thirty-eight stones, ten of which form a rectangle within the ring. It is called the Castlerigg Stone Circle or Druids Circle.

Keswick Park Museum and Art Gallery open Apr to Oct Mon to Sat. **Lingholm** open Apr to Oct daily. Parking and refreshments available. **Castlerigg Stone Circle** open any reasonable time. AM and NT.

Kidwelly Castle

Dyfed *p212 C4*

Roger, Bishop of Salisbury, built the castle in about 1130, which was subsequently deeply involved in the struggle between the rebellious Welsh and the English Crown. A well known incident here was the battle between the Normans and Welsh in which the Welsh army was led by a woman, Gwenllian. At the time the Normans were in occupation, and during her unsuccessful attack,

A long colourful herbacious border runs along the hillside arboretum in Killerton House Gardens

Ashness Bridge, near Keswick, is one of the many marvellous viewpoints found in this area

she and one of her sons died. The battlefield still bears her name, Maes Gwenllian, and Welsh bitterness for her 'murder' remained strong for centuries.

Strategically placed above a steep slope leading down to the river Gwendraeth, the extensive ruins of the castle stand in lovely countryside. The twelfth-century plan consisted of a rectangular inner ward in which there was a great hall and a chapel.

In the fourteenth century a semi-circular outer ward was added including the three-storeyed south gatehouse. Also built between the inner and outer wards at this time was another hall and kitchen, and the great ovens can still be seen here.

See AM info. Also open Sun am Apr to Sep.

Killerton House and Gardens

Devon *p212 D2*

Home of the Acland family since the Civil War, the property was given to the National Trust by Sir Richard Acland in 1944. Visitors can see here the Paulise de Bush costume collection, shown in a series of rooms furnished in different periods from the second half of the eighteenth century to the present day.

Imaginative use of the natural landscape provides Killerton House with attractive hillside gardens sweeping down to open lawns. Delightful walks can be taken through a fine collection of trees and shrubs. On the east side of the garden is a neo-Norman chapel modelled on the Lady Chapel of Glastonbury.

Open Apr to Oct daily. Gardens all year. NT.

Kilmarnock

Strathclyde *p220 C3*

The busy industrial centre and market town of Kilmarnock is the home of the Burns' Federation and it was here that Scotland's national poet had his first collection of poems published in 1786 by John Wilson.

The Burns' Museum in Kay Park contains an outstanding collection of original manuscripts and relics, including a copy of the first Kilmarnock edition. The museum is housed in a Victorian tower built of red sandstone, to commemorate the poet. From the top are panoramic views of the town and distant Arran.

Situated in Elmbank Avenue is the Dick Institute, a fascinating museum of rural life including an art gallery and collections of Scottish arms and armour.

About one mile to the north of the town is Dean Castle, set in some forty-two acres of gardens and parkland which include nature trails. The castle, beautifully restored, contains exhibitions of armour and early musical instruments.

Burns' Museum open by prior arrangement with curator.
Dick Institute open all year daily (except Sun). Parking available.
Dean Castle open mid May to mid Sep daily, pm only. Country Park all year. Refreshments available.

Kilverstone Wildlife Park

Norfolk *p213 D5*

Displayed in the very attractive grounds of seventeenth-century Kilverstone Hall are several birds and mammals from North and South America. The Hall is the home of Lord and Lady Fisher, who, with the curator, have collected all the animals and hope to breed some of the rarer species.

There is also a pleasant riverside walk, a picnic area and a walled garden in which a water tower was built at the beginning of the century. In the park are Chinese water deer as well as Fallow and Sika deer. Of particular interest are the miniature horse stud, pets corner and adventure playground.

Open all year daily. Parking and refreshments available.

King's Lynn

Norfolk *p217 D1*

The low-lying Norfolk coast sweeps in a great arc from Gorleston-on-Sea to The Wash. Some two miles south of the mouth of the Great Ouse, which flows into the Wash, lies the ancient port and market town of King's Lynn, formerly called Bishop's Lynn before it became royal property.

Once a walled city of considerable importance, King's Lynn received its first charter from King John in the twelfth century. Parts of the old city walls remain and the town's medieval streets contain many attractive buildings, such as the timber-framed Hampton Court in Nelson Street. The tall octagonal tower of Greyfriars in St James's Street is all that survives of an original thirteenth-century building. Adjoining the twelfth-century St

Margaret's Church is the Saturday Market Place and to the north-east of the large Tuesday Market Place stands the later Church of St Nicholas. It was around these two markets that the town gradually expanded and, although now car parks, markets are still held here on Saturday and Tuesday.

The elegant Customs House was built by local architect Henry Bell in 1683. The town was a glass making centre between the seventeenth and nineteenth century and visitors may still see glass being manufactured at the Wedgwood Glass Factory in Oldmeadow Road.

Lynn Museum in Market Street contains items of natural history and local archaeology. Temporary exhibitions are held throughout the year and of special interest is the collection of medieval pilgrims' badges.

Located in King Street, the Museum of Social History displays costume, ceramics, glass, toys and domestic items.

Lynn Museum open all year Mon to Sat (except Good Fri, Christmas New Year's Day).
Museum of Social History open all year, Tue to Sat (except Good Fri, Christmas and New Year).

Knebworth House and Country Park

Hertfordshire *p213 B4*

Knebworth house was first built amidst its vast park in 1492, but the present house was largely rebuilt in 1843 by the statesman Lord Lytton, author of *The Last Days of Pompeii*.

The interior is full of treasures, spanning 500 years of English history, such as furniture, family portraits and personal relics of past inhabitants, including some

of Lytton's manuscripts. The great hall is a magnificent room – the plasterwork of the ceiling and the carved screen are both Jacobean, whereas the panelling in the hall is seventeenth century.

The seemingly boundless grounds provide picnic areas, riding facilities, a children's narrow-gauge railway and museum, and the Fort Knebworth adventure playground.

Open Apr to May Sun, Bank and school hols, then end May to late Sep daily (except Mon). House pm only. Parking and refreshments available.

Knole

Kent *p213 C2*

Knole, one of the largest private houses in England, is a great mansion of grey-brown Kentish stone on the outskirts of the ancient town of Sevenoaks. Knole is

Knebworth House was decorated with battlements, gargoyles and heraldic symbols when it was transformed into a Gothic mansion in the 19th century

Now a Tudor house, Lacock Abbey was originally an Augustinian nunnery. It was the last religious foundation to be dissolved at the Reformation

a house of complicated architecture with irregular roof lines, topped by slim brick chimney-stacks, battlemented towers, turrets and gables. The building is spread out over some four acres on the contours of the rounded hill, or knoll, from which it takes its name. The house consists of seven courtyards, corresponding to the days of the week, fifty-two staircases for the weeks in the year, and 365 rooms for the days of the year.

It dates mainly from the fifteenth century and was both an archbishop's and a king's palace before becoming the home of the Sackville family for ten generations. Its magnificent state apartments with their richly plastered ceilings are furnished mainly with original Jacobean and Caroline furniture together with priceless art collections, carpets, tapestries and silver. The mansion's unique interior includes three long galleries – each with their own state bedroom; two state beds; a great hall; the ornamental great staircase; a crimson drawing room; the old billiard room and the ballroom.

The garden plan has changed little since the seventeenth century and covers some twenty-six acres enclosed within its massive Elizabethan wall. The gardens are laid out with formal walks and flower beds, shrubs and trees. Beyond the gardens lies the large park which is open to the public and covers some 1,000 acres. Here, among its hills and valleys, are clumps of broad oaks, tall beeches and herds of Fallow and Japanese deer.

Open Apr to Oct Wed to Sat and Bank Holiday Mon, Sun pm only. House closed Nov to Mar. Gardens open first Wed in the month, May to Sep. Parking available. NT.

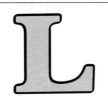

Lacock

Wiltshire *p212 F4*

Lacock is a village of cobbled streets, old mellow houses, many medieval, and none later than eighteenth century. Old inns, weavers' houses, a King John hunting lodge, a pack horse bridge and ford and a fifteenth-century tithe barn, together with a fourteenth-century church, blend together charmingly.

The abbey, founded in 1232 by Ela, Countess of Salisbury, stands on the banks of the river Avon. The cloisters and chapter house survive from the original building, but most is the responsibility of Sir William Sharington, who converted it into a Tudor dwelling house shortly after its suppression in 1539. Notable additions made by him include the octagonal tower, in which there is kept a photostat of the Lacock Magna Carta of 1225, and the stable court, in which the six-

teenth-century brew house has been restored.

The house passed to the Talbot family in the seventeenth century, and a century later they added the Gothic-style entrance hallway and great hall.

Near the abbey gates, in the sixteenth-century barn, is the Fox Talbot Museum dedicated to W. H. Fox Talbot whose experiments advanced photography here in 1835.

House open Apr to Oct Wed to Mon, pm only. Grounds also Apr to Oct but daily, pm only. Parking available. NT.

The east side of Knole. Vita Sackville-West was born here in 1892

Lake District Cumbria

Some of the deepest lakes, the highest mountains, the quietest valleys and the most dramatic panoramas in England are to be found within this diverse landscape covering an area of 900 square miles.

Five hundred million years ago there were no mountains or lakes – but a trough, choked with sediment, lying under a muddy sea. Since then the land has undergone immense changes. Volcanic activity buried it under two miles of ash and lava, earth movements buckled it into a mountain range, which was in turn gradually eroded and drowned in a coral-rich sea. This slowly silted up to create a marshland of pools and mudbanks upon which giant ferns grew. Yet another phase of mountain building followed, and again was the victim of extensive erosion, which this time produced a vast, arid wind-blown desert.

Finally, about twenty-six million years ago movements within the earth's crust raised the land in a great dome, which formed the basis of today's lakeland. The lakes themselves are the most recent addition to the scenery, and will perhaps be the first to change. River sediment is gradually filling the lakes, and in thousands of years time the lakes may have disappeared altogether.

The Lake District has a reputation for being more wet and cold than dry and sunny and it is true that Seathwaite, at the head of Borrowdale, is the wettest place in the country. Yet often the Lake District basks under blue skies while the rest of England shivers beneath rain and fog, and the weather changes quickly – a rainy, overcast morning may be followed by a gloriously sunny afternoon. However beautiful the fells may appear in the sunshine, they take on a wild grandeur in bad weather – the peaks are wrapped in cloud, the rocks running with raindrops.

The great attraction of the lakes, which enthralled the early tourists of the late eighteenth century, is of course the scenery. This is best seen by the walker, but for the less energetic sightseer there is an almost unlimited fund of places to visit which are reasonably accessible to the motorist. There are Wordsworth's homes at Grasmere and Rydal, his birthplace at Cockermouth, Beatrix Potter's home at Hilltop, near Sawrey, there is the tiny Bridge House at Ambleside, the third highest inn in England on top of Kirkstone Pass, the famous Bowder Stone in Borrowdale, the Ruskin Museum at Coniston, numerous old churches and the Roman Fort on Hardknott.

Local customs and events provide plenty of alternative entertainment, such as the rush-bearing ceremonies at Grasmere and Ambleside, or country dancing in the Langdales. There are sports meetings during the summer months where Cumberland and Westmorland wrestling, fell racing and pole leaping can be watched. Hound trailing is a great Lakeland favourite. Specially bred trail hounds are set to follow a course marked by an aniseed-scented trail across the fells. The first dog to return wins, and all are rewarded with a bowl of meat as soon as they finish. There are frequent fox hunts,

Ambleside, Westmorland.

usually followed on foot over such rugged terrain, carrying on the tradition of John Peel, who hunted this region and lived at Caldbeck.

The lakes themselves offer their own variety of pastime. There is water skiing on Lake Windermere and Ullswater – the former also boasts a yacht club and a motor boat racing club, as well as canoeing and other aquatic sports. Skating is often possible on many of the lakes during the winter months, and the sport of curling is still popular.

However the activity most commonly associated with the Lake District is fell walking. Every summit can be reached by walking, although some are more difficult than others; Lord Rake on Scafell is perhaps the hardest. Well trodden paths mark routes on the popular mountains, which are sometimes marked by cairns –

Tarn Hows – a scene typical of Lakeland's tranquil landscape combining water, woods and fells

piles of stones – along the way. However, caution is needed, some clear paths lead straight to the edge of a precipice, worn by those wishing to enjoy the view.

The hard way up the fells provides the rock climber with ample opportunities, and although not on such a grand scale as many other mountainous areas in Europe, the Lake District has several climbs generally respected among the mountaineering community. Skiing is possible on the north-east slopes of Helvellyn during the right conditions, and the Lake District Ski Club have a hut and a ski tow high above Glenridding.

For the naturalist there are Red deer in Gowbarrow Park and Fallow deer in the woods, such as those between Windermere and Coniston Water and in the numerous Forestry Commission plantations. Foxes thrive despite the hunts, and otters and badgers are present although seldom seen. The now rare Red squirrel has one of its few refuges in the Lake District, and can be seen in the Windermere woods and in Borrowdale. Of all the Lakeland birds the Golden eagle must be the most publicised and, in recent years, this magnificent creature has returned to breed after an absence of about 200 years. The

buzzard, often mistaken for the eagle, is common, and the resident falcons are the kestrel and the rarer peregrine. The raven is the most characteristic bird, its sombre plumage and coarse cry typify the brooding wildness of the high fells. Of the smaller birds, the Meadow pipit and

wheatear are the most interesting, although along the stream valleys the delightful dipper may be seen.

Around the lakes the stalking heron is a familiar sight fishing in the shallows, and coots and moorhens are probably the commonest birds on the lakes.

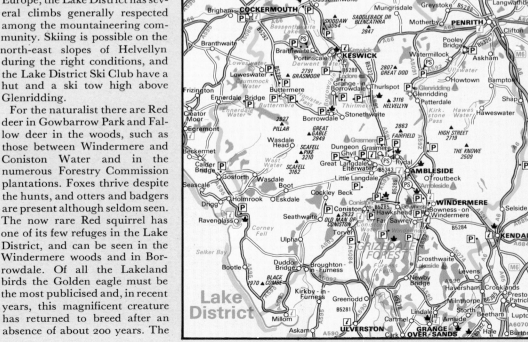

One of the Haverthwaite Railway's two Fairburn 2-6-4 tank engines

Lakeside and Haverthwaite Railway

Cumbria *p216 D5*

This steam operated railway carries passengers through the lovely wooded hills of south lakeland between Haverthwaite and Lake Windermere. Most of the trains connect at Lakeside Station with the popular Lake Windermere steamers. The railway's collection of twelve steam and two diesel locomotives includes two rare 2-6-4 class 4 Fairburn tank engines, together with both passenger and freight rolling stock.

Trains operational Easter then May to Sep daily, also Apr and Oct Sun only. Parking and refreshments at Haverthwaite station.

Lamport Hall

Northamptonshire *p213 A5*

Lamport Hall, situated in the small village of Lamport was the home of the Isham family for over 400 years. However, since 1976 it has been the property of the Lamport Hall Trust.

The Hall, most of which dates from the 17th and 18th centuries, is of particular interest for its South-West front. It is a rare example of the work of John Webb, a pupil and son-in-law of Inigo Jones, and was built in 1655 with wings added in 1732 and 1740.

The interior of the building features a Music Hall which has a fine stone chimney piece by Webb, a High Room with plaster ceiling by John Woolston, an outstanding library and a fine collec-

tion of family portraits. There are also paintings by such artists as Van Dyck, Maratti and Lely, plus a collection of china and furniture.

An attractive parkland surrounds the Hall and its garden contains one of the earliest Alpine rock gardens in England.

Open Easter to Sep, Sun and Bank Holiday Mon, also Thu Jul and Aug, pm only. Parking and refreshments.

Lancaster

Lancashire *p216 E5*

The old, grey city of Lancaster lies westwards of the lovely moorland scenery of the Trough of Bowland, to the east of Morecambe Bay, with the mountains of the Lake District as an impressive backdrop. Essentially Georgian in appearance, the city nestles at the foot of its Norman castle and ancient priory which look down from the vantage point of Castle Hill. The castle was built in the eleventh century, and, although much altered since medieval days, has been used as a prison for centuries. The great Shire Hall has an impressive display of heraldry and the drop room contains the brutal relics of early prison life.

Standing side by side with the castle is the ancient fourteenth-century parish church of Lancaster, which was founded as part of an eleventh-century Benedictine priory. It is notable for its Saxon doorway and magnificent oak-canopied stalls from Cockersand Abbey.

In the Old Town Hall, an outstanding Georgian building, are the exhibits of the City Museum

which include archaeology, maritime history and local paintings. The early uniforms, medals and photographs of the King's Own Royal Lancaster Regiment are on display here as well.

Judges' Lodgings, a seventeenth-century town house, formerly the home of visiting Assize Judges, now contains two museums. The Gillow and Town House Museum displays the work of the famous Lancaster cabinet-making firm of Gillows, while the Museum of Childhood incorporates the Barry Elder Doll Collection.

To the east of the city in Williamson Park stands the Ashton Memorial, the gift of Lord Ashton in 1909 who also provided the city with its magnificent Town Hall. The green dome of the memorial is a well-known landmark and its higher galleries provide panoramic views of the surrounding countryside.

Shire Hall open Easter to Sep daily.
Priory and Parish Church open daily all year.
City Museum open daily (Nov to Mar pm only).
Judges' Lodgings open Apr to Oct Mon to Fri, also Sat Jul to Sep; (Apr to Jun, Oct and Sat, pm only).

Lanhydrock House

Cornwall *p211 B2*

The simple lines and warm brown stone of Lanhydrock House present a pleasing image of a seventeenth-century great house. Yet only the north wing and a part of the west wing are truly seventeenth century, as the rest of the house was rebuilt after a disastrous fire in 1881.

The showpiece of the house is the 116-foot long gallery in the original north wing, with its outstanding plaster ceiling vividly illustrating early scenes from the Old Testament. The ceiling was created by local craftsmen in about 1650.

Inside is delightfully informal, hats and coats hang on hatstands, photographs are proudly displayed on desks – the atmosphere is that of a private home. The kitchen and buttery, full of curios, are particularly fascinating.

Great magnolias grace the outside walls and to the front and one side formal gardens of lawns, rose beds, clipped cypresses and shrubberies are splendidly laid out and immaculately kept. Pleasant walks give access to the parkland which slopes gently away from the gardens, and here stands a half-mile avenue of beeches and sycamores – a landmark among the many other flowering trees and shrubs.

Open Apr to Oct daily. Gardens only Nov to Mar during daylight. Refreshments available (except Christmas to Mar.) NT.

Launceston Castle

Cornwall *p212 C2*

Launceston Castle stands in a dominating position on a hill above the town, surrounded by a public garden. It is a well known local landmark and the topmost wall provides fine views over the wild expanse of Bodmin Moor.

The remains of the circular shell keep and central tower have stood on this spot since the thirteenth century. The original castle here was a primitive motte-and-

Oak timbers with clay and wattle fillings characterise Lavenham

Leeds Castle, where Henry VIII's first wife, Catherine of Aragon, lived, and where the diarist John Evelyn guarded French and Dutch prisoners in 1665

bailey, established by William the Conqueror's half-brother, Robert of Mortain, when he became Earl of Cornwall shortly after 1066. Richard, a subsequent Earl of Cornwall, is thought to have built the present structure between 1227 and 1272.

Although the castle fell into disrepair after the Civil War one tower was kept in use as a prison. It was, it appears, an evil, filthy place and its most famous inmate, George Fox, the Quaker leader, was unfortunate enough to be incarcerated there for eight months during 1656, on a charge of distributing 'subversive' literature. Public executions were carried out below the castle walls until 1821.

See AM info. Also open Sun am Apr to Sep. Parking available.

Lavenham

Suffolk *p 213 D4*

The attractive little town of Lavenham is probably one of the most photographed in England. It is noted for its ornate timbered houses, some of which date back to the fifteenth century when the town was an active centre of the Suffolk wool trade. Lavenham blue cloth became famous and a

certain sort of horse blanket is still called a Lavenham rug, but the trade declined during the period when the more notable worsted industry sprang up in neighbouring Norfolk. The Angel Hotel, containing fourteenth-century wall paintings, and the Swan Hotel, which incorporates the old Wool Hall, have survived from this period and a number of ancient weavers' and merchants' houses are to be found near Church Street.

The Church of SS Peter and Paul, with its 141-foot square-buttressed tower, stands at the top of the High Street. It is considered to be one of the finest in the county, with a spacious nave containing some early Flemish carving, notably that adorning the tomb of Thomas Spring who, together with the 14th Earl of Oxford, contributed to the building costs of the church. The church bells are another well-known feature, and the tenor bell, made in 1625 by Miles Graye of Colchester, is famous for its almost perfect tone.

The half-timbered Guildhall, built in 1529, was originally the headquarters of the Guild of Corpus Christi which was responsible for the local cloth trade, and a full length figure of the 15th

Lord de Vere, founder of the Guild, is set into one of its corner posts. The Guildhall has since, in turn, been used as an almshouse, a workhouse and a prison and Dr Rowland Taylor, Archbishop Cranmer's chaplain, was held captive there in 1555 before he died at the stake. Inside are exhibits relating to the history of Lavenham and the local wool trade.

Little Hall (fifteenth century) is the only furnished house open to the public in Lavenham and contains the Gayer-Anderson collection of antique furniture, pictures and books.

Guildhall open Apr to Oct daily; Nov, Sat and Sun only. NT.

Little Hall open Easter to mid Oct Sat, Sun and Bank Holidays, pm only. Parking available.

Leeds Castle

Kent *p 213 D2*

Two islands in a lake formed by the river Len provide a picturesque setting for Leeds Castle. It was named after Led, the chief minister of Ethelbert IV, King of Kent, who inhabited the area during the ninth century, given to the Crèvecoeur family by William the Conqueror, and rebuilt by them in stone in 1119 to form an

unassailable fortress. The castle reverted to the Crown in the late thirteenth century and earned the name Lady's Castle, following its occupation by a number of Queens of England. Eleanor of Castille and Margaret, the first and second wives of Edward I, Philippa of Hainault, queen of Edward III and Catherine of Valois, wife of Henry V, were some of its well-known occupants. In 1926 Leeds Castle was acquired by the Hon. Olive, Lady Baillie, who, until her death in 1974, was responsible for a great deal of renovation. She finally bequeathed the castle to the Leeds Castle Foundation, a charitable trust concerned with the furtherance of medical research.

Features within the castle of particular interest include the twelfth-century Norman cellar, Impressionist paintings and house-keeping records for the year 1422 – kept by Joan of Navarre (second wife of Henry IV), the King's private chapel and Henry VIII's banqueting hall. The surrounding parkland contains rare swans, geese and ducks, aviaries and a golf course.

Open Apr to Oct daily; Nov to Mar Sat and Sun pm only. Parking and refreshments available.

Leicester

Leicestershire *p213 A5*

The railway of 1832 linked Leicester to the coalfields, thus transforming an ancient, compact, county town into a sprawling industrial city.

Early remains include an impressive memorial to Roman times – Jewry Wall, believed to date from AD 130. It once formed part of a complex which included a public bath and shops. The Jewry Wall Museum contains finds from the excavation carried out here as well as other items ranging from the prehistoric period to 1500.

Little remains of the Norman castle with the exception of the motte and great hall; the latter is preserved behind a façade built in 1695 and is now used as a law court.

There are many fascinating museums in Leicester. Near the old castle is Newarke Houses Museum, which contains a social history of the county from 1500 to the present day. The fifteenth-century Magazine gateway close by houses the Museum of the Royal Leicestershire Regiment and displayed here is a collection of mementoes, battle trophies and other relics.

Three other museums in the town are of special interest. In the museum of Technology in Corporation Road giant beam engines can be seen, whereas in contrast, the Wygston's House Museum offers English costume ranging from 1769 to 1924 shown in a late medieval building with some later additions. The Leicestershire Museum and Art Gallery in New Walk, with its display of eighteenth- to twentieth-century English paintings and drawings, also houses a unique collection of German Expressionist paintings and exhibitions of ceramics, natural history and Egyptology.

Ecclesiastical buildings of special interest include the beautiful church of St Mary de Castro, which is of Norman origin but was enlarged in the thirteenth century. Of particular note here are the five sedilia, or priests seats. St Martin's Cathedral, a thirteenth- to fifteenth-century church became a cathedral in 1926. The splendid bishop's throne reaches almost to the roof in diminishing tiers adorned with tracery.

On the south-eastern outskirts of the city are the University Botanic Gardens, which include amidst their sixteen acres rock gardens, rose beds and a herb garden.

Jewry Wall Museum and Site open all year daily (except Fri and Christmas), Sun pm only.
Newarke Houses Museum open as above.
Museum of the Royal Leicestershire Regiment open as above.

Leighton Hall

Lancashire *p216 E5*

In 1822 Leighton Hall was acquired by Richard Gillow of the famous furniture-making family, whose descendants still own it today. It is a fine example of a neo-Gothic mansion with an elegant staircase, a series of family portraits and wood panelling. However, the feature which distinguishes Leighton Hall from many other houses is the superb collection of Gillow furniture. Unusual pieces include the altar in the private chapel, a games table and a unique cabinet decorated with religious panels and Italian ivory statuettes.

Many birds of prey are kept and flown in the grounds when the weather is suitable.

Open May to Sept Tue to Fri, Sun and Bank Holiday Mons, pm only. Parking and refreshments available.

Lelant

Cornwall *p211 A1*

South of the charming village of Lelant, situated on the estuary of the river Hayle, is this interesting model village. Standing in landscaped grounds are scale models of historic Cornish buildings and a museum displaying various crafts from the county's colourful history; special attention is given here to smuggling, shipwrecks and tin-mining. Other features within the grounds include water gardens and a junior assault course. An art gallery exhibits paintings by local artists, which are for sale.

Open Easter to Oct daily. Parking and refreshments available.

Levens Hall

Cumbria *p216 E5*

This fine Elizabethan mansion was developed from a thirteenth-century pele tower – a border defence tower. Much of its character today can be attributed to James Bellingham who bought the Hall in 1580 and had it decorated with richly carved panels and superb moulded plaster ceilings. A substantial part of the furniture also dates from this time and there are some interesting family relics including a pair of the earliest English-made pistols in existence.

Levens Hall Gardens are famous in their own right for their wealth of topiary work and they remain very much as they were laid out in 1692. The former brewhouse now houses a unique steam collection and on certain days traction engines can be seen working. There is also a plant centre and a gift shop here.

House and Gardens open Easter Sun to Sep Sun to Thu. Parking and refreshments available.

The yew topiary at Levens Hall is a survivor of the formal gardens so popular before the 18th century

stands in the market square. Here, too, is a statue of Johnson's friend and biographer, James Boswell. Dr Johnson is buried in Westminster Abbey but there is a bust of him in the south transept of Lichfield Cathedral.

Johnson Birthplace Museum open all year (except Public and Bank Holidays, other than Late Summer Holiday) Mon to Sat, also Sun pm May to Sep.

Lilford Park

Northamptonshire *p213 B5*

Deer herds roam freely over the 240 acres of parkland which surrounds a magnificent Jacobean Hall. Although the Hall is not open to the public, the grounds are and hold many attractions for the visitor.

At the end of the last century the Hall was the home of the 4th Baron Lilford, who created the great aviaries and gardens out of his love for birds. Now the aviaries have been rebuilt and stocked with hundreds of birds, including the Lilford crane and the Little owl – a native of Europe

A magnificent display of daffodils offsets the grandeur of Lilford Park

which was first established in Britain through birds released from here.

The park also contains a flamingo pool, a children's farm, an adventure playground, ponies for riding and pleasant riverside walks with picnic spots along the banks of the Nene.

In the stable block and old coaching house is a museum, crafts and antiques centre, and other facilities include a gift shop and log cabin cafeteria.

Open Easter to Oct daily. Parking and refreshments available.

Lichfield

Staffordshire *p216 F2*

The city's beautiful red sandstone cathedral dates from about 1200 to 1340 and is dedicated to St Mary and St Chad. It has the distinction of being the only English cathedral with three tall spires, and, known as the Ladies of the Vale, they are a beloved local landmark. One hundred and thirteen statues grace the grand west front, although only five of them are the originals.

Inside, just before the Lady Chapel, is a sculpture by Chantrey known as the *Sleeping Children*, a memorial to children of the cathedral cleric who perished in a fire in 1812. The Lady Chapel itself contains a lovely sixteenth-century stained glass window. The St Chad Gospels (seventh-century manuscripts) are the cathedral's most treasured possessions.

An old house in the cobbled market square of Lichfield is the birthplace of one of the town's most notable characters, Dr Samuel Johnson, man of wisdom and wit, and compiler of the first Dictionary of the English Language in 1755. The house is now a museum dedicated to Johnson's life and works, and a statue of him

The three spires of Lichfield Cathedral, the tallest almost 260-feet-high, can be seen from every approach

Lincoln Lincolnshire *p217 C2*

The three majestic towers of Lincoln's cathedral dominate the sky line of this ancient city and rise as a spectacular landmark above the Lincolnshire plain. Narrow cobbled streets wind down through quaint old buildings and antique shops, to the banks of the Witham.

The Romans called the town *Lindum Colonia*, used it as the centre of their control over east England, and turned it into one of the finest towns in Britain. They built colonnaded streets and a stone built sewerage system unique in Britain. They encouraged agriculture by draining fenland and boosted trading opportunities by digging the Fossdyke canal, which links the rivers Witham and Trent.

During the Middle Ages Lincoln prospered on the wool trade, as the city had a right to tax the wool merchants. However, after the fourteenth century when the wool trade began to decline, the city's fortunes fell with it and it was not until the mid nineteenth century with the advent of the Industrial Revolution, that Lincoln's second boom period began.

Lincoln has many ancient buildings of interest. On Steep Hill stands the oldest domestic building still in use in Britain, the twelfth-century house known as Aaron the Jew's House, named after a well-known money lender of that period. Close by is the Jew's House, built about 1170; it is a fine Norman house notable for its superb decorated doorway and chimney.

Leading off The Strait is an attractive timbered black and white building called The Cardinal's Hat, probably named in honour of Cardinal Wolsey, who was Bishop of Lincoln in 1514.

Newport Arch spans the ancient Roman road – Ermine Way, and is unique in being the only Roman gateway still used by traffic. The remains of another Roman gate, the east gate, are visible in the forecourt of the Eastgate Hotel. Here is the massive north tower, once part of a double carriageway gate, built in the third century AD. Further relics of a Roman past are indicated

A survivor of the Roman wall, Newport Arch, is still used by traffic

by inscriptions in the roadway at Bailgate, which mark the positions of the columns of a façade 275 feet long. This was cut by the road linking the east and west Roman gates.

The Cathedral

Completed in 1092 by the Normans, a fire destroyed the roof in 1141, and in 1185 an earth tremor brought down the main structure.

Bishop Hugh began the rebuilding in 1192, building five chapels behind the high altar and worked his way towards the west front which had survived. When the nave was completed and joined to the Norman front, the alignment of the vault wasn't accurate, and the irregularity can be seen to this day. The five chapels were later demolished to make way for the beautiful Angel Choir and to create a setting for the shrine of St Hugh.

The present cathedral tower was completed in 1310. It was originally crowned with a wooden spire which reached 540 feet above ground level, but this fell during a storm in 1547.

Notable are the two Eyes (windows) of the cathedral. Dean's Eye at the north end of the transepts dates from 1225, and contains vividly coloured glass. Bishop's Eye at the south end is fourteenth century and is filled with a mosaic of eighteenth-century glass fragments.

The arcading was designed by Christopher Wren, and above it is Wren's library, containing first editions of *Paradise Lost* and *Don Quixote*.

The Castle

This castle featured in the struggle between King John and his barons, and the cathedral holds one of the four original copies of the Magna Carta. It was stormed for the last of many times in 1644 during the Civil War, when the Royalists surrendered to the Roundheads.

The building encloses about six acres of lawn and trees with a wall up to ten feet thick and double that in height. There are two artificial mounds within the grounds, on top of one is the Observatory Tower, on the other Lucy Tower, which formed the main stronghold of the castle. At the northeast corner is Cobb Hall, added in the fourteenth century as a prison cell. Its roof remained a place of public execution until 1868.

Greyfriars and City Museum

Originally a two-storey church of the thirteenth century, and made a free school in 1574, this oldest surviving church of the Franciscan order is now a fascinating museum of local antiquities and natural history. Special exhibits include a prehistoric boat found buried near the Witham, and a huge punt gun used by wild fowlers on the fens.

The Museum of Lincolnshire Life

Here the visitor obtains an insight into the county's social and industrial history from Elizabethan times to the present day. The exhibits also include the traditional devices of poachers.

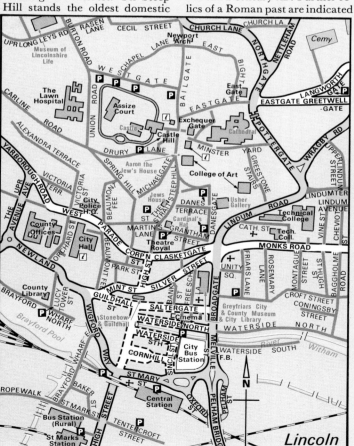

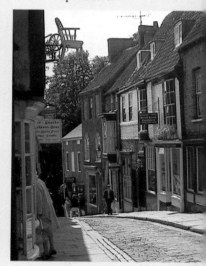

The Usher Gallery

The gallery contains a remarkable collection of antique watches, glass, ceramics, exquisite miniatures and over fifty paintings by Peter de Wint, the artist who was born in Staffordshire and worked in Lincoln.

Stonebow and Guildhall

The Stonebow is a 500-year-old Tudor Gothic gateway, above which stands St Marys Guildhall, popularly known as John of Gaunt's Stables. Built about 1180, it was the meeting place of medieval social and religious guilds.

In one of the rooms some of the city's treasures are kept, including a sword probably presented by Richard III, and another given by Henry VII. Also here are the Mayor's Mace and other trappings of state. The City Council still meets in the hall and are summoned as they have been for centuries by the Mote Bell, cast in 1371.

Castle open all year daily (except Christmas and Sun Nov to Mar).

Greyfriars City and County Museum open all year (except Good Fri and Christmas) daily, Sun pm only.

Museum of Lincolnshire Life open all year daily. Sun pm only. Parking available.

Usher Gallery open all year (except Good Fri and Christmas) daily, Sun pm only.

Stonebow and Guildhall open all year, first Sat in each month, other times by arrangement with the Publicity Officer of Lincoln.

Right: A view of Lincoln Cathedral. The building before the west front is the ancient Exchequer Gate

Below: One of the many cobbled streets which are fascinating to explore in this ancient city

Little Moreton Hall, 400 years old, retains its original furnishings

Littlecote House

Wiltshire *p213 A3*

Flowing through the lovely gardens and parkland of Littlecote House is the river Kennet, and in the spring and summer the rich water meadows are alive with the blooms of wild flowers and the voices of birds.

Henry VIII is thought to have courted Jane Seymour at Littlecote, a legend substantiated by their initials entwined in a stained glass window of the Tudor great hall. Another legend concerns the ghost of a lady-in-waiting. She bore a child of the master of the house, Wild Darrell, who promptly threw it on the fire. Her spirit is said to walk still, looking for her child.

The house is a building of enormous size, and it was Wild Darrell who built the magnificent long gallery, 110 feet long, hung with buff coats, arms and armour which belonged to a garrison of soldiers who stayed here during the Civil War.

The chapel is distinctly Puritan, reflecting the beliefs of the Pophams, who succeeded Darrell, and is the only one of its kind to survive intact.

The house of mellow stone and flint lies in woodland, and in the grounds excavations have uncovered the remains of a Roman villa and a large mosaic which was lifted in 1978 and is now a permanent display.

Today the house is being imaginatively transformed by its new owner, Peter de Savary. A company of knights and their ladies are in permanent residence, recreating a medieval atmosphere.

Open all year, daily. Main rooms on ground floor only open for viewing. Refreshments available.

Little Moreton Hall

Cheshire *p216 E3*

This black and white timbered building is probably one of the best known of its kind. Little Moreton Hall, or Moreton Old Hall as it is sometimes known, rises majestically above the surrounding countryside, its slightly leaning gabled walls casting a picturesque reflection in the waters of the moat which surrounds it. The house is reached by an arched stone bridge and a timbered gatehouse guards the entrance to a cobbled courtyard. From the quadrangle there are lovely views down to the immaculately kept gardens and a small grassy hill upon which a watch tower once stood.

The Hall was originally built by William Morton the elder in the early fifteenth century, roughly in the shape of a capital H with the great hall as its central feature. His son added the gatehouse a few years later and in turn his son John was responsible for the magnificent Elizabethan long gallery, which is probably the most impressive part of the building. The gallery measures sixty-eight feet by twelve feet, and particularly fine are its huge fireplaces, oak beamed roof and leaded windows. Another special feature of the interior is the enormous kitchen with its open range and collection of pewter utensils.

Open Mar and Oct Sat, Sun pm only, Apr to Sep daily, (except Tue) pm only. NT.

Llanberis

Gwynedd *p216 C3*

Llanberis, a little grey town in the shadow of Snowdon, attracts thousands of visitors each year who come to explore this popular mountain area. Just outside the town stand the ruins of Dolbadarn Castle which once commanded the valley. It is thought to have been built by Llewelyn the Great, but fell into disrepair after Edward I established his supremacy in Wales.

More recent history has left a greater mark on Llanberis, for this was one of the major slate-producing areas in North Wales. The Vivian Quarry Trail follows the footsteps of the quarrymen, including the splitting and dressing sheds and blast shelters. The Welsh Slate Museum goes one step further and here, in the former central workshops, much of the original machinery is preserved. There is also the fifty-four-foot diameter waterwheel which at one time supplied most of the power needed for the workshops. The cinema/gallery provides a film and photographic illustration of the quarrying industry and many aspects of the social history of the nineteenth-century workers.

Llanberis is also the terminus for two of the famous railways of North Wales. Undoubtedly the best known is the Snowdon Mountain Railway, established in 1896 specifically for the purpose of carrying tourists to the top of Snowdon. It is the only rack and pinion steam railway in Britain and Swiss locomotives provide the power for the easiest, if not the cheapest, way to the summit. In contrast the Llanberis Lake Railway follows the valley along the north bank of Llyn Padarn, using the old Dinorwic Quarries to Port Dinorwic line.

Dolbadarn Castle See AM info. Also open Sun from mid morning July to Sep. Parking available.
Welsh Slate Museum open daily Easter to Sep. Parking available. AM.
Snowdon Mountain Railway operates from week before Easter to early Oct daily. Parking and refreshments.
Lake Railway operates from Easter to Sep, trains run frequently (except Sat). Parking and refreshments.

Llandaff Cathedral

South Glamorgan *p212 D4*

During the latter half of the eighteenth century Cardiff began expanding, gradually incorporating a whole series of communities within its boundaries. One such community was the tiny cathedral city of Llandaff which became a part of Cardiff in 1922.

Tightly grouped around its ancient cathedral and lying some two-and-a-half miles from the city centre, Llandaff has nevertheless retained the air of a separate community. Bounded by the river Taff and busy main roads, the cathedral occupies the site of an earlier sixth-century church founded by St Teilo. The present cathedral was began in the twelfth century on the instructions of Urban, the first Norman Bishop of Llandaff, and continued down the centuries. At various times over the years the cathedral has suffered from periods of abuse and neglect, from storm damage and from devastation by a German landmine in 1941. Its history has been chequered with misfortune to such an extent that its survival is surprising. An impressive feature of Llandaff Cathedral is the sculpture by Sir Jacob Epstein, *Christ in Majesty*, which dominates the interior. Cast in aluminium, the inspiring figure soars above the nave. Outside the cathedral, to the south-west of the presbytery aisle, stands a tenth-century Celtic cross discovered in 1870. Also to be seen in the cathedral grounds are the remains of a thirteenth-century bell-tower and the ruins of the former bishop's palace. Sacked by Owain Glyndwr in 1402, the ground within the palace ruin has been developed into a public garden.

Llandudno

Gwynedd *p216 C3*

In the mid-nineteenth century Llandudno developed from a cluster of mining and fishermen's cottages to a Victorian seaside resort. The town was the brainchild of Liverpool surveyor Owen Williams, who planned the great sweep of its promenade and its majestically wide streets.

This classic little resort lies on a curving bay, flanked to the west by the massive limestone headland of the Great Orme and on the other side by the smaller headland of Little Orme. The Great Orme towers some 679 feet above sea level, dominating the town and separating its two superb beaches. The summit of this massive headland offers panoramic views and can be reached in a variety of ways; either by Edwardian tramway; a funicular or cable railway almost a mile in length; by modern cabin lift; by foot or by road. A toll road called Marine Drive encircles the Great Orme.

Set on the Orme's northern slopes overlooking the sea is the ancient church of St Tudno, from which the town derives its name. The church dates back to the twelfth century, but it is thought that St Tudno began a Christian Mission here back in the sixth century. Features of interest in the church are the stigmata in the roof above the altar representing the five wounds of Christ, together with the font dating from the Middle Ages.

Just above the town on the lower slopes of the Orme are the Happy Valley Rock Gardens containing rare plants, shrubs and trees interlaced with footpaths overlooking the sea. Nearby Haufe Gardens also overlook the town from the Orme's lower slopes and provide sweeping views over Conwy Bay and Estuary from its terraced gardens.

Tucked away in the town is the Dolls Museum and Model Railway which exhibits a delightful collection of over 1,000 dolls, depicting the different eras and fashions of yesteryear. There is also a collection of prams, cradles and toys together with intriguing lace, chain items and bead purses. Contained in the same building is a large model railway and displays of old tin plate. Also of interest is the town's other museum, the Rapallo House Museum and Art Gallery, which is situated at Craig-y-Don. Standing among ornamental gardens, the museum contains a traditional Welsh kitchen, Roman relics, armour, weapons and porcelain, together with its art collection and sculpture.

There is a memorial stone of the white rabbit from *Alice in Wonderland* consulting his watch on the west promenade, because Lewis Carroll decided to write his famous story whilst holidaying in Llandudno.

Cabin Lift operates from Happy Valley to Great Orme summit.
Great Orme Tramway operates from Victoria Station, Church Walks in the town to Great Orme summit. Continuous daily service May to Sep.
Dolls Museum and Model Railway open Easter to Sep daily, Sun pm only.
Rapallo House Museum and Art Gallery open Apr to Oct Mon to Fri.

Llywernog Silver-Lead Mine

Dyfed *p216 C1*

It is about 200 years since the first prospectors began to dig in these Welsh hills for ore, but the real boom occurred during the 1870s and that era that is now being re-created at Llywernog. A Miners' Trail has been laid out around the seven-acre site with information plaques near the main features. Although most of the tunnels are still flooded or clogged with rubbish, one underground section, Balcombes Level, can be visited as part of the trail. However the roof is very low, the floor uneven and the tunnel narrow, so only the sure-footed should attempt this section. The rest of the trail is above ground and includes several waterwheels, winding gear, the main engine shaft and head-frame and gunpowder magazine. The Crusher House contains the last of the Cornish roll-crushers in Wales and in the Jigger Shed is a triple-compartment jig, powered by a fourteen-foot diameter water wheel.

The main building on the site is the nineteenth-century Count House which contained the office, workshops for carpenters and blacksmiths, stores and secondary power supplies. The building has been restored as a museum and includes reconstructions of underground scenes, a working smithy and, upstairs, the California of Wales Exhibition which illustrates all types of metal mining in Wales.

Open Easter to Oct daily. Parking and refreshments available.

Loch Lomond

Strathclyde *p220 C4*

This Queen of Scottish Lakes is in fact the largest lake in Great Britain and is said to have inspired the song 'Loch Lomond', composed by a prisoner of prince Charles Edward on the eve of his execution – the 'low road' being the path that his spirit would take back to its native land when released by death. It stretches for twenty-four miles, its width varying between three-quarters of a mile and five miles. Of its thirty islands, the most significant are Inchmurrin with its ruins of Lennox Castle and Inchcaillach where a former nunnery stands in ruins near the burial place of the MacGregor clan. Gentle slopes in the south give way to more dramatic mountain scenery further north. Amongst this is Ben Lomond, which can be climbed from Rowardennan, a long rather than a difficult climb, but well rewarded by the superb views from its summit. A pleasant way to view the loch is by taking one of the popular steamer trips from Balloch.

Situated at the southern end of the Loch is Balloch Castle Country Park, a large area of grassland suitable for picnics and surrounded by extensive woodlands. The park has wooded walks, a nature trail, specimen trees and a magnificent walled garden. From the castle terrace there are fine views of the Loch.

Balloch Castle Country Park open daily.

Tarbet Pier on Loch Lomond. The loch is one of three famous for the rare powan, or freshwater herring

London

No other area of Britain is as rich in history, traditions, and cultural associations as London. Throughout the capital there are great mansions, venerable old buildings, quaint houses, unrivalled collections of art treasures, tremendous sweeps of glorious parkland, and colourful ceremonies to suit every possible taste and mood.

The palace of Hampton Court stands majestically on the river Thames

British Museum

The collection which began one of the world's largest and most varied treasure house was founded in 1753 and, since then, has grown to include every conceivable kind of artefact from all over the world.

Exhibits not to be missed include the superb Elgin Marbles from Athens, the mummies and sculpture in the Egyptian Galleries, two of the four existing original copies of the Magna Carta, and the beautiful seventh-century Sutton Hoo Treasure from a ship burial discovered in Suffolk.

Open all year daily (except Christmas, New Year's Day, Good Fri and May Day Holiday), Sun pm only. Refreshments available.

Buckingham Palace

Originally built in 1703 for the Duke of Buckingham, this most famous of royal homes was purchased by George III in 1762. On her accession to the throne in 1837, Queen Victoria moved the Court here from the Palace of St James, and it has been the London home of the reigning monarch ever since.

The imposing east wing of the building, which faces down The Mall, was added in 1847, and the façade was redesigned in 1913. The Royal Standard flies above the building when the sovereign is in residence. At 11.30 am every day the ceremony of the Changing of the Guard takes place in the palace forecourt.

Although the palace is not open to the public, many of the art treasures belonging to the royal family can be seen in the Queen's Gallery, whose entrance is in Buckingham Gate. The Royal Mews, in Buckingham Palace Road, is also open to the public. It houses the state coaches and the beautiful horses which draw them.

Queen's Gallery open all year daily (except Mon) Sun pm only.
Royal Mews open Wed and Thu pm (except at certain times) and at other times as published.

Courtauld Institute Galleries

Most famous for its magnificent Impressionist and Post Impressionist paintings, this gallery also contains an excellent collection of Old Master drawings and Italian primitive paintings.

Open all year daily (except Christmas and most Bank Holidays), Sun pm only.

Greenwich

It is from the Thames that the splendid buildings of Greenwich are best appreciated. Nearest to the river, on the site of a palace that was used by successive

monarchs from the fifteenth to the seventeenth centuries, are the buildings of the Royal Naval College, which were mainly the work of Sir Christopher Wren. Beyond this complex is the National Maritime Museum, housed in the Queen's House and its wings. The Queen's House was begun by the architect Inigo Jones in 1618, and is the oldest example of an Italianate house in England. Exhibits in the museum include some of the best seascapes ever painted and many reminders of the great days of British seafaring. On the hill in the centre of Greenwich Park is the old Royal Observatory, now a museum. The park is a royal one and owes much of its elegant charm to the seventeenth-century landscape artist Le Notre. It has areas of wild as well as formal gardens, a great many mature trees, and excellent sporting facilities. Near the Thames are two further reminders of Britain's seafaring tradition – the lovely clipper ship *Cutty Sark*, and *Gypsy Moth IV*, in which Sir Francis Chichester sailed round the world.

Cutty Sark open daily (except Christmas and New Year's Day), Sun pm only.
Gipsy Moth IV Apr to Oct daily.
National Maritime Museum open as *Cutty Sark*.
Old Royal Observatory open all year daily (except Christmas, New Year's Day, Good Fri and May Day Holiday), Sun pm only.
Royal Naval College open all year daily (except Thu) pm only.

Hampton Court

The extensive grounds of Hampton Court Palace comprise one of London's royal parks. There are wide areas of grass crossed by avenues of stately trees and beautiful, varied formal gardens. In springtime the wilderness garden is a carpet of daffodils, and at all times of the year the herb garden, in the shadow of the tremendous palace buildings, exudes marvellous scents. Near to the famous maze is the rose garden, growing in what was once Henry VIII's tiltyard.

The palace itself is breathtaking both in its size and its beauty. It was built for Cardinal Wolsey during the early part of the sixteenth century, but he did not have long to enjoy it, for in 1529 he felt impelled to give it to Henry VIII for political reasons, and less than a year later was imprisoned for high treason.

Henry considerably enlarged the palace, and it became his favourite residence. No further extensive changes were made until the reign of William and Mary, who commissioned Sir Christopher Wren to rebuild it. In fact, he only rebuilt the eastern and southern parts of the palace, and the rest was left virtually untouched. Today the palace is a vast storehouse of treasures that range from domestic utensils to great works of art.

Open all year daily (Sun pm only Oct to Mar). Parking available. AM.

Hampstead

Hampstead owes much of its character to the Heath. An area of open grassland dotted with trees and interspersed with formal gardens, it covers nearly 800 acres. From Parliament Hill there are extensive views over the whole of the London basin. On the northern edge of the Heath is Ken Wood – the grounds of seventeenth-century Kenwood House. It was enlarged during the eighteenth century by Robert Adam and makes a magnificent setting for the Iveagh collection of Dutch and English paintings.

Hampstead, with its elegant old houses, historic inns, and literary associations, retains a village-like atmosphere that has been lost in

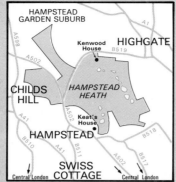

much of the rest of London. One of England's greatest poets, John Keats, lived at Wentworth Place, Keats Grove, for nearly two years, and it was here that he wrote his best poems. The house,

and the one next door – lived in by Keat's lover Fanny Brawne – are open to the public.

Kenwood House open **all year** daily (except Christmas **and Good Fri**). Refreshments available.
Keats House open all year daily (except Christmas, New Year's Day, Easter and May Day Holiday) Sun pm only.

HMS *Belfast*

Moored just above Tower Bridge, this 11,000-ton cruiser was the largest ever built for the Royal Navy. She was built in 1939 and has functioned as a floating museum since 1971.

Open all year daily (except Christmas, New Year's Day. Good Fri and May Day Holiday). Refreshments available in summer.

Elegant 18th-century Kenwood House stands in its own grounds on the edge of Hampstead Heath

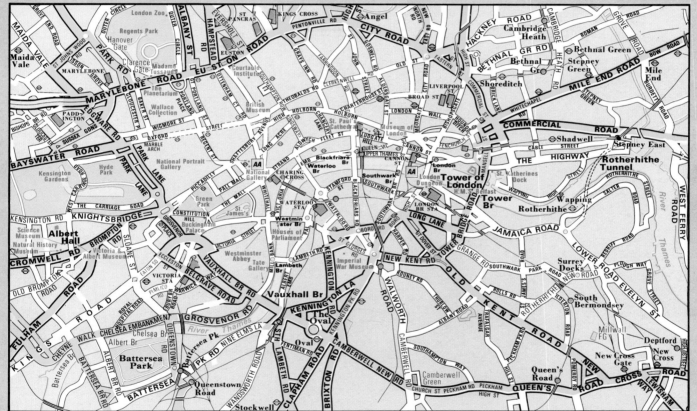

Houses of Parliament

Officially known as the New Palace of Westminster, this forest of towers, turrets and spires rising from a vast honeycomb of courts, corridors and chambers, stands on the site of a palace which was a royal residence from the time of Edward the Confessor until the reign of Henry VIII.

In 1834 the whole rambling complex was destroyed by fire. A competition was held at once for the design of a new Parliament building. It was won by Sir Charles Barry, whose designs, in an imposing Gothic style, were immeasurably improved by Augustus Pugin – an architectural genius then only twenty-three years old.

During World War II the House of Commons and adjacent chambers were destroyed by bombs, and were rebuilt in 1950 in an uninspired Gothic style.

Westminster Hall, incorporated in the western part of the complex, somehow escaped the fire of 1834, and has what is said to be the finest and earliest hammer-beam roof in Europe. The Hall was originally built by William Rufus, but was virtually rebuilt at the end of the fourteenth century by Richard II, from which time the roof dates. It has been the scene of many great moments in British history, including the forced abdication of Edward II in 1327, the deposition of Richard II himself in 1399, and the trial of Guy Fawkes in 1606.

At the northern end of the Houses of Parliament is the magnificent gilded Clock Tower universally known as Big Ben. In fact, the name Big Ben only belongs to the thirteen-and-a-half ton bell which strikes the hours.

The most important parts of the Houses of Parliament, including the Queen's Robing Room, House of Lords, Central Hall, and House of Commons, may be seen on conducted tours.

Palace of Westminster To gain admission to Strangers' Galleries queue at St Stephens entrance; 16.30 Mon to Thu, 9.30 Fri (House of Commons). From 14.30 Tue, Wed and some Mons, 15.00 Thu and 11.00 Fri (House of Lords), or by arrangement with MP or Peer.

Westminster Hall open Mon to Thu am only. Tours by arrangement with an MP only.

Imperial War Museum

This museum illustrates and records all aspects of the two world wars and other military operations involving Britain and the Commonwealth since 1914. Exhibits include tanks, aeroplanes, models of ships, and reconstructions of famous battles. The collection of paintings and drawings by official and unofficial war artists is unsurpassed in Europe.

Open all year daily (except Christmas, New Year's Day, Good Fri and May Day Holiday), Sun pm only.

The famous Palm House in Kew which is at present being rebuilt

Kew Gardens

The superb Royal Botanical Gardens at Kew were begun more than 200 years ago by Princess Augusta, George III's mother. From the small nine-acre garden she planted, the gardens have grown to be one of the largest and most extensive of their kind in the world. Every kind of plant, from tiny alpine flowers to huge trees and delicate exotics that will only thrive in the magnificent palm houses are to be found here.

Kew even has a royal palace. It is a relatively modest seventeenth-century town house, but for George III it meant escape from the Court life which he so heartily detested. It is now open to the public and houses mementoes of the King and an excellent collection of furniture.

Kew Gardens open all year daily (except Christmas, New Year's Day). Refreshments available.

Kew Palace open Apr to Sep daily. Parking available (AM).

Big Ben dominates the complex of buildings known as the Houses of Parliament

London Zoo

Opened to the public in 1849, London Zoo has established a reputation as one of the world's leading collections of animals. Over 8,000 species, ranging from tiny sea creatures to the largest land mammals, are kept in environments as natural to them as possible, yet giving the public the best possible chance of seeing them. Of special merit are the lion terraces, the elephant and rhino pavilion, the night-time world of the Charles Clore pavilion for small mammals, and the Snowdon aviary, where birds nest, feed and fly as they would in the wild.

Open all year daily (except Christmas Day). Parking and refreshments available.

Madame Tussaud's

One of London's most famous and lasting institutions, this collection of waxworks was opened in 1835. Exhibits include historical figures, politicians, entertainers, and in the Chamber of Horrors reconstructions of hideous crimes.

Open all year daily (except Christmas Day). Refreshments available.

Maritime Trusts Museum, Historic Ship Collection

Set in the elegant surroundings of the restored nineteenth-century St Katharine's Docks, this floating collection comprises a number of British sailing and steam-powered vessels.

Open all year daily (except 25, 31 Dec and 1 Jan).

The Museum of London

This museum, opened in 1976 in the ultra-modern Barbican complex, illustrates, by means of brilliantly-displayed exhibits, models, and audio-visual effects, London's continually evolving and fascinating story. The museum is arranged chronologically, and the exhibits include a relief model

Polar bears breed happily at London Zoo and the cubs are particularly popular

showing the archaeological levels of the Thames Valley, a reconstruction of the Great Fire – complete with realistically-crackling flames, and the lavishly decorated Lord Mayor's State Coach, which was made in 1757.

Open all year (except Mon and Christmas), Sun pm only. Refreshments available.

National Gallery

Housed in this handsome Classical-style building is one of the finest collections of paintings in the world. The works include examples from all the great European schools of art, including a choice selection of British masterpieces.

Open all year daily (except Christmas, New Year's Day, Good Fri and May Day Holiday), Sun pm only. Refreshments available.

National Portrait Gallery

The aim of this gallery is to illustrate British history by means of portraits, sculpture, engravings and photographs. It is almost incidental to the gallery's function that many of its works are masterpieces.

Open all year daily (except Christmas, New Year's Day, Good Fri and May Day Holiday), Sun pm only.

Natural History Museum

Dinosaurs, whales, fossils, insects, butterflies, mammals, and birds are all to be found in this museum. The creatures are so well displayed that they could well be alive. The Botanical Gallery on the second floor has beautifully-made dioramas illustrating many different types of habitat and landscape.

Open all year daily (except Christmas, New Year's Day, Good Fri and May Day Holiday), Sun pm only. Refreshments available.

The Planetarium

Spectacular representations of the heavens are projected on to the inside of the Planetarium's great copper dome and are accompanied by a commentary.

Open all year daily (except Christmas Day). Refreshments available.

Richmond Park

This vast royal park, over 2,000 acres in extent, was enclosed by Charles I as part of a hunting estate and still has large herds of Red and Fallow deer. It has kept its feeling of wild countryside, but several gardens – notably the Isabella Plantation Woodlands and the grounds of Pembroke Lodge – have been laid out. Pen Ponds are popular with skaters in the winter and fishermen during the season.

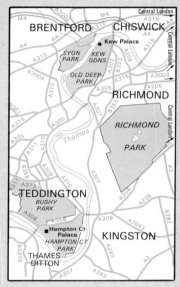

Stretching across the bottom of the London pages is J C Visscher's *Long View of London*. This engraving, depicting London along the Thames from St Katharine's Docks to Westminster, dates from 1616

Wren's greatest achievement – St Paul's – took 35 years to complete

Royal Parks

Five of London's nine spectacular and unique royal parks are in the very heart of the capital and each has a special character of its own.

St James's is, in some respects, the most attractive of the parks; perhaps because so much is crammed into so comparatively small a space. It has a lake enlivened by water birds of all sorts, flower beds, many kinds of trees, and affords beautiful views of the towers and pinnacles of West-minster through the foliage.

Green Park is principally a place of stately avenues of trees among grass that is bestrewn with crocuses and daffodils in spring. Beyond Hyde Park Corner is Hyde Park itself. Its most outstanding feature is undoubtedly the Serpentine, but it is the feeling of great space and freedom which characterises it. Kensington Gardens are separated from Hyde Park only by a road, but the difference in character is marked. It is a more formal, more enclosed and gentle area than Hyde Park. It shares the Serpentine with Hyde Park, but here it is called the Long Water.

Regent's Park is set apart from the other four royal parks in central London. If Primrose Hill is included in its area, it is, at 670 acres, the largest of the central parks. It was originally a hunting ground (like the others) and was given its present appearance in the early nineteenth century by the great architect John Nash. At the heart of the park is Queen Mary's Garden, a lovely place of water, rock gardens, beautiful roses and overhanging trees. To the north is London Zoo, bounded on its far edge by the Regent's Canal.

St Paul's Cathedral

Sir Christopher Wren drew up plans for a new cathedral on this site almost before the ashes of the old cathedral (razed to the ground during the Great Fire of London in 1666) had grown cold. The building that rose from those ashes is Wren's masterpiece and has a dignity which the surrounding tower blocks cannot diminish.

It is crowned by a beautiful central dome, 365 feet above ground level at its highest point and 112 feet in diameter, which contains the famous Whispering Gallery. There are several hundred monuments in the cathedral, as well as the imposing tombs of such notables as the Duke of Wellington and Lord Nelson.

Science Museum

Of all London museums this is the one most loved by children and their fathers. There are knobs to press, handles to turn, and all kinds of functioning exhibits. The museum has a serious aspect in that it traces the application of science to technology and the development of engineering and industry from their beginnings to the present day.

Open all year daily (except Christmas, New Year's Day, Good Fri and May Day Holiday), Sun pm only. Refreshments available.

Tate Gallery

The Tate Gallery houses the national collection of British works from the sixteenth to the twentieth century, and also traces the development of British and foreign art from the mid 1800s to the present day. British artists represented include Hogarth, Blake, Turner, Constable, and the Pre-Raphaelites. All modern schools of painting and sculpture are superbly represented; and because the Tate buys works almost before they are finished it is often many years ahead of generally accepted tastes in art.

Open all year daily (except Christmas, New Year's Day, Good Fri and May Day Holiday), Sun pm only. Refreshments available.

Tower of London

William the Conqueror built the Tower of London as a reminder to the citizens of the City of his unassailable power. At the heart of the complex is the White Tower, or keep, looking much as it has done for the last 900 odd years. It is one of the earliest and largest buildings of its kind in Western Europe and contains the Chapel of St John, which displays Norman architecture at its simplest and most dramatic.

Over the centuries a powerful and complicated series of walls and towers were built up round the White Tower, gradually transforming the original Norman motte-and-bailey castle into

the most important medieval fortification in Britain.

The Tower has been used as palace, treasure house, menagerie and – most famously – prison. Many of the prisoners entered the Tower through the infamous Traitors' Gate and eventually went to their deaths at the block on Tower Green.

The Crown Jewels – most of which were melted down during the Commonwealth and had to be remade for the coronation of Charles II – are displayed in vaults beneath the Waterloo Barracks and a wealth of armour and other military equipment in the White Tower, Waterloo Barracks, and the Tower's Museum.

The Tower is also famous for its Beefeaters, splendidly attired officers; and for its ravens, sinister black birds that strut over Tower Green – scene of many executions.

Open all year daily (except Christmas, New Year's Day and Good Fri) Sun pm only from Mar to Oct, closed Sun from Nov to Feb. Jewel House closed Feb.

Victoria and Albert Museum

Exhibits ranging from great works of art to items whose function is simply to entertain and amuse are displayed in this vast box of delights. Among the items on display in the museum's seven miles of galleries are paintings, sculpture, furniture, costumes, armour, locks, ceramics, and, of all things, a large wooden model of a tiger eating a British officer. It was made in the eighteenth century and emits sounds intended to imitate the soldier's groans of agony.

Open all year daily (except Christmas, New Year's Day, Good Fri and May Day Holiday) Sun pm only. Refreshments available.

Wallace Collection

Perhaps the most famous work of art contained in this elegant eighteenth-century town house is *The Laughing Cavalier* by Frans Hals, but it is also packed with a huge variety of other treasures. These include French paintings and furniture of the eighteenth century, works by Titian and Rubens, and objects ranging from the finest and most delicate porcelain to assorted bric-a-brac.

Open all year daily (except Christmas, New Year's Day, Good Fri and May Day Holiday) Sun pm only.

Westminster Abbey

Henry III began this magnificent abbey church in 1245 to replace a church which had been built during the reign of Edward the Confessor. After Edward's death in 1065, his successor, Harold, was crowned here, and every English sovereign since that time has been crowned in the abbey (with the exception of Edward V and Edward VIII, who were never crowned).

Henry III's church was completed in 1269, and from then until the reign of George III it was the burial place of all English kings and queens. During the late fourteenth and early fifteenth century the nave was rebuilt, but without altering Henry III's overall conception. Between 1503 and 1509 the Lady Chapel was replaced by the majestic Henry VII Chapel – perhaps the supreme example of Perpendicular architecture. The 225-foot-high towers at the abbey's west end were added in the mid eighteenth century by the architect Nicholas Hawksmoor.

The interior of the abbey is one of the finest achievements of English architecture, and over a thousand monuments

The shrine of St Edward the Confessor lies within Westminster Abbey

are crowded into the building; they not only commemorate prominent men and women from every walk of life, but also give a breathtaking view of English monumental sculpture. However, it is perhaps the simple grave of the Unknown Warrior near the west entrance which is the most poignant. His Tomb symbolizes the sacrifice of more than a million British who lost their lives in World War I.

Beneath the cloisters of the abbey there is an undercroft originally used by the monks of the abbey as a resting room, but now housing a museum. Among the many fascinating exhibits here are several wax funeral effigies which figured in the elaborate funerals of famous people buried in the abbey. The oldest is believed to be an actual death mask belonging to Edward II.

Longleat

Wiltshire *p212 F3*

The Marquess of Bath claims there is something for everyone at Longleat and there is certainly enough entertainment to choose from on his country estate.

Longleat House, still the family home, and one of the most famous stately homes in England, is a magnificent Elizabethan building set in sweeping parkland landscaped by Capability Brown. The interior is filled with treasures including tapestries, Spanish leather, Genoese velvet and paintings by famous artists including Titian, Reynolds and Lawrence. The magnificent Venetian ceilings and ornate Italian décor are the results of alterations carried out by Sir Jeffrey Wyatville during the last century. The state bedroom suite, last used by the Duke of Windsor, and the Victorian bathroom, are amongst smaller rooms on view. Many possessions of the household can be seen, including the family's state and garter robes, state coach, and a waistcoat worn by Charles I at his execution.

The fully equipped Victorian kitchens give a glimpse of what life was like 'below stairs'. The scullery is now a kitchen shop selling culinary goods and gifts.

Perhaps the most famous of the attractions at Longleat now is the extensive Safari Park, home of the Lions of Longleat. However, these are by no means the only exotic animals here, and visitors can observe at close range from the safety of their car Siberian tigers, elephants, rhinos, zebra, buffaloes and antelopes.

During the summer months, the Safari boat weighs anchor regularly, and one can cruise amongst wallowing hippos and frolicking sealions, and sail past the Ape Islands.

For the non-seafaring visitor there is a fifteen-inch gauge railway running alongside the lake.

Amusements for children include camel and donkey rides, nineteenth-century dolls houses, a pets' corner with a chimps' tea party, and Leisureland – an exciting adventure playground. The Garden Centre sells many plants actually grown at Longleat.

Open all year daily (except Christmas Day). Safari Park closed in winter.

A view of 16th-century Longleat House through some of the more informal parkland on the estate

Melford Hall was sacked by Parliamentary forces during the Civil War

Long Melford

Suffolk *p213 D4*

One of the most outstanding small towns in Suffolk, Long Melford has a delightful main street, lined with fine old shops and houses. Dominating the street is the magnificent church of the Holy Trinity, a huge fifteenth-century building occupying the site of a Roman temple. Many windows illuminate the church, and beautifully worked pillars, columns and stained glass make the interior particularly striking.

At the upper end of the triangular Melford Green is Melford Hall. Completed in 1578, this turretted Tudor manor house was built in brick with attractive contrasting stone decorations. The rooms date from varying periods, and contain collections of fine furniture, porcelain and paintings.

To the north of the village is Kentwell Hall, a mellow Tudor manor surrounded by a moat and beautiful grounds. A 300-year-old avenue of lime trees forms a picturesque approach to the tranquil setting of the Hall. Among the attractions here is the brick-paved mosaic Tudor Rose Maze and an interesting exhibition of Tudor Style costumes.

Melford Hall open Apr to Sep Wed, Thu, Sun and Bank Holiday Mon pm. NT.
Kentwell Hall open Apr to mid Jun, Wed, Thu and Sun; mid Jul to Sep Wed to Sun; pm only. Also Easter and Bank Holiday weekends, pm only. Parking and refreshments available.

Loseley House

Surrey *p213 B2*

An elegant Elizabethan mansion of Bargate stone, tall white windows and decorative chalk corner stones beneath right-angled gables, Loseley is the home of the descendants of Elizabethan statesman, Sir William More.

Elizabeth I and James I stayed here on more than one occasion, and further royal connections are suggested by the painted panels in the great hall, one of them bearing the initials of Henry VIII and Catherine Parr. The hall has a lofty, flat-beamed ceiling and the gallery is made up with various carvings and panelling said to have come from Henry VIII's Nonsuch Palace. Here also is a notable portrait of Edward VI.

The drawing room has a handsome plaster ceiling and an extraordinary chimneypiece, made from a single piece of chalk, and excellent Elizabethan carving is to be found in the library.

The beautiful parkland which surrounds the house can be viewed from the garden terrace and the moat walk. Delicious products of the dairy farm are on sale in the house shop.

Open end May to Sep, Wed to Sat pm only. Also Spring and late Summer Bank Holidays.

Lotherton Hall

North Yorkshire *p217 B3*

This early eighteenth-century house was the home of Sir Alvary and Lady Gascoigne. It now houses the admirable Gascoigne collection and English and oriental objets d'art. Of particular interest are the exquisitely decorated gold and silver pieces and the excellent costumes of the fashion display.

Among the collection of eighteenth and nineteenth-century furniture is an octagonal table beautifully inlaid with ivory, mother-of-pearl, various woods, copper and brass. A grand piano and dressing table housed here are also fine examples of the cabinet makers' skill.

Nearby is a small chapel notable for its beamed roof and richly carved pulpit.

Open May to Sep, Tue to Sun and Bank Hol Mon. Parking and refreshments available.

Ludlow

Shropshire *p216 E1*

Ludlow, former capital of the Welsh Marches, stands on high ground overlooking the river Teme at its junction with the river Corve. Above the town rises the impressive red-stone ruin of Ludlow Castle and the 135-foot-high tower of the parish church of St Laurence.

Famous for its black and white buildings, Ludlow has a regular pattern of intersecting streets. Parts of the old town walls are still visible and Broad Gate, complete with its portcullis slits, is the only original town gate still surviving. Broad Street, considered one of the finest streets in England, has a mixture of Georgian houses and timber-framed buildings including the Angel Hotel, a splendid coaching inn. Other buildings of note include the sixteenth-century Feathers Hotel in the Bull Ring, the fine thirteenth-century Reader's House and the Hosyers Almshouses dating from the fifteenth century but rebuilt in 1758. The church of St Laurence has some very fine carving, including a famous series of misericords, and a fine fifteenth-century window. The ashes of A. E. Houseman, author of *A Shropshire Lad*, are buried in the churchyard.

The eighteenth-century Butter Cross houses the town museum in a room once used as a school. Displaying a fascinating collection of Ludlow's past, the exhibits include examples of arms and armour, geology and Georgian and Victorian domestic items.

Dating from the twelfth-century, Ludlow Castle was built by Roger de Lacey and formed part of a chain of castles erected along the border between England and Wales. During its troubled history it was a royal palace and residence of the President of the Council of the Marches. Although the castle is now in ruins, an unusual circular Norman chapel has survived.

Museum open Easter to Sep. Mon to Sat. Sun, June to Aug only.
Castle open daily (except Dec, Jan).

Lullingstone Castle

Kent *p213 C3*

The large sixteenth-century gatehouse with its crenellated towers and parapet could aptly be described as a miniature castle, whilst the castle itself is a large eighteenth-century mansion. The most decorative feature of the exterior is the entrance with its false pillars and open stonework parapet.

Worth noting inside is the panelling and carved balustrade of the staircase incorporating crests of the Hart family. Also of interest is the state drawing room with its plasterwork, barrel vaulted ceiling and portrait of Queen Anne who was a regular visitor here. The extensive grounds have sweeping lawns, shrubs, trees and a lake. About half-a-mile to the north are the remains of a Roman villa with a particularly fine tessellated pavement.

Castle open Apr to Oct, Sat, Sun and Bank Holidays pm only. Parking available.
Villa see AM info. Also open Sun am Apr to Sep. Parking available.

Luton Hoo

Bedfordshire *p213 B4*

This palatial mansion on the southern outskirts of Luton was built in 1767 by Robert Adam, but has been considerably altered over the years. The most significant changes were made at the beginning of the twentieth century, when it was completely remodelled in the French style for Sir Julius Wernher, a South African diamond magnate. His architect, C. F. Mewes, created a perfect setting for Wernher's remarkable collection of works of art and although a part of the house is now a private residence, the major part is laid out as a museum for the collection. Paintings include works by Rembrandt and Titian and the splendid *St Michael* by Bartolomé Bermejo (c 1480). There are also fine collections of English porcelain and china – with a few pieces from Dresden and China; ivories, metal-work and enamels and superb Fabergé jewels. In the Russian room are the Court Robes and personal mementoes of the Russian Imperial Family and in the dining room Beauvais tapestries are hung in specially designed marble wall insets. The house stands in the 1,500 acre park which was skilfully landscaped by Capability Brown.

Open late Mar to mid Oct Mon, Wed, Thu, Sat (Sun pm only) and Good Fri. Parking and refreshments available.

Lydford

Devon *p212 C2*

Lydford, a secluded moorland village, lies on the edge of Dartmoor, where the river Lyd has cut a deep wooded gorge into its valley. It was once an important town and the headquarters of the tin-miners who virtually ruled Dartmoor until the decline of the industry in the seventeenth century.

The village is dominated by the remains of its Norman castle, which was built by the omnipotent tin-miners in 1195 as a prison to house offenders against its mining laws. The castle's lower floor was once the prison, whilst its upper floor was the Stannary Court. Lydford's role as a prison lasted for many centuries and was notorious for its rough and ready justice, where it is said men were tried after being hanged.

Lydford Gorge is one of Devon's outstanding beauty spots. This deep wooded ravine, about a mile in length, offers a dramatic and unforgettable walk beside the seething waters of the Lyd, with its boulders, dark pools, cascades and long rapids. On either side huge oaks almost roof the gorge and wild garlic, lichens, moss and ferns carpet its sides, flourishing in the humid atmosphere. At its southerly end the Lyd is joined by a tributary at the spectacular ninety-foot-high White Lady Waterfall. In the seventeenth century the gorge was inhabited reputedly by the fearsome family of highway robbers called the Gubbins. The gorge is best approached from the car park beside the bridge at the southern end of the village.

The village church is worth visiting too, just see its fine screen and carved bench-ends. In the churchyard is an epitaph to George Routleigh, the watchmaker.

Castle open at all reasonable times. Parking available. AM.
Gorge open Apr to Oct daily. NT.

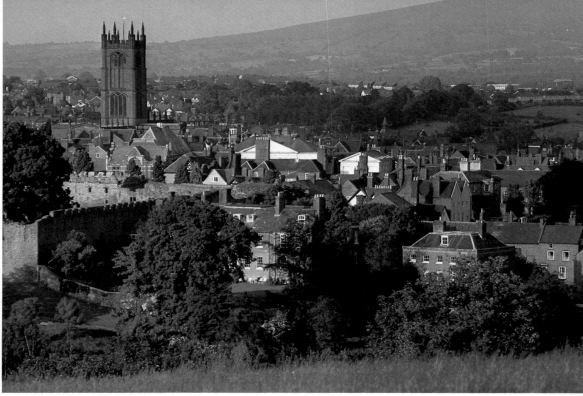
Ludlow stands in the boundary area of England and Wales known as the Marches

Lyme Park

Cheshire *p216 F3*

Lyme Park was the home of the Legh family for 600 years until Richard Legh, 3rd Lord Newton, gave the estate to the National Trust. The house is a splendid example of Palladian architecture built around a central courtyard, and from the outside there is little evidence of the Elizabethan building upon which it was based. The notable exception is the huge Tudor gateway on the entrance front.

Contained within Leoni's enlargement of 1726 is the Tudor drawing room and the long gallery, stretching 120 feet, which has remained unchanged since 1541. The house contains a fine collection of pictures and furnishings and the state rooms are richly panelled with some superb wood carving and tapestries. In the parlour there are four interesting chairs made by Thomas Chippendale and upholstered with the cloth from the cloak worn by Charles I at his execution in 1649. The exterior of the house is imposing, particularly the south front with its huge Ionic portico which looks out across the lake. Surrounding the building is a 1,300-acre park, nine miles in circumference, which is home to a herd of Red deer.

House open Apr to Oct daily pm (except Mon but including Bank Holidays). Park and gardens open all year daily. Parking available. NT.

Lympne

Kent *p213 D2*

The Romans built a fort at Lympne as part of their coastline defence. At that time it was a coastal village, but the sea has since receded.

Built 300 yards from the ruins of the fort, known as Studfall Castle, is Lympne Castle, a fourteenth-century fortified manor house. Although greatly restored in 1905, it retains its Norman appearance. Romney Marsh, the Channel and the Military Canal – dug in fear of invasion from Napoleon – are overlooked by the castle.

Just west of the village is Port Lympne Wildlife Sanctuary and Gardens covering some 270 acres – several of the more exotic animals kept here include wolves, rhinos, African leopards, Siberian and Indian tigers, monkeys and bison.

Within the grounds is a Dutch-colonial-style mansion which is the work of the architect Sir Herbert Baker. Many of the original features still survive, including an hexagonal library where the Treaty of Paris was signed after World War I. The house is set in fifteen acres of elaborate terraced gardens, from where on clear days the French coast is visible.

Castle open Jun to Sep and Bank Holidays, daily. Parking available. **Port Lympne Zoo Park, Mansion and Gardens** open all year daily (except Christmas Day). Parking and refreshments available.

Mapledurham

Oxfordshire *p213 A3*

This peaceful, unspoilt village beside the river Thames, backed by wooded hills, is noted for its old cottages and contains a particularly attractive row of early seventeenth-century alms-houses.

Mapledurham House stands majestically beside the river, and is probably the best known feature of the village. Built in pink brick by Sir Michael Blount during the sixteenth century, it is a fine example of Tudor architecture and is said to be the model for the home of Soames Forsyte, in John Galsworthy's novel *The Forsyte Saga*. An interesting feature of the house is the small chapel which, when built in 1789 during a period of strong anti-Catholic feeling, was required by law to have an exterior which could not be easily recognised as an ecclesiastical building.

Mapledurham's other main historic building, also dating from the Tudor period, stands on the river near the weir. The watermill is the last working corn and grist mill on the Thames. One of its two great waterwheels was replaced by a water-driven turbine in 1926 but the other is still in operation and has been restored and still grinds wholemeal flour which may be purchased.

The village church, dating from the late fourteenth century, has a fine oak-timbered arcaded ceiling and contains memorials to local families, including the Blounts, and the south aisle is still walled off as a Roman Catholic chapel where many of the Blounts are buried.

Mapledurham House open Easter to Sep Sat, Sun and Bank Holidays, pm only. Parking and refreshments available. **Mapledurham Watermill** open Easter to Sep, Sat, Sun and Bank Holidays, pm only. Also winter Sun pm.

Margam Park

West Glamorgan *p212 D4*

Margam Park is a delightful place in which to wander – whether over open parkland, through woods, beside quiet lakes or around the orangery, abbey, castle and gardens.

The ruins of the chapter house and abbey church are all that are left of what was once the largest Cistercian abbey in Wales. Close-by is the orangery, reputed to be the largest in Britain. It was built of local stone to house orange and other citrus trees (highly prized in the eighteenth century) with tall, elegant windows and a parapet adorned with numerous stone urns, paralleled by a balustrade of open stonework. In the surrounding gardens many rare and unusual trees and shrubs flourish.

Margam Castle, now an empty shell, was built in the nineteenth-century, and is a fanciful compilation of turrets, mock battlements, Gothic doorways and windows. In complete contrast, overlooking the castle, is a hill-fort called Mynydd-y-Castell, built by Iron Age people over 2,000 years ago.

The castle park is a haven for wildlife. Wild flowers flourish, and the woods and water attract all manner of birds and beasts, from buzzards to dragonflies. One of the greatest attractions is the herd of Fallow deer, established since the fifteenth century and a delight to watch grazing among the trees.

There are facilities for boating and putting, children's donkey and pony rides, an adventure playground and marked walks. Gymkhanas, horse trials, pony and carriage events, band concerts and archery competitions take place throughout the year.

Open Apr to Oct Tue to Sun. Also Mon in Aug and Bank Hol. Nov to Mar Wed to Sun. Parking and refreshments available.

Marwell Zoo

Hampshire *p213 A2*

Opened in 1972, Marwell quickly became established as one of Britain's major wild animal collec-

The splendid library of Mellerstain House – little altered in 200 years

The Living of Mapledurham Church was much sought after, and is now in the possession of Eton College

tions and now specialises in conservation and breeding. Over 1,000 animals of a hundred or so species are kept in spacious enclosures which once formed part of the park surrounding Marwell Hall (not open). The many varieties of big cats here include Asian lions, and a magnificent pair of Siberian tigers. There are also camels, giraffes, monkeys, cattle, Przewalski wild horses and several species of deer.

For younger visitors, there is a delightful children's zoo and a playground. The gently sloping site of the park has good walking surfaces, for those who do not wish to drive, and there are pleasant picnic areas around the perimeter.

Open all year daily. Parking and refreshments available.

Melbourne

Derbyshire *p217 B1*

This pretty village gave its name to Lord Melbourne – nineteenth-century statesman and first prime minister to Queen Victoria – and through him to Australia's city.

Lord Melbourne's home was Melbourne Hall, a charming stone mansion, now owned by the Marquess of Lothian and filled with superb family portraits.

The formal gardens are probably more famous than the house itself. Landscaped by Henry Wise, they form a delightful mosaic of well-cut lawns, terraces and tree-lined avenues scattered with elegant fountains and statues of lead cupids and embracing cherubs. One of the most attractive features of the gardens is the delicate wrought iron 'birdcage' summer-house by Robert Bakewell, the great Derby ironsmith. Another feature to look out for is the hundred-yard tunnel of yew.

Hall open Jun to Oct Wed pm.
Gardens Apr to Sep Wed, Sat, Sun and Bank Hol Mon, pm only. Parking and refreshments.

Mellerstain House

Borders *p220 E3*

Robert Adam designed this great Georgian house of honey-coloured stone. When he began his work in 1770 there were already two lower wings built by his father, but the mansion which was to join them was never begun. The result is rather forbidding and rigid, very square and built in an E-shape with a castellated roof line.

However, it is interior decoration for which Adam is most famous, and here he excelled himself. Little has been altered, and the ceilings, friezes and fireplaces are just as Adam designed them. A particularly fine room is the library. It has a fireplace of green and white marble, white carved wood bookcases, and the white plaster relief of the ceiling stands out against pale green and pink, with medallions in slate grey.

Among the treasures within the house are a Van Dyck portrait, an early painting by Gainsborough, and other paintings by Ramsay, Van Goyen and Constable. They are all hung in Adam's immaculate rooms which are furnished with fine eighteenth-century pieces, and separated by beautifully finished mahogany doors.

The garden terraces were created in 1909 by Blomfield, and look out across the sweeping lawn which slopes to a distant lake fed by Eden Water, with the distant Cheviot Hills as an attractive backdrop.

Open Easter then May to Sep daily (except Sat), pm only. Parking and refreshments available.

Melbourne Hall was rebuilt from ruins of Melbourne Church in the 17th century

Melrose

Borders *p220 E3*

This small, quiet town is best known for what must be the most famous abbey ruins in Scotland, Melrose Abbey – owing much of its fame to the glamour given it by the romantic writings of Sir Walter Scott. Its position on one of the main routes into Scotland meant that during the Wars of Scottish Independence, both the abbey and town suffered repeated plunder and burning by the English armies. Nevertheless, the well-preserved stone ruins, mainly of fifteenth-century origin, give an indication of just how grand and beautiful the abbey was in its prime. The elaborate stonework, flying buttresses, pinnacles and the rich tracery of the windows are among its finest features. The abbey contains the remains of King Alexander II, and the heart of Robert the Bruce is buried near the High Altar. The fifteenth- to sixteenth-century Commendators House has been adapted as a museum to display many items excavated in and around the abbey.

Close to the abbey ruins are the unusual Priorwood Gardens, which grow flowers suitable for drying. The National Trust for Scotland run the gardens and have set up a regional visitors centre, shop and picnic area here.

Abbey see AM info. Parking available.
Priorwood Gardens open Easter to Oct daily, pm only on Sun. Nov to 24 Dec daily except Sun. NTS.

Mevagissey

Cornwall *p211 B1*

Sprawling up the cliff in typical Cornish style, Mevagissey maintains a sense of timelessness that eludes many of the neighbouring fishing villages. Its real charm has to be discovered by walking through the narrow streets between the wooden slatted houses and along the quay, rather than viewing it from a distance. The traditional trade of Mevagissey has always been pilchard fishing and this reached its height in the nineteenth century when the town became very prosperous. Smuggling would have undoubtedly contributed to this wealth too. Now Mevagissey relies mainly on tourism, although after Looe it is still the main centre for shark fishing in Cornwall. In a small folk museum on the north

Melrose Abbey was saved by the Duke of Buccleuch in 1822

quay can be seen local handicrafts, fishing tackle, a cider press and agricultural implements. There is also an indoor model railway in the village, laid out through realistic terrain.

Folk museum open Easter to Sep. (Easter to May pm only).
Model railway open two weeks Easter, then Spring Bank Hol to Sep daily. Winter, Sun pm.

Milton Abbas

Dorset *p212 F2*

In this picture-postcard village, identical pairs of picturesque, square, thatched and whitewash cottages are set behind immaculate wide mown verges and rowan trees, strung out along the curving village street. The Park Farm Museum is housed in the old brewery here and contains a marvellous collection of local relics, including agricultural implements, bygones and a collection of old photographs.

A short distance from the village is Milton Abbey, its mansion and abbey church standing side by side in Gothic splendour, in a delightful bowl of farmland and woods. The beautiful Benedictine abbey church dates from the fourteenth and fifteenth centuries, but only part of it remains today – the choir, crossing and transepts, and fifteenth-century tower. The church was sensitively restored by Sir Giles Gilbert Scott and contains good vaulting under the tower and a carved altar screen, together with the white marble monument to Lady Milton (1775) which Robert Adam designed; Lord Milton lies beside his wife.

The fifteenth-century Abbot's Hall of the former abbey was incorporated into today's eighteenth-century mansion by architects Sir William Chambers and James Wyatt, for the owner, Lord Milton. The mansion is now a school and the abbey church its chapel. There is a rewarding walk from the abbey up a hundred or more grassy steps to the Norman St Catherine's Chapel which stands surmounting the hill above the abbey. Lord Milton completely cleared the original village as it spoilt his view although he did subsequently build the present village, which has all the balance and symmetry of an integrally planned village.

Park Farm Museum open all year daily. Parking available.
House open daily during school Easter and summer holidays.

All the atmosphere and excitement of a working fishing port can be found in the harbour of Mevagissey

Monmouth Gwent *p212 E4*

Monmouth, lying at the centre of the Lower Wye Valley, has many interesting buildings and retains much charm from the Georgian era, while maintaining the hectic life of a market town.

Monmouth was probably the site of the Roman fort of *Blestium*, on the route from Gloucester to Caerleon, and Roman pottery and coins have been found at Overmonnow and near the river crossing. The town's recorded history, however, begins with the Normans who established a castle and a priory here within a few years of the 1066 conquest. Eventually the Lordship passed into the Duchy of Lancaster, and so it was as a Lancastrian that Henry V was born in Monmouth Castle in 1387. The walled town which grew up has lasted almost unchanged to this day, although the castle was practically destroyed by Parliamentary forces during the Civil War.

The town became prosperous during the eighteenth and nineteenth centuries, when it benefitted from the vast trade up and down the Wye. Coaching inns were turned into hotels to cater for travellers from England to Wales, or for followers of the fashionable Wye Tour, and the many attractive domestic and religious buildings in the town date from this period. Markets in both agricultural produce and livestock developed, and each year Monmouth holds an agricultural show which is one of the best in the country.

Local History Centre and Nelson Collection

The centre provides information on all aspects of the history of the town and the surrounding neighbourhood, including such articles as the Monmouth Cap and the Borough Weights, Measures and Seals. There is also a good deal of information about C. S. Rolls, co-founder of Rolls-Royce, together with a model of the plane in which he was killed in 1910. He was born at the nearby village of Rockfield and his statue stands in Agincourt Square outside Monmouth's Shire Hall.

Left: The statue of pioneer aviator Charles Rolls of Rolls Royce, and on Shire Hall, one of Henry V, who was born in Monmouth

Monmouth was renowned in medieval times for the Monmouth Cap. The town was prominent in the art of knitting which originated on the Continent.

The Nelson Collection was the gift of Lady Llangattock to the Borough of Monmouth. It contains a very fine and varied collection of Nelson relics, and his fighting sword is the most prized exhibit. There are also several letters, log books, naval documents, prints, engravings and paintings here.

Great Castle House

This was built by the first Duke of Beaufort in 1673, and in about 1875 it became the HQ of the Royal Monmouthshire Royal Engineers, the senior non-regimental unit of the Army. The speciality of the house is the plasterwork on the ceilings.

Monnow Gateway

Guarding the bridge over the river Monnow, the gateway is probably the most famous building in the town. It was constructed at the end of the thirteenth century for use as a toll house, watchtower and prison.

St Mary's Church

Except for the tower and spire, the church was rebuilt in 1736 on the site of the Church of the Benedictine Priory, founded here in 1075. Medieval tiles, a cresset stone, and fragments of a piscina are the only remains of the former priory church.

In the wall of the nearby old priory is a fifteenth-century oriel window, named Geoffrey's Window, after the celebrated Geoffrey of Monmouth who, in about the year 1135, wrote *History of the Kings of Britain*, the origin of much of the Arthurian legend.

Dixton Church

At the entrance to the chancel of this church, small brass tablets show the height to which Wye floods have reached in the past. It was consecrated between 1066 and 1070, and still bears traces of Saxon work.

Castle and Great Castle House exterior freely accessible at any reasonable time. AM. Parking available.
Museum (Nelson Collection and Local History Centre) open all year daily, Sun pm only. Closed Christmas and New Year.

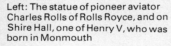

The Elizabethan stone balustrade and Lodge of Montacute House

Montacute House

Somerset *p212 E3*

This must be one of England's loveliest Elizabethan houses, built of locally-quarried golden Ham stone at the edge of a medieval village. It is adorned with carved statues, open-stone parapets, fluted columns, twisted pinnacles, oriel windows and a decorated entrance porch. The gallery, reputed to be the largest of its kind in England, houses a collection of Tudor and Jacobean portraits on permanent loan from the National Portrait Gallery. Of particular note is the stained glass and stone screen in the great hall.

The formal garden with its pavilions is walled with a stone balustrade which looks beyond to open parkland.

Open Apr to Oct daily (except Tue) pm only. Gardens open daily. Refreshments available. NT.

Morecambe

Lancashire *p216 E5*

The shoreline known as Morecambe Bay is one of the most spectacular stretches of coastal scenery in Britain. The bay stretches for some four-and-a-half miles, and when the tide goes out several miles of sand are revealed. These have been crossed on foot at low tide since Roman times, when the route provided a short cut to the Furness Peninsula – twenty-seven odd miles round the coast. Later the Cartmel monks guided travellers along this 'roadway'. Much later it was traversed by stage coaches and during that time 140 people died. This gives some indication of the dangerous nature of the journey, due mainly to the three tidal rivers and treacherous quicksands which have to be negotiated.

Today the sands can be crossed for fun as an adventure trek between Hest Bank and Grange-over-Sands, under the guidance of the official Sand Pilot appointed by the Chancellor of the Duchy of Lancaster.

Situated on the southern shores of the bay is the huge holiday resort of Morecambe – sometimes called the Naples of the North. As a resort, it dates back to the start of the 20th century, when holiday-makers from industrial towns in the North of England discovered it. It has grown from two villages, Poulton-le-Sands and Heysham. The former was an ancient fishing village until just over fifty years ago. Now there are all the usual seaside attractions, including the huge Marineland. As well as daily dolphin and sea lion shows, there are collections of turtles, penguins and alligators – quite apart from hundreds of kinds of local fresh and salt water fish.

Close to Marineland is the Leisure Park, one of the North-West's foremost entertainment centres where, among many attractions, the swimming pool with a wave machine, and the Superdome attract the crowds.

The village of Heysham is best known as the departure point for the ferry to the Isle of Man, but to locals it is also known as the home of an original nettle drink. Just as intriguing, upon the promontory, is the site of ancient St Patrick's Church where some unique stone coffins are still to be seen.

Home of the Miss Great Britain contest, with heats held weekly throughout the season, Morecombe's other great attraction is its illuminations. In the autumn the whole Promenade and Happy Mount Park are ablaze with colour.

Marineland open daily Easter to Oct

Morwellham

Devon *p212 C2*

This small village on the river Tamar has served as a port to Tavistock since the twelfth century. Morwellham reached its peak of activity in the first half of the nineteenth century as a mining centre and an underground canal was built between town and village as a valuable link from Tavistock to the Tamar.

Now some hundred years later Morwellham Quay has been set up as an outdoor museum and recreation centre. Old workings of the port can be seen, including lime kilns and copper chutes. In the original wheel pit stands a thirty-two-foot water-wheel

The pier and attractions of this major seaside resort are enhanced on summer evenings by the spectacular sunsets over Morecambe Bay

which was brought from Dartmoor. There is also an indoor museum depicting the life and industry of the nineteenth century. Visitors can meet workers dressed in period costume or ride underground into a copper mine.

Open-air Museum open all year daily. Parking and refreshments.

Muncaster Castle and Bird Garden

Cumbria *p220 D1*

The Pennington family have owned the land here since the thirteenth century, but the present castle is mainly a nineteenth-century structure which incorporates an ancient tower.

Some Tudor fireplaces were installed and the castle has a fine collection of sixteenth- and seventeenth-century furniture, pictures and embroidery. The most interesting piece in the castle is the Luck of Muncaster – a gold and white enamelled glass bowl given by Henry VI to bring luck to the

family, after he was given refuge here following his defeat at the Battle of Hexham in 1464.

From the castle terrace there are magnificent views down the lovely Esk Valley and the gardens are superb. Rhododendrons and azaleas create a riot of colour in the spring, which is rivalled by a collection of startling ornamental and tropical birds. There is also a bear garden with Himalayan bears and a flamingo pool.

One mile from the castle is the interesting Muncaster Mill, where water from the river Mite is carried three-quarters of a mile to turn a thirteen-foot water wheel. This provides the power for the three pairs of millstones, two elevators, flour separators and a sackhoist. Flour milled here can be bought, and a new feature is a fish farm selling trout.

Castle and Garden open from Easter to Sep, Tue to Sun and Bank Holidays pm. Parking and refreshments available.
Muncaster Mill open Apr to Sep daily (except Sat). Parking available.

Newby Hall

North Yorkshire *p217 B3*

Newby Hall, a Queen Anne house built for wealthy mine owner Sir Edward Blackett at the end of the seventeenth century, lies on the north-east bank of the river Ure.

One of Yorkshire's smaller country houses, and now the home of Major R. E. J. Compton, Newby Hall is set in extensive grounds of parkland and beautifully planned gardens with their flower beds, shrubberies and rare ornaments sloping gently down to the river's edge. The house is famous for its magnificent Roman sculpture galleries, with pride of

William Weddell, owner of Newby Hall in the mid 18th century, filled the house with sculpture collected during his Grand Tour

place going to the beautiful Venus from the Barberini Palace in Rome. No less renowned is the sumptuous tapestry room, as planned by Robert Adam and hung with a complete set of Gobelin tapestries.

Other features of the house include the fine entrance hall and the furniture, much of it made by Adam and Thomas Chippendale.

Situated within the grounds of Newby Hall is the nineteenth-century village church of Christ the Consoler, noted for its Victorian stained glass windows. A miniature steam passenger-carrying railway runs through orchards and alongside the river, from which a small steam launch operates in suitable weather.

House and Garden open Easter to Sep daily, pm only. Closed Mon except Bank Holidays. Parking and Refreshments available.

New Forest Hampshire

For many centuries a royal game preserve, the area is no more a natural forest than the regimented plantations of the Forestry Commission, but was planted by order of William the Conqueror in AD 1078 for his favourite sport of deer hunting.

William I's successor, William Rufus, was also addicted to hunting, and the Rufus Stone at Stoney Cross marks the place where legend has it the arrow of one Sir Walter Tyrell, loosed at a fleeing deer, glanced off the trunk of an oak tree to mortally wound the king.

Seven hundred years ago the forest stretched from the Avon on the west to Southampton Water on the east, and from the borders of Wiltshire to the English Channel. That area is now considerably reduced, but the forest still covers 144 square miles and measures twenty miles across at its widest point. The term 'forest' is misleading, as about half of the total area termed forest is open heath, and the area is a delightful mixture of streams, green lawns shorn by ponies, rivers, ponds, cottages, leafy villages and ancient churches.

The forest divides naturally into three areas, each with a different character. The northern area is mostly open moorland covered in heather, furze and bracken – split into five parallel ridges by streams bound for the river Avon.

Here and there thickets, pine woods, old woods and Forestry Commission plantations replace the heather and gorse.

The middle region is truer to what is commonly understood by forest. It is an area of woodlands interspersed with glades – old woods in every state of maturity and decay. Complementing these old woods are thickets and plantations, or enclosures, of young trees. The exceptions are the cultivated lands around Lyndhurst, Minstead and Burley, and a heathland that stretches from Brockenhurst to Thorny Hill to Burley, and then on to Bratley Plain. The woods provide many pleasant walks, and it is only on foot or horseback that the forest can be truly appreciated. The woods are splendid in any season. In the winter they are carpeted with fallen leaves, the branches hang with grey lichen and gnarled roots are covered with vivid green moss hiding fungi and ferns. Spring revitalises the forest with young green and in summer the woods produce flowering honeysuckle, foxgloves and banks of tall, cool bracken. New Forest ponies and deer wander freely about the woods.

Bounded on the southern side by a low-lying stretch of cultivated land beside the Solent, the southern part of the Forest lies inland from Sway Common to Butts Ash. It consists of bare heathland, overgrown in places by Scots Pine, cut by well-wooded valleys of numerous streams. Farther inland the land dips down above sea level, and bogs stretch from Hinchesley, Brockenhurst and Beaulieu Road to Ashurst. From here the ground gradually rises northwards to Ramnor Park Hill woods and on to Lyndhurst. Birch and holly are found in the lowlands, the holly once cropped for its berries at Christmas and sent by rail to London.

The Rufus Stone records the death of William II on August 2, 1100

The forest is unique in retaining the ancient Court of Verderers, which administers the laws of the forest. The ten members directly protect the well-being of the commoners and animals – their laws, for example, give wildlife priority on the roads, and there are strict

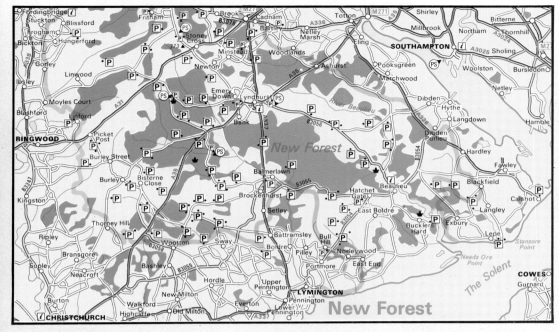

hunt them during the winter.

Otters inhabit the river Avon and several of the smaller streams, while the solitary badger lives under the big oak and beech woods. The Grey squirrel has here, as in many places, replaced the native Red squirrel, but all the British species of bats, save one, live within the New Forest.

It is a paradise for the bird-watcher, and houses species scarce elsewhere in Britain. The common buzzard, the legendary Dartford warbler, occasionally Montagu's harrier, siskin and pied flycatcher number among the many unusual nesting birds. Green woodpeckers can be heard in the woods, and the jaunty jay and magpie are forever present. Woodlarks, nightjars and nightingales, gold crests, redstarts and marsh tits are a few of the numerous species breeding within the boundaries of the forest in a variety of habitats. Winter visitors include siskins and bramblings, and the coastal haunts of the forest play host to waders and occasionally to rarely seen birds such as osprey, avocet and spoonbills.

The area is also renowned for its butterflies, and species include the Queen of Spain fritillary, Camberwell Beauty, Brown Argus and Silver-Studded Blue.

rules against the public feeding the animals.

The forest officers, called Agisters, patrol the forest on horseback dressed in traditional green, watching over the land and enforcing the laws. One of their duties is to cut the tails of the New Forest ponies, to show that the owners have paid their dues – any

found unmarked are impounded and the owner fined. By careful selection of those stallions allowed into the forest, the Verderers have greatly improved the New Forest breed, established since Norman times. All the ponies are annually rounded up in the spring for the marking of any foals and selling at auction.

Right: Market day in Ringwood – a pretty town on the edge of the forest and an ideal touring centre

The variety of wildlife in the forest can rarely be matched in Britain. Matley Bog is an example of an area which is still a sanctuary for rare plants and insects. Red deer, Fallow deer, Roe and Japanese Sika deer live in the forest, and are kept in check by the Forestry Commission and the New Forest Buckhounds which

Newquay

Cornwall *p211 B2*

The town first became prosperous during the sixteenth century as a centre for pilchard fishing. Huer's Hut, on the western headland, dates from this period when the 'Huer' kept watch for pilchard shoals and alerted the fishermen when one was sighted. It was not until the late nineteenth century that Newquay realised its potential as a holiday centre and exploited its 650 acres of beautiful white sands. In spite of a certain lack of character in its buildings, it is now established as Cornwall's largest resort, and is probably the best place for surfing in Britain, attracting international surfing champions.

The main part of the town overlooks Towan Beach which is somewhat sheltered from the Atlantic breakers, and therefore especially suitable for children. It is illegal on any beach to swim when red danger flags are flying. There is a paddling pool at the foot of 'the Island' – a rocky outcrop connected to the mainland by a suspension bridge – and rock pools and caves here fascinate both children and adults. High cliffs make most of the beaches accessible only to the young and fit.

Periodically throughout the summer, several thirty-foot boats race each other round a six-mile course in the bay. These were once Newquay pilot gigs that competed for the lucrative job of landing a pilot on an incoming ship. Deep-sea fishing boats may be chartered at the harbour, which is enclosed by cliffs and two granite piers.

The main amusement area is around Trenance Park, where a boating lake, miniature railway, outdoor swimming pool, trampolines and a zoo are to be found.

Towan Beach and the Island at Newquay

Other attractions include a golf driving range, a toboggan run, and facilities for bowls, pitch-and-putt and tennis and a golf course on the cliffs above Fistral Bay. There are opportunities for pleasant coastal walks, especially around East Pentire which has lovely views; and the rocky headlands such as Porth, with its island which was a prehistoric camp, are interesting to explore.

Zoo open Apr to Oct daily. Parking and refreshments available.

Newstead Abbey

Nottinghamshire *p217 B1*

Founded as an Augustine Priory around 1170 by Henry II, possibly as part of his atonement for the murder of Becket, Newstead Abbey now stands resplendent as a stately home.

After the Reformation, the abbey was sold by Henry VIII to Sir John Byron for the sum of £810. Documentation of this sale has been preserved, along with other deeds relating to the abbey's history. Successive generations of Byrons adapted the monastic buildings into a comfortable dwelling, incorporating much of the medieval architecture into their designs. The west façade of the thirteenth-century priory church, the fifteenth-century cloister and the old chapter house, now converted into a chapel, have survived virtually in their original form.

By far the most famous occupant of the house was the 6th Lord, the poet, who owned the abbey from 1798 until 1817. Many relics of Lord Byron have been retained, including his bedroom containing the gilt four-poster bed which he had at Trinity College, Cambridge, and his writing table. The Byron Gallery houses many of the poet's treasures, such as the helmet he designed for the Greek campaign of liberty against the Turks, in which Byron fought and died.

Newstead Abbey is justly famous for its fine gardens with lakes, waterfalls, rock gardens and a Japanese garden representing the design on a willow-patterned plate. A monument to Boatswain, Lord Byron's beloved Newfoundland dog, stands near the Eagle Pond, with lines composed by the poet engraved on its pedestal.

Open Easter to Sep daily, pm only. Garden open all year daily (except 25 Dec). Parking and refreshments (summer only) available.

Norfolk Broads Norfolk

The Norfolk Broads have become one of the most popular holiday haunts in England – not too far from London and the hinterland of Great Yarmouth. They have become a haven for amateur sailors and all those who enjoy 'messing about in boats'.

The 200 miles of waterways, part lakes and part rivers, weave their way through a quiet and charming countryside in an area bounded by Norwich, Beccles, Lowestoft, Great Yarmouth and North Walsham. In general, the waterways lie away from the roads and often private land separates the motorist from the water's edge. Indeed, between Acle and Yarmouth, where the country is flat, the only evidence of the Broad's existence is the appearance of sails apparently gliding over the flat fields.

However, the land is not in fact entirely flat. In many places steep banks rise from the rivers, and below Norwich, hills rise to the south of the river Yare, and a ridge of high ground to the north separates it from the river Bure where many of the Broads are grouped. Higher ground to the south-east of Norwich causes the river Waveney to make a wide sweep before it joins the Yare at Breydon Water. It is the area west of Great Yarmouth, as far inland as Acle on the river Bure, which is virtually uninhabited, flat marshland, broken only by the sails of boats and the stark silhouettes of windmills – at Horsey, Reedham and Herringfleet there are particularly fine windmills.

Surprisingly, the Broads are man-made. It was not until the post-war years that it was realised that these natural-looking lakes were the result of extensive peat digging by the Anglo-Saxons, who used the peat as a source of fuel. A change in the land and sea levels caused the pits to flood, so creating the shallow lakes known as the Broads. The process of peat formation has resumed, and since the nineteenth century it has been noticed that the 'meres' are shrinking by silting up with dead vegetation. The exception is Breydon Water, the largest of the Broads, which is a tidal landlocked estuary of the rivers Yare and Waveney, separated from the sea by a sandbar upon which stands Great Yarmouth.

The Broads vary considerably in character. Wroxham and Salhouse are surrounded by woodlands and gently sloping

grassland leading down to the water's edge, while the northern Broads and Rockland Broad, connected with the river Yare, are fringed by reedbeds. The upper reaches generally are wooded and unspoilt.

In the past, the villagers utilised the Broads for trade, and built trading wherries – broad shallow draught boats with a single tall mast which sailed under the power of one huge brown or black sail. The word wherry comes from the Scandinavian, and betrays the past presence of the Danes, who colonised East Anglia. One of the cargoes these craft carried was possibly the harvested reeds which grow in abundance around the shores of the northern Broads. Many people associate the Broads with the famous local thatching and although not as finely worked and decorative as straw thatch, it lasts a good deal longer. With the mini-revival of thatch as a roofing material, the small band of remaining craftsmen in Norfolk are in great demand, so the craft may well be saved from dying out.

Many of the villages in the area stand back a mile or two from the water and are easily missed, which is a pity as several of them are extremely attractive and nearly all have ancient churches of interest.

Those villages near to the water

have developed thriving boat building and hiring industries, and cater to the amateur yachts'-man's every need. A place of particular interest is the site of the ruins of St Benet's Abbey, which is only accessible by water. Founded in AD 955 on the banks of the river Bure, the Bishop of Norwich still travels there by boat every August Bank Holiday to hold an open-air mass.

The wildlife of the Broads is plentiful, and a number of unusual creatures inhabit the reedbeds, woods and marshland. On the open water the great crested grebe, mallard and teal are a common sight, and semi-tame Greylag and Canada geese are present all the year round. The reedbeds conceal some unusual birds. The rare bittern is not often seen, but its strange booming call heard at night time has sent shivers down many a spine. The charming bearded-tit, or reed pheasant, also makes its home amongst the reeds and lapwing and snipe live on the marshland. In the woods the Green woodpecker can often be heard hammering at bark in search of small insects and grubs, and the noise echoes about the tree-tops. An unusual animal, and something of a pest, is the coypu. Originally from South America this largest of rodents (the size of a small dog) is a strong swimmer, and does

much damage to crops. Due to its semi-aquatic life, a curious adaption is the row of teats along the female's back, allowing the young to cling there and feed while the mother is in the water. For the fisherman, roach, perch, pike, rudd, bream, tench, eels and the occasional trout can be taken.

A bonus for the holiday-maker is the climate. The area boasts the least rainfall in England, although the evening breezes can

be chilly. Because of the mildness of the weather, the Broads are one of the few habitats where the exotic swallowtail butterfly breeds.

Boats are easily hired, and the tourist afloat is well catered for, whether for the day or a fortnight. Few waterways are restricted, and as long as channels are followed and safety rules obeyed, there is no better way to explore this charming corner of East Anglia.

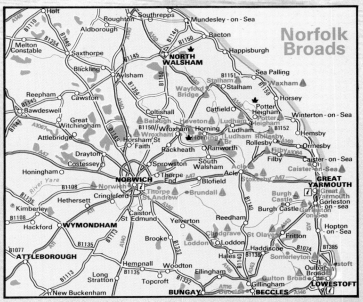

Hickling water nature trail in Norfolk Wildlife Park

Norfolk Wildlife Park

Norfolk *p218 E1*

Founded in 1962 by the famous naturalist Philip Wayre, the Norfolk Wildlife Park is now regarded as the largest collection of European animals and birds in the world. The park tends to specialise in breeding and it can boast a number of firsts in this field – for example, it produced the first European otters bred in captivity in Britain since the nineteenth century, and the first lynx for over thirty years. Rare Eagle owls have also been bred here for a number of years. Animals include beavers, bison, bears, ibex, seals, wolves, Barbary apes, badgers and a large number of European birds, which are displayed in specially constructed aviaries.

The park is also the home of the Pheasant Trust which safeguards rare and endangered species. Swinhoe's pheasant, from the island of Taiwan, and the Mikado pheasant are two whose continued existence has been ensured.

Open all year daily. Parking and refreshments available.

Norham Castle

Northumberland *p220 F4*

The river Tweed, winding its way past the ruins of Norham Castle, marks the boundary here between England and Scotland. A stone fortress called Norham Castle was built during the twelfth century. It replaced a wooden one, and continued to defend this strategic position by a ford in the river. However, border skirmishes over the centuries took their toll, and today the castle stands in ruins with only parts of the lofty keep, gates and inner and outer baileys remaining. Enough remains though to indicate the former strength of the castle with the keep walls rising up to some ninety feet. Towers and turrets are still in evidence around the outer walls.

See AM info.

North Norfolk Railway

Norfolk *p218 E1*

From its headquarters at Sheringham Station, the North Norfolk Railway operates over three miles of track to Weybourne, once part of the Midland and Great Northern Joint Railway, and it is hoped to extend the line as far as Holt. Sheringham station has a collection of steam locomotives and rolling stock, some undergoing and some awaiting restoration. There are several industrial tank engines and two examples of ex-Great Eastern Railway main line engines. Rolling stock includes many suburban coaches, the Brighton Belle, Pullman cars and directors' private saloons, and there is a railway museum – including a model railway.

Sheringham Station open Easter to Sep daily. Steam-hauled trains operate Easter and Spring Bank Holiday weekends, then Sun and certain weekdays throughout the summer until Sep. (daily in Aug).

Right: A replica of *Locomotion* in steam at the Beamish Open Air Museum – the original ran in 1825

Below: The evocative ruin of Norham Castle is set high up on rocks above the winding river Tweed

North of England Open Air Museum

Co Durham *p217 B5*

Covering some 200 acres of park and woodland, this fascinating open-air museum at Beamish was the first of its kind in England. It consists of a large collection of buildings imaginatively reconstructed and grouped into areas to illustrate the past way of life in north-east England.

The Town has co-operative shops, Georgian town houses, a Victorian pub and stables, a printers' workshop and its own park. Various shops and buildings house small exhibitions, including Victorian toys and games, a nineteenth-century school classroom and traditional crafts such as Durham quilting and slipware pottery.

Rowley Station, first built in 1867, has been rebuilt here in the railway area and includes the station office, furnished as it would have been during the latter days of the North Eastern Railway Company. An N.E.R. Class C locomotive is regularly kept in steam during the summer months. The station is complete with weighbridge, signals, ticket office, waiting room and footbridge.

A Victorian colliery has also been recreated here in another area, complete with traditionally furnished pitmens cottages. It features a typical north-east steam-winding engine of 1855. Boilers, originally from Shotton colliery, provide the steam for all the colliery engines. A full-scale working model of *Locomotion No. 1*, a replica of the original built by Stephenson in 1825, can also be seen in the colliery, and there are even guided tours down a 'drift' mine.

The Home Farm, established for some 250 years, houses a collection of agricultural machinery and tools. A cart collection is housed in the rebuilt cartshed to the rear of the farm.

It is also possible to ride on an old electric tramcar from the museum's large transport collection, which carries the visitor between the different areas

Open all year daily. Closed Mon from Sep to Easter. Parking and refreshments available.

Norton Priory

Cheshire *p216 E3*

Norton Priory, the most fully excavated monastic site in Britain, is situated close to Astmoor on the eastern outskirts of Runcorn.

Founded by Augstinian monks in the twelfth century, it flourished until the Dissolution of the monasteries brought about its closure in 1536. Some years later it was acquired by the Brooke family who made it their home, building a Tudor mansion in the outer courtyard. This was replaced in the eighteenth century by a Georgian house which remained until 1928, when it fell into decay. In 1970, work started on the excavation of the site which proved to be far more interesting than anyone had realised. The remains included a medieval vaulted room in which exhibitions are held and a very large model of the priory church may be seen in the cloister. The sandstone coffins which were uncovered during the excavation of the church, the east cloister walk and the chapter house are vivid evidence of the fact that many people were buried at Norton.

Norton Priory is surrounded by some seven acres of woodland and a museum here displays excavated floor tiles, carved stonework, ceramics and an exhibition about medieval monastic life. Excavation work still continues at certain times of the year.

Open daily (except Christmas) pm only.

Norwich   Norfolk   *p213 D5*

Over 1,000 years old, Norwich is a truly English city with an individuality and independence born of isolation. It is still a pleasure to wander among the medieval streets — particularly Elm Hill, the evocative cobbled thoroughfare which is now the centre of the city's flourishing antique trade.

Market day in Norwich, with the castle beyond rising above the town

A large and important city since the Norman conquest, Norwich prospered as a textile centre in the fourteenth century and this industry was revived some 200 years later when settlers came over from the Netherlands and introduced their crafts and skills.

Prosperity and forward-looking attitudes have always characterized Norwich, and the vast modern shopping centre of Anglia Square, and the unusual new buildings of the University of East Anglia, testify to this. However, the preservation of old Norwich is a prime concern of the city, and its different architectural styles complement, rather than detract from, each other. A link between the two is the colourful open-air market that has taken place every weekday since Norman times, and is still very much part of the city's life.

Norwich's Norman Cathedral

The Cathedral

Rising in Norman splendour from the spacious surrounds of the Cathedral Close, the Church of Holy and Undivided Trinity is as magnificent and awe-inspiring as it must have appeared to those who saw it consecrated in 1278.

Apart from the stone vaulting and clerestory windows, the architecture is purely Norman. The survival of the semi-circular east end is unique in northern Europe and houses a stone bishop's throne, possibly 1,000 years old. Beautiful gilded and painted bosses decorate the vaulting and those in the cloisters are particularly outstanding examples of medieval craftsmanship.

Within the Close, which leads down to the river, are many medieval buildings. Some now house a school established in 1553 as the Edward VI Grammar School. Perhaps the most famous scholar here was Horatio Nelson, whose statue stands in the close.

Pull's Ferry, a great beauty spot on the river, is a fifteenth-century watergate which once marked the entrance to a small canal which was built especially to transport building materials to the cathedral.

Strangers' Hall

This ancient merchant's house, the earliest parts dating from about 1320, is now a fascinating museum depicting English domestic life. Built around three courtyards, the house was constantly enlarged and rebuilt by successive wealthy owners, resulting in a delightfully rambling place of many different periods. Twenty-three of its rooms are open to the public, furnished in periods ranging from early Tudor to late Victorian.

Two of the finest rooms have special attractions. The great hall

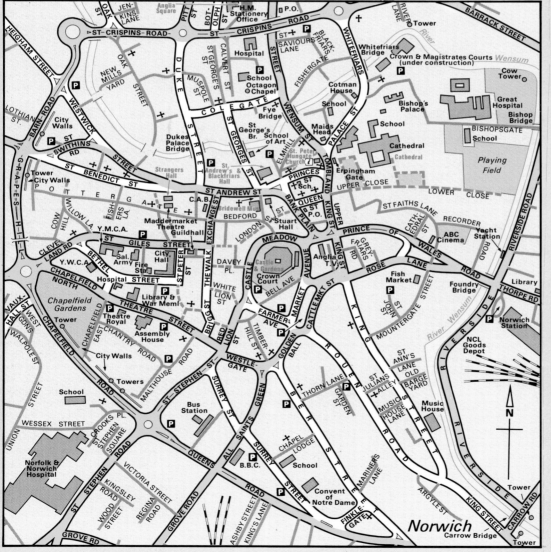

Norwich

– the most impressive – has a crown-post roof, a minstrel's gallery, an early Tudor bay window, a staircase of 1627 and on its walls hang superb Flemish tapestries, woven about 1485. Adjoining the great hall is the Georgian Room, the dining room of the Assize Judge, who had his official lodgings here. The room is notable for the fine furniture it contains, and the magnificent chandelier made of Irish glass.

Stranger's Hall derives its name from the building's association with Flemish weavers, who were encouraged to settle in Norwich at the end of the sixteenth century to revitalise the textile industry.

St Andrew's Hall
This was the home of the Dominican Friars up until the Reformation, when the Norwich Corporation bought the Hall for use as a public building. The Blackfriars Hall at the east end was originally the chancel of the Friar's church. Events which have occurred here since the sixteenth century include Charles II's knighting of Sir Thomas Browne; the celebration of the opening of the city's railway; and the entertainment of King Edward VII, George V and George VI. The Triennial Music Festival began here in 1824, and has played host to many notable names in the world of music.

Bridewell Museum
The Bridewell Museum is housed in part of a fourteenth-century merchant's house – used as a prison for tramps and beggars in 1583. In the courtyard can be seen various dates and initials scratched by prisoners. Now a museum of local industries, there is a room devoted to agriculture, a room displaying cloths and looms of the old textile industry, and another room of exhibits relating

The water-gate at Pull's Ferry.

to the boot and shoe industry, including footwear from Tudor times to the present day. Other industries recalled here are metalwork – partly represented by a smithy; the building industry, demonstrating traditional techniques; and clockmaking.

The Castle
Norwich's castle, built in the twelfth century, has one of the finest Norman keeps in England. It consists of a great stone tower seventy feet high decorated by tiers of blank arcading which were carefully restored in 1834.

The castle was adapted as a splendid museum, after being a county jail from 1220 to 1887. In the art galleries of the museum is an unrivalled collection of paintings by John Sell Cotman, and works by other artists of the Norwich School, such as John Crome.

Other exhibits reflect the history and culture of the Norwich region over the centuries. In the Geology Gallery can be seen the fossilised foot of a plesiosaur. The Archaeological Gallery contains beautiful Iron Age gold necklaces, and a wonderfully decorated Roman parade cavalry helmet and visor of gilding metal.

In the keep is a case of bones from local sites – one skull shows the effects of a battle axe. On a more festive note are two large brightly painted snapdragons, built of wickerwork and canvas, once used for state processions.

Weapons, coins, stamps, domestic trivia, glass and many other collections, cater for every interest.

St Peter Hungate
Early this century, the medieval church of St Peter Hungate was threatened with demolition, but fortunately was saved to be used as a Museum of Church Art and Craftsmanship. It now provides an apt setting for the exhibits which include illuminated manuscript service-books, Russian icons, musical instruments (once played in church) and, most unusual, a fourteenth-century coffin complete with a skeleton.

Strangers' Hall open all year (except Christmas, New Year, Good Fri and Sun).
Bridewell open as above.
Castle open all year (except Christmas New Year and Good Fri) daily, Sun, pm only. Refreshments available.
St Peter Hungate Church Museum Open all year daily (except Christmas, New Year, Good Fri and Sun).

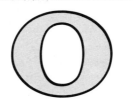

Oakhill Manor
Somerset *p212 E3*

The little village of Oakhill lies high in the Mendip Hills. Close by is Oakhill Manor, incorporating The World of Models at Oakhill Manor – a display of models paying tribute to great British engineers of the past, and the British craftsmen who brought their dreams to fruition. A small, private country estate of some forty-five acres, the manor is a fine example of one of England's smaller country houses. Attractively furnished, all the principal rooms and many of the lesser ones have been used to display the magnificently comprehensive collection of models and pictures embracing land, sea and air transport.

The house itself is set in eight acres of wooded and formal gardens, and a miniature railway, complete with stations in Mendip stone, transports visitors from the car park to the manor. The three-quarter-mile scenic route incorporates cuttings, embankments, bridges and even its own miniature Cheddar Gorge.

Open Easter to early Nov daily. Parking and refreshments available.

Oban
Strathclyde *p219 B5*

Oban was no more than a small fishing village with a single inn when Dr Johnson and Boswell stayed there in 1773 on their famous tour of the Highlands, but it

has since grown considerably in size and importance. It is now both the Gateway to the Western Isles, with regular ferry services, and a centre for those attracted by the grandeur of the western Highlands. The town has much to offer those who enjoy natural beauty and traditional entertainment, and its magnificent setting combines the delights of a busy harbour with views across the Sound of Mull to a backdrop of blue mountains.

The town stretches along a flat seafront, backed by a wooded escarpment with more buildings on a higher level. Behind these terraces stands Oban Hill with the skeleton of an abandoned Victorian hydro, and Battery Hill with its strange semi-completed edifice resembling Rome's Colosseum. This was built in the 1890s by a Mr MacCaig to provide work for the town's unemployed, but his worthwhile, though eccentric, project was abandoned when he died.

The bay is a popular yachting and boating centre, and is home port to a fishing fleet. Fish auctions are held on Railway Pier, and motor boats take sightseers out to a seal island, and short cruises are available to such places of interest as Iona.

Oban is also the centre of an agricultural area, with a thriving livestock market. Local industry includes MacDonalds Mill, a tweed mill with a historical display and showroom open to the public, a glass factory, and a whisky distillery. At the end of August the Argyllshire Highland Gathering draws the crowds, and other events with a Scottish flavour are the game of shinty, a game similar to hockey, in Mossfield Park, and performances by the Oban Pipe Band.

MacDonalds Mill open Mar to Oct daily. Demonstrations Mon to Fri only. Parking and refreshments.

Car ferries sail for the Hebrides from the harbour at Oban

Moated Oxburgh Hall was fortified against possible civil unrest

Oxburgh Hall

Norfolk *p213C5*

Surrounded by a formal moat, this building resembling a fortress was built in the late fifteenth century by Sir Edmund Bedingfeld, whose descendants still live here. The outstanding feature of Oxburgh Hall is the magnificent eighty-foot-high gatehouse which, unlike the rest of the house, was spared from Victorian restoration. Two wings, built around a central courtyard, are decorated with battlements, decorated chimneys, oriels and elaborate windows. The interior is mainly Victorian except for the rooms in the gatehouse which have retained their original form; the King's Room where Henry VII was lodged in 1487 is furnished with a bed dated 1687, and wall hangings with panels worked by Mary Queen of Scots and by Elizabeth, Countess of Shrewsbury. The Queen's Room is hung with an elaborate tapestry of Oxfordshire and Buckinghamshire. A spiral staircase links the chambers and the roof, from which there are fine views over the surrounding countryside. The contrasting Victorian rooms, dark and richly patterned, are filled with memorabilia of the Bedingfelds.

In the grounds outside the moat is an interesting parterre garden of French design, laid out to the designs of Alexandre le Blond.

Open Apr and Oct weekends. May to Sep, Sat to Wed, pm only. Also Bank Hol Mon. NT.

Oxford Oxfordshire *p213A3*

Bounded by the Isis and willow-lined Cherwell, this city of ancient spires scattered with high walls, medieval gateways and enchanting college precincts, glories as the oldest and most respected academic seat in Britain.

The history of Oxford's university is almost as old as the origins of the city itself. Although a Saxon settlement (called Oxenford) developed around the place where ox-drovers crossed the river Thames, it was not until the twelfth century that the town really began to grow. This came about when Henry II ordered all English students studying abroad to return to England immediately. For various reasons, many of them converged at Oxford and so the scholarly character of the town was established.

Today there are twenty-eight colleges in Oxford and most of them are within walking distance of the High Street. Student life is always apparent in the city, the streets teeming with students on bicycles, and during summer, the rivers are alive with boats. These are either punts, or rowing boats practising hard for the numerous summer river events.

Ashmolean Museum

The Ashmolean Museum of Art and Archaeology first opened its doors in 1683 and the collection expanded to such an extent that in 1845 the stately New Ashmolean was built to house it.

This, the oldest museum in the country, is famed throughout Europe. The main exhibits are archaeological, of British, European, Mediterranean, Egyptian and near-Eastern origins. Coin collections and medals from all countries and periods are kept in the Heberden Coin Room, and other rooms hold examples of European ceramics, English silver, Chinese and Japanese porcelain, painting and lacquer, Tibetan art, Indian sculpture and paintings, Islamic pottery and metalwork, and Chinese bronzes.

The galleries are hung with Italian, Dutch, Flemish, French and English oil paintings; Old Masters and modern drawings; watercolours; prints; miniatures; and the Hope collection of engraved portraits.

St Edmund's Hall

This delightful small college is everyone's idea of an Oxford College. Once through the little archway this, the last of the medieval Halls appears as a world in miniature. It is a gentle and scholarly place, giving the impression of having been rather haphazardly planned, the buildings surrounding a green square overlooked by mullioned windows and golden stone. The little Classical chapel has above it the original college library, which still continues the medieval tradition of chaining up its books.

Magdalen College

Beneath Magdalen Bridge runs the river Cherwell, and beside it stands the college, founded in 1458. From the top of the striking bell-tower, choristers sing at sunrise on Mayday to tired but happy crowds below, in celebration of the beginning of summer. The peaceful haven of the quadrangle is surrounded by cloisters, and above the west walk, venerable manuscripts lie in the library.

The New Buildings of 1773 merge exceptionally well with the old and overlook the Grove – the deer park within the grounds where open-air plays are performed every summer.

Museum of the History of Science

This first home of Elias Ashmole's collection, in which the Ashmolean Museum has its origins, is among the foremost Classical buildings of the city, and has been used since 1939 as the Museum of the History of Sci-

Magdalen Tower and Bridge – the scene of Oxford's May Day celebrations

ence. Here is the finest collection of early astronomical, mathematical and optical instruments in the world. Many of the exhibits are artistic as well as scientific, such as the sun-dials and the orreries – mechanisms which represent the motions of planets.

The Sheldonian Theatre

This was designed by Sir Christopher Wren in likeness to a Roman theatre in 1669. From the cupola, practically all the important buildings in Oxford can be seen. The interior of the theatre, with its tiered seats, gallery and Vice-chancellor's chair, is elegantly decorated beneath a beautifully painted ceiling. The university awards its degrees here.

The Radcliffe Camera

The Bodleian Library

The Bodleian Library, second only in size to the Vatican's library, holds in excess of three million volumes and possesses many of the oldest manuscripts in existence. These include a seventh-century manuscript of the Acts of the Apostles, used by the Venerable Bede. Founded by Humphrey, the Duke of Gloucester, in 1480, and reformed by Sir Thomas Bodley in 1598, the library consists of 'Duke Humphrey', the oldest part on the upper storey of the glorious Tudor Divinity School, the huge New Bodleian building, and the Radcliffe Camera of 1737, beneath which great subterranean bookstacks store 600,000 books.

Merton College

Merton is one of the three oldest colleges in Oxford, founded in 1264. The old city wall encloses part of the college, and, like many of the colleges, has beautiful gardens. The original Hall, though much altered, still stands but the outstanding buildings are the library and chapel. In the library is the helmet of Sir Thomas Bordley, founder of the Bodleian library, and the chapel is renowned for its thirteenth and fourteenth-century glass, and its choir.

Christ Church College

Cardinal Wolsey founded the college in 1525, on one of the loveliest sites in Oxford, overlooking lush water meadows which sweep down to the rivers Thames and Cherwell. From Christopher Wren's Tom Tower, high above the gateway, rings Great Tom, an ancient bell taken from Osney Abbey. The college has amongst its buildings the smallest cathedral in England, which contains architectural features from the twelfth to fifteenth centuries.

Trinity College

Trinity is the traditional academic rival of Balliol College. The mainly nineteenth-century building stands at the end of Broad Street, a pleasant, wide road where Oxford's leading booksellers are found.

One of the most notable features of the college is its chapel, which holds an alabaster tomb of Sir Thomas Pope (the founder), and has a screen and altarpiece carved by Grinling Gibbons.

Ashmolean Museum open all year (except Mon, Christmas, New Year, Easter and during St Giles Fair in early Sep). Sun pm only.

Colleges open to the public most afternoons though some restrictions during term times.

Museum of the History of Science open all year Mon to Fri (except Christmas and after Easter weeks).

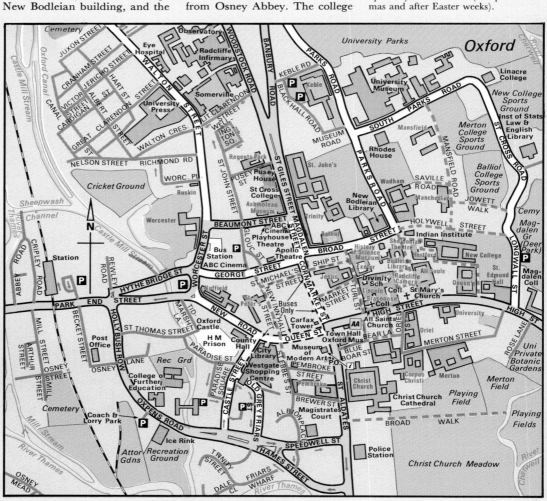

P

Packwood House

Warwickshire *p216 F1*

Originally a sixteenth-century farmhouse of modest proportions, Packwood House was extended during the seventeenth century and a large range of outbuildings was added to it. The result is a pleasing blend of two styles, carefully restored by the National Trust.

Interior furnishings, both interesting and valuable, include Jacobean panelling, seventeenth-century furniture, Italian needlework and French and Flemish tapestries. The gardens are particularly famous for the layout of clipped yew trees of various sizes, which represent the Sermon on the Mount. Another interesting feature of the gardens is a wall with a series of niches designed to hold beehives.

Open Apr to Sep Wed to Sun and Bank Holiday Mon pm only. Oct Sat and Sun pm only. Refreshments available. NT.

Paignton

Devon *p212 D2*

Paignton has a mild climate, gently-sloping reddish sands, and plenty to offer by way of entertainment. Lawns, play areas and beach huts line the front, with hotels and guesthouses galore on the other side of the esplanade.

The town has developed very swiftly over the last century, effectively obliterating the original village. The Church of St John, on the site of a Bronze Age settlement, was established in Saxon times, and has a Norman font and west door, although the present structure dates mainly from the fifteenth century. Next to it is all that remains of the erstwhile palace of the Bishops of Exeter, known as Coverdale Tower after the sixteenth-century Bishop who translated the Bible into English. Fifteenth-century Kirkham House, which is open to the public, was the home of the family responsible for building the chantry of St John's Church. Oldway

The pretty walled flower gardens of Packwood House

Mansion, built by Isaac Singer and his son with some of the millions derived from their sewing machine company, has a hundred rooms and was modelled on Versailles and the Paris Opera.

Floats and diving rafts, as well as deck chairs, can be hired from the beaches, and pleasure trips run from the small harbour. South of the pleasure pier is the Festival Hall, surrounded by gardens with a mini-golf course, and beyond the harbour and Roundham Head are the well-kept gardens of Goodrington Cliff, with its zig-zag path leading to a holiday centre and amusement area.

Other delights include the Torbay and Dartmouth Railway with steam trains running between Paignton and Kingswear; opentopped double-decker buses along the front; the Torbay Aircraft Museum just inland at Higher Blagdon, which contains eighteen aircraft dating from 1924 to 1954, an indoor aeronautic exhibition, and a section devoted to World War I aces. Paignton Zoo, set amidst seventy-five acres of grounds full of exotic plants, contains a world-wide collection of birds and animals.

Kirkham House open Apr to Sep daily, pm only on Sun. AM.
Oldway open May to Sep daily, Sun pm only, Oct to Apr Mon to Fri only. Closed occasionally for Council purposes. Parking and refreshments (in summer) available.
Torbay Aircraft Museum open late Mar to early Nov daily. Parking and refreshments available.
Torbay and Dartmouth Railway open Easter Bank Hol and June to Sep daily. Parking available.
Zoological and Botanical Gardens open all year (except 25 Dec) daily. Parking and refreshments available.

Pembroke Castle

Dyfed *p211 B4*

The castle stands on a rocky promontory lapped by the tidal waters of Milford Haven on three sides. Its towers and circular defensive walls encompass a seventy-five foot high, round keep, unique in its design, with walls some nineteen feet thick at the base. Another unusual feature is the Wogan cavern, a high natural cave in the limestone rock below the Northern Hill, probably used as a store room and boat house.

The wood and turf forerunner of this massive fortress was established by Arnulf of Montgomery towards the end of the eleventh century, as a base from which to subdue the turbulent Welsh. Arnulf retained it until 1102 when his part in the unsuccessful rebellion launched by his brother, Robert of Bellême, against Henry I, led to his possessions being confiscated by the Crown. Pembroke passed into the hands of the Clare family, who were the first Earls of Pembroke. They enlarged and strengthened the castle and a subsequent Earl, William Marshall, Marshal of England, was probably responsible for the construction of the fortress in its present form, building the keep and the Norman hall between 1189 and 1245.

Perhaps the most famous occupants of the castle were the Tudors. Jasper, half-brother of Henry VI, was created Earl of Pembroke in 1453 and his nephew, Henry Richmond, was born there in 1456, probably in a room on the first storey of what is now known as the Henry VII Tower near the gatehouse. Although the young Henry and his uncle were forced to flee the country during the Wars of the Roses, they returned in 1485, gathered their forces and seized the crown of England on Bosworth Field.

After the Civil War the castle fell into disrepair until 1880 when Mr J. R. Cobb spent three years carrying out restoration to the original design.

Open daily all year (except Sun, Oct to Easter, Dec 25 and 1 Jan).

The impressive fortifications of Pembroke Castle

Pembrokeshire Coast National Park Dyfed

The most westerly peninsula in Wales is scattered with relics of past peoples, and around every little village or chapel are woven curious legends and often stranger facts. Along the coasts grey seals gambol in grey-blue waters, and fulmars battle with the heady winds. Inland walls, built at the dawn of the Christian era, divide the rich, fertile countryside.

Whitesand Bay near St David's is typical of Pembrokeshire's coast

Over one third of Pembrokeshire is designated a National Park. The area includes the coastal belt, outlying islands and the Preseli Hills. It is a wonderfully varied countryside of imposing cliffs, secret coves and sandy beaches, hills and moorland, wooded valleys and fast flowing streams.

The coast is easily and enjoyably accessible by way of the coastal path which stretches 167 miles from the old fishing village of St Dogmaels on the estuary of the Teifi to Amroth.

Working from north to south, the path first climbs to Cemaes Head and follows high cliffs to Newport, passing by an Iron Age hill-fort at Pen-Castell and fulmar breeding grounds, with fine views over the Newport Sands and the Nyfe estuary. At Newport the town clusters beneath a Norman Castle and the Iron Age hill-fort which crowns the summit of Carn Ingli, where St Brynach is said to have communed with angels.

Heading towards Fishguard the path takes the line of rugged cliffs, and once past the sheltered harbour, near the place where the last invasion of Britain took place in 1797), it continues along the indented coastline of Strumble Head, weaving its way towards St David's Head, a bare, windswept plateau whose coast is the breeding ground for seals, and where peregrine falcons and choughs may be sighted.

The path sweeps round Whitesand Bay with its sixth-century sailor's chapel – one of several from which St Patrick is supposed to have set out from on his last journey to Ireland. Just beyond Porth Clais is the chapel of St Non, mother of St David, where the patron saint is said to have been born during a great gale. Past the tiny inlet and village of Solva, a gay assembly of colour-washed cottages typical of

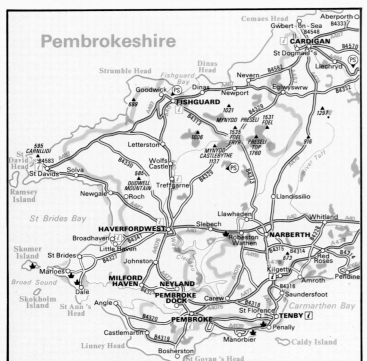

many along this stretch, the path arrives at Newgale, which has the largest beach in Pembrokeshire, some two miles of golden sands, and at low tide the fossilised remains of the forest which once covered the area can be seen. Beyond, the path turns south along St Bride's Bay to the popular little resorts of Broad Haven and Little Haven.

To the south-west the path rounds the Marloes-Dale Peninsula and takes in Martin's Haven and Marloes Sands on its way to St Anne's Head. Then the path turns northward for Dale, the sunniest place in Wales and a busy yachting centre, and across the estuary to St Ishmael's. There is a second crossing at Sandy Haven, both of which can only be crossed at low tide. The path follows the shores of the vast natural harbour of Milford Haven. Once past the town, the path continues on to the Cleddau Bridge and the southern shore of the estuary, via Pembroke Dock and Pembroke. The path returns to the shore at Pwllcrochan. It continues on round Angle Bay, and the Angle Peninsula to turn eastwards for the home straight.

Before St Govan's Head, a little inland, is Bosherston, famous for its water-lily ponds and its mere, out of which it was believed came Arthur's sword, Excalibur. Deep in a cleft in the cliffs is St Govan's Chapel, probably St Gawaine's cell. A rock by the chapel is said to hold a silver bell, which rings out when the rock is struck.

Past St Govan's Head the path continues along the towering cliffs, until it arrives at Tenby, the only sizeable resort along the coast. Beyond, the path follows the shores of Carmarthen Bay through Saundersfoot to the path's end at Amroth, where ebonised stumps revealed at very low tides are all that are left of a great forest in which some of the earliest men to reach these shores hunted.

A completely different aspect of the park is found on the Preseli Hills. This ridge of rounded hills made up of moorland, heath and bog is a landscape of gorse, heather and bilberry in which the curlew and skylark make their home, noted for its many prehistoric remains. A prehistoric track, known as the Flemings Way, was probably the route along which the 'bluestones' of Stonehenge were transported from the outcrops of igneous rock found in this region. Near Mynachlog-ddu is Garn Fawr, a stone circle of sixteen stones and Moel Drygarn, near Crymmych, is the site of a huge Iron Age hill-fort, within which are three Bronze Age cairns.

An area of outstanding beauty is the Gwaun Valley, which runs from Newport to Fishguard. Along its length are the churches of Cilgwyn, Portfaen, Llanychllwydog, Llanawer, and Llanychaer. Near Llanawer is Parc y Meirw (Field of the Dead) which contains the largest Megalithic alignment in Wales, over 140 feet in length with four of eight pillars standing. The ghost of a lady in white is said to walk among them at night.

Pendennis Castle

Cornwall *p211 B1*

Falmouth, with its important harbour, grew up under the protection of Pendennis Castle, which has seen the town evolve from a tiny hamlet into Cornwall's largest port.

The castle was built in about 1540 by Henry VIII, as part of his coastal fortification against the Continent. It stands on a promontory 200 feet above sea-level – an ideal position from which to defend Carrick Roads. The original castle consists of a circular tower or keep, surrounded by a curtain wall. A large outer enclosure was added by Elizabeth I in 1598, when the Spanish were rumoured to be preparing to launch another armada against England. The castle was in use by the military as late as World War II when it became a coastal defence post. The well-preserved keep is now open to the public, and is entered through an impressive gateway over which the Royal Arms are carved into the stone. Above the entrance is the room from where the drawbridge and portcullis were operated, and the two slots through which the chains passed can still be seen.

Penshurst Place has not had any major alterations since the long gallery was completed in 1607

The two main floors of the round tower housed guns which fired through ports provided with smoke vents. Heavy guns were also mounted on the roof and from the battlements the view of the estuary is dramatic.

A museum of arms and armour is housed in a separate building within the complex.

See AM info. Also open Sun am Apr to Sep. Parking available.

These sturdy walls of Pendennis Castle withstood a Civil War siege

Penrhyn Castle

Gwynedd *p216 C3*

Overlooking the Menai Strait, Penrhyn Castle commands splendid views of Beaumaris Bay, Great Ormes Head and Anglesey. G. H. Dawkins Pennant, the wealthy owner of the Penrhyn slate quarries, commissioned Thomas Hopper to build this massive neo-Norman castle, which was completed in 1840. The result is a dramatic and remarkable structure, built of local materials wherever possible: slate from the nearby quarries; oak from the estates' forest; and Mona marble from Anglesey.

The vast and extravagant interior reflects the lavish, opulent hand of the architect, who completely decorated and furnished the castle, mostly in Norman style. The great hall, modelled on Durham Cathedral, is floored with polished slate; the splendid library has deeply recessed windows, and a marvellous ribbed and bossed ceiling. A large collection of nineteenth-century paintings can be seen in the house and in the stables, there is an industrial railway museum and an exhibition of dolls. The castle is set amidst beautiful grounds, and a walled garden contains a variety of rare trees and shrubs.

Open Easter to late Oct daily (except Tue), pm only. NT.

Penshurst Place

Kent *p213 C2*

Penshurst Place stands unobtrusively in the corner of a wooded park, amid gardens laid out in authentic Tudor style. It is the seat of the Viscount De L'Isle, whose ancestors, the Sidneys, gradually converted Penshurst from a medieval manor house into a sumptuous estate, while still managing to retain most of its original character. Sir Philip Sidney, the well-known soldier and writer, was born at Penshurst in 1554 and writers such as his sister, Lady Pembroke, and Ben Johnson, were associated with the estate during the early seventeenth century.

The oldest feature is probably the great hall, with a sixty-foot-high timbered roof and an octagonal central hearth which can still provide an adequate form of heat. It was built by John de Pulteney, a wealthy wool merchant who was Mayor of London no less than four times.

Next to the great hall is the state dining room where a table is permanently laid with a Rockingham dinner service, made for William IV. A complete tour of Penshurst includes a number of other rooms and galleries containing some fine examples of Elizabethan architecture and furniture, and a collection of historic family documents is on display in the Nether Gallery. An unusual museum of nineteenth-century toys and games is to be found in the stable wing.

A public restaurant overlooks the Italian garden, and the home park, which adjoins the north front of the house, contains varied rare breeds of sheep and a venture park and nature trail, recently commissioned by Lord De L'Isle.

Open Apr to early to Oct daily (except Mons, but open Bank Hol Mons), pm only. Parking and refreshments available.

Perth Tayside *p220 D5*

The aptly named Fair City of Perth straddles the banks of the river Tay on the very edge of the Highlands. In ancient times it played an important role in Scotland's affairs, and was the country's capital for a century.

Few of the ancient buildings remain intact, but the city nevertheless retains a unique character with Georgian terraces overlooking the river and parkland. Today, it is the commercial and cultural centre for a wide surrounding area and has a major livestock market famous for its Aberdeen Angus bull sales, whilst its repertory theatre, which is housed in the Victorian Perth Theatre, is reputed to be the oldest in Scotland.

Branklyn Garden
Described as the finest garden of its size in Britain, it covers little more than two acres and contains a unique collection of rare plants from all parts of the world.

Black Watch Regimental Museum
The museum is housed in Balhousie Castle, a restored tower house reputed to be older than the Burgh of Perth itself. It contains treasures of the 42nd/73rd Highland Regiment from 1725 and includes paintings, silver, colours and uniforms.

The Fair Maid's House
This restored house was the former home of Catherine Glover, as described in Sir Walter Scott's famous novel, *The Fair Maid of Perth*. It was a guildhall for over 150 years and a recently uncovered wall here is said to be the oldest visible wall in Perth. The house is now an antique and craft centre.

Museum and Art Gallery
The Classical portico of this purpose-built museum and art gallery houses a varied and interesting collection of items, including natural history, social and local history and a collection of fine and applied art.

St John's Kirk
This imposing kirk is one of the noblest of the grand Scottish burghal churches, and is one of the few buildings to survive from Perth's medieval past. Consecrated in 1243, the choir dates from 1450, the central tower has a fifteenth-century steeple and the nave is c1490. It was here in 1559 that the fiery preaching of John

Perth from the bridge over the Tay. The tower belongs to St John's Kirk

Knox kindled the Reformation in Scotland. In the 1920s the church was restored as a memorial to those who fell in World War I.

The church boasts a set of thirty-five bells, together with fine examples of stained glass. Also on view is a priceless collection of old pewter and silver sacramental dishes.

Kinnoull Hill
The 739-feet summit of this hill commands a fine view of the city and the Tay estuary towards the Ochil and Lomond Hills. A nature trail and numerous wooded paths make this a popular spot.

Branklyn Garden open Mar to Oct daily. NTS.
Black Watch Regimental Museum open all year, Mon to Fri. Sun and Public Hols, Easter to Sep.
Fair Maid's House open all year Mon to Sat.
Museum and Art Gallery open all year Mon to Sat.

Peterborough

Cambridgeshire *p213 B5*

The geographic position of Peterborough, its fertile surroundings and handy raw materials, have made it a place of importance since Neolithic man first settled here.

The focal point of the old city is the magnificent cathedral, founded as a monastic abbey in 655, although the present fabric dates back to 1118. It is a massive Norman structure with a remarkable early Gothic west front. Its height, the light colour of the local Barnack stone and the double arches which admit daylight to the nave, prevent it from being gloomy. It retains its ancient wooden roof with an odd variety of figures in its painted decoration. Catherine of Aragon was buried here, as was Mary Queen of Scots until her son, James I of England, had her body moved to Westminster. On the west wall of the nave is a memorial to Old

Scarlet who dug the Queens' graves. Behind the altar is a carved stone, known as the Hedda Stone because it was thought to commemorate Abbot Hedda who, with his monks, was

The triple-arched west front of Peterborough Cathedral

murdered by Norsemen in 870, though it is now believed to be of an earlier date.

Other old buildings of note are Longthorpe Tower – a fortified medieval house with rare wall paintings, and Thorpe Hall, built during the Commonwealth period. The City Museum and Art Gallery in Priestgate covers local history, and includes articles made by prisoners during the Napoleonic wars.

Multi-purpose leisure centres, swimming pools, a theatre, stadium, and a complex of facilities for outdoor recreation at Orton Mere, are some of the developments connected with the city's expansion. For railway lovers, the Nene Valley Railway operates on a five-mile track between Wansford and Orton Mere, using a variety of steam and diesel locomotives, some of them from the Continent.

Longthorpe Tower see AM info.
Museum and Art Gallery open all year (except Good Fri and Christmas) Tue to Sat. Oct to Apr pm only.
Nene Valley Railway open Easter to Sep Sat and Sun, also Wed and Thu June to Aug. Also Bank Hols and Christmas specials every Sat and Sun in Dec. Parking and refreshments available.

Petworth

West Sussex *p213 B2*

Petworth is a charming small country town dominated by Petworth Park, its walls some thirteen miles long. Within these walls is a beautiful deer park and the impressive mansion of Petworth House.

Rebuilt from the former Percy mansion by the sixth Duke of Somerset between 1688 and 1696, only the fourteenth-century chapel remains of the former building. The magnificent 320-foot west front faces a lake and the great park; the south front was reconstructed between 1869 and 1872 to the designs of Anthony Salvin. One of the finest art collections in England can be seen in its state rooms and galleries including works by Gainsborough, Rembrandt and Van Dyck. Perhaps the most notable collection is that of the artist Turner who was a frequent visitor to Petworth House. The most impressive room in the house is probably the carved room with its lovely decoration by Grinling Gibbons.

Open Apr to Oct, Tue Wed, Thu, Sat, Sun and Bank Holiday Mon (closed following Tue), pm. Deer park open all year. Refreshments. NT.

Pickering

North Yorkshire *p217 C4*

Lying on the edge of the North York Moors National Park, Pickering is an ancient market town with some interesting old buildings and historic coaching inns. The parish church is particularly notable, with its huge entrance porch and some of the best preserved fifteenth-century wall paintings in the country.

Agriculture has always been, and still is, important to the area and one of the great pioneers of farming development, William Marshall, lived in Pickering. He converted his home into one of the first agricultural colleges; today the Georgian building houses the Beck Isle Museum of Rural Life. The rooms illustrate, with bygones and folk exhibits, the history of Pickering and the surrounding area.

On the northern edge of the town the castle stands high on its mound. In the twelfth century it was a hunting lodge for medieval kings and a centre for all administration of their forests. Only fragments remain today, but there is still a good deal to see.

A stretch of the Tay, the longest river in Scotland, near Pitlochry

Sections of the wall with towers enclose a now grassy area, and upon the forty-three-foot high motte there are remains of the keep. The chapel is the only structure that has been restored.

One of Pickering's most popular attractions is the North York Moors Railway, which operates out of Pickering Station to Grosmont, some eighteen miles away. Diesel and steam-hauled trains carry passengers northwards, following Pickering Beck through the beautiful forest and moorland countryside of the National Park, including the outstanding Newton Dale. At the station in Pickering visitors can see the loco sheds and viewing gallery.

Museum open Apr to Oct daily. **Castle** see AM info. Also open Sun am Apr to Sep. Parking available. **North Yorkshire Moors Railway** open Easter to early Nov. Parking and refreshments available.

Pilkington Glass Museum

Merseyside *p216 E3*

With the natural resources of coal and fine sand available in the area, St Helens became an important glass-producing centre in the eighteenth century and has continued to be so. Attached to the headquarters of the Pilkington Company in Prescot Road is an interesting museum of the history of glassmaking. The displays on two floors include some which show how glass was made, as well as the development of glass-making techniques, decorating glass, clear and coloured glass, plate glass, mirrors, optical glass and uses of glass in science, technology, transport and building.

Open all year (except Christmans and New Year) daily, pm only Sat, Sun and Bank Holidays. Parking available.

Pitlochry

Tayside *p221 D1*

Pitlochry, lying almost exactly in the centre of Scotland, is a popular base for touring. The origins of Pitlochry go back to prehistoric times and evidence of this may be seen on the present golf course where the remains of a 2,000-year-old Pictish fort are to be found.

The town of today is a well-known holiday resort with notable manufacturing interests, namely tweed and whisky. Its Festival Theatre, Scotland's Theatre in the Hills, is internationally famous for its summer presentations of drama, music and art.

To the north of the town lies the Pass of Killiecrankie, notorious site of a seventeenth-century battle. Also to the north lies the picturesque village of Moulin with its ruined fourteenth-century Black Castle. Some one-and-a-half miles south of the town, at the entrance to the Dunfallandy House mausoleum, is the Dunfallandy Stone, a Pictish sculptured slab from the eighth century.

Pitlochry dam, situated some ten minutes walk from the town centre, has a public walkway along the crest which links up with Forestry Commission footpaths. The power station is not open, but there is public access to an exhibition area which contains a viewing gallery and an illustrated history of the development of hydro-electricity in the Highlands. Observation chambers in the 900-foot long fish ladder provide close-up views of salmon returning upstream to their spawning grounds.

About two miles to the northwest of Pitlochry lies the Faskally Wayside Centre, on the shores of the idyllic man-made Loch Faskally. The centre incorporates woodland, picnic facilities, a children's play area and a nature trail.

Power Station Dam and Fish Pass Exhibition area open Easter to Oct daily. Fish Pass observation chambers open during daylight hours. **Faskally Wayside Centre** open Apr to Sep Daily. Parking available.

The west front of Petworth House looks out onto a 2,000-acre estate

Plymouth Devon *p212 C2*

An historic seaport with a great maritime tradition — it was from here that Captain Cook sailed round the world; so, many years later, did Sir Francis Chichester, and the Pilgrim Fathers put into Plymouth for repairs before finally departing for the New World.

Sutton Pool beside the Barbican – the old town of Plymouth Drake knew

By far the most famous of all the seafarers connected with Plymouth is Sir Francis Drake, the local boy who became a national hero and of whom the city has been justifiably proud for 400 years. From the Hoe, which he made famous with his legendary game of bowls, his statue looks out across the sea he loved. The Hoe is still a pleasant open space of lawns and flower beds, backed by a row of cannons.

However, Plymouth's maritime heritage is not confined to the history books, for it is still a major base for the Royal Navy at their Devonport dockyard. While the presence of the Navy ensured Plymouth's prosperity over the years, it also brought about the devastation of the 1941 Plymouth Blitz. Nevertheless, from the rubble of bomb damage has risen a new city centre with good shops and civic offices. Fortunately not all of the historic buildings were destroyed, and the area known as the Barbican is an attractive Old Quarter with narrow streets, old houses and a busy harbour.

Drake's statue, Plymouth

City Museum and Art Gallery
This interesting museum covers local history, archaeology and natural history. The art gallery has a collection of West Country scenes by local artists, including Sir Joshua Reynolds, together with portraits and collections of porcelain and silver.

Royal Citadel
Charles II built this impressive fortress and its remaining buildings include the Guard House, the Governor's House and the Chapel. The entrance gateway is still magnificent, and from its ramparts there are superb views across the city and along the coast.

Elizabethan House
An attractive sixteenth-century house in the heart of the old Barbican area has retained most of its original features and contains period furniture.

The Merchant's House
The largest of Plymouth's old buildings to have survived, the Merchant's House now contains a museum which illustrates the development of Plymouth in the Middle Ages.

Prysten House
This was the Priest's House of the nearby St Andrews Church and was built in 1490. One room is dedicated to the Mayflower story, and there is also a model of Plymouth as it was in 1620, and a herb display.

Drake's Island
A prominent feature in Plymouth Sound, this was a fortress and a prison before becoming an Adventure Training Centre.

Mount Edgcumbe House and Country Park
Across the Sound from Plymouth is a Tudor-style mansion, extensively restored following bomb damage during World War II and now the home of the seventh Earl of Mount Edgcumbe. Unfortunately the contents and many works of art were also destroyed

and only a few examples remain of a once-large collection of Reynolds portraits. The grounds include formal gardens, over 800 acres of woodland and lovely scenic walks along some ten miles of coastline.

Museum and Art Gallery open all year daily (except Sun, Good Fri and Christmas).
Royal Citadel open May to Sep. pm only. AM.
Elizabethan House open all year Mon to Sat, also Sun pm form Apr to Sep.
Merchants House open all year daily, (except Good Fri and Christmas) Sun (summer only), pm only.
Prysten House open Apr to Oct, Mon to Sat.
Drake's Island open end May to mid Sep, daily. Ferries depart every 1½ hours. Refreshments available.
Mount Edgcumbe House House and Higher Gardens open May to Sep Mon and Tue pm. Park and Lower Gardens open all year daily.

Poldark

Cornwall *p211 B1*

This area was mined for tin even before the Romans came and gave many Cornishmen their livelihood over several centuries. Vast amounts of tin were extracted before the industry finally went into a decline, but here at Poldark Mining visitors can see the old workings and a remarkable collection of historic engines and machinery.

The site covers some three acres and the underground tour shows where the miners worked, the tools they used and the shafts which were their access to the world above.

A somewhat unexpected feature is the underground postbox, and souvenir postcards sent from here carry a special postmark. The tour progresses through a series of museum chambers where there are a large number of steam engines, many of which can be seen working. These include beam engines, pumps, a Horizontal Tandem steam engine and an Overhead Grasshopper engine. Not all of the exhibits are associated with mining, however.

There are also printing presses, some tools of the cobbler's trade, cream, butter and cheese making equipment, and such household items as clothes mangles and ranges.

The mine entrance is within the confines of Ha'Penny Park, a major fun park with circurama from America. The Park contains a display of historic machines, a Cornish mining cinema, picnic gardens and many attractions for the children.

The admission charge is one ha'penny, with a Cornish ha'penny given in return for one penny, but once inside many of the attractions are free.

Mine and Ha'Penny Park open Apr to Oct daily. Parking and refreshments available.

An industrial steam locomotive at Poldark Mine

Polesden Lacey

Surrey *p213 B2*

Polesden Lacey is situated on high ground with fine views from its south terrace across to Ranmore Woods. Thomas Cubitt built his Regency 'villa' here between 1821–23, on the site of the original house, and over the years a succession of owners have altered and enlarged the property. In 1906 Polesden Lacey was purchased by Captain Grevelle and his wife became a celebrated hostess. She entertained many famous people over a period of forty years, and even lent the house to King George VI and Queen Elizabeth for part of their honeymoon.

The house contains a fine collection of furnishings, painting, porcelain, tapestries and other works of art. The estate of over 1,000 acres is a delightful mixture of woodland and formal gardens and there is an open-air theatre here.

House open Mar and Nov, Sat and Sun pm only, Apr to Oct Wed to Sun, pm only. Open Bank Holiday Mon all day.
Gardens open all year daily. Refreshments available. NT.

Polesden Lacey, where George VI and Queen Elizabeth honeymooned

Polperro

Cornwall *p212 C1*

Picturesque little colour-washed cottages huddle together in a deep cleft cut from the cliffs by the river Pol, making Polperro one of the most popular and frequently photographed of the Cornish fishing villages. Its streets are narrow and winding, often with no pavements, and in the height of the season it is necessary for visitors' cars to be left outside the village.

The most attractive part of the village is the little harbour, still used by local fishermen, but now also offering pleasure trips out to sea. Before the rest of the world discovered Cornwall, these were secluded beaches for the local smugglers to land their contraband.

Also of interest here is a model village, a replica of old Polperro set amidst lovely gardens.

Model Village open Mar to Oct Sun to Fri. Refreshments.

Poole

Dorset *p212 F2*

Poole is a modern resort with a large natural harbour which has four tides a day as the sea ebbs and flows around the Isle of Wight. The tides keep the golden sands clean and are a great boon to the many pleasure craft entering and leaving the port. The beaches and amusements of the Sandbanks peninsula are attractive, especially for families. Between there and the Town Quay, are the headquarters of several yacht clubs and colourful craft swarm in the harbour. Boats can be hired from Sandbanks and ferries run from there across to Shell Bay.

The town has had a colourful history. In the Middle Ages it was the county's main port, it became popular with smugglers in the eighteenth century and during the Civil War became a Roundhead stronghold. Some of the first settlers in Newfoundland came from Poole in the nineteenth century and a lucrative trade developed, mostly in timber. This reached a peak at the time of the

Napoleonic Wars, and, as an expression of its wealth and civic pride, the town was almost completely rebuilt. To preserve the Georgian buildings and the few older houses which survive, fifteen acres near the Quay have been designated a Historic Precinct. Amongst the interesting buildings are the Customs House of 1813, the Harbour Office and St James Church, both built in 1820, and the former Guildhall of 1761, now a museum illustrating Poole's social history during the eighteenth and nineteenth centuries.

Also on the quay is the Maritime Museum, housed in the Town Cellar which dates from the late fifteenth century. The exhibits depict Poole's strong links with the sea since prehistoric times up until this century.

Here too is the world-famous Poole Pottery which was founded in 1873, although the characteristic pottery known today began in 1921. The various stages involved are demonstrated by craftsmen.

For leisure facilities Poole Park, with its large boating lake, miniature railway, and small zoo is deservedly popular. The more unusual animals in the zoo include wild cats, otters and porcupines.

Guildhall Museum open all year daily (except 1 Jan, Good Fri, and Christmas), Sun pm only.
Maritime Museum open as above.
Poole Park Zoo open daily (except Christmas Day). Parking available.
Poole Pottery open all year (except Christmas week and Bank Holidays). Refreshments available.

The harbour scene at Polperro, typically and unmistakably Cornish

Portchester Castle

Hampshire *p213 A2*

On a long spit of land projecting into Portsmouth Harbour stands Portchester Castle. It was built as a fort by the Romans in the third century as one of the many defences strung around the south and east coasts of England. The original twenty-foot high wall still stands, as do fourteen of the twenty round bastions, covering some nine acres.

A priory and its church was built in 1133 outside the inner walls of the castle, although only the church has survived, of which its west front and carved font are particularly fine features.

The great tower was added in the fourteenth century by Sir Robert Assheton, Constable of the Castle, and it became known as Assheton's Tower.

Buildings within the inner courtyard were converted into a palace by Richard II at the end of the fourteenth century and the ruined remains of the kitchen, hall and great chamber can still be seen.

The castle had been popular as a residence with royalty visiting Portsmouth including King John, Henry V who embarked from here for Agincourt and Henry VIII who came to the castle with Anne Boleyn.

During the seventeenth century the castle gradually fell into disrepair, although prisoners from the Napoleonic Wars were kept here.

See AM info. Also open Sun am, Apr to Sep. Parking available.

Sited between the estuaries of the Glaslyn and the Dwyryd, Portmeirion resembles a Mediterranean village

Portmeirion

Gwynedd *p216 C2*

This unique, fairy-tale village is situated on a rocky tree-clad peninsula on the shores of Cardigan Bay. Here, Welsh architect Sir Clough Williams-Ellis built his own dream village amidst exceptionally beautiful scenery.

At the nucleus of the estate is a sumptuous waterfront hotel – rebuilt from the original house and still containing a fine eighteenth-century fireplace, and a library which was moved here from the Great Exhibition of 1851. All around are many architectural fancies, among them an Italianate campanile (detached bell-tower), castle and lighthouse. Colonnades, a watch tower, grottoes and cobbled squares all combine harmoniously with pastel-shaded picturesque cottages. The buildings have been sited to the best advantage of the natural heights and slopes, with much of their materials being rescued from demolished buildings throughout Britain.

One - hundred-and-seventy-

five acres of sub-tropical coastal, cliff and wooded gardens surround this harbour village occupying a mile or so of the Portmeirion peninsula. The estate encompasses the sixty-acre Gwyllt Gardens, considered to be one of the finest wild gardens in Wales. They include miles of dense woodland paths, and are famous for their fine display of rhododendrons, hydrangeas, azaleas and sub-tropical flora. Among the many varieties of trees here are palms, eucalyptus, cypresses and magnolias, together with various ferns and lilies.

The village has been used as a film set on numerous occasions and was the setting for the successful television series *The Prisoner*. Here, in one week, Noel Coward wrote his comedy *Blithe Spirit*. The village is run as a holiday complex but is open to toll-paying visitors. Apart from the hotel itself, accommodation is mainly self-catering in the cottages.

Village and Gwyllt Gardens open Apr to Oct daily. Parking and refreshments available.

Portsmouth

Hampshire *p213 A1*

There has been a harbour at Portsmouth since Roman times, and the city has been important in the history of the Navy since the fourteenth century.

Although 'Pompey' was heavily bombed during World War II, much of the original town survives. Old Portsmouth, the area around the Isle of Wight car-ferry embarkation point, is particularly interesting with its cobbled streets, narrow lanes and tall slim houses.

The city has several literary ties, and amongst these is H. G. Wells who worked as a drapery assistant in a local shop, and Charles Dickens, who was born in the town in 1812. His Georgian house, furnished in the style of the 1800s, contains the author's personal relics and an extensive library of his works, including many rare first editions.

Refurbished in 1972, the City Museum and Art Gallery houses the Fine and Decorative art collections, together with social his-

tory material and a display on the history of Portsmouth.

HMS *Victory*, Lord Nelson's famous flagship at the Battle of Trafalgar, which is moored in the harbour, has been described as 'the proudest sight in Britain', and because of her age and historic significance the ship is unique as the world's most outstanding example of ship restoration. Nearby is the Portsmouth Royal Naval Museum. It complements the ship by housing those relics of Nelson and Trafalgar which cannot be conveniently displayed on board as well as exhibiting a large collection of ships and figureheads. The interesting Nelson-McCarthy Collection consists of prints, paintings, ceramics, medallions, letters and miniatures. Also within the Naval Base is the preserved hull of Henry VIIIs warship, the *Mary Rose*, which sank in the Solent in 1545 and was raised in 1982. Viewing galleries allow visitors to watch the beginnings of the work to conserve the hull and replace many of the timbers, decks and cabins. A boathouse nearby houses many of the 'treasures' of the vessel.

Dickens Birthplace Museum open Mar to Oct daily.
City Museum and Art Gallery open all year daily (except Christmas). Parking and refreshments available.
HMS Victory open all year daily, Sun pm only. Closed Christmas Day.
Royal Naval Museum open all year daily. Refreshments available.
The Mary Rose open all year daily (except Christmas Day).
Royal Marines' Museum open all year daily.

HMS *Victory* in Portsmouth Harbour

Powderham Castle

Devon *p212 D2*

The ancestral home of the Earls of Devon, Powerham Castle is delightfully set in beautiful parkland beside the Exe Estuary.

The original fourteenth- to fifteenth-century building was more a defensive manor than a castle, and was converted into today's stately mansion during the late eighteenth century, after suffering damage during the Civil War. Today's structure is therefore a blend of styles, the term castle being well suited though to Powderham's solid masonry and embattled towers.

Of particular interest inside are the medieval chapel, the elaborately decorated staircase and the music room. The very pretty chapel is the only medieval room to be seen and has an arched and braced timber roof, along with excellent old carved bench ends. The magnificent staircase rises the entire height of the building. The plasterwork by John Jenkins has drops of fruit and flowers modelled and arranged between panels. The music room was designed by James Wyatt in the 1790s and has a central dome and musical instruments modelled in its fine plasterwork, all lit by the room's bow window.

Outside there is a fine terraced garden and the mansion's extensive wooded parkland, with its deer, almost reaches the river. The parkland was once part of the marshland and bogs of the river Exe before it was reclaimed during the eighteenth century and planted with cedar, lime and oak trees.

Open late May to mid Sep Sun to Thu, pm only. Parking and refreshments available.

Prinknash Abbey and Bird Park

Gloucestershire *p212 F4*

There are two abbeys at Prinknash, both set among the trees on opposite sides of the lovely parkland. The old abbey, which dates in parts from the fourteenth century, spent some 400 years in private ownership, following the Dissolution, until it was given back to the Benedictine monks in 1928. It is a pleasant building of mellow stone, and much of its history can be traced through the heraldic features in its carved woodwork and stained glass. An attractive feature of the old abbey is the charming medieval chapel. When the monks returned to Prinknash in 1928 they found the original building hopelessly inadequate for their expanding community, and in 1939 the foundation stone was laid for the new abbey. Completed in 1972, it is a bright, clean and modern building of total simplicity.

During the excavation of the foundations for the new building a bed of clay was discovered which prompted the monks to establish a pottery and today Prinknash Pottery is world-famous. Visitors can see the monks and their employees at work in the pottery and guides are available. The pottery is just one of the industries followed by the monks which include farming, ironwork stained glass and incense making.

Nine acres of the park have been set out as a Bird Park with many varieties of birds and waterfowl. Several types of swans and geese, notably a flock of Snow geese, are free flying and can be fed by visitors. There are also Pygmy goats and Jacob sheep, and the monk's fish ponds which were built before the Reformation, are still alive with trout.

Abbey open all year daily.
Pottery Mon to Sat and Sun pm (shop open all day)
Bird Park open Easter to Oct daily. Parking and refreshments available.

A thatched replica of an Iron Age Dorset dwelling

Queen Elizabeth Country Park

Hampshire *p213 A2*

The park covers 1,400 acres of forest and downland including level plains, deep valleys and woodland which shelter numerous varieties of wildlife. Several marked routes throughout the park guide the visitor amongst forests and hills, over plains and down valleys; the length and stamina required for each differs according to the trail chosen.

A nineteenth-century shepherd's hut can be seen in the sheep management area, and many items used in the farming of these hills throughout the centuries are kept in the forest craft demonstration area.

The Butser Ancient Farm is a working reconstruction of an Iron Age settlement, operated according to the methods used around 2,300 years ago. The largest building on the farm is a thatched round house, made of oak stakes, woven with hazel rods, and daubed with clay. This house was based upon an Iron Age dwelling found in Dorset. The animals being raised on the farm are Exmoor ponies, Dexter cattle and Soay sheep, the nearest equivalent to historic breeds. Two fields are planted with crops commonly grown during Iron Age times, these were spelt and emmer, primitive varieties of wheat. A hand mill, weaving loom and kiln are amongst working replicas to be seen at the farm.

Open all year daily. Parking and refreshments available.

The last Abbot of Gloucester rebuilt an old hunting lodge into this lovely manor house – Prinknash Abbey

Raby Castle

Co Durham *p217 B4*

Dating from the latter part of the fourteenth century when Sir John Neville, High Admiral of England fortified it, Raby Castle is reputed to incorporate a tower built by King Canute in the eleventh century. The most notable features of the castle are the nine towers, including the Neville Tower, which was built in such a way that carriages were able to drive up to an inner staircase.

An outstanding collection of paintings from English, Dutch and Italian schools are contained within the castle, as well as numerous pieces of French furniture and porcelain. There is also a collection of horse-drawn vehicles from the eighteenth and nineteenth centuries, and a superb medieval kitchen.

Open Easter to Sep daily, pm only, Easter weekend including Tue; Wed, Sun and Bank Holiday weekends until June then daily except Sat until Sep. Parking and refreshments available.

Raglan Castle

Gwent *p212 E4*

This fine example of a medieval castle was probably the last of its kind to be built in Wales, and although damaged during the Civil War, remains impressive.

The walls of the castle enclose the Pitched Stone Court, named after its cobbled surface, and the Fountain Court, where only the foundations remain of the large marble fountain which once sent water as high as the walls themselves. Dividing the two courtyards is the great hall and the adjacent buttery – both parts of the later additions which made the castle more comfortable.

When the castle was first built in the fourteenth century, there was still a certain amount of unrest in Wales, and the main keep, known as the Yellow Tower of Gwent, was built outside the castle walls with its own moat and drawbridge. In this way the five-storey hexagonal keep watched over the two gateways to the castle and could, at the same time, be isolated from the main part of the building. The Cromwellians set charges under the tower, but even they could not completely destroy it. From the top of its staircase there are superb views of the surrounding countryside.

See AM info. Also open Sun am Apr to Sep. Parking available.

Ragley Hall

Warwickshire *p216 F1*

Ragley Hall stands at the highest point of a 400-acre park. It is a magnificent seventeenth-century porticoed Palladian mansion with an imposing exterior which is more than matched by the craftsmanship displayed within.

It was the 1st Marquess of Hertford who commissioned James Gibbs to design the great hall, some seventy feet long and forty feet high. With its exquisite rococo plasterwork on the walls and ceiling, it is considered to be one of the finest baroque rooms in England. Many great artists have contributed to the decoration of the house over the centuries and the whole atmosphere is one of wealth and luxury.

Ragley Hall is filled with treasures, including collections of Sèvres porcelain, period furniture and fine paintings, such as the *Raising of Lazarus* by Cornelis van Haarlem. There are also portraits of the Hertfords' ancestors, among them Horace Walpole, a cousin of the 1st Marquess.

The Prince Regent visited the Hall during the late eighteenth century and the bedroom he occupied has been preserved.

The park was laid out by Capability Brown in 1750 and, despite nineteenth-century alterations, has retained most of its original

pattern. More recent attractions include a children's adventure wood, a country trail and pleasant lakeside picnic areas.

Open Easter to Sep, Tue, Wed, Thu, Sat, Sun and Bank Holidays, pm only. Park daily Jul and Aug, closed Mon and Fri rest of year. Parking and refreshments available.

Ravenglass and Eskdale Railway

Cumbria *p216 D5*

Ravenglass lies on the Cumbrian coast, at the mouth of the river Esk. Once a Roman port, this delightfully unspoilt little fishing community is the starting point of the Ravenglass and Eskdale Railway. Originally constructed in 1875 to carry iron ore, this miniature fifteen inch narrow-gauge railway, known affectionately as L'aal Ratty has carried passengers since 1876. Its steam and diesel locomotives, open and saloon coaches, operate over seven miles of beautiful scenery. Running from Ravenglass to Dalegarth, near the attractive village of Boot in Eskdale, the train stops at both Irton Road and The Green en route. There is a small railway museum at Ravenglass.

Open late Mar to early Nov daily. Late Feb to late Mar and Nov, weekends only. Parking and refreshments available.

Rhuddlan Castle

Clwyd *p216 D3*

This great castle ruin stands on a mound overlooking the banks of the river Clwyd, which was diverted into a channel so that the garrison could be supplied from the sea, two miles away. The present structure was built on the orders of Edward I as part of his plan to subdue the Welsh Princes, and he used it as his headquarters during campaigns. It continued in use until the Civil War, when it was wrecked by order of Parliament and subsequently used by the local people as a quarry.

It is still possible to appreciate the power of this once substantial fortress. One of four strictly concentric castles in Wales, it was built to a diamond-shaped plan with round towers, gatehouses, and nine-foot-thick curtain walls. In the east gatehouse near the centre of the passage, are the holes which accommodated the portcullis and gate.

See AM info. Also open Sun am, Apr to Sep. Parking available.

The baron hall at Raby Castle is 136 feet long and used to hold as many as 700 knights

Riber Castle Fauna Reserve

Derbyshire *p217 B1*

Standing at a height of 853 feet overlooking the delightful town of Matlock, is Riber Castle – a prominent landmark for many miles around. Although its turrets and battlements give the impression of an ancient fortress, the castle was built in 1862 by Mr John Smedley, a local textile manufacturer who developed Matlock as a spa. For a good many years the castle was utilised as a school, but following this, between 1930 and 1950, it lay empty and fell to ruins. However, in 1962, a group of zoologists acquired the grounds, which cover over twenty acres, and established a nature reserve in them.

A comprehensive collection of British and European birds and animals live here now in natural surroundings. Of special interest are the breeding colonies of European lynx, whose kittens can be seen from June to September. The large collection of domestic animals include rare breeds of sheep, pigs, cattle, goats and poultry. Other features of the reserve are a nature centre, a model railway, models of prehistoric creatures, and some vintage cars and motor cycles.

Open all year daily (except 25 Dec). Parking and refreshments available.

Richmond

North Yorkshire *p217 B4*

Richmond is a pleasant mixture of narrow, twisting lanes and large open spaces. It contains examples of many architectural styles, incorporating buildings of the medieval, Georgian and Victorian periods. Two of the town's oldest features are the castle, which towers above the river Swale, and Grey Friars Tower. The latter dates from the fourteenth century and stands in Friary Gardens; it was once part of a Franciscan Friary and a curfew bell is still sounded.

The castle is an impressive example of early military architecture with a hundred-foot-high keep, built, curiously enough, on top of the gatehouse, and surrounded by some of the oldest defensive walls in the country. From the roof of the keep there are fine views of the river Swale. Scollards Hall, beside the east wall, dates from around 1080 and is probably the most ancient

It is easy to see why Richmond's castle, 100 feet above the river Swale, was an ideal military stronghold

domestic building in England.

Holy Trinity Church, which stands in the cobbled market place, is the oldest church in Richmond and, in 1971, was converted into the Green Howards Museum. The museum covers the history of the regiment and contains a collection of uniforms, weapons and medals, some of which date back as far as 1688. A separate chapel has been retained so that services may still be held in Holy Trinity.

Apart from its historical associations, Richmond is a popular touring centre, lying in a superb position at the entrance to Swaledale, and within easy reach of the rest of the Yorkshire Dales National Park. It is a favourite starting point for walkers and cyclists and there is a very pleasant local walk beside the Swale, which ends near the remains of twelfth-century Easby Abbey to the south-east of the town.

Castle See AM info. Also open Sun am, Apr to Sep.
The Green Howards Museum Open all year (except Dec and Jan); Apr to Oct daily, Sun pm only: Mar and Nov Mon to Sat; Feb Mon to Fri.

Although moated on three sides and bounded by the Clwyd on the fourth, Rhuddlan Castle fell in the Civil War

Rievaulx Abbey

North Yorkshire *p217 B4*

The grandeur of the setting and the considerable remains of this beautiful abbey, make Rievaulx one of the most magnificent monastic ruins in the country. The lofty walls of the abbey church and monastic quarters occupy a secluded and sheltered site in the valley of the river Rye, from which it took its name in 1131 on becoming the first Cistercian foundation in northern England.

On the hill above the abbey is Rievaulx Terrace, now the property of the National Trust. This is a winding, landscaped terrace of some half-a-mile in length, which was laid out in the mid-eighteenth century for Thomas Duncombe of nearby Duncombe Park. There are Classical temples at either end and the landscaping has been cleverly designed to reveal superb views all along the terrace.

Abbey see AM info. Also open Sun am Apr to Sep. Parking available.
Terrace open Apr to Oct (except Good Fri) daily. Parking available. NT.

Ripon

North Yorkshire *p217 B3*

Standing at the confluence of the rivers Ure, Skell and Laver, Ripon is often referred to as the Gateway to the Dales.

The large Market Square is dominated by a ninety-foot-high obelisk, where a forest horn is still sounded at each corner every night at 9.00 pm. At the south-west corner of the square is the Wakeman's House, a fourteenth-century half-timbered building. Formerly the official residence of the Wakeman and later the Mayor, it now houses a small museum of local history.

Built on an east-facing ridge in the middle of this busy market town is the small, but very impressive, cathedral. There has been a church on this site for over 1,300 years, but it was not until 1836 that Ripon was granted cathedral status.

The thirteenth-century west front is quite plain in contrast to the east, with its magnificent fifty-foot-high window in Decorated style, supported by gabled buttresses.

Inside, the notable fifteenth-century choir stalls are the work of local carvers. Above the south transept is the library, which contains books dating from before 1500 – including a twelfth-century manuscript copy of the Bible. Beneath the grand sixteenth-century Gothic nave is the oldest part of the cathedral, a seventh-century Saxon crypt, now a strongroom in which ancient silver and other church treasures are displayed.

Wakeman's House Museum open Easter then May Day to mid Sep daily, Sun, pm only.

Roche Abbey

South Yorkshire *p217 B2*

This Cistercian house was named after a rock formation which resembled a cross and was a place of pilgrimage. Founded in the twelfth century by two local land-owners, the abbey was colonised by monks from Newminster Abbey near Morpeth. During the sixteenth century the Dissolution of the monasteries led to the surrender, and subsequent plundering, of Roche Abbey. Centuries later the ruins were placed in the care of what was then the Ministry of Public Building and Works, by the 10th Earl of Scarborough.

In the valley of the river Ryton, close to Sandbeck Park, the ruins lie amidst lawns and woods landscaped by Capability Brown. The vaulted gatehouse, partly rebuilt in the fourteenth century, is particularly well preserved, and parts of the transept walls still stand to their full height.

See AM info. Parking available.

Rochester

Kent *p213 C3*

The strategic importance of Rochester was recognised by the Romans – who first fortified it, the Saxons – who incorporated the remains of Roman walls into their own fortifications, and the Normans – who built a castle of which the walls and an enormous keep survive. At the top of the spiral stairway there are superb views of the area. Just across the road from the castle is the great cathedral. Bishop Gundulf of Bec, chief castle builder to Wil-

In its heyday, Rievaulx, one of the great abbeys of the north, housed a community of over 600; for more than 400 years it has stood in ruins

Rockingham Castle, once a royal hunting lodge, looks down on the pleasant old houses of Rockingham village

liam the Conqueror, was responsible for replacing the Saxon church, but only the lower part of the tower remains from the eleventh century. The rest of the cathedral is largely twelfth-century, with additions from the thirteenth and fifteenth centuries – all much restored and rebuilt after the depredations of the Civil War. Of particular interest is the elaborate Romanesque carving of the west door, the choir stalls, the chapter house doorway of 1340, and a series of bishops' tombs spanning seven centuries.

The city has many associations with Charles Dickens, who spent his boyhood here. In his story *The Seven Poor Travellers*, he describes the Watts Charity building. The charity, founded in 1579 by Sir Richard Watts, provided for any poor travellers, who were given dinner, accommodation for one night, and fourpence to help them on their way. Other buildings described in his books include the Royal Victoria and Bull; Restoration House – so called because Charles II stayed a night there on his return to London; the Tudor Eastgate House – now a museum with a display of Dickensia; and Chertsey's Gate – one of three surviving monastic gates.

Another person closely associated with Rochester was Admiral Sir Cloudsley Shovell. He built the Corn Exchange and paid for renovations to the Guildhall which dates from 1687 and has a 1780 copper weathervane in the form of a ship.

Castle see AM info, but closed all day Tue and pm Fri. Parking available.
Eastgate House open all year daily (except Good Fri, Christmas and New Year).

Rockingham Castle

Northamptonshire *p213 B5*

Many old thatched cottages line the steep hill of the pleasant village of Rockingham. High above it on a hill stands Rockingham Castle, commanding scenic views ranging over five counties. First built by William the Conqueror, the castle occupies the site of an earlier fortification. Almost every style of architecture from the eleventh century blends harmoniously together, although the present house within the Norman walls is mainly Tudor. The sixteenth and seventeenth centuries saw considerable modernisation of the castle, transforming what was once dilapidated fortification into a comfortable country house.

Many treasures are to be found within, including two chests, one belonging to King John, the other to Henry V. Indeed, it was believed that King John had hidden his jewels on the castle premises, but excavations carried out in 1935 to find the hoard proved fruitless.

The servants' hall and great kitchen give the visitor a glimpse of what life must have been like 'below stairs'; other domestic buildings include a brewhouse, woodshed, dairy, and servants quarters.

Within the grounds is a famous 400-year-old yew hedge shaped in the form of elephants. Charles Dickens is reputed to have seen Lady Dedlock's ghost behind it on one occasion. An iron gate leads to the delightful Wild Garden, a ravine containing some 200 varieties of trees and shrubs. A vast expanse of lawn, called the Tilting Ground, is headed by a beautiful avenue of sycamore trees, providing a majestic setting for this once royal castle.

Open Easter to Sep, Thu, Sun, Bank Holiday Mon and following Tue pm only. Parking and refreshments available.

Romsey

Hampshire *p213 A2*

Lying on the banks of the river Test – one of England's finest trout and salmon streams, is this ancient market town which grew up around its now famous abbey.

Founded in the tenth century, the abbey church is a splendid Norman construction built in the shape of a cross. A carved (possibly Saxon) seven-foot-high crucifix can be seen outside against the south transept wall, and an early sixteenth-century painted wooden reredos standing

Rochester, onetime guardian of the river Medway, is still a major port

in the north transept. Within the vestry is the Romsey Psalter (a fifteenth-century illuminated manuscript). Today the abbey is a popular place of pilgrimage, for it is here that the much loved Lord Louis, Earl Mountbatten of Burma, who was horrifically assassinated in August of 1979, is laid to rest.

Not far from the abbey is King John's House, a thirteenth-century flint building which was used as his hunting lodge, and is now a museum.

Broadlands, home of the late Lord Mountbatten, lies just south of the town, and is one of the finest examples of mid-Georgian architecture in England. The elegant eighteenth-century house is set in lovely landscaped grounds beside the river Test which remain a tribute to the genius of Capability Brown. Robert Adam, William Kent and Henry Holland the Younger, all contributed to the creation of this masterpiece, with its richly decorated interior and fine works of art. Broadlands has many historic associations and has long been famous as a centre of hospitality for royalty and distinguished visitors. It was once the country house of the great Victorian Prime Minister, Lord Palmerston, and Queen Elizabeth II and Prince Philip began their honeymoon here.

Broadlands open Apr to Sep daily. Closed Mon except Aug, Sep and Bank Holidays. Parking and refreshments available.
King John's House open Spring Bank Holiday to end Sep, Tue pm only; Thur, Fri and Sat all day.

Rufford Old Hall

Lancashire *p216 E4*

One of the finest examples of its type, this medieval black and white timbered building stands on the banks of the Leeds and Liverpool canal. The only additions to the building were the brick wings, one was added 1662 (now demolished), and the other in 1821. The original great hall is of particular interest, as it has an ornate hammerbeam roof and an intricately carved sixteenth-century wooden screen.

Inside the manor is some excellent period furniture, tapestries, armour and arms which, together with the house, were presented by Lord Hesketh to the National Trust in 1936. Also housed here is the Philip Ashcroft museum of country life.

Open Apr to Oct, Sat to Thu, pm only. Closed Good Fri. Refreshments available. NT.

The great hall at Rufford – the blocked doors once led to the other brick service wing

One of Wordsworth's lakeland homes – Rydal Mount

Rydal Mount

Cumbria *p220 E1*

This sixteenth-century yeoman's house was the home of William Wordsworth from 1813 until his death in 1850. The house stands on a hill above the small village of Rydal, overlooking the lower extremities of Rydal Water, and is surrounded by four-and-a-half acres of gardens laid out under the personal supervision of the poet. Wordsworth became Poet Laureate whilst living here, and, with his fame and popularity reaching its height, received a constant stream of admiring visitors – the forerunners of the tourists who throng the area today.

The house is now owned by a descendant of Wordsworth, and contains a collection of family portraits and many relics of the poet's life, including furniture and first editions of his works. A neighbouring meadow, Dora Field, (National Trust property) is named after Wordsworth's daughter who was particularly fond of the area.

What was once Wordsworth's favourite walk, is now a well-trodden footpath leading from Rydal Mount around Rydal Water – a small lake dotted with islands lying below the 2,000 foot Rydal Fell – to Grasmere, where the poet previously lived.

Rydal village has other literary connections. De Quincey and Hartley Coleridge were both former occupiers of Nab Cottage, situated near Rydal Water, and St Mary's Church has a memorial window dedicated to the poet Dr Arnold and his family.

Open daily all year (except Wed). Parking available.

Ryedale Folk Museum

North Yorkshire *p217 C4*

This fascinating museum superbly illustrates the life and work of an agricultural community from the sixteenth to twentieth centuries. Tools, implements, domestic appliances and furniture are on show in authentic settings, which include a mock smithy and cobbler's shop. Sometimes there are demonstrations of various old country crafts. Outside are many reconstructed cruck buildings, including a medieval longhouse, a manor house, crofters' cottages, a barn and a wheelshed. There is also a particularly interesting medieval glass kiln, believed to be unique.

The museum is within one of the most enchanting villages in the country – Hutton-le-Hole. Its houses face each other across the wide grassy banks of the picturesque Little Beck.

Open late Mar to Oct, daily.

St Albans Hertfordshire *p213 B3*

St Albans, named after Britain's first Christian martyr, Alban, has developed over a period of 2,000 years. Present day St Albans combines narrow, medieval streets where some half-timbered houses with overhanging upper storeys survive, with wide roads of elegant Georgian residences and modern buildings.

The massive tower of the Norman cathedral can be seen from most parts of the town, and there are pleasant gardens and open spaces such as Verulamium Park, with its large ornamental lake. French Row is where French mercenaries were quartered in 1216, whilst employed by the Barons in their squabbles with King John. Here stands the fifteenth-century Fleur de Lys Inn, partly built of timbers from an earlier inn where King John of France was imprisoned in 1356. Situated in Abbey Mill Lane is Ye Old Fighting Cocks, an unusual octagonal timber-framed building, claimed to be the oldest inhabited licensed house in England, although originally a monastic fishing lodge.

The Cathedral

The Paul de Caen, a Norman abbot, reconstructed the original Saxon abbey, built in the eighth century of flint and brick from the ruins of the Roman town. Parts of the Norman structure which have survived include the transept (the pillars of which may be Saxon), the choir, the tower, and the bays to the east of the tower. The 300-foot nave and aisles, built in the thirteenth century, make the abbey one of the longest in the country. Particularly noteworthy are the thirteenth and fourteenth-century paintings on the piers of the nave; the Purbeck marble Shrine of St Alban (a Roman soldier beheaded for concealing a Christian priest) which was reconstructed from shattered pieces discovered in the nineteenth century, and above this the chamber of the monk who kept watch over it. Interesting brasses include one of a fourteenth-century abbot, and monuments dating back to the fifteenth century.

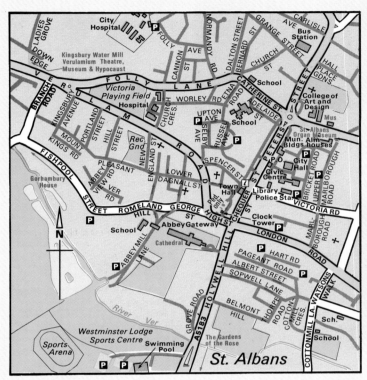

City Museum

The Natural History section of this museum also includes some live specimens, whilst in the Social History and Folk Life section there is a remarkable collection of craft tools, set in reconstructions of craftsmen's shops.

Verulamium Theatre, Museum and Hypocaust

The Roman town was built on the banks of the river Ver to the west of the town centre – a site now occupied by Verulamium Park. Although much of the remains were plundered for building materials in Saxon times, excavations have revealed parts of the third-century walls, foundations of a street of shops and a section of a hypocaust – the Roman system of underfloor heating. Nearby is the Roman theatre, the only known example in Britain to have a stage, rather than an amphitheatre. It has been excavated and restored and measures some 180 feet across. The Verulamium Museum contains the best collection of Roman decorated wall plaster in Britain, and there are also sections of mosaics, a painted ceiling and Roman artifacts. A model shows how the town would have looked during the third century.

Kingsbury Water Mill

This sixteenth-century water mill in St Michael's Street has been restored to working order and is now open as a museum. There is also an art gallery, and a craft shop displaying woodwork, pottery, pewter, jewellery and lace.

St Albans Organ Museum

A colourful collection of fairground and other mechanical organs and musical instruments is housed in this museum. There is also a saleable selection of records and books about various mechanical instruments.

Gorhambury House

This late Georgian mansion – home of the Earl of Verulam – contains Chippendale furniture, Grimston portraits and sixteenth-century enamelled glass. Francis Bacon, Viscount St Albans, philosopher and statesman, lived in the previous house on this site, and there are several mementoes of his family on show.

St Albans' clock tower from the church gateway

The Gardens of the Rose

Lovely rose gardens here incorporate a trial ground for new species. The fragrant and colourful displays include 30,000 plants of some 1,650 varieties.

City Museum open all year daily (except Sun and Bank Holidays).
Verulamium Theatre open all year daily (except Christmas). **Museum** open all year daily, Sun pm only.
Kingsbury Water Mill open all year daily (except Mon, Tue and Christmas week). Sun pm only. Parking and refreshments available.
St Albans Organ Museum open for recitals Sun pm.
Gorhambury House open May to Sep, Thu pm only. Parking available.
The Gardens of the Rose open mid June to Sep daily. Parking and refreshments available.

St Michael's Mount – an early centre of Christianity in these isles

St Mawes Castle

Cornwall *p211 B1*

One of Henry VIII's coastal defence fortifications, St Mawes Castle was completed in 1543 and together with Pendennis Castle on the opposite bank, guarded the entrance to Falmouth harbour. It follows the trefoil, or cloverleaf, pattern much favoured by Henry VIII, with circular bastions protecting the round central tower. It has been well restored, and is more or less complete with some carvings, Tudor fireplaces, and Latin engravings on the walls. The slots in the walls where the drawbridge mechanism was operated, and where soldiers could defend the walls are still visible. Below the castle are some nineteenth-century gun emplacements. The whole site is now surrounded by extensive gardens, and there are superb views across Carrick Roads, Falmouth harbour, and out to sea.

See AM info. Also open Sun am, Apr to Sep. Parking available.

St Michael's Mount

Cornwall *p211 A1*

Rising 230 feet out of the sea in Marazion Bay, is a rocky island crowned by a building of fairytale battlements and pinnacles. It was called St Michael's Mount because legend has it that St Michael appeared in a vision on the outcrop in 710, and Benedictine monks from Brittany subsequently built a monastery there. This accounts for its resemblance to Mont St Michel in France.

After the Dissolution of the monasteries it was a royal fortress until, in 1659, it became the home of the ancient Cornish St Aubyn family, and has remained so ever since. The Mount can be reached either by a causeway at low tide or, during the summer at high tide, by boat from Marazion or Penzance. The interior has some beautiful Georgian Gothic decoration, some intricately carved wooden and period furniture, and a collection of armour and pictures.

Open all year Mon, Wed and Fri, Jun to Oct Mon to Fri. NT.

St Osyth

Essex *p213 D4*

The little village of St Osyth is a charming old-world community, centred around the Norman church and the ancient ruins of St Osyth Priory. Founded in the twelfth century by Augustinian Canons, the priory was named after the martyred daughter of Frithenwald, first Christian king of the East Angles. Only a few fragments of the original building remain, but they include an impressive late fifteenth-century flint gatehouse, complete with battlements and patterned with stone. St Osyth Priory is set in extensive and beautiful grounds of parkland and gardens. Red and Fallow deer roam free in the deer park, and peacocks grace the shady lawns. The gatehouse building contains apartments which house a collection of ceramics and jade.

Gardens and original priory remains open May to Sep daily. Private apartments, ceramics and jade, Aug daily, pm only.

Salisbury Wiltshire *p212 F3*

This great city, county town of Wiltshire, situated at the confluence of the rivers Avon, Bourne, Nadder and Wylye, spans the centuries with architecture from all periods.

The roots of Salisbury lie in Old Sarum, now on the outskirts of the city. Originally a cathedral and a castle stood at Old Sarum, with attendant town, but the close proximity of Church and State gave rise to friction. This, combined with the high winds which were damaging the cathedral, and a shortage of water near the site, compelled the clergy to leave Old Sarum, and rebuild their cathedral two miles away, down in the meads. Gradually the townspeople followed, and Old Sarum fell into decay although until 1832 it retained two members of parliament, despite the electorate numering only ten.

Today Salisbury is a thriving market town, and people from all over the south-west come to meet and trade. Apart from the normal market, there is a large cattle market and a Corn Exchange.

Salisbury and South Wiltshire Museum

A visit to this museum is a valuable precursor to exploring the city. There is a large collection of local exhibits, among the most exceptional are a group of mounted Great Bustards, all shot on Salisbury Plain and now a bird extinct in this country and models of Stonehenge and Old Sarum with a fascinating collection of objects found on these sites. There are also exhibits of finds from the city's past, such as Guild relics, including a processional giant, used in Guild pageants.

The Cathedral

On Easter Monday, 1220, the first foundation stones were laid, and thirty-eight years later the main building of the cathedral was finished. Before the end of the century the towering spire was added, which with the tower, soars 404 feet above the surrounding plain. Unlike many medieval cathedrals, Salisbury, because of the short time it took to build, has a uniformity of style unmatched anywhere else. It has an entrance for every month of the year, a window for every day, and a column for every hour – 8,760 altogether. The imposing west front has tier upon tier of niches in which statues once stood, but most have disappeared disappeared and those left are mainly nineteenth century.

There are many impressive tombs within the cathedral, the earliest, with a magnificently

An open-air market is held in Salisbury every Tuesday and Saturday

mailed and armoured figure reclining upon it, is that of William Longespere, who witnessed the signing of the Magna Carta and was laid here in 1226. In the north transept is the oldest clock in working order in Britain. Made in 1386, it has no dial, but strikes the hour.

The thirteenth-century roof painting in the choir has been restored, and beautiful sculptures decorate the walls of the octagonal chapter house. The cloisters, the largest of any English cathedral, contain some medieval glass, and in the library over the east walk one of the four remaining copies of the Magna Carta is kept.

Mompesson House

On the north side of Chorister's Green stands one of the finest houses in the cathedral Close. Mompesson House was built in 1701 for Thomas Mompesson, a rich merchant. A restrained, dignified building, the plain well-proportioned exterior contrasts with the lush interior decoration. It contains a finely carved staircase, elaborate plaster ceilings and overmantels, and some original panelling.

The House of John A'Port

Six times Mayor of Salisbury, John A'Port built this half-timbered, three-storeyed house in 1425. In 1930 restoration began and the plaster and paint removed to reveal the original beams. Alterations to the building were slight, and none of the old timbers had to be replaced.

Today it is a shop, but visitors are welcome to look at the stone fireplaces, the old staircase, Jacobean oak panelling of the upstairs room, and the carved oak mantel piece made in 1620.

Poultry Cross

Built to provide shelter for vendors at market, this octagonal building was probably erected as an act of penance by a wealthy citizen which was the custom at the time. It is the only one of four market crosses left, and is still used by market folk as it has been since the fifteenth century.

St Thomas of Canterbury

The original church was built in 1238, but the building as it stands is fifteenth century, with some of the earlier features retained. Notable here is the Tudor roof of the nave, and the remarkable, if crude, painting above the chancel arch. Restored in the nineteenth century, this sixteenth-century work shows Christ atop a rainbow, the Virgin Mother and St John with saints beneath sending the damned to hell below.

Salisbury and South Wilts Museum open all year Mon to Sat, also Sun pm July and Aug. Closed Christmas and Good Fri.
Old Sarum see AM info. Also open Sun am Apr to Sep. Parking available.
Mompesson House open Apr to Oct daily (except Thu and Fri) pm only. Parking available. NT.

Sandringham House has been a favourite royal residence since 1862 and it is the present Royal Family's traditional New Year venue

Samlesbury Hall

Lancashire *p216 E4*

This fine old half-timbered building was first built in 1325, but restored in the sixteenth and nineteenth centuries. Particularly interesting is the banqueting hall, complete with a minstrels' gallery and several valuable antiques and paintings.

Throughout the year a wide variety of exhibitions are held at the Hall, sometimes with craftsmen demonstrating their work.

Open mid Jan to mid Dec daily (except Mon). Refreshments available.

Sandringham

Norfolk *p218 E1*

Sandringham was purchased in 1862 by Queen Victoria, following the wishes of her husband, Prince Albert, who felt that their eldest son Edward, Prince of Wales, should have his own home. The house had many additions and alterations made to it in order to accommodate the Prince's family and household. Amongst the many treasures contained within the mansion are several paintings of the Royal Family, and members of European royal families.

Well laid out routes through the grounds surrounding the house provide a good way to appreciate their colourful beauty. North of the mansion is a lovely flower garden created by King George VI, and nearby stands an eighteenth-century statue of Father Time – purchased by Queen Mary in 1950. Also within the grounds is the Church of St Mary Magdalene, which contains many memorials and gifts connected with the Royal Family.

A former Royal Retiring Room used specifically by kings and queens en route to Sandringham can be seen at Wolferton Station, about two miles west. Built in 1898, the rooms contain fine oak panelling, the original fittings (some gold plated), period posters, important small railway relics and Edwardian curios – including some from royal train journeys.

Sandringham House, Grounds and Museum open Apr to late Sep (except mid July to early Aug), Mon, Tue, Wed and Thu; Sun pm only. Parking and refreshments available.

Wolferton Station (down side) open Apr to Sep (plus Bank Holidays) daily (except Sat), Suns pm only. Parking available.

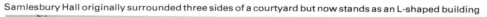

Samlesbury Hall originally surrounded three sides of a courtyard but now stands as an L-shaped building

Scarborough North Yorkshire *p217 C4*

Scarborough – historic town, working fishing port and host to various national festivals, is nevertheless best known as a large, popular east-coast holiday resort.

The old harbour at Scarborough and the lighthouse which guides vessels

Scarborough first began to develop as a spa in about 1649, when water from a stream flowing across the South Sands was discovered to have curative properties. The next century saw the first bathing machine here (local people claim it was invented here), and since then crowds have flocked to Scarborough in order to enjoy the invigorating North Sea air.

The twin bays either side of Scarborough's promontary provide great stretches of sandy beaches. North Bay, backed by beautiful gardens, is studded with rocks which dry out at low tide and provide numerous pools to explore, although north-easterly gales result in exceptionally heavy surf which makes swimming dangerous. However, the main part of the resort is centred along South Bay, and here there are sheltered sands and safe bathing. Around the old harbour, still used by commercial vessels carrying timber, stand picturesque eighteenth-century buildings, including Customs House,

King Richard III's house (now a café) and some interesting old pubs, including the Three Mariners Inn in Quay Street. This dates from the fourteenth century and, once the haunt of smugglers and, although no longer a licenced premises, it can be viewed by the public.

The several Victorian villas which remain in the town include the Medicinal Baths, Londesborough Lodge and the Art Gallery which contains a permanent collection by local artists – all three are in The Crescent. The Rotunda Museum, situated in Vernon Road, has an interesting collection of regional archaeology and Scarborough bygones.

Wood End Museum

This is the home of the Sitwell family, who all became famous writers. The house is set in charming gardens and contains a collection of first editions, portraits belonging to the family, natural history and geology exhibits.

St Mary's Church

The novelist Anne Brontë, a frequent visitor to the town with her sister, Charlotte, is buried in the churchyard. The church, built in the early twelfth century, was rebuilt in the fifteenth, but severely damaged during the Civil War. However, it still retains its medieval arcades, piers and south-aisle chapels.

The Castle

Scarborough Castle has dominated the town for 800 years, and stands on the magnificent headland between the two bays. The Normans built the large keep, the barbican and the curtain wall

which can still be seen today. Although besieged six times, the castle was never taken by force.

Three Mariners Inn open daily.
Art Gallery open all year Tue to Sat and Sun pm, Spring Bank Holiday to Sep only.
Wood End Museum open all year Tue to Sat; Sun pm only Spring Bank Holiday to Sep.
Castle see AM info. Also open Sun am Apr to Sep. Parking available.

Scone Palace

Tayside *p220 D5*

Scone was the capital of the ancient Pictish kingdom until 843, after which Kenneth MacAlpine, King of the Scots, overthrew the Picts and united the two nations. MacAlpine brought the Stone of Destiny to Scone, and Scottish kings were crowned on it for 400 years before it was removed to Westminster Abbey.

The present palace is an enlargement of the house built in 1580 by the Earls of Gowrie. By 1805 the architect had completed the Gothic restyling of the palace, with its turrets and castellations which were reminiscent of the medieval royal abbey that once stood here.

Among the many treasures within the Palace is fine French furniture from the eighteenth and nineteenth centuries, including a piece made for Marie Antoinette shortly after her wedding, and a superb collection of china (housed in the library) including an armorial tea service from the 1700s. Beautiful family portraits adorn the walls of the long gallery, a room measuring some 168 feet – an unusual feature in Scottish homes. Other items of interest include a collection of French and English clocks, and a rare set of Vernis Martin vases.

The spacious grounds of the Palace are famed for the beautiful walks they afford through giant oaks, limes, copper beeches and sycamore trees. Magnificent displays of colour are provided throughout the seasons by daffodils, azaleas, and rhododendrons.

A huge collection of conifers grows in the Pinetum, some reaching a height of 140 feet. Giant sequoias and Sitka spruces are just two of the varieties to be seen here. Also in the grounds is an agricultural machinery exhibition, and a children's adventure playground set in a small wood.

Open late Mar to mid Oct daily, Sun pm only (all day Jul and Aug). Parking and refreshments available.

Severn Valley Railway

Shropshire *p216 E2*

The famous Severn Valley Railway is the foremost standard-gauge railway in the country, and has one of the largest collections of former British Rail locomotives. Over thirty are on show at the terminuses at Bewdley and Bridgnorth, and as many as five can be seen in steam when the service is in operation. There is also a vast amount of rolling stock, much of which is ex-Great Western, restored to its original livery.

The line runs for sixteen miles, following the winding river Severn through some beautiful scenery. North from Bewdley it crosses the edge of the Wyre Forest where wooded slopes reach right down to the river, then across the massive Victoria Bridge, a 200-foot span, high above the river. With superb river views, the line passes through several village stations before entering Bridgnorth, a pleasant town built on two levels, with a strangely leaning castle keep.

Passenger services operate at frequent intervals every weekend Mar to Oct and most weekdays from mid May to early Sep, plus all Bank Holidays. Parking at Bewdley and Bridgnorth. Refreshments available.

Sewerby Hall, Park and Zoo

Humberside *p217 D3*

This fine Georgian mansion was built between 1714 and 1720, and now serves as an art gallery and museum. Its collections include historical and archaeological items, and paintings by local artists. However, the principal feature here is the Amy Johnson Room. Exhibits include the pilot's awards and trophies, and her pilot's log book which spans 1928 to 1938.

The Severn Valley Railway travels through gloriously open country

The grounds extend to some fifty acres and are attractively laid out with gardens, notably an Old English walled garden. Deer and wallabies can be seen in the park and there is also a mini-zoo and aviary. Recreational facilities here include a miniature golf course, archery, croquet, bowls, putting, and a children's corner.

Grounds open all year daily.
Museum open Easter to Sep daily, Sat pm only.

Shaftesbury

Dorset *p212 F3*

Perched high on the edge of the Mendip Hills, this ancient town looks down over the wide expanse of Blackmoor Vale. Shaftesbury's famous Gold Hill, a steep cobbled street lined with old cottages, is one of the most photographed street scenes in the country, and at the top of this hill the Local History Museum is to be found. Exhibits include agricultural and domestic items, toys, needlework,

Picturesque Gold Hill in Shaftesbury – originally a West Saxon town where Edward the Martyr was buried in 981

fans, pottery and finds from local excavations. Some of the relics relate to the old Benedictine Abbey for nuns, which was founded here in the ninth century by King Alfred. Although the abbey was demolished after the Dissolution, its foundations can still be seen near the Town Hall.
Abbey Ruins and Museum open Good Fri to Oct, daily.

Sheffield Park Gardens

East Sussex *p213 C2*

The credit for these beautiful gardens, situated in the heart of Sussex, can be laid at the feet of two people. The original design with its trees, swards and serpentine water was landscaped by Capability Brown in 1775 and thus was greatly modified in the early part of this century by A G Soames. It was Soames who introduced the exotic trees and shrubs which changed the face of the 150 acres of woodland garden and parkland.

Lakes spanned by ornamental bridges, waterfalls and watery vistas recall the spirit of the original layout and the views across the water owe much to the introduction of dark conifers, pampas grasses and white-stemmed birches.

Autumn, especially the second half of October, is a magnificent scene with hundreds of trees and shrubs planted specially for their autumn colour. Tupelo trees, azaleas, maples, birches and larches contribute to the spectacle. Due to the high trees growing to the west, the colour is best seen in

the morning or early afternoon. By contrast spring comes almost modestly, yet the greensward is covered with Lent lilies and later types of daffodils, narcissi and bluebells; great belts of rhododendrons, azaleas and other early-flowering shrubs. Also hundreds of water lilies float their blossoms on the surface of the lakes.

Also of interest is an avenue of hardy palms, displays of autumn gentians and trees such as Wellingtonias, Eucalyptus, redwoods and cedars.

Open Apr to early Nov Tue to Sat; Sun and Bank Holiday pm only. Closed Good Fri and Tue after Bank Holiday. Parking and refreshments available.

One of the four landscaped lakes in Sheffield Park Gardens

The 15th-century St John's almshouses at Sherborne from the abbey gate

Sherborne

Dorset p212 E3

The quiet country town of Sherborne stands on the edge of the lovely Blackmore Vale, on the north bank of the river Yeo. Sherborne school is famous, founded in the sixteenth century and now occupying some of the former abbey buildings. Adjacent to the school is the beautiful abbey church, burial place of the ninth-century kings Ethelbald and Ethelbert, which possesses some fine fan vaulting and old monuments. The abbey gate house contains the Sherborne Museum, with local history and Roman material, local photographs and natural history. Particularly interesting are a model of a Norman castle and a Victorian dolls house.

Sherborne has two castles. The Old Castle, built by Roger, Bishop of Salisbury, in the early twelfth century, is now a ruin. In 1592 Sir Walter Raleigh acquired the castle, but his attempts to modernise it for his own use proved futile, and soon afterwards he began the New Castle. This is more of a stately home than a castle, and is surrounded by lovely woods and parkland. In the seventeenth century the Earl of Bristol, whose descendants still live at Sherborne today, added two wings to the castle, creating an ornate and impressive exterior. Capability Brown planned the twenty acres of pleasure grounds which include a lovely lake, a cascade and an orangery. Special events take place here on Sundays during the summer.

Museum open all year, Apr to Oct daily (except Mon), Sun pm only, Nov to Mar Tue, and Sat.
Old Castle see AM info. Also open Sun am Apr to Sep. Parking available.
New Castle open Easter Sat to Sep, Thu, Sat, Sun and Bank Holidays, pm only. Parking and refreshments available.

Shrewsbury *Shropshire p216 E2*

This charming old county town is famous for its superb setting, its half-timbered buildings and its picturesque streets. Magnificently set on a virtual island in a huge loop of the river Severn, no less than nine bridges connect the town to the opposite bank of the Severn.

Shrewsbury was traditionally founded by the Britons who abandoned Wroxeter, the Roman City of *Viroconium* lying just five miles to the south-east, and subsequently adopted this strategic site.

Much of the character of this historic town has been retained in its narrow old streets. Gullet Passage and Grope Lane exemplify the bizarre alley and street names here which have changed little from the days of Elizabeth I; with their quaint, narrow passageways and leaning upper storeys almost meeting over them. Everywhere there are superb black and white buildings of plaster and weathered timber. Among some of the numerous notable examples of these are: Rowley's House in Baker Street; Bear Steps in St Alkmund's Square; Abbot's House in Butcher's Row; the tall gabled Ireland's Mansion and Owen's Mansion in the High Street; Rooke's House in Dogpole; King's Head in Mardol and the Old Council House Gateway.

The Castle

Commanding the once vulnerable north-eastern approach to the town, the castle was built soon after the Norman Conquest, but the present structure dates chiefly from about 1300. In 1790 the building was refurbished as a house by the engineer and architect, Thomas Telford. The keep is square, with circular corner turrets and a good proportion of its walls and inner bailey still survive, together with a Norman gateway.

Bear Steps

This group of picturesque buildings is of considerable antiquarian interest, and consists of a recently restored timber-framed fourteenth-century cottage with shops and a lovely old meeting hall. The hall itself has a mid-fourteenth-century crown post roof.

Clive House Museum

An interesting eighteenth-century Georgian town house, this was once occupied by Clive of India, during his period as Mayor of Shrewsbury in 1762. It now houses a collection of Caughley and Coalport china, maw tiles, costume, and church silver, together with a Georgian room and the Regimental Museum of the 1st Queen's Dragoon Guards.

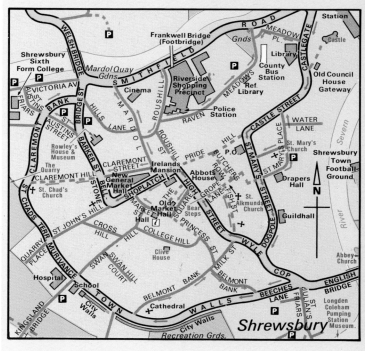

Shrewsbury Castle defends the river approaches to the ancient capital

Rowley's House

Rowley's House is a restored sixteenth-century timbered house which contains impressive Roman remains from Wroxeter, and a collection of Shropshire bygones.

Longden Coleham Pumping Station

Situated on the south side of the river, facing the town, is this fine old pumping station. Now a museum, it preserves its two compound beam engines which were originally installed in 1900 and are now restored to working order.

St Mary's Church

The fine stone spire of the largest church on the Shrewsbury skyline is one of the three tallest in England. St Mary's is Norman, with Early English and later work. Its stained glass is particularly beautiful and the fourteenth-century jesse window in the chancel is especially rich in colour.

St Alkmund's Church

The other major spire of the skyline belongs to St Alkmund's, which was built in the late eighteenth century on the site of a medieval church. This, too, has good stained glass, with an east window portraying an adaptation of Reni's *Assumption of the Virgin*.

St Chad's Church

The most unusual-looking of the town's churches and one of the very few round churches in the country is St Chad's. It has an oddly-shaped tower – the top half being shaped like a minaret crowned with a dome.

Abbey Church

Some Norman work is preserved in this impressive abbey church, founded in about 1080 by Roger de Montgomery. The west tower has a fine Perpendicular window and the font is reputedly made from a Roman capital. There are also some interesting tombs and monuments dating from about 1300 onwards.

The Quarry

On the town side of the river lies this huge park, which bears witness to the talents of famous gardener Percy Thrower. The splendid formal gardens of The Dingle, near its centre, are his great work.

Statues commemorate two great men associated with the town; Charles Darwin (1809–82), born and educated in Shrewsbury, together with Robert Clive (1725–74). Whilst among the famous nineteenth-century visitors at The Lion – a Georgian coaching inn – were Charles Dickens, the singer Jenny Lind and the violinist Paganini.

Castle and Regimental Museum open Easter Sat to Oct daily. Oct to Easter, Mon to Sat only.
Bear Steps open all year daily (except Sun).
Clive House Museum open all year (except Sun and Bank Holidays).
Rowley's House open all year daily (except Bank Holidays). Sun, mid May to Sep, pm only.
Longden Coleham Pumping Station open all year Mon to Sat, pm. only.

Shugborough

Staffordshire *p216 F2*

The white colonnaded mansion, lying in a shallow valley on the northern edge of Cannock Chase, is the ancestral home of the Earls of Lichfield.

The house was built in 1693 and greatly enlarged in the eighteenth century. Along with the 900 acres of grounds it passed to the National Trust in 1966, and is now a museum – although the present Earl still lives in part of it.

The Staffordshire County Museum takes up the kitchen wing and stable block, and has displays illustrating agricultural development, rural crafts and social history. Among the exhibits is the Shrewsbury collection of horse-drawn vehicles, and an eighteenth-century brewhouse and laundry. The house itself contains a fine collection of French furniture and much porcelain and silver. Drawings and sketches by Landseer are on display, as well as a long series of portraits of the Earl's ancestors.

The gardens and park, landscaped by James Stuart, are decorated with temples and follies, and at the park farm rare breeds of livestock are reared.

Open mid May to Oct Tue to Fri and bank Holidays, Sat, and Sun pm only. **Museum and Park Farm** only open winter Tue to Fri; Sun pm only. Parking and refreshments. NT.

Sissinghurst Castle Gardens

Kent *p213 D2*

Situated in the Weald between the North and South Downs, this magnificent garden has been created around the remaining buildings of the original medieval castle. They are the result of work in the 1930s by the writers Vita Sackville-West and her husband Sir Harold Nicolson. Extensive and colourful, the enchanting gardens are a collection of varying shapes and sizes, interspersed with beautiful lawns and separated by a yew, lime and a moat walk. The white garden in front of the old Priest's house features, as its name implies, plants which have a profusion of white blooms. Borders of flowering shrubs, trees, bulbs and the orchard, with its dogleg moat, all add to the beauty of Sissinghurst, and the rose garden is at its best in June and July.

The Priest's House at Sissinghurst seen from the unique garden which contains white flowers only

The long library and the Elizabethan tower, from which there is an excellent panoramic view of Kent, are also open to the public. A delightful room in the tower was Vita Sackville-West's study.

Open Apr to Oct daily (except Mons) pm only. Sat, Sun and Good Fri all day. Parking and refreshments available. NT.

Sizergh Castle

Cumbria *p220 E1*

Home of the Strickland family for more than 700 years, Sizergh Castle was begun in the mid fourteenth century as a simple pele tower (defensive border fort). Later additions have created a sizeable property, one of the largest, in fact, of the border fortresses which were built in the turbulent days before the Union of Crowns. The exterior, surmounted by battlements, is still impressive, although eighteenth-century modifications considerably softened its appearance.

Inside the castle there is particularly fine wood panelling and carving, decorated plaster ceilings and seventeenth-century Flemish tapestry. The furniture is both English and Continental, and items collected by the family over the centuries include Stuart and Jacobite relics, a fourteenth-century two-handed sword, a collection of family portraits and a medieval document describing Sir Walter Strickland's allegiance to the Earl of Salisbury in 1448. The grounds extend to more than 1,500 acres and contain gardens, terraces, a lake and rock garden with pools and waterfalls.

Open Apr to Oct. House and garden open Sun, Mon, Wed and Thu; pm only. NT.

Skegness

Lincolnshire *p217 D2*

'Skegness is so Bracing' was the slogan advertising the Great Northern Railway's trips to this seaside resort in 1908, and it was the coming of the railway that led to the development of the resort. Today, its wide sandy beach, attractions and entertainments, are as popular as ever.

Although it is a vastly different place from the tiny fishing village so loved by the poet Tennyson in the early nineteenth century, its history is not forgotten. The Church Farm Museum is housed in a farmhouse and outbuildings which have been restored to show the life and work of a Lincolnshire farmer at the end of the nineteenth century. Displays include the Bernard Best collection of farm implements and machinery, and an interesting exhibition of veterinary equipment. Also on display are a re-erected timber-framed cottage and barn. During the summer craftsmen demonstrate their skills at weekends.

The promenade at Skegness is very attractive with its large areas of colourful gardens and seafront attractions. At North Parade is the popular Natureland Marine Zoo. Seals, sea lions and penguins are kept here in modern enclosures; a tropical house features creatures such as snakes, scorpions, and crocodiles, and the aquarium has both tropical marine tanks and a large fresh water fish collection. The Floral Palace is a riot of colour with its exotic plants and free-flying tropical birds, while more familiar animals can be found in the pets corner. The zoo also cares for baby seals which have been orphaned and washed up locally.

Church Farm Museum open May to Oct daily. Parking available, refreshments at weekends.
Natureland Marine Zoo open all year daily (except Christmas Day). Refreshments available.

Skipton

North Yorkshire *p217 A3*

To the north of Skipton lie the Yorkshire Dales, to the south rugged moorland extends along the Pennine chain into Derbyshire. Skipton stands near the northernmost point of the Leeds and Liverpool canal on the banks of the Eller Beck, a tributary of the river Aire.

A variety of interesting buildings in the town include the Old Town Hall, or Toll-Booth, with its remains of the town stocks. Popularly regarded as The Gateway to the Dales, Skipton is essentially a market town although even the introduction of textile manufacturing in the eighteenth century, which is now giving way to light industry, did nothing to lessen its rural atmosphere.

Standing on high ground, with an impregnable ravine to the north, are the few remains of the original castle. Built by the Normans in the twelfth century, it suffered extensive damage in the thirteenth century and was largely rebuilt by the Clifford family. Today it provides a fine example of a medieval fortress. Fully roofed, it has a picturesque interior courtyard and a massive

gatehouse flanked by six fourteenth-century round towers.

The Town Hall contains the Craven Museum which includes exhibits of folk life, lead mining and prehistoric and Roman remains, with special reference to the Craven District.

Situated in the High Corn Mill, parts of which date from the thirteenth century, the George Leatt Industrial and Folk Museum is built on a site where milling has been carried out since before the Normans came to England. Both restored and operational machinery includes two waterwheels, and flour milled on the premises may be purchased. Other points of interest here are a working blacksmith's forge and a collection of horse-traps and carts.

Some two miles to the northeast of Skipton, the Yorkshire Dales Railway Society have created the Embsay Steam Centre. Attractions here include steam locomotives, vintage carriages, and a shop selling models.

Castle open all year (except Sun am, Good Fri and Christmas Day) daily.
Craven Museum open Apr to Sep daily (except Tue), Sun pm only, Oct to Mar open daily (except Tue and Sun) pm only, Sat all day.
George Leatt Industrial and Folk Museum open most Wed, Sat and Suns, pm only.
Embsay Steam Centre open weekends, Bank and school holidays.

Right: Seaside entertainment is the trademark of Skegness

Skipton Castle was the last Royalist stronghold to surrender in the north

Skye

Highlands *p221 A2*

Skye, an historic isle of romance, is a wild area of mountains and lochs, inhabited by gaelic-speaking crofters and fisherfolk. This loveliest of Scottish islands is quickly reached from the mainland; but, beyond Skye, scattered islets streach away to the ocean. Its mountains are slashed by sea lochs up the western coast and in the north-west and south-west lie fertile areas with farms and woods. The land is often shrouded in mist, and when the sun shines on the red granite and black gabbro of its peaks, blue waters, and whitewashed crofts, it presents a timeless picture.

There are two ways of enjoying Skye: to feast the eyes and breathe in the atmosphere; or, for the strong and active, to walk, climb and explore. The island's natural phenomena include the Lealt Falls, where salmon may sometimes be seen leaping; the Old Man of Storr, a remarkable basalt column on the Trotternish ridge; and the Kilt Rock and waterfall where the rock has been eroded into pleats, all of which lie north of the island's capital of Portree.

In the southern part of the island, the magnificent Loch Coruisk is encircled by the famous Cuillin hills, best reached by boat from the hamlet of Elgol. Dunvegan Castle is the home of the Chief of Clan Macleod, where Rory Mor's two-handed sword and the MacLeod's Fairy Flag are preserved.

Two folk museums of note are

The ruin of Caisteal Maol stands guard over the waters between Skye and the mainland

the Skye Cottage Museum at Kilmuir and the Skye Black House Folk Museum at Colbost. The former consists of four one-hundred-year-old thatched croft cottages. The museum also houses a fine selection of implements and tools used by the people of the Highlands, together with interesting collections of old letters, papers and pictures.

The Skye Black House Folk Museum is housed in a well-restored typical nineteenth-century Black House, and contains implements and furniture of bygone days. Behind the museum is a replica of a whisky still.

Also of interest is the Skye Watermill, situated at Glendale on the shores of Loch Pooltiel. This grain mill and kiln (200 years old) has recently been restored to working order and is open to the public. At Armadale, the visitor can find the Clan Donald Centre which is located in the recently restored north wing of Armadale Castle, the seat of the Macdonalds. Although the main part of the building is now derelict, it was originally built in 1815 in the Gothic style and is set in romantic grounds. These sheltered woodland gardens overlook the waters of the Sound of Sleat.

Skye Cottage Museum open mid May to Sep daily (except Sun). Parking available.
The Skye Black House Folk Museum open Easter to Oct daily. Parking available.
Skye Watermill open Easter to Oct daily (except Sun.). Parking and refreshments available.
Dunvegan Castle open Easter to mid Oct Mon to Sat pm only, late May to Sep all day. Parking available.
Clan Donald Centre open Easter to Oct Mon to Sat, also, Sun pm from Jun to Sep. Gardens always open. Refreshments available.

Sledmere House

Humberside *p217 C3*

This handsome, solid looking Georgian building has been the home of the Sykes family since it was originally built in the late eighteenth century. In 1911 a fire gutted the entire building, although much of the furnishings were rescued. It was restored to its original state by the architect W H Brierly. The park that surrounds the house was laid out in a semi-formal design by Capability Brown, and includes formal gardens, vast lawns, a lake and an Italian fountain.

The rooms are large and airy, the largest being the enormous library which has a semi-circular vault and is divided into three compartments. The contents include furniture by Chippendale and Sheraton, a set of Louis XVI

A vast sweep of park in front of Sledmere House makes the house look shorter than it actually is – 120 feet

seat furniture, and an early eighteenth-century tea table in Canton enamel. Paintings and portraits, including one by Benjamin West, adorn the walls. Of particular interest is the Turkish Room (built after the fire) which is decorated with tiles obtained in Damascus.

Special events take place here some weekends during the summer, and a children's playground is in the grounds. One unusual feature is the organ recital held on the second and last Sundays of each month and on Bank Holiday Sundays.

Open early Apr then Sun only till early May; mid May to Sep daily (except Mon and Fri, but open Bank Holiday Mon) pm only. Parking and refreshments available.

Slimbridge Wildfowl Trust

Gloucestershire *p212 E4*

Sir Peter Scott founded the Trust in 1946, in order to aid the conservation of birds, and the centre at Slimbridge was the first of seven to be opened. Over 3,000 birds are kept here, making this the largest collection of wildfowl in the world.

Some seventy-three acres of landscaped pens, lakes and paddocks are open to visitors, where numerous species of ducks, geese and swans can be watched at close quarters. Observation towers and hides afford a closer look at the more wary birds. Appropriate food for wildfowl can be purchased from the gatehouse, and binoculars may be hired.

The collection includes many rare and exotic varieties, and has the largest flock of flamingos in captivity. In the tropical house several fascinating species of birds sensitive to the British climate live amidst jungle foliage and exotic flora.

The visitor reception area houses a permanent exhibition centre, a cinema and a gift shop.

Open all year daily (except Christmas). Parking, refreshments and picnic facilities available.

Flamingos in characteristic pose at Slimbridge Wildfowl Trust

Snowdonia National Park Gwynedd

'There is no corner of Europe that I know which so moves me with awe and majesty of great things as does this mass of the northern Welsh mountains'. These sentiments of the novelist Hilaire Belloc echo a response which has stirred visitors for centuries.

The Snowdon Mountain Railway was first opened on Easter Monday, 1896

Snowdonia National Park comprises 840 square miles of beautiful and varied countryside – mountains, lakes, forests, estuaries and twenty-five miles of coastline. Within its boundaries are sixteen nature reserves, which testify to the unusual store of wildlife, stark villages whose people still make their living off the hillsides, and numerous relics of ancient tribes and cultures.

Nearly all the early remains of man's settlement in Snowdonia are found along the northern coastline – from near Bangor to Conwy – and from the estuary of the Traeth Mawr to that of the Dyfi. People settled upon these slopes facing the sea because of the milder climate and the wind, which kept tree growth down. The valleys were uninhabitable, due to marshes and impenetrable forest.

Between 4,000 and 2,000 BC, settlers arrived either by way of St George's Channel, or by the land which once linked southern Britain with Ireland. These people left behind them great Megalithic tombs, built of huge slabs of stone. Examples can be seen a little inland between Harlech and Barmouth, and at Maen Y Bordel and Capel Garmon in the Conwy Valley.

Inland from Aber to Penmaenmawr, and from Talsarnau to Tywyn are many round cairns, or barrows, dating from 2,000 BC, in which the ashes of the cremated dead were placed in pottery vessels. This form of burial persisted for well over 1,000 years. Druids Circle above Penmaenmawr is the best example of a stone circle. Simple standing stones are frequent, and probably marked ancient pathways over the mountains from the ports on the coasts.

With the arrival of iron and the weaponry that accompanied it, came the necessity to build hill-forts, fortified by walls of earth and stone. There are examples on Conwy Mountain, at Pen y Gaer, half a mile south-west of Pont Aberglaslyn, and in western Merioneth. These date from about 500 BC, and probably played a major part in the struggle against the Romans, who held Wales as a frontier for over three centuries from AD 73. They built a series of forts linked by roads. From the fort at Caerhun, four miles south of Conwy, the Roman road known as Helen's Causeway

runs through the centre of the National Park, linking Caerhun to forts at Bryn y Gefeiliau near Capel Curig, Tomen y Mur, a well-preserved example, Brithdir and Pennal. Another fort is Caer Gai, on the shores of Bala Lake.

The principal remains of early Christian settlements are the gravestones of the founding missionaries of the sixth and seventh centuries, who arrived shortly after the Romans left. A collection of these can be found in the church at Penmachno. At Beddgelert and Tywyn, parts of the existing churches date back to the twelfth and thirteenth centuries, and many parish churches in Snowdonia show work from the thirteenth to sixteenth centuries.

Snowdonia's highest point is a mere 3,650 feet above sea level, yet it appears a mountainous area, perhaps because of the abrupt nature of the landscape – its sudden rise from the coast, deep valleys and great bare slopes, a ruggedness left by the ice-age glaciers. Consequently there is an enormous variety of habitat, from the milder coastal regions to the spectacular eroded peaks upon which grow alpine plants, such as purple and mossy saxifrage, found on the north facing lock ledges of Cwms.

An easily identifiable upland bird is the raven, which makes its home among the crags, and can frequently be seen throughout Snowdonia wherever there are sheep. The buzzard also nests in the high crags and shares the raven's diet of beetles, worms, carrion sheep and voles. The peregrine, though rarely seen, still lives here and it is hoped, will recover its numbers – so drastically cut as a result of them eating prey poisoned by insecticide. The ring ouzel and wheatear are the two most interesting small upland birds, and of course the wren, which is a true mountain bird and can live at a height of 2,000 feet. On heather moors, such as Berwyn, are grouse, and where young conifer plantations meet the heatherland the black-cock is found.

The competition of cattle and sheep has banished deer from the hillsides, although Fallow deer which have escaped from parks are spreading in the larger Forestry Commission plantations. Farmers blame the forests for harbouring foxes, of which there are many. Due to limited game keeping, other predators have survived here which have been persecuted to the point of extinction in most other areas of Britain. The polecat, hardly known outside Wales, is quite common, and the rare pine marten, whose dark red-brown fur is known as sable in the fur trade, still exists in the remoter woods. The otter is also rare, although weasels, stoats and badgers are fairly common. These predators feed on an

abundant supply of field voles, bank voles, water voles, wood mice, shrews and hedgehogs.

Walking, climbing, skiing, canoeing, sailing, fishing and pony trekking are popular activities in the National Park of Snowdonia and there are several facilities for these throughout.

The Carneddau and Rhinog ranges provide challenging walks in mountainous scenery, whereas walks through the easier terrain of the Gwydyr, Beddgelert, Coed y Brenin and Dyfi forests, the Cregennen lakes and the north side of the Mawddach estuary, avoid high mountains but reveal fine views, moorlands, valleys, trees and open water.

Snowdon itself is the most popular summit, and was the attraction of North Wales which drew the first tourists in the eighteenth century. There are six major routes to the top, and for the less energetic, the Snowdon Mountain Railway climbs to the 3,650-foot peak at a steady 5mph. Beginning at Llanberis, the track runs nearly five miles to a bar, restaurant and shop at the summit, each train consisting of a single coach propelled by a Swiss-designed rack and pinion engine – the only one in Britain.

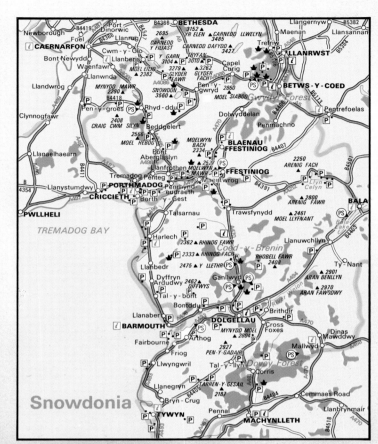

Snowshill Manor is a treasure house
of curios and a tiny model village
is laid out in the terraced gardens

Snowshill Manor

Gloucestershire *p212 F5*

This small manor house built of
warm Cotswold stone is Tudor in
origin, and once belonged to
Catherine Parr – wife of Henry
VIII. The interior reflects the
character of its last owner,
Charles Wade, who was a com-
pulsive collector of a wide variety
of items, and it is these collections
which make Snowshill Manor
particularly remarkable. Some
take over whole rooms, such as
the nautical collection of old com-
passes, the model ship and the
telescopes. Another is devoted to
early forms of transport – old
bicycles, sedan chairs, models of
farm carts and hobby-horses.
There are also old musical instruments, weaving and lacemaking

A wealthy Victorian railway
magnate rebuilt Somerleyton
Hall in the 19th century

exhibits, and many other fascinating, unusual, rare and valuable objects.

Open Apr to Oct, Wed to Sat and
Bank Holiday Mon, (Apr and Oct,
only open Sat, Sun and Bank Holiday
Mon). NT.

Somerleyton Hall

Suffolk *p214 E5*

The magnificent red brick and
mellow stone mansion, rebuilt in
Anglo-Italian style in 1846,
stands surrounded by twelve
acres of beautiful gardens.

On the east side of the house
there is a French Renaissance arcade, and the north end supports
a charming campanile, or bell-
tower. The west, or garden, side
has an ornate three-storey,
square porch, inset with a fine

oriel window and topped by pinnacles at each corner. These, combined with the stone parapets and stone-faced dormer windows, present a delightful façade.

The interior has some rich carved panelling, particularly in the oak parlour and on the staircase, and there are some superb pieces of antique furniture, tapestries and big game trophies.

The gardens, including a statuary, are well laid out with lawns, flowering shrubs, rare trees, shaped hedges, and the remains of a winter garden surrounds a sunken garden. A fine pagoda stands in the centre of the maze, and there is a nature trail and miniature railway.

Open Easter Sun to Sep Thu, Sun and Bank Holidays pm only; also Tue and Wed also in July and Aug. Refreshments and parking available.

Southampton

Hampshire *p213 A2*

Southampton is a modern commercial port with a fine shopping centre, new civic buildings, a good deal of industry, a splendid university, fine sports and leisure facilities. However, the secret of its character is that it has been a modern port for upwards of a thousand years – always adapting to change, rebuilding, strengthening, growing. The docks, situated where the rivers Itchen and Test join Southampton Water, have expanded over the centuries into the giant passenger and container services for which the city is now famous. The liner *Queen Elizabeth II* moors here.

Southampton has had the status of city since 1964, although it has no cathedral. The mother church is St Mary's, a handsome late-nineteenth-century building, and the oldest church is St Michael's which dates back to Norman times. The base of the tower is the earliest part and inside is a twelfth-century French font. The tower of Holy Rood, a fourteenth-century church which was badly damaged by bombing in 1940, has been preserved as a memorial to men of the Merchant Navy. Other memorials are the Mayflower column commemorating the Pilgrim Fathers who sailed from Southampton in 1620, and a sculpture in East Park dedicated to the crew of the *Titanic*.

Tudor House, now used as a museum of antiquarian and historical interest, is a fine example of a timber-frame town house with overhanging upper storeys. The Bargate, a striking medieval gateway and now the focal point of the city centre, was originally the northern entrance to the medieval town. Its upper floor, once the Guildhall, contains a museum of local history. An interesting maritime museum is housed in a fourteenth-century wool warehouse which has buttressed stone walls and old roof timbering.

The Southampton Hall of Aviation, dedicated to R J Mitchell, houses historic aircraft, including the Spitfire Mk 24 and the Seaplane S6A which made world speed records in 1929. There is also a Sandringham Flying Boat and displays depicting aviation production and engineering in the South of England.

The Art Gallery housed in the Civic Centre includes a collection of eighteenth to twentieth-century English paintings, Continental Old Masters of the fourteenth to eighteenth centuries, and modern French paintings, including works by the Impressionists. There is also a small collection of sculpture and ceramics here.

Tudor House Museum open all year Tue to Sat, Sun pm only (closed Christmas and Bank Holiday Mons). **Bargate Guildhall Museum** open all year (except Christmas and Bank Holidays) Tue to Sat, Sun pm only. **Wool House Maritime Museum** open all year Tue to Sat, Sum pm only (closed Christmas). Parking available. **Southampton Hall of Aviation** open all year Tue to Sat, Sun pm only (closed Good Fri and Christmas). Parking and refreshments available. **Art Gallery** open all year (except Christmas) Tue to Sat, Sun pm only.

Southend-on-Sea

Essex *p213 D3*

Within easy reach of London's east end, Southend has extended its reputation as a day-tripper's paradise to become a commuter colony, at the same time retaining its position as a favourite holiday resort. In the process it has swallowed a number of villages, encouraged industry, and undertaken a good deal of rebuilding and development, including a shopping centre which attracts a new variety of day-tripper – Continental shoppers who fly in to Southend Airport or come by ship. The town is situated on the Thames estuary and the tide goes out a long, long way, uncovering

Vessels ranging in size from ocean-going liners to hydrofoils ply up and down Southampton Water

mud which is said to have curative properties. To provide enough depth of water for ships, the pier has to stretch out beyond the sand and silt and is, at one-and a quarter miles, the longest in the world.

The pierhead is the focal point of an area devoted to fun – amusement park and entertainment centre rolled into one, with facilities for a variety of sports into the bargain.

To the east, Thorpe Bay has a quieter atmosphere, with a beach of sand and shingle. There are ornamental gardens and an Edwardian bandstand at Westcliff, and further up the estuary is the fishing village of Old Leigh, where cockle boats can be watched unloading.

One mile from Southend is Prittlewell which is reputed to be one of the oldest villages in Essex. In fact, it is thought that the name of the resort originated from its being established at Prittlewell's south end. Set among the extensive gardens of Priory Park is the old priory, erected in the 12th century and rebuilt in 1470. It now houses a museum which contains displays of natural and social history of south-east Essex.

At Southchurch there is a fourteenth-century moated manor house called Southchurch Hall. This has been restored and is furnished as a medieval manor house, although one wing is Tudor in style.

Prittlewell Priory Museum open all year Tue to Sat (except Good Fri and Christmas). **Southchurch Hall** open all year Tue to Sat (except Good Fri and Christmas).

Southend's pleasure pier – packed with amusements

Southport

Merseyside *p216 D4*

Donkeys still take children jig-jogging along the sands of Southport, and in the mornings race-horses are exercised on the beach. This combination of traditional entertainment and refinement is typical of the town. Amusement areas such as Happiland (for children) and Pleasureland contrast with beautiful parks and gardens; kiosks and shops along the front are complemented by boulevards of select emporiums; sporting facilities include a skate-board rink and a golf club; and entertainment varies from ballet to brass bands, and from zoos to steam engines.

Southport Zoo in Princes Park, covering three-and-a-half acres, contains aviaries and an aquarium as well as an assortment of mammals and reptiles. In Churchtown, the older part of Southport, are thatched cottages, old pubs, and the splendid Botanic Gardens, where there is a section specialising in ferns, a pets' corner and a small museum. The town's most distinctive feature is Lord Street, which runs parallel to the sea front and for more than a mile forms a wide boulevard with attractive shops on one side, and gardens, fountains and public buildings on the other. These include the Atkinson Art Gallery, which has both permanent and temporary exhibitions of painting and sculpture, and an Arts Centre which caters for theatre and music lovers.

The Steamport Transport Museum houses ex-BR locomotives and also buses, tram-cars and traction engines, while the Model Village and Model Railway on the promenade is marvellously detailed.

Southport Zoo open all year daily (except 25 Dec). Refreshments available.
Atkinson Art Gallery open all year daily (except Sun), Thu and Sat am only.
Botanic Gardens Museum open all year, Tue to Sat and Bank Holiday Mon, Sun pm only. Closed Good Fri, Christmas and New Year's Day and Fri following Bank Holiday Mon.
Model Village and Railway open Mar to Oct daily.
Steamport Transport Museum open June to mid Sep, Mon to Fri pm only. Also open from mid morning on Sat and Sun, May to Sep, and during July and Aug daily. Oct to Apr Sat and Sun pm only. Parking and refreshments available.

Above: Wayfarers' Arcade – a shoppers' paradise – typifies Southport's Victorian elegance

Spalding

Lincolnshire *p217 D1*

Spalding stands in a flat landscape interwoven with dykes and streams, which make it very similar to parts of Holland. Both ancient and modern buildings blend harmoniously together in this delightful town – world famous for its bulb and horticultural industry.

One of the outstanding features of the town is the impressive Ayscoughfee Hall. Dating back to the fifteenth century, the house was later restored in the Gothic style. Many rare and beautiful stained glass windows can be seen here, encompassing all periods from fourteenth to the eighteenth centuries. The Hall is also the home of a bird museum, and contains several hundred British specimens.

The most famous of Spalding's attractions however must be Springfields, a unique twenty-five-acre spring flower park on the eastern out-skirts of the town. Over a million bulbs flower here in springtime amidst lawns and lakes, and under glasshouses. The summer rose gardens, a recent addition, are a collection of over 12,500 rose bushes, in a hundred varieties. The flower parade takes place here each spring, a spectacular procession

of floats decorated with numerous colourful tulip heads, watched by crowds of some 200,000 people. After the procession, the floats are displayed at a four-day exhibition, together with many other exhibits of both an educational and commercial nature.

Ayscoughfee Hall and Gardens Limited opening due to redevelopment. Due to reopen fully in 1987.
Springfield Gardens Flower parade and exhibition usually mid May. Spring gardens open late Mar to mid May, summer gardens open Jul to Sep daily. Parking available.

Speke Hall

Merseyside *p216 E3*

Speke Hall, a particularly fine half-timbered, black and white house, stands in a wooded park on the north bank of the river Mersey. It was started in 1490 by Sir William Norreys, but it was not until the sixteenth century that it assumed its present form. A red sandstone Elizabethan bridge, which once spanned the moat, leads to the gloomy inner, cobbled, courtyard where two yew trees, over 400 years old, grow.

The interior of the house presents a fascinating blend of styles ranging from the seventeenth century to the mid nineteenth century. Among the furniture there are some fine antiques, and of particular interest are the Mortlake tapestries. The great chamber, or hall, has a sixteenth-century plasterwork ceiling of inimitable quality, fine wainscoting of Flemish origin and an Elizabethan chimney-piece. The kitchen has stone mullioned windows and contains a display of polished brass and copper cooking implements, a collection of smoothing irons, and some interesting early vacuum cleaners.

Open all year daily (except New Year, Good Fri and Christmas), Sun pm only. NT.

Spetchley Park

Hereford and Worcester *p212 F5*

The lovely early nineteenth-century neo-Classical home of the Berkeleys, although not open to the public, adds a great deal of charm to the gardens which sur-

The Dutch introduced the tulip industry to Spalding over 60 years ago and now the area grows more than half Britain's bulbs

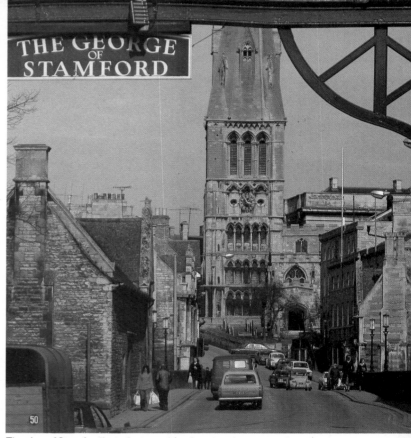

The sign of Stamford's ancient coaching inn stretches across the street

round it. These extend to more than thirty acres with many rare trees, shrubs and plants, and a lake inhabited by ornamental wildfowl. Springtime at Spetchley is particularly delightful, although the gardens are colourful throughout the summer. In the park wander herds of Red and Fallow deer and there is a garden centre selling plants and shrubs.

Open Apr to Sep daily (except Sat), Sun pm only. Garden centre also open in Mar. Parking and refreshments (Sun and Bank Holiday Mons only) available.

Stamford

Lincolnshire *p213 B5*

Stamford's Town Bridge, just by the ford used since prehistoric times, is the heart of a town whose position has brought it importance and prosperity. It is quieter since a bypass took through-traffic away from its streets and retains so much charm that it is now a conservation area.

During the Middle Ages it had six religious houses; little remains of these but five out of fourteen medieval churches are still used. In Red Lion Square are All Saints, an Early English building which has a separate fifteenth-century tower with a tall spire, and St John's, which also dates from the fifteenth century. St Mary's has a thirteenth-century tower with a fine fourteenth-

century spire, and a chapel which has a roof decorated with stars. St Martin's, south of the river, is late fifteenth century and contains a monument to the first Lord Burleigh.

Nearby are almshouses founded by Burleigh in 1597, the year before his death. Brasenose Gate, a pointed arch in the old grammar school wall, is a reminder of those Oxford students who set up a short-lived rival university in the fourteenth century.

Browne's Hospital, founded in the fifteenth century by a rich wool merchant, enlarged in 1870 and now modernised, is one of the finest examples of medieval almshouses in the country. Riverside meadows, an open-air swimming pool, and the Friday Market are other attractions of the town.

About one mile south, is Burghley House, the largest and grandest Elizabethan house in existence. Arranged around a courtyard, it has towers, turrets, and the tall decorated chimneys which typify Tudor architecture. The interior is equally magnificent, containing over 700 works of art. In the grounds are a lake, a rose garden and an orangery.

Browne's Hospital open all year by appointment.
Burghley House open Good Fri to early Oct daily. Parking and refreshments available.

The river Avon provides a lovely setting for distinguished Stanford Hall

Stanford Hall

Leicestershire *p213 A5*

This fine William and Mary mansion was built in about 1690 on a lovely site overlooking the river Avon. The Hall remains largely unaltered and contains some fine antique furniture, family portraits and a collection of Italian works of art. Seventeenth-century Flemish tapestries adorn the walls and the ballroom has particularly good decorative plasterwork with hunting scenes painted on the walls.

The stable block which stands next to the house, now houses a collection of old cars and motorcycles. There is also an aviation museum set up to commemorate Lt. Percy Pilcher RN, who was the first man in the country to get a flying machine off the ground. The centre-piece of the museum is a replica of his plane, *The Hawk*, which took to the air in 1898. Unfortunately Pilcher died the following year when his plane crashed in the park and a memorial erected by the Royal Aeronautical Society now marks the spot.

Other interesting features at Stanford Hall include an old forge, and a working craft centre which operates at weekends. There is a colourful walled rose garden, and the park has a nature trail and facilities for fishing.

Open Easter to Sep Thu, Sat and Sun pm only; Easter, Spring and Late Summer Bank Holiday Mon and Tue pm only. Parking and refreshments available.

Steamtown Railway Museum

Lancashire *p216 E5*

Once the meeting point of three of the old railway company lines, Carnforth is now the home of the Steamtown Railway Museum. The engine shed, covering thirty-seven acres with almost four miles of track, is the home of thirty steam locomotives of various sizes. They have been collected here, not only from Great Britain, but also from France and Germany and range from the little *Gasbag*, formerly in use at Cambridge Gas Works, to the magnificent *Flying Scotsman*. The museum also has a restored automatic electric coal plant, a 75,000-gallon water tank, a carriage and wagon repair shop and a seventy-foot turntable. A fifteen-inch gauge miniature passenger railway also operates on this site. Locomotives can be seen 'in steam' on Sundays from Easter to October and daily during July and August.

Open all year daily (except Christmas Day). Parking and refreshments available.

Stirling Central *p220 C4*

Stirling is a very pleasant town of lovely gardens and great historical interest. It is a busy shopping centre and a junction of several of Scotland's main highways lying at the heart of an area of great beauty.

Known as the Gateway to the Highlands, the town is surrounded by fertile agricultural land which is watered by the meandering river Forth. It is overlooked by the lovely wooded Ochil Hills and even loftier peaks appear away on the horizon. In the past Stirling has paid the price for its strategic position and battlefields such as Sauchiburn (1488), Stirling Bridge (1297) and Bannockburn (1314) can be seen nearby. An equestrian statue of Robert the Bruce looks over Bannockburn and a presentation by the National Trust for Scotland illustrates this decisive battle in Scotland's struggle for independance. Today Stirling is a centre of learning, with its new university built on the banks of the loch within the Airthrey estate to the north of the town. The public are free to wander in its parkland setting and its MacRobert Centre provides opera, concerts and exhibitions for all.

Although the town is dominated by its castle, there are many other historic buildings. Argyll's Ludging (Lodging), now used as a Youth Hostel, is a remarkable example of seventeenth century domestic architecture. Cowane's Hospital, or Guildhall, was built for 'the support of twelve decayed gild breithers' by John Cowane, Dean of Guild. The Tollbooth was the work of the famous Scottish architect, Sir William Bruce, and features a fine pavilion roof and clock tower. Nearby is the Mercat Cross, a tall column surmounted by a unicorn and flanked by cannons. Standing in the middle of the road, this was for many centuries the focal point of the town for events, announcements and public punishments. More ancient than all of these is Stirling's Auld Brig (Old Bridge) over the Forth which was built in 1415 and is now pedestrianised.

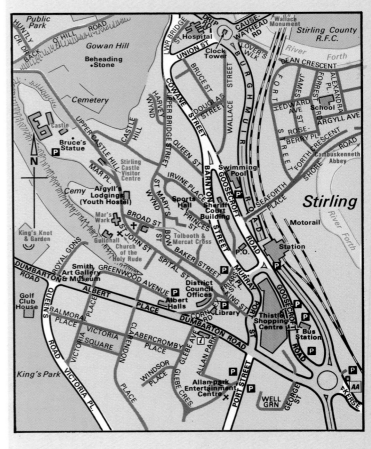

The Castle

Perched on a 250-foot sheer crag dominating the town, this imposing castle seems to have grown from the stone on which it is built. It figured prominently in the wars of Scottish succession during the thirteenth and fourteenth centuries, passing back and forth between Scots and English until it was finally won by the Scots in 1342. From 1370 to 1603 the castle was the home of the Stuart Kings and it was they who shaped the castle as it is seen today, replacing an earlier wooden structure. It was an era during which the castle was witness to coronations, festivities and all the intrigue which surrounded the Royal Court. It was the birthplace of James II and James V and both Mary Queen of Scots and James VI (James I of England) spent several years in the castle. It was James V who created the magnificent Renaissance palace within the castle walls, one of the best examples of its type in the country. From the castle's lofty position there are some splendid views extending well into the highlands, particularly from the 420-foot high Queen Victoria's lookout and from Ladies Rock. The upper rooms of the palace contain the Museum of the Argyll and Sutherland Highlanders, the castle's 'home regiment', and items on display include the regiment's silver and plate, uniforms and a collection of medals from the time of Waterloo to the present day.

King's Knot

This ancient mound is thought to be an Iron Age burial mound but was long ago incorporated into the castle garden. Bordering the old jousting grounds, it was used as a sort of medieval grandstand for royal spectators of the tournaments. It is now a popular picnic area amid wooded lawns.

Stirling Castle Visitor Centre

A multi-screen presentation, complete with sound effects, traces the history of Stirling and brings to life such events as the Battle of Bannockburn, a tournament at the castle and the commercial life in the town. There is also an exhibition of life in Stirling one hundred years ago and a shop with Scottish crafts, books and records.

For over 800 years Stirling has looked up to a protective castle

Mar's Wark

These ruins were once the magnificent palace built by the Earl of Mar in the fifteenth century but never completed. It was a building which went from riches to rags for it housed the newly-wed James VI and his bride soon after it was built, but later became a workhouse.

Church of the Holy Rude

This impressive fifteenth-century church has an unusual open timber roof and a five-sided apse in the choir. Its 90-feet-high tower bears the scars of hostilities which may have occurred during the Civil War or the Jacobite rebellion. Mary Queen of Scots was crowned here as a child and, following her abdication, it was the scene of the coronation of her son James VI, also an infant monarch.

Wallace Monument

To the north of Stirling, overlooking Causewayhead, is this famous pinnacled monument to Sir William Wallace, who defeated the English at the Battle of Stirling Bridge in 1297. It is a tall tower on top of the 362-feet-high Abbey Craig and incorporates a bronze statue of the patriot. The Tower Hall contains a display of armour which includes Wallace's 5ft 4in two-handed sword, together with a collection of portrait busts of famous Scots such as Robert the Bruce, Robert Burns, Sir Walter Scott and many more. Over 200 steps lead up to the top of the monument from where there are magnificent views.

Cambuskenneth Abbey

The remains of this Augustinian abbey, founded by David I in the eleventh century, lie beside the river Forth to the east of the town. It was the scene of Bruce's first Scottish parliament in 1326 and is the burial place of James III and his wife. The abbey was dissolved during the Reformation and some of its masonry was used for new buildings in the town.

Castle open all year daily (Sun pm only from Oct to Mar). AM.
Museum of the Argyll and Sutherland Highlanders open Easter to Oct daily. Parking and refreshments.
Stirling Castle Visitor Centre open all year daily (except Jan); Sun pm only Oct to Dec. Refreshments.
Mar's Wark open at all times. AM.
Wallace Monument open Feb to Oct.
Cambuskenneth Abbey open Apr to Sep daily, Sun pm only. AM.

It is remarkable to think that the massive stones at Stonehenge were moved using only levers and ropes

Stokesay Castle

Shropshire *p216 E1*

Stokesay Castle, reputed to be the oldest fortified manor house in England, dates back to the eleventh century. Many additions were carried out during the thirteenth century and during the Civil War the house was surrendered to Parliament, but survived relatively unscathed.

The courtyard is oblong in shape and surrounded by a wide moat. The oldest part of the house is thought to be a wing projecting into the moat in the north-west corner. The beautiful sixteenth-century gatehouse has an ornately timbered upper section, and replaces an earlier drawbridge house. Good examples of Early English windows can be seen in the fine thirteenth-century hall, heated by means of a central brazier.

Open early Mar to Oct daily (except Tue), Nov weekends only. Parking available.

Stonehenge

Wiltshire *p212 F3*

To the west of Amesbury on the broad expanse of Salisbury Plain lies Stonehenge, one of the most impressive Megalithic monuments in Europe. Uncertainty shrouds its purpose, but it is believed that this was the site of ancient sun-worshipping ceremonies. The pattern consists of an outer ring and an inner horseshoe of sarsen, or 'foreign', stones which came from the Marlborough Downs. Some of the larger sarsens are over twenty-one feet in height and embedded to a depth of more than eight feet. Set up inside and outside the horseshoe are eighty bluestones with the largest, the so-called Altar Stone, at the centre of the horseshoe. The bluestones are thought to have been brought from the Preseli Hills in Dyfed. An outer ditch, banking, and fifty-six late-Neolithic holes mark the outer perimeter of the stones.

Open all year daily. Parking and refreshments available. AM.

Stourhead House and Gardens

Wiltshire *p212 F3*

This fine Palladian mansion was built for the wealthy banker, Henry Hoare, in the early eighteenth century. Although the interior is superb, the whole

house is somewhat overshadowed by the magnificent gardens – acknowledged as having one of the finest layouts in Europe.

It was the second Henry Hoare who was responsible for the original landscaping, and he devoted many years to its development. The area covered is vast and the combination of water, lawns, trees, shrubs and Classical temples is delightful. Carefully designed vistas have been made to appear completely natural, whilst others which are more obviously

Wellington chose Stratfield Saye House, an unpretentious country retreat, as his home

contrived are no less enchanting. Each generation made useful additions to the flora at Stourhead, notably the many varieties of rhododendrons and azaleas, but the basic landscape remains the same.

House open daily (except Fri) between May and Sep, pm only. Mon to Wed, Sat and Sun, pm only, Apr and Oct.
Gardens open all year daily. NT.

Stratfield Saye House

Hampshire *p213 A3*

Originally built in 1630 by Sir William Pitt, Stratfield Saye was later purchased by the Nation in 1817 for the first Duke of Wellington after his victory at Waterloo.

The Duke's life and work is reflected throughout the rooms of this Jacobean-styled house: Napoleon's Tricolours hang from marble columns; the library con-

Stone Bridge and the Pantheon at Stourhead

tains leather volumes from his early days in India, and paintings and bronzes portray his beloved Copenhagen – the charger who carried the Duke at Waterloo, and whose grave is marked in the grounds. The house is full of beautiful pieces of French furniture, Sèvres china, silver, and a fine art collection. Of particular historic interest is the Roman mosaic pavements excavated from nearby Silchester.

Open Easter and weekends in Apr, May to end Sep daily (except Fri).

Stratford-upon-Avon

Warwickshire *p216 F1*

Famous as Shakespeare's birthplace, Stratford is a charming old market town in its own right. Mellowed buildings, many half-timbered, line broad streets. Lush meadows lead to the gently flowing river Avon, and brightly-coloured boats on the canal lend a holiday atmosphere to this pleasant town in the heart of England.

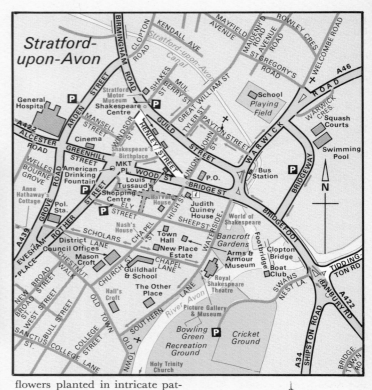

The town first grew from a Bronze Age settlement, was succeeded by a Romano-British village, and then in Anglo-Saxon times a monastery was founded. Recognition as a town came when it was granted the right to hold a weekly market in about 1196. In the thirteenth century, the powerful Guild of the Holy Cross built its chapel and hall, and virtually ran the town. When Henry VIII suppressed such religious organisations, the municipal power went to a bailiff, fourteen aldermen and fourteen burgesses. John Shakespeare, William's father, held the office of bailiff in 1568.

Stratford is surprisingly unspoilt, for there is no doubt that since the first Shakespeare Festival, 200 years after his death, a large part of the town's prosperity is due to its Shakesperian connections. This medieval and Georgian town is now second only to London as a tourist attraction.

A portrait assumed to be of Shakespeare, our greatest dramatist

Holy Trinity

Approached down a long avenue of limes, this partly thirteenth-century building stands in quiet, pleasant grounds beside the river Avon. The great panelled door has a sanctuary knocker; any criminal who reached it could gain thirty-seven days' grace. In the chancel set, in the wall above his gravestone, is a bust of Shakespeare. It was made within a few years of his death and is supposedly a fairly accurate likeness. His wife lies on one side and his daughter Susanna on the other.

Particularly beautiful features of this church are the choir stalls, richly carved with figures. Among them is a scolding wife pulling a man's beard, a monkey drinking from a jug and a mermaid with a mirror, combing her hair.

Nash's House

The name of this splendid half-timbered building comes from Thomas Nash, who was the husband of Elizabeth Hall, Shakespeare's grand-daughter. It is now

a museum depicting Stratford's history since prehistoric times, and provides an accurate record of England in Shakespeare's day.

Behind Nash's House is the Knott garden, with herbs and flowers planted in intricate patterns, and the Great garden. A mulberry tree, said to have been grown from a cutting of a tree Shakespeare planted, shades the lawn.

180

Royal Shakespeare Theatre, Picture Gallery and Museum

The red-brick block of the theatre's buildings was the country's first National Theatre. Built from a public fund and completed in 1932, it is best seen at night when its riverside position is enhanced by floodlighting. The Royal Shakespeare Company which performs here is world famous, and the auditorium and huge stage, with its mechanical contrivances, were designed specifically for Shakespeare's plays.

The gallery contains portraits of Shakespeare, famous Shakespearian actors and actresses, scenes from plays performed at the theatre, and theatrical relics.

Harvard House

From this house John Harvard left his parents and set out for America. Educated at Cambridge, he died at the age of thirty but left a legacy of £779 17s 2d for the founding of Harvard University. His grandparents, Thomas and Alice Rogers, whose initials are carved on the front of the house, built it in 1596. The rambling interior is full of passages and winding stairs with rough beams in the rooms.

The rambling cottage at Shottery where Anne Hathaway's family lived

Now the property of Harvard University, it contains some interesting exhibits, including the walking stick of Jefferson Davis, the Southern leader in the Civil War.

Shakespeare's Birthplace

The house in Henley Street where Shakespeare was born is visited by more than 500,000 people every year. It has been restored to its old condition as far as possible and is a typical middle-class home of the period. The stone-paved living rooms open straight on to the street, and in the kitchen the great fireplace with its roasting spit and cast-iron pots includes an unusual feature, a seventeenth-century 'baby-minder', which prevented children from getting too close to the fire.

Upstairs is the room Shakespeare was born in. The walls and ceiling, even the glass in the windows, are scratched with the names of visitors. These include those of Walter Scott, Robert Browning, Isaac Walton and other literary figures. Among the treasures in the house are a sword and a ring said to be Shakespeare's, his school desk, documents, portraits and a letter sent to him by his friend Richard Quiney asking for a loan of thirty pounds.

Hall's Croft

Perhaps the most impressive medieval house in Stratford, Hall's Croft was the home of John Hall, an eminent local doctor and husband of Susanna, Shakespeare's elder daughter. The house contains an exhibition illustrating sixteenth- and seventeenth-century medical practice. The walled garden is a delight, and the house is seen at its best from here. When Susanna's daughter, Elizabeth, died in 1670, Shakespeare's direct line of descendants came to an end.

Stratford-upon-Avon Motor Museum

This pleasant Victorian building, once a church and school, is the home of an excellent motor museum, recommended to every

vintage motoring enthusiast.

The vintage cars and motorcycles are displayed in a setting with a theme of the Roaring Twenties – the Golden Age of Motoring. Specialities include exotic sports cars and grand tourers from that age – often recovered from places like India, and professionally restored to showroom condition. Also here is the music, fashion and decor of the twenties; a replica of one of the early roadside garages; and many collections of motoring memorabilia. A shop, picture gallery and picnic garden complete the attractions.

Elizabethan England is recreated in the World of Shakespeare building with life-size tableaux combining dramatic light and sound techniques and original music.

Ann Hathaway's Cottage

Two miles from the centre of Stratford is the village of Shottery. The Hathaway family lived here, and did so until 1892. Shakespeare married Ann in 1582, and the house is kept much the same as they must have known it. The fifteenth-century building with its country garden looks like a typical English cottage, although in fact it has twelve rooms. One of these has a settle beside a large fireplace where Shakespeare is said to have courted his bride-to-be. The kitchen is a fascinating place where old cooking utensils, tableware and other tools of a working Elizabethan kitchen are kept.

In one of the bedrooms is an oak bed over 400 years old. It has five carved figures at its head, the original rush mat beside it and a needlework cover made by Ann Hathaway's sister.

Nash's House open all year Mon to Sat, also Sun pm Apr to Oct. Closed 25 Dec, 1 Jan and Good Fri am.
Royal Shakespeare Theatre, Picture Gallery and Museum open all year daily, Sun pm only. Parking.
Harvard House open Apr to Sep Mon to Sat and Sun pm; Oct to Mar certain weekdays only.
Hall's Croft open all year (except Good Fri am, Christmas and New Years Day am) Mon to Sat, also Sun pm Apr to Oct.
Shakespeare's Birthplace open all year daily. Closed Sun am Nov to Mar, Good Fri am, Christmas and New Years Day am.
Motor Museum and World of Shakespeare open all year daily.
Ann Hathaway's Cottage open all year daily (except Good Fri am, Christmas, New Years Day am and Sun am Nov to Mar). Parking available.

Sudbury Hall

Derbyshire *p216 F2*

Sudbury Hall, a seventeenth-century Jacobean mansion set in attractive parkland, was the home of the Vernons until 1967.

Its fine 138-foot long gallery is decorated with murals by Laguerre, Grinling Gibbons carvings and an elaborately carved staircase by Edward Pearce. The east wing of the house contains the Museum of Childhood which has a permanent exhibition entitled Exploring Childhood; each room has activities for children and there are galleries for temporary exhibitions of arts and studies.

In the grounds is the twelfth-century All Saints Church which has a stained glass window presented by Queen Victoria.

Open Apr to Oct Wed to Sun and Bank Holiday Mon pm only. Parking and refreshments. NT.

Sudeley Castle and Gardens

Gloucestershire *p212 F5*

This very large and very grand castle has a history stretching back for over 1,000 years, but owes its present grandeur to the extensive restoration undertaken during the nineteenth century. The exterior was treated most sympathetically and adheres to the style of the remaining parts of the fifteenth-century edifice, with towers and battlements.

The interior, however, is almost completely nineteenth-century, with occasional reminders of the illustrious past of Royal Sudeley. The chapel contains the tomb of Catherine Parr, sixth wife of Henry VIII, who out-lived her husband and came to Sudeley as wife of its owner, her second husband Sir Thomas Seymour. She died soon afterwards, followed shortly after by her husband who was executed for treason. The tomb of the dowager queen is not the original, which was destroyed by Parliamentarians, but is a nineteenth-century replacement. The castle contains a magnificent art collection including works by Constable, Poussin, Van Dyck and Turner. There is also some fine period furniture, tapestries, one of which is reputed to have belonged to Marie Antoinette, an exhibition of costumes and the largest private collection of toys on public view in Europe. The grounds are extensive and include formal gardens and a lake. A more recent addition is the large adventure playground for young visitors, complete with its own replica castle.

Open Apr to Oct daily, grounds from late morning, castle and exhibitions pm only. Parking and refreshments available.

Suffolk Wildlife and Country Park

Suffolk *p214 E5*

In a gently sloping, part-wooded country park just outside Kessingland, is this interesting collection of birds and animals. Some will be familiar to all, such as the goats, sheep and waterfowl; others include the more elusive native species such as Red and Fallow deer. Animals from far off continents are the monkeys, llamas, wallabies and, most impressive of all, the big cats. There are many varieties of birds in the park including colourful parrots, macaws, owls, toucans, stately peacocks, cranes, rheas and the sacred ibis. Many of the birds and animals are free-roaming and special food can be purchased to feed the ducks and geese on the lake.

Open all year daily. Parking and refreshments available.

Sulgrave Manor

Northamptonshire *p213 A4*

The oldest part of Sulgrave Manor was built in the sixteenth century by Lawrence Washington. At that time it was a modest building and additions were made during restoration in the early part of this century. It was the ancestral home of George Washington; his great-grandfather, John Washington departed from Sulgrave Manor for America in 1656. After having several owners the house was eventually bought by a body of British subscribers in 1914, then restored and refurnished by American subscription for the peoples of Great Britain and America to celebrate the hundred years of peace.

The house is now a museum containing portraits, contemporary furniture and many relics associated with George Washington and his family. The most treasured possession in the manor is an original oil painting of George Washington which hangs in the great hall. Above the main door is the Washington coat of arms.

Sulgrave's fourteenth-century church contains many memorials related to the manor, including the tomb of Lawrence Washington and the Washington family pew.

Open all year daily (except Wed and Jan). Parking available.

Sutton Park

North Yorkshire *p217 B3*

This is an elegant seventeenth-century building, much influenced by the Palladian style of architecture. The interior is for the most part light and extremely attractive with rooms of modest proportions and some superb plaster ceilings. Much of the contents originated from the ancestral home of the Dukes of Buckingham at Normanby Park in Lincolnshire, including some fine pieces of furniture and a large array of family portraits. In the entrance hall is a drawing of the first Duke's London home which is now Buckingham Palace. Throughout the house there are a large number of attractive and valuable clocks, and collections of enamelwork and porcelain. The latter collection is housed in the porcelain room, which has a particularly lovely porcelain chandelier. An interesting feature is the Chinese room with its rare Chinese wallpaper.

The house is surrounded by parkland, landscaped by Capability Brown, and delightful gardens.

Open Easter Fri, Sun and Mon, then Suns in Apr. From early May to early Oct Sun, Tue and Bank Holiday Mon, pm only. Parking and refreshments.

Sweetheart Abbey

Dumfries and Galloway *p220 D2*

The tiny, picturesque village of New Abbey is situated in a wooded setting on the Pow Burn. Overlooking the village is Sweetheart Abbey, one of the most beautiful monastic ruins in Scotland. Dating from the thirteenth century, it was constructed of red sandstone brought from the quarries at Caerlaverock, and colon-

The Jacobean front of Sudbury Hall, with diapered brickwork and a Baroque porch designed by Sir William Wilson

ised by monks from nearby Dundrennan Abbey.

This, the last pre-Reformation Cisterican abbey to be built in Scotland, was founded by Devorgilla, Lady of Galloway. She also founded Oxford's Balliol College in memory of her husband, John Balliol the elder. Upon her husband's death, Devorgilla kept his embalmed heart in a casket and it was from this that the abbey got its name.

Lying in a secluded hollow, the roofless remains of the abbey include the ninety-foot-high central tower and much of the nave and transepts. The short choir is dominated by a great rose window and the precinct wall is amazingly well-preserved. This encloses about thirty acres and was built from particularly large stone boulders.

Devorgilla was buried in front of the abbey altar, together with her husband's heart, in 1289. The original monument fell into decay but a replacement was set up in the south transept chapel in 1933.

The isolated Abbot's Tower stands to the north-east with the estuary of the river Nith and Solway Firth beyond.

See AM info. Parking available.

Above: Sulgrave Manor kitchen, with its great fireplace, contains old cooking implements and antique guns
Below: Sudeley Castle dates from the 14th century and once belonged to Yorkist kings Edward IV and Richard III

Talyllyn Railway

Gwynedd *p216 C2*

The small seaside town of Tywyn is the terminus for the narrow-gauge Talyllyn Railway which was once used to carry slate and passengers from the Bryn Eglwys Quarry, south of Abergynolwyn, to the coast at Tywyn. It now carries visitors for some seven miles up a beautiful valley, close by the Dolgoch Falls to Nant Gwernol, near to the foot of the Cader Idris range.

Maintained by the Talyllyn Railway Preservation Society since the early 1950s, it was the first railway in Britain to be saved by volunteers – and the first to provide a continuous public service since 1866. Adjacent to Talyllyn Wharf Station is a museum which contains one of the finest collections of relics representing narrow-gauge railways, including a number of locomotives and wagons.

Railway open Easter to late Sep regular daily services, Oct to early Nov Tue to Thu, Sat and Sun, late Dec to New Years Day daily. Time tables available. Refreshments.
Railway Museum open Easter to Oct daily, Nov to Mar by arrangement.

Tamworth Castle Museum

Staffordshire *p216 F2*

In 1897, the Corporation of Tamworth acquired the castle to commemorate the Diamond Jubilee of Queen Victoria, and to establish a museum. So it remains today – a remarkably well-preserved building in a variety of styles which show something of its long history. The oldest part is a section of early Norman herringbone masonry which leads to the keep, a remnant of the days when the Marmions, Royal Champions of the Kings of England, lived here.

One of the finest rooms in the castle is the fifteenth-century banqueting hall with its lofty open-timbered roof and mullioned windows. The majority of the castle buildings are of seven-teenth- and eighteenth-century construction and contain richly carved woodwork, period furniture and there is a painted heraldic frieze in the state apartments.

Many of the rooms contain art exhibitions and items of local history.

Adjacent to the castle is a sixty-five-acre park on the banks of the rivers Tame and Anker. Three-and-a-half acres have been laid out with lawns and flower beds – the rest is laid out with a playground and sports and swimming facilities.

Open all year daily (except 25 Dec and Fri), Sun pm only. Parking available.

The great tower of Tattershall Castle once housed about 100 servants

Tattershall Castle

Lincolnshire *p217 D1*

Both the village of Tattershall and the surrounding flat fenland are dominated by the massive square keep of Tattershall Castle, which rises to a height of over a hundred feet. It was built in the fifteenth century of locally made bricks as an extension, to provide more comfortable accommodation than the existing castle offered. At the end of the seventeenth century the castle was left empty and subsequently fell to ruin. At the beginning of this century is was rescued by Lord Curzon from transportation and re-erection in America, and he restored the keep before donating it to the National Trust in 1926.

Today, the keep stands alone, the earlier buildings having all gone, surrounded by smooth lawns and two moats. It is a solid and impressive structure with four corner turrets, the walls surmounted by battlements which enclose five storeys and forty-eight rooms. Particularly interesting are the stone fireplaces, carved with heraldic detail, which were recovered and reinstated by Lord Curzon.

Open all year (except 25 and 26 Dec) daily. Nov to Mar and Sun pm only. NT.

Tatton Park

Cheshire *p216 E3*

In a magnificent deer park of some 1,000 acres, stands Tatton Hall. The grounds were landscaped by Humphry Repton in the middle of the eighteenth century and today leisure pursuits, such as horse riding, exploring nature trails and picnicking, can be enjoyed in them. On a large lake called Tatton Mere there are facilities for sailing, fishing, swimming and model yachting; whereas Melchett Mere is the home of many species of wildfowl.

Home of the Egerton family since the late sixteenth century, the present house was designed by the architect Samuel Wyatt at the end of the eighteenth century; after his death in 1807, his nephew Lewis Wyatt completed the work. There are spectacular views of the gardens and park from the state rooms and bedrooms. The interior is entirely furnished with the Egerton family collection, which includes furniture by Gillow, china, glass and silver. There are also many excellent paintings, including works by Van Dyck and Canaletto. A family museum has been established in the tenants hall, and the last Lord Egerton's remarkable collection of curiosities and hunting trophies, veteran cars, estate fire engines and a state coach can be seen here as well.

The fifty acres of grounds with an orangery, Japanese and Italian gardens and a hundred-yard-long broad walk of tall trees leading to a replica of a Greek monument, complete the attractions of Tatton Park.

Park and Gardens open all year daily, (except Christmas Day).
House open Easter to Oct daily, pm only. Mar and Nov Sun and Bank Holidays pm only. NT.

Tenby

Dyfed *p211 B4*

The centre of Tenby, with its charming Georgian houses and winding narrow streets enclosed by well-preserved medieval walls, has as much appeal as the beautiful stretch of Welsh coastline on which it is built.

Prominent from all angles is the ruined Norman castle on its hill; a statue of Prince Albert surveys the fragmented castle walls and there is a museum in the renovated keep. To the north of Castle Hill lies the little harbour – now a popular yachting centre – the lifeboat station and North Sands.

Beyond these high limestone cliffs are broken by a series of coves. To the south are Castle Sands and South Sands backed by low cliffs and dunes. All the beaches provide safe bathing.

A small zoo is housed in a Napoleonic fort on St Catherine's Rock which can be reached on foot at low tide, and ferries run to Caldy Island where there is a Cistercian monastery

The municipal buildings, station and new housing estates lie outside the old walls, and camp-

High cliffs and sandy beaches spread out on either side of Tenby's old fishing harbour

Tatton Hall is one of England's best pieces of Regency architecture still in existence

ing and caravanning areas on the outskirts are evidence of Tenby's popularity as a holiday centre, but the town's expansion has not interfered with the attraction of the older part. In the town centre the Tudor Merchant's House, with its gabled front, and Plantagenet House, are both National Trust properties. The former houses a small museum. Laston House in Castle Square was designed as a public baths when Tenby was a fashionable watering place in Victorian times, and

North Bay House, built to a design which won an award at the 1851 Exhibition, is known as Prize House.

St Mary's Church is the largest parish church in Wales. It is Perpendicular in style. Tenby Museum has, amongst other exhibits, items from caves which indicate that they were inhabited by prehistoric man.

Castle open at all times.
Tudor Merchant's House open Easter Sun to Sep Mon to Fri, Sun pm only.
Tenby Museum open daily all year. Nov to Apr Mon to Sat am only.

A Bristol Fighter, built in 1917, during one of Shuttleworth's summer flying displays. All the exhibits in the collection are kept in working order

Tewkesbury

Gloucestershire *p212 F5*

The ancient town of Tewkesbury occupies a delightful site at the confluence of the rivers Avon and Severn, where several smaller tributaries join them. It is a small town of half-timbered buildings and historic inns, including The Black Bear, which is one of the oldest in the country, and The Royal Hop Pole, associated with Dickens' *Pickwick Papers*. Tewkesbury's literary connections are many, for it was featured as Nortonbury in Mrs Craik's *John Halifax, Gentleman* and was the home of the author, John Moore. Mementoes of both are collected in the John Moore Museum in Church Street. Adjacent to this museum is the Little Museum, and both are housed in particularly interesting old buildings. The latter has been restored as a medieval merchant's cottage. Tewkesbury's third museum, the Town Museum, is in Barton Street and contains items of local history and archaeology. There is also a reconstructed carpenter's workshop here and a model of the Battle of Tewkesbury – one of the bloodiest events of the Wars of the Roses. These are housed in an

equally interesting building which, formerly a merchant's house, contains fine wood panelling and decorated ceilings.

The town is dominated by its magnificent abbey church which has the largest Norman tower in existence. The climb to the top is well rewarded with panoramic views over such local landmarks as Bloody Meadow, named after the terrible battle which took place there, and Gupshill Manor, which was used as a headquarters during the battle. The tower was, in fact, a lookout point throughout the hostilities. The abbey, which was once part of an extensive Benedictine monastery, is most noted for its superb vaulted ceilings, its vast Purbeck marble altar and the organ, which is the oldest in the country. There are a large number of monuments and memorials within the abbey, including a plaque which marks the burial place of Prince Edward, son of Henry VI, who was brutally murdered by the Yorkists within the abbey when he took refuge from the battle.

Museums open daily Apr to Oct, John Moores Museum and Little Museum closed Sun and Mon.

The Shuttleworth Collection

Bedfordshire *p213 B4*

The aerodrome at Old Warden holds this fascinating collection of historical aircraft, cars, bicycles and other items of transport.

Founded more than half a century ago by the late Richard Shuttleworth, it was his aim that each exhibit must work, and this still applies today. The aviation exhibition includes a Blériot similar to the model used for the world's first crossing of the English Channel in 1909, a reproduction of a British Boxkite of 1910 – especially designed for the film *Those Magnificent Men in Their Flying Machines* – and the famous de Havilland Moth. Genuine veterans of World War I are represented, as are fighters of World War II, such as Spitfires and Hurricanes.

There is an extensive programme of road vehicle restoration and those already restored include a 1903 de Dietrich racer and a 1902 Baby Peugeot. An old fire engine dating from 1780 is among the many other interesting exhibits.

Visitors now have the chance to see servicing and restoration

being carried out on exhibits as an area of the workshops has been opened to the public. During the summer there are several flying displays and pageants featuring aeroplanes from the collection.

Open all year daily (except Christmas). Special flying days on last Sun in month, Apr to Oct. Two special pageant days July and Sep. Parking and refreshments available.

Thetford

Norfolk *p213 D5*

Thetford was the capital of the Saxon Kings of East Anglia and for a short period after the Norman conquest was the seat of the Bishopric of East Anglia. Its ecclesiastical importance continued until the Reformation, and there were four religious houses and twenty churches during the reign of Edward II.

After the Dissolution of the monasteries its importance waned, but as a market town in an agricultural area it remained reasonably prosperous. In the early nineteenth century an attempt was made to turn it into a spa – the pump house in Spring Walk was built in 1818 – but this was unsuccessful. With the closure in the 1930s of the long-established engineering firm which had been Thetford's main industry, the town's population dwindled. It was in these circumstances that Thetford became an overspill area for London.

Only three of the medieval churches survive, the most interesting being the part-Saxon, part-Norman Church of St Mary the Less; all three have been much rebuilt and renovated. The mound of a motte and bailey castle is preserved in Castle Park, and the remains of the twelfth-century Cluniac Priory stand amidst mature trees, contrasting strangely with new houses which overlook the area. The Ancient House, now a museum, has carved beams in the main room and is believed to have been a Tudor merchant's house. The Georgian King's House (now the Council offices) stands on the site of a house used by James I, and other buildings of interest include an old lock-up behind the Guildhall, the gaol of 1816 in Old Market Street, and almshouses. There is a riverside promenade in the town centre.

Ancient House Museum open all year (except Good Fri, Christmas and New Year's Day) daily, also Spring Bank Holiday Sun pm only.
Castle accessible at any time.
Priory see AM info. Also open Sun am Apr to Sep.

The Thursford Collection

Norfolk *p218 E1*

This is a memorable museum containing perhaps the best collection of engines and organs to be found anywhere in the world. Each exhibit has been lovingly restored, and today's visitors can experience the sight, sound, fun and excitement of the heyday of the fairground.

Exhibited here are many mechanical and keyboard organs ranging from huge, carved and richly decorated fairground, cinema and dance organs, to small barrel organs, all to be heard demonstrating the variety and richness of their nostalgic music. Among these exhibits is the mighty Wurlitzer cinema organ, the fourth largest in Europe, which was built by the Rudolf Wurlitzer Company in New York for the Paramount Cinema in Leeds. It boasts 1,339 pipes, arranged in nineteen ranks half an inch to sixteen feet in length.

After the Dissolution of the monasteries part of Tewkesbury Abbey was used as the parish church

Forming the centrepiece of the main museum building is the Savage's Venetian Gondola switchback ride, a unique example from the traditional travelling fair. Some fifty-six feet in diameter and thirty feet high, this amazing Gondola ride is covered in beautiful ornate decoration carved in solid wood. Its musical accompaniment is provided by a Gavioli organ.

The museum also has a considerable collection of magnificent engines, ranging from showman's engines, traction and ploughing engines, and steam road locomotives. An outstanding example of this age of steam is portrayed here by the King Edward VII Showman's Engine, weighing some twenty tons with drive wheels of eight feet diameter.

During the summer season there are rides on a narrow-gauge steam railway which runs around the beautiful grounds of Thursford. The engine is a traditional saddle tank steam engine (built during the late nineteenth century) which spent much of its working life in the Dinorwic Slate Quarry in Wales. There is also a picnic area, a children's adventure playground and a souvenir shop in the grounds.

Open all year, Easter to Oct daily pm only, rest of year Sun pm only.
Midsummer musical evenings Tue mid June to Sep.
Parking and refreshments available.

A musical organ from The Thursford Collection's bizarre assortment of fairground exhibits

The Vyne's Classical portico is the earliest example of this style to be found on an English country house

The Vyne

Hampshire *p213 A2*

This beautiful Tudor manor house was built early in the sixteenth century by William Sandys, who later became Lord Chamberlain. Woodland surrounds three sides of the H-shaped house and the north side, to which John Webb added a Classical portico a century later, overlooks lawns and a lake stocked with waterlilies. The small private chapel in the grounds has some excellent stained glass which depicts Henry VIII and Catherine of Aragon amongst its nobilities; the screen and canopies are also noteworthy. After the Civil War, the Chute family bought the mansion and were responsible for the interior alterations during the eighteenth and early nineteenth centuries. The most outstanding is the Palladian-style staircase hall, with its fluted columns, panelling and decorative plasterwork ceiling. The long gallery was altered by the addition of beautiful oak linenfold panelling. The furnishings have been collected over the centuries, and include elegant porcelain figures and Venetian painted glass plates.

Open Apr to Oct pm only. Closed Fri and Mon, open Bank Holiday Mon but closed Tue following. Refreshments available. NT.

Thoresby Hall

Nottinghamshire *p217 C2*

Around the pretty little village of Edwinstowe, in Sherwood Forest, is an area known as The Dukeries because of its stately homes. Some three miles to the north of the village, deep in the heart of the forest, is Thoresby Hall, until recently the only Dukeries mansion still occupied by descendants of the original owners. Now the property of the National Coal Board, it is the third house to have been built on the site. Lady Mary Wortley Montagu, one of the greatest English women letter writers, occupied the first one which was destroyed by fire in the eighteenth century; the second, demolished in the nineteenth century, was the residence of the Duchess of Kingston. The present Thoresby Hall, built between 1864 and 1875, was designed by Anthony Salvin for the Pierrepont family.

Standing in 12,000 acres of parkland, this impressive Victorian mansion with some 200 rooms has retained much of its original character. The state apartments are open to the public, and include the great hall with its portrait of Lady Montagu; the historic library with its carved fireplace and statues of Robin Hood and Little John; the Rococo blue salon and the state dining room. The grounds consist of gardens, river walks, fine avenues of chestnut trees and an ornamental lake. To the west of the lake there is a folly called Budby Castle, and a miniature steam railway. Other attractions include the Thoresby Hall Pottery, a deer park and an adventure playground.

Open Easter Sun and Mon, then May to Aug, Sun and Bank Holidays pm only. Parking and refreshments available.

Thorpe Park

Surrey *p213 B3*

Converted gravel pits have been attractively landscaped to provide a lake and parkland setting

A castle has faced the wild Atlantic at Tintagel for over 800 years

for this unusual new 500-acre leisure park.

Elaborate displays record the bited Britain through the ages. For example, there is a reconstruction of a Celtic farm and a Saxon hall; a Norman motte and bailey castle; a Roman galley; and a Viking long ship.

There are over fifty attractions, including Space Station Zero, a family rollercoaster ride, Phantom Fantasia ghost ride and many more, plus a shire horse centre and a craft centre. Free transport is available around the park by train or waterbus.

Open mid Mar to early Nov daily (closed mid week early and late season). Parking and refreshments available.

Tintagel

Cornwall *p211 B2*

Legend has it that Tintagel Castle was the stronghold of King Arthur, but in fact the castle was built 600 years after the romantic King's supposed lifetime. The rock on which it stands, known as The Island, was connected to the mainland by a natural bridge of rock, but this collapsed long ago and was replaced by a footbridge.

There are traces of a settlement in AD 500, but this is believed to have been monastic. Built in the twelfth century by the Earl of Cornwall, a bastard son of Henry I, the castle later belonged to the Black Prince. It then became a prison for a while but eventually fell into decay. However, the Arthurian legend, first mentioned in 1145, persists; but Tintagel is exciting whether or not Arthur lived here. Waves crash in Merlin's Cove and a waterfall drops forty feet into Tintagel Cove, from which great cliffs rise with dark slate caverns at their base.

The village itself has expanded in recent years, with new bungalows outnumbering the thick-walled stone houses. However, the old Post Office, a small fourteenth-century manor house, remains a rare survival of domestic building from the Middle Ages with many interesting features. It was used as a receiving office for post during the nineteenth century and is now owned by the National Trust.

Castle see AM info. Also open Sun am Apr to Sep.
Old Post Office open Apr to Oct daily. NT.

Tintern

Gwent *p212 E4*

One of the finest relics of Britain's monastic age, the abbey owes almost as much of its beauty to its idyllic setting as to the serene beauty of its roofless walls. It is set in the Wye Valley, amid peaceful meadows by the river and is flanked by steep-sided wooded slopes.

The noble ruins of the abbey church date back to the thirteenth century and still preserve an aura of sanctity. Its walls, almost intact, display Gothic architecture at its best. Particularly noteworthy are the majestic arches, fine doorways and elegant windows, including a fine traceried rose window over sixty feet high, set in the east end. Remains of many of the domestic buildings also survive and include the sacristy, chapter house, parlour, refectory and kitchen.

The abbey was founded in 1131 by the Cistercians, the monks

Tintern Abbey became a favourite haunt of William Wordsworth in the 18th century and its beauty inspired him to write a poem about it

from Citeau in France, and was suppressed by Henry VIII's Dissolution of monasteries during the sixteenth century. The monks of this order were noted for their austere lives and farmed on a large scale, maintaining lay brothers to do all their manual labour. The Anchor Inn, near the river, is connected to a slipway by a thirteenth-century arch, and was probably once the abbey's water gate.

Tintern's former railway station now houses a small exhibition telling the story of the old Wye Valley railway line. Here there are also refreshment facilities together with a picnic site. At Wyndcliff, some two miles south, a walk leads to a 770-foot-high hill which offers exceptional views. Walkers can also enjoy fine views of the Wye Valley from the Tintern Forest, Chapel Hill and Barbadoes Forest trails – controlled and waymarked by the Forestry Commission.

Abbey see AM info. Also open Sun am Apr to Sep. Parking available.
Tintern Station Railway Exhibition open Easter to Christmas daily. Parking and refreshments available.

Torquay Devon *p212 D2*

Torquay's setting of natural beauty and mild climate have helped to make it the Queen of Watering Places, famous holiday resort and favoured residential area. Terraces of elegant houses encircle lushly-vegetated hillsides, palm trees stand amid gardens of blossom and pleasure craft ride at anchor in the harbour.

Wooded slopes and terraces encircle Torquay's colourful harbour

Until the Napoleonic Wars Torquay was a fishing village, but while Europe was in upheaval wealthy Britons had to find a substitute for holidays abroad and Torquay offered a gentle climate and beautiful surroundings. The Palk family, who owned much land in the area, were quick to see the possibilities of this sudden popularity and employed architects to lay out the town, consciously choosing an Italianate style to enhance its Mediterranean appearance. Their plan, with its fine houses and gardens, is the core of the present-day Torquay.

Boat trips and fishing expeditions start from the harbour, and regattas and powerboat races are held at intervals throughout the year. Tennis and bowls championships are held in Torquay and other sports are well-catered for.

Kent's Cavern

The natural cave contains weird formations of stalactites and stalagmites, now effectively illuminated. It is one of the oldest known caves to be inhabited by man and bones were found here, along with those of bears and a sabre-toothed tiger believed to date from the Ice Age.

Torquay Museum

Founded in 1844, the museum contains archaeological finds from Kent's Cavern and other caves in South Devon, as well as natural history exhibits.

Babbacombe

Over 400 models and 1,200 feet of model railway are laid out here in four acres of ingenious miniature landscaped gardens. Modelled to represent the English countryside, the gardens show a comprehensive range of conifers, flowering shrubs and trees, with an emphasis on dwarf conifers, and the buildings have the smallest details.

Torre Abbey Mansion

This eighteenth-century house is used as an art gallery and museum and has some interesting pictures and furniture. Nearby are the ruins of Torre Abbey, founded by monks from northern France who were responsible for building the first quay. The twelfth-century tithe barn is known as Spanish Barn because sailors from the Spanish Armada were imprisoned there in 1588.

Aqualand

This is the largest aquarium in the West Country and its speciality is tropical marine fish. Aqualand also has a fine exhibition of various types of local marine life, tropical freshwater fish and even a pair of otters from Asia.

Kent's Cavern open all year daily (except Christmas Day).
Torquay Museum open all year (except Good Fri, Christmas and New Year Mon to Fri, also Sat Mar to Oct). Parking available.

Babbacombe Model Village open all year daily (except 25 Dec). Parking available.
Torre Abbey Mansion open daily Easter to Oct.
Aqualand open Apr to Oct daily.

Totnes

Devon *p212 D2*

Folklore has it that Brutus, grandson of Aeneas, came from Troy to found Totnes and the British race. Verifiable fact shows that Totnes was mentioned in Domesday Book and by the thirteenth century was a Borough with a Merchant Guild and a town wall. The East Gate and North Gate remain from those times, and the former has a flight of steps leading to the Rampart Walk, which follows the line of the medieval wall. The curfew and angelus bells are still rung, and every Tuesday in summer Elizabethan history comes to life when the people of Totnes create a colourful spectacle by wearing Elizabethan dress.

There are many old buildings in the town centre, among them the Guildhall, an ancient stone building of great charm where the Council has met since 1624. Here are kept samples of Saxon coins minted in Totnes, a list of Mayors back to 1359, and other historical items. Elizabethan House, a half-timbered, gabled building with overhanging upper storeys, is now the Totnes Museum and has an exhibition on the development of computers. The red sandstone parish church of St Mary, mainly reconstructed in the fifteenth century although founded much earlier by the Normans, contains a superb stone rood screen and a winding stairway which led to the rood-loft. The Butterwalk and Poultrywalk have projecting upper storeys supported on pillars, providing a covered area where produce was displayed for sale. Nowadays a pannier market is held here on Fridays.

Inhabited since 950, Traquair House is occupied now by a descendant of the 1st Laird of Traquair – James Stuart

The Normans built a castle to defend the crossing place of the river Dart at the northern end of the town, but only parts of the keep and walls remain.

Totnes also has a Motor Museum which covers sixty years of motoring with a collection of vintage, sports and racing cars.

There is splendid walking country both in the immediate environs of Totnes and on Dartmoor. Sports facilities include bowls and tennis in the Borough Park and a covered, heated, swimming pool.

Guildhall open Easter to Sep Mon to Fri, Oct to Mar by appointment.
Totnes Museum open Apr to Oct Mon to Fri (also occasionally during winter).
Castle see AM info. Also open Sun am Apr to Sep. Parking available.
Motor Museum open Easter to Oct daily. Parking available.

Tramway Museum

Derbyshire *p217 B1*

This most unusual and fascinating open-air museum is situated in the hill village of Crich. Once an important mining centre, the village is now famed for its unique museum, set in a disused limestone quarry. The quarry itself was the site of a former narrow gauge mineral railway, built by the great railway pioneer, George Stephenson, to link the quarry with the main line railway at nearby Ambergate.

Here vintage tramcars from all over Britain and abroad have been painstakingly and beautifully restored, many of them to working order, by volunteer members of the Tramway Museum Society. The museum is a live one, with a number of lines laid out so that the trams can still run, and visitors may ride them along one mile of electric tramway, following part of the track-bed of the original railway. An air of authenticity has been created by the museum's period setting. This is achieved by the use of the reconstructed façade of Derby's Georgian Assembly Rooms, an Edwardian bandstand, gates from London's Marylebone Station, Victorian gas lamps, street furniture, a pillar box, stone paving and granite setts laid between its tram rails, together with many other tram relics from this bygone era. All this has enabled the trams to be shown today in the surroundings in which they once operated. At the passenger-loading island there is an elegant cast-iron tram shelter and at the Wakebridge terminus one can see a replica of an old Derbyshire lead mine.

High above the Tramway Museum is the 940-foot summit of Crich Stand, a lofty vantage point crowned by a monument to the Sherwood Foresters – the Nottingham and Derby Regiment.

Open Easter week to end Oct Sat, Sun and Bank Holidays. Also Mon to Thu, May to Sep. Tram services operate at frequent intervals when the museum is open. Parking and refreshments available.

Traquair House

Borders *p220 E3*

Traquair House, the oldest consistently inhabited house in Scotland, originally dates from the tenth century, although much of it was rebuilt in the seventeenth century.

The main staircase leads to an eighteenth-century library which remains as it was some 250 years ago, and contains an original collection including a fourteenth-century bible and Nuremberg Chronicle, hand-printed in 1493. Other treasures to be seen in the house are tapestries, silver, glass, embroideries from the thirteenth century, and relics of Mary Queen of Scots – one of twenty-seven monarchs who have stayed at the house. Among exhibits connected with her are a rosary and a cradle – reputed to have been used for her son, James VI of Scotland, James I of England.

Outside an eighteenth-century brewhouse is still used to produce ale which is bottled and sold to visitors. In an old farm workman's hut there is a wood workshop; the adjacent old stables house the pottery; a screen printing workshop is in the old grain loft and nearby Bachelors Hall has a weaving workship. Here also are cottage tea rooms, a small antique shop, nature trails and woodland walks by the river Tweed and Quair Burn.

Open Easter to mid Oct pm only (except Jul to early Sep when open daily). Parking and refreshments available.

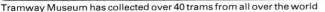

Tramway Museum has collected over 40 trams from all over the world

Trelissick Gardens

Cornwall *p211 B1*

This beautiful wooded park affords splendid views of the river Fal and Falmouth Harbour. A fine collection of trees such as magnolias, cedars, maples and great beeches surround the spacious, well tended lawns which are so much a feature of Trelissick. Throughout the seasons, the garden is alight with colourful flora, and a comprehensive range of rhododendrons, azaleas, fuchsias and hydrangea provide a glorious display. Many winding walks lead through tunnels of foliage, under massive trees, and eventually to a summer house and a Saxon cross.

A house has stood in the gardens since 1280, but the present building (not open) dates from 1750. It was subsequently altered and extended during the course of its varied ownership.

Gardens open Mar to Oct daily, Sun pm only. Refreshments available. NT.

Trentham Gardens

Staffordshire *p216 F2*

These gardens surround an elongated lake and cover 800 acres. They are particularly renowned for their formal sections, originally created by Capability Brown, and believed to be the largest in Europe.

The various gardens make a blaze of colour throughout the year; in the spring over a quarter of a million bulbs burst into bloom and the famous Italian gardens are best seen in summer, whilst the autumnal colours of the trees reflected in the waters of the lake create a marvellous spectacle. There are also rock, peat and woodland gardens, together with a perfumed garden for the blind, and demonstration gardens.

Trentham has an attractive woodland setting, a children's adventure playground, pony and trap, and donkey rides. For those who prefer more leisurely entertainment, rides are available on a miniature railway through trees along one side of the lake, or a trip on a motor launch around the lake.

Open Easter to mid Sep daily. Parking and refreshments available.

Trerice

Cornwall *p211 B2*

Situated in some fourteen acres of grounds, Trerice, partly screened by elm trees, is approached along narrow Cornish lanes. A picturesque Elizabethan mansion, it is the second house to occupy the site (although no records remain of its predecessor) and dates from 1573, when it was rebuilt by a member of a famous Cornish family, Sir John Arundell.

The house has unusually distinctive curved gables which crown its silvery grey limestone façade. A popular theory is that Sir John may have got the idea for them when soldiering in the Netherlands and Belgium. Now a National Trust property, it was purchased in 1954 with money bequeathed by Mrs Annie Woodhouse. Restored by the Trust, with help from various quarters, the house remains much as it did in the sixteenth century.

Its turfed forecourt enclosed by high walls leads into an E-shaped entrance front beside which is the vast latticed window of the main hall. The house follows a familiar medieval pattern of a passage from the porch leading to the great hall beyond, and contains tapestries and oak and walnut furniture.

A notable feature of Trerice is the fine quality of its plasterwork which was probably modelled by the same master craftsman who plastered Buckland Abbey. The main hall contains a contemporary fireplace, dating from 1572, and beyond the row of recessed arches above the screens passage

The châteaux of the Loire inspired the architect of Waddesdon Manor, and the splendid gardens were laid out by a French landscape artist, Lainé

lies a little musicians' gallery. The principal sitting room on the first floor has a barrel ceiling and the Arundell arms are incorporated into both the frieze and the main house and a small museum tracing the development of the lawn mower.

Open Apr to Oct daily. Refreshments available pm only. NT.

Tucktonia

Dorset *p212 F2*

Tucktonia is a model landscape featuring the famous, and not so famous, buildings and landmarks of Britain. A network of old and modern railways, roads, canals and rivers connect over 200 faithfully reproduced buildings which are accurate to the smallest detail.

The city of London, with its fascinating sights, is recreated here at Tucktonia. St Paul's Cathedral, the Tower of London, Buckingham Palace and Tower Bridge are amongst many that have been scaled down to form this impressive miniature of England's capital.

Here also a typical Cornish fishing village, complete with fishing boats, forms a picturesque part of the model coastline, along which is moored a perfect scale replica of the famous liner *Queen Elizabeth 2*. Other models depict places of Scottish historical interest, including the romantic Eilean Donan Castle, the cottage where Robert Burns was born, and Hadrian's Wall.

Britain's heritage, from prehistoric Stonehenge to an ultra modern nuclear power station, is delightfully illustrated and after dusk the models are illuminated to provide the visitor with a spectacular last glimpse of this world in miniature. There is also a leisure complex here with amusements for all ages.

Open All year daily. Parking and refreshments available.

Twycross Zoo Park

Leicestershire *p213 A5*

This modern zoo, set in fifty acres of parkland, specialises in breeding animals in danger of extinction. The only group of proboscis monkeys in the country are included in one of the finest collections of primates. Other larger animals at the zoo are elephants, camels, giraffes, lions, tigers,

Ruined Tynemouth Priory stands with the castle built to protect it

cheetahs and leopards. Attractive waterfowl and flamingos can be seen in large pools, and a bird house contains a colourful display of tropical birds. Also of interest is the butterfly house and the modern reptile house.

Open all year (except 25 Dec) daily. Parking and refreshments available.

Tynemouth Priory and Castle

Tyne and Wear *p217 B5*

These majestic ruins stand on a headland, with excellent views of the coastline, the harbour entrance and Tyne estuary. The eleventh-century priory occupies the site of a previous monastery, destroyed by the Danes in 865. The fourteenth-century castle and curtain wall was originally built to protect the Benedictine priory, but served later as a coastal defence.

The mellow old ruins, which include the grave of Malcolm III of Scotland and fine lawns, are reached through the ruined gatehouse with its towers and keep. Hiding behind the ruins is the coastguard station. An excellent view of the ruins can be had from the end of the north pier.

See AM info. Also open Sun am Apr to Sep. Parking available.

Waddesdon Manor

Buckinghamshire *p213 A4*

This mock French Renaissance château was built between 1874 and 1889 by Destailleur, for Baron Ferdinand de Rothschild.

Inside there is a fine collection of furnishings, paintings and personal mementoes of the family. Items of particular interest in the collection are two writing tables, one made for Marie Antoinette and another for Louis XVI. Paintings include works by Gainsborough, Reynolds, Romney and Rubens. A museum of small arms can be seen in the bachelors' wing.

The grounds, decorated with fountains and sculptures which have been collected from France, Italy and the Netherlands, include two deer enclosures and a well-stocked aviary.

Open mid Mar to mid Oct, Wed to Sun, pm only. Open from late morning on Good Frid and Bank Holiday Mon (closed Wed following Bank Holiday). Parking and refreshments available. NT.

London Bridge, as it appeared in medieval times, perfectly reconstructed in the model world of Tucktonia

The picture gallery at Wallington, with pre-Raphaelite wall-paintings

Wakehurst Place Garden

West Sussex *p213 C2*

The estate of Wakehurst Place was bought in 1903 by Gerald Loder, and later by the first Lord Wakehurst, who was a president of the Royal Horticultural Society, and he began to create the gardens as we see them today. They were bequeathed to the National Trust and later leased to the Royal Botanical Gardens at Kew as an extension of their scientific and experimental work. Much of the estate is given over to woodlands, but about a hundred acres is cultivated and contains many exotic plants and rare species. The flowering shrubs give a superb show and a picturesque water course links a series of ponds and lakes.

Open daily (except Christmas Day and New Year's Day). Parking and refreshments available. NT.

Wallington

Northumberland *p220 F2*

Although it was built in 1688, this fine mansion has a predominantly eighteenth-century flavour, owing to the considerable alterations which were made at that time. Originally owned by the Blackett family, it passed by inheritance to the Trevelyans and both families are much in evidence in the many portraits which adorn the walls here. Much of the furniture is Dutch and there are also some fine pieces by Chippendale, Hepplewhite and Sheraton. The extensive collection of porcelain, including Oriental, Bow, Meissen, Wedgwood and Sèvres, are on show in specially constructed cabinets. There is also some fine silverware and an enchanting collection of old dolls houses now kept in the common room. Nearly twenty of these are on show, with pride of place given to a particularly large model of a mansion. This has thirty-six rooms, all with electricity and some with running water, and is populated with more than seventy dolls. The adjacent store is now a children's room with old toys, games and books and a fascinating Noah's Ark. Elsewhere in the house a large number of model soldiers can be seen.

Having seen the main part of the house with its lavish furnishings and beautiful plasterwork, a visit to the kitchen provides an interesting contrast. It is furnished as it would have been around the turn of the century, with a scrubbed pine table and huge dresser. All the old cooking utensils and clothes-washing equipment can be seen too. The house is set amid wooded park and moorland with three lakes and some lovely gardens, much still adhering to the formal layout of the eighteenth century. An interesting feature is a set of four stone dragons' heads, which were once a part of the old Bishopsgate – one of the entrances to the City of London.

Open Apr and Oct Wed, Sat and Sun, May to Sep daily (except Tue), pm only. Grounds open all year dialy. Refreshments available. NT.

Walsingham

Norfolk *p218 E1*

Walsingham, or Little Walsingham, a market town beside the river Stiffkey, has always been famous for its Shrine of Our Lady of Walsingham. The town arose around the shrine and later its Augustinian priory, sometimes referred to as an abbey. The shrine was built in about 1061 to commemorate a vision of the lady of the manor and became a famous medieval place of pilgrimages. Richeldis de Favraches founded the priory in the twelfth century, incorporating the shrine into its church. In the fourteenth century a Franciscan friary was established, but a century later all the monastic buildings were destroyed and the statues from the shrine burnt at Smithfield. Walsingham again became a place of pilgrimages in 1922 and there are now two modern shrines: an Anglican and, a mile to the southwest, the Roman Catholic. The most striking aspect of the priory ruins is the east wall of the fourteenth-century church which is now a handsome archway with elaborate buttresses and turrets. The noble fifteenth-century gatehouse led from the church into the town. It is thought that the original chapel lay inside the precinct wall near the north aisle, but nothing remains today. The surviving walls of the refectory, rebuilt in the thirteenth-century, lie to the south. Adjacent to the former precinct walls of the priory is the Anglican church built in 1931.

Shirehall Museum – a Georgian building, formerly a courthouse where Sessions Courts were held, has now been converted into a museum. Its former courtroom has retained its original fittings including the prisoners' lock-up.

Abbey grounds open Apr to Sep, pm only Wed only in Apr. May to July and Sep, Wed, Sat and Sun. August, Mon, Wed, Fri, Sat and Sunday. Also Bank Holidays from Easter to Sep.
Museum open Apr to Sep daily; Oct: Sat and Sun only. Parking available.

Warkworth Castle

Northumberland *p220 F3*

The builders of Warkworth Castle in the eleventh century, found here a site with remarkable natural defences. The river Coquet loops protectively around the castle and the village, and its steep banks provide additional defences. The castle occupies the highest point on this little peninsula and towers over the quaint village below. The remains are extensive with an impressive gatehouse and an unusual keep which still retains a vivid picture of its former strength.

Not far away, and accessible by boat from the castle, is Warkworth Hermitage – a tiny chapel with living quarters which were hewn out of the sandstone by an unknown hermit. Another interesting feature of Warkworth is the ancient fortified bridge which spans the Coquet across to the northern end of the village.

Castle and Hermitage see AM info, but Apr to Sep only. Parking available at castle.

Warwick Warwickshire *p216 F1*

Warwick, the historic county town of Warwickshire, grew around its impressive castle. This turreted fortress rises above the lovely river Avon which flows past the castle and lends Warwick much of its charm.

Although the town was devastated by fire in 1694, when over two hundred buildings were destroyed, there are some notable survivors from the Tudor period. The High Street, Mill Street, Bridge End and Castle Street have some fine examples of the characteristic half-timbered and gabled buildings. Two of the old town gates also survive, both surmounted by chapels. The West Gate bears the chapel of the nearby Lord Leycester Hospital and at the other end of the High Street the East Gate carries the fifteenth-century St Peter's Chapel.

The Castle

The present castle, one of Britain's most splendid castle-mansions, dates from the fourteenth-century and was built on the site of a Norman castle, which itself replaced a Saxon motte and bailey. The gatehouse bears the crest of the Earls of Warwick, a bear and a ragged staff. Within are the Bear Tower and Clarence Tower, built by that Duke of Clarence who was reputedly drowned in a butt of malmsey. Below is a dungeon with a horrific display of torture instruments, the walls bearing graffiti attributed to Royalist soldiers during the Civil War.

The armoury contains the sword of Guy of Warwick, a Saxon knight who slew the Danish champion, the giant Colbrand. A suit of armour of particular interest is that made for a son of the Earl of Leicester, who was only three years old when he died in 1584; it is displayed in the great hall of the state apartments overlooking the river. The armour collected here includes Oliver Cromwell's helmet, and his death mask may also be seen. The furnishings and paintings in the hall are of great interest.

Lord Leycester Hospital

This group of buildings dates from the twelfth-century and had been used as Guildhall, council chamber and grammar school before 1571, when Robert Dudley, Earl of Leicester, had them renovated and extended. He endowed the hospital for occupation by men wounded in the service of the Queen and her successors. The hospital is still the home of ex-servicemen.

Collegiate Church of St Mary

The nave and tower of this cathedral-like church were built after the disastrous fire of 1694, to a design by Sir William Wilson. The Beauchamp Chapel houses the tomb of Richard Beaumont who died in 1439, one of the most perfect medieval tombs extant. On a Purbeck marble base lies an effigy of Beaumont, his hands raised to a figure of the Virgin in the roof. The Chapel also houses the tombs of Ambrose Dudley, created Earl of Warwick by Elizabeth I when the Beauchamp line died out, and his brother, Robert Dudley, Earl of Leicester.

Market Hall and St John's House

Originally built on arches to provide space for stalls underneath, the Market hall, which dates from 1670, is used as the Warwickshire County Museum, the arches now being filled by doors and windows. A branch of the County Museum, specialising in crafts, costume and musical instruments, together with the museum of the Royal Warwickshire Regiment, is housed in St John's House, a lovely seventeenth-

The tower of Warwick Church

century building with gardens and beautiful wrought-iron gates.

Warwick Doll Museum

This fascinating collection of antique period dolls and toys was put together by Mrs Joy Robinson and is now housed in one of Warwick's best surviving medieval buildings. The black and white Tudor Oken's House was the home of Thomas Oken, one of the foremost sixteenth century-citizens of Warwick.

Castle open all year daily (except 25 Dec). Parking and refreshments.
Lord Leycester's Hospital open all year daily (except Sun, Good Fri and 25 Dec). Parking and refreshments (Easter to Sep) available.
Warwickshire County Museum open all year Mon to Sat. Also Sun, May to Sep only.
St John's House open Tue to Sat and Bank Holidays. Sun pm May to Sep only.
Warwick Doll Museum open Mar to Nov daily, Dec to Feb weekends.

Winkhurst House at the Museum

Weald and Downland Open Air Museum

West Sussex *p213 B2*

Historic buildings re-erected on a magnificent forty-acre site of wood and parkland make up this museum. Among these buildings, which were threatened by demolition, are farmhouses from the fifteenth and sixteenth centuries, a large aisled barn (particularly well preserved) and a working tread-wheel dating back to Elizabethan times. A charcoal burner's camp has been recreated here, together with a blacksmith's forge and wheelwright's shop. Most of the buildings are accessible and are authentically furnished and equipped.

The Hambrook Farm houses an introductory exhibition with information on the type of people who would once have inhabited these buildings, plus a brief outline of the building techniques and materials used in their original structure. A nature trail runs through the woodland area.

Open Apr to Oct daily. Nov to Mar Wed and Sun only. Parking and refreshments available.

Wedgwood Museum and Visitor Centre

Staffordshire *p216 F2*

This centre has been especially designed to give visitors every opportunity to see the skills of the craft of pottery being performed, using the traditional and modern techniques that have made Wedgwood so famous. The museum contains a comprehensive collection including works by Josiah Wedgwood, made when he founded his first factory in 1769. Exhibits dating from the eighteenth century to present day include the famous Queens Ware, Jasper and Black Basalt, as well as the development of bone china in the nineteenth century and interesting examples of Josiah Wedgwood's experimental designs.

Open all year Mon to Fri. Also Sat Apr to Oct (closed two weeks Christmas and first week Feb.) Parking and refreshments available.

Wells Somerset *p212 E3*

Wells is England's smallest city and it nestles below the sometimes gentle, sometimes dramatic scenery of the Mendip Hills. It takes its name from the underground streams which rise to the surface here, watering the moat of the Bishop's Palace before joining the river Sheppey. Were it not for its magnificent cathedral and the adjoining ecclesiastical buildings, Wells would be no more than a country market town.

In spite of its traffic and the thousands of visitors who flock to the city, Wells retains an unusual air of tranquillity, a characteristic which has held true throughout the centuries for it has seen none of the hostilities which have beset other cities. The worst disturbance would seem to have been when William Penn, founder of Pennsylvania, USA, attracted a crowd of around 2,000 to his preaching in the courtyard of the Crown Hotel, for which he was forcibly removed.

The area around the cathedral is the most peaceful of all and the Vicar's Close is particularly picturesque. This is a row of fourteenth-century buildings (the only complete medieval street remaining in Britain) whose exteriors have changed little from the original. The street is oc-cupied now by the singers of the cathedral and is linked by a bridge to it. Access from the street is via the Chain Gate, above which is the communal dining room, still with much of its original furniture.

Other historic buildings include the Guildhall and some fifteenth-century almshouses; the City Arms – a gaol until the nineteenth century; and St Cuthbert's Church which dates from the fifteenth century and has an imposing tower, a tie-beam roof and a carved font cover.

The Cathedral

Thought by some to be the world's finest example of a secular church with its subordinate buildings, the present cathedral was begun by Bishop de Bohun in 1174 and was one of the first at-tempts in English Gothic architecture. It was extended during the following centuries and the cloisters and some of the subsidiary buildings date from the fifteenth and sixteenth centuries.

The west front is superb with its canopied statues of saints, angels and prophets, and although depleted in number during the Civil War, many survive looking down over the vast lawn which spreads before the entrance. The central tower was built in the fourteenth century and led to the addition of the inverted support arches at the east end of the nave which, though practical in origin, are one of the visual delights of the cathedral. The two squat, yet elegant, towers at the west end were later additions. On a smaller scale, the amusing and beautifully executed carvings in the transepts reward study. The sweeping double staircase, its worn stone treads eloquent of succeeding communities of monks and clergy in procession from the cathedral, leads to the bridge which crosses the public road to the houses of the vicars choral and, by its second branch, to the thirteenth-century polygonal chapter house. This is elevated on an undercroft once used as a

The 14th-century gateway to the moated Bishop's Palace at Wells

treasury, and has a fan-vaulted roof supported by a ribbed central column.

A great attraction within the cathedral is the fourteenth-century astronomical clock, one of the oldest working clocks in the world, which features jousting knights among its moving parts. Other points of interest include medieval window glass and the carvings under the misericord choir seats.

Wells Museum
Alongside the cathedral is a row of old buildings which includes the former Deanery and it is here that the Wells Museum has its home. Several rooms contain its collections which include finds from the nearby Wookey Hole and items of local history. There is also a collection of samplers.

Bishop's Palace
To the south of the cathedral lies the beautiful moated Bishop's Palace, one of the oldest inhabited houses England and home of the Bishop of Bath and Wells. Access from the town market place is through a medieval gateway known as the Bishop's Eye. The Palace is surrounded by a high wall, which dates back to the beginning of the thirteenth century, and the lovely wide moat upon which swans glide. They are famous for their habit of ringing a bell for food, a trick which they seem to have inherited from their Victorian ancestors who were taught to do this by the daughter of the Bishop. The earliest parts of the Palace are the undercroft, the Bishop's chapel and the banqueting hall ruin. Portraits of past Bishops hang on the walls of the long gallery.

Wells Museum Apr to Sep daily, Oct to Mar, Wed, Sat and Sun, pm only. (Closed Christmas).
Bishop's Palace open Easter to Oct Wed, Thu, Sun and Bank Holiday Mon pm only; daily during August, pm only. Refreshments available.

Welney Wildfowl Refuge
Norfolk *p213 C5*

Over 800 acres of the Ouse Washes have been designated as a refuge for migratory birds and native species under the protection of the Wildfowl Trust. Thousands of Bewick's swans have their winter home here, together with tens of thousands of ducks which include wigeon, teal, shoveler and mallard. In springtime the refuge is alive with nesting birds including redshank, snipe, ruff black-tailed godwit and mallard. Wild flowers also benefit from the seclusion here and provide a lovely show in summer. The birds can be watched undisturbed from the hides and from the spacious observatory. During the winter a lagoon containing hundreds of swans is floodlit for the benefit of visitors.

Open all year daily (except Christmas). Evening visits Nov to Feb and May to Aug for parties (prior booking).

Welsh Folk Museum
South Glamorgan *p212 D4*

This open-air museum has old buildings from all over Wales which have been reconstructed to illustrate the Welsh way of life over several centuries. It occupies the grounds of St Fagans Castle which is itself interesting – a fine Elizabethan mansion with beautiful furnishings and a fascinating kitchen. The gardens are formal with fishponds, statues, topiary work and a lovely avenue of lime trees.

The castle out-buildings now house the workshops of a wood-turner, a blacksmith and a cooper – barrel maker – who can be seen at work.

The modern main block of the museum contains four separate galleries. The gallery of material culture has an enormous range of exhibits from Welsh dressers to medical equipment; from Eisteddfod chairs and crowns, to carved love-spoons. The costume gallery not only displays a variety of modes of dress but sets them out in authentic surroundings. The other two galleries are devoted to agriculture, the first illustrating the development of farming methods with implements, machinery and photographs and the second housing a collection of old carts and wagons from the horse-drawn era.

The remainder of the site, which extends to about a hundred acres, is dotted with the reconstructed buildings in lovely settings. They include a number of farmhouses, the earliest of which dates from the fifteenth century, a North Wales quarryman's cottage and a toll-house displaying its eighteenth-century tariffs.

More unusual items are a circular pigsty and a cockpit, which once provided gory entertainment in the yard of a Denbigh inn. The fishermen of Wales are not forgotten and the boat house contains a unique collection of coracles, a wide variety of freshwater and sea fishing equipment in the net house and, at the end of the pool, several salmon traps.

Open all year daily (except Christmas, New Year's Day, Good Fri and May Day Holiday). pm only on Sun. Parking and refreshments.

The old smithy is one of many traditional buildings that have been re-erected in the grounds of St Fagan's Castle. The interior is authentic

Powis Castle was built in 1250 by Owain ap Gruffydd. Capability Brown landscaped the grounds which contain oak trees many centuries old

Welshpool

Powys *p216 D2*

The little town of Welshpool is situated to the south-east of Lake Vyrnwy on the Shropshire Union Canal. Lying in the Severn river valley close to the border with England, it is an important agricultural and market centre with a long and stormy history. The site of an early Celtic settlement, the town was called Y Trallwng in Welsh, which means pool, because of the surrounding water-logged countryside. It received its first charter in the thirteenth century, and became known as Welshpool in the nineteenth century to distinguish it from Poole in Dorset. A compact town – its north-western edges skirt steep hillside, whilst the heights of Long Mountain rise to the east beyond the river. In recent years Welshpool has been extensively modernised, but a few of its original narrow streets still survive along with some interesting half-timbered buildings. High on a bank at the north end of Church Street stands the parish church of St Mary of the Salutation, notable for its roof and tower architecture. In the churchyard lies a great stone known as the Maen

Llog. Once used as a throne by the Abbot of Strata Marcella, a Cistercian monastery to the north-east of Welshpool, it was brought to the town upon the Dissolution of the monastery. Other interesting buildings include the railway station and the nineteenth-century Town Hall.

Set amidst terraced gardens and lawns, reputed to have been landscaped by Capability Brown, Powis Castle stands on the south-west outskirts of Welshpool. This well-preserved red sandstone medieval castle with twin towers has been continuously occupied for more than 500 years. The interior contains some fine sixteenth-century plasterwork and panelling, along with tapestries, paintings and late Georgian furniture. Many relics and possessions of Clive of India are also on display and the castle was given to the National Trust in 1952 by a great-great-great grandson of Lord Clive.

Powysland Museum, started in 1874 by Morris Jones, displays a striking collection of relics illustrating the social history of Powysland. Its archaeological, domestic, agricultural and craft exhibits include an Iron Age shield and Roman antiquities.

The Welshpool and Llanfair Light Railway was originally built to carry general goods, and it ran from the 1930s to 1956 when it was closed by British Railways. However, after being rescued by railway enthusiasts, the eight mile stretch between Llanfair Caereinion station and Welshpool station was opened in 1963.

Powis Castle open Easter to mid Apr, then May to Sep Wed to Sun pm only. Tue also in Aug. Also open Bank Holidays. Parking and refreshments available. NT.
Powysland Museum open all year daily (except Sun), pm only on Sat. Closed Wed Oct to May.
Welshpool & Llanfair Light (Steam) Railway open at weekends from Easter to Oct. Spring Bank Holiday, mid Jan to mid Jul Tue, Wed and Thu, Jul and Aug, daily. Parking and refreshments at Llanfair Station.

West Midland Safari and Leisure Park

Hereford and Worcester *p216 E1*

The West Midlands park was established in the early 1970s and is now one of the most popular Safari Parks in Britain. It covers some 200 acres and includes drive-through reserves of lions,

monkeys, bison, tigers, giraffes, zebra, elephants and rhinos. Outside the reserves there is an extensive leisure park with a pets' corner, sea lions, boating ponds and children's amusements. These include a playground, roundabouts, trains, rocket rides and a skatepark. The park is attractively laid out with landscaped picnic areas.

Open Apr to Oct daily. Parking and refreshments available.

Westonbirt Arboretum

Gloucestershire *p212 F4*

One of Europe's most comprehensive collections of trees can be seen here at the Westonbirt Arboretum. Some of the trees date back as far as 1829, when Robert Holford began planting in what was then open pasture. Set in 247 acres of gently rolling parkland, the arboretum is incorporated into a 600-acre Forestry Commission estate. Each season brings a different beauty; budding trees in spring, summer flowering shrubs, the russet tones of autumn leaves, and the severity of winter. Many kinds of rare specimens can be seen here, and particularly impressive are the large varieties of conifers, maples, birches and oaks.

Open all year daily. Refreshments available Apr to mid Nov. Parking available.

Weston Park

Staffordshire *p216 E2*

This lovely Classical mansion is the home of the Earl and Countess of Bradford and has been in their family for some 300 years. The interior has been considerably altered since it was built, emphasising the fact that Weston Park is a home as well as a great historic house. It contains a fine collection of furniture and paintings, which include works by Holbein and Van Dyck, and there is a large collection of letters on show which were written by Disraeli to the 3rd Countess. The tapestry room contains a late eighteenth-century Gobelin tapestry.

The house is the centre of an estate which covers about 14,000 acres. Much of this is given over to forestry and farming, but the area around the house was laid out by Capability Brown in one of his famous landscape gardens. Mature sweeping lawns, watered by three lakes were embellished in 1760 with the addition of the Roman Bridge and the Temple of Diana, which looks back towards the house. The park is also the home of a herd of Fallow deer and some rare breeds of sheep, and visitors can enjoy rides in horse-drawn vehicles. For the younger visitor there is a woodland adventure playground, a pets' corner and an aquarium, while their parents will probably enjoy seeing a potter at work in the Taurus Pottery, or a visit to the garden centre. Each year there is a programme of special events.

Open Apr, May and Sep weekends and Bank Holidays; Jun and Jul daily (except Mon and Fri), daily in Aug. House pm only. Parking and refreshments available.

Weston-super-Mare

Avon *p212 E3*

Weston has expanded rapidly since the Victorians started to develop this small fishing village into a seaside resort, and it is now the largest town on this stretch of coast.

The town is well laid out with wide roads and lawns along the seafront and plenty of open spaces. The tide goes out a long

The view from the Grand Pier across the bay to the famous Winter Gardens at Weston-super-Mare

way over the beach, leaving mud exposed as well as the golden sands. This type of beach is ideal for ball games and sun-bathing, but at high tide swimmers have a long walk to deep water. However, the sea-water pool on the beach caters for bathers of all ages and abilities and has a multi-stage diving board; there is an indoor pool too, if the weather is inclement. In the attractive Winter Gardens are tennis courts,

bowling and putting greens; there is a seafront golf course and good facilities for other sports. Two piers provide traditional seaside amusements and there are two theatres offering year-round entertainment, regular concerts in the Rozel Music Garden, a three-screen cinema, several discothèques and ten-pin bowling. Children are well catered for too; amongst the many pleasures are donkey rides and pony carts on

the beach, a model boat pond, paddling pools and mini-zoo.

The Woodspring Museum, housed in workshops of the old Gaslight Company, has a wide variety of exhibits including an old chemist's shop, a dairy, and a display illustrating Victorian holidays.

Woodspring Museum open all year Mon to Sat (except Good Fri, Christmas Day and New Year's Day). Parking and refreshments available.

The east front of Weston Park; the present house was designed by Lady Wilbraham in the 17th century

Whipsnade Park Zoo

Bedfordshire *p213 B4*

Originally planned as a sort of convalescent home for sick animals from London Zoo, Whipsnade has developed into a major zoo in its own right. It now covers some 500 acres of lovely Chilterns countryside and is home to over 2,000 animals. When the zoo opened in 1931, it was quite revolutionary in that it provided large open enclosures for animals that would previously only have been kept in heated cages. The experiment was a resounding success and the creatures from warmer climes adapted well to their new surroundings; so well in fact that the zoo has achieved a remarkable breeding record, and about eighty per cent of its inhabitants have been born at the zoo.

One of the zoo's major successes is in the conservation of endangered species, including North American bison, Père David's deer, Przewalski's horses, Great Indian rhinos, African Black rhinos and, of course, the White rhino which now form a sizeable herd at Whipsnade. As well as these rare breeds the zoo contains all the usual mammals and birds, far too numerous to list, a delightful children's zoo and the ever popular animal rides. It is possible to take vehicles into the zoo and a novel way of seeing part of it is via the Whipsnade and Umfolozi Railway, a two-foot-six-inch gauge steam operated line which follows a circular route through the African region.

Open all year daily (except 25 Dec). Steam Railway Apr to Oct. Parking and refreshments available.

Although the great Thomas Telford designed Wick harbour, large steamers can only dock here at high tide

Whitby

North Yorkshire *p217 C4*

For hundreds of years gulls have screamed over the incoming fishing boats of Whitby, and fishermen and their families have lived under the East Cliff on the banks of the river Esk. Terraces of cottages still rise tier on tier from the water's edge, a fishing fleet plies from Whitby harbour, and nets are mended outside cottage doors. The Victorians started to develop the town as a resort, building hotels and houses to the west of the river mouth, and now the town relies on holidaymakers for its prosperity.

Much of the provision for outdoor activity is on the West Cliff and the Spa complex, which includes a theatre and Floral Pavilion (often used for dances) can be found here. A lift links the cliff top with Whitby Sands, where there are a number of chalets for hire, donkey rides and safe bathing.

On West Cliff is a statue of Captain James Cook, who learnt his seamanship sailing colliers from the port, making his home at a house in Grape Street which bears a memorial plaque. Another sailor remembered in the town is Captain William Scoresby, who invented the 'crow's nest' and is reputed to have captured 533 whales in his lifetime. Relics of Cook and Scoresby are displayed in the Whitby Museum, which also has a fine collection of fossils.

Adding to the sense of timelessness which gives Whitby its especial character, are the abbey ruins on East Cliff. The first abbey, founded by St Hilda in 657, was destroyed by Danes in 867, and the buildings of the later Benedictine monastery, dissolved in 1539, have disappeared. Stripped of its roof, battered by the elements, and shelled by the Germans in 1914, the ruins are nevertheless austerely impressive. Close by is the medieval parish church of St Mary with a squat Norman tower, and it is approached by a flight of 199 steps.

Museum open all year (except Christmas and New Year's Day). May to Sep daily, pm only on Sun. Oct to Apr daily am only Wed and Sat open all day, pm only on Sun.
Abbey see AM info. Also open Sun am Apr to Sep. Parking available.

Wick

Highland *p222 E4*

The townspeople of Wick said harsh things about Thomas Stevenson's ability as a civil engineer when a breakwater he constructed was smashed by a violent storm, so perhaps his son, Robert

Louis (who wrote *Treasure Island*), was feeling disgruntled when he described Wick as 'the bleakest of God's towns on the baldest of God's bays'. It is true that the cliffs are forbidding, the hilltops windswept and devoid of tree or shrub, yet the coast and surrounding countryside have a fascination of their own.

The town does not deserve to be called bleak these days, and it welcomes holidaymakers.

Swimming from the beach is safe only in the calmest weather, but there are two open-air swimming pools, and facilities for bowls, tennis and putting, with a golf course at the nearby village of Reiss. There are boats for hire on the river, and sea angling is popular – though it needs an expert to navigate around this coast.

The obelisk on the South Head honours James Bremner, a great engineer, and there is a plaque commemorating Robert Louis Stevenson on the Customs House. This is a land of castles, most of them now gaunt ruins. A landmark, nicknamed by seamen Auld Man O' Wick, is the ruined fourteenth-century Castle of Old Wick, also known as Castle Oliphant; to the north are the ruins of seventeenth-century Sinclair Castle and Girnigoe Castle, dating from 1500. The latter has a dungeon where the 4th Earl of Caithness held his son until he died of 'famine and vermin'.

Until 1800 the herring fleet was based at Staxigoe a few miles to the north, where the old red-tiled houses can still be seen. Then the building of Pulteneytown harbour to the south of the river signalled the expansion of Wick and a boom period for fishermen. The

Shakespeare's mother, Mary Arden, spent her childhood here at Wilmcote

people of Wick have sought new industry and the town is now famous for Caithness glass. Both industries have great appeal, the fishing fleet bringing life and colour to the harbour, and a visit to the glassworks, where the manufacture of subtly-coloured handblown vessels can be seen, being both informative and interesting.

Castle of Old Wick accessible except when adjoining rifle range is in use. AM.
Castles Girnigoe and Sinclair accessible at all times.

Wilmcote

Warwickshire *p216 F1*

This village of local stone cottages and timber-framed houses, set on the Stratford-Upon-Avon Canal, is famous as the birthplace of Shakespeare's mother, Mary Arden. Her birthplace is the picturesque Tudor farmhouse of the Arden family, now owned and preserved here by the Shakespeare Birthplace Trust. The interior of the house, laid out as it might have been during her day, has a huge fireplace with one of the largest ovens to be seen in England, and a table believed to have been used by monks in the fifteenth century. Outside there is a cider-mill and dovecote, along with other attractive stone outbuildings housing a museum of farming and rural life.

Mary Arden's House open all year (except 24 to 26 Dec, New Years Day am and Good Fri am, Apr to Oct daily, Nov to Mar, Mon to Sat only. Parking available.

Wilton House

Wiltshire *p212 F3*

Standing on the banks of the river Wylye, Wilton House has been described as one of the most beautiful houses in England. The mansion was started by Inigo Jones with the aid of his nephew John Webb, in the sixteenth century, and later additions were made by Holbein and James Wyatt in the eighteenth century. It has been the seat of the Earls of Pembroke for 400 years. Inside the house is a world famous collection of paintings and furniture, including pieces by Kent and Chippendale. There are magnificent double and single 'cube' rooms, elaborately decorated with bundles of fruit, flowers and foliage gilded in gold. Paintings include works by Rembrandt, Rubens and Van Dyck. An interesting exhibit of 7,000 nineteenth-century miniature model soldiers can be seen here.

The grounds are beautiful, with their superb setting of twenty acres of cedar-shaded lawns, with Cedars of Lebanon and an eighteenth-century Palladian bridge which spans the river Nadder.

Open Easter to mid Oct daily (except Mon, but open Bank Holidays) Sun pm only. Parking and refreshments available.

Wimborne Minster

Dorset *p212 F2*

This ancient town once owed its prosperity to the wool trade, but now its wealth comes from market gardening. One of the great churches of Dorset is situated here; the twin-towered Church of St Cuthberga, built of brown and grey stone, and encompassing almost every architectural style from Norman to Gothic. The quarter-jack clock on the minster's west tower features a grenadier wielding a hammer in each hand with which to strike the bells on each quarter-hour.

Many items of local interest are contained in the Priest's House Museum in the High Street. Items from Roman times are exhibited here, together with a sec-

The 18th-century whalers saw Whitby's greatest days as a seaport

tion devoted to rural implements. The museum houses some of the best horse brasses in the country.

West of the town centre is Kingston Lacy House which has recently been acquired and renovated by the National Trust. The seventeenth-century house, designed by Sir Roger Pratt but altered by Sir Charles Barry in 1835, contains one of the finest private picture collections in the country with works by Titian, Van Dyck, Reynolds, Lely, Rubens and Velasquez. It is set in two hundred and fifty acres of wooded parkland.

About one-and-a-half miles south of Wimborne are the Merley Tropical Bird Gardens. Three acres of lawns and gardens, enclosed by an eighteenth-century wall, contain large cages of a wide variety of birds, including many tropical species.

Priest's House Museum open Easter Mon to Sep daily (except Sun).
Kingston Lacy House and Park open late Apr to Oct, Sat to Wed pm only. Refreshments available. NT.
Merley Bird Gardens open all year daily. Parking and refreshments available.

Winchester

Hampshire p213 A2

When the Romans left Winchester – having made it one of their largest towns – King Alfred designated it capital of England. Since then the city has continued to be an important administrative centre and, having the oldest public school in England, a venerable seat of learning.

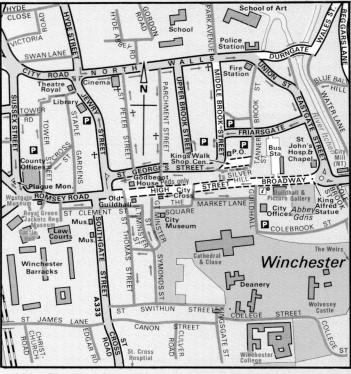

Like so many English cities, the heart of Winchester is its cathedral and its precincts. However, the whole of this compact city is a delight to explore, with its architecture spanning over eight centuries and the river Itchen flowing through its charming back streets. There are many reminders of Winchester's history scattered around its streets; a bronze statue of King Alfred faces up the High Street, and near to it is the City Mill. This sixteenth-century building stands across the river Itchen and, now a youth hostel, is a good starting point for riverside walks to both the north and south. A stretch known as The Weirs is particularly pleasant and this runs alongside the old city walls. The High Street (now mostly pedestrianised), apart from having a number of good shops has many interesting features. These include the Victorian Old Guildhall and, although now occupied by a bank, echoes the past daily at 8.00 p.m. by sounding the bell which rang out the curfew in Norman times. Close to it is the old Butter Cross – a Gothic monument with a fifteenth-century statue of John the Baptist set in to it.

The Cathedral

The history of the cathedral dates as far back as the seventh century to St Peter's Church which oc-

Winchester Cathedral, interior

cupied the site. When the Normans arrived in Britain they brought with them their own distinctive architectural style and the tower, transepts and the crypt of the present cathedral built by William the Conqueror reflect this. As one of the longest cathedrals in Europe, it measures 556 feet and stands majestically in the spacious Close. Here can be seen Pilgrims' Hall, where pilgrims used to rest on their journey to Canterbury in the Middle Ages; the Deanery and the attractive half-timbered Tudor Cheyne Court. One of the cathedral's bishops in the ninth century was St Swithun, and the legend goes that he wished to be buried in the churchyard where the rain would fall on him. However he was not, and to express his anger he caused rain to fall for forty days – hence the expression that if it rains on St Swithun's Day (July

15th) it will rain for the next forty days. In any event there is a shrine to St Swithun in the cathedral. Treasures to be seen inside include a square font made of black marble, which is carved with scenes depicting the life of St Nicholas; medieval wall paintings and elaborate tombs dedicated to such notable people as King Canute, Jane Austen and Izaak Walton.

Wolvesey Castle

Near to Cathedral Close lie all that remain of the former residence of the Bishops of Winchester – Wolvesey Castle. Built in the twelfth century, it was reduced to ruins during the Civil War.

The present Bishop's Palace, standing next to the castle, was built to the designs of Christopher Wren in 1674. Only one wing of

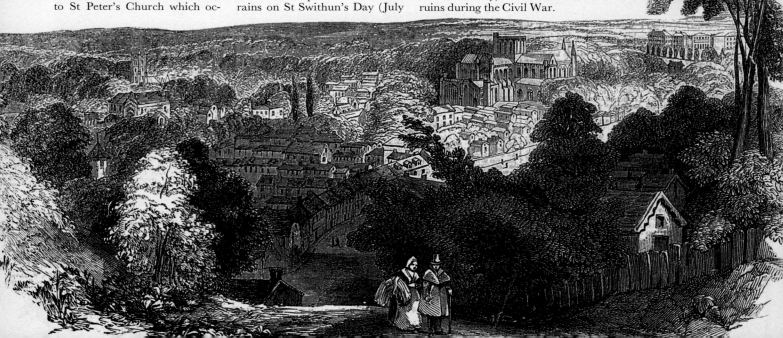

the original building still stands, and incorporated in to this is a Tudor chapel that was once part of Winchester Castle.

Winchester College

When founded by the Bishop of Winchester, William of Wykeham, in 1382, the school was for poor scholars only. However fee paying pupils gradually began to attend and by the end of the nineteenth century had increased to such an extent that many new boarding hostels had to be established and it became England's first public school. The college is made up of a number of buildings grouped around a quadrangle and they vary in age from a hundred to 600 years. Inside the chapel are a sixteenth-century Flemish tapestry, seventeenth-century altar rails and fourteenth-century carved stall ends. Other buildings include the cloister, where summer lessons used to be held, and the hall where boys used to eat from wooden platters. Pupils today are still called Wykehamists, after the college founder.

Castle Hall

The Hall stands on the site of William the Conqueror's defence point and is all that remains of the castle which Henry III built, but was later demolished during the Civil War by Cromwell's armies. Inside hangs the famous Round Table which was made to commemorate King Arthur and his knights. The Tudor rose was painted on it in 1522 to honour the visit of Emperor Charles V when Henry VIII entertained him here. The Hall has seen many royal personages and a number of trials have taken place here, including the one at which Sir Walter Raleigh was condemned to death.

Westgate Museum

Westgate, at the western end of the High Street, is one of the five gates of the city walls that enclosed the city in the thirteenth century. At one time Westgate was used as a prison, but it is now a museum with exhibits that include weaponry, armour, and weights and measures that were used in Tudor and Elizabethan times.

St Cross Hospital

Founded by Bishop Henry de Blois during the twelfth century, this establishment is still used as

We know that this table has existed since at least the 15th century

almshouses today and is therefore the oldest in Britain. The inhabitants are dressed in two different distinctive robes. Those belonging to the original order founded by de Blois wear black and are decorated with a silver cross; those belonging to the other Order, founded by Cardinal Henry Beaufort around 1445, wear purple cloaks. These elderly gentlemen can often be seen walking around the city. Hospitality is still extended to visitors at St Cross by the offering of the Wayfarer's Dole, which consists of a piece of bread and a mug of ale.

The Royal Green Jackets' Museum

This specialist museum is divided into three sections. One is devoted to the Rifle Brigade, one to the King's Royal Rifle Corps and one to the Oxfordshire and Buckinghamshire Light Infantry. Incorporated in to all the displays are collections of uniforms, weapons, regimental silver and medals.

Pilgrim's Hall open all year daily (except when closed for private functions).
Winchester College accessible all year daily Sun pm only. Guided tour available (except Sun am).
Castle hall open all year daily (except Good Fri and 25 Dec).
Westgate Museum open all year daily (except Mon Nov to Mar, Good Fri, Christmas and New Year); Sun pm only.
St Cross Hospital open all year daily (except Sun and Bank Holidays).
The Royal Green Jackets' Museum open Apr to Sep, Mon to Fri. Sat pm only. Oct to Mar, Mon to Fri only.

Windermere

Cumbria *p220 E1*

Nineteenth-century conservationists protested that a railway would ruin the peace of Lake Windermere and its environs, as a result of which the line was terminated at the hamlet of Birthwaite, and the station was called Windermere. The present town of Windermere grew up around the station, expanding until it joined with Bowness to make a lakeside town devoted to tourism. The invention of the internal combustion engine further popularised the area, and roads, towns, places of interests, and even the lake itself, suffer from congestion during the holiday season.

However, no influx of people can spoil the beauty of Windermere. To the north, where the lake is fed by the rivers Brathay and Rothay, the country is mountainous, affording protection from the colder winds, and ten miles to the south the lake waters join the river Leven on its way to the sea. The banks of the lake are well-wooded, so that from the road the water is rarely glimpsed, and conversely, from a boat one is almost unaware of road traffic. In fact the best way to enjoy the scenery is by boat, whether from a ferry plying between the major towns, a hired motor cruiser, a rowing boat, or one of the yachts which add colourful movement to the scene. There are often as many as 1,500 craft on the lake and wardens enforce a strict code of conduct.

One of the best overall views of Lake Windermere can be obtained from Orrest Head (reached by a footpath from the station).

The biggest island in the lake is Belle Isle, where an eighteenth-century circular mansion, built on the site of a Roman villa and surrounded by landscaped grounds, is open to the public. This unique house was the first completely round house built in England and contains portraits of the Curwen family, views of Lake Windermere by Philip de Loutherburg and specially designed furniture by Gillow of Lancaster.

The Steamboat Museum has a covered dock where Victorian and Edwardian craft are preserved. The oldest exhibit is *Dolly* of 1850, salvaged from Ullswater in 1962 and restored. Situated in the village of Near Sawrey, is Hill Top, where Beatrix Potter worked on many of her *Peter Rabbit* stories. However visitors often have a long wait to enter this charming little seventeenth-century house which contains some of her original drawings, furniture, china and pictures.

The parish church of Windermere is St Martin's at Bowness and was founded in the tenth century. The present church dates from 1484 and was restored in 1870. It contains chained books and some interesting stained glass windows. One depicts a packhorse, and in the east window is the coat of arms of John Washington, an ancestor of the American President.

Steamboat Museum open Apr to Oct, daily but pm only on Sun. Parking and refreshments available.
Belle Isle (Motor Launch runs continuously from far end of Bowness promenade) open May to Sep, Sun to Thu. Refreshments available.
Hill Top open Apr to early Nov daily (except Fri) pm only on Sun.

Passenger boats ply from end to end of Lake Windermere, a 10-mile trip

Windsor Berkshire *p213 B3*

Royal Windsor, a town which has given its name to the Royal Family, owes its existence to the great fortress, the largest inhabited castle in the world, upon the chalk bluff high above the bend of the river Thames.

Saxon kings had hunted the forests in this area for centuries, based in a settlement known as Windelsora. When the Norman kings built the first fortress on Windsor's present site, four miles upstream from the old settlement, and Henry I held his court there in safety from the hostile Saxons, the town began to grow.

The architecture of Windsor today is largely Georgian and Victorian, but there are buildings far older. One mile from the castle is Clewer parish church, which was virtually completed by the eleventh century. The font is Saxon, and there is also a tomb with Saxon lettering.

Windsor parish church, rebuilt in 1820 although dating from 1168, records in its register the burial of Charles I. The Three Tuns Hotel was built in 1518 and in St Alban's Street is the seventeenth-century home of Nell Gwynne, mistress of Charles II.

There are many narrow cobbled streets in Windsor, especially between Church Lane and Castle Hill, lined with seventeenth- and eighteenth-century buildings. The river too lends its own special atmosphere to Thames-side towns and Windsor is no exception. Boating is to be had and there are pleasant riverside walks, gardens and pubs.

The Castle

For nearly nine centuries Windsor Castle has been the home of kings and queens, and it is the oldest royal residence still in use.

The thirteen-acre site was chosen by William the Conqueror who built a concentric castle of earthworks and wooden defences here. Because it lay near a large tract of forest which provided good hunting, the castle soon became a residence of Norman kings, who loved the hunt as much as their Saxon predecessors. However, it was not until the reign of Henry II that stone buildings were erected as the royal apartments.

Open to the public are the precincts, the state apartments and Queen Mary's Doll's House.

The state apartments are in the upper ward, and the sixteen magnificent rooms hold a remarkable collection of furniture, porcelain and armour. The carvings of Grinling Gibbons are everywhere, and on the walls hang many masterpieces, especially those by Van Dyck and Rembrandt.

Everything in the remarkable Doll's House works, even the minute light bulbs the size of dewdrops. The scale of this house, built by Sir Edwin Lutyens, is one inch to one foot. Famous artists, craftsmen and writers (the library has real leather-bound books of original works) contributed to this gift to Queen Mary in 1924. The detail is amazing, even the linen in the pantry is initialled – a task which took 1,500 hours of work, and the cars in the garages are constructed to run 20,000 miles to a gallon of petrol!

The Chapel of the Order of the Garter, St George's Chapel, was begun in the reign of Edward IV and completed by Henry VIII. It forms the setting of the ceremonious annual service of the Sovereign and Knights Companion of the Order. Here, among the magnificent architecture, heraldry and decoration, Charles I, Henry VIII and Jane Seymour are buried.

Within the walls of Windsor Castle lies St George's Chapel

Eton College

Eton, north of the river, is linked to Windsor by Windsor Bridge. Henry VI founded Eton in 1440 as a collegiate church with a grammar school and almhouse attached. The epitome of the public school, it has produced a string of famous names, and still clings to the traditions which have made it famous.

College Hall and the kitchen survive from the original design, and most of the rest is fifteenth century. College Chapel is the choir of the original Founder's Church, whereas the west range of the cloisters, the great gatehouse, and Lupton's Tower were added in the early sixteenth century; Upper School was built in about 1690.

Guildhall

Built in 1689 by Sir Thomas Fitz, but finished by Wren, the Guildhall houses an exhibition of local history from the Palaeolithic period to the present day. Notable is the collection of royal portraits from the time of Elizabeth I, and a series of dioramas showing historical events at Windsor from early times to the celebration of George III's Jubilee in 1809. There is also a natural history display.

Madame Tussaud's Royalty and Empire Exhibition

This exhibition is housed in the original buildings of the Central Station. It depicts Queen Victoria's Diamond Jubilee celebrations with a full-size replica of the Royal Train and a theatre presentation.

Household Cavalry Museum

This is one of the finest military museums in Britain. Situated in Combermore Barracks, it traces the history of the Household Cavalry from the Monmouth Rebellion in 1685 to the present day. Exhibits include uniforms, weapons, horse furniture and armour.

Windsor Great Park

This royal park covers approximately 4,800 acres south of the castle, and includes parkland, woods and magnificent gardens.

The Long Walk stretches from the towers of Windsor to Snow Hill, a distance of three miles. On Snow Hill stands a huge bronze of George III on horseback, erected in 1831. Queen Anne added the three mile ride to Ascot in the eighteenth century. In George III's reign Thomas Sandby and his brother laid out the two-mile-long lake of Virginia Water. It has a fine cascade and on the banks stand a group of Roman columns brought from Tripoli.

Lodges in the park include Cumberland Lodge, named after 'Butcher' Cumberland of Culloden. From here the famous Rhododendron Walk stretches for a mile to Bishop's Gate, where the poet Shelley once stayed.

The Savill Gardens started by Eric Savill in 1931, show to their best advantage rhododendrons, magnolias, cherries and camel-

The Long Walk, lined with chestnut and plane trees, was created in 1685

lias, and beside the ponds and streams grow primulas, irises and lilies. There are beds of roses, rock plants and alpines – almost every manner of plant found in English gardens. The Valley Garden, near Virginia Water, is similar, and the Kurume Punch Bowl is an amphitheatre of thousands of Japanese Kurume azaleas.

Castle Precincts open all year daily. State apartments open, Mon to Sat and Sun pm late Jun to late Oct (closed Dec to early Jan, Mar to early May and Jun). Queen Mary's Doll's House open all year daily, Sun May to late Oct only pm (except Good Fri, 22 to 26 Dec, 1 and 2 Jan). Castle is subject to closure at short notice. **Eton College** open daily pm only, but also am during school holidays. Chapel closed Sun during school holidays. Parking available. **Madame Tussaud's Royalty and Empire Exhibition** open all year daily (except Christmas). **Household Cavalry Museum** open all year Mon to Fri, except Bank Hol, also Sun from mid May to Sep. **Savill Gardens** open all year (except Christmas) daily. Parking available. **Valley Gardens** open all year daily.

Wisley Gardens
Surrey *p213 B3*

These are the famous and extensive gardens of the Royal Horticultural Society. At all seasons there is something to enjoy at Wisley: crocuses in early spring; a sudden flourish of rock plants; glorious rhododendrons in bloom; tranquil green lawns set with formal rose beds; cheerful borders; the mellow colours of the heather garden – particularly lovely in autumn.

The gardens cover 300 acres and include testing grounds for fruit and vegetables, as well as flowers, shrubs and trees, and there are also a number of glasshouses. At the information centre gardeners can obtain advice about horticultural problems, and there is a shop selling books, gifts, preserves, and, in season, fruit from the gardens.

Open all year daily (except 25 Dec). Sun, pm only. Parking and refreshments available.

Woburn Abbey, Wild Animal Kingdom and Leisure Park
Bedfordshire *p213 B4*

Probably Britain's most famous stately home, Woburn Abbey is the ancestral home of the Dukes of Bedford and has been open to the public since 1955. One of the world's greatest private collections of works of art, including paintings by Rembrandt, Gainsborough, Reynolds, Van Dyck, Franz Hals, and many other famous and important works are housed in the palatial mansion of Woburn. The magnificent state apartments are decorated in the superb elegance so typical of the seventeenth and eighteenth centuries, and contain an abundance of treasures. The state bedroom is particularly impressive, with its fabulous ceiling and furnishings, and it was here, in the splendid four-poster state bed, the newly married Queen Victoria and Prince Albert once slept. The exquisite Chinese room is hung with hand-painted oriental wallpaper, and contains a host of beautiful Chinese porcelain and furniture.

Some 300 acres of the surrounding woodland has been given over to a superb Wild Animal Kingdom. The drive-through safari park includes a lion reserve, tiger range, and monkey jungle, where animals can be seen roaming in almost natural habitats. Amongst other species to be seen in the Kingdom are brown bears, giraffes, rhinos, elephants, and bison.

Amongst other animal life to be seen here at Woburn are the many species of deer in the park. There is also an extensive Leisure Park and a fairground with various rides, including the Carousel, Rainbow ride and Cabin Lift. The pets' corner is another feature.

Within the grounds of Woburn there are many recreational facilities. A Chinese dairy overlooks a pond where Chinese ducks can often be seen swimming; a pottery, art gallery and craftshop display work by international artists.

Abbey and Deer Park open early Jan to late Mar Sat and Sun; daily late Mar to Oct.
Animal Kingdom and Leisure Park open daily mid Mar to early Nov.

Woburn Abbey was built on the site of a medieval monastry in the 17th century

Robert Smythson, who also worked at Longleat, designed Wollaton Hall

Wollaton Park and Hall

Nottinghamshire *p217 B1*

Lying on the outskirts of Nottingham is the 774-acre Wollaton Park, with its formal gardens, deer park and nature trail set around a lovely lake.

Standing within the park is the striking sixteenth-century Wollaton Hall. This is now a natural history museum, exhibiting mammals, birds and fishes arranged in natural habitat groups. Also displayed here is a large series of insects, and various archaeological finds.

The eighteenth-century stables house an industrial museum connected with printing, engineering, pharmacy and mining. Machinery connected with agriculture, lace, hosiery and tobacco-making can also be seen. In the courtyard is a colliery horse-gin, once used to wind both men and coal up and down a mine.

Industrial Museum open all year daily from Apr to Sep, Sun pm only; Oct to Mar Thu and Sat, also Sun pm. Refreshments available Apr to pm. Parking available.
Natural History Museum open all year daily (except 25 Dec) but pm only on Sun. Parking and refreshments (Easter to Sep) available.

Woodstock

Oxfordshire *p213 A4*

Woodstock is a charming busy place on the river Glyme – full of hotels, pubs, teashops and lovely old stone houses. The town has many royal links, but is most famous for its magnificent Blenheim Palace.

This palatial Italian-style mansion by Sir John Vanbrugh was started in 1705 for John Churchill, the 1st Duke of Marlborough. The enormous palace took seventeen years to build at a cost of £300,000, of which £240,000 was defrayed by Parliament as a reward for the Duke's victory over the French and the Bavarians at Blenheim. Unfortunately it was not completed until after the Duke's death in 1722.

The palace is rich in exotic furnishings and art treasures and it was here that Sir Winston Churchill was born in 1874. He was buried in the nearby Bladon churchyard on the southern fringe of the park and within sight of Blenheim.

The immense grounds, covering some 25,000 acres, were originally conceived by Henry Wise but later exquisitely remodelled and landscaped by Capability Brown. He created an artificial lake from the river Glyme, with its unfinished bridge, and a column 134 feet high in honour of Marlborough, the victor of Blenheim. Trees surrounding the column were planted in groups to represent the battle.

The grounds also play host to a butterfly house, adventure playground, a narrow-gauge railway and there are launch trips on the lake. The deer park is always open to walkers.

Also of interest in Woodstock is the Oxfordshire County Museum which is located in the sixteenth to eighteenth-century Fletcher's House and houses an exhibition of Oxfordshire from earliest times to the present day.

Blenheim Palace open daily mid Mar to Oct. Garden Centre open daily. Refreshments available.
Oxfordshire County Museum open all year daily (except Good Fri and 25, 26 Dec and Mon Oct to Apr); pm only on Sun. Refreshments available.

Wookey Hole Caves and Mill

Somerset *p212 E3*

Over many thousands of years the river Axe has worn away the rocks here to form the vast underground caverns in the heart of the Mendips at Wookey Hole. The guided tour leads through several of the caverns and they are truly spectacular. Unlike the caves at nearby Cheddar, there are no pretty rock formations here, but the immense size of the caverns more than compensates for this. The only exception is a strangely shaped rock known as the Witch of Wookey which casts an eerie shadow and is associated with morbid legends of child-eating and suchlike. The tour proceeds deeper into the more recently opened seventh, eighth and ninth caverns, crossed by high metal bridges, with the river Axe rushing far below. On emerging from the caves which gave shelter to man more than 2,000 years ago, the path passes the Hyena Den once occupied by those predatory creatures between 35000 and 25000 BC.

The circular tour continues by entering the old paper mill where high quality paper has been hand made since the seventeenth century. The recently restored works now make paper again and the long process of pulping, pressing, drying and finishing can be seen in operation.

Further rooms in the mill have been given over to some colourful and unusual collections, for example, Lady Bangor's Fairground collection of bygone fairground items from the age of steam. The superbly carved and painted figures from the old-time rides are an art form of their own and can be viewed to the accompanying music of a Marenghi fairground organ.

In 1973 Madame Tussaud's bought the caves and mill and the most unusual attraction of the tour is the fascinating storeroom of moulds and figures from the famous waxworks. The moulds are a strange collection of heads, limbs and torsos. Other shelves contain row upon row of familiar faces such as Henry VIII, Diana Dors and Harold Wilson. The 'Old Penny Pier Arcade' houses a large collection of vintage one penny slot machines. The final display before re-emerging from the mill is an exhibition of archaeological finds from the caves.

Open all year daily (except one week before Christmas). Parking and refreshments available.

The damp, chilly caverns of Wookey Hole are still being explored

Worcester
Hereford and Worcester *p216 F1*

*The ancient cathedral city of Worcester lies within an area of rich
farmland and meadows, of apple and cherry orchards and hopfields.
It is famous for sauce and china; for having the country's oldest
surviving newspaper; and for its fine cricket ground.*

In medieval times, the eastern boundary of Worcester was marked by defences which ran parallel to City Walls Road. These have been excavated and Worcester's oldest buildings lie between them and the riverfront. Friar Street and its continuation, New Street, contain several historic houses including the sixteenth-century Nash House and the fifteenth-century Greyfriars, one of the few monastic buildings to survive the Dissolution of the monasteries.

The Cathedral
The cathedral was founded as a Saxon monastery by St Oswald in 983. The crypt, one of the most inspiring parts, was constructed by St Wulston, the only Saxon bishop to keep his office after the Norman invasion in 1066. In the centre of the exquisite chancel, in front of the high altar, is the tomb of King John. Above, in the choir, is the oldest royal effigy in England. This is made of Purbeck marble and was originally painted and bejewelled. The arches of the Lady Chapel behind the high altar are perhaps among the most beautifully proportioned thirteenth-century work to be found in the country.

Prince Arthur's Chantry, an elaborately carved chancel, was built in 1504 by Henry VIII in memory of his son Arthur, who had died at Ludlow. It is remarkable for its fine tracery, heraldry and sculptures.

The cathedral library, over the south aisle of the nave, contains a large collection of early manuscripts, including fragments of an eighth-century Gospel and deeds of land from the same period. A thirteenth-century gateway opens out on to College Green. It leads on to the cloisters, the King's School and the chapter house as well as the ruins of the old Guester Hall – the guesthouse the monks built in 1320.

Just to the west of the gateway (also called the Edgar Tower) is the deanery, an early eighteenth-century house with a particularly beautiful pedimented doorway.

The Commandery
Founded in 1085 as a hospital by St Wulston, this timber-framed building with its most impressive great hall, was used by Charles II as his HQ during the Battle of Worcester in 1651. The magnificent Elizabethan staircase leads to upper rooms, one of which has fine sixteenth-century wall paintings.

Royal Worcester Porcelain Works and The Dyson Perrins Museum
The porcelain industry was started in 1751 by Dr Wall and a group of local businessmen. Their factory soon produced its own successful lines of Chinese blue-printed ware, and later richly ornamented ware, that ranks with some of the world's greatest. Dr Wall died in 1766, but the royal seal of approval was given by King George III some twelve years later.

Adjacent to the factory is the Dyson Perrins Museum, which contains the finest collection of Worcester china in the world. Exhibits cover the period from 1751 (when the factory was founded) to the present day.

Tudor House
This 500-year-old timber-framed building, once an inn, has been turned into a folk museum which depicts daily life in the city from Elizabethan times. Amongst its exhibits is an old-fashioned kitchen with a cast-iron cooking range.

King Charles's House
King Charles II hid in the house after his defeat in the Battle of Worcester in 1651 outside the city walls, and fled through the back door as Parliamentary troops entered at the front. The house is now a shop.

Guildhall
One of the most gracious Queen Anne buildings in the town is the Guildhall. It was designed in 1721 by Thomas White, a pupil of Sir Christopher Wren. Inside the building is a beautifully decorated assembly room and a heritage centre where the history of Worcester and its personalities are vividly portrayed.

City Museum and Art Gallery
This museum has a collection of Civil War relics together with archaeology and natural history. One section of the museum is devoted to the Worcestershire Regiment raised in 1694, and the county's Yeoman Cavalry.

The Commandery open all year daily; Sun pm only. Open Bank Holiday Mon.
Dyson Perrins Museum open all year Mon to Fri, also Sat Apr to Sep. Parking and refreshments available.
Tudor House open all year Mon to Sat (except Thu).
Guildhall open all year Mon to Fri, occasional Sat in summer. (Closed Bank Holidays).
City Museum and Art Gallery open all year daily (ex Thu and Sun).

Worcester Cathedral occupies a commanding site above the river Severn

Ancient remains of a Roman wall

Wroxeter

Shropshire *p216 E2*

A Roman legionary fortress was established at Wroxeter in about the middle of the first century, but later the garrison moved further north to Chester and a new town – the fourth largest in Britain during the Roman occupation and tribal capital of the Cornovil – grew up on the site. Aerial surveys show that this town – *Viroconium Cornoviorum* – covered about 180 acres, most of which is now farmland. The town was inhabited long after the Roman legions were withdrawn, probably in to the eighth century.

Although the forum was excavated in the 1920s, it has since been covered in except for a line of column stumps. On the site which is now open to the public were a market hall, a public latrine, a baths complex, and a *palaestra*, or exercise hall. The largest remaining section of masonry is an old arch, part of the wall which divided the hall from the baths. These consisted of a series of rooms providing hot baths, moist heat, dry heat, and cold plunges. A swimming pool was also built, but never seems to have been used – possibly because an extension to the baths, providing a second set of rooms which may have been for women, blocked access to the pool. Visitors can see the *pilae* (some of them modern reconstructions) which supported the floors, stoke holes, and furnace chambers.

A museum contains, besides an assortment of interesting artifacts, a cast of the inscription stone from the forum which shows that the building was dedicated to Emperor Hadrian in AD 130. Another inscription stone mentions Cunorix, believed to be an Irish settler, probably one of the *foederati*, or allies, brought to Britain by the Romans in their endeavour to protect the country from invaders when the military occupation came to an end. The original forum inscription stone and many other finds from the Wroxeter site, are in Rowley's House Museum in Shrewsbury.

See AM info. Also Sun am Apr to Sep. Parking available.

The Romans called York *Eboracum*, and, as capital of Lower Britain, became one of the leading cities of the Roman empire. Emperor Hadrian used it as a base, and when Emperor Constantine died here, in AD 306, his son became the only Emperor proclaimed in Britain – Constantine the Great, one of the most famous men in history.

During Saxon times York declined, because the Saxons did not like living in the old Roman cities, and it was not until AD 867, when the Danes took York, that it once more became an important trading centre and port.

The three-mile circuit of the medieval walls, which enclose the old city, stands on earth ramparts erected by the Anglo-Danish kings. It takes two hours to walk the walls, and they provide a fascinating sight of the tight-knit, jumbled centre of a medieval town. Close to the Minster is a maze of narrow streets of ancient shops and inns. The Shambles is perhaps the most famous street – here are still the shelves and hooks in front of shops used to

York North Yorkshire *p217 B3*

Two thousand years of history are crammed within the walls of York – one of Europe's most interesting and historic cities. It is a city to be walked in, so the alley ways and corners of medieval domesticity can be discovered, and the glory of the Minster can be wondered at.

York Minster from the south-east, a superb example of English Gothic

display meat beside the cobbled thoroughfare. Many of the old houses have boot-scrapers outside their doors, harking back to the days when the unsurfaced streets were often a sea of mud, and others display firemarks – badges which proved a property was insured with a company possessing fire-engines, before the days of a municipal fire brigade.

The Minster

The Gothic cathedral of York was begun in 1220, but was not completed until 250 years later. The earliest part is the south transept, and then came the beautiful octagonal chapter house, the nave, the choir, the finely carved twin west towers and finally the massive central lantern tower, completed by about 1480 in replacement of an earlier one which had collapsed. One of the Minster's greatest treasures is the wealth of stained glass, spanning the ages between the twelfth and twentieth centuries. About eighty of the 130 windows were taken down for safety reasons during World War II, and this gave re-

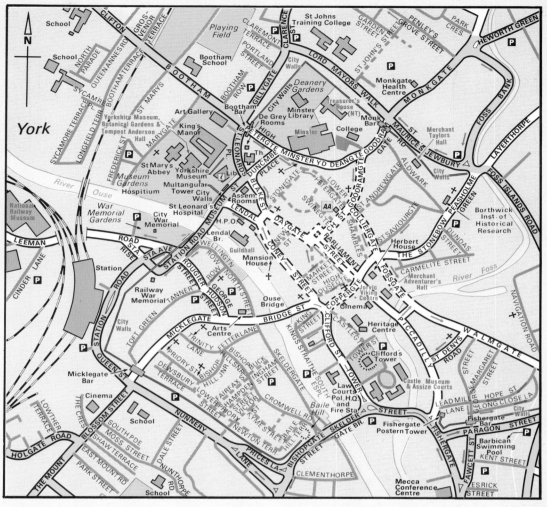

Some of the houses in the Shambles almost touch across the street

storers a chance to put right the mistakes of past glaziers, where the wrong glass had been put in to replace broken pieces, or had been put in the incorrect place. The great east window is approximately the size of a tennis court and was created between 1405 and 1408. At the apex God is depicted with the words 'Ego sum Alpha et Omega' – I am the beginning and the end – which is the theme of the whole window.

Jorvik Viking Centre

Jorvik was uncovered by archaeologists below Coppergate shedding a totally new light on the northern Viking kingdom based at York. The Viking city has been lavishly recreated beneath the streets of modern York and the tenth-century buildings replaced where they were found. Visitors are transported by 'time-car' through a bustling market place, dark smokey houses and a busy wharf; even the sounds and smells have been recreated. Many of the magnificent objects found are also on view in a treasure hall.

Merchant Adventurers' Hall

This fourteenth- and fifteenth-century hall was the meeting place of the powerful Company of the Merchant Adventurers. It is a superb example of a medieval guildhall, with the banners of the various guilds still displayed. The building is made almost entirely of wood as the Black Death killed the majority of masons in the city. The Pancake Bell in the under-

croft, where guild pensioners lived, was rung every Shrove Tuesday to tell the apprentices it was pancake time.

Yorkshire Museum and Gardens

The museum, founded in 1827, is housed in a fine neo-Classical building in grounds containing the Botanical Gardens and the majestic ruins of St Mary's Abbey. It houses large collections of archaeology, geology, pottery and natural history. Among the unique finds from Roman York is the head of a statue of Constantine the Great. The sixteenth-century guesthouse of the abbey is a separate museum exhibiting relics of prehistoric, Viking and medieval times. Also here is an extensive and important geological collection, including dramatic twenty-five-foot-long fossils of ichthyosaurs and pleisiosaurs – animals which lived 160 million years ago.

The Botanical Gardens, laid out in the early nineteenth century,

form York's most beautiful park – full of fascinating trees and plants, pleasant lawns and walks.

Castle Museum

Dr J. L. Kirk presented his outstanding collection of bygones to the City of York in 1935. It is displayed in the Female Prison, designed in 1780. There are among the reconstructions a Victorian parlour, moorland kitchen, Georgian dining room and Jacobean hall. The outstanding attraction is Kirkgate and Alderman's Walk in the prison exercise yard. This is a Victorian cobbled street complete with shop fronts and waiting hansom cab.

Across the circular lawn from the Female Prison is the Debtors Prison. Upstairs is kept a collection of firearms, armour, uniforms, medals and decorations, and general militaria. Downstairs there are costumes, period rooms and toy collections.

National Railway Museum

This museum is the largest rail-

way collection in Britain. Housed in a former British Railways steam locomotive shed, the central hall covers two acres and contains twenty-five locomotives and twenty items of rolling stock. The museum also illustrates railway history through uniforms, posters, models – every conceivable thing connected with railway development.

Jorvik Visitors Centre open all year daily.
Merchant Adventurers' Hall open all year Mon to Sat (also Sun, Apr to Oct) and Bank Holidays (except New Years' Day, Good Fri and Christmas). Closed when Hall is in use.

Yorkshire Museum open all year daily (except Christmas) but pm only on Sun. Hospitium open Mon to Sat in summer only. Gardens open all year daily (except Christmas).
Castle Museum open all year daily (except Christmas and New Year's Day).
National Railway Museum open all year daily (except New Years' Day, Good Fri, May Day Holiday, Christmas and some other public holidays); pm only on Suns. Parking.

Key to Location Atlas

The cities and towns in the gazetteer which have a street plan are underlined in red.

221
Stornoway
Portree
Thurso
Wick

222
Banff
Inverness
Peterhead
Aberdeen
Fort William
Montrose
Pitlochry
Dundee
Oban
Perth
Inverary
Stirling

219
Glasgow
Edinburgh
Berwick
Peebles
Ayr
Dumfries
Stranraer

220
Newcastle
Carlise
Durham

Hadrian's Wall
See Pages 88, 89
Workington
Isle of Man
Kendal
Scarborough

Lake District
See Pages 108, 109
Lancaster
217
York
Blackpool
Bradford
Leeds
Hull

Manchester
216
Grimsby
Liverpool
218

215
Anglesey
Chester
Stoke
Lincoln
Caernarvon
Derby
Nottingham

Snowdonia National Park
See Pages 170, 171
Shrewsbury
Leicester
King's Lynn
Norfolk Broads
See Pages 134, 135
Norwich
Aberystwyth
Birmingham
Peterborough

Pembrokeshire Coast National Park
See Page 143
Warwick
Bury St Edmunds
Worcester
Stratford-upon-Avon
Cambridge
Ipswich
Fishguard
Carmarthen
Hereford
Cheltenham
Pembroke
Oxford
St Albans
Colchester
214
Swansea
Gloucester
213
Newport
London
Cardiff
Bristol
Reading
Windsor
Maidstone
Canterbury
Bath
Dover

211
212
Salisbury
Winchester
Brighton
Taunton
Southampton
Chichester
Bournemouth

Dartmoor
See Pages 64, 65
Exeter
Isle of Wight
New Forest
See Pages 132, 133
Plymouth
Penzance

Motorway
Motorway under construction
Primary route single carriageway
Primary route dual carriageway
Other A roads
Motorway junction ㉒
Motorway junction with limited entries or exits. ㉒
Place of Interest   The Vyne
Overlaps and numbers of continuing pages   212
Scale   16 miles to 1 inch
0   10   20 mls
0   10   20   30 kms

Newlyn, near Penzance, in the days when fish, not tourists, were Cornwall's livelihood and visitors to these picturesque coasts were a rarity

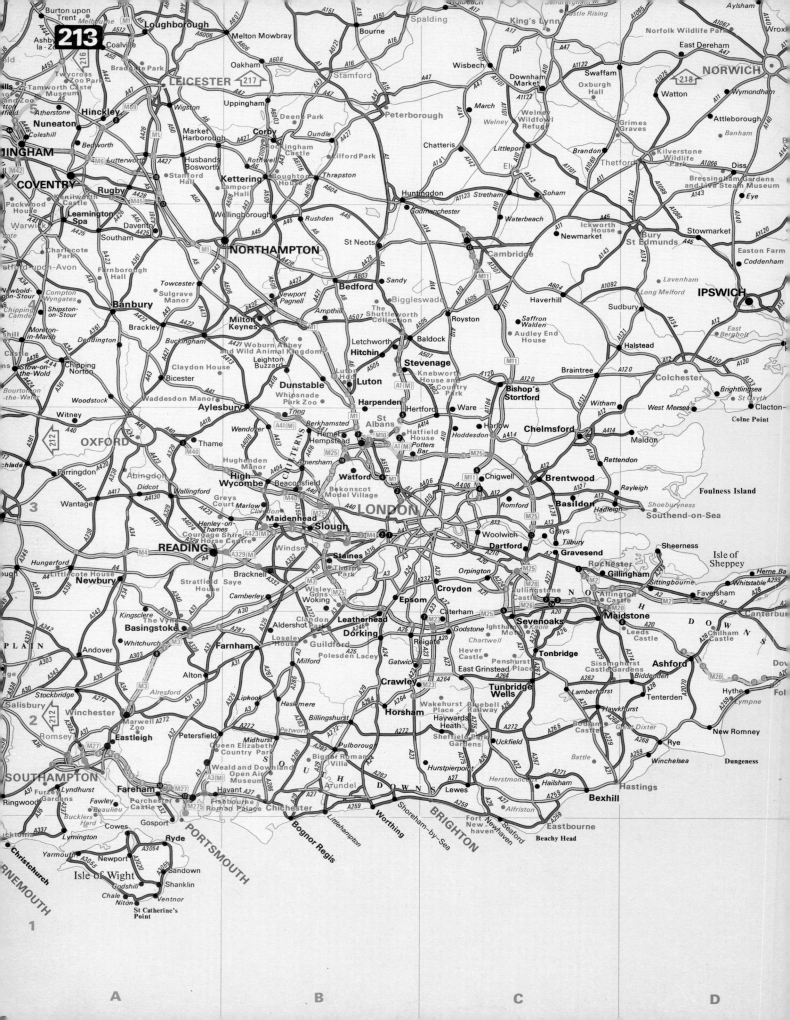

Once a thriving Kentish port, Deal is now a modern town and a favourite week-end haunt for Londoners

The setting has not changed since Victorian times but Beddgelert's traditional costumes and occupations are a thing of the past

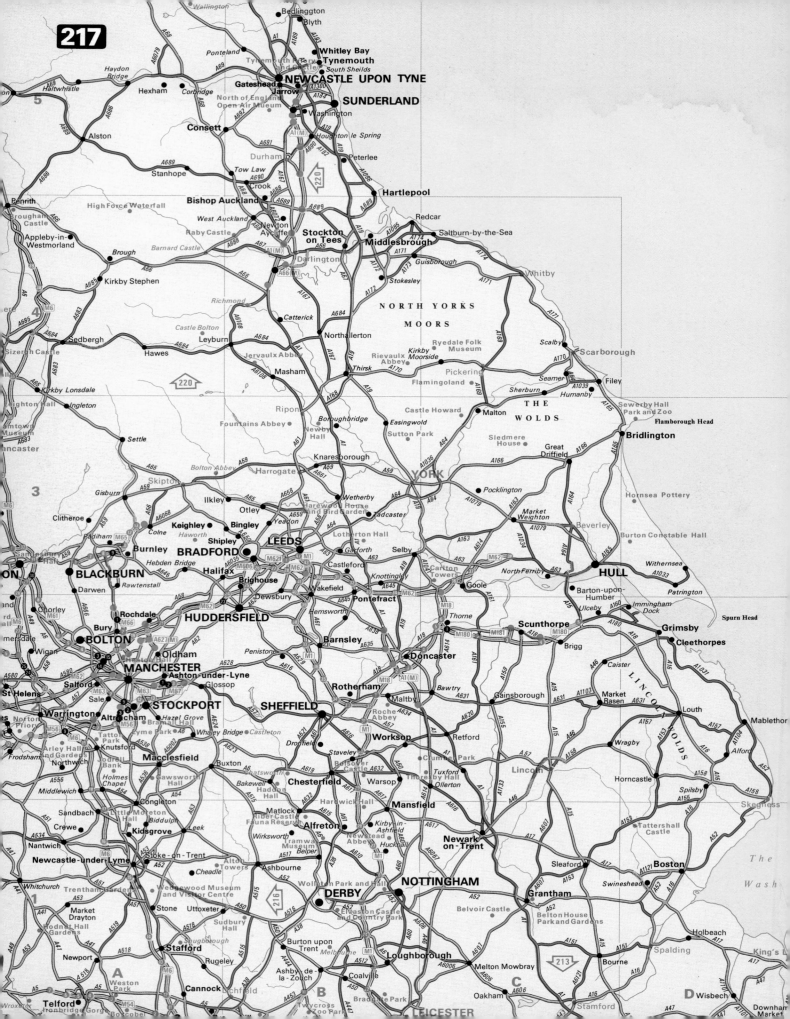

An idyllic view of rural life in the last century in a remote valley not far from Barnard Castle, County Durham

A 19th-century view of Derwentwater, looking towards the high peaks of Skiddaw

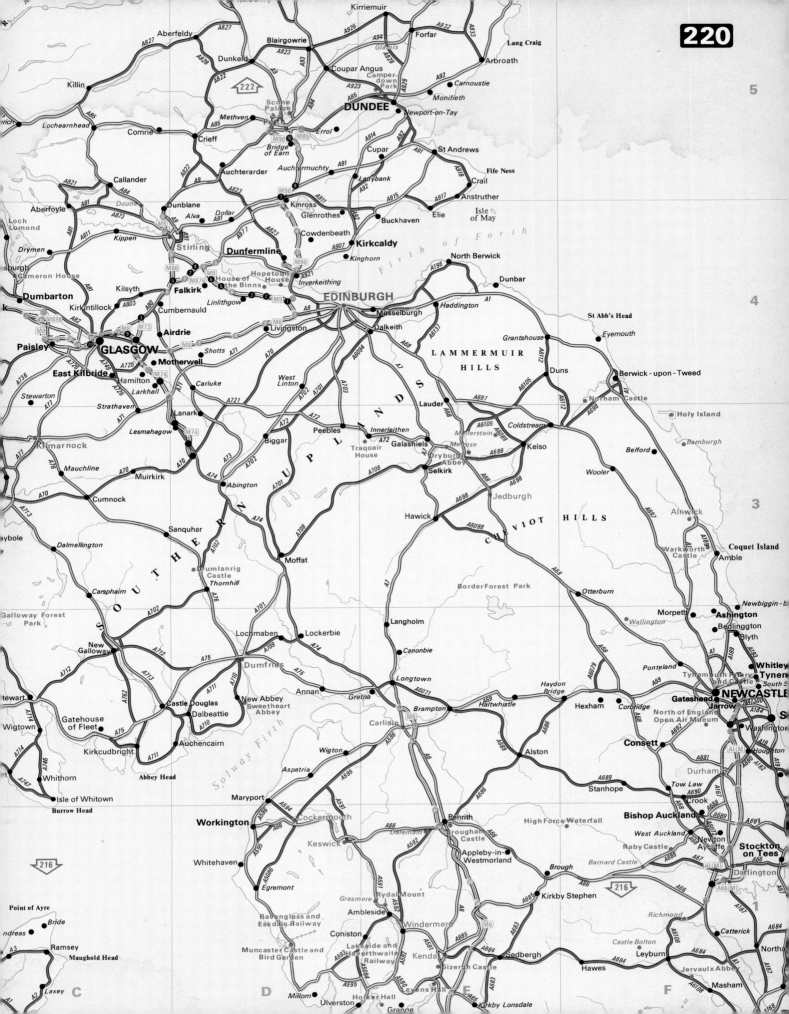

5

4

3

2

1

DUNDEE

Kirriemuir
Aberfeldy
Blairgowrie
A827
A926
A94
Forfar
A932
Lang Craig
A827
A926
Dunkeld
Glamis
A933
A826
A923
Coupar Angus
A929
Arbroath
Killin
A822
222
A9
A85
A92
Carnoustie
Camper-down Park
Monifieth
Methven
Scone Palace
Newport-on-Tay
Lochearnhead
A85
Comrie
Crieff
A85
Errol
Cupar
A914
A92
St Andrews
Auchterarder
A91
Ladybank
A918
Fife Ness
Callander
A823
Auchtermuchty
Crail
A821
A9
Bridge of Earn
A92
Anstruther
Dounee
A90
Dunblane
Kinross
Buckhaven
A915
A917
Elie
Aberfoyle
A873
Dollar
A91
A911
Isle of May
A81
A84
Alva
Glenrothes
A92
Loch Lomond
Kippen
A877
Cowdenbeath
A81
A811
Stirling
Dunfermline
A907
Kirkcaldy
Drymen
M9
A823
M90
Kinghorn
North Berwick
Cameron House
A921
A198
Dumbarton
Kilsyth
Hopetoun House
Inverkeithing
Dunbar
Kirkintilloch
A803
Falkirk
House of the Binns
EDINBURGH
St Abb's Head
A81
A80
Cumbernauld
Linlithgow
Musselburgh
Haddington
A1
Eyemouth
M898
M73
Airdrie
M8
Livingston
Dalkeith
A1
Grantshouse
A6137
M8
GLASGOW
Shotts
A71
A68
A6094
LAMMERMUIR HILLS
Berwick-upon-Tweed
Paisley
Motherwell
A70
A7
Lauder
Duns
A6112
A736
Hamilton
West Linton
A702
A701
A697
Norham Castle
East Kilbride
Larkhall
Carluke
A103
A68
Coldstream
Holy Island
Stewarton
Strathaven
Lanark
A72
Peebles
Innerleithen
A6105
Bamburgh
Kilmarnock
A71
Lesmahagow
A721
A72
Mellerstain
A6089
Belford
A77
M74
Biggar
Traquair House
Galashiels
Melrose
Kelso
A76
Mauchline
A70
Dryburgh Abbey
A699
Muirkirk
A70
Abington
A708
Selkirk
A698
Wooler
A713
A74
A702
A701
Hawick
A6088
Jedburgh
CHEVIOT HILLS
Alnwick
Cumnock
Sanquhar
A74
A68
A189
Dalmellington
A708
Moffat
A7
A69
Otterburn
Warkworth Castle
Drumlanrig Castle
Border Forest Park
Coquet Island
Carsphairn
Thornhill
A76
Amble
Galloway Forest Park
A701
Langholm
Newbiggin
New Galloway
A712
A75
Lochmaben
Lockerbie
Wallington
Morpeth
Ashington
A712
A713
A709
A74
Canonbie
Bedlinggton
Dumfries
A75
Longtown
Ponteland
Blyth
Castle Douglas
New Abbey
Annan
Gretna
A6071
Haydon Bridge
Whitley Tynemouth Priory and Castle
Gatehouse of Fleet
Dalbeattie
Sweetheart Abbey
Brampton
A69
Haltwhistle
Corbridge
Gateshead
NEWCASTLE
Wigtown
A711
Carlisle
M6
A69
Hexham
North of England Open Air Mueum
Jarrow
Kirkcudbright
Auchencairn
Wigton
A6
Alston
A68
Washington
Whithorn
Abbey Head
Aspatria
A595
A686
Consett
Durham
Houghton
Isle of Whitown
Solway Firth
A689
A691
Burrow Head
Maryport
A596
Cockermouth
A66
High Force Waterfall
Stanhope
Tow Law
Crook
A690
216
Workington
A594
A591
Penrith
Brougham Castle
Bishop Auckland
Keswick
Dalemain
A66
West Auckland
Raby Castle
Newton Aycliffe
Whitehaven
A595
Appleby-in-Westmorland
A689
A66
Stockton on Tees
Egremont
A592
Brough
Barnard Castle
A66(M)
Darlington
A6086
216
Ravenglass and Eskdale Railway
Grasmere
Rydal Mount
A685
A66
Kirkby Stephen
Richmond
Catterick
Ambleside
Windermere
M6
A684
Castle Bolton
Leyburn
A684
Point of Ayre
Coniston
Kendal
A685
A683
Sedbergh
Hawes
Jervaulx Abbey
Bride
Muncaster Castle and Bird Garden
Lakeside and Haverthwaite Railway
Sizergh Castle
A6108
Andreas
Ramsey
Millom
Ulverston
Levens Hall
Kirkby Lonsdale
Masham
Maughold Head
A3
Holker Hall
Grange
Laxey

C
D
E
F

SOUTHERN UPLANDS

5

Cape Wrath
Faraid Head
Whiten Head
Strathy Point
Butt of Lewis
Durness
A838
A838
Bettyhill
Melvich
A836
Tongue
A836
Tolsta Head
A838
A836
Handa
Laxford Bridge
Gallan Head
Tiumpan Head
ISLE OF LEWIS
Broad Bay
Stornoway
A834
Altnaharra
A836
Kinbrace
A897

4

Point of Stoer
Unapool
H
A837
Lochinver
Rubha Coigeach
Ledmore Junction
A835
A837
Lairg
A839
Brora
Summer Isles
A837
A836
A839
Golspie
Dunrobin Castle
Priest Island
Horse Island
Bonar Bridge
A9
Dornoch
Greenstone Point
Ullapool
A835
Tarbert
Toe Head
Rubha Reidh
Inverewe Gardens
A832
Braemore Junction
Tain
Sound of Harris
Longa
Gairloch
A835
Invergordon
Lochmaddy
Rubha Hunish
A832
Kinlochewe
A832
Garve
Alness
Cromarty
Vaternish Point
Torridon
A896
A8 32
Achnasheen
Dingwall
Nairn
BENBECULA
Uig
A856
Rona
Shieldaig
A890
A832
Cawdor Castle
A835
A832
A9
Dunvegan
Portree
ISLAND OF SKYE
Raasay
Inner Sound
Lochcarron
A896
A862
Inverness
Culloden Battlefield
A863
Stromeferry
A890
Cannich
A831
Drumnadrochit
A833
A82
Granton-S
Scalpay
Kyle of Lochalsh
A87
Dornie
A831
Carrbridge
A938
Broadford
A850
Kyleakin
Shiel Bridge
Invermoriston
Bo Ga
Soay
A87
A887
A82
MONADHLIATH MOUNTAINS
Aviemore
Canna
A851
Fort Augustus
Highland Wildlife Park
Glen M Forest
Ardvasar
Sound of Sleat
Invergarry
A87
Kingussie
RHUM
Mallaig
Newtonmore
Eigg
Arisaig
A830
Spean Bridge
A86
Laggan
A86
A889
Kinlochmoidart
Corpach
A82
Dalwhinnie
Salen
A861
Fort William
A9
Blair Atholl
TIREE
COLL
Tobermory
Drimnin
219
Glencoe
South Ballachulish
Aberfeldy
A827
Lochaline
A848
Portnacroish
A827
Killin
Salen
A848
ISLAND OF MULL
Lismore
Connel
Taynuilt
A822
Dunke

Exploring the Mysteries of Science

by Deborah Crotts

illustrated by Janet Armbrust

cover illustration by Matthew Van Zomeren

Publisher
Instructional Fair • TS Denison
Grand Rapids, Michigan 49544

ISBN: 1-56822-619-5
Exploring the Mysteries of Science
Cover Photograph © Corel Corporation
Copyright © 1998 by Instructional Fair • TS Denison
2400 Turner Avenue NW
Grand Rapids, Michigan 49544

Table of Contents

Introduction

Many of the wonders and curiosities of the natural and scientific world have a simple explanation. The activities in this book investigate and explain some of these wonders and curiosities. Each activity is safe, uses easily obtainable materials, and requires a minimum of teacher supervision. Each topic is a self-contained, reproducible unit and may be used individually to support the student text or may be developed as a separate unit of study to augment the text. The activities are a simple explanation of the mystery or curiosity presented but they are also an introduction or launching point for further study. The activities invite further research and give the student some suggestions for further investigation.

Each activity has clear, concise directions. Any cautionary information is highlighted. The materials list is given at the top of each activity. Research topics and suggestions for additional activities and parallel topics for investigation are suggested at the bottom of the activity sheets. The answer keys for the activity sheets are found in the back of the book.

The activities in this book cover a wide range of topics spanning the disciplines of science. The topics correlate with student textbook topics. The major themes are introduced with an introductory overview page which contains interesting facts pertaining to the subject and some research topics. The individual activities relating to this topic follow the overview page. Each activity challenges the student to discover interesting scientific facts while utilizing the basic procedures necessary for obtaining accurate results and employing clear scientific reasoning.

The Wonderful Human Body

Your body is an incredible machine. It is a combination of the most delicate camera, the most advanced computer, the most sensitive audio equipment, the most efficient fuel system, and the most durable and easily renewable structural support system. The whole body works because of the delicate balance of the interrelated small parts. For example, we have miles of tiny *capillaries*, the small blood vessels which carry the blood to the outer portions of our bodies. If we placed all of the capillaries on the ground side by side, they would cover a 1½-acre area. If all of the capillaries, veins, and arteries were placed end to end, they would stretch 60,000 miles. These capillaries have tiny valves or sphincters at their entrance. The sphincters are smooth rings of muscle which open and close to allow the blood to flow into the capillaries. If we did not have these sphincters or if they did not work properly, all of the blood would drain out of our veins and arteries into these capillaries.

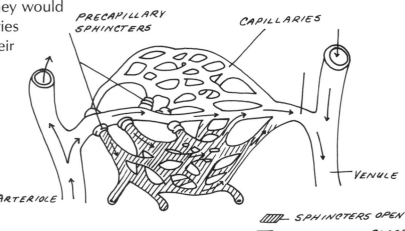

PRECAPILLARY SPHINCTERS

CAPILLARIES

VENULE

ARTERIOLE

SPHINCTERS OPEN
SPHINCTERS CLOSED

Our remarkable bodies contain approximately 206 bones. (Babies are born with 305 bones, but some of these fuse together.) We have 650 muscles to move these bones and more than 100 joints to allow the whole skeleton to move and bend at different angles. Each adult body contains enough fat for seven bars of soap. Each fat cell contains only 10 percent water, but 60 percent of the whole body is water. Each adult human contains about 10 gallons of water.

This remarkable body is covered with almost 20 square feet of waterproof, flexible, constantly renewable skin. The skin is decorated with approximately five million hairs. Each individual hair lasts for almost three years.

This mobile wonder is fueled by 50 tons of food and at least 11,000 gallons of liquid. A person's diet must include certain essential elements and compounds to keep the body functioning and healthy. The average body contains enough phosphorus to make 2,200 matches. To keep the phosphorus content even, we must eat foods which contain phosphorus, such as bananas. The red in our blood is from iron. What foods contain iron? What other minerals and substances does your body need? Use your library resources to help you answer these questions and write your answers on a separate sheet of paper.

Name _____

The Brain

Your brain weighs approximately three pounds (males have slightly heavier brains because they usually have slightly heavier bodies). The grayish-white brain has ridges and folds and is soft and smooth to the touch. Different sections of the brain control different things. Some parts of the brain below are already labeled. Label the other parts to help you understand which section of the brain controls each kind of activity.

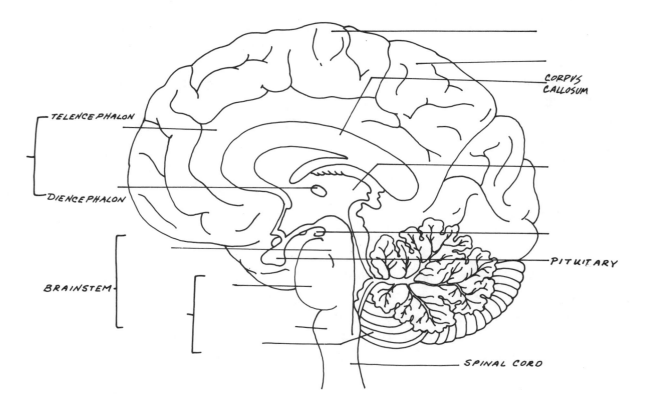

The lowest part of the brain is the *medulla oblongata*. It controls several of the autonomic body functions, such as breathing, swallowing, vomiting, digestion, and the activities of the heart and blood vessels. The pons is just above the medulla oblongata. The *pons* works with the medulla in controlling the body functions that are automatic. In addition, all of the sensory and motor neurons from the upper parts of the brain pass through these two brain parts. The *hindbrain* is the main information conductor and also controls large body movements such as walking.

Most of the neurons that go from the upper parts of the brain through the medulla cross from one side to the other. Because of this crossing, the right side of the brain controls movement in the left side of the body and vice versa. What hand do you write with? Which side of your brain are you using when you write? ___left___

The *cerebellum* is the third part of the hindbrain. The cerebellum controls movement, such as eye-hand coordination. The *midbrain* is the upper part of the brainstem. It receives sensory information and sends messages to regions of the forebrain.

The *forebrain* is the largest part of the brain and contains the most complex processing centers. The *hypothalamus* is the lowest region of the forebrain, located just above the midbrain. This small area controls body temperature, hunger and eating, thirst and drinking, and many other basic functions necessary to our survival. The *thalamus* is just above the hypothalamus. The thalamus relays information from one part of the brain to another.

The *cerebrum* is the major structure of the forebrain. The outside of the cerebrum is called the *cerebral cortex*. The cerebral cortex has many folds or convolutions. The cell bodies of the cerebrum are in this outer layer or cortex and the folds allow room for more of these cells than a flat, smooth surface allows. This means that brains with folds or convolutions have more of the cell bodies than smooth brains. The cerebral cortex contains sensory and motor areas, areas that process information, and areas that integrate information from other parts of the brain. The four parts of the cerebral cortex are labeled in the diagram below. Write the associated functions in the blanks in each section. The frontal lobe controls speech. The parietal lobe controls both speech and reading ability. The section that controls speech in the frontal lobe is called *Broca's area,* and the part that controls speech in the parietal lobe is called *Wernicke's area*. If Broca's area is damaged, a person has difficulty talking but can speak sensible words. If Wernicke's area is damaged, the person's words do not make sense or are nonsense syllables. The occipital lobe controls vision. The temporal lobe controls smell and hearing.

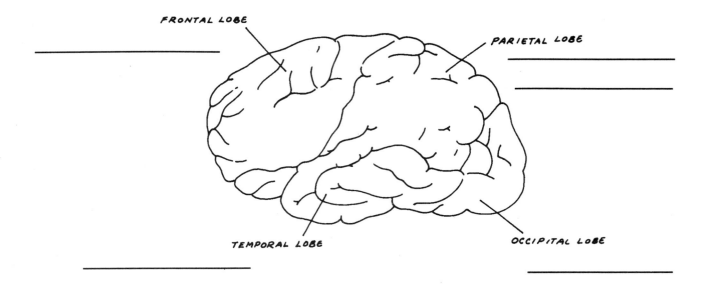

Are All Brains Alike?

Look at the pictures of the animal brains below. The shaded area in each skull is the brain.

1. How is the brain of a human different from that of a fish or frog or duck?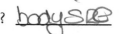

2. How is the brain of the cat similar to ours? How is it different? _____

   _____

3. Which animals are more intelligent? What characteristic do the brains of more intelligent animals share? _____

4. Primates (lemurs, monkeys, and apes) and porpoises have much larger brains relative to their body size than other animals (with the exception of humans), and their brains are much more complex, with many folds or convolutions. Porpoise brains are larger and more complex than primate brains in proportion to their body size and are second only to the human brain. Which animal is probably more intelligent, a porpoise or an ape?

   _____

   _____

The Nervous System

What can carry messages as fast as 300 miles per second, is more elaborate than the most complex computer circuit board, and has electrically charged components? You guessed it— your nervous system. The central nervous system, or CNS as biologists like to call it, helps you respond and react to stimuli. When a ball is flying toward your head, your nervous system helps you respond appropriately and raise a hand to catch the ball instead of standing still until the ball hits you in the head.

The nervous system contains two kinds of cells—neurons and supporting cells. The neurons are the message conductors. Each neuron has a large *cell body,* which contains the nucleus and long tentacle-like extensions which are called *processes.* The processes may be one of two kinds. *Dendrites* are short and branched, like a tree. *Axons* are long and have few branches; they are more like a taproot. Schwann cells often cover the axon. The *Schwann cells* form a layer of insulation, known as the *myelin sheath,* along the length of the axon. This sheath insulates crowded neurons from the electrical impulses of neighboring neurons. A person with multiple sclerosis shows deterioration of this myelin sheath and suffers from a loss of coordination. Label the cell body, dendrites, axon, and Schwann cells in the diagram below.

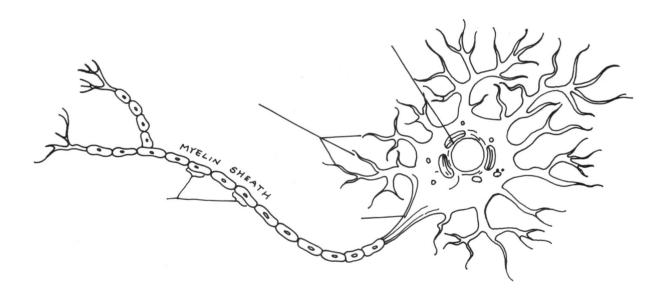

All living cells are electrically charged. Cells contain potassium and sodium ions, and these ions have an electrical charge. The ions move back and forth through the cell membrane to make the charge positive or negative inside or outside of the cell. Neurons are called *excitable cells,* because, when a neuron is stimulated, the electrical composition of the cell is changed and the cell can conduct a signal.

Moving That Body

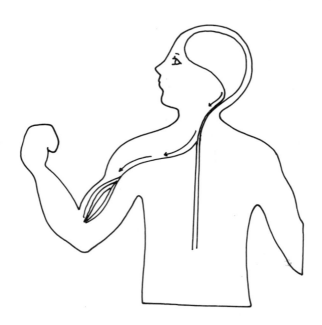

What makes your body move? How does the brain tell the muscles to move? How do the muscles make the bones and body move? When you decide to move a body part or respond automatically to a situation or stimulus, your brain cells transmit a tiny electric impulse to your spinal cord. Your spinal cord carries this impulse to the appropriate nerves. The nerves in turn transmit this impulse directly to your muscles. The impulse causes the muscles to contract. Muscle contraction causes movement.

What happens when your muscles contract? How does this cause movement?

Materials
2 thin rubber bands
bendable wire

Procedure:

1. Cut two pieces of wire two inches longer than the rubber bands. Fasten the wire and rubber bands together as shown in the diagrams below.

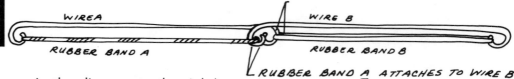

RUBBER BAND _B_ ATTACHES TO WIRE _A_

WIRE A   WIRE B

RUBBER BAND A   RUBBER BAND B

L RUBBER BAND _A_ ATTACHES TO WIRE _B_

2. At the joint (as shown in the diagram to the right), pull one side of one rubber band. What happens?

_____

_____

3. Release the rubber band. What happens? _____

_____

_____

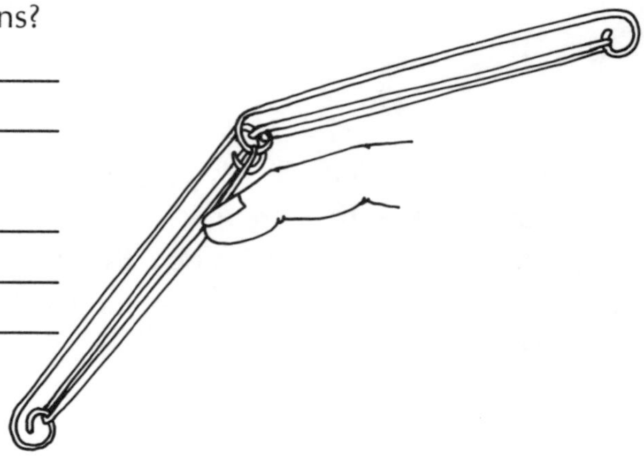

The Eyes at Work

The human eye consists of several parts. The outer layer is tough, white connective tissue. It is called the *sclera*. In the front, this sclera is clear and forms the *cornea*, which is the transparent part you see through. Directly underneath this is a thin layer called the *choroid*. The choroid contains pigment or color cells which give the eye its color in the front. This colored front part is called the *iris*. The iris is donut-shaped and the round, black hole in the middle is called the *pupil*. The iris changes size to regulate the amount of light that enters the eye, and this makes the pupil change size. The inside layer of the eye is called the *retina*. In the back of the retina is the blind spot or *optic disc*. This disc contains no photoreceptors and therefore does not detect light. This is the place where the *optic nerve* attaches. The optic nerve carries visual information from the photoreceptors in the eye to the brain. Label the sclera, the cornea, the choroid, the iris, the pupil, the optic disc, the optic nerve, and the retina in the diagrams below. Color the iris in the diagram on the right.

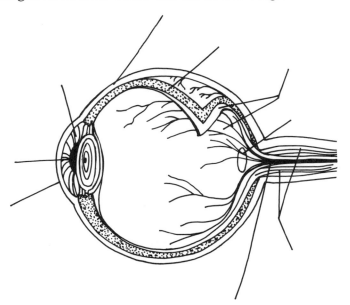
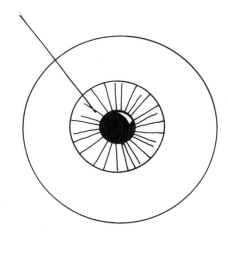

To see your pupil in action, darken the room and then look at your eyes in a hand mirror. Switch on the lights and quickly examine your eyes again. What has happened to the pupil?

_____

For Research: Humans have camera-type eyes. How is this different from the compound eyes of crustaceans and insects? We focus our eyes by changing the shape of the lens. How do fish focus their eyes?_____

_____

Name _____

A World of Color

The retina of each human eye has approximately 125 million *rod cells* and 6 million *cone cells*. These cells are named for their shapes. Rod cells and cone cells are the two types or photoreceptors which relay visual information to the brain.

Rods are sensitive to the brightness of the light, but they do not respond to color. That is why we do not see colors in the dark, we see only black and white. Cone cells respond to color, but they require a large amount of light to detect the color. The *fovea*, a spot on the back of the retina just above the optic disc, contains the most cone cells (about 150,000 per square millimeter). For this reason, you see color and daylight objects best when you stare directly at them. Hawks and some other birds have a larger number of cone cells per millimeter (1,000,000 or more). This gives the hawk sharper vision and enables it to spot a tiny mouse from high up in the sky.

Cone cells come in three types—red, green, and blue. Each contains a different kind of *photopsin*, a protein which has the ability to absorb light. The colors refer to the color the particular photopsin absorbs. If the red and green cone cells both absorb light, the person sees either orange or yellow depending on whether more green cone cells or more red cone cells are stimulated. If a person is missing one kind of cone cells or has too few of one kind, he or she will have color blindness and be unable to see a certain color or colors.

Color the patterns below to see how color blindness would affect your vision. Color the circles with the dots light orange. Color all the other circles green.

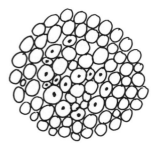   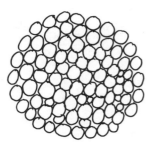

For Research: What other animals have color vision? What animals do not detect color? Which animals need more cone cells, nocturnal or diurnal animals?

Name _____

Your Ears and Balance

Your ears have two functions. You use them to hear and you also need them to help you keep your balance. The inner ear is the section of your ear which helps you keep your balance. The *outer ear*, the *pinna* or *auricle*, is the part which you see. The *middle ear* consists of three small bones called the *hammer*, the *anvil*, and the *stirrup*. The *inner ear* is made up of three looped tubes called the *semicircular canals* and a snail-shaped organ called the *cochlea*. Label the parts of the ear on the diagram below. The semicircular canals and two tiny chambers called the *utricle* and the *saccule* are the parts of the ear which help you keep your balance.

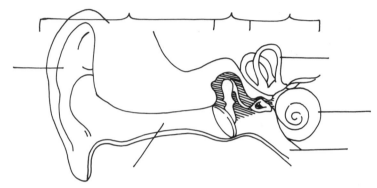

The utricle and the saccule contain many tiny hairs. These hairs grow in clumps and protrude from the walls of the two chambers into a jelly-like substance. This jelly contains many small calcium carbonate particles known as "ear stones" or *otoliths*. Gravity pulls this substance and the small hairs downward. When the position of the head changes, the position of the hairs changes and sends a signal to the brain. How does this work?

Materials
florists' wire
modeling clay

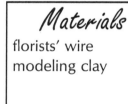

_____
_____
_____
_____
_____
_____

Procedure:

1. Cut six pieces of florists' wire each 6½ inches long.
2. Anchor one end of each piece of wire in the modeling clay so that the six pieces are in a straight line, close together like hairs.

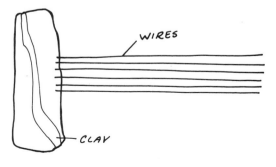

WIRES

CLAY

3. Hold the apparatus under a water faucet so the wires are running in a line perpendicular to the flow of the water (see the diagram to the right) and turn the water on full force. What happens?

_____

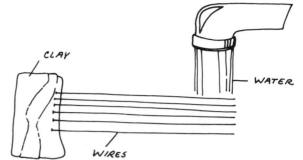

In your ear, the tiny hairs are pushed downward as the force of gravity pulls the jelly downward. When you move your head, the hairs change position and a new message is relayed to your brain indicating that "down" is in a different spot.

Why do you feel dizzy if you spin rapidly in a circle? When you spin, these hairs are changing position rapidly, and the message your brain receives from your eyes is different from the message it is receiving from your inner ear. Your brain is confused and responds with the feeling of dizziness.

Do other animals hear like we do?

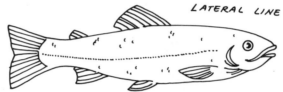

Most mammals have ears that work very much like ours. Many mammals, particularly bats, can hear much higher frequency sounds than humans, but the basic structure of the ear is very similar to ours.

Many kinds of fish and aquatic amphibians have what is called a *lateral line system*. This consists of a long tube which runs the length of the animal on each side and opens to the outside water with small pores. Water flows in through the pores and flows the length of the tube past many neuromasts that detect movement. The *neuromasts* have tiny hairs like our semicircular canals. The neuromast hairs have a gelatinous cap called the *cupula*. As water flows past, it pushes on the cupula and bends the hair. This system works only in water. Some amphibians have this system as tadpoles but not as adults.

Many invertebrates also have a sense of hearing. Many insects have body hairs that vibrate with sound waves. Mosquitoes have hairs on their antennae. Some caterpillars have body hairs that detect sound and many insects have "ears" on their legs! These ears consist of a tympanic membrane with receptor cells inside to transmit the impulses to the insect's brain.

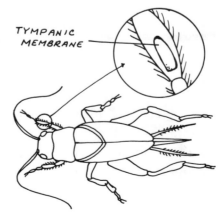

Taste and Smell

1. Can you taste something you cannot smell? Cut several small pieces of onion and apple of equal size and shape. Mix them on a plate. Close your eyes, hold your nose and grab a bite. Can you tell which is which? Try this experiment with a friend. Can the friend tell which is which? _____

The senses of taste and smell depend on *chemoreceptors*, or tiny cells that respond to specific chemicals. Insects have tiny hairs called *setae* on their mouth parts and feet. These hairs contain the chemoreceptors which allow the insect to taste or smell its food. Each chemoreceptor responds to one certain taste, such as salt or sugar.

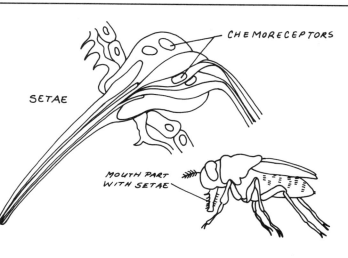

CHEMORECEPTORS

SETAE

MOUTH PART
WITH SETAE

HYDRA

Even animals as tiny as the microscopic hydra have chemoreceptors that respond to certain chemicals. The hydra reacts to a chemical called *glutathione*. When it detects this chemical, it responds by swallowing.

2. In humans, the chemoreceptors are found in *taste buds* on the tongue and in the mouth. The taste buds on the tongue are grouped in different areas with different taste perceptions for each area. The taste buds can detect four kinds of tastes—bitter, sweet, salty, and sour. Repeat the experiment above, first using small amounts of sugar and salt and second using vinegar and lemon juice. Does it make a difference what part of the tongue touches the food? _____

Salmon use a keen sense of smell to guide them back to the streams where they were born. They leave the streams as small fish and swim to the sea. As adults, they use the smell of the plants and soil from their stream to guide them back to the stream to spawn and hatch their own young. How do other animals use their sense of smell? Which animals have the keenest sense of smell? Use your library resources to help you answer these questions.

Name _____

The Wonderful Skin

Your skin is the primary organ for the sense of touch. Skin consists of three layers. The bottom layer is fat called *subcutaneous tissue*. The middle is called the *dermis*, and it contains blood vessels, nerves and nerve endings, hair roots, and sweat and oil glands. The top layer is a tough layer called the *epidermis*. Label these layers in the diagram below. The epidermis protects the body against infection and seals water and heat inside the body. Most of the mechanoreceptors for touch are located in the dermis, as you can see in the diagram below. Read the paragraph below and use it to help you write the name of each mechanoreceptor on the line beside it in the diagram.

Nociceptors, which are naked nerve endings, are found in the epidermis. Nociceptors detect pain. *Meissner's corpuscles* and *Merkel's discs* are right below the surface of the epidermis. They both detect light touch and pressure. *Ruffini's end organ* detects heat, and the *end-bulb of Krause* detects cold. *Pacinian corpuscles* are found deep in the dermis very close to the fat layer. They detect deep pressure. Hairs also function as mechanoreceptors. They detect movement.

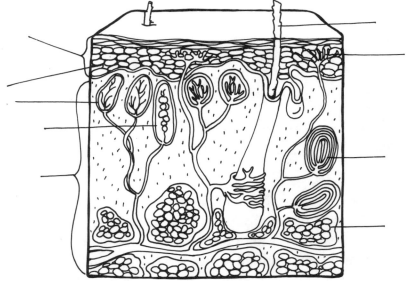

Which parts of your body are most sensitive to touch? Rub your fingertips over a piece of fine grain sandpaper. How does it feel? _____

Next, rub the sandpaper gently against your upper lip. How does it feel? _____

Rub your fingertips across the back of your hand. How does it feel? _____

Rub the back of your hand against your upper lip. How does it feel? _____

Which is more sensitive, your fingertips or your upper lip? _____

Name _____

The Germ Fighters

The *immune system* is the body's main defense against disease. Bacteria and viruses are lurking everywhere waiting to attack, but the immune system has several different methods of thwarting the attackers. The first line of defense is the *skin* and the *mucous membranes*. The *epidermis*, the outer layer of the skin, is too tough for most bacteria and viruses to penetrate. In addition, oil and sweat glands give the skin an acidic coating which kills many bacteria. Perspiration contains an enzyme called *lysozyme*, which destroys the cell walls of a number of bacteria. Gastric juices in the stomach kill most bacteria which are swallowed. The hairs in the nose filter small particles which might carry bacteria and any that do get through are trapped by the slimy *mucus* that covers the respiratory tract. Tiny, hair-like cilia move the bacteria-laden mucus out of the lungs. The tiny, black dots in between the cilia in the illustration to the right are influenza viruses. The *cilia* are sweeping them out of a human windpipe. Label the cilia and the *viruses*.

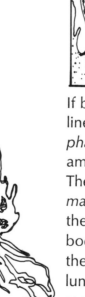

If bacteria and viruses do penetrate these lines of defense, they have to face the *phagocytes*. These are specialized amoeba-like cells which eat the intruders. The leaders of this group are the *macrophages*, or "big eaters." Some of these are wanderers, floating through the body, and some are permanent residents of the organs such as the heart, brain, and lungs. The picture to the left shows a macrophage eating a rod-shaped *bacterium*. Label the macrophage and the bacterium.

Name _____

Sometimes, the attack on the body comes from within as in the case of cancer. The white cells of the body adapt to the job of fighting infection from without and within. In the picture to the right, *cytotoxic T cells* attack a cancer cell. Label the cancer cell and the cytotoxic T cells.

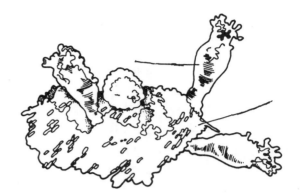

The *inflammatory response*, which means "setting on fire," is another means of combatting infection. Have you noticed that the area around a wound is often red and swollen? The small blood vessels or *capillaries* near the wound dilate and supply more blood. This means that more white cells are available to swallow the invading bacteria and to devour the remains of the damaged cells. The pus that can be found around a wound is mostly dead cells and fluid that has leaked from these capillaries.

Our bodies also produce proteins that block the growth of microorganisms. Interferons are one group of these proteins. *Interferons* "interfere" with the growth and reproduction of viruses.

How do we become immune to certain viruses and bacteria? The immune system in your body recognizes your body's own cells and distinguishes between those cells and foreign cells. When a foreign substance, which is called an *antigen*, enters the body, your immune system produces *antibodies* which attack the antigen. Once your body produces these antibodies, they stay in your body and wait for the next attack by the same antigen, which makes your body *immune* to the next attack by the same virus, and you do not catch that particular virus a second time. Unfortunately, each antibody is effective against only the one antigen which triggered it. Smallpox, chickenpox, measles, mumps, and diphtheria are all diseases which trigger this immune response.

You can develop immunity to these diseases by having them and then recovering from them, but an easier and less dangerous way of developing immunity is by getting a *vaccination*. What is a vaccination? (Use a dictionary or other library resources if you do not know.)

_____
_____

How does a vaccination work?

_____
_____

© Instructional Fair • TS Denison   14   IF87012 Exploring the Mysteries of Science

Name _____

The Biological Clock

Plants and animals have certain rhythmic behaviors. Your blood pressure, your temperature, your pulse, and your mental alertness are some of the traits that fluctuate according to the time of day. Plants also show different responses to the time of day. Some plants have leaves or blossoms that open and close, depending on the time of day. This is not just a response to light. You would feel sleepy at night even if you were in a fully lit room and awake during the day even if you were in a dark cave. A plant has the same kind of responses. Bean plant leaves droop at night. Do you think they would droop if they were kept in the light at night? Prove whether your hypothesis is correct with this experiment.

Materials
a bean seed
potting soil
a flowerpot
water

Procedure:

1. Fill the flowerpot with potting soil, and plant the bean seed in the center of the pot. Water the soil and place the bean in a warm, sunny window.
2. Water the plant regularly and keep the plant in the sunlight until the seed has sprouted and the small bean plant has at least four leaves. Observe the plant in the sunlight at noon. In the space below, draw the position of the leaves relative to the stem.
3. Place the plant in a dark room for 24 hours. Observe the plant at noon the next day. In the space below, draw the position of the leaves relative to the stem.

4. Place the plant under a lamp. Turn the lamp on and leave it on for 36 hours. Observe the plant at midnight. In the space below, draw the position of the leaves relative to the stem.

5. Place the plant in the dark. Leave the plant for 24 hours. Observe the plant at midnight the next day. In the space below, draw the position of the leaves relative to the stem.

Observations:

1. What did you observe about the position of the leaves? Did the leaves tend to droop at a certain time of day? _____

2. Did light or darkness affect the plant's actions? Did the position of the leaves change when the light changed? _____

_____

A response which is based on a 24-hour cycle is called a *circadian rhythm*. The name comes from the Latin words *circa* for "approximately" and *dies* for "day." These rhythms can be changed slightly. In outer space or any constant, unchanging environment, the 24-hour cycle will change to what is called a *free-running period*, where the response will be on a cycle other than 24 hours, but somewhere between 21 and 27 hours. When a person travels across several time zones, this biological time clock can be reset and adjusted to the new time zone, but it takes several days. During the adjustment period, the person feels a tired feeling known as "jet lag."

For Research: How can human beings counter the feeling of jet lag? What can be done to lessen the effects and make the adjustment time easier?

Wonders of the Animal Kingdom

Every animal has special adaptations and special features that make it particularly suited to its environment. In addition, the size of an animal is important. One of the most important factors for warm-blooded or *endothermic* animals is keeping a constant body

temperature. Look at the two "cube animals" in the illustration to the right. The one on the left has a larger external surface area in proportion to its body size. Because of this, it loses body heat twice as fast as the larger animal. If we were as small as hummingbirds, we would be constantly searching for high-energy, fatty foods to stay alive and, without feathers or dense fur, we would die of *hypothermia* within minutes on a sixty-degree day. If we were the size of elephants, we would have difficulty staying cool and would have to spend warm summers wallowing in the mud the way elephants do to stay cool or migrate to cooler climates.

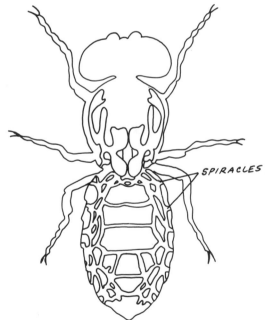

SPIRACLES

Size affects animals in other ways, also. Small insects do not have lungs. They "breathe" or take in oxygen through *spiracles,* which are tiny pores on the surface of their bodies. In small insects, such as spiders, the air naturally flows in and out of these holes. If these spiders were suddenly enlarged to the size of a bear, they would need a constant hurricane-force wind to breathe. (Some larger insects move air in and out of their bodies by rhythmic body movements that act like bellows, drawing the air in and out.)

Another difficulty with being large is that larger bodies require more food. The blue whale, which weighs in at a whopping 100 tons, needs to eat 4 tons of food every day! This whale survives on *krill*, a microscopic animal which is found in great abundance in the ocean. If its diet were something less abundant, it could not survive. Do you think there are a huge number of these giants? Why or why not?

_____

_____

_____

Animals That Glow

When a light bulb is on, it grows very hot. Ninety-six percent of its energy is heat and only six percent is light. Fireflies are much more efficient. They produce ninety percent of their energy in the form of light. It takes only six large fireflies in a small enclosure to provide enough light to read a book! In Brazil and China, fireflies are caught and caged in pierced gourds to serve as sources of light.

Both male and female fireflies produce this light. They have light-producing organs at the base of their tail. Color the light organs in the fireflies to the right a pale green/yellow.

The firefly and its close relative the glowworm both produce their light from chemicals, but this *bioluminescence,* or "living light," can come from another source. Some animals do not have their own chemical source of bioluminescence, but are host to bacteria that are luminescent. The photoblepharon, a fish that lives in the Indian and Pacific oceans, has a white spot under each eye which contains luminescent bacteria. The bacteria glow constantly and cannot be shut off like the chemical luminescence of the firefly. Since the continual glow could be a hazard for the fish, it has a fold of skin above the spot which can be lowered to close off the light when danger approaches.

To help you see how bright and showy the luminescent fish can be, color the spots of the lantern fish yellow and the rest of the fish blue-grey.

1. Why do you think this luminescent characteristic would be useful for an animal?

   _____

2. Do plants also have this quality of bioluminescence?

   _____

For Research: How do the bathysphere fish, the lantern fish, and the hatchetfish use their bioluminescence?

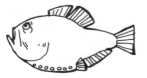

Coral Reefs

Reef corals are colonies of living animals. Sea anemones and leather corals have soft bodies with no skeleton. *Madreporarians,* or true stony corals, have a hard calcium skeleton which remains as a base for the next generation after the animal has died. These coral reefs are important to us as sea barriers which protect the beaches from erosion. Reef corals live from the low tide area to a depth of approximately 150 feet. They cannot live out of water for much more than an hour. The true reef-forming corals live primarily in tropical waters. The corals shown at the left in the illustration below are reef corals. Both the brain coral and the staghorn coral consist of thousands of tiny *polyps,* as each individual coral animal is called. The tiny buttons of coral are solitary coral animals. The top button picture shows the upperside of the animal and the lower picture shows its underside. The treelike coral to the far right is a red coral. It is bright red when it is living but loses its color when it dies.

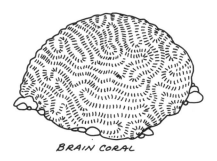

BRAIN CORAL

STAGHORN CORAL

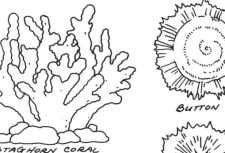

BUTTON

RED CORAL

Not all corals are stationary. The coral to the right is a mushroom coral and it can move. If another animal turns it over, it can move to turn itself upright. The mushroom coral is not a colonial coral; the skeleton of this coral was created by one large, single polyp.

MUSHROOM CORAL

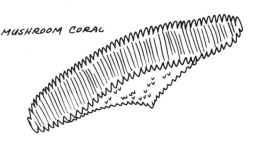

For research: How is coral important to the Great Barrier Reef? What are the natural enemies of this reef?

Whale Tales

What weighs 3,000 pounds or more, has a 30-year life span, and likes arctic waters? The beluga whale. These huge animals can swim faster than scientists predicted they could, because the top layer of their skin sloughs off constantly and forms a slippery layer that acts as an extra lubricant, allowing them to literally slip through the water. Stories tell of belugas swimming up beside a boat, rising up out of the water to peer inside, and then sliding back into the water without moving the boat off course. They have flexible, jointed bones and can turn their heads from side to side without turning their bodies, just as you can. Like you, they breathe air, and they can survive underwater because they can hold their breath for as long as 20 minutes.

Belugas eat a variety of sea creatures including sandworms, fish, and octopuses. Their flexible neck allows them to sweep the ocean from side to side vacuuming in their lunch. They can also squirt a jet of water to loosen the grip of a reluctant dinner item. A group of belugas will work together to round up a school of fish for a shared meal. A hungry beluga can consume 60 pounds of seafood in one day.

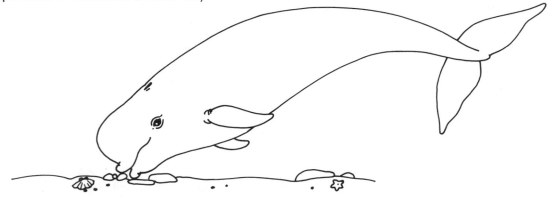

Belugas are very conversational and communicate with each other through squeaks, squawks, and whistles. Early sailors called them "sea canaries" because they make so many different bird-like sounds. To make these sounds, they move the large lump or "melon" on the front of their heads.

MELON

Underwater Communication

Why does sound work well as a means of communication under water?

Materials
a large bowl full to
  the brim with water
a metal spoon

Procedure:
1. Tap the side of the bowl with the spoon. Listen carefully to the sound.

2. Place one ear in the water in the bowl and tap the outside of the bowl again. Which tap sounded louder? _____

Conclusion:
3. Does sound travel better in water or air? _____

4. Do you think sound would travel better (and be louder) on a dry night or a damp, humid night? _____

Test your hypothesis on the next damp, foggy night.

Belugas are very curious and friendly around humans and tend to be very trusting until their friendship is abused. They become very fond of their zookeepers when they are in captivity. In the wild, they will come right up to boats until they are threatened. When one individual in the group has been hurt or killed, they avoid human contact. In the previous two centuries and as recently as the 1930s, the belugas were hunted and killed to catch other whales or to protect fish supplies. Today, there are only 60,000 to 90,000 belugas left, and they are protected by an international treaty in an attempt to rebuild their population. Unfortunately, hunting is not the only source of danger to the belugas. The belugas consume hundreds of fish and many of the fish contain high quantities of toxic wastes from living in polluted water. The wastes, such as DDT, PCB, and Mirex, have run off into the water from farms and industries. In addition, oil rigs heat the water that the belugas need to survive. What can we do to help?

The Last Dragon

The Komodo monitor is not technically a dragon and it does not breathe fire or fly, but it is definitely an awesome species of lizard. Male Komodos can be up to 10 feet long and weigh as much as 200 pounds. They live for more than 25 years and their home habitat is the islands of Indonesia. Komodo monitors eat any animal they can catch. They eat virtually everything from grasshoppers to 1,300-pound water buffaloes. They have shark-like, sharp teeth and long claws which help them hold and devour their prey. Their short legs make them slow runners, but they can go as fast as eight miles

KOMODO MONITOR

per hour for a 2,000-foot sprint. They can also stand on their hind legs and walk upright, and they climb well, using their claws to grip the bark on trees. They are at home in the water as well as on land and dive down more than six feet in the water looking for dinner.

Young Komodos spend much of their time avoiding larger Komodos and stay in trees as much as possible. They dine on geckos and insects. When they are about three feet long, they move to the ground and start catching larger prey such as rats and birds. The smaller Komodos are very careful to defer to the older, large monitors. They stay on the edge of the group while larger monitors feed on deer and water buffalo. The full-sized adult Komodo can open its jaws wide enough to encompass the entire hind-quarters of a deer.

1. Komodo monitors eat dead animals as well as living ones. They tend to eat the sick and weaker members of the population, leaving the strong, healthy ones to reproduce. How does this help the ecology of the islands?

   _____

2. The islands of Indonesia, especially the monitor's home island of Komodo, are rich in minerals and oil. How may this be harmful to the monitors?

   _____

The Electric Eel

Several species of fish produce electric impulses which they can pass into the water which surrounds them. The electric eel, which can grow to a length of ten feet, is one of the most astonishing. The electric impulse from an electric eel can measure as high as 650 volts of electricity, equivalent to 50 car batteries and enough to stun or kill its prey and give a severe shock to a man or large animal. Interestingly, these eels are born with normal eyesight but become blind as they grow older.

The organs which produce electricity in the eel consist of electroplates which line each side of the tail. These organs contain thousands of tiny electroplates and compose almost half of the body weight of the eel. While the eel is resting at the bottom of the sea, it does not emit electric impulses. As it starts to swim about, it emits low-voltage electric discharges which help it locate its prey. The eel prefers to dine on living victims and adjusts the electric discharge from its electroplates to match the size of its prey so that the animal is stunned but not killed.

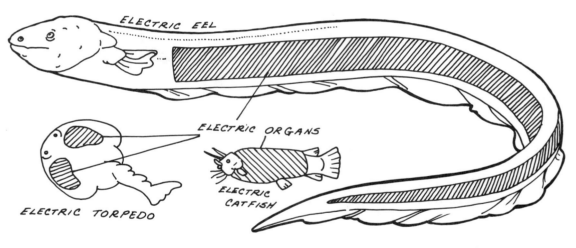

Electric eels are not the only fish with this electric capability. Certain species of knife fish, morymyroid fish, catfish, and torpedo fish can also produce this electric shock. The *Gymnarchus* has a constant electric field which it uses in a method very similar to radar to detect its prey and avoid obstacles. It also uses impulses to threaten other members of its species and protect its territory. Some of the electric fish are saltwater species and some are freshwater species. The torpedo rays are cartilaginous fish related to the skates and rays. The freshwater electric fish are all bony fish, but only one marine species is a bony fish.

Is it likely that these electric fish all came from a common ancestor? What evidence seems to support your answer?

_____

_____

The Hugging Anaconda

The giant anaconda, which can measure up to 37½ feet in length and weigh in at a whopping 400 pounds, is a fearsome adversary. This snake is a strong swimmer who lives in rivers and swamps in South America and can kill and eat a six-foot caiman alligator. It has difficulty swallowing anything larger than 100 pounds, but its strong, muscular body is quite capable of strangling something larger.

The anaconda starts its attack with a bite. The anaconda does not have any venom, but the bite gives the snake a grip. It wraps itself around the diaphragm of the animal and tightens its grip every time the prey exhales. As the grip tightens, the victim loses its air supply and becomes unconscious. The snake holds its grip until the heart stops beating and then swallows its victim whole.

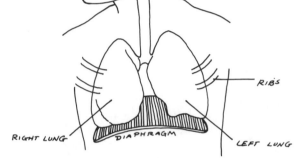

1. How does the anaconda do this? Your diaphragm is directly under your rib cage. Sing a long "ah" sound on one note and push against your diaphragm. What happens?

   _____

   _____

2. Why do you think this happens?

   _____

   _____

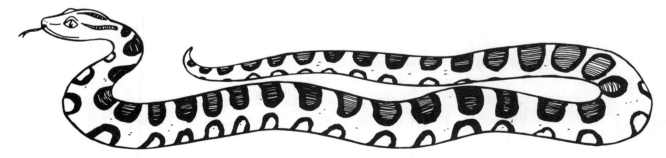

3. How does the anaconda fit a large meal into its mouth? The anaconda has a detachable jaw, and its jawbones have a left and a right section attached by stretchy ligaments. How is this different from your jaw?

   _____

   _____

Flee Flea

When you hear the term "flea circus," you may think that it is imaginary. Actually, in the 1500s to 1800s, people actually paid money to see fleas decorated with tiny costumes and collars and lifting what seemed by comparison to be huge loads. Actually, a flea can drag an object that weighs as much as fifty times as much as itself and can jump as high as 13 inches, or more than 130 times its own height! Multiply your height by 130. How far could you jump if you were a flea? _____

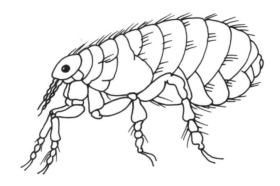

Besides delivering an itchy bite, these little pests are dangerous as disease carriers. Although there are more than 1,500 species of fleas and each species has its preferred host, the fleas are flexible. The fleas that prefer to have dogs, rats, and chickens as hosts (that is three different species) also are quite willing to bite humans. There is a human flea, but it is also willing to bite pigs, dogs, squirrels, skunks, and badgers. Rat fleas are the most dangerous because they tend to carry diseases that are fatal to humans. They carry typhus, bubonic plague, and tapeworms, among other things.

1. Where does the flea get the germs that cause typhus and bubonic plague? _____

_____

2. How can we prevent the spread of these diseases?_____

_____

For Research: What do tapeworms look like? What do they do? How do fleas spread tapeworms? Do humans get tapeworms?

Owls

1. Locate an object on the wall in back of you. Stand so that the object is directly in back of you and turn your head as far as you can to the right without moving the rest of your body. Can you see the object?_____

2. Turn your head as far to the left as you can without moving the rest of your body. Can you see the object? _____

Owls can turn their heads all the way to the back and stare directly in back of them. Owl eyes are large for the size of their heads and pushed into their skulls. The eyes can move very little and the owl can follow moving objects only by turning its whole head.

3. Owl eyes have a large cornea and lens. The iris can dilate very wide at night. Why would this be useful for a nocturnal animal? _____
_____

Otherwise, owl eyes are very similar to ours and not much more sensitive. Owls do not rely on vision alone to catch their prey. Owls have sensitive ears as well as good eyes. Sound coming from one direction takes slightly longer to reach the ear on the opposite side of the head than the near ear.

Owls which fly primarily in the daytime have smooth flight feathers, but nocturnal owls have fluffy, fringed flight feathers. These fluffy feathers are quieter than the stiff flight feathers of the other birds. Test this for yourself.

Materials

scissors
2 pieces of typing paper

Procedure:

1. Fold each piece of paper in half the long way. Cut the open edges of one piece of paper into narrow fringes.

2. Hold the uncut piece of paper by one end and flap it so it makes a snapping sound in the air. Repeat the procedure with the fringed paper. Can you make as loud a sound?

_____

_____

Name _____

The Lazy Sloth

1. The sloth is a relative of the anteater. Originally, these animals were classified as *Edentata*, which means "toothless." The anteaters are the only members of this group that do not have teeth, however. Armadillos, which are another cousin of the sloth, have as many as 100 teeth! How does this compare to humans? _____
_____

Sloths and their relatives have been reclassified as *Xenarthra*, which means "extra-jointed," because they all have an extra vertebra in their necks.

Sloths usually sleep for 18 hours out of every 24, using long claws on their feet to hang upside down from trees. They wake up for six hours in the night but do not change position. They eat and sleep hanging upside down. These animals are mammals and feed on leaves and fruits.

2. Sloths have become so adapted to living upside down that their hair grows from their bellies to their backs, allowing the rain to slide off. The individual hairs are grooved, and a type of algae grows in the grooves and gives the sloths a greenish color. How would this green color be helpful to a slow-moving animal that lives in the trees?
_____
_____

3. Sloths are found only in the Western Hemisphere, in Central and South America. There are approximately 30 species, and these are divided into two groups. Look at the pictures below. Can you guess how these animals might be grouped?
_____
_____

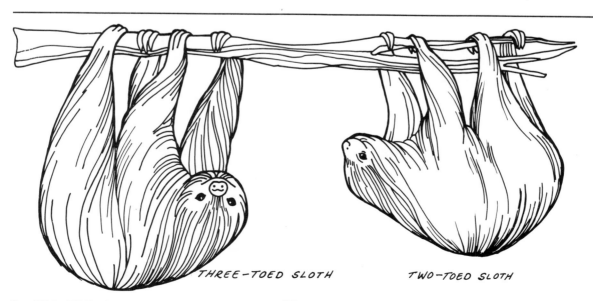

THREE-TOED SLOTH   TWO-TOED SLOTH

Octopus Intelligence

We learn by observing others, not just by doing something ourselves. Humans and other mammals often use this method. Lions and wolves teach their young to hunt. By their example, adult chimpanzees show their children how to fish termites out of holes with a twig. We expect this behavior from mammals, particularly our pets, but this behavior can also be found in the octopus, an ocean-dwelling *invertebrate*.

Octopuses have been trained to lift the lid off a sealed jar to get to a treat. They first learn to enter the jar through the open hole. This is a feat in itself, because a twelve-inch octopus can squeeze through a one-half-inch hole. An octopus this long has a body as big as a tennis ball, so this is not an easy task. The octopus next learns to move a loose stopper and finally to pull a tight stopper out of the hole. Experiments have shown that octopuses can tell one shape from another, find their way through mazes, and remember the things that have happened to them.

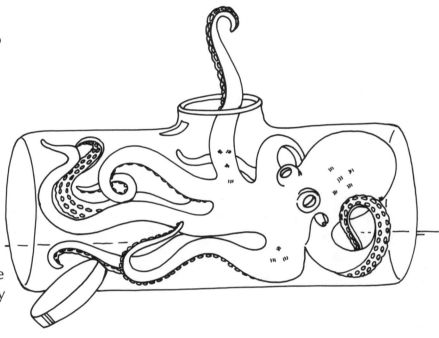

1. What is an invertebrate? (Use your library resources if you do not know.)_____
   _____

2. How is an invertebrate different from you?_____
   _____

3. How would being an invertebrate help the octopus fit into small places? _____
   _____

4. Why can't you make your body squeeze into a space that is as small (relatively) as the bottle the octopus can squeeze into? _____
   _____

Name _____

How do the octopus' sucker feet help it to grip things?

Materials
suction hooks
sandpaper
a flat glass surface
   such as a window
   or door

Procedure:

1. Place the suction hook against the dry glass surface. Press the hook firmly against the glass. Does it stick? Try to remove the hook. Does it pull off easily? _____

_____

2. Clean the glass surface and dampen it slightly. Stick the suction hook to the surface. Does it stick? Try to remove the suction hook. Does it pull off easily? _____

_____

3. Place the sandpaper on a hard, flat surface such as a floor or table. Press the suction hook against the sandpaper. Does it stick? Try to remove the suction hook. Does it pull off easily?_____

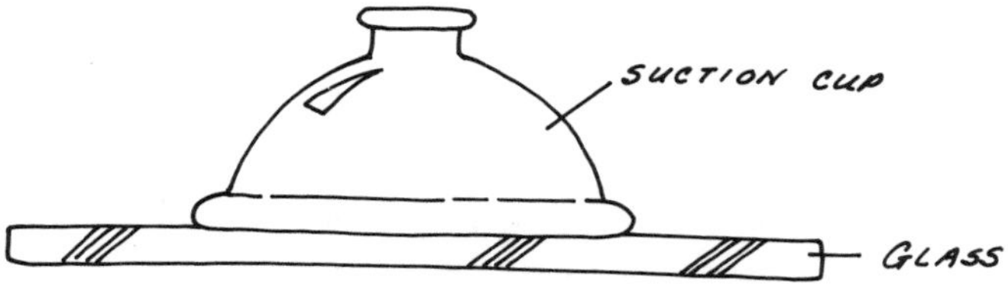

_____

SUCTION CUP   AIR HOLES   SAND PAPER   SUCTION CUP   GLASS

4. Study the diagrams above. Why do you think the suction hook sticks best on the glass surface? _____

_____

5. If a suction hook does not stick well on a glass surface, what could you do to make it adhere better?_____

_____

Hide and Seek in the Animal World

Many animals have *protective coloration*; they mimic other animals or their surroundings to hide from predators. Spotted fawns, striped tigers, and mosaic-patterned pheasants are all hard to spot against their respective backgrounds. A patterned coat or skin helps the animal blend with a background of grass or leaves as you can see in the illustrations below.

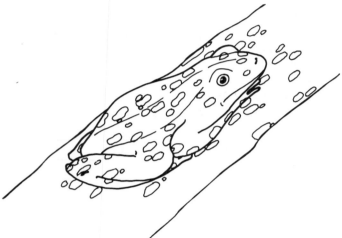

The pootoo of Central and South America goes even further with its disguise. The bird is a mottled brown, gray, and black and resembles the bark on a tree. It is a nocturnal bird and roosts in trees during the day. Instead of perching flat so that its body is horizontal, it perches with its body held upright, making it look very much like a broken branch. When it is scared, it closes its eyes and raises its head high with the beak pointed upward so it resembles a broken branch even more closely.

Protective coloration is most effective when the animal is motionless. Look at the two illustrations of the plover chick on the next page. The one on the left shows the chick standing in its natural habitat, a sandy beach.

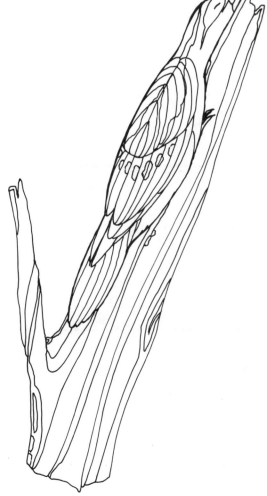

Why is the chick not as well camouflaged if it is standing or moving as it is crouching against the ground as in the picture at the right?

_____

African Flattid bugs lie in a line up the stalk of plant stems so that they closely resemble flowers. Depending on the species, these bugs are bright green, yellow, pink, or white. Color the bugs on the stalk at the left to see why they so closely resemble flowers. Color the stalk and leaves green and the bugs yellow or pink.

The blue-tailed skink uses its bright blue tail to advantage in another way. When it is attacked, the bright blue tail breaks off easily. The predator is distracted by the bright blue color of the tail and the striped body slips away quickly. The skink regenerates a new tail in a short time. Color the skink's tail a bright blue to see what an attention-getter it is.

For Research: How do other animals such as zebras, snowy owls, and mantids use protective coloration? What other animals use protective coloration? How do we use protective coloration?

Name _____

Special Defenses

Many animals have special defenses to protect themselves from predators. Skunks have a *strong odor*, porcupines have *quills,* and bees have *stingers*. The animals shown below have special defenses, also.

1. The box-fish exudes a strong poison when it is attacked. It also has a bony exterior which makes it difficult for predators to swallow or crush. Color this fish a bright yellow.

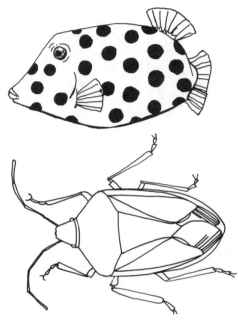

2. This is the nymph of a stink bug from Borneo. It gives off a very unpleasant odor when it is attacked. Color it a bright pink.

3. The blister beetle produces a liquid which contains a caustic substance. It causes blisters on any animal that attacks it. Color the body of the beetle bright yellow-orange and the head rusty brown.

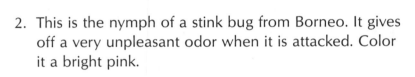

4. The European fire salamander secretes a milky substance on its skin which is very poisonous. Color it black with bright yellow spots.

5. What trait do each of these animals share?_____

6. If an inexperienced predator came in contact with a blister beetle and was hurt, what do you think it would do the next time it saw an insect that looked like a blister beetle?

_____

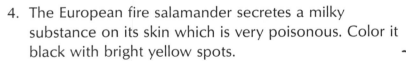

Wonders of the Plant Kingdom

The plant kingdom is as varied and unique as the animal kingdom. Plants vary in size, rate of growth, appearance, and habitat. The common ground for plants is their need for sunlight and their ability to manufacture their own food.

Seed plants, or the group of plants that reproduce from seeds, include the *flowering plants* and *conifers*. *Conifers* are plants that produce cones. All other seed plants are *flowering plants* or *angiosperms*, including grasses, flowers, and trees such as the maple and oak.

The seed of each plant is a storehouse, with a protective coat called the *seed coat*, a tiny *embryo* or future plant, and a food store for the embryo. The embryo of each seed consists of a *radicle* or tiny root, a *plumule* or miniature shoot, and one or two *cotyledons* or seed leaves. Flowering plants are classified based on whether they have one or two of these cotyledons in the seed. *Monocots* have one cotyledon and the seed will not easily split in half. *Dicots* have two cotyledons and the seed will easily split in half. Corn is an example of a monocot and beans are dicots. Look at the seeds of an apple and a peanut.

1. Are apples monocots or dicots?_____

2. Are peanuts monocots or dicots? _____

Seeds have an incredible ability to survive. They can remain dormant for months, years, and even centuries in some cases and withstand extremes of heat, cold, and drought that would destroy an animal embryo. The seed stays *dormant* or "sleeping" until it is watered. Once it begins to soak up water, it starts to *germinate* or produce a new plant. Is the seed as strong and durable when it is germinating?

Materials
grass seeds
paper towels
three plastic
  containers with lids
water

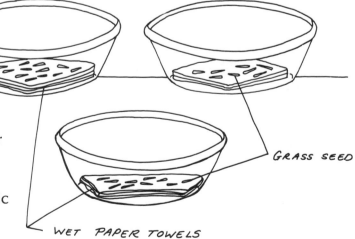

GRASS SEED

WET PAPER TOWELS

Procedure:
1. Soak three paper towels with water and fold them so they fit the bottoms of the plastic containers. Line the bottoms of the three plastic containers with these wet towels. Cover the towels with grass seeds.

2. Place one container in the freezer. Place the other two containers in a warm, dark place. Check the seeds daily until they germinate. Check the seeds in the freezer. Did they germinate? _____

3. Place one container of germinated seeds in the freezer. Observe them after 48 hours. What happens? _____

Conclusions:

1. Will grass seeds germinate when they are frozen?_____

2. Can a grass seed withstand freezing temperatures once it has germinated? _____

3. Do germinated seeds have the same ability to withstand adverse or harsh conditions that dormant seeds do?_____

All seeds need certain conditions in order to germinate. They all need:

1. water
2. air
3. a certain temperature, depending on the kind of plant
4. some seeds require light or total darkness, most plants will germinate in either light or dark
5. soil

The seed itself needs only water until it germinates. The plant requires air and minerals from the soil, but the seed itself requires neither. As the seed germinates, it *sprouts* or produces a tiny new plant. A tiny new plant includes a stem and roots.

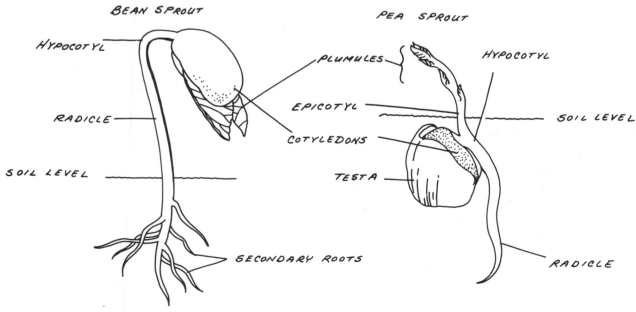

> **Materials**
>
> mung, soy, or alfalfa beans
>   (found in Oriental or health
>   food stores)
> a wide-mouthed glass jar
> a double thickness square of
>   cheesecloth
> water
> a piece of string or a thick
>   rubber band

Procedure:

1. Rinse two tablespoons of beans and soak them in cold water overnight.

2. Remove any beans that are floating on top of the water; they will not germinate.

3. Drain off the water and rinse the beans.

4. Place the drained, rinsed beans in the jar. Cover the jar with cheesecloth and fasten the cloth with the string or rubber band. Place the jar on its side in a warm, dark place such as a closet. The next morning, rinse the beans and return them to the closet. Repeat this procedure for four or five days or until the sprouts are one to three inches long.

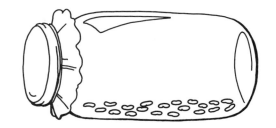

5. Remove one sprout from the jar and draw what you see in the space to the right. What parts does this young plant have? What color are the parts of the young sprouts? Place two sprouts on a damp paper towel on a saucer. Place the saucer in a sunny place for two days. Keep the towel damp. What happens to the sprouts?

6. Rinse all of the remaining sprouts under a strong stream of cold water. These sprouts are rich in vitamin C and are ready for you to eat. Serve them in a salad or cook them in an Oriental dish or fry them slightly and add them to an omelet or scrambled eggs. Enjoy!

Name _____

Hairy Roots

Some plants have a large, main taproot with some small root hairs; others have fibrous root systems with a mass of small root hairs. Each root hair is one enlarged cell. The root hairs absorb water and nutrients from the soil and bring them into the plant. The root hair must have water, but not too much. It also requires oxygen.

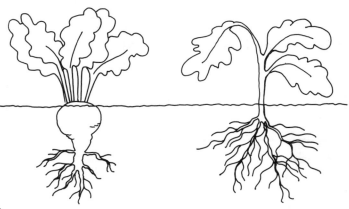

Materials

radish or tomato seeds
paper towels
two saucers
water

Procedure:

1. Soak one paper towel and fold it on the bottom of one saucer. Sprinkle 10 or 15 seeds on the paper towel and cover them with water.

2. Soak the second paper towel and fold it on the bottom of the second saucer. Drain off any excess water. Sprinkle 10 or 15 seeds on this paper towel.

3. Place both saucers in a warm, dark place. Check the saucers daily. Make certain that the first saucer always has standing water to cover the seeds and do not let the paper towel on the second saucer dry out.

Observations:

1. Which seeds germinate first?

_____

2. Do the soaked seeds germinate?

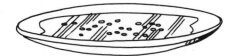

_____

3. Which seeds develop root hairs?

_____

Osmosis

Both plant and animal cells have walls made of *semipermeable membranes*. These membranes have tiny holes in them that allow molecules which are small enough to pass through to the other side. The molecules pass from the side with a higher concentration to the side with a lower concentration. For example, if you have salt water on one side of a semipermeable membrane and fresh water on the other side, some freshwater molecules will slip through the membrane to the salt water until both sides are equally salty. This process is called *osmosis*. This is the method by which plants move water from one cell to another within the plant.

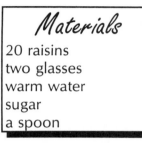

Materials
20 raisins
two glasses
warm water
sugar
a spoon

Procedure:

1. Fill each glass with water. Stir sugar into one glass until no more will dissolve. This will be glass "A." The plain water will be glass "B." Allow the water in both glasses to cool, and then place ten raisins in each glass.

2. Allow the raisins to stand in the water overnight.

3. How do the raisins look the next day?

   _____

4. Taste the water in glass B. What does it taste like?

   _____

5. Taste the raisins in glasses A and B. Do the raisins taste the same? If there is a difference, what is it?

   _____

6. What has happened to the raisins in glass A? _____

   _____

Ex-osmosis

Every plant and animal must maintain a balance of the salts and other chemicals in their cells. Saltwater plants and animals cannot survive in fresh water because they absorb too much of the fresh water. Some microscopic marine organisms absorb so much water when they are put in fresh water that they actually swell up and burst. Conversely, freshwater fish and animals cannot survive in salt water because the water flows out of their systems into the salt water. This loss of water is called *ex-osmosis*.

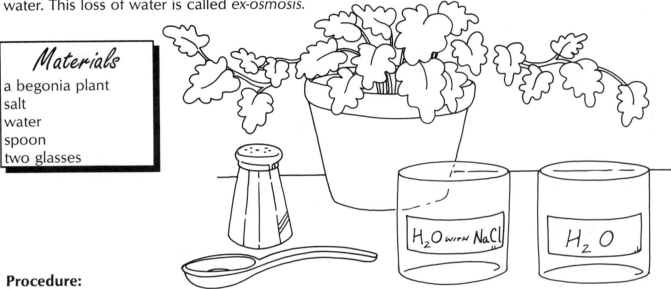

Materials
a begonia plant
salt
water
spoon
two glasses

Procedure:

1. Fill the two glasses with water. Dissolve salt into one glass of water a teaspoonful at a time until salt crystals remain on the bottom of the glass.

2. Place one stem of the begonia plant in the saltwater glass and another stem of the begonia plant in the freshwater glass. Allow both glasses and stems to sit undisturbed overnight. Observe the stems. What has happened? _____

_____

Conclusion: What happens to the water in a begonia stem when it is allowed to stand in saltwater overnight? _____

_____

Transpiration

We lose moisture through the pores in our skin in the process known as sweating. For us, this process is a way of cooling our bodies and preventing overheating. Plants lose moisture through the pores or *stomates* in their leaves. This process is called *transpiration*. Transpiration does not serve to cool the plant, but causes suction in the stem of the plant pulling water and minerals up from the roots. Which side of a leaf has the most stomates, the top side or the underside?

Materials
six philodendron
  leaves
scissors
thread
nail polish

Procedure:

1. Cut six pieces of thread approximately 10" long. Tie a piece of thread around the stem of each leaf.

2. Cover the top side of three leaves with nail polish. Cover the underside of the other three leaves with nail polish. Hang all six leaves to dry.

Observations:

1. Which leaves curl first? _____

   _____

2. Does the nail polish let water vapor escape more easily from the leaf or less easily?

   _____

Note: leaves shrivel because they have lost water.

Conclusion:
Which side of a leaf has more stomates? _____

_____

Flower Giants

Rafflesia arnoldii
deep peach with cream spots

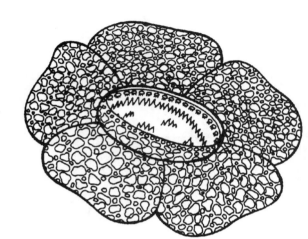

Amorphophallus titanum

yellow spadix

deep maroon
spathe

light green

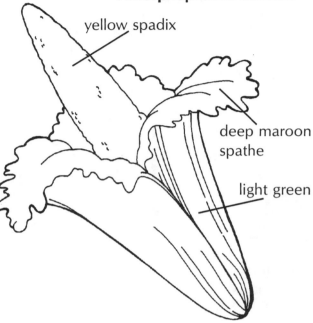

Sunflowers are relatively large compared to other garden flowers, but they are dwarfs compared to some of the wild plants that flower on this planet. The *rafflesia arnoldii* is a parasite which grows on the vine tetrastigma and has no leaves or stem. The flower, which is approximately one yard in diameter, grows directly on the vine. The flower is a deep peach color with pale cream speckled patches. The flower is anchored directly to the root of the host plant and part of the host plant grows into the flower to "feed" it. The flower has a fetid, unappealing smell.

The *amorphophallus titanum* is another flower giant. It is four feet in diameter and over six feet high, but this bloom is really a collection of flowers which look like a single flower. Inside the *spathe* or "large leaflike part enclosing the flower cluster" of the plant are hundreds of male and female flowers. As it blooms, the plant emits a smell that is described as a combination of burning sugar and rotten fish. To help you visualize these flowers, color the illustration above according to the labels beside each flower part.

Flowers need to be pollinated to produce seeds for more plants. Bees, butterflies, and many other insects and animals pollinate flowers. Bees and many insects are attracted to the sweet smell of flowers such as magnolias, jasmine, lilacs, lilies, and roses. What sort of insect or animal would be attracted by the scent of the flowers described above?_____

Edible Wild Plants

Dandelion

The name *dandelion* comes from the French *dent de lion* or "tooth of the lion." No one knows whether the plant is named for its fluffy, yellow flower which looks like a lion's mane or its sharply toothed leaves. Dandelions are not native to North America but were brought here by early colonists. Dandelions are composite flowers. Each yellow head is actually many tiny flowers. They do not need to be pollinated to produce seeds, but the seeds which are produced without pollination yield plants that are identical to the parent. The roots of a dandelion may be roasted and then boiled to make a coffee substitute or sliced in a salad or boiled and eaten. The young leaves of dandelion make good salad greens or may be boiled and eaten like spinach, and the young buds are also tasty. Dandelions are rich in vitamin A. The blossoms are used to make dandelion wine.

Chicory

Roasted chicory roots provide another coffee substitute and its greens, like the dandelion, are good for salads. It is similar in looks and taste to the dandelion, but the flowers are a bright blue. The flowers usually close by noon on bright, sunny days. The mature leaves of the chicory are very tough and bitter, so only tender, early leaves are worth gathering for food.

Clover

The tiny pink or white florets of clover contain nectar, which is a favorite of bees. The young leaves and flowers of clover may be eaten raw or they may be steamed or boiled. The dried blossoms and seeds make a good bread. The roots of the clover have a sweet flavor and may be eaten. In addition, the flowers may be dried and then crumbled and used to brew a kind of tea.

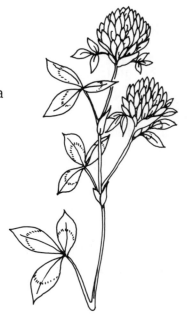

Plantain

Plantain is found in almost every lawn. This plant has broad green leaves which are excellent greens. The darker the leaf, the more vitamins A and C and minerals they contain. Boil the leaves until they are tender but still slightly crisp. The leaves may also be used for tea. Steep half a handful of leaves in a cup of boiling water for ½ hour. In addition, these leaves are astringent and may be used to treat cuts, scratches, and open wounds. For this purpose, mash fresh leaves and apply them directly to the open wound.

Many garden flowers are also edible. The blossoms of the nasturtium are edible and make a fine and beautiful addition to a salad. Sunflower seeds are particularly tasty and nutritious. Rose hips, the round, smooth fruit of the rose which follow the flower on the stalk, are full of vitamin C. Three rose hips are reported to have as much vitamin C as one orange. They also contain iron, calcium, and phosphorus. These rose hips can be squashed, boiled, and added to sugar to make jelly. The petals of the rose are tasty if you discard the greenish or white base portion. The dark red and bright colors are strongest-tasting and the pastels are more delicately flavored.

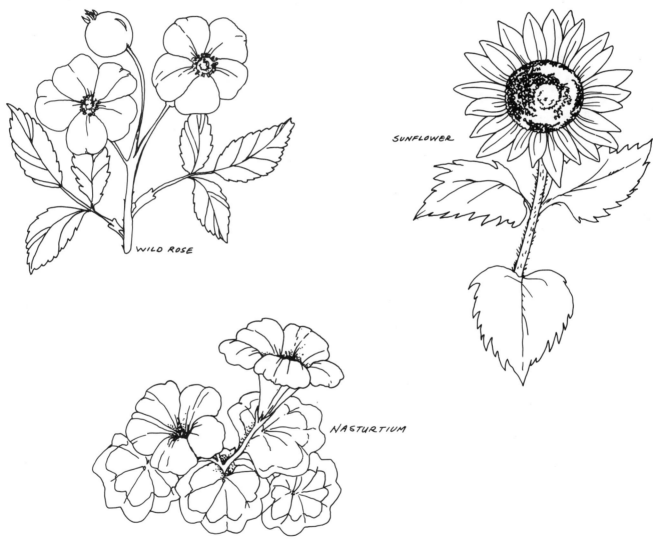

WILD ROSE

SUNFLOWER

NASTURTIUM

For Research: Read books by Bradford Angiers (*Feasting on Wild Edibles* and *Free for the Eating*) and Euell Gibbons (*Stalking the Wild Asparagus*) for more edible wild plants and some recipes for cooking these plants. Always consult a botanist before you attempt to eat a plant that you have identified. There are many look-alikes in the plant world.

Carnivorous Plants

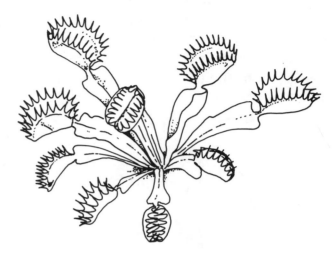

While herbivorous or plant-eating animals are common and carnivorous or animal-eating animals are equally common, carnivorous plants are more unusual. The Venus flytrap is one of the more well-known carnivorous plants. It grows wild in the bogs of North Carolina but has been cultivated as a houseplant and grows well indoors if it is carefully tended. The Venus flytrap, as you might expect from its native habitat, likes damp soil. When you purchase a specimen, follow its growing instructions carefully.

Materials

a potted Venus flytrap
some flies or hamburger

The insides of the lobes of a Venus flytrap leaf contain a sweet nectar which in the wild attracts flies and other insects. The small hairs which line each of the leaves generate an electrical current if an animal touches two of these hairs at one time. The current causes the motor cells at the middle of the lobes of the leaf to lose water and go limp. The leaf closes with the dinner inside.

Procedure:

1. Lightly touch the outside spikes of the leaf with the hamburger or fly. What happens? __

   _____

2. Place a fly or some hamburger in the center of the leaf. What happens? _____

   _____

3. When a Venus flytrap leaf reopens after it has eaten its meal, is anything left? _____

   _____

4. Test the Venus flytrap on other kinds of food, such as tiny bits of vegetables or fruit. Is the Venus flytrap an omnivore? Will it eat other plants?_____

   _____

More Carnivorous Plants

Carnivorous plants grow in wet, soggy places where the soil is low on nitrogen. All living things, plants and animals, contain nitrogen, so these plants get the extra nitrogen they need from the animals they trap. The Venus flytrap is not the only carnivorous plant. Read the descriptions below; then identify all four plants by writing the correct name next to each picture.

The bladderwort is an underwater carnivore. It has tiny bladders, which are little balloon-like containers, on its leaves. These bladders swallow any small animals that come in contact with them.

The sundew has sticky droplets on its leaves. Insects are attracted to this syrup and land on the leaf. They stick to the droplets and the leaf curls up, trapping the insect inside.

The pitcher plant has a long hollow tube lined with downward pointing hairs. The rim of the plant contains a sweet liquid which attracts insects. They crawl inside to get the liquid, slide down the hairs, and cannot crawl back up. They eventually become tired and fall into the rainwater inside the tube. There they drown and are digested by the plant.

Carnivorous plants are nearing extinction because many of their swampy habitats have been drained by developers. What can we do to save the remaining plants? _____

_____

_____

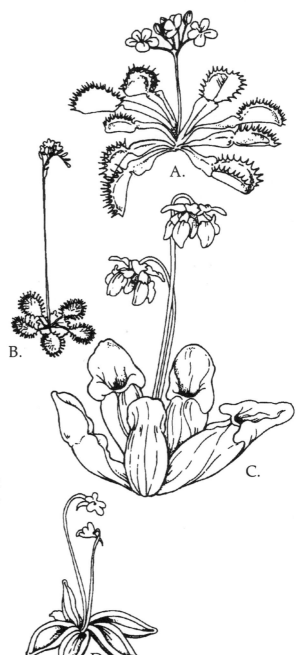

Name _____

Poisonous Plants

Many plants are dangerous, for a variety of reasons. Some plants are dangerous to touch and some are dangerous when eaten. Many of the plants can be dangerous or fatal if eaten in large amounts but may have medicinal value if only a small amount is swallowed. Read the descriptions below and match the description to the correct picture on the right. Label each picture with the correct name of the plant.

The foxglove is a garden plant. Its tall spires of pink and white blossoms are often seen in flowerbeds. This plant is the source of digitalis, a common medication for strengthening the heartbeats of cardiac patients. In large doses, digitalis causes heart failure.

Poison ivy contains an oil called urushiol. Those who are allergic to this oil break out in itchy blisters when they come in contact with this plant. Remember the rule: "Leaves of three, let them be."

The poison hemlock is a pretty flower which closely resembles Queen Anne's lace or wild carrot. It can grow up to five feet tall and, unlike Queen Anne's lace, it has smooth, hairless stems with purple spots. When its leaves are squashed, they emit a foul odor. All parts of this plant contain the alkaloid coniine, the source of the poison that killed Socrates.

All parts of the mountain laurel are poisonous. Even honey made from its nectar is poisonous. The small, pink flowers resemble tiny pink skirts turned upside down. This gives it its alternate name, calico bush.

A.

B.

C.

D.

Name _____

Seaweed

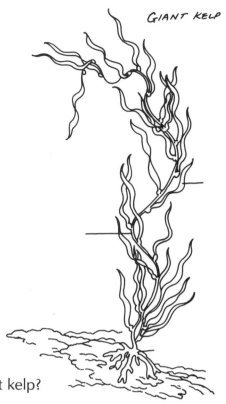

GIANT KELP

What plant can grow as much as a foot a day and can grow up to 160 feet in one year? Does it sound like an over-fertilized bamboo plant? No. This plant is the California giant kelp, huge seaweed. It is really a form of algae. Seaweed, like other algae, does not have flowers. It reproduces by spores. It has a *stipe* instead of a stem and *fronds* instead of leaves. The stipe is strong, rubbery, and flexible and allows the seaweed to bend and sway with the ocean currents. At the base of the stipe is a *holdfast,* a rootlike projection that allows the kelp to clamp onto a rock or shell to keep it anchored to the ocean floor. The fronds often contain gas-filled bladders that help the seaweed to float in the water. Label the stipe, fronds, and holdfast in the giant kelp illustration to the right and color the giant kelp light brown.

For research: How does the sea otter use the giant kelp?

Seaweeds are green, brown, or red. All seaweeds contain chlorophyll, and the color pigments in brown and red seaweed mask the green color of the chlorophyll. Everything that looks like seaweed is not seaweed, however. *Bryozoans* or moss animals are tiny colonies of animals that closely resemble seaweed. The illustrations below show two bryozoans. The one on the left shows a colony or group of these bryozoans attached to a rock to anchor them to the ocean floor. These moss animals have thin *filaments* which help them trap food in the water. The bryozoans on the right have broad, flat fronds with folds which help them filter food from the seawater.

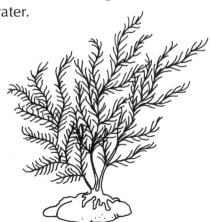

Wonders Under the Microscope

The earliest residents of our planet were primitive bacteria or *prokaryotes*. Evidence of ancient prokaryotic life has been found in rocks called *stromatolites*. The term *stromatolites* comes from the Greek words *stroma* or "bed" and *lithos* or "rock." Stromatolites are mound-shaped rocks. They can be as small as a pea or as large as a football field. They are made of layers of very fine rock, each layer about a millimeter thick. The layers were made by and are the fossil record of colonies of microscopic organisms. These organisms are *bacteria* and *cyanobacteria*.

We have no record of the very first living organisms because the first living things had no cells; they were like a drop of oil. These first life forms were probably *anaerobic*; they did not need oxygen. A bolt of lightning or electricity may have produced organic compounds, the *primordial soup* as scientists like to call it. Simple organisms evolved from this primordial soup and used it to maintain themselves and develop.

Scientists use three methods to study stromatolites. Before they apply one of these methods, however, they label the rock to make certain that they can track its origins. An unlabeled rock is useless. Next, they divide the rock into pieces. The first piece is ground to a fine powder and undergoes chemical studies. The second piece is dissolved in acid. Some bits of organic material will remain, and these are studied under a microscope to see whether there are any cells. The third chunk is sliced into paper-thin pieces and studied under a microscope. Label the three methods shown in the illustrations to the right.

How can the methods used to find fossilized bacteria on earth help us to find out whether there are or were living organisms on other planets?

_____
_____
_____
_____

1. _____

2. _____

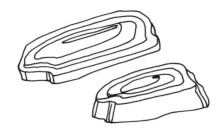

3. _____

What Are Bacteria Like?

The number of bacteria in your mouth is greater than the number of all the human beings that have ever lived. Numerically, bacteria are by far the dominant organisms, but in size they are no match. They are called the kingdom *Monera* because they are single-celled, although some kinds of bacteria group together. They do not have a true nucleus, but have a *nucleoid region* that contains a tangle of *DNA* in fibers. This is actually a ring-shaped, double-stranded DNA molecule. Some bacteria have smaller rings of DNA called *plasmids* in addition to the nucleoid region. Plasmids give the cell extra resistance to antibiotics, allow the cell to live on nutrients that are not present in the normal environment, and give it other special abilities. Most bacteria have *cell walls* which protect them, give them shape, and keep the cell from bursting in a saltwater environment. Label the cell walls, nucleoid region, and plasmids in the illustration below.

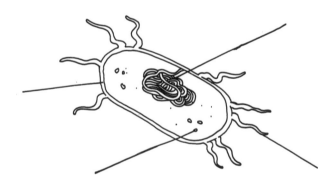

Many bacteria have an extra layer of sticky material outside of the cell wall. This layer is called a *capsule* and comes from substances the cell secretes. It forms an extra protective barrier for the bacteria and helps the bacteria stick to other bacteria in a colony or to another organism or *substratum* on which the bacteria is growing. The substratum is a layer of material or a structure on which the bacteria is growing.

Some bacteria have *appendages* or parts that allow them to attach to other things. These appendages are called *pili*. Pili look like fat, short hairs. Label the pili on the illustration above.

Bacteria and Cyanobacteria Shapes

Bacteria and cyanobacteria are prokaryotes. They belong to the kingdom *Monera*. Besides being the most prolific, they are the most far-ranging of any organism. They live in extremes of heat, cold, wet, dry, and salty, basically anywhere there is life. Most species are useful or at least not harmful and many are essential to the survival of higher organisms, but some are extremely harmful. Most bacteria come in one of three basic shapes: spherical or *cocci*, rod-shaped or *bacilli,* and spiral or *spirilla.* Cocci may come in pairs which are called *diplococcus,* or chains of many cells in a row which are called *streptococcus,* or in clusters like grapes which are called *staphylococcus.* Rod-shaped bacilli are usually solitary but occasionally form chains. Spirilla may be either comma-shaped which are called *vibrios,* corkscrew-shaped which are called *spirilla,* or curly, ribbon-shaped which are called *spirochetes.* Label the bacteria below by their shapes.

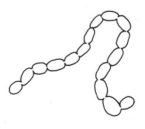

1. _____   2. _____   3. _____

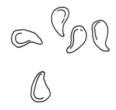

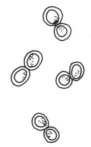

4._____   5. _____   6. _____

What shape are the cyanobacteria Chroococcus? _____
_____

Identifying Bacteria

Since bacteria are very small, how do scientists identify the different kinds? One method is to use what is called the *Gram stain*. This method is named for Hans Christian Gram, a Danish doctor who devised this technique in the late nineteenth century. The bacteria are first stained with a violet dye and iodine. Next they are rinsed in alcohol. Third, they are restained with a red dye.

The Gram stain identifies bacteria based on their cell walls. *Gram-positive* bacteria have simple cell walls that contain large amounts of a substance called *peptidoglycan*. The violet stain sticks to their walls and they keep a violet color. *Gram-negative* bacteria have a more complex outer membrane. Their membrane contains less peptidoglycan. The alcohol rinses the violet dye off their cell walls, and the red dye replaces it and gives them a red color. *Pathogenic* or harmful bacteria (from the Greek words *pathos* or "suffering" and *gignomai* or "cause") may be either Gram-positive or Gram-negative, but the pathogens that test Gram-negative tend to be more harmful and more resistant to antibiotics.

Color the bacteria on the left violet and the ones on the right red. Label them Gram-positive or Gram-negative according to their color. Which bacteria are more likely be harmful and resistant to antibiotics? _____

A.

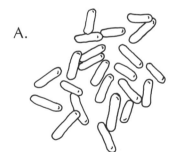

B.

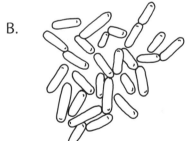

To classify bacteria, scientists use two main categories: *archaebacteria* and *eubacteria*. The name for archaebacteria comes from the Greek word *archaio* for "ancient." This group of bacteria developed as a separate strain early in the evolutionary tree. Most archaebacteria live in very harsh conditions where other forms of life could not survive. They are found in the super-hot deep sea vents in the ocean, for example, and in the extremely salty Dead Sea and Great Salt Lake.

Archaebacteria are one of three types: *methanogens, halophiles,* and *thermoacidophiles.* *Methanogens* use hydrogen to change carbon dioxide to methane, which is where they get their name. They are the bacteria found in swamps and marshes. They live where there is no oxygen and the "swamp gas" they produce is methane. They are also the bacteria which convert sewage and garbage to methane and are very useful in sewage treatment. One species of methanogens lives in the stomachs of cows and other herbivores that live on a diet of cellulose.

Halophiles are salt lovers, which is what their name means. Some require salt for survival; some will live in more or less salty conditions and tolerate the salt. A large colony of halophiles looks like a pink scum on the surface of the salt water.

Thermoacidophiles need heat and acid. They prefer temperatures of 60 to 80 degrees Celsius and a pH between 2 and 4, which is very acidic. *Sulfolobus* bacteria live in hot, sulfur springs in Yellowstone National Park. They oxidize sulfur to get their energy.

Label the archaebacteria below according to their habitats.

1. _____

2. _____

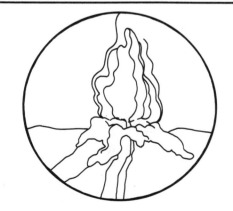

3. _____

4. _____

Eubacteria

The *eubacteria* are the modern bacteria, the more recently evolved members of the kingdom *Monera*. There are many different kinds of bacteria and only a few of them are portrayed below. Match the descriptions with their portraits to the right.

Cyanobacteria are commonly called blue-green algae. Most of these organisms live in fresh water, but a few of them are saltwater species. They use sunlight and chlorophyll to synthesize their food the way plants do and, like plants, they release oxygen into the atmosphere. They form a "scum" on the surface of ponds and, in contrast to their common name, they come in a variety of colors, including red, black, yellow, brown, and green.

Phototrophic bacteria also use sunlight to manufacture food, but they do not release oxygen into the atmosphere. Instead, most are anaerobic and grow in the sediment at the bottom of ponds, lakes, and oceans. They are green or purple in color.

Pseudomonads may live in soil or water. Some of the soil species decompose pesticides and other substances that no other organism can use as food. Some can also survive in hot tubs and in the medicines and cleaning solutions that were designed to eliminate bacteria.

Spirochetes are curly-shaped and move like twisting corkscrews. This species includes the infamous *Treponema pallidum* which causes syphilis and the pestiferous *Borrelia burgdorferi* which causes Lyme disease.

1. _____

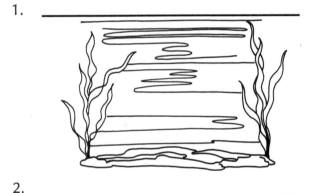

2. _____

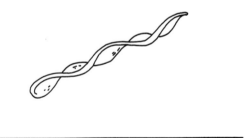

3. _____

4. _____

Endospore-forming bacteria are bacteria which form endospores or very thick cell walls which protect the organisms against extremely harsh conditions. The bacteria dehydrate and may remain dormant inside the thick wall for centuries until conditions are favorable for growth. They must be heated to temperatures higher than 120 degrees centigrade to be killed. *Clostridium botulinum,* the bacteria which causes botulism, is an endospore-forming bacteria.

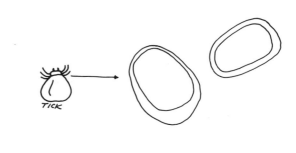

5. _____

Enteric bacteria live in the intestines of animals. Most of them are harmless under normal circumstances, with the exception of *salmonella*. One genus of salmonella causes *typhoid* and several other varieties of salmonella cause food poisoning. *Escherichia coli,* the infamous *E. coli bacteria,* which is commonly spread when people do not wash their hands after using the toilet, is a member of this group.

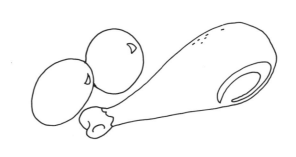

6. _____

Rickettsias and chlamydias are the very smallest bacteria. They live as parasites inside the cells of other organisms. Rocky Mountain spotted fever and typhus are both caused by different rickettsias bacteria and are transmitted through the bites of ticks and other insects.

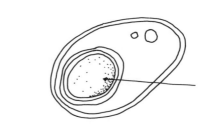

Myxobacteria live in colonies. These bacteria glide through soil by secreting a slippery substance. Their name comes from *myxa,* the Greek word for "mucus." If the soil becomes dry or they run out of food, they gather together and form a mass which becomes a stalk with a fruiting body. This fruiting body produces very durable spores. When they are released, they vegetate until conditions are favorable for them to grow into a new colony of myxobacteria.

7. _____

8. _____

Bacteria in Motion

Bacteria that can move, or *motile* bacteria, use one of three mechanisms. Spirochetes have *axial filaments*. These are tiny fibers that spiral around the outside wall of the bacteria and cause it to spin like a corkscrew. A second kind of bacteria has a *flagella* which is attached to the surface of the cell. A flagella is a long, whip-like appendage which protrudes from the surface of the prokaryotic cell. The third way that bacteria move is to secrete a slime and glide along the surface. Label the flagella in the illustration below.

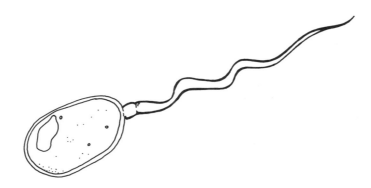

If the environment is uniform throughout, the bacteria wander around randomly. If the environment consists of dissimilar ingredients, many bacteria can *taxis* or move away from or toward a stimulus. Some bacteria respond to a chemical stimulus. They move toward food or away from some poisonous material. These bacteria are *chemotactic*. Some bacteria use sunlight for *photosynthesis*. These bacteria are *phototactic*. Some bacteria are sensitive to magnetism and contain crystals of *magnetite,* which is a kind of iron oxide. The magnetic field of the earth is strongest at the poles, so magnetotactic bacteria in the Northern Hemisphere are north-seeking.

1. Which direction do the magnetotactic bacteria in the Southern Hemisphere seek?

   _____

2. The marine bacteria *Aquaspirillum magnetotacticum* contains magnetite. What kind of bacteria is it? _____

   _____

3. In the Northern Hemisphere, which direction does this bacteria point? _____

Viruses

Unlike bacteria, viruses can not be cultivated on a nutrient media in a test tube or Petri dish and are not affected by alcohol, which usually kills bacteria. Viruses are very small and can be seen only with an electron microscope. Viruses can be *crystallized* or dried and formed into a crystal. A virus, or *virion*, is not a cell, but just nucleic acid inside a protein shell.

Most DNA is double-stranded, in a double helix form as shown in the top illustration to the right. Viruses are different. A virion may contain double-stranded DNA, single-stranded DNA, or double or single-stranded RNA. Some of the smallest viruses have only four genes. This genetic material is called *genomes*. The protein shell that surrounds the genomes is called the *capsid*. The individual protein units which make up the capsid are called *capsomeres*. Some viruses, such as flu viruses, have *envelopes* around these capsids. The membranes are made partly from the membrane of the host cell and partly from proteins and material from the virus. Label the capsid, genomes, and envelope in the second diagram to the right.

Viruses have different shapes. Read the descriptions below and label the illustrations to the right with the correct names.

Tobacco mosaic virus, or TMV, has a helical capsid, but the whole virus is shaped like a cylindrical rod.

The influenza virus also has a helical capsid, but the overall shape is spherical with glycoprotein spikes sticking out around the outer envelope.

1. _____

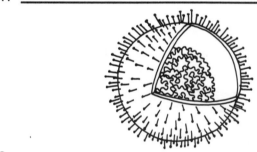

2. _____

3. _____

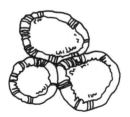

4. _____

The *adenovirus* has a polyhedral capsid also, but it has a spike-like protein projection at each vertex.

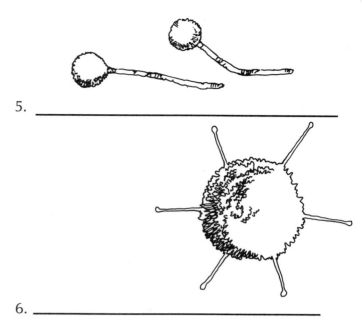

5. _____

Some viruses are *bacteriophages* or "bacteria eaters." The bacteriophage lambda has a capsid with a polyhedral head and flexible, rod-shaped tail. The tail helps the virus attach to a bacteria.

6. _____

Viruses can infect only specific cells, called their *host range*. Viruses fit into their host cells like a piece of a puzzle. Proteins on the outside of the virion fit into a certain spot on the surface of the host cell called the *receptor site*. Since the virus can infect only specific cells, this means that sometimes they can infect a part of a larger organism without affecting the rest of the organism. For instance, the cold virus infects the respiratory tract of humans but not the toes or the fingers.

Some bacteriophages kill their host cells. These virions are said to be *virulent*. They reproduce themselves by what is known as the *lytic cycle*.

Read the descriptions and then number the steps of the lytic cycle in the diagram to the right below.

1. T4 phage attaches to cell surface.
2. The sheath of the virion's tail contracts and thrusts a hollow core through the cell wall of the bacteria, injecting its DNA into the bacteria.
3. The virion injects its DNA into the bacteria and leaves its shell outside on the surface.
4. The virion chops up the host's DNA and protein and reforms them into phage DNA and protein components. These parts form new phage virions.
5. The phage virion produces an enzyme that weakens the host's cell wall. The cell wall bursts or "lyses" and the new phage virions are released, ready to start the cycle again.

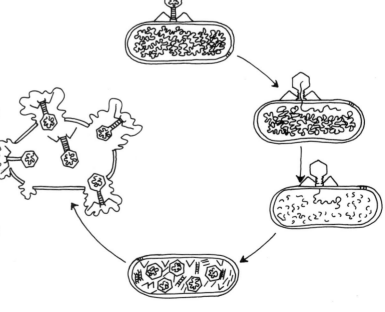

Viruses and Cancer

Cancer is a cell or group of cells gone wild. When normal cells differentiate into specific types of cells, control mechanisms keep them growing and dividing in a specific way. When they reach a certain number and size, they stop growing. They do not inhibit the growth or function of other cells. Cancer cells do not have these constraints. They keep growing and form a *tumor* and continue to grow indefinitely. One particular cell line, called HeLa because it was taken from the tumor of a lady named Henrietta Lacks, has been growing in a laboratory culture since 1951! *Benign tumors* do not move from their original site in the body and can usually be removed. *Malignant tumors,* or cancerous tumors, often have abnormal cell surfaces that allow them to move from their original position in the body and duplicate themselves in numerous places. They spread to different sites in the body in a process known as *metastasis.*

Some viruses cause cancer in animals. These viruses are called *tumor viruses* and are members of four virus groups: the retrovirus, papovavirus, adenovirus, and herpesvirus groups. The virus that causes hepatitis B seems to cause liver cancer in people who have chronic infections of the liver. Retroviruses are major causes of cancer. HTLVI causes adult T-cell leukemia and HIV causes AIDS or Acquired Immune Deficiency Syndrome, which is a weakening of the immune system and makes the individual more susceptible to cancer. The diagram below shows a cross-section of a model of the HIV virion. Label its parts.

In the center of the virion are two dots of *transcriptase,* an unusual enzyme which uses RNA to make DNA. Touching the *reverse transcriptase* are two Z-shaped *RNA molecules.* The *core* of the virion is thimble-shaped. The core is surrounded by the knobs of the *viral envelope* which project inward. The outside of the viral envelope has bean-shaped projections of *envelope protein.*

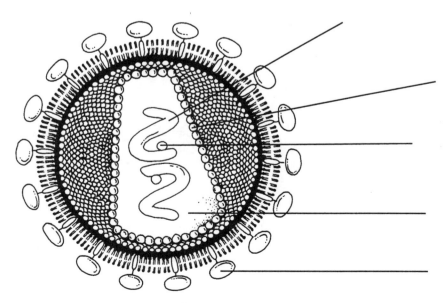

Protozoa

Protozoa are part of the kingdom *Protista*. Protists are *eukaryotic*—they have membrane-enclosed nuclei and organelles. The name *protozoa* means "first animals" and is a relic from the two-kingdom classification system.

Rhizopoda are all unicellular. Amoebas are members of this group. Some have shells and some do not. All have *pseudopodia* or cellular extensions which may bulge out from any part of the cell surface. These "false feet" are their method of locomotion. Amoebas live in fresh water, salt water, and soil. Some are parasites, like the amoeba *Entamoeba histolytica,* which causes amoebic dysentery in people. Label the amoeba and its pseudopodia in the illustration on the next page.

Actinopoda means "ray feet" and refers to the needle-like projections called *axopodia* that radiate from this spherical protist. Label the actinopod and its axopodia in the illustration on the next page.

Foraminifera or *forams* are marine protists. Some live in the sand and others attach themselves to rocks or algae or float as plankton. These protists have porous shells and, as the organisms die, these shells sink to the bottom and form sediment. The chalky cliffs of Dover are formed from the shells of these protists. Small extensions of cytoplasm extend through the holes in their shells and they use these for locomotion. Label the foram.

Zoomastigina or *Zoomastigotes* use their whip-like *flagella* to propel themselves. One member of this group is the *Trypanosoma,* which is spread by the bite of the tsetse fly and causes African sleeping sickness. Label the zoomastigote.

Apicomplexa are parasites, and they cause several important human diseases, including malaria. They spread through microscopic cells called *sporozoites* and cause the deaths of a million or more people each year. Label the apicomplexa.

Ciliophora use cilia to move around and feed. Cilia are hairlike projections. Some ciliates are almost covered with rows of them, and some have small clumps of cilia. Some have cilia bonded together to form leg-like projections. Most ciliates are solitary organisms and they possess two kinds of *nuclei,* a large *macronucleus* and many tiny *micronuclei.* The macronucleus controls everyday functions and asexual reproduction. The micronuclei are used in *conjugation* when the ciliates exchange genetic material. The slipper-shaped *Paramecium* and the trumpet-shaped *Stentor* are both ciliates. Label the Paramecium, the Stentor, their cilia, and their macronuclei and micronuclei.

Name _____

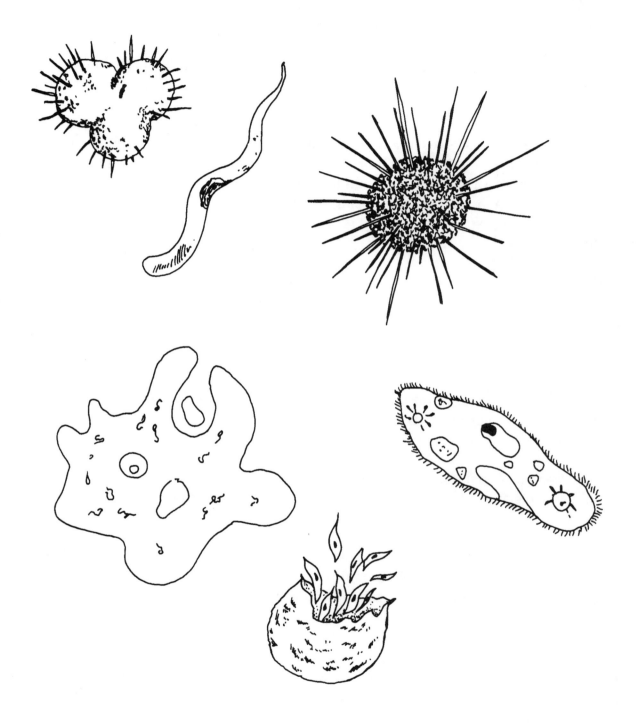

Algal Protists

Most members of this phyla are photosynthetic; they manufacture their own food using sunlight and chlorophyll. Photosynthetic protists contain chlorophyll a, the pigment found in plants and cyanobacteria. The members of this phyla include the organisms described below and many other organisms. Use the information below to label the organisms and their parts on the next page.

Dinoflagellata are a large part of the seas of phytoplankton that provide food for many aquatic animals. Dinoflagellates cause red tides in warm, coastal waters. These organisms have a pair or more of flagella which are seated in a perpendicular groove in cellulose plates. The beating of the flagella makes the cell spin as it swims. Label the dinoflagellates and their flagella.

Chrysophyta are named for their golden color. The word *chrysos* is Greek for "golden." They live in freshwater and are colonial protists. They form hardy cysts to survive freezing in winter or drought in summer. *Dinobryon,* which looks like slender golden flower buds clumped on stalks, is a colonial form of this phylum. Label the Dinobryon.

Bacillariophyta are *diatoms,* yellow or brown protists with a unique cell structure. The cells store their food as an oil, which helps them float near the surface where they get plenty of sunlight for photosynthesis. Diatoms have glasslike walls made of silica and organic material. Each shell is formed of two halves that fit together like a pillbox. Tiny pores allow gases and other material to flow in and out of the cell. They are classified by the shape of their shells and the pattern of pores in their shells.

Euglenophyta are the tiny *Euglenas,* tiny green flagellates. They are photosynthetic if they are in sunlight except for needing a small quantity of chlorophyll B and are heterotrophic if they are in the dark. Some members of this group do not have chloroplasts and chlorophyll. They move by means of their long flagella.

Chlorophyta contain bright green chloroplasts. There are more than 7,000 species in this phylum and they live in both fresh and salt water. This phylum is also known as *green algae.* Many of these protists are colonial, often forming a gooey mass known as "pond scum." *Volvox* are colonial chlorophytes that live in freshwater. Each colony is a round ball which consists of hundreds of thousands of individual cells in a gelatinous matrix. Each individual volvox has two flagella. Label the volvox colony.

Name _____

Phaeophyta or *brown algae* and *Rhodophyta* or *red algae* are also members of the kingdom Protista, although people often think of them as plants. The giant kelp and coralline algae (which contribute to the coral reefs) are both colonial protists.

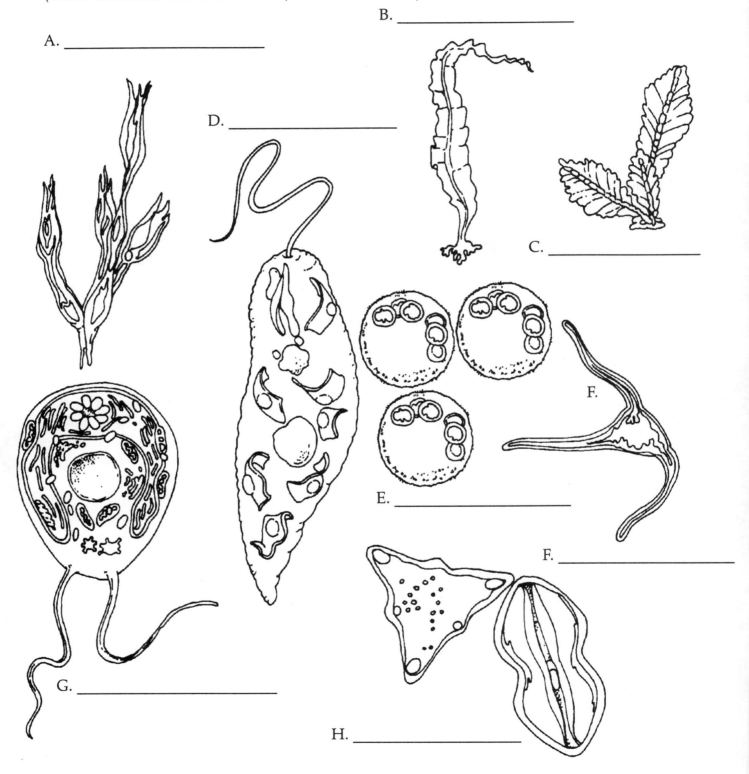

A. _____

B. _____

C. _____

D. _____

E. _____

F. _____

F. _____

G. _____

H. _____

Slime Molds

Slime molds are different from most protists, but they are not really fungi, although they resemble fungi. Some taxonomists prefer to regard the water molds as fungi and, by the old two-kingdom classification, both the water and the slime molds were considered fungi. They are different from and similar to both protists and fungi in some respects.

Myxomycota are the *plasmodial slime molds,* which makes them sound like some creepy, alien life form. Many species are brightly colored, often orange or yellow. They are not photosynthetic. Instead, they have a feeding stage in their life cycle in which they form a one-celled amoeboid mass called a *plasmodium*. This mass has many nuclei but only one cell wall. It extends pseudopods through damp soil or rotting vegetation and engulfs food. Often, the plasmodium has a weblike appearance. When the soil dries up or the food supply is gone, the slime mold forms a fruiting body or *sporangia* and reproduces itself. Label the plasmodium and the sporangia in the illustration below.

A.   B.

Acrasiomycota are *cellular slime molds*. When this organism is in its feeding stage, it functions as a solitary cell. When the food supply runs out, the cells gather together in a clump that functions as a single unit.

Oomycota or *oomycetes* are water molds, white rusts, and downy mildews. They look like fungi, but their cell walls are usually made of cellulose, unlike the chitin cell walls of fungi. They also develop flagellated cells as part of their life cycle, unlike fungi. *Oomycota* means "egg fungi," referring to the fact that oomycetes reproduce by means of a large egg cell fertilized by a smaller sperm cell. Most oomycetes are saprophytes which grow as a cotton-like mass on dead algae or animals, usually in fresh water. Some are parasites which attach to the injured skin and gills of fish in ponds or aquariums.

For Research: Use your library resources to learn more about the Irish potato famine of the 1800s, which was caused by an oomycete which caused a potato blight.

Our Wonderful Planet

The planet earth has an incredible number of unique formations, interesting rocks and minerals, and spectacular sights. They range in size from the Grand Canyon to the delicate snowflake. We have the power of Niagara Falls and the quiet beauty of the aurora borealis.

One of the most interesting features of our planet is its basic composition—a sphere with a dense, heavy, and hot core, probably composed of iron and other heavy elements, such as nickel. The temperature in this hot center ranges from 7,200 to 9,000 degrees Fahrenheit, which is almost as hot as the surface of the sun. The core is approximately 2,200 miles in diameter. The *mantle* surrounds the core and is about 1,802 miles thick. It is composed primarily of silica and metals. A 20-mile-thick *crust* floats on top of the mantle and forms the continents on which we live. This crust is broken into six large and more than a dozen small *plates,* which are constantly shifting and bumping into one another.

The plates which form the crust of the earth move in four different ways. Sometimes they slide past each other. This is called a *transform boundary plate*. When this happens, no plate is broken or destroyed and no new plates are created. An example of this is the San Andreas Fault in California. Part of California is on the Pacific plate and part of California is on the North American plate. The Pacific plate is moving northwest at the rate of half an inch a year. Under the oceans, several plates are spreading apart. This causes *seafloor spreading* where the two plates are separating. An example of this is the Mid-Atlantic Ridge. *Subduction* is the term used to describe one plate sliding under another. The bottom plate breaks apart in this process. An example of this is the *Japan Trench*. Label the examples of *transform boundary plates, sea-floor spreading,* and *subduction* below. The fourth kind of plate movement is *colliding plate boundaries*. This occurs when two plates ram directly into one another. This causes the crust to buckle and bump up, forming mountain ranges such as the *Himalayas*.

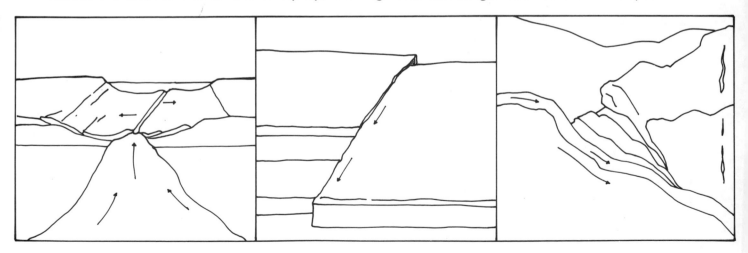

1. _____   2. _____   3. _____

1. As the plates of the crust move and shift over the surface of the earth, they form new mountains and valleys. What else is caused by the movement of these plates? (Hint: Think of Alaska in 1964, California in 1971, and Mexico City in 1985.) _____

2. The crust is of two types, continental and oceanic. The continental crust, composed largely of light rocks such as granite, is thicker, with a range of between 12 and 40 miles in thickness. The thinner oceanic crust is composed primarily of basalt and ranges in thickness from 3 to 6.8 miles. Basalt is a dark, fine-grained rock which has been formed from molten rock or *magma*. The layers of rock on the continental crust contain the best record of the earth's history. Inside different layers of rock are the fossil records of all the living things that have inhabited this earth. There are fossil records of palm trees in Great Britain, marine life in Kansas, and glaciers in Brazil, as well as whale bones on mountain tops! What would these fossil records tell you about life in Great Britain, Kansas, and Brazil thousands of years ago? _____

   _____

   _____

3. How is that different from life in those places today? Have there been climate changes? What other changes have occurred?_____

   _____

   _____

4. The Grand Canyon is one of the geological wonders of our world. This enormous canyon, which is approximately one mile deep, from 4 to 18 miles wide, and 280 miles long, was caused by erosion from the Colorado River over a period of roughly ten million years. The canyon contains the fossil records of all the life that has existed in that region over that period of time. The walls of the canyon contain bands of rock in different colors, depending on the type. At the bottom is blackish *schist*, a very heavy, old rock. About halfway up are layers of sandstone (white and brown) and shale with many fossils of ferns, insects, and prehistoric frogs. Above this is a pale, sandy layer of desert-like sand and then a limestone layer full of marine snails, sponges, and corals. What does this tell us about that area and its geologic history? _____

   _____

Name _____

Earthquake Zones

Most earthquakes occur along one of two main belts, the *Ring of Fire* and the *Alpine belt*. The Ring of Fire runs from Japan and the East Indies up through the Aleutian Islands to Alaska and southward through California to Mexico and South America. This belt or *fault* occurs where the American and Pacific continental plates meet on the east and the Pacific and Eurasian and Australian plates meet on the west. Mark this circle in red on the map below. The Alpine belt runs from Spain through the Mediterranean to Turkey and from there through the Himalayas to the East Indies. This fault line occurs where the African and Indian plates are bumping against the Eurasian plate. Mark this belt in blue on the map below. Crustal plates are named for the continents or oceans located on their surfaces. Label the unmarked plates on the map below. Use a library reference source to help you find these plates: Eurasian, Pacific, Australian, African, South American, North American, and Antarctic.

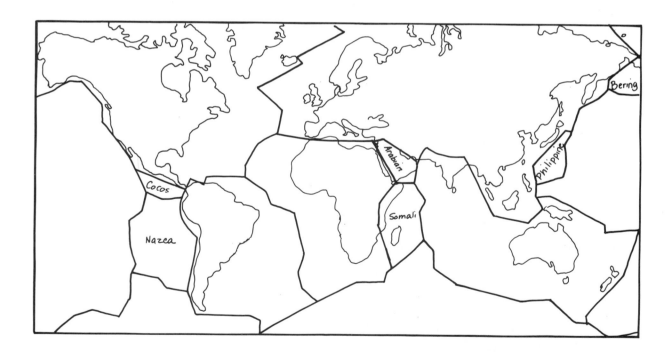

Volcanoes

Volcanoes form when *magma,* hot, molten rock from under the surface of the earth, bubbles out between *tectonic plates* or through *hot spots,* which are weak areas in the earth's surface. The magma is contained in a *magma chamber.* The pressure builds in this magma chamber as the temperature rises, and the weaker areas of rock above the chamber allow the magma to rise. When the pressure builds to a certain point, the surface can no longer contain it, and the magma spews forth, erupting on the surface. When the magma flows out to the surface of the earth, it is called *lava.* Volcanoes can remain *dormant* or inactive for hundreds or thousands of years and then erupt violently. Label the magma chamber, the magma, and the lava in the diagram below.

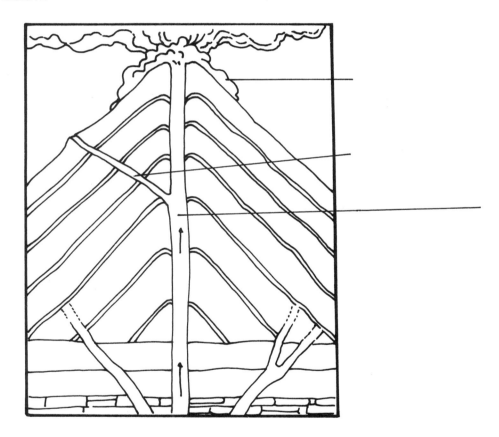

Like earthquakes, volcanoes occur at tectonic plate boundaries. The Ring of Fire is one of the main sites of volcanic activity, but other plate boundaries are equally likely sites of volcanoes, some active and some dormant.

Name _____

Locate each recently active volcano site by placing its number (on the left) and a star on the world map below:

Location	**Date of Recent Activity**
1. Tanzania	1993
2. Zaire	1992
3. Ross Island, Antarctica	1990
4. Heard Island, Antarctica	1986
5. South Shetland Island, Antarctica	1970
6. Japan	1993
7. Indonesia	1993
8. Philippines	1993
9. Russia	1993
10. Costa Rica	1994
11. Guatemala	1994
12. Costa Rica	1992
13. Italy	1994
14. Iceland	1991
15. Alaska	1994
16. Hawaii	1993
17. Washington	1991
18. Mexico	1991
19. Indonesia	1994
20. Papua New Guinea	1993
21. New Zealand	1992
22. Colombia	1993
23. Ecuador	1993
24. Argentina	1992
25. Chile	1992

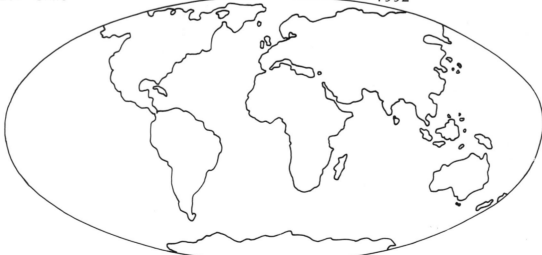

Compare the marks you have made on the map above to the map of the tectonic plates on page 66. How do the marks compare? What are the marks near? _____

Hot Vents, Geysers, and Hot Springs

Hot vents are basically undersea volcanoes. They are also called *smokers,* because clouds of black or white precipitated minerals billow up from them. This mineral-rich seawater is home to many organisms, all of them adapted to the extremely hot environment, where temperatures range up to 750 degrees Fahrenheit and the pressure can be almost 300 times that of the air pressure on earth's surface. High-temperature bacteria such as *Pyrococcus furiosus,* large mussels, tube worms over a meter long, and red-bodied clams inhabit this world. These organisms are adapted to a world that would crush a more fragile organism and instantly hard boil an egg. In the illustration below, label the organisms that would live around a hot vent.

Geysers are also associated with volcanic activity. Geysers are natural hot springs that periodically spout hot water and steam from cracks or weak spots in the earth. A geyser has a narrow *feeding tube* near the surface. Below the surface are wider *branches.* The tube starts off filled with water. The branches are surrounded by hot rock and the water in them heats first. The bubbling hot water works its way upward, building pressure until it explodes out of the feeding tube in a jet of water. Much of this water cools and drains back into the feeding tube to start the process again. Most *hot springs* are also found near active volcanoes. They are formed when magma is pushed up near the surface of the earth and heats the ground water. Iceland has many hot springs and geysers. Label the *feeding tube* and *branches* in the diagram on the right.

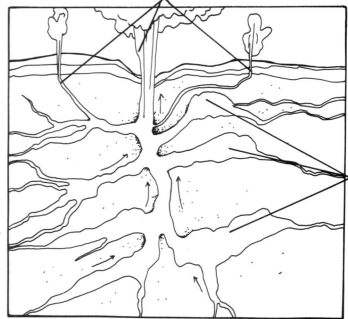

Glaciers

Glaciers are huge rivers and sheets of ice which cover the poles and the tops of the highest mountains. These mounds of ice are more than two miles thick in some places, and they make up three quarters of the earth's fresh water supply. If all the glaciers of the world melted, the sea level would rise 200 feet and New York, Paris, and London would be under water, along with hundreds of other seaside towns and cities. Three percent of Alaska is composed of glaciers, some of them rising to 10,000 feet in towering mountains of ice.

Glaciers are formed when more snow falls in winter than melts in summer. The snowflakes at the bottom are squashed down by the weight of the snow on top and are compressed into a denser snow, then granules of ice, and finally a rock-hard mass of solid ice. This mass of ice starts to slide on the surface of the earth below it. Most glaciers move only a couple of inches a day, but, in 1966, Mount Steele in the Yukon was moving at the rate of two feet an hour. As the glaciers move, they carve U-shaped valleys. As the glaciers melted in some areas, they left water trapped behind in the valleys. The Great Lakes in the United States and the Lake District in Britain were formed this way. Mark an "X" by the land formations below which were caused by glaciers.

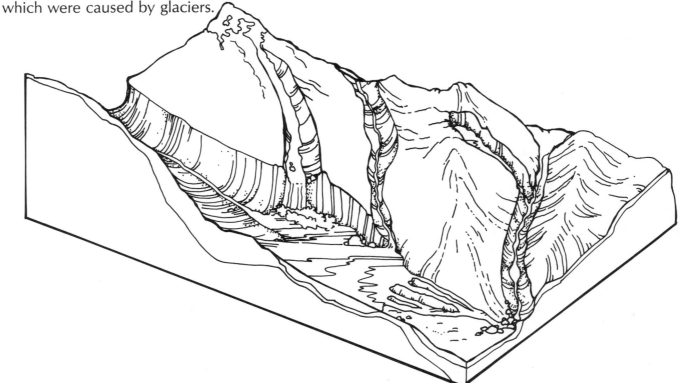

Glaciers increase during an Ice Age when the temperature over the earth is colder than usual. A temperature drop of between 7 and 21 degrees Fahrenheit is enough to bring on an *ice age*. This has happened at least 20 times over the last 2.5 million years. What could cause this to happen again? _____

Name _____

Waves, Tides, and Tsunamis

Waves are caused by the wind blowing on the surface of the water, movement of animals and objects in the water, earthquakes, the gravitational force of the sun and the moon, and other disturbances of the surface and body of the water. Ocean waves at sea tend to remain lower and the water itself does not move with the wave; it simply rises and falls as the waves pass by. The wave rises as it approaches the shore because it meets the hard surface of the land, which does not yield to the force of the wave. Test this for yourself.

Materials

a large, shallow
   baking pan
a brick
water
a small cork

Procedure:

1. Place the brick at one end of the baking pan. Fill the pan half full of water. Place the cork in the water at the end opposite the brick.

2. Use the palm of your hand to gently push the surface of the water toward the brick from the opposite end of the pan. Keep the cork between your hand and the brick and be careful not to hit the cork.

Observations:

1. What did the "wave" do when it met the brick? _____

2. Did the cork move closer to the brick? _____
_____

The entire surface of the earth is affected by the gravitational force from the moon and the sun, but it is particularly noticeable in the oceans, where the pull of these two bodies causes *tides.* You can observe tide marks along the shoreline, where the periodic rise and fall of the ocean leaves its mark. The moon has the greatest effect on the tides because it is closest to earth. The size of the tide varies, because the distance of the moon from the earth varies. When the moon is closer, the tides are higher. The solid part of the earth pulls away from the ocean at the same time that the gravity of the moon pulls the water outward, causing high tides on opposite sides of the world at the same time. The water rushes in to fill the spaces, causing low tides on the other two sides of the earth.

Kinton

The sun exerts less than half as much gravitational pull as the moon, but when they are aligned on the same side of the earth, their combined effect produces what is called the *spring tide,* an exceptionally high tide which occurs twice a year, at the spring and fall equinoxes. Lower tides are called *neap tides,* and they occur approximately 15 days later, when the sun and the moon are on opposite sides of the earth. Label the spring and neap tides in the diagram below.

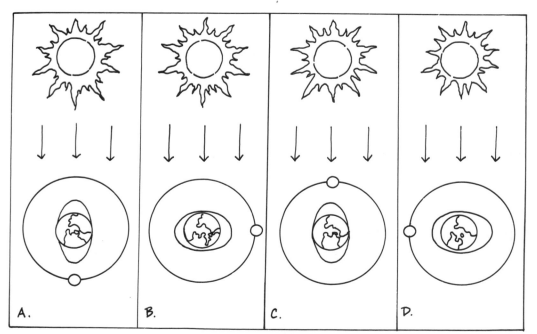

A.   B.   C.   D.

Tsunamis are named for the Japanese words for harbor (*tsu*) and wave (*nami*). These waves are often called tidal waves, although tides do not cause or influence them in any way. These waves are caused by volcanic eruptions or earthquakes which push against the nearby water with a massive force. The wave of a tsunami is deceptive at sea, because it is low and long. The height of the tsunami comes when it hits land. The land does not move with the wave and instead forces it upward, sometimes to a height of 200 feet. This huge wave can be moving at speeds of 150 miles per hour, making it a major destructive force. Perform the following experiment outdoors, in a bathtub, or in an area where spilled water will not damage anything.

Materials

a large, clear glass
  baking pan
water

Procedure:

1. Fill the pan half full of water.

2. Gently push against the surface of the water at one end of the baking pan. Allow the surface of the water to become still. Then repeat this step but give one firm shove to the surface of the water. How are the waves different from the first time?

_____

_____

Deserts

We think of deserts as blistering hot stretches of open sand. Actually, deserts are simply dry places with little vegetation. The Great Basin Desert, which occupies part of Nevada, Utah, and Oregon, is a relatively cold desert. In the hot deserts, such as the Mojave, Sonoran, and Chihuahuan deserts, the days are scorchingly hot but the nights are cool. Animals hide in the shade or in dark holes underground until the sun goes down and then they come out. Sagebrush is the primary vegetation of the cool Great Basin Desert, but the hotter deserts have the cactus, mesquite, and creosote bush, all of which are specially adapted to the hot desert habitat. Many plants, like the California poppies, remain dormant during times of drought and then spring into bloom after a rain. Use your library resources to help you identify the plants and animals of a desert habitat in the illustration below and answer the questions. You will find a *sidewinder snake*, a *kangaroo rat*, a *Joshua tree*, the *cactus wren*, a *giant saguaro cactus*, a *prickly pear*, and a *century plant*.

1. Which of the plants above provides a fruit eaten by humans? _____

2. Which of these plants usually grows 50 feet or taller and absorbs up to a ton of water during the rainy season, causing it to swell to twice its width? _____

3. Which of the animals lives on seeds and receives enough water from the seeds so that it never needs to drink water? _____

Stalactites and Stalagmites

Many areas of the world have large deposits of a mineral called *calcite*. Calcite or $CaCO_3$ is a component of marble, chalk, pearls, coral reefs, and seashells and is also the main mineral in *limestone*. Calcite does not dissolve in pure water, but it will dissolve in slightly acidic water or water which contains carbon dioxide. Rainwater and surface water which flow underground through limestone deposits dissolve the calcite, producing what is known as *"hard water."* Hard water is water which contains calcium or magnesium deposits. This water does not react well with soap and forms a scum. It affects the cleaning ability of detergents. In addition, the calcium leaves a crust on pots and pans and hot water tanks when the water is heated.

If the limestone deposit is deep underground, the water dissolves the calcite and leaves a cave. As ground water continues to seep through the remaining limestone deposit and into the cave, the water containing the calcite drips down one drop at a time from the roof of the cave. As it comes through the roof of the cave, it forms a tiny, ring-shaped deposit which gradually lengthens into a tube that forms a huge icicle shape made of calcite. This formation is called a *stalactite*. Sometimes the dripping water hits the floor of the cave, and the water evaporates, leaving a calcium deposit. As drop after drop falls in this same place, a formation that looks like an upside-down icicle is created. This formation, which is attached to the floor of the cave, is called a *stalagmite*. If the two meet, they form a *column*. Stalactites and stalagmites grow at different rates. Some grow an inch a year; some grow one inch every century. Although the natural color of calcite is white, other minerals or impurities may color it red, yellow, or black. Label the stalactites, the stalagmites, and the columns in the illustration.

Rocks, Minerals, and Crystals

A *crystal* is formed when the atomic structure of a substance is arranged in an orderly manner. Crystals have a certain shape defined by the kind of elements the material contains. Crystals come in one of seven basic shapes. The shapes and an example of each shape are shown below. Use the illustrations to answer the questions below.

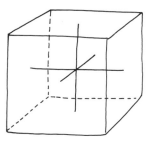
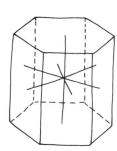
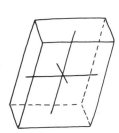

Cubic   Hexagonal   Monoclinic

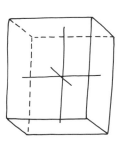
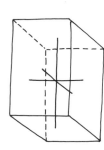
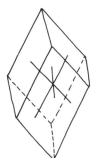
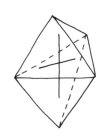

Orthorhombic   Tetragonal   Triclinic   Trigonal

1. What shape are tetragonal crystals? _____

_____

2. Classify the crystals shown below. What shapes are these crystals? _____

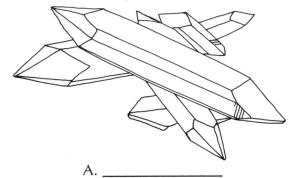
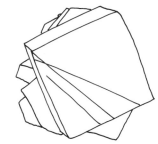
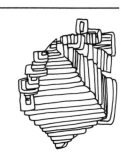

A. _____   B. _____   C. _____

Name _____

A *mineral* is a naturally forming, usually inorganic crystalline substance which has characteristic physical and chemical properties that conform to its composition and structure. Minerals have these physical properties:

Cleavage - A mineral tends to break in certain directions along a smooth surface.
Color - Minerals have characteristic colors that differentiate them from other minerals.
Crystal shape - Minerals have a special shape according to the type of crystal.
Fracture - Fracture is the way a mineral breaks when it does not have cleavage.
Hardness - Minerals have a certain hardness depending on the kind of mineral. They can be scratched by harder minerals, but not by softer minerals.
Specific gravity - Specific gravity is the weight of a certain mineral by unit of volume. If the mineral weighs more, it has a higher specific gravity.
Streak- Streak is the color a mineral has when it is ground to a powder.
Striations - Striations are thin lines or bands that run across the surface of some minerals.

For Research: Use your library resources or other resources to learn how to identify minerals using the Moh's Hardness Test, the streak test, and other tests to classify minerals.

Rocks are *aggregates* of minerals or groups of different minerals bonded together. *Igneous* rocks are the most common rocks; they make up 95 percent of the earth's crust. Igneous rocks are formed from the magma from volcanoes. They are classified based on their texture and their mineral composition. Less than 5 percent of the earth's crust is made of *sedimentary* rock, although about 75 percent of the top land surface of the earth is made of sedimentary rock. These rocks form from hardened layers of sediment which have been eroded from other rocks. *Metamorphic* rocks are rocks that are formed from other rocks which have been changed by great heat or pressure. Label the pictures below to show which depicts the formation of each kind of rock: igneous, sedimentary, or metamorphic.

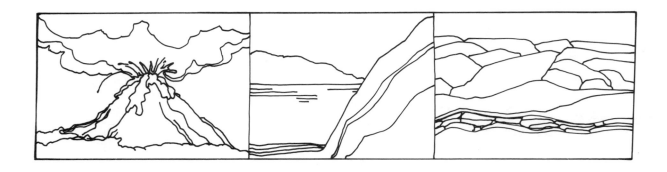

1. _____   2. _____   3. _____

Name _____

Water

Over 70 percent of the earth's surface is covered with water. Water is a very special and unique substance. Water molecules are attracted to each other and, when water comes in contact with air, a "skin" forms on the water. This is called *surface tension*. This surface tension makes a single drop of water pull together into a spherical shape. Test this property.

Materials

water
an eyedropper
a magnifying glass
a piece of dark
  plastic

Procedure:

1. Use the eyedropper to drop water onto the plastic.

2. Observe the drops through the magnifying glass.

3. What shape are the drops? _____

4. Try to flatten the drops. Will they stay flattened? _____

_____

This surface tension makes it possible to float things in water, even if they are actually heavier than the water.

Materials

a glass of water
a clean, steel
  needle
small piece of
  paper towel

Procedure:

1. Drop the needle into the glass of water, point first. Does it float? _____

_____

2. Take the needle out of the water and carefully place the piece of paper towel on the surface of the water with the needle on top of the paper towel. What happens? _____

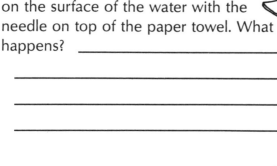

_____

_____

_____

This surface tension causes water to cling to the side of a container. In a container that is not quite full, the water molecules cling more on the sides than in the middle, so the shape of the surface of the water is concave. In a completely full glass of water, the water bumps up in the middle, forming a convex, "bubble" shape. The water actually sticks up slightly above the rim of the glass. The concave shape is difficult to see in the partially full glass, but you can easily see the convex shape in a very full glass.

Materials

water
3 oz. or 5 oz.
  plastic cup

Procedure:

1. Place the cup on a level surface and fill it with water to the very brim.

2. View the top of the cup exactly at eye level as shown in the illustration to the right. What do you see?

   _____

   _____

Water is also interesting because, unlike many materials, it is lighter and larger when it is a solid. The molecules in water form a very rigid crystalline structure with more space between each molecule as a solid than as a liquid. This allows more empty space between each molecule and makes the water occupy more space as a solid than as a liquid, as shown in the diagrams below.

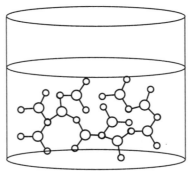 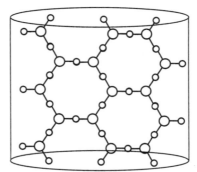

3. Does ice float or sink in a glass of water? ____ Why? _____

   _____

   _____

Tornadoes and Hurricanes

Tornadoes and hurricanes are both the result of extremely strong winds circling around an area of very low pressure. The difference between the two is size and wind speed. Tornadoes are usually 300 feet or less in diameter. Hurricanes may be 300 miles in diameter. Wind speeds in a tornado may top 360 miles per hour. Hurricane winds do not usually exceed 120 miles per hour.

Hurricanes start out as *tropical depressions* or *tropical storms*. Tropical depressions have sustained winds of less than 39 miles per hour. Tropical storms have wind speeds that range from 39 to 74 miles per hour. When the wind speed exceeds 74 miles per hour, the storm becomes classified as a *hurricane*.

Hurricanes gain their strength from warm, moist air, which they must to keep their strength. They form over tropical oceans in the summer when the sun heats enormous masses of air. As the hot air rises, it spirals, and as it rises higher and more hot air rises to join it, it gains power and speed. Most of a hurricane's destructive power is from its winds, although heavy rains from a hurricane can cause flooding.

1. Why do you think hurricanes usually lose their strength as they move inland? _____

_____

Even though tornadoes are much smaller than most storms, their impact can be deadly. Tornadoes usually affect only an area from ⅛ of a mile to a mile wide and two to five miles long. The air pressure in the center of a tornado is considerably lower than the pressure outside the tornado. When the tornado strikes, it can cause the pressure in an area to drop up to 10 percent in a few seconds. This sudden drop in pressure causes buildings to explode. The rapidly rising hot air, swirling in a circular motion, also pulls loose items upward.

Meteorologists can predict hurricane paths much earlier and much more accurately than tornado paths because of the size, speed, and duration of the storm. For this reason, hurricane warnings are usually quite accurate. When a *tornado warning* is issued, this means that a tornado has been sighted. When the meteorologist simply thinks a tornado may form, he or she issues a *tornado watch*. Which is more dangerous?

2. _____

Name _____

Lightning

Lightning contains an enormous amount of electricity. One bolt of lightning contains enough electric energy to supply the power for one small town for one year! Lightning starts inside a cloud where air currents toss ice crystals and water droplets around so hard that they knock electrons off on one another's atoms as they collide. The droplets that lose the electrons become positively charged. The extra electrons fall to the bottom of the cloud and accumulate, building up a *charge* or electrical potential of about 300,000 volts per foot. Lightning neutralizes this charge by allowing the electrons to flow back to the positively charged droplets or crystals.

If two adjacent clouds have opposite charges, the lightning jumps from cloud to cloud. If not, the lightning jumps from cloud to ground. Lightning always seeks the best *conductor* to reach the ground, such as a lightning rod, a tall building, or a tall tree.

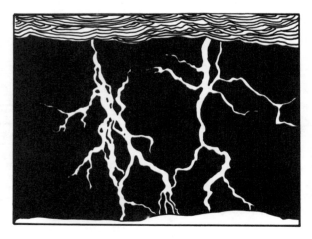

1. Why is it a bad idea to stand under a tree in a thunderstorm? _____

   _____

2. Would it be better to stand out in an open field in a thunderstorm? Why or why not? _____

   _____

3. Is a car a safe place to be in a thunderstorm? Why or why not? _____

_____

When lightning strikes sandy ground, the heat of the bolt of lightning actually melts the sand. When it cools, it fuses together into a root-like lump called a *fulgurite*.

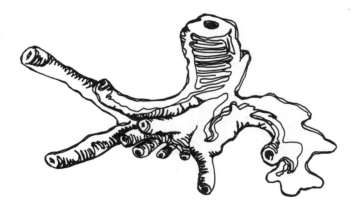

Auroras and Sunspots

The *aurora borealis* or northern lights and the *aurora australis* or southern lights are colorful, shimmering lights which occur at various times of the year at their respective poles. The colors vary from a grayish color, to green, to bright red and multicolored ribbons of light. They occur most frequently during times of heavy *sunspot activity.*

Sunspots are cooler regions on the sun's surface which appear as *dark spots.* These dark spots usually last a few days and have temperatures of approximately 6,700 degrees F instead of the customary 9,750 degrees F of the rest of the *photosphere,* which is the visible surface of the sun. Usually, when these sunspots occur, the surface of the sun also has *solar flares,* which are great bursts of energy that spew particles and radiation out into space. These particles and radiation are what cause the auroras on earth.

The aurora borealis is often visible in the lower 48 states, although it is brightest in Alaska and near the pole. Sunspots, however, may be observed from anywhere on the globe. **DO NOT EVER look directly at the sun or its reflection in a mirror. The light from the sun can damage your eyes without your even being aware of it.** Instead, use this device to observe sunspots.

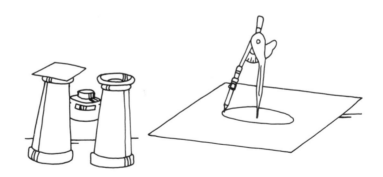

Materials
binoculars
3" square of black
  paper
typing paper
pencil
compass

Procedure:

1. Cover one lens of the binoculars with the black paper.

2. Draw a circle three inches in diameter on the typing paper.

3. Do not look directly at the sun, but hold the binoculars so that the light from the sun shines through the open lens and is reflected onto the circle on the paper. Move the binoculars and the paper until the image fills the circle. Trace the dark spots and marks you see on the paper. These are sunspots.

The universe is unimaginably immense. We can see only our sun, moon, solar system, and a small percentage of the stars in the universe with our naked eyes. Much more lies within the scope of large telescopes such as Hubble and Mount Palomar, but even they do not give us a view of everything in the universe. More is being discovered as we send space probes and satellites into outer space. What lies beyond our solar system and galaxy can only be guessed at; it is the fuel for science fantasy and the frontier for scientific investigation.

The first enigma concerning space is how it was formed. How did our sun and solar system come into being? One theory is the "Big Bang" theory. This was suggested in 1930 by Georges Lemaître, a Belgian scientist. His theory stated that all the matter in the universe was contained in one primal atom and that this "atom" exploded about ten billion years ago into many fragments. These fragments became the galaxies which moved away from the source of the explosion at a rapid rate and are still moving outward today.

A second theory was proposed by three British scientists in 1948. These three scientists, Hermann Bondi, Thomas Gold, and Fred Hoyle, said that the explanation was the "Steady State" theory. They said that the universe is eternal and has always existed. Matter is created from nothing and forms new galaxies to fill in the spaces created as old galaxies spread farther apart.

In 1965, the American scientist Allan Sandage developed the "Pulsating Universe" theory, which is an adaptation of the "Big Bang" theory. He suggested that the universe is created, destroyed, and recreated in cycles. Each cycle lasts about eighty billion years. First the universe expands, then it contracts. When it has contracted fully, it explodes and starts to expand again. Another name for this theory or model of the universe is the *oscillating universe*.

Study the diagram below and label each part with the appropriate theory.

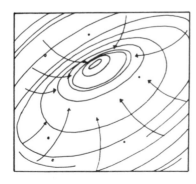 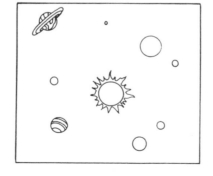 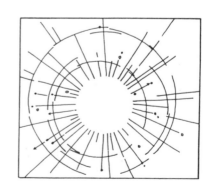

1. _____ 2. _____ 3. _____

The universe is spreading out and galaxies do seem to be pulling away from one another. Several other explanations have been advanced to explain what has happened and what will happen. The *open universe* model suggests that the universe is expanding infinitely. The galaxies, stars, and planets will all grow farther and farther apart. The *closed universe* theory states that the universe is expanding but at some point gravity will take over and cause the universe to collapse. The *balanced universe* theory says that the force of expansion and the force of gravity are equal and eventually the universe will just stop expanding. The *inflationary universe theory* states that the universe will keep expanding or it will stop expanding, depending on whether there is "dark matter." This dark matter is a special kind of matter which keeps the universe from expanding. Dark matter consists of dead stars, black holes, and unknown particles. This matter is so dense and has such incredible gravitational force that not even light can escape from it, hence the name "dark matter." Study the models below and then label each with the correct theory.

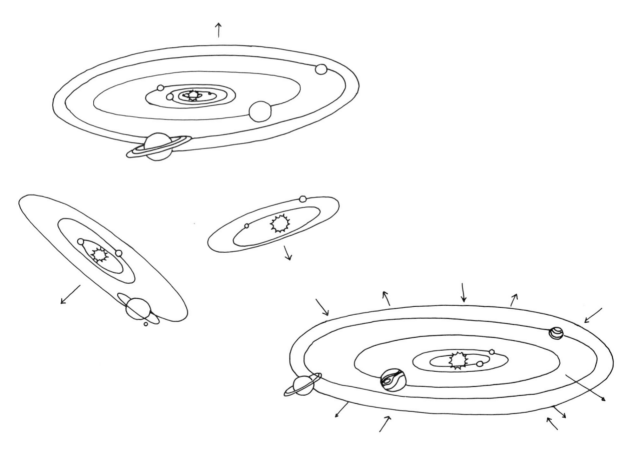

What is your theory of how the universe came into being? _____

_____

_____

Aliens and UFOs

Many people believe that the existence of life on other planets is possible. Evidence suggests that many of the stars in our galaxy and in other galaxies might have orbiting planets similar to our own. If these planets have conditions similar to earth, they could support life.

People have been seeing strange things in the sky since the dawn of recorded time. Ezekiel, the Biblical prophet, reported seeing a large bronze vessel with four human-like beings. In A.D. 747 a huge, flame-breathing dragon and airships were seen in China. In A.D. 900 three men and a woman supposedly exited a spaceship in Lyon, France. In 1561 over 200 UFOs were sighted in Nuremberg, Germany. In 1666 villagers in Robozero, Russia, saw a strange, fiery ball in the sky as they came out of church in the middle of the day.

The modern era of UFOs began with Kenneth Arnold's sighting of nine silver-colored, crescent- or saucer-shaped objects flying at a high speed over the Cascade Range in Washington on June 24, 1947. Kenneth Arnold was a trained pilot and his report of the sighting has never been explained. After his report, many other people began to come forward with accounts of aliens and spacecraft. Some of the aliens and UFOs that people have described are illustrated above.

In response to citizen concern, the military set up Project Sign on January 22, 1948. Its name was changed to Project Grudge and then Project Blue Book before it was finally phased out in December 1969. This project investigated approximately 15,000 cases of UFO sightings, many by military personnel. Many were explained scientifically, and the few which were not explained were lacking the data to make any accurate conclusions. Currently, the French group, GEPAN, is the only government-funded group of UFO investigators in the world. Their name in English means "Study Group into Novel Atmospheric or Aerospatial Phenomena." The group is based at the Space Center in Toulouse, France, and only investigates cases that are recommended to them by the police. Very few of their cases remain unexplained.

Dr. J. Allen Hynek, who died in 1986, was one of the founding fathers of ufology. His group, the CUFOS (the J. Allen Hynek Center for UFO Studies) and the group MUFON (Mutual UFO Network) are two responsible groups which take a scientific, investigative approach to reported sightings.

What is your opinion of UFOs and aliens? Do you believe in them? Why or why not? _____

_____

_____

Many UFOs may be the result of seeing unusual cloud formations such as those shown below. Lenticular or "lens-shaped" clouds and oddly shaped cumulus and altocumulus clouds may resemble a person's vision of a spacecraft. At night, beaded, ribbon, or ball lightning might easily be confused with a UFO. Color the backgrounds in the pictures below blue or black to help you see the image more clearly. Leave the cloud and lightning shapes a bright white.

Comets

Most comets are discovered not by professional astronomers, but by amateurs, ordinary people watching the sky through binoculars, small telescopes, or with their naked eyes. There are two reasons for this. First, professional astronomers are often viewing the sky through large telescopes which are not as easy to move as small telescopes and binoculars. Astronomers are often concentrating on one section of the sky and miss the rest of the view. Second, there are very few professional astronomers and many amateurs. In addition, comets such as Hale-Bopp are more spectacular when viewed through binoculars. The large telescopes enlarge the image and make it look blurred and fuzzy compared to the bright, sharp image of the binoculars. An English woman named Caroline Herschel discovered eight comets during the period of years from 1786 to 1797!

Comets are usually named for the people who discover them. The Hale-Bopp comet was discovered on July 23, 1995, by two separate people at the same time. The two men who discovered the comet were Alan Hale and Thomas Bopp. Hale was looking through his own small telescope in his driveway in New Mexico when he sighted the comet. Bopp was using a friend's telescope at an astronomy club meeting in Arizona. They both reported their findings to an observatory to register their discovery and, since they discovered it at the same time, the comet was named for both of them. Halley's comet is not named for its discoverer, but for the English astronomer, Edmund Halley. This comet had been returning to earth for thousands of years, and he was the first to realize that it was the same comet returning at regular, predictable intervals.

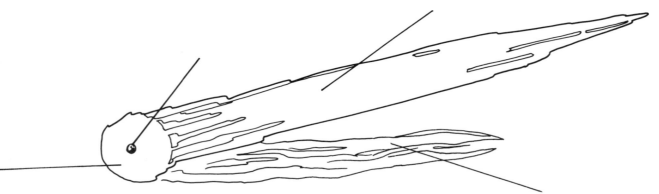

Use the information in the paragraph below to help you color and label the diagram above.

A comet is a frozen mixture of ice, dust, gases, and rocks. The *nucleus,* or core, is frozen and may be from one mile to twenty-five miles wide. The *coma* which surrounds the nucleus looks like a cloud or halo and is formed of dust and frozen water particles. The *tail* extends out from the coma. It is a gaseous cloud of frozen particles. The tail always blows away from the sun because of the solar wind (gases which blow outward from the sun). This means that when the comet passes by the sun, the tail is in front of the comet, not behind it. The tail has two parts. One part is the yellow *dust tail,* which is made of tiny dust particles which shine yellow in the sunlight. The *gas tail* is made of electrified atoms or ions from the coma. Some of them are carbon monoxide atoms which glow with a blue color.

1. There are about 800 comets whose orbits are known. The comets fly by the sun with a frequency called the *period* of the comet. The comet Encke has the smallest orbit and the shortest period, a mere 3.3 years. How long does it take Encke to circle the sun?

   _____

2. Kohoutek has one of the longest orbits. It was last seen in 1974 and may not return to earth for a million years or more. Halley has a period of 75 to 76 years. It was last seen in 1985 and 1986. When will it return? _____

As the comets loop out past the sun, they return to the *Oort Cloud,* a huge region of perhaps some 100 billion or more comets and pieces of comets. This is the origin of the comets we see. The force of gravity from a passing star snatches a comet out of this cloud and starts it on its elliptical orbit around the sun. Some comets stay in this orbit; others are flung out into deep space.

3. Look at the diagram of the orbits of the comets shown below. Which comets have the shortest periods? _____

4. Which comets have the longest periods? _____

   _____

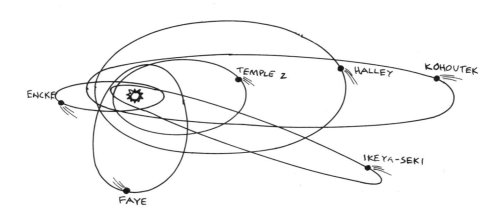

Name _____

Meteoroids, Meteors, and Meteorites

Meteoroids, meteors, and meteorites are all names for pieces of comets. *Meteoroids* are pieces of a comet that have broken off its nucleus and are still orbiting the sun. *Meteors* are meteoroids that have entered earth's atmosphere. Large meteors are called *bolides*. Bolides sometimes make a hissing, crackling sound as they enter the atmosphere. Exceptionally bright meteors are called *fireballs. Meteorites* are meteors that have actually landed on earth. Meteor Crater in Arizona, which would more accurately be named Meteorite Crater, is the impact crater or depression left when a very large meteorite crashed into the earth about 22,000 years ago. It would have hit the earth at a speed of approximately 30,000 miles per hour and produced an explosion as powerful as half a million tons of TNT. Any living things would have died instantly from the force of the explosion and the heat, and trees would have been flattened for miles around. The meteorite which formed this crater is buried deep in the walls of the crater.

Sometimes the meteorite is small and imbeds itself on the surface of the earth. Meteorites are made of either iron (siderites) or rock (aerolites) or both iron and rock (siderolites).

In the twentieth century, only two large meteorites have been recorded and both fell in uninhabited parts of Siberia. One fell in 1908 in the region known as Tunguska. When expeditions reached the site years later, they observed that the pine trees had been flattened to the ground in a large radius. The second meteorite fell in 1947 in the region of Vladivostok. This meteorite broke apart as it descended.

1. Will meteorites hit the earth again? _____

2. What could happen if a meteorite struck a populated area? _____

Asteroids

Asteroids are the planets that never were. They are lumps of rock and metal that orbit the sun between Mars and Jupiter. There are tens of thousands of them, but all the known asteroids lumped together would not be as big as the moon. They are pitted with craters and are usually not spherical, because they bump into each other so much. Asteroids are named by their discoverers. One honors Queen Victoria of England; another is named after the mythical Icarus. The largest asteroid is Ceres, measuring 500 miles in diameter. Most of the asteroids are much smaller. The difference between an asteroid and a meteor is primarily size. Asteroids are larger.

Most of the asteroids move in the wide gap between the orbits of Mars and Jupiter and keep to strict orbits of their own. Some of the asteroids move in orbits far outside this zone. The Trojans move in the same orbit as Jupiter, either following or preceding the planet in its trip around the sun. Some of the asteroids are inside the orbit of Mars. Eros is a sausage-shaped asteroid, 18 miles long by nine miles wide, which came within 15,000,000 miles of Earth in 1975. Apollo crossed the orbit of both Mars and Earth. Hermes came closest to us in 1937. It passed by at a distance of 485,000 miles, or twice the distance to the moon, away from us.

If one of these asteroids collided with us as has happened in the past, it would cause major damage. An asteroid the size of Apollo would create 100-foot tidal waves if it landed in the ocean. If an Apollo-sized asteroid landed on a continent, it would leave a crater at least 12 miles across and the impact would cause damage for miles around that. The impact of a really large asteroid would have the effect of 20,000 megaton hydrogen bombs all exploding at once. Scientists think that an asteroid collision like this may have wiped out the dinosaurs.

How could we protect ourselves from one of these unwelcome visitors? _____

_____

_____

_____

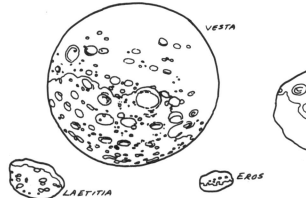
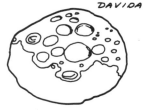

Stars

Stars are grouped by their size, color, and brightness. There are four main classes of stars: stars of much smaller mass than our sun, stars of about equal mass to our sun, stars of much larger mass than our sun, and super giant stars with relatively short lives. These stars have different surface temperatures, different luminosity, and different *absolute magnitudes*. The absolute magnitude is the apparent magnitude that a star would have if it were seen from a standard distance of 32.6 light years.

The smallest stars are of Class I and are between ⅟₁₆ and ⅟₁₀₀ the size of our sun. These stars condense into a ball of hot gases from the force of gravity, but they never become hot enough for a nuclear reaction to occur in the core. These stars heat to a temperature of 10,000,000 degrees Celsius. If they do not reach this temperature, they glow feebly and then die out to a cold, dead mass.

Our sun is a Class II star. The core temperature rose high enough to support nuclear reactions using the huge amounts of hydrogen in its core as fuel. As the hydrogen "burns," it becomes helium. Our star is a *Main Sequence* star.

Ejnar Hertzsprung of Denmark and Henry Norris Russell of the United Stated devised the Hertzsprung-Russell Diagram, which is a way of comparing stars by their luminosity and their spectral types. The classes of stellar spectra are designated by letters of the alphabet: O, B, A, F, G, K, and M. O, B, and A stars are the hottest and have a white or bluish color, F and G stars are yellow, K stars are orange, and M stars are red. M stars are the coolest. Use the diagram below to help you answer the questions on the next page.

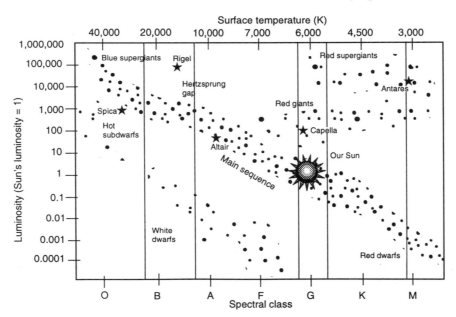

Name _____

1. What color is the star Antares? _____

2. What color is the star Spica? _____

3. Is Rigel more or less luminous than the sun? _____

4. Which star is closest in absolute magnitude and luminosity to the sun? _____

A star's supply of hydrogen eventually burns out and the helium core which is left shrinks and heats up again. The outer shell still contains enough hydrogen to burn again, with the stable helium core. The star expands, squeezing the core to the point where the helium reacts. The helium nuclei combine to make carbon and oxygen. Energy pours out and the surface cools to what is called a *Red Giant.*

When the helium is used up, the star shrinks again and the temperature rises again. The carbon-and-oxygen core remains inert, but the outer shell of hydrogen and the inner shell of helium both react. The star starts to pulsate and finally both rings are thrown off, leaving a core and a ring of gas. This is known as a *planetary nebula.* The ring Nebula in Lyra and the crab Nebula in Taurus are planetary nebulas. The star's core is very small, very dense, and very bright and is called a *White Dwarf.*

Circular-shaped *planetary nebulas* are just one kind of nebula. *Emission* nebulas are a mass of dust, gas, and ionized gases that give off their own light. The Lagoon Nebula in Sagittarius is an emission nebula. The material in this nebula glows because of an exceptionally bright star known as 9 Sagittarii which is inside it. Dark nebulas are made of opaque dust and gas that often hide the star behind them from view. *Reflective* nebulas are a collection of dust and gas that reflect light from nearby stars.

The Orion Nebula is visible to the naked eye, though a pair of binoculars will give an even better view. It is located in the Hunter's sword close to the three bright stars of the Belt. It can be seen from every inhabited continent. It is officially known as M42, because it was the 42nd object listed in the catalog of clusters and nebula made by the eighteenth-century French astronomer, Charles Messier. Use the diagram to the right to help you locate the constellation on a clear night.

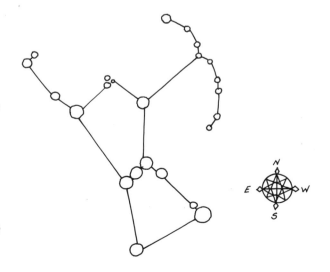

Pulsars

Pulsars are thought to be rotating *neutron stars*. A neutron star is much heavier and has a much higher density than the White Dwarf star. It starts out following the pattern of other stars, shrinking and becoming unstable, then burning. In a neutron star, this process happens much more quickly and the temperature climbs much higher to a toasty 700 million degrees Celsius. At this temperature, the carbon and oxygen in the core react and form silicon. The star keeps heating and, at 3,000 million degrees Celsius, the silicon reacts and forms iron. Iron will not burn and the pressure in the core increases. Finally, the star implodes or pulls inward (the opposite of an explosion) and releases masses of energy and then explodes. At this point, the protons and electrons smash together in the core to form neutrons. Neutron stars have very powerful magnetic fields, so radio waves can escape only at the poles. In this last stage, some neutron stars spin very rapidly and this causes them to emit regular bursts or pulses of radio waves from their poles. This is a *pulsar*.

Dr. Jocelyn Bell-Burnell found the first pulsar by using a radio telescope. A team of astronomers at Steward Observatory visually located a pulsar in the Crab Nebula in November of 1968. This pulsar releases radiation in all wavelengths. The Vela Pulsar is the second pulsar to be detected by eyesight. Most pulsars are detected by radio telescopes. The Vela Pulsar appears as a tiny, faint speck which flashes at the rate of thirty times a second because it is spinning so rapidly. The pulses emitted by these stars are very regular and rapid.

At first, when people heard that radio waves were being sent from outer space, they worried about aliens, but the scientists who studied pulsars quickly dismissed that notion. They were certain that the emissions were not being produced by alien life forms. Why do you think they came to this conclusion even before they sighted a pulsar? (Hint: When people type or move keys on a keyboard, how regular and fast is the rhythm?) _____

_____

The illustration below shows how a pulsar emits its radiation pulses.

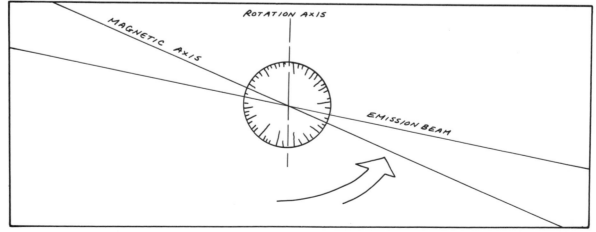

The Inner Planets

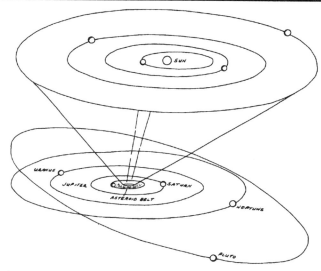

Mercury, Venus, Earth, and Mars are the four *inner planets,* circling closest to the sun. They orbit much closer to the sun and much closer to each other than the outer planets do. If you made a diagram of the planets' orbits and made Pluto's orbit the size of a bicycle tire, Mars would have to have an orbit the size of a quarter to be to scale, and the other three planet orbits would fit inside that. Label the four inner planets on the diagram above.

The four inner planets are also much smaller than the outer planets, with the exception of Pluto. Earth is the largest of the four and Mercury is the smallest. Earth is almost equal in size to the other three planets and the moon all together. Because of this, Mercury, Mars, and Venus have less gravitational force than Earth. Venus' gravity is about 90 percent of Earth's, but Mercury and Mars have only about ⅓ as much gravity. That means that a person would weigh only ⅓ as much on Mercury or Mars.

1. How much would a hundred-pound person weigh on Venus? _____

   _____

2. How much would a hundred-pound person weigh on Mercury or Mars? _____

   _____

Mercury is the innermost planet, circling within 285,000,000 miles of the sun, and it circles the sun about 1½ times more rapidly than Earth. That, combined with the fact that it is much closer to the sun, gives Mars a year that is only 88 Earth days long. A person who is fifteen years old on Earth would be 62 years old on Mercury! It rotates more slowly on its axis, however, so one day on Mercury is as long as six months on Earth. This means that the temperature on Mercury's surface jumps from extreme cold of almost 300 degrees below zero Fahrenheit to an incredibly warm 800 degrees Fahrenheit. Mercury's temperatures are in the Earth temperature range for only a short period in the mid-morning and another short period in the middle of the afternoon.

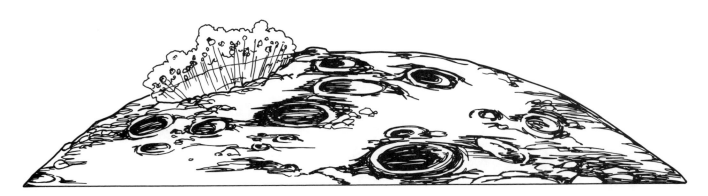

Mercury has a magnetic field and may have some gases drawn from the sun because of this magnetism, but it has no true atmosphere. On Earth the thick atmosphere blocks out some of the sun's radiation, keeping the days cooler than they would be otherwise. The same atmosphere acts as insulation, keeping the warmth in at night. Mercury's thin covering of gas does not block out the sun's radiation, making the side that is facing the sun even hotter. Mercury rotates so slowly that the shaded side of the planet is in the dark for many days, and it cools off rapidly without an atmosphere for insulation.

Mercury has steep, rocky cliffs and lumpy plains formed by volcanic lava. The planet's rocky surface is pockmarked with craters ranging in size from 100 yards to holes the size of Texas. These craters were formed early in the history of Mercury, when the planets were being formed and rock fragments such as those now found in asteroid belts were bombarding the planets. Large chunks of this rocky material crashed on the surface of Mercury, making the surface material and some of the bedrock of Mercury fly up in the air from the impact. Some of the material which spewed out was smaller and white in color and formed powdery-looking rays around the crater. These craters are called *rayed craters*. As the large chunks of rock came back to Earth, they made secondary craters.

3. What problems would face a manned spaceship trying to land on Mercury? What would an astronaut need to have to walk on the planet Mercury? _____

_____

4. What problems would we face in building a space colony on Mercury?_____

_____

Venus is the second planet from the sun. It is almost the same size and density as Earth, and it was once thought to be a paradise of lush vegetation and sparkling water. Venus in fact is more of a nightmare. Thick, yellow clouds of poisonous sulfuric acid swirl across the face of the planet, pushed by winds faster than our worst hurricanes. These clouds never produce rain, but lightning and thunder fill the eerie sky day and night. The carbon dioxide atmosphere under this canopy is so thick that you could almost swim in it.

Venus orbits the sun in an almost perfect circle, the only planet to do so. The other planets' orbits are elliptical. To see the difference in these shapes, follow the instructions below.

Materials

a sheet of thick,
  corrugated cardboard
two thin nails
a pencil
12 inches of string
2 sheets of paper

Procedure:

1. Place one sheet of paper on top of the cardboard. Stick one nail through the center of the paper so that it is fastened to the cardboard.

2. Tie the ends of the string together to form a loop and slip the loop over the nail. Insert the pencil inside the opposite side of the loop and pull the loop taut. Keeping the loop tight, draw a circle around the nail. Hold the nail steady for support if necessary.

3. Remove the paper and replace it with the clean sheet of paper. Stick the nail through the center of this second sheet of paper, nailing it to the cardboard as you did in step one. Stick the second nail in the cardboard about 3 inches below the first nail.

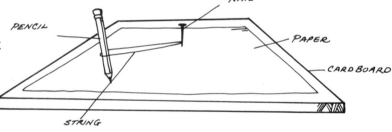

4. Loop the string around both nails and insert the pencil. Again, pull the string taut and draw the shape that forms as you pull the pencil around both nails.

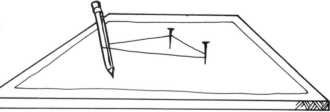

On the first sheet of paper, you have drawn a circle. On the second sheet of paper, you have an ellipse.

Mars is the fourth planet from the sun. Its red color comes from rustlike dust which covers its surface. Violent winds sometimes whip this dust into a huge cloud. Mars had a very active geological past. Its surface is dotted with volcanoes. Three large volcanoes line up north to south near the equator to form the Tharsis Montes. Nearby is one even larger volcano named Olympus Mons. These volcanoes are two times larger than the island of Hawaii and twice as high as the distance from the sea floor to the top of Hawaii's highest peak. The surface of Mars is dotted with craters. To the east of the Tharsis Montes is a long system of canyons which in places is four times deeper than the Grand Canyon. In addition, Mars is crisscrossed with dried-up stream channels.

A day on Mars is almost the same length as a day on Earth—24 hours and 37 minutes—but each Martian year lasts 687 Earth days. Two small moons fly around Mars. Deimos, the larger of the two, orbits about once every 30 hours, but tiny Phobos orbits every 8 hours. This means Phobos rises and sets twice a day.

Mars does have water, but most of it is frozen in the ground and at the polar caps. Much of the "ice" at the poles is frozen carbon dioxide or "dry ice." Mars has a carbon dioxide atmosphere. The force of gravity on Mars is about ⅓ that of Earth, because Mars has only 1/10 as much mass as Earth and only ⅔ its density. Its interior is rocky, not metallic like Earth's, and the rocks are much less dense.

1. Could Mars support life? Explain your position using the information above to support your argument. _____

   _____

2. Would Mars make a good space colony? Explain your answer. _____

   _____

The Outer Planets

The four inner planets are all *terrestrial* or earth-like, with metal cores covered with a rocky crust. All but Mercury have thin atmospheres. (Mercury has no atmosphere.) The first four of the *outer planets* are the *gas giants*. They are huge balls of gas with thick atmospheres which condense to liquid surfaces and rocky cores. Pluto is the exception. It is the smallest planet and seems to be primarily a ball of ice. Pluto has one moon and Neptune has two, but Uranus, Jupiter, and Saturn have many moons, including some very large moons, much larger than ours.

Jupiter is the largest planet, a whopping 318 times the mass of Earth. It contains ⅔ of the matter in our solar system outside of the sun. It circles the sun much more slowly than Earth, with a year that is equal to 11.86 Earth years. It revolves faster than any other planet, however, giving it a short day, only 9 hours and 55 minutes. It has sixteen moons, Ganymede being the largest.

The most prominent feature on Jupiter is its *Great Red Spot.* This spot is actually a storm, like a fierce hurricane, that has been going non-stop for at least 300 years. Locate this spot on the illustration below and color it bright red. Most of Jupiter is made of hot, liquid hydrogen. Other gases, including methane, water vapor, and ammonia, swirl in the thick atmosphere. These gases give Jupiter a mixture of colors ranging from cream and yellow to deep orange and rust. Color the swirling patterns around the Great Red Spot these colors. The three oval spots below the Great Red Spot are storm areas. Leave them a bright white.

The top atmosphere of Jupiter crackles with huge bolts of lightning. This area is cold with icy clouds, but the liquid surface may be more than 1,000 degrees Celsius. This is so hot that the hydrogen near Jupiter's surface acts like molten metal and sets up electrical currents. These currents may give Jupiter its tremendous magnetic force. When Jupiter's moon, Io, moves through this magnetic field, it sets up an incredibly strong electrical current equal to the current flowing through five million 100-watt light bulbs. This electrical current is gradually wearing away Io's surface.

Jupiter's atmosphere is made up primarily of hydrogen with some helium (about 10%) and traces of methane, water, and ammonia. Jupiter probably does not have a solid crust but, beneath the swirling clouds of dense gas and molten hydrogen, there may be an earth-sized ball of rock and ice. Since temperatures near the surface are high, they may both be liquids.

Icy particles make a wide ring around Saturn. The ring is less than 100 meters thick, but it stretches about 73,300 kilometers out from the planet. Saturn's gases are the least dense of the gas giants; in fact, Saturn would float if you could put it in water. Only Jupiter is larger than Saturn. It rotates rapidly, giving it a 10-hour and 39-minute day, but, like Jupiter, it has a long orbit, giving it a year equal to 29.46 Earth years.

Saturn has at least 17 moons. (*Voyager* uncovered evidence of others.) The outermost moon, Phoebe, revolves backwards around the planet. Saturn's fourteenth moon, Titan, is the largest moon and has a thick atmosphere. It may be the most earthlike body in the solar system. Larger than the planet Mercury, it is about twice as dense as water, and scientists think it is about half ice and half rock and metal. Ethane lakes probably cover the region around the equator. The top atmosphere is a combination of methane and nitrogen and the lower atmosphere is primarily nitrogen, like Earth's. The planet is very similar to the early years in Earth's history with one difference: surface temperatures on Titan are a frigid 180 degrees below zero Celsius. Find Phoebe and Titan on the diagram below and label them.

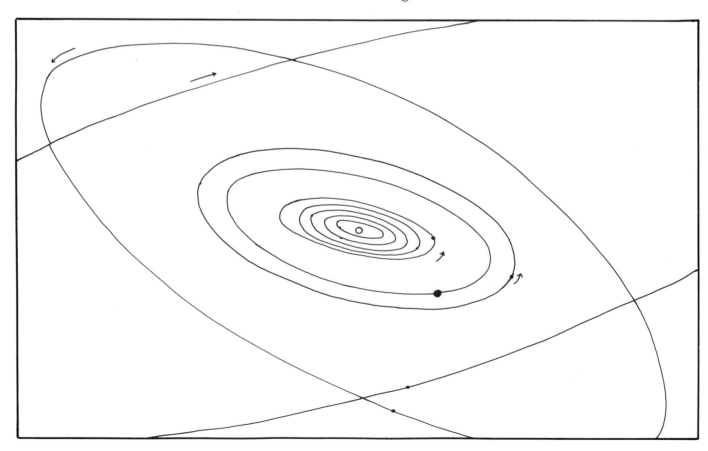

Uranus is nineteen times as far away from the sun as Earth is. It has a year equivalent to 84 Earth years and a 17.3-hour day. Uranus is tipped sideways on its axis, so one pole is in constant sunlight for 42 years and then, as the planet shifts around the sun, the other pole is in sunlight for 42 years. Briefly, at these change points, both poles experience day and night. Because of this tilt, the rings at the equator of Uranus are perpendicular to its orbit, making the giant blue-green planet look as if it has fallen on its side. These rings are made of chunks and boulders a meter wide or larger. The rocks are coal black, making them hard to spot with a telescope.

Methane in the upper atmosphere gives Uranus its color, but the atmosphere below is mainly hydrogen with a little helium. The thick atmosphere cools slowly, so the dark side is as warm as the light side. Below the frigid upper atmosphere, the inner part of the planet is about 7,000 degrees Celsius, possibly even hotter than the sun! The winds on Uranus are fierce. At about 70 kilometers per hour, they blow approximately four times the speed of high-altitude winds on Earth.

Uranus has at least 15 moons, with five of them visible from Earth. Ten of the moons were discovered by *Voyager* as it passed by the planet. Miranda, the smallest and innermost moon, is the most interesting. It has craters, deep valleys, high ridges, and canyons ten times deeper than the Grand Canyon. The next moon, Ariel, has scars that look like those left by ancient glaciers on Earth. The third moon is Umbriel, with a bright circular spot which scientists call the "fluorescent Cheerio." Titania is the largest of the moons of Uranus. It is split with long fissures which have jagged edges, as if frost had formed from material which had splashed out of the fissures and frozen. The outermost moon is Oberon. Its surface is dotted with craters and one huge mountain. All of the moons except Umbriel have whitish markings. Label the two major moons in the illustration below.

A.

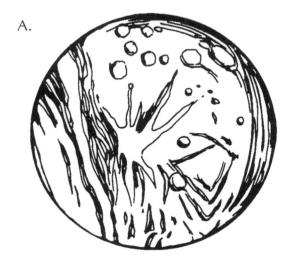

B.

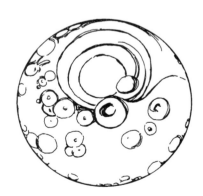

Neptune is 4,504,000,000 kilometers from the sun and takes 165 Earth years to orbit it. It has a 17-hour and 50-minute day. It has seventeen times the mass of Earth and is one and a half times as dense as water. Neptune has two moons and both of them are unusual. Tiny Nereid is only 200 kilometers wide and takes one Earth year to complete a very elliptical orbit. Triton is a giant, even larger than our moon, and circles Neptune in six days—traveling backwards! Neptune, like Saturn and Jupiter, gives off more heat than it receives from the sun. Neptune and Uranus are considered twin planets because they are similar in size, density, mass, and rotation. They are both very similar to Saturn and Jupiter except in size.

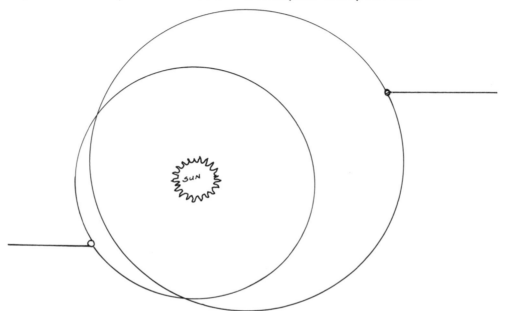

Pluto is the oddball. Pluto and its moon Charon are the farthest from the sun. Pluto follows the most elliptical orbit of the planets, ranging from 4,400,000,000 to 7,400,000,000 kilometers from the sun. From 1979 to 1999, Pluto is closer to the sun than Neptune. Label Neptune and Pluto in the diagram above. Pluto takes 248 Earth years to orbit the sun. When was it last in this position of being closer to the sun than Neptune? _____

Pluto's moon, Charon, is almost half as big as its planet and only 19,640 kilometers away from it. In comparison, our moon is 384,000 kilometers away and Earth is 81 times larger. Pluto seems to be an iceball of frozen gases with little or no atmosphere, and the temperature on its surface is near *absolute zero,* the point at which molecules stop moving.

Are there any other planets? Possibly. Some astronomers think that Pluto is an escaped moon of Neptune. There may be a tenth planet hiding out beyond the viewing range of telescopes. So far, there is no concrete evidence to support this theory, but no telescopes or cameras have traveled to all the limits of the solar system yet. There may be more worlds to discover, and there are many things we have yet to learn about the worlds we have discovered.

Engineering Feats and Great Inventions

People are builders and inventors. Since the beginning of time, we have records of different tools and utensils that humans have made. The cavemen made spears, axes, knives, and other simple tools to assist them in daily life. As their knowledge grew, the tools and instruments became more complex and larger—men built boats and chariots and buildings. Some of the inventions were practical and gave people solutions to simple problems, such as using a bucket to draw water from a well. Other inventions were more fanciful, such as the hand mirror to show a person's reflection. Some of the inventions were great successes. The bow and arrow survived through centuries of use in different cultures because this was a successful way to launch a sharp object toward a target. The first slot machine was invented by the Greek scientist, Hero, in the first century after Christ. His invention was actually a holy water

dispenser for the temple. Parishioners fed a coin into the slot at the top and it slid down a chute to the end of a bar that moved like a seesaw. The coin pushed the bar down, which lifted the stopper at the other end of the seesaw and allowed a few drops of water to run down the drain hole. We use a very similar machine for dispensing candy, gum, and other products. Draw arrows in the diagram below to show the path of the coin and the movement of the "seesaw."

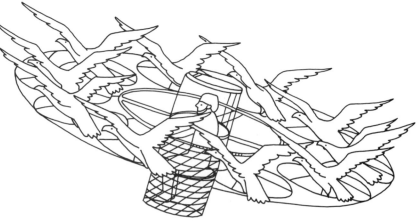

Other inventions were less successful. Greek mythology gives us the myth of Icarus, who made wax-and-feather wings so that he might fly to the heavens. According to the myth, the heat of the sun melted the wax and he fell back to earth and his death. In 1865 a creative person designed a flying machine powered by ten eagles. The eagles were supposed to be harnessed to frames around a cage which held the human passenger. There is no record of this design having flown.

Name _____

Gliders

A German named Otto Lilienthal made some of the first successful gliders, starting in 1891. His gliders were graceful, bird-like things with scalloped wings and tailpieces. He made more than 2,000 successful flights of up to 250 yards. In 1896, his last glider fell sideways to the ground, killing him.

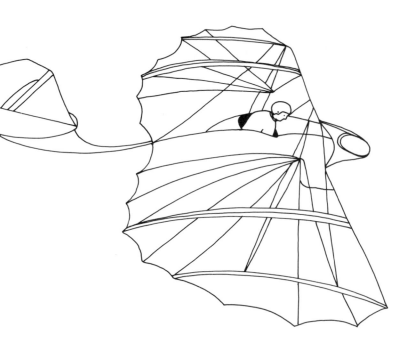

Gliders are still popular. Gliders are lightweight and require no fuel. They are held up by air currents and are guided by the shifting weight of the rider. The modern hang glider is a descendent of Lilienthal's earlier craft. To see for yourself how gliders work, fold the airplane shapes shown below. Test the different shapes to see which works best. Attach paper clips to the underbody of each craft.

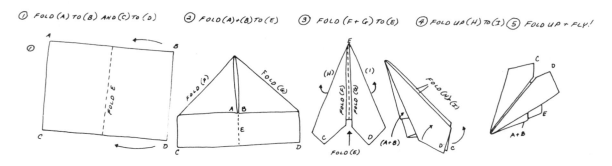

① FOLD (A) TO (B) AND (C) TO (D)   ② FOLD (A) + (B) TO (E)   ③ FOLD (F + G) TO (E)   ④ FOLD UP (H) TO (I) ⑤ FOLD UP + FLY!

1. Which can carry the heaviest load?_____

2. Which flies the farthest? _____

Helicopters

Helicopters can fly straight up, forward, backward, or hover in space. Air flowing over the rotor blades causes a low pressure area above the blades and a high pressure area under the blades, pushing the helicopter up. To see how a helicopter functions, try this experiment.

Materials
short pencil with an eraser
a thumbtack
posterboard
scissors
string

Procedure:

1. Using the pattern at the right, cut a rotor from the posterboard.

2. Attach the rotor to the eraser end of the pencil, using the thumbtack to hold it in place as shown in the diagram (A).

3. Wrap 36 inches of string around the pencil, leaving one end of the string free (B).

4. Stand the pencil on its pointed end and pull the string like a top (C). What happens? _____

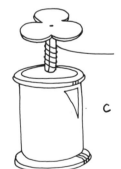

The Pyramids

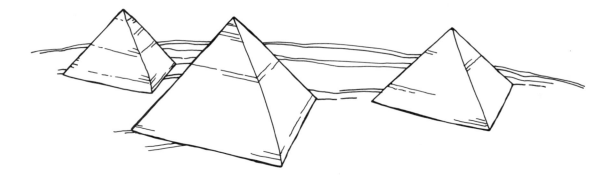

The pyramids of Egypt were built over 5,000 years ago without the use of cranes or any of the heavy equipment we take for granted. The people who built the pyramids relied on manual labor and ingenuity to construct these wonders out of huge blocks of stone. The Great Pyramid of Cheops was built around 2,700 B.C. It stands 42 stories high and covers 13 acres at the base. It contains enough stone to build a ten-foot-high wall around the entire country of France.

To construct this wonder, the Egyptians first had to have level land. They didn't have a modern level instrument, so they cut channels in the rocky ground and filled them with water. They cut the surface rock down to the level of the water in the channels to make it all level.

It took 20 years to build this pyramid, and they used 2½ million rocks weighing between 2½ and 15 tons each. These enormous blocks were cut, moved, and raised into position using only a lever, a roller, and an inclined plane. The finished corners of this pyramid are almost precise right angles and each face of the pyramid faces a compass point: north, south, east, or west.

What were these tools and how did the Egyptians use them?

LEVER

Materials
a ruler
a fist-sized rock
3 heavy books

Procedure:

1. Pile the books in a stack and try to lift them with one finger. How easy is it? _____

2. Place one end of the ruler under the stack of books. Place the rock under the ruler. Press down on the other end of the ruler. Can you lift the books more easily now? _____

_____

_____

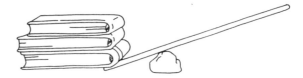

3. Repeat this experiment using a different length of ruler or yardstick. Does changing the length make a difference?_____

_____

_____

4. Move the rock nearer to or farther from the end of the ruler. Does this make a difference? _____

_____

_____

ROLLER

Materials
5 smooth, round pencils
3 heavy books

Procedure:

1. Place the books in a stack on a flat surface and try to push the stack with one finger. Are the books easy to move?_____

_____

2. Place the five pencils side by side, an inch apart. Place the stack of books on top of the pencils. Push the stack with one finger. How easy is it to move the books? Is it easier than before? _____

_____

_____

The Inclined Plane

An inclined plane is a ramp. A slide on a playground and a stairway are both inclined planes. The Egyptians used the inclined plane or ramp to slide the massive blocks up to the proper level on the pyramid. As they finished each layer, they built the ramp higher and longer, so that the building dimensions remained constant.

Materials
a long board
an assistant
a cardboard box
  filled with heavy
  items such as
  bricks or books

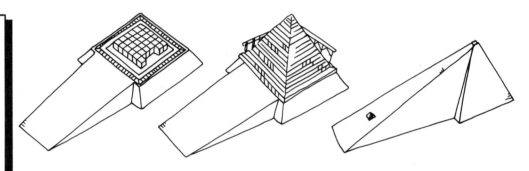

Procedure:

1. Lift the carton off the ground using only one hand. Is this easy to do? _____

   _____

2. Place one end of the board on a chair or large rock so it tilts at an angle.

3. Place the cardboard box at the lower end of the board. Push it up the board with one hand. Is this easier than lifting it with one hand? _____

   _____

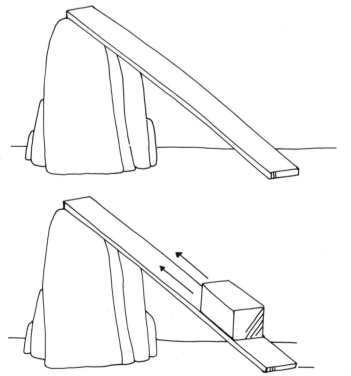

The Giant Lady

Ancient peoples built many large statues to honor their leaders, their heroes, their gods, or their nation. The Colossus of Rhodes stood a mighty 105 feet tall, guarding the harbor of the ancient Greek island of Rhodes. In 292 B.C., an earthquake toppled the statue and it lay in fragments until A.D. 672, when people carted pieces of the bronze away to sell for scrap metal. The Roman Emperor Nero was extremely impressed with his own importance and commissioned a sculpture of himself by the sculptor Zenodorus. When it was finished, the sculpture of Nero measured 106 feet tall from top to bottom.

The beautiful Statue of Liberty, whose official title is "Liberty Enlightening the World," stands a stately 151 feet and 1 inch tall. She is outclassed in the height division by a statue to the "Motherland" which stands on Mamayev Hill outside Volgograd in Russia. It was designed by Yevgeyi Vuchetich in memory of the Battle of Stalingrad and stands a lofty 270 feet tall from the base to the tip of the sword in her right hand.

What sort of difficulties do sculptors have making these statues? To find out for yourself, try this experiment. Use potter's clay from a ceramics supplier, not modeling clay for this experiment, because you need clay that will dry out and harden. If you are successful with your statue, take it to someone with a ceramics kiln and have it fired so you can keep it permanently.

Materials
clay
newspaper

Procedure:
Build a statue of the clay as tall and elaborate as possible. You may make something realistic or totally abstract, but it must be one piece and it must be able to stand alone. Do not have thick chunks of clay, but hollow out the inside and stuff it with newspaper. Leave an opening so the piece can dry and will not explode if you have it fired. Wad the newspaper and use it to brace your sculpture until it dries. Have at least one piece of your sculpture extend from the main body of the piece. Example: a person's hand sticking up in the air or an elephant's trunk extending out to the front.

What difficulties did you encounter? _____.

Name _____

Architect's Dream

People have constructed some remarkable pieces of architecture. The immense cathedrals of medieval Europe were built by stonemasons, bricklayers, and carpenters using the type of tools used in ancient Rome. Some of these tools are illustrated below. How many of them are still in use today? _____

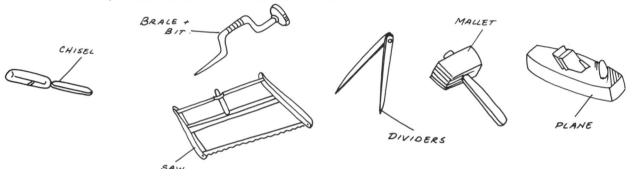

CHISEL

BRACE + BIT

SAW

DIVIDERS

MALLET

PLANE

In the 1800s, engineers and architects discovered that much larger, airier, and stronger buildings could be constructed of steel and concrete. In addition, many of the pieces for these buildings could be constructed off site or *prefabricated* and then brought to the site and assembled. This meant that buildings could be built much more quickly. The Eiffel Tower is 1,000 feet high and weighs 7,000 tons. It was constructed in less than two years (1887-1889).

Sometimes an architect's dream is hard to execute. The Sidney Opera House in Sydney, Australia, was designed by Danish architect, JØrn Utzon in the 1950s but was not finished until 1973, after 15 years of work and at a cost of 100 million dollars. The sail-like roofs of this remarkable building are made of concrete arches and ribs covered with concrete panels, which were covered with white tile.

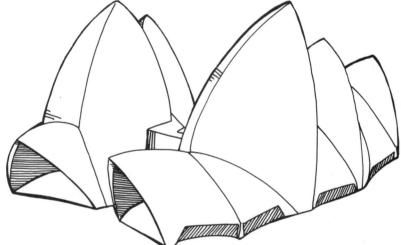

Buildings such as these and tall skyscrapers do not simply sit on the surface of the ground. They have heavy, strong, and often deep *foundations*. The foundations are often made of *piles* or posts sometimes hammered or drilled as deep as 200 feet in the ground. What does a foundation do? Why would a tall building need a deep foundation? _____

Building Bridges

Ancient peoples built bridges from logs and ropes to span rivers so they could cross. The Romans built massive stone arches and created some of the most durable roads ever built. Some of them still survive and are still in use. The use of steel and steel-reinforced concrete made it possible to build longer and stronger bridges.

Bridges come in three basic types or shapes: *beam, arch,* and *suspension.* A *beam* bridge is a straight, log-shape. It is supported from below with posts or *pillars.* An *arch* bridge may have one or many arches. The arch shape is very strong as long as the ends of the arch are anchored so that it cannot move. A *suspension* bridge is hung from tall towers by steel cables. Label the different kinds of bridges shown in diagrams A-C below.

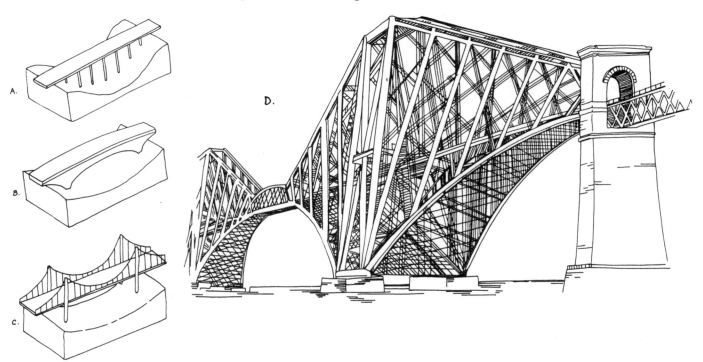

A.

B.

C.

D.

A bridge must be strong and able to support its own weight and the weight of whatever traffic is crossing over it. It also must be able to withstand the stress of high winds. Cable bridges can carry huge loads, and arch bridges are extremely strong. Illustration D, above, shows the steel girder cantilever design of the bridge across the Firth of Forth in Scotland. This bridge carries a railroad. How does it combine features of both the arch and the suspension bridge?

_____

_____

Name _____

Expansion

One of the problems engineers have to deal with when they are constructing a bridge is expansion. A bridge can be three feet longer in summer than in winter. Why is this so?

To test your theory, try this experiment.

Materials

a 12"-long copper wire
a short, votive candle
masking tape
two bricks
a ruler

Procedure:

1. Suspend the wire between the two bricks with the candle under the center of the wire as shown in the diagram.

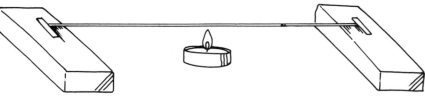

2. Mark the ends of the wire with masking tape.

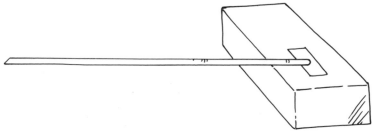

3. Light the candle and observe the ends of the wire as the wire heats up. DO NOT LEAVE THE CANDLE UNATTENDED. BLOW THE CANDLE OUT AS SOON AS YOU FINISH THE EXPERIMENT.

Observations and conclusions:

1. What happens to the wire as it heats up? _____

_____

2. Why do bridges expand in summer?_____

_____

The Shape of a Dam

Like bridges, dams have been being built for thousands of years. Over 5,000 years ago, ancient peoples were building dams to control river flooding. Today, dams are used to create water reservoirs, harness water for energy, and to control the flow of a river.

There are two basic types of dams: *embankment* and *concrete*. *Embankment* dams are made of earth and rock and have a thin concrete covering. An embankment dam is the largest and cheapest kind of dam. It is made from massive mounds of earth and the concrete shell holds this earth in place. The highest dams are embankment dams.

Concrete dams may be either *arch* dams or *gravity* dams. A gravity dam is simply a straight piece of concrete which holds back the water. It is braced between the two sides of a river. The arch dam is a curved concrete shell which pushes the river so that the weight of the river pushes against the banks of the river instead of against the dam.

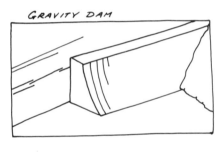

GRAVITY DAM

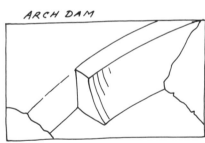

ARCH DAM

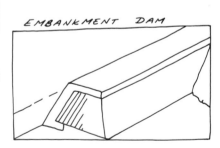

EMBANKMENT DAM

Materials

a foil bread-baking pan
water
modeling clay
two paper cups

Procedure :

1. Cut the bottom off of one paper cup and slit the top at the side seam to flatten it into a trapezoid as shown below.

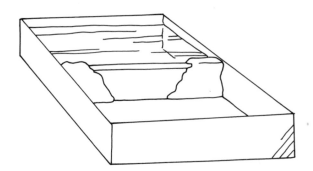

2. Anchor the trapezoid shape between layers of clay so that it forms a dam across one end of the baking pan as shown above. Fill the space behind the "dam" with water. What happens? _____

3. Remove the "dam."

4. Cut the second paper cup in half as shown in the diagram below.

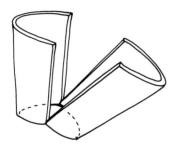

5. Use modeling clay to anchor the second paper cup half between one end of the baking pan as shown in the diagram below. Fill the space behind the "dam" with water. What happens? _____
    _____

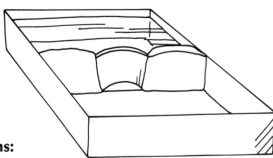

Observations and conclusions:

1. Which kind of dam can hold back more water? _____

2. Which kind of dam is stronger? _____

Name _____

Winning Idea

Often, times of crisis bring out the most creative ideas and solutions to problems. World War II was just such a crisis for the Allied forces. Hitler had won many victories in the early years of the war. One particular prize eluded him—the island of Britain. The British forces were weak compared to the German forces, but the English Channel was a major barrier. The Allies faced an even stronger barrier when they decided to launch the reverse attack in 1944 on the coast of Normandy. They had to face the fierce channel and land their troops and reinforcements in heavily fortified harbors. Since the Allies did not have a harbor, they decided to make one to take with them. The code name for this harbor was "Mulberry." Mulberry was a series of floating ramps, concrete-and-steel pontoons, breakwaters, and jetties. The Allies took two Mulberries with them to Normandy. The total length of these portable "harbors" was seven miles. Each harbor weighed 750,000 tons. Sixty ships were positioned to block the harbor from enemy attack and then were scuttled to make an outer harbor wall.

In the first six days of the invasion, which began on June 6, 1944, the Allies landed over 300,000 men, 54,000 vehicles, and more than 100,000 tons of supplies on the coast of France. On June 19 a storm destroyed the American Mulberry and damaged the British one, but the British one was soon restored and the Americans used it to capture Cherbourg.

1. Why did the Allies need to make the Mulberries out of heavy material such as concrete and steel? _____

   _____

2. Why did they need to make them so large and long? _____

Name _____

Ultrasound

Sound travels in waves. Sound waves are very similar to water waves in their behavior. What happens when a water wave bumps into a flat surface?

Procedure:

1. Place the pan of water on a flat, level surface and let it sit until the surface is quiet and unmoving.

2. Gently push the surface of the water at one end of the pan toward the other end of the pan so it forms one wave. Watch the wave closely.

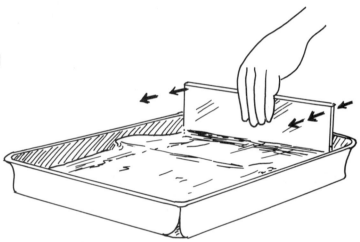

Observations:

What does the wave do when it hits the other side of the pan?

_____

_____

Some sounds are too high for us to hear. Ultrasound is a very high-frequency sound used for SONAR, or *Sound Navigation and Ranging,* to help ships locate schools of fish or underwater obstacles. Ultrasound has other uses as well. It is used in the medical profession to make a scan or picture of an unborn baby. Ultrasound is used in industry to detect faults in metal parts. The ultrasound bounces off faults in the metal and can show where breaks are likely to occur. To do this, a transmitter sends a wave of sound toward the object. A receiver or detector records the echoes as the wave is bounced back. Ultrasound has one other interesting use. Ultrasound waves vibrate very quickly, up to 20,000 vibrations per second. They can make the material they bounce against vibrate as well. If the ultrasound beam is focused on one point, it can make the material vibrate so fast that it heats up. Ultrasound can be used this way to weld plastic parts together.

Microphones, Amplifiers, and Tape Recorders

A *microphone* has a thin, conical-shaped piece of metal or cardboard inside it. This object is called the *cone*. As sound waves from a person or instrument bounce against this cone, it vibrates. This vibration is passed to a moving coil, which moves when the cone moves. The coil is near a magnet and, as it moves in the magnetic field, it sets up a current. The current is passed through a wire to an amplifier, which works exactly opposite to a microphone.

The *amplifier* takes the current through a coil which is near another electromagnet. As the coil passes the magnet, it vibrates. The coil is attached to a cone and, as it vibrates, it makes the cone vibrate.

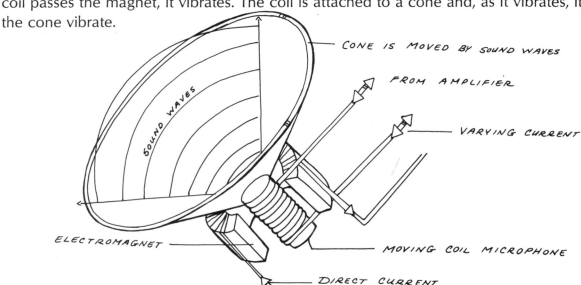

To see how sound makes something vibrate, perform this experiment.

Materials
a surgical glove
a thick rubber band
pepper
scissors
a tin can

Procedure:

1. Cut the fingers off the glove and slit the glove up the side on the thumb side.

2. Spread the glove over the open end of the can and pull it tight. Secure it with the rubber band to make a tight "drum head."

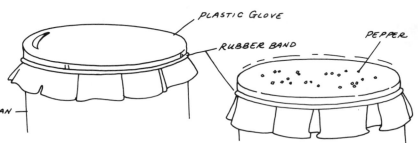

3. Sprinkle pepper on the "drum head."

4. Tap the side of the can to make a ringing sound. Observe the pepper closely. What happens? _____

_____

Observe the vibrations of sound in other things. Place your hand on the body of a guitar and strum it with the other hand. Place your hand on your throat and hum.

A *tape recorder* takes the electrical signals from the amplifier and sends them to the record/play head. This consists of coils of wire wrapped around a core of metal with a small space cut in it. The space is for the tape to pass through.

The signals from the amplifier set up a magnetic field in the space. The tape is a thin, plastic ribbon covered with magnetic particles. As the particles pass by the head, the magnetic field aligns them in a pattern that represents the original sound. To play the recorded sound back, the tape passes back through the gap and the pattern makes a weak electrical current in the head, which passes back to the amplifier.

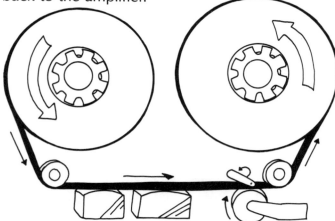

5. To see how magnets affect a tape, use an old, unwanted tape and a magnet. Rub the magnet against a portion of the tape. Play that portion of the tape. What has happened?

_____

Lasers

Lasers are machines which produce a special type of light. Ordinary light is made of many different colors or wavelengths of light. Laser light is all one wavelength. Ordinary light waves travel in different directions and at different speeds. Unlike ordinary light, laser light waves travel in the same direction and at the same speed. Because of this, laser light can travel long distances without fading.

Laser light is used in surgery in place of knives because this sterile, sharp light can cut small blood vessels and seal them shut. Lasers can be used to reattach the retina in a person's eye without cutting into the eye.

To see how laser light can be directed, try this experiment.

Materials
cornstarch
4 small mirrors
a laser penlight

PEN LIGHT

Procedure:

1. Place the mirrors so that the beam from the penlight can bounce from one mirror to another, hitting all the mirrors.

2. Test your arrangement by darkening the room and sprinkling cornstarch on the light beams.

Observations:

1. Did your arrangement work? _____

2. Repeat your experiment using other arrangements of the mirrors. Will other arrangements work? _____

Circuits and Microchips

A circuit is simply a circle of electrical conductors. There are two kinds of circuits, *parallel* and *series*. The diagram on the left shows a parallel circuit; the one on the right shows a series circuit. How are they different? _____

_____

_____

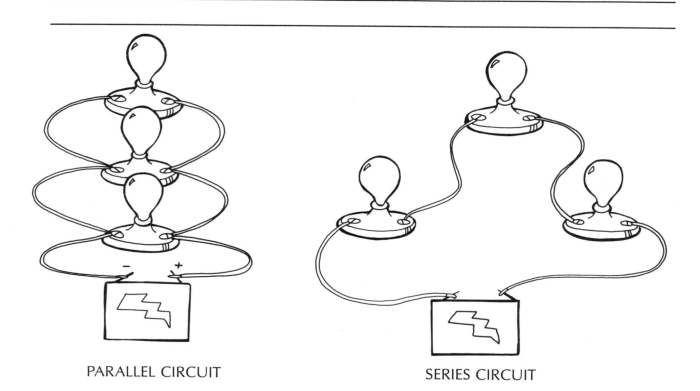

PARALLEL CIRCUIT   SERIES CIRCUIT

Circuits need a force, called the *electromotive force* or *emf,* which must overcome *electrical resistance* to make the current flow. A light bulb is a resistance. The electromotive force may come from a battery or a mechanical generator.

Circuits used to be large. Computers, which need many circuits, used to be as large as a room. The *microchip* revolutionized the computer industry. A microchip is made from a wafer-thin slice of silicon taken from a larger silicon cylinder. The *components* or parts of the microchip are etched on the wafer by a chemical process. These components are built up in layers using a complex pattern based on a larger original design. Next, the wafer is cut into tiny blocks. The chip is sealed inside a plastic block with metal contacts trailing out from the central circuit to connect it to a printed circuit board. Because a microchip contains many different links, it can carry out many different functions at one time. One special chip is the *microprocessor,* which controls the computer. Label the metal contacts and the silicon chip in the illustration below.

The Wonderful Human Body   **Page 1**
Eggs, lean meats, legumes, whole grains, and green leafy vegetables all contain iron.

In addition to iron, your body needs the vitamins B1, B2, B6, B12, A, C, D, E, and K and niacin, folacin, biotin, calcium, phosphorus, sulfur, potassium, chlorine, sodium, magnesium, fluorine, zinc, copper, manganese, iodine, and cobalt.

The Brain   **Page 2**
The diagram should be labeled as follows:

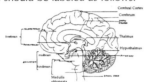

                                                              Page 3
If you write with your left hand, you are using the right side of your brain. If you write with your right hand, you are using the left side of your brain.

Frontal lobe controls speech.
Parietal lobe controls speech and reading ability.
Temporal lobe controls smell and hearing.
Occipital lobe controls vision.

Are All Brains Alike?   **Page 4**
1. The human brain is much larger than that of a fish, duck, or frog in relation to their body size
2. The brain of a cat is larger in proportion to the body, but does not have the enlarged cerebrum section.
3. Primates and porpoises are more intelligent animals, and they have much larger brains in relation to their body size.
4. The porpoise is probably more intelligent.

The Nervous System   **Page 5**
The diagram should be labeled as follows:

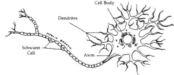

Moving That Body   **Page 6**
2. As you pull one side of the rubber band, the wire pulls up.
3. As you release the rubber band, the wire goes back down.

The Eyes at Work   **Page 7**
The diagram should be labeled as follows:

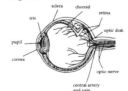

When you turn on a light, your pupil quickly starts to contract. Compound eyes see many different images at one time—like a mosaic. In a fish's eye, the lens actually moves.

A World of Color   **Page 8**

Your Ears and Balance   **Page 9**
The diagram should be labeled as follows:

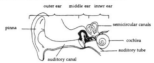

                                                              Page 10
3. As you turn the water on, the wires bend away from the force of the water.

Taste and Smell   **Page 11**
1. Usually, if a person holds his or her nose, the apple and the onion are indistinguishable to the taste buds.
2. Yes, different parts of the tongue detect different flavors.

The Wonderful Skin   **Page 12**
The diagram should be labeled as follows:

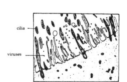

Your fingertips are sensitive, but nowhere near as sensitive as your lips.

The Germ Fighters   **Page 13**
The diagrams should be labeled as follows:

                                                              Page 14
The diagram should be labeled as follows:

A vaccination is an inoculation of a fairly harmless virus to produce immunity to that virus. The vaccination gives your body a small dose of the virus and allows it to develop antibodies to fight off future attacks from that virus.

The Biological Clock   **Page 15**
The plant leaves should droop at night even if they are kept in the light. The drawings should reflect the student's own accurate observations.

OBSERVATIONS: **Page 16**
1. The leaves tend to droop at a certain time of day.
2. The leaves droop even when the light is on.

Wonders of the Animal Kingdom   **Page 17**
There are not huge numbers of the blue whales because the food supply is limited. There is not enough krill to support a huge number of blue whales.

Animals That Glow   **Page 18**
1. The luminescence is useful as a lure to attract prey and a lure to attract mates. It is also useful to scare away predators.
2. Some plants do have bioluminescence.

Underwater Communication   **Page 21**
  2. The tap sounds louder when your ear is under water.
CONCLUSION:
  3. Sound travels better in water than in air.
  4. Sound travels better on a damp, humid night.
We can clean up toxic wastes and limit our hunting. (Any reasonable answer is acceptable.)

The Last Dragon   **Page 22**
  1. The Komodos keep the environment clean and allow the strong, healthy animals to reproduce and produce more strong, healthy animals.
  2. Industrial development may produce toxic waste and destroy the habitat of the Komodos.

The Electric Eel   **Page 23**
It is not likely that the electric fish all came from the same ancestor because they are not all bony fish.

The Hugging Anaconda   **Page 24**
  1. When you push on your diaphragm, you cannot sing as loudly.
  2. When you push on your diaphragm, it squeezes some of the air out of your lungs and does not allow as much space in your lungs for more air.
  3. Our jaws are not stretchy. Our jaws are firmly attached and allow our mouths to open a limited amount.

Flee Flea   **Page 25**
  1. The flea bites infected animals and spreads the germs to healthy animals through the bite.
  2. We can prevent the spread of these diseases by disposing of refuse properly to prevent infestations of rats, by preventing infestations of fleas, and by observing good rules of sanitation.

Owls   **Page 26**
  1. and 2. You cannot see a small object that is directly in back of you by turning your head.
  3. The dilated pupil lets in extra light, making the images easier to detect.
PROCEDURE:
  2. The fringed paper does not make as loud a sound.

The Lazy Sloth   **Page 27**
  1. Adult humans have 32 teeth.
  2. The green color helps camouflage the sloth.
  3. The sloths are grouped by the number of toes: two-toed or three-toed sloths.

Octopus Intelligence   **Page 28**
  1. An invertebrate has no backbone.
  2. People are vertebrates; they have backbones.
  3. Being an invertebrate means the octopus is soft-bodied and extremely flexible, so it can bend its body to fit different sizes and shapes.
  4. Our bodies have hard, inflexible bones that cannot be squeezed or bent to fit such small spaces.

PROCEDURE: **Page 29**
  1. The suction hook will adhere to a glass surface if it is clean. It will not pull off easily. It will not adhere well to a dirty glass surface.
  2. The suction hook will adhere easily to a clean, slightly damp, glass surface. It will not pull off easily.
  3. The suction hook will not adhere to the sandpaper. It will fall off.
  4. The suction hook sticks best on the glass surface because it forms a seal. The glass is smooth and, once the suction hook is pressed against the glass, the air goes out of the area under the suction hook and forms a vacuum. The vacuum holds the hook in place.
  5. Cleaning and dampening the glass makes the suction hook adhere better.

Hide and Seek in the Animal World   **Page 31**
The chick is not as well camouflaged if it is standing or moving because it cannot blend in with the background.

Special Defenses   **Page 32**
  5. Each animal has a special defense to protect itself.
  6. The next time it saw a blister beetle or an insect that looked like a blister beetle, it would avoid it.

Wonders of the Plant Kingdom   **Page 33**
  1. Apples are monocots.
  2. Peanuts are dicots.

PROCEDURE:
  2. The seeds in the freezer will not germinate.
  3. Freezing will usually kill the germinated seeds.
CONCLUSIONS:
  1. Grass seeds will not usually germinate when they are frozen, but they will germinate when they are thawed out.
  2. Freezing will kill germinated grass seeds.
  3. Germinated seeds are much more fragile than dormant seeds.

            Page 35
  5. Sprouts placed in the sun turn green.

Hairy Roots   **Page 36**
OBSERVATIONS
  1. The seeds on the damp towel should germinate first.
  2. The soaked seeds should not germinate.
  3. The damp seeds should develop root hairs.

Osmosis   **Page 37**
  3. The raisins swell up.
  4. Accept student response.
  5. The raisins in glass A are sweeter.
  6. The raisins in glass A absorbed the sugar from the water.

Ex-osmosis   **Page 38**
PROCEDURE:
  2. The begonia in the glass of salt water wilts.

CONCLUSION: The water in a begonia stem leaves the cells if the stem is placed in salt water.

Transpiration   **Page 39**
OBSERVATIONS:
  1. The leaves which were painted on the upperside should curl first.
  2. The nail polish lets the water vapor escape less easily.

CONCLUSION: The underside of a leaf has more stomates.

Flower Giants   **Page 40**
Flies, insects, and animals which feed on rotting vegetation would be attracted to these flowers.

Carnivorous Plants   **Page 44**
  1. When you touch the outside spikes of the leaf, or its "teeth," it usually does nothing.
  2. When you place a fly or hamburger on the center of the leaf, it touches the tiny sensory hairs and triggers the closing response.
  3. When the leaf reopens, a small husk may be left or nothing at all.
  4. Response should reflect accurate student observation.

More Carnivorous Plants   **Page 45**
We can save habitats and create new habitats.
  A. Venus flytrap   C. northern pitcher plant
  B. sundew   D. bladderwort

Poisonous Plants   **Page 46**
  A. poison hemlock   C. poison ivy
  B. mountain laurel   D. foxglove

Seaweed   Page 47

The illustration should be labeled as follows:

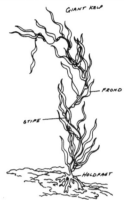

Wonders Under the Microscope   Page 48
1. Ground to a powder for chemical studies.
2. Dissolved in acid.
3. Sliced into thin pieces and viewed under a microscope

We can use the same methods when we are studying the rock samples from other planets.

What Are Bacteria Like?   Page 49

The illustration should be labeled as follows:

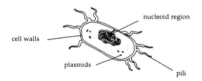

Bacteria and Cyanobacteria Shapes   Page 50
1. cocci   4. vibrios
2. bacilli   5. diplococcus
3. spirochete   6. streptococcus

Chroococcus are round or spherical, as you can tell from the word *coccus* which is part of the name.

Identifying Bacteria   Page 51
A. Gram-positive (violet color)   B. Gram-negative (red color)
Gram-negative or red-stained bacteria are more likely to be harmful.

Page 52
1. methanogens   3. methanogens
2. halophiles   4. thermoacidophiles

Eubacteria   Pages 53 and 54
1. pseudomonads   5. rickettsias and chlamydias
2. phototrophic   6. enteric
3. spirochetes   7. endospore-forming
4. cyanobacteria   8. myxobacteria

Bacteria in Motion   Page 55

The illustration should be labeled as follows:

1. In the Southern Hemisphere, magnetotactic bacteria seek the south pole.
2. Aquaspirillum magnetotacticum is a magnetotactic bacteria.
3. In the Northern Hemisphere, magnetotactic bacteria point to the north pole.

Viruses   Pages 56 and 57
1. DNA   3. flu virus
2. TMV   4. adenovirus
                           5. bacteriophage lambda

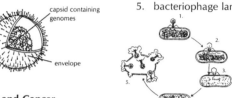

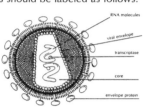

Viruses and Cancer   Page 58

The Illustrations should be labeled as follows:

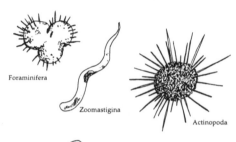

Protozoa   Page 60

The illustration should be labeled as follows:

Algal Protists   Page 62
A. dinobryon   E. volvox colony (chlorophyta)
B. phaeophyta   F. dinoflagellate
C. rhodophyta   G. chlorophyta
D. euglenophyta   H. bacillariophyta diatoms

Slime Molds   Page 63
A. plasmodium   B. sporangia

Our Wonderful Planet   Page 64
1. sea-floor spreading
2. transform boundary plates
3. subduction

Page 65
1. The shifting of the plates causes earthquakes.
2. The fossil record tells us that Great Britain once was a tropical climate, Kansas was under an ocean, and Brazil was a frozen wasteland under a glacier.
3. Britain now is a temperate climate, Kansas is a grassy plain, and Brazil is a subtropical climate. These are very large climate changes. New animals and plants are living in each of the areas.
4. It tells us that there have been major climate changes and major land changes (the area was once under an ocean) over time.

Earthquake Zones   **Page 66**
The plates should be labeled as follows:

Volcanoes   **Page 67**
The diagram should be labeled as follows:

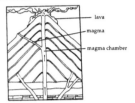

Page 68
The map should be labeled as follows:
The marks are near the edges of tectonic plates or the places where two plates abut each other.

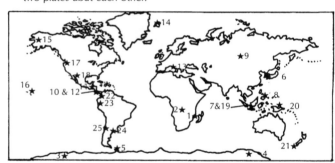

Hot Vents, Geysers, and Hot Springs   **Page 69**
The illustrations should be labeled as follows:

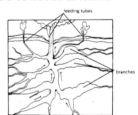

Glaciers   **Page 70**
The illustration should be marked as follows:

Global cooling could result from major volcanic activity or anything else that puts large amounts of dust or foreign particles in the air which block the sunlight.

Waves, Tides, and Tsunamis   **Page 71**
1. When the "wave" hits the brick, it makes a much taller wave or splash.
2. The cork does not move much nearer the brick.

Page 72

A. spring
B. neap
C. spring
D. neap

2. A firm shove makes a much higher and stronger wave.

Deserts   **Page 73**
The illustration should be labeled as follows:

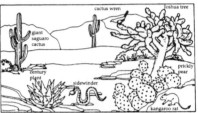

1. The prickly pear can be eaten by humans.
2. The saguaro cactus grows 50 feet or taller and absorbs up to a ton of water during the rainy season.
3. The kangaroo rat lives on seeds and never needs to drink water.

Stalactites and Stalagmites   **Page 74**
The illustration should be labeled as follows:

Rocks, Minerals, and Crystals   **Page 75**
1. Tetragonal crystals are a prism with a square top and bottom and rectangular sides.
2. The crystals should be classified as follows:
   A. calcite
   B. quartz
   C. bismuth

Page 76

1. igneous
2. metamorphic
3. sedimentary

Water   **Page 77**
3. Drops are circular or spherical.
4. The drops will not stay flattened.

1. The needle drops to the bottom of the glass if it is put in point first, because steel is heavier than water.
2. The needle floats.

Page 78
2. The center of the top of the water curves upward above the rim of the glass.
3. Ice floats in a glass of water because the molecules of the ice are spread farther apart than the molecules in water, making the ice lighter or less dense than water.

Tornadoes and Hurricanes   **Page 79**
1. Hurricanes lose strength as they move inland because they lose their warm, wet air. As they cool and dry out, they slow down.
2. A tornado (or any other storm) **warning** is much more dangerous, because the storm has formed and has been sighted.

Lightning   Page 80
1. Lightning always seeks the best and nearest conductor. Tall trees are nearer the clouds.
2. If you stand in an open field, you become the nearest and best conductor—a very bad idea.
3. A car is a safe place in a thunderstorm because the metal body conducts the electricity safely around you and to the ground.

The Wonders of Space   Page 82
1. Pulsating Universe
2. Steady State
3. Big Bang

                                  Page 83

The diagram should be labeled as follows:

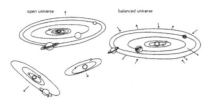

Aliens and UFOs   Page 85
The illustration should look like this:

Comets   Page 86
The illustration should be labeled as follows:

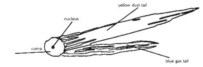

                                  Page 87
1. It takes Encke 3.3 earth years to circle the sun.
2. Halley should return between 2060 and 2063.
3. Encke and Tempel 2 have the shortest orbits.
4. Kohoutek has the longest period, but Halley and Ikeya-Seki also have long periods.

Meteoroids, Meteors, and Meteorites   Page 88
1. Meteorites will definitely hit the earth again; it is a question of when.
2. If a meteorite struck a populated area it could cause great destruction and loss of life.

Asteroids   Page 89
Any reasonable response is acceptable.

Stars   Page 91
1. Antares is red.
2. Spica is blue.
3. Rigel is more luminous than the sun.
4. Capella is closest in magnitude and luminosity to the sun.

Pulsars   Page 92
The emissions from a pulsar are very quick and very regular, unlike deliberately keyed life form transmissions.

The Inner Planets   Page 93
1. A person who weighs 100 pounds on earth would weigh 90 pounds on Venus.

2. A person weighing 100 pounds on earth would weigh only 33 pounds on Mercury or Mars.

                                  Page 94
3. A manned spaceship landing on Mercury would have to deal with extremes of heat and cold, no atmosphere, and lower gravity.
4. To have a space colony, we would have to deal with the same problems as listed in question three plus the problems of keeping a food supply and water. Plants and animals both need an atmosphere and water.

                                  Page 96
1. Accept any reasonable answer.
2. Accept any reasonable answer.

The Outer Planets   Page 98
The diagram should be labeled as follows:

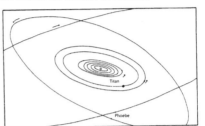

                                  Page 99
A. Titania
B. Umbriel

                                 Page 100

The diagram should be labeled as follows:

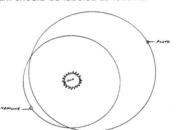

Pluto was last in the position of closer proximity to the sun than Neptune in 1731 to 1751.

Gliders   Page 102
1. Answer should reflect accurate student observation.
2. Answer should reflect accurate student observation.

Helicopters   Page 103
4. The "helicopter" rises in the air.

The Pyramids   Page 104
1. The books are not easy to lift.

                                  Page 105
2. The books are easier to lift using the lever (ruler).
3. Changing the length does make a difference.
4. Changing the fulcrum (rock) does make a difference.

ROLLER PROCEDURE:
1. The books are not easy to move.
2. It is easier to move the books with the roller (pencils).

The Inclined Plane   Page 106
1. It is not easy to lift the carton.
3. It is easier to move the carton using an inclined plane (ramp).

The Giant Lady   **Page 107**
One of the difficulties in building any large sculpture is supporting the structure. Statues such as the Statue of Liberty also have to deal with the effects of wind, rain and weathering, the weight of people walking inside, and erosion at the base.

Architect's Dream   **Page 108**
All of these tools are in use today.
A tall building needs a deep foundation to anchor it. The foundation gives weight and stability to the building to keep it from falling over in high winds and storms.

Building Bridges   **Page 109**
A. beam
B. arch
C. suspension

The Firth of Forth bridge is shaped like an arch, but the railroad bed is suspended from the arches.

Expansion   **Page 110**
The metal and asphalt expand in the heat of the summer sun.

OBSERVATIONS AND CONCLUSIONS:
1. When a wire heats up, it expands and lengthens.
2. Bridges expand in summer because they heat up.

The Shape of a Dam   **Page 112**
2. The flat "dam" will hold water.
5. The curved "dam" is stronger and will hold more water longer.

OBSERVATIONS AND CONCLUSIONS:
1. The curved dam can hold back more water.
2. The curved dam is stronger.

Winning Idea   **Page 113**
1. They needed strong materials to support the weight and traffic of the heavy materials and the amount of men and materials they were moving.
2. The Mulberries had to be long to allow all of the ships to dock and unload.

Ultrasound   **Page 114**
When the wave hits the other side of the pan, it bounces back.

Microphones, Amplifiers, and Tape Recorders   **Page 116**
4. As the can is tapped, the pepper jiggles.
5. Rubbing a magnet across a tape erases it.

Lasers   **Page 117**
1. The answer should reflect accurate student observation.
2. Other arrangements will work.

Circuits and Microchips   **Page 118**
The parallel circuit shows light bulbs connected to separate, parallel wires. The series circuit shows light bulbs connected in a line along one, single path.
The illustration should be labeled as follows:

silicon chip
metal contacts

$$12 \times 6 = 72$$